TABLE OF CONTENTS

S0-CSZ-075

Highest Individual League Averages

Men

251	Russ Hunt, Ogden, Utah, 1995-96, two-player league
247	Jeff Phipps, Salem, Ore., three-player league, 1992-93
246	Marc Crawford, York, Pa., 1995-96, four-player league
245	Doug Vergouven, Harrisonville, Mo., four-player league, 1989-90
	Paul Geiger, Jamestown, N.Y., five-player league, 1989-90
	Doug Vergouven, Harrisonville, Mo., five-player league, 1989-90
	Timothy Zelger, Red Lion, Pa., five-player league, 1988-89

Women

234	Liz Johnson, Niagara Falls, N.Y., doubles league, 1993-94
232	Patty Ann, Arlington Heights, Ill., singles league, 1983-84
231	Patty Ann, Arlington Heights, Ill., singles league, 1991-92
230	Patty Ann, Arlington Heights, Ill., singles league, 1984-85
	Patty Ann, Arlington Heights, Ill., singles league, 1992-93
	Jodi Hughes, Greenville, S.C., singles league, 1996-97

Highest Individual Three-Game Series

Men

900	Jeremy Sonnenfeld, Lincoln, Neb., Feb. 2, 1997
899	Tom Jordan, Union, N.J., March 7, 1989
	Ron Prettyman, Newark, Del., Feb. 10, 1996
	Steve Lewis, Xenia, Ohio, Sept. 19, 1996
898	Steve Lickers, Nanticoke, Pa., Nov. 16, 1996

Male Youth

888	Brentt Arcement, Kenner, La., Jan. 20, 1990
878	Jason Johnson, Novi, Mich., Dec. 7, 1993
867	John Delp, Sinking Spring, Pa., Jan. 22, 1990
	Steve Wiley, Muscatine, Iowa, Feb. 11, 1995
866	Thomas Robards, San Jose, Calif., 1974-75
	Walter Hastings III, North Brunswick, N.J., Jan. 31, 1995
	Travis Carr, St. Louis, Nov. 18, 1995

Women

877	Jackie Mitskavich, Van Wert, Ohio, Aug. 10, 1997
865	Anne Marie Duggan, Edmond, Okla., July 18, 1993
864	Jeanne Maiden-Naccarato, Tacoma, Wash., Nov. 23, 1986
	Diane Guttormsen Northern, Kenosha, Wis., Jan. 3, 1996
859	Patty Ann, Arlington Heights, Ill., April 2, 1985

Female Youth

838	Kelle Renniger, Williamsport, Pa., Nov. 20, 1994
825	Tiffany Stanbrough, Oklahoma City, Sept. 25, 1994
	Lisa McCardy, Troy, Mich., June 18, 1997
824	Cindy Shipman, Endicott, N.Y., Dec. 20, 1986
	Diandra Hyman, Dyer, Ind., Nov. 4, 1995

Highest Team Three-Game Series

Men Five Player

3,868	Hurst Bowling Supplies, Luzerne, Pa., Feb. 23, 1994
3,858	Budweiser Beer, St. Louis, March 12, 1958
3,834	Ansted-Schuster Florist, Toledo, Ohio, Sept. 26, 1994
3,820	Wally's Gang, Susquehanna, Pa., April 12, 1981
3,813	Vince Gance Agency, Endicott, N.Y., Feb. 18, 1993

Women Five Player

3,536	Contour Power Grips, Detroit, Aug. 29, 1994
3,509	Goebel Beer, Detroit, Jan. 3, 1994
3,504	Contour Power Grips, Detroit, Nov. 13, 1994
3,474	Goebel Beer, Detroit, Dec. 13, 1993
3,466	Strike More Spareless, Lincoln, Neb., Nov. 5, 1996

Highest Team Games

Men Five Player

1,410	Golden Harvest No. 4, Springfield, Ill., May 1, 1993
1,387	Eden Lanes, Tinley Park, Ill., Oct. 7, 1996
1,384	Soutar's Pro Shop, Kansas City, Mo., March 1, 1990
	Steve's Delivery, Richmond, Va., Oct. 25, 1996
1,382	Sunset Bowl, Kansas City, Kan., Sept. 8, 1987

Women Five Player

1,292	Women's Central State Association Tournament, Akron, Ohio, March 2, 1994
1,262	Drug Package Inc., St. Louis, Jan. 5, 1993
1,252	River Liquors, Minneapolis, March 16, 1995
1,244	Chamberlain Wholesale, Detroit, 1987-88
1,242	Goebel Beer, Detroit, April 4, 1994

Highest Mixed Four-Player Records

Highest Mixed, Two Women, Two Men Game

1,067	Supreme Casting, Coloma, Mich., Nov. 15, 1996
1,066	Fleming, Ft. Worth, Texas, April 9, 1996
1,055	KFCEMF's Team, Brick, N.J., Feb. 24, 1993
1,052	Yattoos, Bedford, Texas, Jan. 7, 1997
1,044	Newell's Bombers, Montoursville, Pa., March 21, 1993

Highest Mixed, Two Women, Two Men Series

2,938	Pro Staff Pro Shop, Marietta, Ga., Dec. 27, 1993
2,910	Right Shop Pro Shop, Saline, Mich., June 10, 1996
2,895	Newell's Bombers, Montoursville, Pa., March 21, 1993
2,894	Auto Dealers Tournament Bowlers Association, Seattle, Oct. 12, 1994
2,885	Red Carpet West Allis, Milwaukee, Dec. 3, 1993
	Grizzly Ranch Production, Spokane, Wash., Dec. 9, 1996

300 Games, Career

Men

54	Bob Learn, Jr., Erie, Pa.
52	Mike Whalin, Cincinnati
	James Johnson Jr., Wilmington, Del.
48	Joe Jimenez, Saginaw, Mich.
43	Robert Faragon, Albany, N.Y.

Women

27	Tish Johnson, Panorama City, Calif.
21	Jeanne Naccarato, Tacoma, Wash.
	Vicki Fischel, Wheat Ridge, Colo.
18	Aleta Sill, Dearborn, Mich.
17	Leanne Barrette, Yukon, Okla.

Male Youth

18	Rory Kalanquin, Davison, Mich.
14	Todd Adams, Sacramento, Calif.
13	Todd Filter, Cedarburg, Wis.
12	Dave Ewald, St. Clair Shores, Mich.
10	Ted Pritts, Garland, Texas
	Shannon Buchan, Waterloo, Iowa

Female Youth

3	Michelle Ewald, St. Clare Shores, Mich.
	Jennifer Petrick, North Canton, Ohio
	Jossett Petrick, North Canton, Ohio

299 Games, Career

Men

19	Woody Crist, Williamsport, Pa.
18	John Chacko, Jr. Larksville, Pa.
15	Jerome Penxa, Detroit
	Carl Chavez, Albuquerque, N.M.
	Jason Queen, Decatur, Ill

Women

6	Dede Davidson, San Jose, Calif.
	Jodi Jensen, Wichita, Kan.
5	Jeanne Naccarato, Tacoma, Wash.
	Paula Drake, Broken Arrow, Okla.
4	Kottie Kemp, Las Vegas
	Dina Manni-Jones, Lake Orion, Mich.

298 Games, Career

Men

6	William Boyd, Warren, Ohio
	Kevin Stabler, Williamsport, Pa.
	Woody Crist, Williamsport, Pa.
5	Terry Rea, Seattle
	Tony Torrice, Wolcott, Conn.
	John Wilcox Jr., Lewisburg, Pa.
	Don Johnson, Las Vegas
	Richard Roberts, San Antonio

Women

3	Aleta Sill, Dearborn, Mich.
	Cindy Coburn-Carroll, Tonawanda, N.Y.

800 Series, Career

Men

40	John Chacko Jr., Larksville, Pa.
28	Steve Gehringer, Reading, Pa.
27	Jerry Kessler, Dayton, Ohio
	Bob Learn Jr., Erie, Pa.
23	Bob Johnson, Dayton, Ohio

Male Youth

15	Rory Kalanquin, Davison, Mich.

Women

9	Tish Johnson, Panorama City, Calif.
7	Aleta Sill, Dearborn, Mich.
6	Nikki Gianulias, Vallejo, Calif.
5	Jeanne Naccarato, Tacoma, Wash.
4	Patty Ann, Kernersville, N.C.

INDIVIDUAL RECORDS

Nine-Game Series, highest
(Some reflect tournament all events totals)

Men		Women	
2,415	Paul Andrew, East Moline, Ill., May 9-10, 1981	2,373	Caren Park, Seattle, 1991-92
2,384	Lawrence Detweiler, Hagerstown, Md., June 1, 1997	2,352	Jeanne Naccarato, Tacoma, Wash., 1986-87
		2,274	Patty Ann, Arlington Heights, Ill., 1990-91
2,367	Randy Lightfoot, St. Louis, Feb. 12, 1995	2,249	Carol Norman, Ardmore, Okla., 1985-86
2,361	Tony Singer, Fort Worth, Texas, May 6-7, 1994	2,240	Alayne Blomenberg, Cranston, R.I., 1983-84
2,332	Taylor Mattox, Columbus, Ohio, Feb. 9-23, 1994		

Eight-Game Series, highest

Men		Women	
2,173	Steve Swearinger, Sacramento, Calif., Aug. 6, 1994	2,203	Tish Johnson, Panorama City, Calif., Sept. 9, 1990
		2,168	Robin Romeo, Newhall, Calif., 1989-90
2,139	Ron Lisher, San Jose, Calif., Sept. 6, 1989	2,063	Betty Morris, Stockton, Calif., 1986-87
2,114	Ken Konczos, Cleveland, Nov. 2, 1980	2,052	Jeanne Maiden-Naccarato, Tacoma, Wash.,
2,112	Jim Stefanich, Redwood City, Calif., June 1969	2,035	Michelle Mullen, Matteson, Ill., Feb. 7, 1989
2,108	Don Collins, Syracuse, N.Y., 1979		

Six-Game Series, highest

Men		Women	
1,659	Dennis Sullivan, Denver, Aug. 10, 1995	1,639	Jeanne Naccarato, Tacoma, Wash., April 7, 1987
1,657	Ken Konczos, Cleveland, Nov. 2, 1980		
1,630	Dan Golobic, Wickliffe, Ohio, May 31, 1994	1,630	Jackie Mitskavich, Van Wert, Ohio, Aug. 10, 1997
1,628	Steve Carson, Oklahoma City, July 23, 1984	1,581	Betty Morris, Stockton, Calif., 1986-87
1,624	John Handegard, Eugene, Ore., 1978	1,565	Donna Adamek, Apple Valley, Calif., Oct. 31, 1989
		1,564	Betty Morris, Stockton, Calif., 1975-76

Five-Game Series, highest

Men Five Games		Women	
1,391	Bob Schumacher, San Jose, Calif., April 10, 1979	1,406	Jackie Mitskavich, Van Wert, Ohio, Aug. 10, 1997
1,385	Timothy Barth, Addison, Ill., Nov. 22, 1981		
1,367	Ken Konczos, Cleveland, Nov. 2, 1980		
1,355	Tom Rippentrop, Belvidere, Ill., Dec. 1, 1968		
1,341	Pat Henry, Wichita, Kan., Oct. 12, 1979		
	Rick Cashell, Boston, May 7, 1987		

Four-Game Series, highest

Men		Women	
1,198	Tom Jordan, Union, N.J., March 7, 1989	1,166	Jackie Mitskavich, Van Wert, Ohio, Aug. 10, 1997
1,167	Chris Riga, Allentown, Pa., May 20, 1992	1,148	Patty Ann, Arlington Heights, Ill., April 2, 1985
1,158	George Pappas, Charlotte, N.C., Dec. 16, 1996	1,142	Anne Marie Duggan, Edmond, Okla., 1983-84
1,155	Chuck Neal, Indianapolis, May 18, 1977	1,109	Marion Ladewig, Grand Rapids, Mich., 1951-52
1,152	Ben Farmer, Fort Worth, Texas, July 6, 1994	1,083	Patty Ann, Arlington Heights, Ill., 1982-83
			Loretta Gedeon, Munroe Falls, Ohio, 1987-88

TEAM RECORDS

Four-Game Series, highest

Men Three-Player		Women Three-Player	
2,867	Hamilton Landscaping, St. Louis, May 22, 1995	2,791	Nemez Sav-A-Lot, Youngstown, Ohio, March 8, 1994
2,782	Tom's Trio, Kansas City, Mo., May 28, 1997		
		2,787	Wichita Billiards, Wichita, Kan., March 5, 1990
		2,778	OO Ready, Arnold, Mo., July 21, 1994
		2,771	Silhouette American, Springfield, Ill., 1988-89
		2,756	Paper Pros, Canoga Park, Calif., 1983-84

Men Two Player

2,202   Tom Jordan-Ken Yonker Jr., Union, N.J., March 7, 1989

1,996   Bud Hodgson-J.B. Blaylock, Los Angeles, June 1964

1,980   Tom Harnisch-Dave Soutar, Detroit, May 16, 1955

1,969   Dick Donahue-Barry Asher, Los Angeles, Sept. 3, 1967

1,954   Dick Weber-Ray Bluth, St. Charles, Mo., May 17, 1964

Mixed Three Player

3,027   Barbara Thorberg, Ron Krippelcz and Austin Nettler, St. Louis, Oct. 12, 1995

3,002   Barbara Thorberg, Ron Krippelcz and Austin Nettler, St. Louis, April 11, 1996

2,972   Debra Kennedy, Glen Gaze and Adam Apo, St. Louis, July 20, 1995

2,923   Brendan Phelan, Bobby Bonds and Shari Griggs, St. Louis, June 29, 1995

2,895   Kurt Thompson, Scott Grupas and Ginger Grupas, St. Louis, June 22, 1995

Women Two Player

1,965   Patty Ann-Paula Mikkelson, Arlington Heights, Ill. -Appleton, Wis., 1990-91

1,960   Jeanne Maiden-Naccarato-Cheryl Shininger, Tacoma, Wash.-Cleveland, 1982-83

1,953   Karen Julien-Brown-Michele Sobin, Albany-Hudson, N.Y., Oct. 10, 1994

1,895   Nancy Hanuschik-Terri Thompson, Trenton, N.J., 1990-91

1,865   Pat Adams-Linda Young, Santa Cruz-Boulder Creek, Calif., 1987-88

Mixed Two Player

2,004   James Geedy-Michelle Frank, Tonawanda, N.Y., Feb. 25, 1994

2,003   Joe Mrenak-Jody Fritschle, Wright Patterson AFB-Fairborn, Ohio, 1986-87

2,000   Ron Stromfield-Vicki Middendorf, Columbus, Ohio, Aug. 10, 1983

1,976   Barbara Leicht-Karl Bieber, Albany, N.Y., Oct. 9, 1989

1,974   Jim Lewis-Kim Julien, Albany, N.Y., Feb. 26, 1990

Three-Game Series, Highest

Mixed, One Woman, Four Men

3,735   Legion of Doom, Dallas, Texas, May 9, 1996

3,685   Texas Sports Palace, Austin, Texas, Dec. 12, 1991

3,647   Team #11, Milwaukie, Ore., April 9, 1997

3,646   U-Turn Ball Cleaner, Des Moines, Iowa, Dec. 5, 1994

3,635   Professional Protection Technologies, Phoenix, April 5, 1990

Men Four Player

3,174   Fireside Lanes, Sacramento, Calif., Oct. 10, 1991

3,163   Ace's Coffeeshop II, Schenectady, N.Y., March 10, 1997

3,154   Ace's Coffeeshop, Schenectady, N.Y., Jan. 13, 1997

3,131   Bob Daubney's, Latham, N.Y., March 17, 1997

3,090   The Dream Team, Davie, Fla., Oct. 20, 1992

Mixed, One Woman, Three Men

3,074   Nadeau's Pro Shop, Las Vegas, Nov. 21, 1996

3,012   Valley Lanes, Portland, Ore., Dec. 23, 1992

2,934   #20, Aurora, Ore., Nov. 6, 1991

2,931   Three Rights and One Wrong, Jacksonville, Fla., Dec. 5, 1996

2,926   Strike Zone Pro Shop, Ft. Worth, Texas, Oct. 17, 1995

Men Three Player

2,423   Two B's, One Shot, West Orange, N.J., Nov. 27, 1991

2,404   Pinky's Lanes, Milwaukee, April 20, 1960

2,381   Lazare Lincoln Mercury, Albany, N.Y., Dec. 16, 1983

2,340   Roxbury Lanes, Seattle, Feb. 19, 1995

2,337   L.J. Carpet, St. Louis, Nov. 17, 1983

Mixed, Two Women, Three Men

3,672   Right Shot Pro Shop, Saginaw, Mich., Oct. 6, 1995

3,613   Smith's 5, Dayton, Ohio, Sept. 9, 1994

3,563   Team 8, Rockford, Ill., Jan. 4, 1994

3,541   Beth and the Buttheads, Mesquite, Texas, March 24, 1994

3,510   The B-L-T's, St. Louis, March 22, 1995

Women Four Player

2,786   Sister Act, St. Louis, Dec. 16, 1993

2,731   Monte's, Minneapolis, April 2, 1991

2,712   Stonehedge Place, Akron, Ohio, 1983-84

2,700   Breed Enterprises, Rochester, N.Y., Nov. 23, 1994

2,662   Dot's Tailoring, Los Angeles, 1975-76

Mixed, Three Women, One Man

2,893   Elsie's, Minneapolis, Feb. 14, 1995

2,858   Buddha's Babes, Wichita, Kan., Oct. 15, 1996

2,743   Camino Seco Bowl, Tucson, Ariz., Oct. 17, 1995

2,710   Andy's Pro Shop, Tucson, Ariz., Feb. 24, 1994

2,652   Minneapolis Athletic Club, Minneapolis, Nov. 11, 1992

Women Three Player

2,205   DDD, New Orleans, Feb. 27, 1997

2,190   John Law Pro Shop, Slidell, Feb. 27, 1997

2,147   Braasch Pro Shop, Garden Grove, Calif., Dec. 20, 1994

2,136   John Law Pro Shop, Garden Grove, Calif., Nov. 22, 1994

2,133   Woodland Construction, Lansing, Mich., Feb. 27, 1995

Mixed Two Men, One Woman

2,324   Tumo's, Belleville, Ill., Dec. 16, 1996
2,314   Trails West, St. Louis, July 18, 1996
2,288   RGD, Inc., St. Louis, April 11, 1996
        One Foot and Two Inches, St. Charles, Mo.,
        Jan. 6, 1992
2,284   Rears, Gears, Discs, Inc., St. Louis, Oct. 12, 1995

Mixed Two Women, One Man

2,313   J & J Fence Co., Wichita, Kan., Dec. 1, 1996
2,222   U.T.A., Kenneth City, Fla. February 20, 1996

Women Two Player

1,547   Jeri Blair Flemming-Linda Kelly, Dayton, Ohio,
        April 18, 1996
1,534   Patty Ann-Paula Mikkelson, Arlington Heights, Ill.
        -Appleton, Wis., 1990-91
1,525   Carol Gianotti-Wendy Macpherson-Papanos,
        Perth, Australia-Henderson, Nev., 1990-91
1,509   Stephanie Thomas-Jodi Musto, Clifton Park, N.Y.,
        April 4, 1995
1,508   Pat Mercatanti-Lisa Wagner,
        Washington Crossing, Pa.-Palmetto, Fla., 1986-87

Men Two Player

1,655   Tom Jordan-Ken Yonker Jr., Union, N.J.,
        March 7, 1989
1,643   William Conrad-Rollie Worman,
        Oceanside, Calif., March 17, 1992
1,642   Joe Golden-Frank Hemberger,
        Oakland, N.J., Aug. 10, 1987
1,639   Bob Perry-Mike Foti, Lodi, N.J., Aug. 27, 1986
        Robert Faragon-Nicholas Misena, Jr. Burlington,
        Vt., April 20, 1997

Mixed Two Player

1,581   Cindy Coburn-Carroll and Mike Neumann, Buffalo, N.Y., March 30, 1995
1,574   Michelle Frank and James Geedy, Tonawanda, N. Y., Feb. 25, 1994
1,567   Linda Rose and Ken Yokobosky, Fairfield, N.J., July 20, 1993
        Marge Kowalski and Stan Kruzel, Toledo, Ohio, Nov. 19, 1994
1,563   Carie Shady and Mike Machuga, Lincoln, Neb., Nov. 8, 1994

Highest Team Games

Mixed Two Women, Three Men

1,311   Patch's IGA, Flint, Mich., Feb. 25, 1995
1,310   Double Trouble, St. Louis, Dec. 7, 1994
1,307   Beth and the Buttheads, Mesquite, Texas,
        March 24, 1994
1,300   Lan Oak Lanes, Hammond, Ind., March 22, 1995
1,298   Right Shot Pro Shop, Saginaw, Mich., Oct. 6, 1995

Mixed Three Women, Two Men

1,298   Right Shot Pro Shop, Saginaw, Mich., Oct. 6,
        1995
        Baker's Dozen, Tulsa, Okla., Dec. 12, 1995
1,295   Thelmal Pro Shop, Louisville, Ky., Oct. 4, 1996
1,215   Fox & Gates, Houston, 1979-80
1,199   Classic Mixed League, Florissant, Mo., 1973-74

Mixed, Three Women, One Man

1,045   Brandt Vending, York, Pa., Oct. 2, 1995
1,027   Bowler Language, Slidell, La., March 3, 1997
982   Elsie's, Minneapolis, Feb. 14, 1995
978   Minneapolis Athletic Club, Minneapolis,
        Nov. 11, 1992
972   Andy's Pro Shop, Tucson, Ariz., April 14, 1995

Mixed One Woman, Four Men

1,340   Mama Tios, North Kansas City, Mo.,
        Aug. 25, 1994
1,330   Last Minute, Kenner, La., Oct. 28, 1995
        Trouble, Dallas, Feb. 5, 1995
1,326   Bowlers Paddock Pro Shop #3, Toledo, Ohio,
        Feb. 25, 1995
1,317   Legion of Doom, Dallas, May 9, 1995

Women Four Player

1,002   Sister Act, St. Louis, Dec. 16, 1993
997   Cove Lounge, St. Louis, Oct. 21, 1993
992   Bedrock Babes, Louisville, Ky., April 21, 1997
991   Three Rights and a Wrong, San Jose, Calif.,
        1988-89
973   Score More Pro Shop, Detroit, Jan. 16, 1995

Men Four Player

1,137   Ace's Coffee Shop, Schenectady, N.Y., March 10,
        1997
1,117   Liberty Vending, Canton, Ohio, Feb. 4, 1994
1,114   The 4 Buds, Monsey, N.Y., Dec. 2, 1986
        The Dream Team, Davie, Fla., Oct. 20, 1992
        Cherry Lanes, Sodus, N.Y., Jan. 23, 1997

Mixed, One Woman, Three Men

1,084	Andy Clark's Pro Shop, Tucson, Ariz., Jan. 11, 1993
1,064	Laura & the Rolos, San Diego, Sept. 17, 1992
1,057	Valley Lanes, Portland, Ore., Dec. 23, 1992
1,053	Northwest Corporate Centre, Tucson, Ariz., Dec. 26, 1995
1,051	Southtowne Lanes, Eugene, Ore., Oct. 31, 1994
	Vaughn Electric Motors, Port Arthur, Texas, Sept. 25, 1995

Mixed, Two Women, One Man

832	J & J Fence Co., Wichita, Kan., Dec. 2, 1996
814	J & J Fence Co., Wichita, Kan., Feb. 17, 1997
803	Team No. 7, Gautier, Miss., July 1. 1996
793	Team No. 15, Pueblo, Colo., May 6, 1996
774	Mark, Marky and the Funky, Cocoa, Fla., Feb. 4, 1997

Women Three Player

803	Canoga Park Motor Inn, Canoga Park, Calif., 1980-81
	Kegler's Korner, Norwalk, Calif., 1988-89
	Woodland Construction, Lansing, Mich., Feb. 27, 1995
799	Goy ABB, Mango, Fla., Dec. 30, 1996
796	John Law Pro Shop, Garden Grove, Calif., Nov. 22, 1994

Men Three Player

877	J.J.'s Pro Shop, Wichita, Kan., Nov. 9, 1992
868	All Event Trophies, Springfield, Ill., April 22, 1986
	Nevada's Pro Shop, Delafield, Ill., Nov. 18, 1996
866	Ace Mitchell, Akron, Ohio, March 30, 1995
	CPS Accounting Services, Endicott, N.Y., Nov. 8, 1994

Mixed Two Men, One Woman

847	Bob Ricciardi, Linda Rose and Dennis Delpome; West Orange, N.J., Dec. 15, 1993
	Todd Hale, Alisia Towles and Roy Kellow; Louisville, Ky.; Dec. 18, 1991
846	Clay Rees, Molly Wadley and Eddie Kesler, Murray, Utah, Feb. 15, 1995
845	Gene Shoup, Lori Branham and Jim Mee; Jamestown, N.Y.; Oct. 22, 1991
843	Doug Buehrer, Angie Goetteland and Chris Taylor, O'Fallon, Mo., April 4, 1994

Mixed Two Player

599	Allison Johnson and Rob Grimmitt, Oklahoma City, July 18, 1994
590	Karen Hayes and Bob Garrity, West Orange, N.J., July 26, 1994
580	Dede Davidson and Doug Becker, Port Richey, Fla., Jan. 9, 1994
579	Jenny Lynn Marczyk and Don Hicks, Bay Shore, N.Y., June 30, 1993
578	Judy Koester and Mike Sadowy, Rochester, N.Y., Aug. 5, 1988
	Linda Ujvari and Jack Jurek, Tonawanda, N.Y., Sept. 3, 1993

Women Two Player

578	Pamela Beach and Cindy Fry, Lansing, Mich., Nov. 21, 1992
576	Kris Gross and Debbie Titus, Sacramento, Calif., Feb. 7, 1993
566	Jeannette Betts and Veronica Wilson, Flint, Mich., 1990-91
	Kathy McNeill and Mary Zalaffi, Johnson City, N.Y., Feb. 26, 1992
565	Debbie Northrup and Willie Spulnik, Albany, N.Y., April 28, 1997

Men Two Player

600	John Cotta and Steve Larson, Manteca, Calif., May 1, 1981
	Jeff Mraz and Dave Roney, Canton, Ohio, Nov. 8, 1987
	William Gruner and Dave Conway, Oceanside, Calif., Feb. 27, 1990
	Scott Williams and Willie Hammar, Utica, Mich., June 7, 1990
	Darrell Guertin and George Tignor, Rutland, Vt., Feb. 20, 1993
	Ken Mayo and Mike Mayo, Peoria, Ill., Jan. 22, 1995
	Keith Nusbaum and Dale Ellis, Toledo, Ohio, Feb. 5, 1995
	Ryan Boyd and Clayton Hicks, Miami, July 27, 1995
	Duke Matties and Dave Frascatore, Albany, N.Y., Nov. 27, 1995

STATE, PROVINCIAL INDIVIDUAL BEST SERIES

The following are the highest ABC three-game series in each state and province. Records should be reported to the Bowling Communications Department at 5301 S. 76th St., Greendale, Wis. 53129, (414) 423-3224.

State	Score	Name, Site, Date	State	Score	Name, Site, Date
Alabama	865	David Wise, Montgomery, 10/16/91	New York	886	Allie Brandt, Lockport, 10/25/39
Alaska	844	Scott Buckingham, Anchorage, 3/26/89	North Carolina	880	Kenneth McNeely Jr., Morganton,
Arizona	873	Eric Hew, Tucson, 4/15/93			5/15/96
Arkansas	855	Rodney Jackson, Texarkana, 11/6/95	North Dakota	856	Dick Schaan, Williston, 1/5/88
California	889	Mark Benavidez, Sacramento, 5/18/91	Ohio	899	Steve Lewis, Xenia, 9/19/96
Colorado	868	Don Meiris, Colorado Springs, 8/27/97	Oklahoma	878	Charles McLean, Oklahoma City, 9/2/97
Connecticut	877	Richard Brietenbach, Milford, 1/5/87	Oregon	876	Alan Stanford, Portland, 4/4/90
Delaware	899	Ron Prettyman, Claymont, 2/10/96	Pennsylvania	898	Kevin Lickers, Nanticoke, 11/16/96
Florida	878	Ken Frymoyer, Hudson, 10/26/96	Rhode Island	889	Bob D'Antuono, Lincoln, 3/5/97
Georgia	887	Bret Dal Santo, Savanah, 10/25/90	South Carolina	884	Blais Mascitelli, Spartanburg, 12/11/90
Hawaii	875	Daniel Maglangit, Ewa Beach, 3/8/82	South Dakota	857	Fred Kiewel, Rapid City, 11/5/96
Idaho	865	Gene Lampe Jr., Boise, 4/13/95			Vito Caputo, Bonesteel, 3/6/97
Illinois	879	Jason McKinney, Centralia, 3/14/97	Tennessee	868	Royce Wallace, Knoxville, 7/23/97
Indiana	887	Kenny Parks, Highland, 3/15/96	Texas	879	Tracy Wadsworth, Dallas, 1/22/93
Iowa	878	Neil Greenwald Jr., Muscatine, 10/21/95			William Henderson, San Antonio,
Kansas	887	Scott Huther, Leavenworth, 2/25/97			7/22/93
Kentucky	878	Steve Guilkey, Newport, 7/20/93	Utah	887	Russ Hunt, North Salt Lake City, 3/18/96
Louisiana	888	Brentt Arcement (YABA), Kenner, 1/20/90	Vermont	841	Donald Gurney Jr., Springfield, 2/17/89
Maine	837	Richard Campbell, Brunswick, 11/1/92	Virginia	857	Paul Zevgolis, Richmond, 3/22/84
Maryland	878	Wayne Webb, Middle River, 3/2/91	Washington	878	Dave Hanson, Tacoma, 12/23/91
Massachusetts	869	Todd Tague, North Attleboro, 12/15/93	West Virginia	870	Jeffrey Gunn, Wheeling, 11/29/94
Michigan	890	Scott Browneye, Grand Rapids, 2/24/97	Wisconsin	896	Mark Munsch, Oshkosh, 1/24/97
Minnesota	889	Wayne Poole, St. Paul, 11/12/90	Wyoming	858	Ivan Weitz, Cheyenne, 2/3/94
Mississippi	851	Thad Land, Jackson, 4/5/92			Justin Moore (YABA), Cheyenne, 4/9/94
Missouri	878	Michael Ferguson, Kansas City, 4/12/90			
		Mike Murkin, Kansas City, 6/22/94			
		Charles Goff, Mexico, 10/11/96			
Montana	858	Ted Bertrand, Butte, 3/28/93			
Nebraska	900	Jeremy Sonnenfeld, Lincoln, 2/2/97			
Nevada	869	Rick Freels, Las Vegas, 2/13/94			
New Hampshire	848	Duane Sanborn, Manchester, 2/19/95			
New Jersey	899	Tom Jordan, Union, 3/7/89			
New Mexico	877	Joe Sanburn, Albuquerque, 3/30/94			

Canada

State	Score	Name, Site, Date
Alberta	794	Joe Lagadyn, Edmonton, 11/15/84
British Columbia	856	Cal Smith, Vancouver, 3/24/88
Manitoba	813	Clem Perreault, Winnipeg, 1/5/94
Ontario	869	Robert Woolley, Sault Ste. Marie, 4/10/96
Quebec	858	Tony Broccoli, St. Leanard, 11/10/95
Saskatchewan	782	Daryl Day, Regina, 4/24/88

STATE, PROVINCIAL TEAM GAME

The following are the highest ABC team games in each state and province. Records should be reported to the Bowling Communications Department at 5301 S. 76th St., Greendale, Wis. 53129, (414) 423-3224.

State	Score	Name, Site, Date	State	Score	Name, Site, Date
Alabama	1,321	Adventure Travel, Mobile, 11/1/94	Iowa	1,343	Gondola Lounge, Des Moines, 4/22/94
Alaska	1,301	The Wilson Agency, Anchorage, 11/22/95	Kansas	1,382	Sunset Bowl, Kansas City, 9/8/87
Arizona	1,317	Sun Pontiac, Chandler, 3/21/89	Kentucky	1,322	KAR Products, Campbellsville, 10/27/94
Arkansas	1,291	Queens EIF, Rogers, 4/17/97	Louisiana	1,299	B&D Pro Shop, Kenner, 10/27/92
California	1,344	Madruga Iron Works, Tracy, 4/6/89	Maine	1,246	The Big Dogs, Portland, 1/15/97
Colorado	1,309	#9, Denver, 4/4/96	Maryland	1,343	Action Auto Center, Baltimore, 3/28/91
Connecticut	1,312	Ken Dunbar's Pro Shop, Woodbridge, 2/1/96	Massachusetts	1,296	Titleist 1, New Bedford, 12/13/95
Delaware	1,283	Ward's, Wilmington, 2/11/81	Michigan	1,359	Dr. Hook's Pro Shop, Kalamazoo, 3/20/95
Florida	1,322	Papa's Puffs, Pensacola, 5/20/93	Minnesota	1,308	Craig's Pro Shop, Sauk Rapids, 10/6/94
Georgia	1,265	TBA of Georgia, Lawrenceville, 2/20/91			Bowler's Choice I, Brainerd, 2/4/95
Hawaii	1,316	Love's Ltd., Honolulu, 3/21/69			Larson's Siding, Rochester, 2/8/96
Idaho	1,250	Plaza #1, Idaho Falls, 2/1/86	Mississippi	1,335	Panorama Lanes, Mehlville, 12/12/84
Illinois	1,410	Golden Harvest No. 4, Springfield, 5/1/93	Missouri	1,384	Soutar's Pro Shop, Kansas City, 3/1/90
Indiana	1,326	Jefferson Manor Lanes, Mishawaka, 11/29/88	Montana	1,273	Bound For Glory, Helena, 5/1/93
		Thwait's Realty, Syracuse, 3/22/95			

STATE, PROVINCIAL TEAM GAME (Continued)

State	Score	Name, Site, Date
Nebraska	1,361	Old Milwaukee, Norfolk, 12/19/90
Nevada	1,214	Reno All-Stars, Reno, 5/22/82
N. Hampshire	1,222	Barns of Bradford, Manchester, 10/28/92
New Jersey	1,350	V. Loria and Sons, Paramus, 4/23/79
New Mexico	1,255	Sandia Bowl, Albuquerque, 4/15/88
New York	1,371	Concord Pools, Scotia, 3/6/95
North Carolina	1,303	Lucky 13, Ashville, 10/13/95
North Dakota	1,256	Midway Lanes, Mandan, 3/22/87
Ohio	1,354	Empire Pro Shop, Oregon, 3/18/97
Oklahoma	1,330	TBA, Tulsa, 3/3/95
Oregon	1,312	PGP, Corvallis, 2/20/88
Pennsylvania	1,374	Concept III, Earlington, 2/5/87
Rhode Island	1,249	Grizzly Bear, Pawtucket, 10/23/85
South Carolina	1,288	Maybe Baby, Aiken, 11/18/93
South Dakota	1,267	Top Line Bowling Supply, Sioux Falls, 1/18/73
Tennessee	1,328	B & H Vending, Nashville, 11/20/89
Texas	1,345	Itty-Bitty-Flashers, Euless, 4/19/90

State	Score	Name, Site, Date
Utah	1,298	Walt Palmer Supply Company, Salt Lake City, 4/4/96
Vermont	1,260	Carpenter's Maintenance, Shelborne, 12/20/93
Virginia	1,384	Steve's Delivery, Richmond, 10/25/95
Washington	1,328	New Frontier Lanes, Tacoma, 2/14/92
West Virginia	1,274	White Oak, Oak Hill, 4/1/90
Wisconsin	1,338	Bluemond Bowl, Milwaukee, 8/29/89
Wyoming	1,264	Sheridan Tent & Awning, Sheridan, 12/17/92

Canada

Province	Score	Name, Site, Date
Alberta		Not Available
British Columbia		Not Available
Manitoba	1,123	Turret, Winnipeg, 1934
Ontario	1,295	All-Star Pro Shop, Windsor, 12/12/94
Quebec		Not Available
Saskatchewan		Not Available

STATE, PROVINCIAL TEAM SERIES RECORDS

The following are the highest ABC recognized team three-game series in each state and province. Records should be reported to the Bowling Communications Department., 5301 S. 76th Street, Greendale, Wis. 53129, (414) 423-3224.

State	Score	Name, Site, Date
Alabama	3,431	McCorveys Sports Shop, Huntsville, 10/30/86
Alaska	3,606	Kings X, Anchorage, 3/29/96
Arizona	3,522	Chandler Truck Rental, Chandler, 11/10/87
Arkansas	3,611	Pleasure Pro Shop, Little Rock, 2/11/82
California	3,769	Williamson Shell, Sacramento, 3/15/73
Colorado	3,674	Western Bowlers Assn., Lakewood, 4/19/91
Connecticut	3,655	Ken Dunbar's Pro Shop, Woodbridge, 2/1/96
Delaware	3,530	Brandywine Club, Claymont, 12/2/80
Florida	3,644	Scott Paint, Tampa, 9/21/95
Georgia	3,479	Atlanta Housing Corporation, Atlanta, NA
Hawaii	3,791	Love's Ltd., Honolulu, 3/21/69
Idaho	3,566	Dietz's Duds, Meridian, 3/29/97
Illinois	3,748	Bel-Air Bowl, Belleville, 1/2/85
Indiana	3,784	Bill Morton's Pro Shop, Hammond, 5/13/94
Iowa	3,774	Hooter's, Des Moines, 2/13/95
Kansas	3,718	Gregg Security, Pittsburgh, 9/5/82
Kentucky	3,672	Kentuckiana Chemical, Louisville, 3/4/93
Louisiana	3,575	B&D Pro Shop, Kenner, 10/27/92
Maine	3,425	The Big Dogs, Portland, 2/11/96
Maryland	3,704	Baltimore Bowling News, Baltimore, 3/2/84
Massachusetts	3,648	PJ's Pro Shop, New Bedford, 1/25/95
Michigan	3,778	Saginaw All-Stars, Saginaw, 5/7/96
Minnesota	3,713	Hamm's Preferred Stock, St. Paul, 2/4/34
Mississippi	3,424	Full House, Jackson, 3/8/93
Missouri	3,858	Budweiser Beer, St. Louis, 3/12/58
Montana	3,588	Montana Jerky Co., Kalispell, 5/18/96
Nebraska	3,628	Old Milwaukee, Norfolk, 4/13/92
Nevada	3,404	Reno All-Stars, Reno, 5/22/82

State	Score	Name, Site, Date
N. Hampshire	3,446	Barns of Bradford, Manchester, 10/28/92
New Jersey	3,754	Faber Cement, Teaneck, 2/25/82
New Mexico	3,593	Sandia Bowl, Albuquerque, 8/28/87
New York	3,813	Vince Gance Agency, Endicott, 2/18/93
North Carolina	3,620	Bryant Realty, Charlotte, 12/6/94
North Dakota	3,645	Midway Lanes, Mandan, 3/22/87
Ohio	3,834	Ansted-Schuster, Toledo, 9/26/94
Oklahoma	3,711	Fistful O Johnson, Tulsa, 2/8/95
Oregon	3,689	Dream Team, Pendleton, 2/2/91
Pennsylvania	3,868	Hurst Bowling Supplies, Luzerne, 2/23/94
Rhode Island		Not Available
South Carolina	3,680	H+B Ball Factory, Greenville, 4/13/97
South Dakota		Not Available
Tennessee	3,746	Get You Summa That, Nashville, 10/6/97
Texas	3,757	Sports Palace, San Antonio, 8/26/78
Utah	3,572	Hilltop Lanes, Salt Lake City, 4/11/97
Vermont	3,523	Bill's Blasters, Plainfield, 5/4/91
Virginia	3,678	Steve's Delivery, Richmond, 10/25/95
Washington	3,619	Kenmore Village Lanes, Tacoma, 1972
West Virginia	3,654	5-Man, Parkersburg, 5/21/88
Wisconsin	3,758	Stack's Bar, Neenah, 1/31/90
Wyoming	3,509	Sheridan Tent & Awning, Sheridan, 12/17/92

CANADA

Province	Score	Name, Site, Date
Alberta		Not Available
British Columbia		Not Available
Manitoba	3,261	Turret, Winnipeg, 1934
Ontario	3,421	Bowlero Bowl, Windsor, 4/23/88
Quebec		Not Available
Saskatchewan		Not Available

STATE, PROVINCIAL INDIVIDUAL BEST SERIES

The following are the highest WIBC three-game series in each state and province. Any women's state or provincial records should be reported to the Bowling Communications Department at 5301 S. 76th St., Greendale , Wis. 53129, (414) 423-3224.

Province	Score	Name, Site, Date	Province	Score	Name, Site, Date
Alabama	812	Sandra Franklin, Birmingham, 12/10/96	New Mexico	833	Dana Miller-Mackie, Albuquerque, 3/20/95
Alaska	823	Jennifer Barron, Anchorage, 8/22/95	New York	856	Kathy Mc Neill, Vestal, 03/01/97
Arizona	822	Robin Tomlinson, Phoenix, 2/4/96			Jodi Musto, Latham, 1/25/95
		Vicki Frizzell, Mesa Valley, 12/10/96	North Carolina	815	Melanie Cooper Miller, Asheville, 4/17/94
Arkansas	827	Cindy Coburn-Carroll, North Little Rock, 7/15/96	North Dakota		Not Available
California	858	Kris Douglas, Garden Grove, 1993	Ohio	877	Jackie Mitskavich, Van Wert, 8/10/97
Colorado	825	Debbie McMullen, Aurora, 1/10/96	Oklahoma	826	Carla Haney, Tulsa, 11/9/93
Connecticut	815	Becky Kregling, Wallingford, 12/13/96	Oregon	812	Kathy Tribbey, Grants Pass, 9/7/96
Delaware	848	Patricia Renshaw, Wilmington, 1/24/96	Pennsylvania	823	Carol Zarr, Milton, 6/13/94
Florida	820	Judi Smimo, Lake Worth, 4/22/92	Rhode Island	822	Teresa Gosselin, Cranston, 1/23/95
Georgia	828	Lisa Wagner, Athens, 4/29/92	South Carolina	847	Jodi Hughes, Spartansburg, 4/11/95
Hawaii	803	Linda Painter, Barber Point, 1993	South Dakota	824	Michelle Soutar, Sioux Falls, 2/5/96
Idaho	797	Cheryl Carlsen, Idaho Falls, 1985-86	Tennessee	815	Shannon Duplantis, Paris, 10/18/97
		Leslie Styls, Idaho Falls, 1991-92	Texas	865	Anne Marie Duggan, Dallas, 7/16/93
Illinois	825	Leann Butts, Rockford, 12/30/96	Utah	793	Pam Sollami, Salt Lake City, 10/31/91
Indiana	834	Julie Meadows, Indianapolis, 3/25/97	Vermont		Not Available
Iowa	823	Stephanie Frey, Dubuque, 1995-96	Virginia	838	Shannon Duplantis, Newport News, 2/27/97
Kansas	823	Jodi Jensen, Wichita, 5/13/96	Washington	838	Kristy Whitcher, Bremerton, 9/11/97
Kentucky	814	Alisia Kellow, Louisville, 03/10/96	West Virginia	805	Diana Howard, Ceredo, 1996
Louisiana	845	Anne Marie Duggan, Alexandria, 2/27/95	Wisconsin	864	Diane Guttormsen Northern, Kenosha, 1996
Maine	755	Melissa D'Alfonso, city, date NA	Wyoming		Not Available
Maryland	826	Debbie Myers , Riverdale, 11/15/96			
Massachusetts	817	Shirley Silva, Brockton, 8/16/96			
Michigan	853	Tamika Glenn, Southfield, 1/30/97			
Minnesota	859	Patty Ann, New Ulm, 1984-85			
Missouri	841	Beth Kramer, St. Louis, 9/7/95			
Mississippi	801	Myra Sly, Ocean Springs, 1/29/97			
Montana	812	Fawn Lyons, Butte, 1/31/96			
Nebraska	837	Cynthia Kesterson, Papillion, 5/3/92			
Nevada	835	Cynthia Abasta, Reno, 10/18/96			
New Hampshire	771	Mary Ellen Thorne, Nashua, 1997			
New Jersey	837	Michele Bruno, Egg Harbor, 1/19/93			

Canada

Province	Score	Name, Site, Date
Alberta		Not Available
British Columbia	745	Sandra Chadwick, N. Vancouver, 1990
Manitoba		Not Available
Ontario	758	Karen Collura, Etobicoke, 1992
Quebec		Not Available
Saskatchewan		Not Available

STATE, PROVINCIAL TEAM GAME

The following are the highest WIBC team games in each state and province. Any women's state or provincial records should be reported to the Bowling Communications Department at 5301 S. 76th St., Greendale , Wis. 53129, (414) 423-3224.

Province	Score	Name, Site, Date	Province	Score	Name, Site, Date
Alabama		Not Available	Iowa	1,095	Dilts Trucking, Council Bluffs, 1985
Alaska	1,047	Flintstones, city, date NA	Kansas	1,215	Thunderbird Bowl, Wichita, 1997
Arizona	1,113	Wayne's Landscaping , Phoenix, 1993	Kentucky	1,115	Pat's Girls, Floyd-Pike Counties, 1993
Arkansas		Not Available	Louisiana	1,178	Sugar Bowl, New Orleans, 1995
California	1,131	Pacific Avenue Bowl, Stockton, 1986	Maine		Not Available
Colorado	1,109	James Drilling, Denver, 1985	Maryland		Not Available
Connecticut	1,047	We Blow Doors, city, date NA	Massachusetts		Not Available
Delaware		Not Available	Michigan	1,244	Chamberlain Wholesale, Detroit, 1987-88
Florida	1,132	JSBMC, Broward County, 1985	Minnesota	1,252	River Liquors, Minneapolis, 1995
Georgia		Not Available	Missouri	1,262	Drug Package Inc, St. Louis, 1993
Hawaii		Not Available	Mississippi	1,176	Here Barely, Gautier, 1996
Idaho		Not Available	Montana	1,032	Skyway Bowl Follies, Great Falls, 1990
Illinois	1,211	B.W. Enterprises, Blue Island, 1996	Nebraska	1,137	McGerr's Pro Shop, Lincoln, 1993
Indiana	1,228	Tatone's, Hobart, 1996			

Province	Score	Name, Site, Date
Nevada		Not Available
New Hampshire	915	Bowlers Annex, Merrimack
New Jersey	1,146	Joe Tolvay's Pro Shop, Bergen County, 1986
New Mexico	1,099	Chackwick Distributor, Albuquerque, 1986
New York	1,123	The Champions, Buffalo, 1985
North Carolina	1,068	The Bowling Center, Wilmington, 1986
North Dakota		Not Available
Ohio	1,209	Ohio Twirling Institute, Cleveland, 1979-80
Oklahoma	1,135	Penn 44 Pro Shop, Oklahoma City, 1986
Oregon	1,189	Bowlers Performance Center, Portland, 1993
Pennsylvania	1,210	Sheraton Inn, Scranton, 1981-82 Veltri & Sons Clothier, Scranton, 1984-85
Rhode Island		Not Available
South Carolina	1,067	Gutter Babes, Spartanburg, 6/8/96
South Dakota		Not Available

Province	Score	Name, Site, Date
Tennessee		Not Available
Texas	1,206	Oakhaven Animal Clinic, Fort Worth, 1990-91
Utah		Not Available
Vermont		Not Available
Virginia		Not Available
Washington	1,098	Daffodil $1111 Invitational, Valley, 1983
West Virginia		Not Available
Wisconsin	1,284	Ber Ben Rec, Green Bay, 1996
Wyoming		Not Available

Canada

Province	Score	Name, Site, Date
Alberta		Not Available
British Columbia		Not Available
Manitoba		Not Available
Ontario		Not Available
Quebec		Not Available
Saskatchewan		Not Available

STATE, PROVINCIAL TEAM SERIES RECORDS

The following are the highest WIBC-recognized team three-game series in each state and province. Any women's state or provincial records should be reported to the Bowling Communications Department at 5301 S. 76th St., Greendale , Wis. 53129, (414) 423-3224.

Province	Score	Name, Site, Date
Alabama		Not Available
Alaska		Not Available
Arizona	3,158	Wayne's Landscaping, Phoenix, 1993
Arkansas		Not Available
California		Not Available
Colorado	3,347	Us and Them, Denver, 1990
Connecticut	3,003	Free Flying Five, Hartford, 1984
Delaware		Not Available
Florida	3,211	Boo's Bowlers, Tampa, 1996
Georgia		Not Available
Hawaii		Not Available
Idaho		Not Available
Illinois	3,384	Cook County Sales, Chicago, 1991-92
Indiana	3,134	Marbaugh Eng. Supply No. 2, Indianapolis, 1993
Iowa	3.,115	Sammy G. Lanes, Davenport-Bettendorf, 1993
Kansas	3,323	Compforms Inc., Wy-Jon, 1986
Kentucky		Not Available
Louisiana	3,016	Sugar Bowl Lanes, Slidell, 1996
Maine		Not Available
Maryland		Not Available
Massachusetts		Not Available
Michigan	3,507	Contour Power Grips, Livonia, 1996
Minnesota	3,122	Diamond Lake Fun Center, Minneapolis, 1985
Missouri	3,446	Drug Package Inc, St. Louis, 1993
Mississippi		Not Available
Montana	2,830	Spare Parts, Great Falls, 1993
Nebraska	3,466	Strike More Spareless, Lincoln, 1997
Nevada		Not Available
New Hampshire	2,681	Let it Be, Merrimack
New Jersey	3,378	Canadian Club, Kenilworth, 1983-84

Province	Score	Name, Site, Date
New Mexico	2,996	Chadwick Distributor, Albuquerque, 1986
New York	3,042	D.W. Christopher Plumbing, Buffalo, 1984
North Carolina		Not Available
North Dakota		Not Available
Ohio	3,416	Plaza Lanes, Dayton, 1997
Oklahoma		Not Available
Oregon	3,405	Bowlers Performance Center, Portland, 1993
Pennsylvania	3,307	Tetterton's Pro Shop, Reading, 1990
Rhode Island		Not Available
South Carolina	2,859	Gutter Babes, Spartanburg, 6/8/96
South Dakota		Not Available
Texas	3,177	Twacy-N-Da-Supwemes, San Antonio, 1993
Utah	2,957	McIntyre Center, Salt Lake City, 1984
Vermont		Not Available
Virginia		Not Available
Washington	3,151	Daffodil $1111 Invitational, Valley, 1983
West Virginia		Not Available
Wisconsin	3,219	S + D Auto Body, Milwaukee, 1983
Wyoming		Not Available

Canada

Province	Score	Name, Site, Date
Alberta		Not Available
British Columbia		Not Available
Manitoba		Not Available
Ontario		Not Available
Quebec		Not Available
Saskatchewan		Not Available

Note: Space limitations prohibit printing more than the top records in many of the following listings. Although some categories are not kept by ABC, WIBC or YABA, all listings that have been compiled are included here. For complete records on any category, or to report any information relating to this section, contact the Bowling Communications Department at (414) 423-3224.

Ages, highest games over 200 *
Women
101 Mollie Marler, N. Kansas City, Mo., 202 game, 1985-86.
85 Bertha Arnold, Amarillo, Texas, 243, March 4, 1995.
84 Gertrude Schoonmaker, hometown unavailable.
81 Zora Evans, Des Moines, Iowa, 239 game, 1987-88.
76 Alma Fields, New York, 277 game, 1954-55.

Ages, oldest doubles teams *
Women
178 Ethel Brunnick, 96, Elsie Spicer, 82, Santa Monica, Calif., 1984 WIBC Championship Tournament.
176 Ethel Brunnick, 98, Elsie Mueller, 78, Santa Monica N. Hollywood, Calif., 1986 WIBC Championship Tournament.
172 Ethel Brunnick, 93, Elsie Spicer, 79, Santa Monica, Calif., 1981 WIBC Championship Tournament.
171 Myrtle Schulte, 85, St. Louis, Theresa Greishaber, 86, St. Joseph, Mo., 1978 Missouri WBA Tournament.

Ages, oldest league bowlers
Women
103 Maude McIntyre, Fresno, Calif., through 1993-94.
102 Mollie Marler, N. Kansas City, Mo., through 1986-87.
101 Mary Wagner, Newport, Ky., through 1984-85.
100 Beatrice Nelsen, Spencer, Iowa, through 1991-92.
 99 Ethel Brunnick, Santa Monica, Calif., through 1986-87.

Men
105 John Venturello, Sunrise, Fla., through 1992-93.
103 Fred Leinhos, Corning, N.Y., through 1995-96.
102 Walter Hargrave, Woodhull, N.Y., through 1994-95.
 Walter Rossow, Green Bay, Wis., through 1996-97.
101 Cecil Thompson, Steubenville, Ohio, through 1983-84
 William McIlvain, Collingswood, N.J., through 1974-75.
 Harry Elliott, Olympia, Wash., through 1990-91.

Ages, oldest teams †
Men
86.0 years Bowlin' Oldies, San Jose, Calif., 1993 California B.A. Tournament.
83.7 years Ray Orf's Pro Shop, St. Louis, 1987-88.
82.3 years Ray Orf's Pro Shop, St. Louis, 1985-86.
82.0 years Kiwanis Club, Indianapolis, 1990 Indiana B.A. Tournament.
81.0 years Legends, Omaha, Neb., 1994-95.

Ages, oldest twin league bowlers *
Women
86 Dorothy Grubbs and Lenora Shea, Hutcheson, Kan., through 1992-93.

All Events Scores, see Nine-Game Series, All-Time Scoring Records

All Events Titles, most by one family in one year
3 Jimmy, Paula and Mike Wilson, Wheatland, Wyo., 1981

All Events Titles, most in state/provincial tournament †
Men
5 Russ Gersonde, Milwaukee, won Wisconsin B.A. in 1943, 1947, 1951, 1953, 1961.
4 Al Toommel, Chicago, won Illinois B.A. in 1905, 1913, 1918, 1922.
 Eddie Meyer, Indianapolis, won Indiana B.A. in 1910, 1916, 1921, 1925.
 Willard Taylor, Charleston, won West Virginia B.A. in 1946, 1951, 1953, 1963.
 Bill Straub, Lincoln, won Nebraska B.A. in 1972, 1977, 1979 and 1980.

All-Spare Games, see Spares

Ambidextrous, 299, 300, and 800 in same season
Bryan Alpert, North Hills, Calif., 1996-97.

Attendance, individual, most years without an absence
Women
43 Nellie Marsura, Sequim, Wash., 1950-1993.
42 Arlene Henderson, Bay City, Mich., 1946-1988.
29 Betty Scott, Moscow, Idaho, 1958-1987.
 Eleanor Ellis, Pottstown, Pa., 1961-1990.
25 Marylou Wheeler, Stillwater, Okla., 1962-1987.
 Lorraine Schroeder, Eldora, Iowa, 1965-1990.
 Beverly Davis, Bradford, Pa., 1966-1992.

Men
45 1/2 Henry Wilz, Appleton, Wis., 1931-76.
45 E. Stanley Porter, White Plains, N.Y., 1931-76.
 George Stahl, Allentown, Pa., 1932-77.
44 Ben Towsley, Miami, 1945-89.
39 Ace Gilliam, San Antonio, 1958-97.

Attendance, team, most games without an absentee †
Men
13,680 Burza's, Amsterdam, N.Y., no games missed 1958-88.
 5,110 Camp Three, Forest Center, Minn., no games missed 1954-64.

Average, champion in league most years †
Men
31 Leonard Lavelle Jr., Scranton, Pa., 1953-84.
30 Boyd Pexton, Salt Lake City, 1958-88.
21 Edgar Roberts, Schenectady, N.Y., 1940-61.
20 John Fazzone, Scotia, N.Y., 1956-74.
17 Harold Krusic, Escanaba, Mich., 1962-77, 1979-81.

* — Men's records not on file   † — Women's records not on file

Average, highest per team, entire league †
Men
1,093	Dominics and Carlitas, Toledo, Ohio, 1993-94 (8 teams).
1,091	Wednesday Night Men's Major, Reading, Pa., 1995-96, 10 teams.
1,090	Bonanza All-Star, Detroit, 1987-88 (18 teams).
1,084	Greater Toledo Cleaning Service Classic, Toledo, Ohio, 1994-95 (10 teams).
1,072	Bluemound Metro, Milwaukee, 1992-93 (8 teams).

Average, individual, highest without a 600 series †
Men
192	Edward Mullen, Schenectady, N.Y., 1932-33. (Best 599)
187	Robert Aspinwall, Ft. Atkinson, Wis., 1939-40. (Best 599)
	Alan DeRicco, Reno, Nev., 1965-66. (Best 599)
	Paul Sander, Great Bend, Kan., 1986-87. (Best 599)
186	Bob Adams, Columbus, Ohio, 1946-47. (Best 589)
	A.M. Hazelgreen, Gary, Ind., 1919-20. (Best 599)
	Glen Squier, Reno, Nev., 1950-51. (Best 599)

Averages, highest by size of league team (See pg. 2 for all-time average records)
Five-Player Team
Women
228	Paulette Karwoski, Taylor, Pa., 1982-83.
	Aleta Sill, Dearborn, Mich., 1987-88.
224	Vicki Fischel, Wheat Ridge, Colo., 1987-88.
	Gayle Racette, San Diego, 1987-88.
221	Paulette Karwoski, Taylor, Pa., 1984-85.
	Stephanie Frey, Dubuque, Iowa, 1990-91.

Men
245.6	Paul Geiger, Jamestown, N.Y., 1989-90.
245.2	Doug Vergouven, Harrisonville, Mo., 1989-90.
	Timothy Zelger, Red Lion, Pa., 1988-89.
244.9	Chris Riga, Allentown, Pa., 1983-84.
244.2	Bob Learn Jr., Erie, Pa., 1987-88.

Four-Player Team
Women
224	Tish Johnson, Panorama City, Calif., 1981-82.
221	Debbie Rainone, Highland Heights, Ohio, 1979-80.
	Debbie Rainone, Highland Heights, Ohio, 1982-83.
219	Jeanne Maiden-Naccarato, Tacoma, Wash., 1982-83.
218	Joann Peworchik, Binghamton, N.Y., 1987-88.

Men
246.7	Mark Crawford, York, Pa., 1995-96.
245.6	Doug Vergouven, Harrisonville, Mo., 1989-90.
244.8	Kirk Gooding, Lancaster, Pa., 1996-97.
242.2	Bill Spigner, Chicago, 1987-88.
241.1	Skip Vigars Jr., Schenectady, N.Y., 1989-90.

Three-Player Team
Women
228	Caren Park, Seattle, 1991-92.
219	Caren Park, Seattle, 1992-93.
217	Mary Martha Cerniglia, Springfield, Ill., 1987-88.
216	Robin Romeo, Newhall, Calif., 1983-84.
	Robin Romeo, Newhall, Calif., 1986-87.
	Caren Park, Seattle, 1987-88.

247.9	Jeff Phipps, Salem, Ore., 1992-93.
241.1	Paul Zevgolis, Richmond, Va., 1991-92.
239.4	James Lewis, Schenectady, N.Y., 1975-76.
238.3	Bob Pinkalla, Milwaukee, 1959-60.
236.5	Mark McClain, Rochester, N.Y., 1986-87.

Two-Player Teams
Women
225	Barbara Thorberg, Florissant, Mo., 1982-83.
223	Sharon Nasta, Kenilworth, N.J., 1981-82.
222	Barbara Thorberg, Florissant, Mo., 1974-75.
	Patty Ann, Arlington Heights, Ill., 1987-88.
221	Barbara Thorberg, Florissant, Mo., 1983-84.

Men
251.0	Russ Hunt, Ogden, Utah, 1995-96.
241.4	Tony Tarsio, Newburgh, N.Y., 1975-76.
239.2	Len Reyngoudt, Albany, N.Y., 1989-90.
236.4	Ron Priester, Albany, N.Y., 1989-90.
236.1	Chuck O'Donnell, St. Louis, 1961-62.

Singles League
Women
234	Liz Johnson, Niagara Falls, N.Y., 1993-94
232	Patty Ann, Arlington Heights, Ill., 1983-84.
231	Patty Ann, Arlington Heights, Ill., 1991-92.
230	Patty Ann, Arlington Heights, Ill., 1984-85.
	Patty Ann, Arlington Heights, Ill., 1992-93.

Men
239.0	David Kowalski, Bay City, Mich., 1983-84.
238.0	Frank Tavella Jr., Denver, 1978-79.
233.4	Woody Crist, Williamsport, Pa., 1984-85.
233.0	Mickey Mariani, Clifton, N.J., 1958-59.

Averages, highest by senior bowlers *
Women
214	E. Lois Morgan, Kansas City, Mo., 1996-97.
212	E. Lois Morgan, Kansas City Mo., 1996-97.
210	E. Lois Morgan, Kansas City Mo., 1995-96.
204	Jean Baggerly, Kansas City, Mo., 1995-96.
201	Gloria Zaesch, Portland, Ore., 1991-92.

Averages, most high average awards *
Women
7	Patty Ann, Arlington Heights, Ill.
4	Millie Ignizio, Rochester, N.Y.
	Marion Ladewig, Grand Rapids, Mich.
	Barbara Thorberg, Florissant, Mo.

Averages, most improved season-to-season in pins *
Women
52	Roe Harper, Aurora, Ill., 1961-62 average 78; 1962-63 average 130.
45	Betty Chambers, Asheville, N.C., 1988-89 average 83; 1989-90 average 128.
39	Theresa Carrington, Southeastern, United Kingdom, 1988-89 average 105; 1989-90 average 144.
37	Cathy Halland, Puyallup, Wash., 1984-85 average 130; 1985-86 average 167.
36	Lee Parkson, Kansas City, Mo., 1984-85 average 98; 1985-86 average 134.

* — Men's records not on file   † — Women's records not on file

Average, most pins below in one game †
Men

152   Anthony Delahanty, Chandler, Ariz., April 21, 1993, rolled 62 with 214 average.

148   George Stieber, Detroit, 1952, rolled 9 with 157 average.

147   Ed Houser, Palmyra, Pa., rolled 39 with 186 average.

134   Fiore Conti Jr., Dunkirk, N.Y., May 19, 1976, rolled 70 with 204 average.

123   Harold Austin, Flint, Mich., Feb. 18, 1954, rolled 17 with 110 average.

Average, most pins difference in two leagues †
Men

48   Jack Hayman, Roseburg, Ore., 1953-54 122 and 170.

47   K.M. Murray, Washington D.C., 1960-61 98 and 145.

46   Glen Stilgebover, Chehalis, Wash., 1953-54 96 and 142. Leigh Hunt Jr., Wilmington, Del. 88 and 134. Joseph Verducci, Hackensack, N.J., 1977-78 139 and 185.

Averages, most 200 averages held in one season *
Women

7   Susan Behr, Clayton, Ohio, 1987-88. Donalda Williams, Independence, Mo., 1994-95.

6   Rose Kotnik, Brook Park, Ohio, 1979-80, 1980-81 and 1982-83. Linda Kelly, Huber Heights, Ohio, 1988-89. Donna Sipniewski, Dayton, Ohio, 1990-91. Cindy Suber, Dayton, Ohio, 1992-93.

Beginner, highest first game †
Men

253   Rollie (Bud) Terrell, Bloomfield, Iowa, Aug. 28, 1974.

234   Bob Pinard, Waterbury, Conn., Dec. 13, 1961.

231   Norris Nevins, Godfrey, Ill., Sept. 4, 1963.

222   John Malyerck, Columbia, S.C., Sept. 28, 1978.

201   Arthur Besen, Scranton, Pa., 1954.

Brothers, highest series by all-brother team †

3,432   Domzalski, Cleveland, Ohio, Dec. 4, 1992.

3,412   Sutter, St. Louis, Feb. 1, 1977.

3,378   Sutter, St. Louis, Sept. 7, 1976.

3,252   Lundberg, Kenosha, Wis., Feb. 22, 1945.

3,234   Fill, Detroit, December 1968.

Duplicate Averages, teammates †
Men

180   Peoria Bowl Recreation, Peoria, Ill., all five men in 1949-50 season.

171   Pete's Bait Shop, Joliet, Ill., all five men in 1985-86 season.

167   Oberle Trailers, Syracuse, N.Y., all five men in 1960-61 season.

Duplicate Games, consecutive †
Men

8   Stan Kodish, Toledo, Ohio, March 1988 (202)

7   Bob Barker, Wayne, N.J., January 1954 (158).

6   Tom Burchard, Wheeling, Ill., April 12-15, 1964 (181). Since then five others have achieved this feat including Lawrence Buller, who bowled six consecutive 180 games March 23, 1992 at the ABC Tournament in Corpus Christi, Texas.

Duplicate Games, individual in same day
Women

190   Ilse Haenish, Warren AFB, Wyo., five consecutive.

Men

180   Lawrence Buller, Corpus Christi, Texas, 1992, six consecutive.

Duplicate Games, individuals on same team
Women

190   The Strikers, St. Louis, April 4, 1993, all four.

178   Capitol Janitorial, Bismarck, N.D., 1979-80, all four.

170   Mayville WBA Team, Mayville, Mich., 1986-87, all five.

144   Lee Lowery Pro Shop, Milwaukee, 1979-80, all four.

Men

201   Kilmer's Flagstone, Clarks Summit, Pa., Feb. 26, 1987, all five.

192   Moffat's Ale, Syracuse, N.Y., 1936, all five. Coors, Miami, Ariz., Oct. 4, 1962, all five.

189   Tony's Truck & Trailer, Pittsburgh, May 4, 1972, all five.

185   Welfare Finance, Cincinnati, 1942, all five.

Duplicate Games and Series, highest by mixed-doubles teams

511   Catherine Nalley and John Augustyn, Trenton, N.J., each bowled 164-182-165, 1961-62.

507   Donna Bronkowski and Jerry Bronkowski, Toledo, Ohio, 186-159-162, 1984-85.

445   Mr. and Mrs. Walter Hauser, Milwaukee, 138-181-126, 1964-65.

Duplicate Series, consecutive in league
Men

5   Dominic Scruci, Philadelphia, Nov. 28-Dec. 26, 1943 (618).
Women

4   Myrtle Richards, Shelby, Ind., September 1966 (374).

Duplicate Series, five-player teams †
Men

528   Rex-King of Discounting, Grand Rapids, Mich., March 26, 1975.

510   Rockets, Hawthorne, Calif., Feb. 22, 1961.

473   Frey's B & G, Brooklyn, N.Y., Dec. 1, 1953.

Duplicate Series, four-player teams †
Men

541   Arlington Legion, Arlington, S.D., April 1, 1962.

531   Geneva Foundry, Geneva, N.Y., March 9, 1966.

516   Ankeny Lanes, Des Moines, Iowa, Oct. 6, 1974.

513   Honiotes Brothers Supermarket, Joliet, Ill., March 6, 1961.

500   Lakeland Ledger, Lakeland, Fla., Nov. 27, 1967.

---

* — Men's records not on file   † — Women's records not on file

Duplicate Series, three-player teams *
Women
523 Tarry Smith, Patty Surface, Deedee Barney, Portland, Ore., Feb. 26, 1993.
464 Lou Gouger, Jack Branigan, Ruth Schultz, Redlands, Calif., 1990-91.
414 Betty Briscoe, Marilyn Talley, Sharon Ringer, Edmond, Okla., 1986-87.

Duplicate Series, identical games
Women
546 Lynne Schmitz, Mukwonago, Wis., bowled 139-169-238, March 5, 1983, and March 9, 1983, Red Carpet West Allis, West Allis, Wis.
385 Ellie Murray, Cleveland, bowled 143-129-113 Jan. 15, 1980, and Jan. 22, 1980, State League, Cleveland Athletic Club.
358 Helen Goodknecht, St. Johns, Mich., bowled 108-129-121 Feb. 8, 1996 and Feb. 15, 1996.

Men
564 Charles Mase, Howard AFB, Canal Zone, bowled 177-184-203 May 22, 1970, Merry Mixers and Friday Night Men's leagues.
561 John Wertz, Chappell, Neb., bowled 170-168-223 Sept. 9, 1974 and Oct. 21, 1974, Monday Night Men's league.
499 Tommy Miller, Ada, Okla., bowled 193-167-139 Jan. 27, 1996 and Feb. 3, 1996, Boomer-Sooner League
471 Harry Van Atten, Fairview, Pa., bowled 147-171-153 Jan. 29, 1974 and Feb. 5, 1974, Tuesday Night Men's league.
468 Paul Metlin, Jacksonville, Fla., bowled 146-145-177 Nov. 8, 1987 and Nov. 15, 1987, Mandarin Strikers league.

Duplicate Series, highest by individual in same day *
Women
489 Deanne McDevitt, Reading, Pa., bowled three identical series on same day, Gem League (two sessions) and Ladies Suburban League, 1979-80.

Duplicate Series, highest in tournaments by individuals *
Women
545 Linda Chenery, Philadelphia WBA Tournament, 1996, (team, doubles and singles)
478 Janet Carter, Eugene, Ore., Eugene WBA Tournament, 1985 (singles, doubles and team events).
404 Bonnie Rail, Chewelah, Wash., Chewelah WBA Tournament, 1978 (singles, doubles and team events).
372 Billie Cutshaw, Kingston, Tenn., Kingston WBA Tournament, 1979-80 (singles, doubles and team events).
363 Margaret Cupp, Chewelah, Wash., Chewelah WBA Tournament, 1981 (singles, doubles and team events).

Duplicate Series, highest with identical games by two-player teams *
Women
521 Nancy Boynton-Mary Lou Reed, Columbia, S.D., (games of 190, 172 and 159), 1969 South Dakota WBA Tournament.

Duplicate Series, highest with identical series by opposing three-player teams *
Women
1,438 Friday Nite Busy Ladies League, Elmira, N.Y., Elmira Bowling Center, November 1980. Elmira Bowling Center team: Myrtle Moran, 145-128-168/441; Marjorie Stroman, 203-145-197/545; and Grace Thomas, 171-145-136/452. Viscelli's Kitchen team: Beverly Querry, 149-155-148/452; Carol McDonald, 146-135-160/441; and Carol Vargeson, 163-171-211/545.

Dutch 200 Games, consecutive †
Men
2 Henry Ostram, Jacksonville, Fla., October 1942. George Paterson, Burbank, Calif., 1949-50. Charles Ciardo, Milwaukee, Oct. 24, 1951. Mark Palmer, Jackson, Wis., March 6, 1997.

Dutch 200 Games, season†
Men
3 William Morland, Detroit, 1943-44. Henry Dodge, Schenectady, N.Y., 1963-64.

Errorless Games, consecutive †
Men
65 Skang Mercurio, Cleveland, 1929. He missed the 10 pin in ninth frame of 66th game.

Errors, fewest in league season †
Men
1 Tom Zavakos, Dayton, Ohio, 1925-26, All-Star, 214 average.
2 Roy Davis, Chicago, 1922-23, Randolph, 188 average.
3 Herman Lehmpuhl, Chicago, 1925-26, Randolph, 190 average. John Blue, Indianapolis, 1931-32, Washington, 200 average.

Fouls, most in league game †
Men
15 Bud Mathieson, Ocean Beach, Calif., Dec. 30, 1946.
9 Art Lundberg, Seattle, 1942.

Fouls, most in league series †
Men
37 Bud Mathieson, Ocean Beach, Calif., Dec. 30, 1946.

Fouls, most in tournament game †
Men
9 Bert (Bill) Allen, Etain, France, Dec. 21, 1963.

* — Men's records not on file   † — Women's records not on file

Game, highest without marks
Women
90   Mildred Gross, Stockton, Ill., 1952-53.
     Alma Kunes, Oakford, Pa., March 26, 1992.

Men
90   Mike Daugherty, Wooster, Ohio, Oct. 29, 1968.
     Bill Chestnut, Springfield, Ill., 1977 ABC Tournament.
89   Glenn Hamm, Middletown, Ohio, April 10, 1984.
88   Jim Dunn, Chicago, May 9, 1964.
87   Ken Larson, Beresford, S.D., March 1965.

Game, lowest in league play †
Men
2   Mike Kappa, Racine, Wis., Sept. 20, 1981,
     Kankakee.
3   Richard Caplette, Danielson, Conn., Sept. 7, 1971,
     Quinebaug Valley.
7   Don Wickenhause, Bloomington, Ill., Sept. 8, 1961,
     G-E Employees.
9   George Stieber, Detroit, September 1952,
     Detroit Post Office.
17   Harold Austin, Flint, Mich., 20th Century.

Game Margins, greatest
Women
212   Lynne Santucci, Rochester, N.Y., 87-299, 1971-72.
204   Kathy Haverland, Miamitown, Ohio, 94-298,
     1985-86.
201   Sandy Stanhope, Boyne City, Mich., 99-300,
     1982-83.
199   Carlen M. Henry, Foresthill, Calif., 101-300,
     1986-87.
193   Kellie Luster, Canyon County, Calif., 300-107,
     1980-81.

Men
213   Jeff Tyler, Phoenix, 299-86, Nov. 5, 1979.
     Reed Townley, Gadsen, Ala., 87-300,
     Jan. 18, 1989
208   Willie Calloway Jr., Detroit, 298-90, Aug. 1, 1975.
203   William Benard, Shreveport, La., 300-97,

Games, greatest game-to-game decrease by team †
Men
430   Seven Up, St. Louis, Oct. 3, 1950 (1,238-808).
368   Reed Bus Co., Kansas City, Nov. 9, 1971 (1,227-859).
351   Melton Motors, Bryan, Ohio, 1967-68 (1,022-671).
341   Cherry Creek Inns, Denver, 1965-66 (1,114-773).
     Raritan Liquors, Bernardsville, N.J., March 12,
     1970 (975-634).

Games, greatest game-to-game increase by team †
Men
420   Regal Window and Door, Green Bay, Wis.,
     Nov. 13, 1992 (795-1,215).
363   Sani-Flush, Canton, Ohio, Jan. 22, 1934
     (926-1,289).
359   Fashion Award Cleaners, Manitowoc, Wis.,
     Nov. 18, 1960 (699-1,058).
348   Spring Partners, Leawood, Kan., Aug. 30, 1995
     (682-1,030).

345   Maple Dale, Bremerton, Wash., Jan. 26, 1961
     (836-1,179).

Games, highest "low game" in a team game †
Men
266   Todd Courtwright, Springfield, Ill., May 1, 1993
     (team had 1,410).
255   Curt Elliott, San Antonio, 1978 (team had 1,324).
     Mark Ivancik, Toledo, Ohio, Feb. 25, 1995
     (team had 1,326).
251   Therman Gibson, Detroit, Jan. 4, 1950 (team had 1,284).
249   Gary Shultis, Levitown, N.Y., Jan. 11, 1982 (team
     had 1,289).
     Bob Buckery, Luzerne, Pa., Feb. 24, 1994 (team
     had 1,351)

Games, highest "low game" in a team series †
Men
234   Tom Cleary Jr., Muscatine, Iowa, Feb. 21, 1995
     (team had 3,739).
     Del Kissinger, Muscatine, Iowa, Feb. 21, 1995
     (team had 3.379).
     Larry Roberson, Muscatine, Iowa, Feb. 21, 1995
     (team had 3,379).
222   Pat Patterson, St. Louis, March 12, 1958 (team had
     3,858).
217   Buzz Wilson, St. Louis, Jan. 27, 1937 (team had
     3,797).
     Chad Wiese, Toledo, Ohio, April 15, 1996
     (team had 3,744)

Games, highest with gutter ball *
Women
290   Mary Ellen Handley, Pompano Beach, Fla., 1980-81.

Games, highest combined match play
Women
567   Dana Stewart, Mountain View, Calif. (300), and
     Ann Harrison, N. Highlands, Calif. (267),
     Western Women Professional Bowlers
     Tournament, April 1978.
556   Lucy Giovinco, Norcross, Ga. (279), and Sharie
     Langford, Canoga Park, Calif. (277), LPBT
     Clearwater Classic, Shore Lanes,
     Clearwater, Fla., February 1982.
Men
600   Steve Carson and Rev. Jim Shifflet, Oklahoma City,
     July 2, 1979 (league). Since then, six
     other duos have achieved this feat.

Games, highest in senior leagues *
Women
300   Josephine Borges, Oakland, Calif., 1973-74.
     Evelyn Culbert, Austin, Minn., April 3, 1992.
     Valerie Gray, Edinboro, Pa., Dec. 10, 1993.
     Dee Sargent, Bakersfield, Calif., April 21, 1994
279   Josie Rosenbaum, Salt Lake City, 1990-91.

Games, most pins over average, individual
Women
188   Diane Ponza, Santa Cruz, Calif., 112 average,
     300 game, 1977-78.
183   Jan Purdy, Minneapolis, 94 average, 277 game,
     1975-76.

---

* — Men's records not on file   † — Women's records not on file

179   Margaret Owens, Beloit, Wis., 111 average, 290
          game, 1969-70.
       Judy Sikes, Denver, 121 average, 300 game,
          1984-85.
178   Wanda Hinton, East Point, Ga., 109 average,
          287 game, 1966-67.

Men

182   Richard Berry, Pontiac, Mich., 299 with 117
          avg. April 8, 1979.
173   Roger Evans, Champaign, Ill., 300 game with
          127 avg. April 12, 1991.
171   Leo Terry, Chicago, 299 with 128 avg., 1939.
167   Larry Senter, Fenton, Mich., 300 with 133 avg.
          Dec. 5, 1988.
164   John Kunz, Plymouth, Mich., 277 with 113 avg.
          April 9, 1973.

Games, most pins over average, team †

Men

412   Hansen Jewelers, Maywood, Calif., Feb. 18, 1944,
          1,262 with 850 avg.
357   S & W Liquor, Trenton, N.J., Sept. 5, 1980, 1,263
          with 906 avg.
346   Tom Long's Bowling Supply, Whittier, Calif.,
          Sept. 29, 1975, 1,199 with 853 avg.
332   Budweiser Beer, Zanesville, Ohio, Dec. 12, 1968,
          1,252 with 920 avg.
314   Wayne Foundry Stamping, Warren, Mich., Oct. 5,
          1973, 1,101 with 787 avg.

Gutter Balls, consecutive †

Men

19   Richard Caplette, Danielson, Conn., Sept. 7, 1971
10   Don Wickenhause, Bloomington, Ill., Sept. 8, 1961

Gutter Balls, game †

Men

19   Richard Caplette, Danielson, Conn., Sept. 7, 1971.
18   Don Wickenhause, Bloomington, Ill., Sept. 8, 1961.
       Mike Kappa, Racine, Wis., Sept. 20, 1981.
12   Bill Lenaburg, Arcadia, Calif., March 30, 1961.
8   Al Fifer, Detroit, 1944.

Hall of Fame, husband, wife and son or daughter
Joe and Marie Fulton and daughter Gene, Indianapolis;
    Stanley and Lena Moskal and son Charles, Saginaw, Mich.

Hall of Fame, three generations
David Luby, Mort Sr. and Mort Jr., Chicago, ABC

League, closest finish at end of season
Men
Moose, Nampa, Idaho, 1953-54:

	W	L
Nampa Neon Co.	50 1/2	49 1/2
Rogers Plumbing	50 1/2	49 1/2
The Schooner	50 1/2	49 1/2
Moose Lodge	50	50
Cash Inn	50	50
Show'r Chevrolet	48 1/2	51 1/2

* — Men's records not on file

League, largest five player †
Men
80   Moslem Shrine, Detroit, 1966-67.
64   MSA Monday Night, Houston, 1982-83.
62   Moslem Shrine, Detroit, 1975-76.
58   Torrington Merchants, Torrington, Conn., 1963-64.
48   Playtime Men's, Toronto, Ont., 1965-66.
       Parson's Recreation League, Columbus, Ohio, 1997-1998

League, largest mixed †
136   World's Largest Couples, Waukesha, Wis., 1983-84.
64   Wood Vending, Indianapolis, 1978-79.
56   Comfort Inn East, Toledo, Ohio, 1994-95.
52   Royal Kings and Queens, Chicago.
       Baskin-Robbins Mixed, Indianapolis, 1978-79.
       Retired Servicemen, Louisville, Ky., 1996-1997

League, largest senior †
Men
56   Windsor Original Seniors, Windsor, Ont., 1993-94.
50   Executive Prime Timers, Louisville, Ky., 1997-1998.

League, most years consecutive
Women
65   Rose Freshley, Coconut Creek, Fla., through 1992-93.
55   Norma Viola Hagen O'Conner, River Grove, Ill.,
          through 1996-1997
53   Beulah Buzzard, Toledo, Ohio, through 1993-94.
50   Polly Grogg, Vancouver, B.C., through 1994-95.
47   Helen Sadler, Central Square, N.Y., through 1993-94.

Men
76   Clarence George, Saginaw, Mich., 1919-1995.
72   Bill Bailey, Hamilton, Ontario, 1906-78.
70   Lewis Saad, Detroit, 1927-97.
69   L.J. Markwardt, Madison, Wis., 1918-86.
66   Fred Fuller, Janesville, Wis., 1920-86.

Leagues, longest schedules in weeks
Women
66   National Record League, Kingston, S.C., Jan. 23,
          1985, through May 7, 1986.
64   Zodiac Christmas League, Del Rio, Texas, Sept. 13,
          1979, through Dec. 11, 1980.
62   Bowlerama Mixed Classic, San Antonio, 1958-59.

Men
64   Zodiac Shirt Christmas, Del Rio, Texas, 1979-80.
62   Bowlerama Mixed Classic, San Antonio, 1958-59.

Leagues, most consecutive championships
Women
9   Jennings Auto Body, Paxton, Ill., 1985-86 through
          1993-94.
8   A & W Drive-In, Wellington, Kan., 1961-62 through
          1968-69.
       A.A. Andersons, Inc., Harvard, Ill., 1965-66 through
          1972-73.
Men
20   L.D. Ranch, Wheatland, Wyo., 1966-67
          through 1985-86.
15   Anderson Motor Sales, Fairview, Pa., 1945-59.
11   Service Iron Steel, Akron, Ohio, 1947-58.
       Howard Sober Trucking, Springfield, Ohio, 1973-84.

† — Women's records not on file

10   U-Hooties, 1942-52.
       T&O Lanes, Oshkosh, Wis., 1963-73.

Leagues, most consecutive losses
Women
132   Peanuts, Hammond, Ind., 1972-73 (105) and
       1973-74 (27).
99   Mead Containers, Denver, 1970-71.
95   TV Times, Kennewick, Wash., 1976-77.
Men
120   Downes Construction, Moravia, N.Y., 1965-66 (96)
       and 1966-67 (24).
113   B & D Printers, South Bend, Ind., 1979-80 (105)
       and 1980-81 (8).
108   Tenny Lumber Co., East Aurora, N.Y., 1974-75 (88)
       and 1975-76 (20).
105   Team No. 8, Denver, 1985-86.
105   St. Leo Foresters, Cincinnati, 1942-43 and 1943-44.

Leagues, most in one center
120   Southland Lanes, Flint, Mich., 1970-71 (76 lanes).
87   Highland Bowl, Moline, Ill., 1990-91 (48 lanes).
81   National Lanes, Dayton, Ohio, 1955-56 (48 lanes).
77   McCook Bowl, Dayton, Ohio, 1955-56 (44 lanes).
65   Gage Park Recreation, Chicago, 1952-53 (38 lanes).

Leagues, most in one day †
Men
5   Si Hewitt, Lincoln, Neb., 1970-71, 1975-76, 1976-77.
       Eric Jensen, Lincoln, Neb. 1995-1996 (2)
4   Si Hewitt, Lincoln, Neb., 1969-70 (2), 1971-72,
       1975-76, 1976-77 (2), 1979-80.
       Eric Jensen, Lincoln, Neb., 1984-85, 1995-1996 (5)

Leagues, most in one week
Women
14   Betty Neely, Anaheim, Calif., 1960-61.
11   Addie Hicks, Los Angeles, 1972-73.
       Pauline Williams, Indianapolis, 1984-85.
10   El Raye Holden, Indianapolis, 1974-75.
       Pearl Giddens, Tampa, Fla., 1964-65.
       Beverly Cass, Slidell, La., 1981-82.
       Joetta Smith, Indianapolis, 1984-85.
       Hallene Walls, Wichita, Kan., 1985-86.
       Vivian Rider, Sheffield Lake, Ohio, 1990-91.

Men
19   Si Hewitt, Lincoln, Neb., 1976-77.
17   Si Hewitt, Lincoln, Neb., 1970-71, 1975-76.
       Arthur Howard, Detroit, 1975-76.
       Eric Jensen, Lincoln, Neb., 1995-1996
16   Si Hewitt, Lincoln, Neb., 1969-70.

Leagues, most in one season
32   Eric Jensen, Lincoln, Neb., 1995-1996.

League, most pins one night (6 teams) †
Men
20,132   Stroh's Major, Detroit (traveling), April 24,
          1988. Average of 3,355 per team and 223.6
          per individual.

League, most pins one night (8 teams) †
Men
27,525   Anheuser-Busch/BPA Masters Traveling,
          St. Louis, Aug. 14, 1984. Average
          of 3,440 per team and 229.37 per individual.

League, most pins one night (10 teams) †
Men
33,911   Wednesday Night Majors League, Reading, Pa.,
          Dec. 13, 1995. Average of 3,391.8 per team
          and 226.07 per individual.

League, most pins one night (12 teams) †
Men
41,253   Budweiser All-Star Traveling, Columbus, Ohio,
          Jan. 23, 1990. Average of 3,437.75 per team
          and 229.18 per individual.

League, most pins one night (14 teams) †
Men
45,619   Bud Light Metro Classic, North Kansas City,
          Mo., 1996-1997. Average of 3,258.5
          per team and 217.23 per individual.

League, most pins one night (16 teams) †
Men
53,752   Stroh's Beer Traveling Classic, Detroit, April 7,
          1994. Average of 3,359.5 per team and
          223.9 per individual.

League, most pins one night (18 teams) †
Men
61,128   Bonanza All-Star Classic, Detroit, 1987-88.
          Average of 3,396.00 per team and 226.44
          per individual.

League, most 700 series, one season †
Men
481   Damerow Ford Classic, Beaverton, Ore.,
       1992-93 (32 teams).
464   Northwest Indiana Classic, Hammond, Ind.,
       1993-94 (18 teams).
459   Northwest Indiana Classic, Hammond, Ind.,
       1992-93 (20 teams).
353   Wednesday Men's Major, Reading, Pa., 1995-1996
       (10 teams).
340   Classic Travel, Sacramento, Calif., 1996-97
       (16 teams).

Leagues, most 800 series, one season
12   Greater Toledo Cleaning Service Classic, Toledo, Ohio,
       1994-95 (10 teams).

Leagues, most simultaneously †
Men
2   Russ Stowell and Herb Spanholtz, San Diego,
       1939-40. Since then, many others have achieved
       this feat.

---

* — Men's records not on file   † — Women's records not on file

Leagues, most years on same teams *
Women

54 Viola Tanke, Erickson Bakery, LaCrosse, Wis., through 1991-92.

53 Betty Bilderbeck, All-American League, Springfield, Ill., through 1993-94.

51 Melba King, Babe's Restaurant, Des Moines, Iowa, through 1991-92.

45 Blanche Gates, Riverside Dress Shop, Pelican Rapids, Minn., through 1981-82.

44 Mae Bolt, Allgauer Restaurant, Chicago, through 1993-94.

Leagues, most years as president †
Men

48 Walter Alinger, Schenectady, N.Y., 1931-79, GEAA Shop.

44 Anthony Iannotti, Amsterdam, N.Y., 1932-76, Sunday Businessmen.

36 Bob Bullen, Miami, 1957-93, Southwest Handicap.

Leagues, most consecutive years as secretary
Women

52 Clara Logemann, Zach's on Friday League, Milwaukee, through 1991-92.

50 Norma Viola Hagen O'Conner, River Grove, Ill., through 1996-1997

46 Pearl Switzer, Regalette Monday Nite Ladies League, South Bend, Ind., through 1976-77.

45 Katie Green, Metro Pinbusters, Louisville, Ky., through 1991-92.

44 Edith Kazmeier, Just Ladies Rainbow League, Flint, Mich., through 1993-94.

Men

61 Emory Krauthoefer, Milwaukee, Nut, through 1969-70.

55 Douglas Ludwig, Stowe, Pa., West End Fire Co., through 1993.
Luther Greenwalt, Allentown, Pa., Commercial, through 1985-86.

53 Herb Hoppe, Racine, Wis., Wednesday Night, deceased.
Carl Cohen, Long Branch, N.J., Carl Cohen "Y", through 1991.

Leagues, most years as secretary
Men

65 Mike Canuso, Omaha, Neb., Booster Graphic Arts, Birchwood and North End Classic, through 1996-1997.

Leagues, most years as treasurer
Women

45 Katie Green, Metro Pinbusters, Louisville, Ky., through 1991-92.

41 Bertha Keenahan, D & H Ladies League, Menands, N.Y., through 1982-83.
Janet Curry, Union City, N.J., through 1995-96.

39 Yuki Koyama, Tues. Nite Wos League, Chewelah, Wash., through 1992-93.

34 Pearl Doll, American League, Bismarck, N.D., through 1986-87.

Men

48 L.K. Harper, Denver, Businessmen's, through 1966.

* — Men's records not on file

44 Arthur Michael, Fairview, Pa., Commerical 'B', through 1980-81.

42 Harold Hart, Peoria, Ill., Calumet, through 1973-74.

41 Tony Novello, Cincinnati, Ohio, Schoolmasters, through 1995-96.

39 W. Harry Zimmerman, Winnipeg, Man., Recreation, through 1964-65.

Leagues, oldest women's

72 Ladies Greater Omaha League, Omaha, Neb., through 1996-97.

70 Ladies City League, St. Paul, Minn., through 1996-97.

69 Palace League, Columbus, Ohio, through 1996-97.

66 Ladies Forest League, Columbus, Ohio, through 1988-89.

56 Ladies Whiteway League, Moline, Ill., through 1994-95.

Leagues, oldest men's

101 Drug Trade, Baltimore, through 1996-97.

100 Metropolitan Traveling, Pittsburgh, through 1996-97.

98 Tri-City Classic, Quad Cities, Ill.-Iowa, through 1996-97.
City, Winona, Minn., through 1996-97.

96 Philadelphia Artisans, Philadelphia, through 1996-97.
City Tenpin, Hamilton, Ontario, through 1996-97.
Westinghouse Tenpin, Pittsburgh, through 1996-97.

Leagues, oldest mixed

60 Suburban Mixed, Hackensack, N.J., through 1996-97.

53 Bird, Neenah, Wis., through 1980-81.

50 Friday Night Mixed, Ill., through 1996-97.

48 Suburban Mixed, Teaneck, N.J., through 1986-87.

45 Western Pacific, San Francisco, through 1981-82.

Lefthanders, highest individual series †
Men

899 Tom Jordan, Union, N.J., March 7, 1989.

898 Kevin Lickers, Nanticoke, Pa., Nov. 16, 1996.

886 Pat Landry, Lansing, Mich., Nov. 22, 1988.

885 John Wilcox Jr., Lewisburg, Pa., Nov. 6, 1972.

879 David Emerich, Lancaster, Pa., June 22, 1987.

Lefthanders, highest team series, league †
Men

3,627 DeLau Fire and Safety, Lansing, Mich., Dec. 4, 1990.

3,606 A/C Electric, Lansing, Mich., March 26, 1996.

3,592 DeLau Fire and Safety, Lansing, Mich., Oct. 3, 1989.

3,488 DeLau Fire and Safety, Lansing, Mich., Oct. 18, 1988.

3,466 DeLau Fire and Safety, Lansing, Mich., March 28, 1989.

Local Associations, most years as secretaries
Women

51 Pack Henry, Mt. Vernon, Ill., 1940-96.

45 Jo Mraz, Cleveland, 1918-63.
Meta Schwarz, Louisville, Ky., 1928-73.

43 Adeline Schoenherr, Neillsville, Wis., 1944-87.

42 Fran Briggs, Olean, N.Y., through 1951-93.

† — Women's records not on file

Men

55 William Mattison, Toledo, Ohio, 1913-67.
50 Ange Bell, Batavia, N.Y., 1948-97.
51 Fred Gutshall, Seven Mountains, Pa., 1942-93.
48 Charles Pacco, Glens Falls, N.Y., 1946-94.
45 J. Nelson Thurston, Lockport, N.Y., 1932-77.

Local Associations, most years as treasurers *
Women

53 Eva Gerleman, St. Louis, 1927-1980.
35 Yuki Koyama, Chewelah, Wash., 1954-1989.
33 Wanda Curry, Athens, Ill., 1961-1993.
32 Mary Elizabeth Davis, Logan, W.Va., through
   1994-95.
31 Rose Erdos, Canton, Ohio, 1962-93.

Losses, most games one season with only one win †
Men

139 Men's Bible Class, Pottsville, Pa., 1957-58.
98 Joyce Tavern, Newark, N.J., 1953-54.
   Sexton Ice Cream, Detroit, 1954-55.
95 Garabaldi Lodge, San Diego, 1948-49.
89 News-Sentinel, Fort Wayne, Ind., 1959-60.
   Hayes Trucking, Buffalo, N.Y., 1949-50.

Mixed Scores, see All-Time Scoring Records

Nine Pin Counts, consecutive †
Men

18 Pete Bland, Bremerton, Wash., Oct. 28, 1976.
17 Jim Margueratt, Stoney Creek, Ontario, Oct. 28, 1991.
15 Wayne Frauhiger, Decatur, Ind., Dec. 11, 1969.
   Owen Kearns Jr., Felton, Calif., Jan. 29, 1986.
14 Michael Emrich, Rochester, N.Y., 1969.

Open Frames, fewest by five player team in three game series †
Men

1 Burghardt Optical, Toledo, Ohio, April 15, 1996
   (rolled 3,744 with one miss).
2 Stroh's Beer, Detroit, Nov. 9, 1971 (rolled 3,671 with
   one split, one miss).
   Manor Bowl, Chicago, Nov. 11, 1972 (rolled 3,479
   with one split, one miss).
3 West Side Barbers, Corsicana, Texas, April 1964
   (rolled 2,960 with three splits).
   Coca-Cola, Detroit, Dec. 2, 1971 (rolled 3,460 with
   two misses, one split).

Open Frames, most consecutive without an open †
Men

244 Merrill Weaver, Columbus, Ohio, May 23-July 25,
   1944.
152 Russ Hunt, Salt Lake City, Oct. 31-Dec. 12, 1994.
119 Joe Accola, Chicago, September 1944.
109 Carl Chavez, Albuquerque, N.M., Nov. 11-Dec. 9,
   1992.
93 Ray Bluth, St. Louis, 1956 ABC Masters.

Perfect Games, (see 300 Games in All-Time Scoring Records)
Pins, individual, three consecutive league series †
Men

2,441 Ray Schanen, Milwaukee, 843, 761, 837,
   November 1958, one section of two
   section league.
2,439 David Frascatore, Fort Johnson, N.Y.,
   802, 824, 813, March 4-18, 1988,
   Amsterdam City.
2,405 Ossie Ragogna, St. Paul, Minn., 782, 802, 821,
   Jan. 21-Feb. 4,1934 , Twin Cities Classic.
2,332 Elvin Mesger, St. Louis, 855 762 715,
   Feb. 22-March 8, 1962, All-Star.
2,295 Bill Golembiewski, Detroit, 801 791 703,
   Dec. 16, 1959, Doubles (regular, makeup and
   advance matches).

Pins, individual, four consecutive league series †
Men

3,180 Ray Schanen, Milwaukee, 739, 843, 761, 837,
   November 1958, one section of two
   section league.
3,164 Elvin Mesger, St. Louis, 855, 762, 715, 832,
   Feb. 22-March 15, 1962, All-Star League.
3,099 David Frascatore, Ft. Johnson, N.Y.,
   March 4-25, 1988.
3,082 Ossie Ragogna, St. Paul, Minn., 677, 782, 802,
   821, Jan. 14-Feb. 4, 1934 , Twin Cities Classic.
3,030 Brian Stempel, Belleville, Ill., Nov. 3-Dec. 8, 1995,
   707, 766, 789, 768.

Pins, five-player team, two series, same night †
Men

7,115 Budweiser Beer, St. Louis, Oct. 10, 1957
   (3,514 and 3,601).

Pins, total by doubles teams in league game †
Men

1,064 Bob Kwolek-Ed Lubanski (568) vs. Joe Joseph-Billy
   Golembiewski (496), Detroit, April 13, 1960.
1,049 Don McClaren-Billy Welu (537) vs. Art Ziern-Ed
   Easter (512), St. Louis, April 18, 1955.

Pins, total by doubles teams in league series †
Men

2,981 Bob Kwolek-Ed Lubanski (1,582) vs. Joe Joseph-
   Billy Golembiewski (1,399), Detroit, April 13,
   1960.
2,952 Art Ziern-Ed Easter (1,483) vs. Don McClaren-Billy
   Welu (1,469), St. Louis, April 18, 1955.
   Luke Leach-Jerry Oster (1,477) vs. Bob Brayman-
   John Ruggiero (1,475), Detroit, Nov. 9, 1960.

Pins, total by five-player teams in league game †
Men

2,613 Riffles (1,313) vs. Leadoff Men (1,300),
   Highland, Ind., April 14, 1995.
2,552 Budweiser Beer (1,293) vs. Pulaski Savings
   (1,259), St. Louis, March 12, 1958.
2,534 Hermann's (1,325) vs. Budweiser Beer (1,209), St.
   Louis, Jan. 27, 1937.
2,505 Faber Cement (1,270) vs. Eclipse (1,235),
   Teaneck, N.J., Feb. 25, 1952.

* — Men's records not on file   † — Women's records not on file

Pins, total by five-player teams in league series †
Men
7,486 Michelob Masters (3,805) vs. Budweiser Eagles
(3,681), St. Louis, April 19, 1994.
7,352 Budweiser Beer (3,858) vs. Pulaski Savings
(3,494), St. Louis, March 12, 1958.
7,322 President Riverboat Casino (3,661) vs. Pro
Connection/Highland Park Bowl (3,661),
Davenport, Iowa, Sept. 19, 1996
7,254 Hermann's (3,797) vs. Budweiser Beer (3,457),
St. Louis, Jan. 27, 1937.
7,187 Faber Cement (3,754) vs. Eclipse (3,433),
Teaneck, N.J., Feb. 25, 1952

Prize Money, most won in one event *
Women
$100,000 Tish Johnson, Northridge, Calif., Super Hoinke
Classic, Cincinnati, 1996
55,500 Catherine Schroeder, Hamilton, Ontario, Hoinke
Classic, Cincinnati, 1979-80.
50,000 Carolyn Anderton, Fort Worth, Texas, Brunswick
Showdown, Las Vegas, 1975-76.
40,000 Carol Norman, Ardmore, Okla., U.S. Open,
Mentor, Ohio, 1987.
Lisa Wagner, Palmetto, Fla., U.S. Open,
Winston-Salem, N.C.,1988.
Robin Romeo, Newhall, Calif., U.S. Open,
Addison, Ill., 1989.

Spares, all-spare games, career *
Women
48 F. Marcille McMicken, Amarillo, Texas
23 Jacklyn Ramsey, Chanute, Kan.
22 Dottie Remick-Bohl, Dayton, Ohio
21 Ruth Vinson, Franklin, Ind.
18 Helen Tschabushnig, Hayward, Calif.

Spares, all-spare games, consecutive, series
Women
3 Mabel Henry, Winchester, Ky., 183-184-155,
April 21, 1987.
2 Jill Blasczak, Westland, Mich., 1978-79
Jackie Lane, Houston, 1979-80.
Anita Robinson, Texarkana, Ark., 1979-80
Pat Scherf, Norwood, N.J., 1979-80.
Nancy A. Malone, Jacksonville, Fla., 1986-87.
Kay Meister, Stanton, Mich., 1986-87.

Men
3 Howard Glover, San Francisco, August 1944.
Charles Claybaugh, Anderson, Ind., Jan. 11, 1952.
Ray Wachholz, Oshkosh, Wis., Jan. 17, 1974.

Spares, all-spare games, season †
Men
4 Gerald Neisess, Jacksonville, Fla., 1964-65.
3 Paul DeMarco, El Paso, Texas, 1952-53.
Howard Glover, San Francisco, August 1944.
Charles Claybaugh, Anderson, Ind., Jan. 11, 1952.
Ray Wachholz, Oshkosh, Wis., Jan. 17, 1974.

Spares, all-spare games with nine-count on all first balls *
Women
Petey Carrigan, Alton, Ill., Feb. 11, 1987.
Dottie Remick-Bohl, Dayton, Ohio, March 8, 1987.

Spares, most consecutive, individual
Women
30 Mabel Henry, Winchester, Ky., 1986-87.
27 Joan Taylor, Syracuse, N.Y., 1973-74.
25 Betty Stewart, San Antonio, 1968-69.
Pat Scherf, Norwood, N.J., 1979-80.
22 Shirley Upchurch, Louisville, Ky., 1981-82.
Jean Barnes, Imlay City, Mich., 1985-86.

Men
30 Howard Glover, San Francisco, August 1944.
Charles Claybaugh, Anderson, Ind., Jan. 11, 1952.
Ray Wachholz, Oshkosh, Wis., Jan., 17, 1974.
27 Larry Martin, Phoenix, February 1977.
25 Charles Barrows, Miami, February 1954.

Spares, most consecutive, team †
Men
21 Speedometer Specialty, Long Beach, Calif., Nov. 14, 1961.
19 Junction Fuel & Supply, Monmouth Junction, N.J.,
April 23, 1962.
Double Cola, Richland Center, Wis., Oct. 3, 1963.
18 Sam Solomon Co., Charleston, S.C., July 5, 1965.
16 Lengels, Canelli, Toledo, Ohio, April 18, 1952.

Spares, most in game, team †
Men
38 Sam Solomon Co., Charleston, S.C., July 5, 1965.
34 Speedometer Specialty, Long Beach, Calif.,
Nov. 14, 1961.

Spares, most in series, team †
Men
101 Sam Solomon Co., Charleston, S.C., July 5, 1965.

Splits, most consecutive, individual
Women
14 Shirley Tophigh, Las Vegas, 1968-69.
11 Catherine Sloan, Alexandria, La., 1969-70.
10 Kathy Pausen, Detroit, 1972-73.
Velma Eggebraaten, Cottage Grove, Ore., 1985-86.
7 Joan Rice, Easton, Pa., 1977-78.
Men
12 Dr. Glyndon Rowe, Detroit, February 1964.
11 Leonard Sisson, Long Beach, Calif., Feb. 15, 1950.
10 Willie Green, Dallas, 1965.
Vincent Meinkoth, Randolph AFB, Texas, Nov. 1971.

Splits, most in one game, individual
Women
11 Catherine Sloan, Alexandria, La., 1969-70.
10 Kathy Pausen, Detroit, 1972-73.
9 Barb Yancey, East Wenatchee, Wash., 1982-83.
Velma Eggebraaten, Cottage Grove, Ore., 1985-86.
Marge Dumold, Eugene, Ore., 1986-87.

Men
11 Don Brayton, Pawtucket, R.I., 1969

Splits, most in one game, team †
Men
37 Lengel Meat Packers, Toledo, Ohio, 1955.
35 Margulis Department Store, Columbus, Ohio,
April 30, 1951.
Mathison Motors, Ames, Iowa, 1952.

* — Men's records not on file   † — Women's records not on file

Lengel Meat Packers, Toledo, Ohio, 1955.
Brazeal-McDaniel, Atchison, Kan., Nov., 12, 1957.

Splits, most in series, individual
Women
19　Lucille Kozul, Troy, Ohio, Jan. 29, 1986.
Men
24　Joe Werner, Pomona, N.Y., Oct. 12, 1962.
21　Tom McCarthy, Racine, Wis., Oct. 22, 1971.
　　James King, Victoria, Texas, Nov. 8, 1972.
18　Thomas Sutherland, Charleston, S.C., Oct. 14, 1963.
　　Harry Branca, Warren, Mich., 1970.

Splits, most in series, team †
Men
50　It's A Fun, North Hollywood, Calif., Oct. 15, 1975.
49　Sam Solomon Co., Charleston, S.C., 1963-64.
45　Sportsman's, Ames, Iowa, Dec. 13, 1951.
　　Gladwin Oil, Gladwin, Mich., Nov. 6, 1975.
43　Texaco Fire Chiefs, Anacortes, Wash., Jan. 17, 1960.
　　No. 3 Team, Pleasant Hills, Pa., Feb. 20, 1964.

Splits, most in series, two teams
Women
53　Timber Lanes & Pantry Shelf, Traverse City, Mich.,
　　Jan. 26, 1984.

Men
76　Gladwin Oil (45) vs. Leo's Place (31), Gladwin, Mich.,
　　Nov. 6, 1975.
75　Underground (40) vs. Accounting (35), Seattle,
　　March 17, 1969.
74　Velma's Supper Club (39) vs. Coors (35), Durango,
　　Colo., Feb. 6, 1962.
72　Amana Food Plan (37) vs. Leo's Cafe (35), Charleston,
　　S.C., Feb. 2, 1961.
　　Field's Roofing (39) vs. Darby's (76), Glendale, Ariz.,
　　March 23, 1962.

Splits, most in one season, individual †
Men
213　Dean Bainer, Lancaster, Ohio, 1978-79.
211　Paul Kabelitz, Lansing, Mich., 1975-76.
205　Fred Hill, Norwich, N.Y., 1974-75.
202　Gottshall Denton, Boyerton, Pa., 1968-69.
198　Merle Glass, Toledo, Ohio, 1966-67.

Splits, most in one season, league †
Men
7,553　Men's Metro, Lansing, Mich., 1975-76.

Splits, most in one season, team †
Men
783　Labus Jewelers, Lancaster, Ohio, 1978-79.
736　Tom O'Brien Associates, Lansing, Mich., 1975-76.
733　Sawyer Pontiac, Lansing, Mich., 1975-76.
719　Sam Solomon Co., Charleston, S.C., 1963-64.

Splits, 4-6-7-10, consecutive †
Men
4　Alvin Hunter, Ogden, Utah, Nov. 28, 1960.
　　William Franklin, Springfield, Ill., Dec. 19, 1961.

Splits, 4-6-7-10, game †
Men
5　Herman Eagler, Decatur, Ill., Feb. 16, 1954.
4　Alvin Hunter, Ogden, Utah, Nov. 28, 1960.
　　William Franklin, Springfield, Ill., Dec. 19, 1961.

Splits, 5-7, consecutive, game †
Men
5　Frank Campbell, Davenport, Iowa, Dec. 15, 1943.

Splits, 5-7-10, game †
Men
4　Virgil Distler, Cincinnati, Nov. 5, 1974.
3　Warren Robinson, Montebello, Calif., June 13, 1961.
　　Richard McDaniel, Montgomery, Ala., Jan. 21, 1978.

Splits, 7-10, consecutive †
Men
6　Payne Rose, St. Louis, September 1962.

Splits, 7-10, game †
Men
6　Payne Rose, St. Louis, September 1962 (consecutive).
5　Ray Nelson, St. Louis, 1946 ABC Tournament.
　　Charlie Allen, South Haven, Mich., Jan. 9, 1954.
　　Herman Eagler, Decatur, Ill., Feb. 16, 1954.

Splits, 7-10, series †
Men
9　Joe Sitzberger, Milwaukee, 1942.
6　Payne Rose, St. Louis, September 1962 (consecutive).
5　Charles Thieson, Omaha, Neb., April 1945.
　　Ray Nelson, St. Louis, 1946 ABC Tournament.
　　Charlie Allen, South Haven, Mich., Jan. 9, 1954.
　　Herman Eagler, Decatur, Ill., Feb. 16, 1954.

Splits, 8-10, consecutive †
Men
5　Arthur Crowe, Miami, Feb. 18, 1965.

Splits, 8-10, game †
Men
6　Ray Dyer, Pico, Calif., May 1962.
5　Gene Raffel, Milwaukee, Feb. 7, 1963.
　　Tom Bennett, Terre Haute, Ind., April 1963.
　　Dan Hill, Pocatello, Idaho, Oct. 14, 1963.
　　Arthur Crowe, Miami, Feb. 18, 1965.

Splits, 8-10, series †
Men
12　John Ermi, Milwaukee, 1937.
8　Oscar Gnadinger, Joliet, Ill., 1942.
7　John Ermi, Milwaukee, 1943.

Splits, most conversions, consecutive †
Men
6　W.F. Hawie, Mobile, Ala., 1972-73.

Splits, most conversions, game, individual †
Men
9　David Williams, Charleston, S.C., November 1964.
7　H.J. Leslie, Muskogee, Okla., 1944-45.

---

* — Men's records not on file　　　　† — Women's records not on file

Splits, most conversions, game, team †
Men
6 Olson Motors, Marquette, Mich., March 4, 1953.
5 U.S. Dry Cleaners, Blair, Ohio, November 1942.
  Smee & Me, Harrisburg, Pa., 1975.

Splits, most 4-6 conversions in same game
Women
2 Fran Coppinger, Hermiston, Ore., Aug. 14, 1982.

Men
2 Art Knighton, Oakland, Calif., Oct. 3, 1944.
  Since then, eight others have achieved this feat
  including Earl Pickle, Baltimore, Jan. 16, 1976 who
  did it in consecutive frames of same game

Splits, most 4-6-7-10 conversions in same game †
Men
2 Raphael Chaika, New Brighton, Minn., Feb. 27, 1960.
  Gene Zotti, St. Louis, 1961.
  Frank Kind, Spartanburg, S.C., Dec. 22, 1971.
  Charles Vidal, Penticon, British Columbia, 1974.

Splits, most 4-6-7-10 conversions in same series
Women
2 Linda Camp, Sonoma, Calif., March 3, 1987.

Men
2 Norman Dybash, Detroit, Dec. 20, 1951.
  Since then, seven others have achieved this feat.

Splits, most 5-7 conversions, consecutive †
Men
5 Morton Confeld, Minneapolis, Feb. 14, 1957.
4 Andy Santors, Detroit, Dec. 5, 1951.

Splits, most 5-7-10 conversions, game †
Women
1 Judy Clark, Modesto, Calif., 1996.
  Lucy Kratzer, Tell City, Ind., March 1996.
  Emily Wissmar, Kenosha, Wis., Feb. 11, 1997.

Men
1 Al Dugay, Toledo, Ohio, Jan. 19, 1956.
  Since then, many other have achieved this feat.

Splits, most 6-7-10 conversions, consecutive †
Men
4 Carl Chavez, Albuquerque, N.M., May 1, 1988.
3 William Sederburg, Cincinnati, 1959.
  Harry Campion, Chicago, 1956.
  Raymond Lamboy, Scotia, N.Y., 1965.

Splits, most 7-10 conversions in careers *
Women
2 Shirley Horn, Cleveland, Wis., 1981-82, 1982-83.
  Lois L. Worthy, Tempe, Ariz., 1976, 1978-79.
  Rosalie Bushick, Bulverde, Texas, 1959-60, 1980-81.
  Jan Krueger, Parkson, S.D., 1985-86.
  Jane Honsowitz, Eagle, Mich., 1991-92.

Splits, most 7-10 conversions in game
Women
2 Jan Krueger, Parkson, S.D., March 25, 1986.
Men
2 Phil Irving, Port Huron, Mich., 1936 was the first.
  Since then, six others have achieved this feat.

Splits, most 7-10 conversions in series
Women
2 Jane Honsowitz, Eagle, Mich., Oct. 2, 1991.
  Jan Krueger, Parkson, S.D., March 25, 1986.

Men
2 Phil Irving, Port Huron, Mich., 1936 was the first.
  Since then, six other have achieved this feat.

Splits, most 8-10 conversions, consecutive †
Men
2 Grantz Meyers, Opelousas. La., 1961.
  Carl Flohrs, Ormsby, Minn., Sept. 12, 1963.

Splits, most 8-10 conversions, game †
Men
2 Tony Bader, Milwaukee, 1943.
  Since then, seven others have achieved this feat.

Sponsors, most years with same team lineup *
Women
30 Tordorf & Son, Jamestown, N.J. Myrtle Schuver,
   Gladys Gilbert, Maude Gilbert, Lucille Johnson,
   Della Tordorf (1946 to 1975).

Sponsors, most years with same league
Women
52 Hiawatha Beauty Shop, Pipestone, Minn.,
   through 1991-92.
41 Babe's Babes, Des Moines, Iowa, through 1987-88.
   Schuber Agency, Big Rapids, Mich., through 1992-93.
39 Gus and Andy's, Tucson, Ariz., through 1992-93.
38 Allgauer's Restaurant, Chicago, through 1987-88.

Men
60 Suburban Chevrolet, Hopkins, Minn., Commercial,
   started 1925.
59 McCracken Box & Label, Chicago, Chicago Drug,
   started 1910.
53 Federal Glass Co., Columbus, Ohio, Federal Glass,
   started 1916.
51 Consumers Sales Agency, Moline, Ill., started 1933.
46 Schumacher Funeral Home, St. Louis, started 1918.

State Associations, most years as presidents *
Women
37 Mildred White, Rockford, Ill., 1942-79.
30 Laura Albrecht, Davenport, Iowa, 1945-75.

State Associations, most years as secretaries *
Women
47 Jeannette Knepprath, Wisconsin, 1924-70.
30 Catherine Sloan, Louisiana, 1950-80.
29 Therese Kelone, Arkansas, 1948-77.

Stepladder, series, one-pin increase per game †
267-268-269 Joe Zechmeister, St. Paul, Minn.,
            Nov. 15, 1955.

* — Men's records not on file   † — Women's records not on file

Strikes, lowest game with nine †
Men
184   Harvey Lemons, Belle Glades, Fla.,
     March 23, 1974 (G-4xxxxG-6xxG-9xxx).
     William Marshino, West Palm Beach, Fla.,
     March 26, 1974 (G-4xxxxG-6xxG-9xxx).
185   Bob Fredrickson, LaCrosse, Wis.,
     Feb. 19, 1964 (xx6-2xx5-0x4-5xxxx).
     James Weller, Charlotte, N.C., 1967
     (xxx6-0x6-2xx7-0xxx).

Strikes, lowest game with 10 †
Men
214   Walter Scott, Shamokin, Pa., 1966
     (xxx3-0xxx7-2xxxx).
218   Thomas Cosgrove, Wallington, N.J., 1960-61
     (xxx6-0xxx6-1xxxx).
221   Leon Mossey, Denton, Mont., Jan. 29, 1961
     (xxxxx1-6x8-0xxxx).
     Chester Burton, Odessa, Texas, March 29, 1961
     (xx6-1xxx5-3xxxxx).
223   Harry Lambert, Santa Clara, Calif., Aug. 22, 1961
     (xxx5-1xxx8-1xxx).

Strikes, lowest game with 11 in a row (from the first frame) †
Men
290   Buck Hasenstab, Dayton, Ohio, 1933.
     Since then, 16 others have achieved this feat.

Strikes, lowest game with 11 (not consecutive) †
Men
240   John Prehm, Bethpage, N.Y., 1980
     (xxx0-0xxxxxxxx).
252   Robert Tkacz, Bloomfield, Conn. (xx0-6xxxxxxxxx).
     Chris Tilli, Canton, Mich., April 19, 1990
     (xx0-6xxxxxxxx).
255   Paul Seabrooke, Grand Rapids, Mich., 1976
     (xx5-0xxxxxxxx).
     Al Brumer, Detroit, Feb. 9, 1989 (xxxxx5-0xxxxx).

Strikes, most Brooklyns, consecutive
Women
11   Mary Sharp, Akron, Ohio, first frame through 10th
     frame, last ball a pocket strike for 300 game,
     Nov. 28, 1980.
10   Thelma Cordier, Tucson, Ariz., from second frame
     through 10th frame for 277 game, March 19, 1972.

Men
16   Leon Kloeppner, Milford, Conn., 1976.
12   Charles Robinson, Studio City, Calif.,
     March 29, 1990.

Strikes, most Brooklyns, game †
Men
12   *Leon Kloeppner, Milford, Conn., April 28, 1976
     (300 game).
     *Charles Robinson, Studio City, Calif.,
     March 29, 1990 (300 game).
11   *Wally McDonald, Green Bay, Wis., 1976.
     Forrest Ward, Dayton, Ohio, 1939.
     *Consecutive

Strikes, most Brooklyns, series *
Women
20   Barbara Freeman, Saginaw, Mich., rolled 23
     total strikes for 709 series, Sept. 30, 1980.

Strikes, most consecutive, individual
Women
40   Jeanne Maiden-Naccarato, Tacoma, Wash.,
     Nov. 23, 1986.*
33   Jeanne Maiden-Naccarato, Tacoma, Wash.,
     1986-87.
31   Patty Ann, Arlington Heights, Ill., 1984-85.
30   Anne Marie Duggan, Edmond, Okla., July 18, 1993.
27   Deborah Thomas, Dallas, March 7, 1997.
* Maiden-Naccarato rolled 40 consecutive strikes during the
Women's Central State Tournament. She finished the doubles
event with seven strikes, before bowling games of 300-300-
264 in the singles event.

Men
36   Jeremy Sonnenfeld, Lincoln, Neb., Feb. 2, 1997.
35   Steve Lewis, Xenia, Ohio, Sept. 19, 1996.
     Kevin Lickers, Nanticoke, Pa., Nov. 16, 1996
     Al Clacer, Jersey City, N.J., Oct. 26, 1997.
34   Ken McNeely, Morgantown, N.C., May 15, 1996.

Strikes, most consecutive, team †
Men
32   Milwaukie Bowl, Beaverton, Ore., 1988-89.
28   Pro Fit, Detroit, 1988-89.
     Fireside Lanes, Sacramento, Calif., Oct. 1, 1992.
26   Sports Palace, San Antonio, March 12, 1980.
     Madden's Lounge, Flint, Mich., Jan. 5, 1995.
     Team #6, Topeka, Kan., Jan. 31, 1996.

Strikes, most in game, team †
Men
53   Eden Lanes, Tinley Park, Ill., Oct. 7, 1996
51   New England Car Sales, Yonkers, N.Y.,
     Feb. 25, 1982 (1,340 game).
50   W.A.D.C., Akron, Ohio, Nov. 13, 1947 (1,320 game).
     Budweiser Beer, St. Louis, March 12, 1958 (1,300 game).
     Swiss Hat Restaurant, Sugar Creek, Ohio,
     Dec. 7, 1963 (1,327 game).

Strikes, most in series, individual †
Men
36   Jeremy Sonnenfeld, Lincoln, Neb., Feb. 2, 1997.
35   Dick Brown, Fresno, Calif., June 22, 1983, was the first
     since then, six others have achieved this feat.

Strikes, most in series, team †
Men
138   Hermann Undertakers, St. Louis, Jan. 27, 1937
     (3,797 series).
     Budweiser Beer, St. Louis, March 12, 1958
     (3,858 series).
     Hurst Bowling Supplies, Luzerne, Pa., Feb. 23, 1994
     (3,868 series).
132   Faber Cement, Teaneck, N.J., Feb. 22, 1952
     (3,754 series).
128   West Lanes, Pittsburgh, Kan., March 5, 1995
     (3,662 series).

* — Men's records not on file   † — Women's records not on file

Strikes, most in 10th frame in series, team †
Men

35   Hermann Undertakers, St. Louis, Jan. 27, 1937.
33   Budweiser Beer, St. Louis, March 12, 1958.
31   Badger Inn, Milwaukee, January 1942.
        West Lanes, Pittsburgh, Kan., March 5, 1995.

Striking Out, in most consecutive games †
Men

14   Emil Joseph, Toledo, Ohio, 1954, three leagues.
9   Sylvester Bykowski, Pittsburgh, March 1947,
        three leagues on consecutive nights.
6   James King, Mt. Prospect, Ill., 1954.

Teams, most years with same lineups
Women

41   De Snyder Plasterettes, Port Huron, Mich., through 1990-91.
30   Tordorf & Son, Jamestown, N.Y., through 1980-81.

Men-Mixed

40   Barton Body Shop, Alpha, Ill., 1954-94
32   Deals Inc., West Monroe, La.-Crossett, Ark., 1964-96
31   Sammons-Bowens, Union City, Pa., 1962-93
25   Crystal Bar, Elkhart, Ind., 1934-59
        Conrad Good Egg, Port Huron, Mich., 1954-79
        Cushman Fruit Company, Palm Beach, Fla., 1961-86

Three-Game Series, highest low player in five-player team series
Men

738   Howard Holly, Luzerne, Pa., Feb. 23, 1994
        (team had 3,868).
736   Pat Patterson, St. Louis, March 12, 1958
        (team had 3,858).
728   Bob Chamberlain, Pontiac, Mich., Feb. 21, 1978
        (team had 3,691).
726   Bill Starnes, Portland, Ore., April 21, 1978
        (team had 3,782).
709   Buzz Wilson, St. Louis, Jan. 27, 1937.
        Bob Granes, Toledo, Ohio, April 15, 1996
        (team had 3,744)

Three-Game Series, highest without a 300 game †
Men

887   Bret Dal Santo, Savannah, Ga., Oct. 25, 1990,
        299, 289, 299.
878   Markus Hartman, Harrisburg, Pa., June 9, 1994,
        299, 299, 280.
877   Peter Victoria, Mattituck, N.Y., Oct. 8, 1994, 288,
        290, 299.

Three-Game Series, highest without a 200 game †
Men

799   Don Hartley, Columbus, Ohio, Sept. 12, 1987,
        300, 199, 300.
798   Bob Theuninck, East Moline, Ill., May 5, 1986,
        300, 198, 300.
795   Richard Cetti, Morris Township, N.J., May 17,
        1983, 195, 300, 300.
791   William Patnode, Fond du Lac, Wis., Sept. 14,
        1983, 300, 300, 300.
781   Bruce Reha, Des Moines, Iowa, Sept. 14, 1990,
        181, 300, 300.

*— Men's records not on file

Three-Game Series, highest by senior bowlers
Women

822   Nadine Oppliger, Wichita, Kan., 66 years old,
        March 4, 1996.
781   Nadine Oppliger, Wichita, Kan., 67 years old,
        Aug. 13, 1997
759   Marilyn Rumple, Omaha, Neb., 58 years old,
        Dec, 11, 1991
750   E. Lois Morgan, Lees Summit, Mo., 71 years old,
        July 9, 1996
746   Donna Zuniga, Tulsa, Okla., 56 years old, 1990-91.

Men

826   Fran Lasee, Green Bay, Wis., Nov. 5, 1992,
        71 years old.
817   George Hougland, Shawnee, Kan., March 9, 1993,
        77 years old.
813   Carl Berger, Chicago, May 28, 1981, 71 years old.
812   Eli Maricich, Normal, Ill., April 5, 1970,
        70 years old.

Three-Game Series, highest by substitute bowlers *
Women

802   Shellie Johnson, Toledo, Ohio, 300-256-246,
        1983-84.
782   Debbie Wilhite, Placentia, Calif., 259-256-267,
        1979-80.
751   Lisa Wilkins, Archbold, Ohio, 1982-83.
742   Sharon Wolf, Defiance, Ohio, 237-258-247,
        1976-77.
739   Sheila Clegg, Chicago, 221-259-259, 1975-76.

Three-Game Series, highest consecutive league series on same days
Women

1,483   Linda Kelly, Huber Heights, Ohio, 754-729,
        1987-88.
1,481   Sandy Sanderson, Dayton, Ohio, 655-826,
        Oct. 15, 1992.
1,477   Betsy Corrigan, Xenia, Ohio, 824-653, 1978-79.
1,466   Sara Clark, Toledo, Ohio, 732-734, 1971-72.
1,451   Cindy Suber, Dayton, Ohio, 793-658,
        Sept. 23, 1993.

Men

1,671   Elvin Mesger, Sullivan, Mo., 846-825,
        June 10, 1967.
1,651   Don Dubro, St. Louis, 831 820, April 26, 1962.
1,603   Bob Bures, Cleveland, 813-790, Feb. 23, 1978.
1,592   Elvin Mesger, St. Louis, 821-771, June 11, 1962.
1,586   Roy Buckley, Columbus, Ohio, 751-835,
        April 3, 1972.

Three-Game Series, lowest in league play †
Men

66   Charles Williams, Chicago, Nov. 28, 1961.
74   Zigmund Hoff, St. Joseph, Mich., 1960.
107   Lee Harper, Jacksonville, Fla., Nov. 12, 1970.
122   Charles Graham Jr., New Milford, Conn.,
        Sept. 8, 1964.
150   Curt Hearnsberger, Valentine, Neb.,
        Sept. 11, 1956.

Three-Game Series, most pins over average, indivdiuals
Women

355   Cindy Hanke, Milwaukee, 1980-81, 736 series
        with 381 avg.

† — Women's records not on file

337   Sandi Clemmer, State College, Pa., April 2, 1995,
763 with 426 avg.

285   Dee Dee Bruehler, N. Olmstead, Ohio,
1982-83, 753 series with 468 avg.

280   Sharon Graff, Cleburne, Texas, 1978-79, 814
series with 534 avg.

273   Ann Splain, Middleton, Ohio, 1979-80, 831 series
with 558 avg.

270   Lynn Wallace, Fort Worth, Texas, 1982-83, 678
series with 408 avg.

Men

337   Chad Allen, South Sioux City, Neb.,
April 15, 1991, 745 with 408 avg.

332   Fred Tucillo, Trenton, N.J., Feb. 6, 1994,
783 with 450 avg.

315   Brett Barry, Oklahoma City, Okla.,
Nov. 3, 1980, 792 with 477 avg.

314   Bob Kerr, Kent, Ohio, Feb. 24, 1994,
719 with 405 avg.

311   Earl Stutz, Norfolk, Va., March 21, 1974,
755 with 444 avg.

Three-Game Series, most pins over average, team †
Men

799   Tom Long's Bowling Supply, Whittier, Calif.,
Sept. 29, 1975, 3,358 with 2,559 avg.

772   Color Chrome Dinette, Milwaukee, Feb. 10, 1965,
3,302 with 2,530 avg.

737   Hermann Undertakers, St. Louis, Jan. 27, 1937,
3,797 with 3,060 avg.

705   Burghart Optical, Toledo, Ohio, April 15, 1996,
3,744 with 3,039 avg.

683   ASPA No. 1, Schenectady, N.Y., Nov. 6, 1972,
3,002 with 2,319 avg.

Tie Games, highest teams in league match †
Men

1,271   Michelob Masters vs. Herrell's Budweiser Eagles,
St. Louis, April 20, 1994 (Masters won rolloff).

1,207   Bill Morton's Pro Shop vs. McCune's Pro Shop,
Highland, Ind., Dec. 10, 1993.

1,205   Barbasol vs. Bowes Seal Fast, Indianapolis,
Oct. 1939 (Bowes Seal Fast won rolloff).

Tie Games, league total for season †
Men

13   Greenbriar Mixed, Brick Town, N.J., 1976-77.

12   Early Bird, Wapello, Iowa, 1962-63.

12   Greenbriar Mixed, Brick Town, N.J., 1982-83.

10   Greenbrier Mixed, Brick Town, N.J., 1975-76 and 1978-79.

9   Greenbriar Mixed, Brick Town, N.J., 165-73.
Friday Niters, Ann Arbor, Mich., 1976-77.

Tie Games, most in league season team †
Men

5   Garber Funeral, Norwalk, Ohio, All-Star.
Lapin Catering, Kansas City, 1963-64,
Country Club Businessmen's.
Jet Drain, Reno, Nev., 1989-90, N.C.S.E.A.

Tie Series, highest in league match †
Men

3,661   President Riverboat Casino vs. Pro Connection
Pro Shop, Highland Park Bowl, Davenport,
Iowa, Sept. 19, 1996

3,357   Marino Rec. vs. Rohr Jewelers, Milwaukee,
Jan. 18, 1955, All-Star.

Ties, for first place at end of season †
Men

5 teams   890, Pasadena, Calif., 1953-54, W56-L43.

4 teams   Alhambra National, Sacramento, Calif.,
1951-52, W26-L16.

3 teams   Capitola Major, Capitola, Calif., 1953-54, W53-L31.
Moose, Nampa, Idaho, 1953-54, W50 1/2-L49 1/2.

Ties, most teams in league standings
Men

8   Gooseberry, Chicago, 1943-44.

7   Cudahy, Omaha, Neb., 1961-62.

6   Fireman's, Chicago, 1941-42.

5   Veterans Mixed League, Waukesha, Wis., 1950.

Titles, state all events won by sisters
Women

Elma Kavonius, Bismarck, N.D., 1951 and 1954; Elna
Kavonius, Bismarck, N.D., 1956 and 1959; and
Helen Kavonius, Bismarck, N.D., 1962, 1969 and 1973;
North Dakota WBA Tournament.

Lil Hofstad, Sioux Falls, S.D., 1972, and Alice Lowell,
Pipestone, Minn., 1964, South Dakota WBA Tournament.
Mary Lou Vining, St. Paul, Minn., 1978, and Judy
Schlukebler, St. Paul, Minn., 1984, Minnesota WBA
Tournament.

Tournaments, largest for a local association in teams *
Women

1,075   Detroit, 1975.

1,020   Detroit, 1978.

995   Detroit, 1977.

976   Detroit, 1979.

944   Detroit, 1974.

Triplicates, duplicates by teammates in same match †
Men

179   Jim Kramer and Allan Milligan, Detroit, March 30, 1966.

146   Joe Minaudo and Ralph Palarino, Stratford, Conn.,
Oct. 24, 1962.

Triplicates, highest games
Women

268   Merrill Alexander, Dallas, 1980-81.
Alecia Kanazawa, Mountain View, Calif., 1990-91.

258   Robin Romeo, Newhall, Calif., 1986-87.

257   Pat Costello, Orlando, Fla., 1979-80.

248   Carol Norman, Ardmore, Okla., 1986-87.

Men

300   Jeremy Sonnenfeld, Linoln, Neb., Feb. 2, 1997

290   Jeffrey Gunn, Wheeling, W. Va., Nov. 29, 1994

289   Joe Heiser, Whitewater, Wis., Feb. 26, 1997

280   Thomas Ferrigno, Foster City, Calif., Feb. 24, 1991

279   Jim Schroeder, Alliance, Ohio, March 21, 1965 (tournament).
was the first. Since then, many others have achieved
this feat.

* — Men's records not on file   † — Women's records not on file

Triplicates, highest, five-player team
Women
848 H. R. Crabb and Son, Arcade, N.Y., 1984-85.
Men
1,144 Stroh's Bohemian Beer, Detroit, Dec. 7, 1950.
1,118 Orchard Lanes, Detroit, April 24, 1980.
1,073 Schoonover Designers, Canton, Ohio, Feb. 23, 1967.
1,064 Antique Kitchen, Kalamazoo, Mich., Oct. 26, 1979.
1,054 Teem Soft Drink, Paramus, N.J., April 6, 1964.

Triplicates, highest, four-player team *
Women
720 Brattain Idealease, Portland, Ore., 1990-91.
668 Oreos, Warren, Mich., 1981-82.
656 Sunset Lanes, Portland, Ore., 1990-91.

Triplicates, highest, senior-league bowler *
Women
200 Mrs. Preston Phillips, 68, Roanoke, Va., 1977-78.

Triplicates, highest individual, one day †
Men
190, 168 H.L. Martinson, Chetek, Wis., April 28, 1963, National Odd Fellows Tournament, Rockford, Ill.
188, 180 Orlo Paculli, North Tonawanda, N.Y., Nov. 7, 1980.
180, 180 Lawrence Buller, Lincoln, Neb., March 23, 1992, ABC Tournament.
180, 149 Williams Jones, Albany, Calif.
180, 162 Dean Waterman, New Bremen, Ohio, Jan. 31, 1958.

Triplicates, identical by opponents in same match †
Men
171 Dave Arnce and Kirt Saulsbury, Ft. Knox, Ky., Sept. 5, 1978.
155 Robert Carlson and Paul Lemke, Clayton, Wis., Sept. 5, 1979.
149 Chuck Harvey and Jack McCumber, Columbus, Ohio, December 1954.
148 Natalie Faryon and Elbert Foster, Redding, Calif., Feb. 21, 1997.
144 Bob Webster and Arvin Powell, Lawrence, Kan., Nov. 15, 1961.
Charles Russo and Greg Kopp, Syracuse, N.Y., April 1964.

Triplicates, individual, season †
Men
3 Steve Geotter, Lansdale, Pa., 1963-64 (207 203 153).
John Gecy Jr., Pittsburgh, 1972-73 (169 171 117).
John Fischer, West Long Branch, N.J., 1978-79 (191 179 158).

Triplicates, individual, career †
Men
10 Gary Schindler, Jackson Heights, N.Y.
8 Tom Tapp, Endicott, N.Y.
7 Jerry Daly, Detroit.
Hubert Hager, Denmark, Wis.
6 Ron Jay, Vista, Calif.
Eric Jensen, Wichita, Kan.

Triplicates, lowest game
Women
131 Vicki Cameron, Norco, Calif., June 4, 1992

* — Men's records not on file

Men
15 Douglass Frack, Flint, Mich., Oct. 15, 1982.
17 Darly Steinar, Mandan, N.D., Feb. 25, 1981.
21 Jeff Cole, Orange County, Calif., Dec. 10, 1980.
22 Charles Williams, Chicago, Nov. 28, 1961, (Williams was blind).
50 Curt Hearnsberger, Valentine, Neb.

Triplicates, oldest bowler †
Men
92 Matt Goduto, East Sparta, Ohio, Sept. 15, 1997 (132).
85 Oscar Solomon, Rock Island, Ill., 1959 (139).
84 Frank Knapp, New Port Richey, Fla., Feb. 23, 1962 (96).
83 Bill Pellam, Lyons Falls, N.Y., Oct. 1, 1985 (134).
82 Charles Myers, Kalamazoo, Mich., Nov. 30, 1966 (160).

Triplicates, same total one season †
Men
2 Wally Dubbs, Rushford, Minn., 1953.
Since then, 12 others have achieved this feat

Triplicates, teammates †
Men
269, 247 Chad Murphy and Lonnie Waliczek, Wichita, Kan., Nov. 30, 1993.
179, 179 Jim Kramer and Allan Milligan, Detroit, March 30, 1966.
180, 173 Ray Pinheird and Marv Heince, Costa Mesa, Calif., Jan. 2, 1974.
190, 167 Paul Basacchi and Alex Bosacchi, Warren, Mich., March 30, 1992 (father and son).
192, 158 Bill Perry and Harold Krause, East Peoria, Ill., Oct. 20, 1949.

Triplicates, team, most in one series †
Men
3 Bickfords, Milwaukee, Jan. 5, 1954
Zimmermans, Murfreesboro, Tenn., Jan. 11, 1955
Wilson Funeral Home, Racine, Wis., Jan. 19, 1959

Victories, team, consecutive †
Men
84 Frank Leonoros, Charleston, W.Va., 1948-49.
72 Lefties, Milwaukee, 1955-56.
45 Mother Truckers Revived, Macomb, Ill., 1979-80.
43 Occidental Lodge, Buffalo, 1943-44.
41 Waugaman's Grill, Tonawanda, N.Y., 1948.

Winning, highest percentage in league †
Men
95.9% Lefties, Milwaukee, 1955-56, W94-L4.
95.0% Air Force Fliegers, Bremerhaven, Germany, 1970-71, W57-L3.
94.4% Borchardt's Food, Chicago, 1952-53, W93[1/2]-L5[1/2].
93.8% Considine Sign, Toledo, Ohio, 1958-59, W90-L6.
91.9% Duckler Motors, Milwaukee, 1951-52, W 94-L8.

Winning Margin, team game (actual pinfall) †
Men
668 Farrell's Bar def. Wild Ones, Groton, N.Y., 1,233-565
652 Farrell's Bar def. Wild Ones, Groton, N.Y., 1,250-598

† — Women's records not on file

490	Williams Novelty def. Schallers Sheet Metal, St. Paul, Minn., April 3, 1952 (1,052-575).
486	Full House def. W.Y.S.C., Hyannis, Mass., Jan. 17, 1977 (1,098-612.)
472	Farrell's Bar def. Wild Ones, Groton, N.Y., Nov. 7, 1995 (1,021-549)

Winning Margin, team series (actual pinfall) †
Men
1,792	Farrell's Bar def. Wild Ones, Groton, N.Y., Nov. 7, 1995 (3,504-1,712)
1,283	Jostens def. Richards, Munster, Ind., March 7, 1980 (3,681-2,398).
1,204	Penalty Box def. Rim Electronics, Sioux City, Iowa, Nov. 29, 1979 (2,845-1,641).
1,137	Alameida's Auto Supply def. Brooklawn Variety, Dartmouth, Mass., March 28, 1984 (3,333-2,196).
1,133	Sacred Heart def. Leopards, Syracuse, N.Y., Jan. 18, 1928 (3,370 to 2,237).
1,123	Stegmaier Beer def. Valley Forge Beer, Scranton, Pa., March 17, 1937 (3,570 to 2,447).

200 Games, consecutive †
Men
77	Rick Parsons, Lexington, Ky., 1992-93.
	Tom Reichmann, Sacramento, Calif., 1992-93.
75	Randy Choat, Granite City, Ill., 1990-91.
64	David Adams, Schenectady, N.Y., 1987-88.
62	Al Cohn, Chicago, 1970-71.
	Dave Ignatius, Cleveland, 1981-82.

200 Games, most in one league, one season, three-game series †
Men
104	Rick Parsons, Lexington, Ky., 1992-93.
97	Ed Dong, Portland, 1969-70.
	Dave Ignatius, Cleveland, 1981-82.
96	Brad Gain, Fairview Heights, Ill., 1994-95.

200 Games, most in one league, one season, four-game series †
Men
128	Russ Sternberg, St. Louis, 1994-95.
119	Harry Polomaine, Schenectady, N.Y., 1975-76.
113	Richard Carney, Schenectady, N.Y., 1975-76.
112	Jack Brown, Evergreen Park, Ill., 1993-94.
110	Al Cohn, Chicago, 1970-71.

200 Games, most in one league, one season, six-game series †
Men
| 163 | Bill McCorkle III, Columbus, Ohio, 1973-74. |
| 156 | Ron Stromfeld, Columbus, Ohio, 1977-78. |

298 Games, career (See pg. 3)

298 Games, youngest ABC members
Men
14	Chad Gulden, Gettysburg, Pa., Oct. 2, 1992.
15	Richard Smock, Huntsville, Ala., June 5, 1974.
17	Harry Zivney, Chicago, Feb. 10, 1948.

299 Games, career, (See pg. 3)

299 Games, most in one series, individual †
Men
| 2 | Peter Kisloski, Wilkes-Barre, Pa., Dec. 10, 1940 was |

the first since. Since then, six others have achieved this feat.

299 Games, teammates, same game †
Men
Ben Garrison Jr. and Jim Henderson, Eureka, Calif., 1962.

299 Games, youngest
| 11 | Matt Mundy, Ventura, Calif., May 1, 1993. |
| | Nicole Johannes, Kansas City, Kan., Sept. 13, 1997 |

299 Games, youngest ABC member †
12	Allen Loch, Nicholson, Pa., Feb. 19, 1984.
13	William Ihrie III, Hickory, N.C., Jan. 9, 1997.
14	Michael Munsch, Oshkosh, Wis., Nov. 11, 1957.

300 Games, ambidextrous, individual †
Men
Gary Thompson, Walnut Creek, Calif., Aug. 24, 1979 (righthanded) and Nov. 24, 1980 (lefthanded). Since then, many others have achieved this feat.

300 Games, by Canadian women *
| 2 | Linda Thompson, Hamilton, Ontario, 1987-88. |

300 Games, career (See pg. 3)

300 Games, consecutive, career †
Men
2	Al Spotts, West Reading, Pa., March 14, 1982 and Feb. 1, 1985.
	Jerry Wright, Idaho Falls, Idaho, Jan. 9, 1992 and Feb. 26, 1992.
	Steve Gehringer, Reading, Pa., Oct. 3, 1991 and Feb. 7, 1992.

300 Games, consecutive by oldest person
| 76 | Bill Bunetta, Fresno, Calif., Oct. 25, 1995 |

300 Games, earliest in adult career
Women
Mary Lou Oldham, 16, Kansas City, Mo., first game of sanctioned competition, 1962.
Men
Pete Weber, 15, St. Louis, first game of sanctioned competition, 1978
Jason Atchison, 16, Bethalto, Ill., June 19, 1997, first game of sanctioned competition.
Joe Jiminez, 18, Saginaw, Mich., fourth game of sanctioned competition, 1984.
Jeff Goble, 17, Downey, Calif., fifth game of sanctioned competition, 1986.
Gary Kunzen, Cleveland, sixth game of sanctioned competiton, 1978.

300 Games, families
300 game family entries are entered under the heading that includes all family members rolling 300 games. For example, the Pollard family from Kansas City, Mo., is entered under "Mothers, Daughters, Fathers and Sons." The feat is entered in the category that denotes the greatest singular achievement for the family.

300 Games, brothers
65	Jeff (40) and Craig (25) Jensen, Wichita, Kan.
60	Joe (48) and Albert (12) Jimenez, Saginaw, Mich.
57	James (52) and Kevin (5) Johnson, Wilmington, Del.

* — Men's records not on file   † — Women's records not on file

56   Keith (33) and Kevin (23) Bruening, St. Charles, Mo.
55   Mike (32) and David (23) Fleming, Leavenworth,
       Kan. and Lansing, Kan.

300 Games, brothers in same league game
Bob and Wayne Pinkalla, Milwaukee, April 20, 1960.
Mike and Dave Fleming, Overland Park, Kan., Sept. 26, 1991.
Joe and Albert Jimenez, Saginaw, Mich., Jan. 20, 1994.

300 Games, brothers in same tournament game
Ken and Mike Mayo, Peoria, Ill., Jan. 22, 1995.

300 Games, brother and sister
28   Mark (21) and Kim (7) Bevevidez, North Highlands,
       Calif.

300 Games, father, daughter and three sons
Bill Pollard Sr., Regina Pollard Snodgrass, and sons Bill
       Pollard Jr., Rick Pollard and, Ron Pollard; Versailles, Ind.
Dick Weber, Paula Darmon and sons John Weber, Pete
       Weber and Richard Weber, St. Louis.

300 Games, father, daughter and son
32   Dick (18), Paula (1) and Pete (13) Weber, St. Louis.
       Bill, Regina and Ron Pollard, Versailles, Ind .
22   Ron (17), Linda (2) and Kevin Woods (3), Hudson, Fla.
21   Bill (2), Regina (2) and Ron Pollard (17), Versailles, Ind.

300 Games, father and daughter
7   Henry Blough (6) and Lisa Farwell (1), Elizaabethtown, Pa.
       Don Ellis (5) and Denise Walker (2), Houston, Texas.
5   Don Mansel (3) and Diane Bowerman (2), Amarillo, Texas.
3   John Ignizio (2) and Mildred Ignizio (1), Rochester, N.Y.
2   Charles Smales and Linda Hudson, Dayton, Ohio were
       the first. Since then, many others have acheived this feat.

300 Games, father and four sons
Chuck Pezzano Sr., Oct. 7, 1951 and Clay Pezzano,
       Aug. 15, 1984; Curt Pezzano, Sept. 17, 1985, Miami,
       Fla., Craig Pezzano, June 13, 1988, and Chuck Pezzano
       Jr., Feb. 2, 1994, Clifton, N.J.
Ron Katona, Oct. 28, 1985 and Tony, Jan. 12, 1987; Scott,
       May 6, 1991; Alex, Oct. 12 1992 and Steve, April 4,
       1994, Daytona Beach, Fla.
Dick Weber (18) and Pete Weber (13), St. Louis, Mo.

300 Games, father and son, same team game
Gary Zakrajsek Sr. and Mark Zekrajsek, Lorain, Ohio,
       Nov. 3, 1993.
Sherman (Bud) and Paul Frost, Wilmington, Ill., Feb. 6, 1995.
       (Note: Bud was righthanded, Paul lefthanded)

300 Games, father and son
50   Jerry (23) and Kris Netherton (27), Sacramento, Calif.
31   Dick Weber (18) and Pete Weber (13), St. Louis.

300 Games, first wife and husband to accomplish
Mazey Laureys and Al Laureys; New Carlisle, Ind.;
       March 26, 1963, and Oct. 28, 1962.

300 Games, first wife and husband to accomplish left-handed
Geri Beattie and Dick Beattie; Dearborn Heights, Mich.;
       March 11, 1979, and April 30, 1968.

                           * — Men's records not on file

300 Games, husband and wife, same night, league and game
Joseph and Jan Wagner, Cleveland, May 8, 1997.

300 Games, mother, daughter, father, and son
Patricia Pollard, Joli Brandt, Williard Pollard and Patrick
       Pollard; Kansas City, Mo.; Dec. 19, 1981; Jan. 25, 1979;
       July 29, 1981; and March 22, 1982.
Kathy, Kathleen, James and Kris Le Croy, Ft. Worth, Texas,
       Feb. 28, 1980, March 6, 1979, Oct. 16, 1994 and
       Feb. 27, 1995.

300 Games, mother, daughter and father
Marjorie Caruso, John Caruso and Cindy Mason; Hayward
       and Sunnyvale, Calif.; Nov. 10, 1977; May 24, 1980;
       and Sept. 21, 1970.
Kathy, Jackie and Doug Edwards, Simi Valley, Calif.,
       Oct. 10, 1989, June 3, 1995 and Jan. 26, 1979.

300 Games, mother, daughter and son
Eloise Vacco, Debbie Rainone and Howard Vacco;
       Cleveland and Downington, Pa.; July 18, 1977; Nov. 15,
       1982; and July 5, 1982.
Betty Bardman, JoAnn Bardman and Dennis Bardman;
       Pottstown, Pa. and Bethesda, Md.; July 30, 1977, April 12,
       1986, and Feb. 3, 1995.

300 Games, mother, father and two sons
Sharon, Wayne and sons Andy and Edward Harnstrom,
       Sept. 19, 1980, Sept. 15, 1992, March 2, 1987 and
       June 1, 1985.

300 Games, mother and two sons
Helen Goodling, Keith Goodling and Kirk Goodling;
       Strasburg, Pa.; March 18, 1977; Sept. 24, 1980;
       and May 7, 1983.
Carolyn Grund, Richie Sposato and Rob Sposato; Syracuse,
       N.Y.; March 8, 1976; Oct. 1, 1985; and
       Dec. 10, 1991.

300 Games, sisters
8   Carolyn Dorin (5) and Cathy Dorin (3); Linden, N.J.
6   Jodi Jensen (5) and Debbie Walker (1), Wichita, Kan.
3   Charita Williams (2) and Michelle Acree (1),
       Indianapolis.
2   Holly Hill and Kelly Wirth; Caro and Vassar, Mich.

300 Games, wife and husband, career
41   Sue Peterson (8) and Rory Peterson (33), Rocklin, Calif.
30   Jodi Jensen (5) and Craig Jensen (25), Wichita, Kan.
27   Judy Soutar (3) and Dave Soutar (24), Bradenton, Fla.
22   Linda Kelly (10) and Bob Kelly (12); Huber Heights,
       Ohio.
14   Debbie Timberlake (5) and Gary Timberlake (9); Blue
       Springs, Mo.

300 Games, first, by countries
Canada—Frank Young, Hamilton, Ont., 1881, open play
England—Jack Vickers, Upper Heyford, Oxon.
       May 22, 1965, sanctioned by British Tenpin B.A.
Finland—Mats Karlsson, Stockholm, Sweden, 1980,
       Ballmasters, Helsinki (First on TV in Europe).

                    † — Women's records not on file

Guatemala—Eduardo Estrada, 1970.

Ivory Coast, Africa—Luc Audemard, 1980.

Japan—Saburo Kasuya, Tokyo, 1960, Nippon Bowling Federation Tournament.

Panama—Robert Balcer, Canal Zone, Nov. 14, 1943, league.

Puerto Rico—Oscar Ulloa, San Juan, April 28, 1972, league.

South Africa—Leo Winters, Durban, 1954, league.

Trinidad—Joe Millay, Port of Spain, 1944, ABC sanctioned league for U.S. Navy personnel.

United States—George Wadleigh, Jersey City, N.J., Jan. 8, 1890.

Virgin Islands—Steve Hector, 1982.

West Germany—Hans Willie Leihr, Mannheim, 1964, Gold Crown tournament sponsored by German Bowling Congress.

300 Games, firsts, other notable

1902 Ernest Fosberg, East Rockford, Ill., March 7, first in five-man league play.

1908 A.C. Jellison, St. Louis, Dec. 15, first to be recognized with an ABC award.

Homer Sanders, St. Louis lost to Jellison in three-game rolloff to determine, medal winner.

1930 Jenny Haverson Kelleher, Madison, Wis., Feb. 12, first women's 300 recognized by WIBC.

1953 Fred Chase, Chicago, first youth 300 recognized by American Junior Bowling Congress.

1953 Bill Phillips, Houston, Oct. 22, first on automatic pinsetting equipment, league play.

1964 Gene Butera, Parma, Ohio, Jan. 10, first on all synthetic pins, league play.

1968 Rick Celotti, San Mateo, Calif., July 9 and 16, first youth bowler with two 300s in one week.

1969 Jeanette Bottorf, Ankara, Turkey, first by WIBC member abroad.

1969 Chuck Seifert and Ralph Emerson, Modesto, Calif., Aug. 17, first on automatic scoring equipment, league play (both games bowled at same time at same establishment).

1977 Jerry Edwards, Itasca, Ill., May 11, first on synthetic lane surface, tournament.

300 Games, most in same league session †
Men

5   Northwest Indiana Classic, Hammond, Ind., March 19, 1993.

4   Westlake Classic, Westlake, Ohio, Dec. 6, 1990.
    Pepsi Invitational, Endicott, N.Y., Dec. 8, 1992.
    Bud Light Metro, Kansas City, Oct. 31, 1996.
    East Valley Open, Mesa, Ariz., Jan. 21, 1997

300 Games, longest time between first and second †
Men

67 years   Joe Norris, San Diego, 1927 and 1994.

47 years   Ferdinand Georgie, Lansing, Mich., 1940 and 1987.

44 years   Fred Wolf, Detroit, 1931 and 1975.

39 years   Dave Tuell Jr., Tacoma, Wash., 1953 and 1992.

* — Men's records not on file

35 years   Paul Zima, Daytona Beach, Fla., 1945 and 1980.

300 Games, lowest series with a perfect game †
Men

476   Reed Townley, Gadsen, Ala., 89 87 300, Jan. 18, 1989.

530   Jim Albanese, Allentown, Pa., 114 300 116, Oct. 11, 1951.

536   Harry Wilson, Bettendorf, Iowa, 111 125 300, Nov. 29, 1940.
      Dick Frueler, Hamilton, Ohio, 121 115 300, Dec. 8, 1966.

546   Jim Phillips, Syracuse, N.Y., 128 118 300, April 28, 1965.
      Gene Rossman, Woodstock, Ill.,121 125 300, Nov. 14, 1974.

300 Games, lowest averages
Women

112   Diane Ponza, Santa Cruz, Calif., 1977-78.

121   Judy Sikes, Denver, 1984-85.

123   Jenny Dallas, Garrett, Ind., 1985-86.

127   Linda Harris, Minot, N.D., 1974-75.
      Kellie Luster, Canyon County, Calif., 1980-81.

Men

127   Roger Evans, Champaign, Ill., April 12, 1991.

133   Larry Senter, Fenton, Mich., Dec. 5, 1988.

300 Games, most consecutive
Women

2   Carol Norman, Ardmore, Okla., 300-300-258/858, April 7, 1986.
    Jeanne Maiden-Naccarato, Tacoma, Wash., 300-300-264/864, Nov. 23, 1986.
    Nancy Seaman, Binghamton, N.Y., 212-300-300/812, Oct. 3, 1990.
    Anne Marie Duggan, Edmond, Okla., 300-300-265/865, July 18, 1993.
    Cathy Henry, New Port Richey, Fla., 182-300-300/782, Sept. 13, 1993.

Men

3   Troy Ockerman, Owosso, Mich., Dec. 18, 1993.
    Norm Duke, North Brunswick, N.J., April 10, 1996
    Jeremy Sonnefeld, Lincoln, Neb., Feb. 2, 1997.

300 Games, most in one day
Women

2   Carol Norman, Ardmore, Okla., 300-300-258/858, April 7, 1986.
    Jeanne Maiden-Naccarato, Tacoma, Wash., 300-300-264/864, Nov. 23, 1986.
    Nancy Seaman, Binghamton, N.Y., 212-300-300/812, Oct. 3, 1990.
    Anne Marie Duggan, Edmond, Okla., 300-300-265/865, July 18, 1993.
    Cathy Henry, New Port Richey, Fla., 182-300-300/782, Sept. 13, 1993.

Men

4   Troy Ockerman, Owosso, Mich., Dec. 18, 1993.

† — Women's records not on file

3   Roger Blad, St. Paul, Minn., July 26, 1981.
    Todd Filter, Cedar Rapids, Iowa, May 8, 1994.

300 Games, most consecutive Brooklyn strikes
Women
11 Mary Sharp, Akron, Ohio, from first frame
    through 10th frame second ball, 12th ball
    pocket strike, Nov. 28, 1980.
Men
12 Leon Kloeppner, Milford, Conn., April 28, 1976
    Charles Robinson, Studio City, Calif.,
    March 29, 1990.

300 Games, most in one season
Women
6   Leanne Barrette, Yukon, Okla., 1989-90.
    Tish Johnson, Panorama City, Calif., 1992-93.
    (11 bowlers have accomplished the feat three times
    in a season.)
4   Jodi Hughes, Greenville S.C., 1995-96.
Men
14 Brett Wolfe, Tempe, Ariz., 1996-97.
12 Michael Whalin, Dayton, Ohio, 1987-88.
11 Jim Johnson Jr., Wilmington, Del., 1987-88.
    Mike Cowley, Dayton, Ohio, 1992-93.
    Tom Sawyer, Green Bay, Wis., 1993-94.

300 Games, most in one season, team †
Men
8   Toby Contreras Pro Shop, Kansas City, Mo., 1993-94.
7   Budweiser Beer, St. Louis, 1957-58.

300 Games, most in one tournament*
Women
3   Paula Vidad, Rancho Cucamonga, Calif., (28 games),
    Jan. 1993.

Men
4   Walter Ray Williams Jr., Mechanicsburg, Pa.,
    Aug. 14-19, 1993.
    Troy Ockerman, Owosso, Mich., Dec. 18, 1993.

300 Games, oldest bowlers
Women
71 years, 5 months, Myrt Kressin, Bremerton, Wash.,
    Feb. 8, 1997.
71 years, 3 months, E. Lois Morgan, Lees Summit, Mo.,
    July 9, 1996
70 Nora Martin, Nashville, Tenn., Jan. 14, 1995.
66 Evelyn Culbert, Austin, Minn., 1992-93.
65 Helen Duval, Berkeley, Calif., June 3, 1982.

Men
86 Joe Norris, San Diego, Dec. 14, 1994.
81 Jerry Wehmann, Port St. Lucie, Fla., April 15, 1992.
80 Leo Sites, Wichita, Kan., April 10, 1985.
    Vince Lucci Sr., Morrisville, Pa., May 16, 1993.
    Marion Boring, Vallejo, Calif., Sept. 17, 1997

300 Games, teammates, right-handed and left-handed, same game †
Men
Robert Rieck (rt.) and Robert Cole Sr., Rome, N.Y., Dec. 13,

1989; Jeff Bertolette (rt.) and Lenny Selby, Columbiana,
Ohio, Oct. 19, 1993

300 Games, three generations †
Men
Jerry Merck, Oct. 24, 1947, Wesley Merck, Oct. 1, 1973
    and Jerry Merck II, July 25, 1973, San Antonio. Since
    then, eight other families have achieved the feat.

300 Games, while pregnant
Audrey Gable, Allentown, Pa., approximately eight months
    pregnant, April 30, 1988.
Denise Welker, Houston, six months pregnant,
    Sept. 13, 1982, .
Eileen Arthur, Sacramento, Calif., five months pregnant,
    April 25, 1997.
Lisa McConkey Cezowitz, Lexington Park, Md., one month
    pregnant, Oct. 2, 1992.
Dusty Barna, North Miami, Fla., six weeks pregnant,
    April 13, 1993.

300 Games, youngest ABC members
13 Allen Loch, Nicholson, Pa., Feb. 8, 1985.
    Chad Gulden, Gettysburg, Pa., Aug. 6, 1992.
14 Kelby Stauffer, Ephrata, Pa., March 10, 1993.
    Joshua Cunningman, Bellflower, Calif., Feb. 8, 1993.
    Cory Lipps, Wichita, Kan., Jan. 23, 1993.
    James Roberts, Richmond, Va., Nov. 22, 1992.
    Jon Goodway, Rio Grande, N.Y., July 9, 1962.
    Rudolf Greenleaf Jr., Hammond, Ind., Sept. 23, 1993.

300 Games, youngest males
10 Scott Owsley, Fontana, Calif., March 26, 1994
    Sean Wyandt, Sinking Springs, Pa., June 5, 1994.
11 Matthew Gilman, Davie, Fla., July 17, 1993.
    Sam Arnone Jr., Ithaca, N.Y., Dec. 19, 1993.
    Alex Cavagnaro, New York City, Nov. 17, 1995
    and Nov. 27, 1995.

300 Games, youngest females
12 Nicole Long, Granite City, Ill., May 27, 1995.
    Tracy Castro, San Mateo, Calif., Jan. 11, 1993.
13 Kimberly Tosseng, Hammond, Ind., Nov. 7, 1993
    (YABA).
    Jennifer Petrick, Canton, Ohio, June 7, 1995.
    Michelle Endress, Staten Isalnd, N.Y., Nov. 5, 1994.

300 Games, youngest WIBC members
16 Mary Lou Oldham, Kansas City, May 11, 1962.
17 Sharon Parmley, Warrensburg, Mo., 1960-61.
    Mary Drew, Cleveland, Oct. 25, 1983.
18 Cathy Dorin, Linden, N.J., Dec. 14, 1984.
    Cindy Mason, Sunnyvale, Calif., May 24, 1980.
    Sybil Case, Madison, Tenn., Dec. 18, 1964.

600 Series, most consecutive
Men
65 Rick Minier, Vancouver, Wash., September 1986-
    May 1988.
61 Rick LaRue, Saginaw, Mich., March 1980-
    February 1981.

* — Men's records not on file

† — Women's records not on file

54   Ron Moore, Louisville, Ky., Jan. 17, 1986-
Nov. 27, 1987.

52   Ron Stromfeld, Columbus, Ohio, August 1977-
March 1978.
Dave Heller, Highland Hills, N.Y., April 1981-
May 1982.

600 Series, most consecutive in one league†
Men

100   Fran Bax, Tonawanda, N.Y., Feb. 25, 1994-April 25,
1997.

91   Chuck Haughn, Columbus, Ohio, Nov. 14, 1991-
Nov. 21, 1996 (did not bowl 1994-95 or 1995-96
season.

87   Rick Parsons, Lexington, Ky., Dec. 11, 1991-April 27,
1994, Greater Lexington Classic.

80   Lloyd Amidon, Syracuse, N.Y., Aptil 11,
1993-Dec. 16, 1994

67   Dan Tarrant, Sacramento, Calif., Jan. 13, 1994-
Dec. 14, 1995, ARC Classic.

700 Series, most consecutive†
Men

16   Randy Choat, Granite City, Ill., 1990-91.

13   Randy Choat, Granite City, Ill., 1987-88.

12   Nelson Burton Jr., St. Louis, 1962-63.
Daryl Wolf, Rock Island, Ill., 1989.

11   Dick Clayton, Beaver Falls, Pa., 1981-82.
Randy Choat, Granite City, Ill., 1986-87.

700 Series, lowest averages to accomplish feat *
Women

127   Cindy Hanke, Milwaukee, 212-256-268/736,
1980-81.

144   Penny Cook, Dayton, Ohio, 257-242-279/778,
June, 1993.

151   Nann Bogunovich, Denver, 247-179-279/705,
1980-81.

163   Millie Brown, Denver, 232-196-277/705, 1976-77.

161   Shirley Goodwin, Lauderhill, Fla., 241-234-246/721,
1992-93.

700 Series, most consecutive in same leagues*
Women

6   Linda Lunsford, Seattle, December 1993/January 1994

5   Jeanne Maiden-Naccarato, Tacoma, Wash.,
November/December 1979.*
Carolyn Trump, N. Ft. Meyers, Fla.,
November/December 1981.
Patty Ann, Arlington Heights, Ill., March/April
1982.

4   Kelly Sparano, Albany, Ore., October 1989.
*Did not bowl in one league session during string.

700 Series, most in season†
Men

98   Scott Tapley, Champaign, Ill.-Appleton, Wis.,
1989-90 (8 leagues).

80   Terry Henson, Salem, Mo., 1984-85 (5 leagues).

72   Arlo Heiland, St. Louis, 1962-63 (13 leagues).

61   Mel Zirzow, Milwaukee, 1967-68.
Rod Bordick, Kingsford, Mich., 1994-95 (4 leagues).

700 Series, most in series†
Men

5   Budweiser Beer, St. Louis, 834 775 759 754 736,
March 12, 1958.
Hermann Undertakers, St. Louis, 709 792 766 771
759, Jan. 27, 1937.
20th Century Lanes, St. Louis, 770 740 726 754 792,
April 21, 1978.

800 Series, ambidextrous
Men

Matt Buxton, Marion, Ohio, Jan. 4, 1982 (left-handed) and
March 19, 1989 and Nov. 15, 1991 (right-handed).

Frank Fitch, Lexington, Ky., Nov. 11, 1987 and Sept. 17,
1992 (left-handed) and Feb. 23, 1991 (right-handed).

Bryan Alpert, North Hills, Calif., May 3, 1990 and Aug. 1,
1996 right-handed) and Feb. 18, 1993 and Feb. 13,
1997 (left-handed).

Timothy Catching, Fresno, Calif., April 28, 1994
(right-handed) and Aug. 1, 1994 (left-handed).

800 Series, brothers, career

23   Jeff (18) and Craig (5) Jensen, Wichita, Kan.

21   Kevin (12) and Keith (9) Bruening, St. Charles, Mo.

800 Series, brothers, same night

Rick Day (803) and Dean Day (814), Wausau, Wis.,
Sept. 19, 1990.

800 Series, career, individual (See pg. 3)

800 Series, father and daughter

Henry Blough (800), 1978 and Lisa Farwell (801), April 23,
1994, Palmyra, Pa.

800 Series, father and son, career

24   Jerry (11) and Kris Netherton (13), Sacramento, Calif.

800 Series, father and son, same league, team and night

John Hatz (811) and son Mike (826), Denver,
Sept. 21, 1990.

Tracy (816 lefthanded) and son Rob (815 righthanded),
Elmira, N.Y., Nov. 22, 1995.

800 Series, father and two sons

Thomas Copp (812), Dec. 12, 1979, son Craig (808),
Dec. 8, 1988 and son Cameron (805), April 11, 1989,
Oshkosh, Wis.

Rick Hommes (800), Aug. 28, 1980, son John (814),
March 17, 1994 and son Chris (803), Dec. 14, 1995,
New Hope, Minn.

Jack Pentek (801), Dec. 15, 1981, son Scott (815), Dec 23,
1996 and son Brian (815), Dec. 30, 1996

Gordy Slauter Sr. (802), April 16, 1990, son Darryl (816),
Dec, 16, 1989 and son Scott (812), April 12, 1994,
Sparta, Mich.

---

* — Men's records not on file   † — Women's records not on file

800 Series, father and three sons
Bill Pollard Sr. (800) Nov. 2, 1994, son Bill Jr. (811),
    March 9, 1988; Rick (836), Jan. 13, 1988 and Ron (800),
    April 24, 1985.

800 Series, father, daughter and son
Kurt Renninger (804), Sept. 17, 1993, daughter Kelle (838),
    Nov. 20, 1994 and son Kyle (802), March 11, 1992,
    Williamsport, Pa.

800 Series, first by WIBC member
Beverly Ortner, South Sioux City, Neb. (818 series on games
    of 267, 264 and 287), Oct. 10, 1968.

800 Series, husbands and wives
12 Rory (9) and Sue (3) Peterson, Rocklin, Calif.

800 Series, most consecutive in same leagues
Women
2 Caren Park, Seattle, Apollo Scratch League, 805
    (279, 247, 279), Feb. 17, 1992. 805,
    (279, 237 and 289), Feb. 24, 1992.

Men
2 Achieved by many people

800 Series, most in same season
Women
3 Tish Johnson, Panorama City, Calif., 1985-86.
2 Caren Park, Seattle, 1991-92.
    Aleta Sill, Dearborn, Mich., 1984-85 and 1990-91.
    Pamela Kiesel, Throop, Pa., 1981-82.
    Patty Ann, Arlington Heights, Ill., 1981-82.
    Tish Johnson, Panorama City, Calif., 1988-89.
    Robin Romeo, Newhall, Calif., 1980-81.
    Tish Johnson, Panorama City, Calif., 1992-93.

Men
7 Ted Long, Wind Gap, Pa., 1980-81.
    Mark Crawford, Red Lion, Pa., 1995-96
    Warren Tam Wasson, Garland, Texas, 1995-96
    John Chacko Jr., Louksville, Pa., 1996-97
    Marv Akers, Stratford, Conn., 1996-97

800 Series, mother, father and daughter
Nadine Opplinger, Dwight Opplinger and daughter
    Jodi Jensen, Wichita, Kan., March 6, 1996.

800 Series, mother, father and sons
Norma Hill, Jerry Hill and sons Gary Hill and Mark Hill,
    Lawton, Okla.; 813, 806, 836 and 812; Dec. 11, 1977;
    Feb. 13, 1975; Aug. 25, 1977 and Aug. 12, 1992.

800 Series, sister and brothers
Tina Jensen and brothers Craig and Jeff, Wichita, Kan.; 800,
    Nov. 19, 1995 and numerous others.

800 Series, sister and brother
Carol Pautsch and Bill Pautsch, Fond du Lac, Wis.; 803,
    800; Apr. 16, 1980 and Dec. 29, 1991.
Patty Patterson and brothers Mike and Gil Daniels Jr.,
    June 13, 1995, El Paso, Texas, March 26, 1994 and
    Oct. 22, 1993.

800 Series, league opponents
1,625 Victor Corbin Jr. (813) and Rob Barton (812),
        Binghamton, N.Y., April 17, 1997, Hilltop
        Classic (both in fifth spot)
1,611 Mike Randesi Jr. (806) and Paul Cannon (805),
        Binghamton, N.Y., Oct. 16, 1977, Man
        Binghamton Press (Both in third spot).

800 Series, most by lefthanders†
Men
40 John Chacko Jr., Larksville, Pa.
21 Tony Torrice, Wolcott, Conn.
18 John Wilcox, Lewisburg, Pa.
 8 Ted Long, Allentown, Pa.
 6 Mike Batchelor, Seattle

800 Series, oldest bowler†
Men
77 George Houghland, Shawnee, Kan., March 9, 1993
    (817).
75 Ferdinand Georgie, Lansing, Mich., Dec. 23, 1987
    (807).
73 Ed Kulasinski, Reading, Pa., Nov. 4, 1995 (800).
    Wilfied Toby, Mansfield, Pa., Dec. 23, 1996 (826)
72 Roger St. Cyr, El Paso, Texas, April 17, 1997 (802)

800 Series, youngest bowler†
12 Matt Mundy, Ventura, Calif., Nov. 6, 1993 (856).
    Carey Patterson, Hyde Park, N.Y., March 4, 1991 (816).
13 Buck Miller, Milwaukee, Wis., Nov. 19, 1986 (826).
    Mike Cyc, Akron, Ohio, Feb. 5, 1989 (806).
    Kyle Renninger, Montoursville, Pa., March 11, 1992
    (802).

800 Series, youngest ABC member
14 William Ihrie III, Hickory, N.C., May 28, 1997 (800).
    Chad Gulden, Gettysburg, Pa., Oct. 2, 1992 (810).
16 Mike Estes, Sheridan, Wyo., March 3, 1987 (844).
    Dick Hoover, Akron, Ohio, Feb. 10, 1946 (847).
    John Santaluccia, Old Bridge, N.J., Aug. 21, 1995.

* — Men's records not on file   † — Women's records not on file

Year	City	Site	Dates	Entries Assns.	From States	Days	Lanes
1997	Huntsville, Ala.	Von Braun Civic Center	Feb. 8-June 8	1,221	50	121	48
1996	Salt Lake City, Utah	Salt Palace Convention Center	Feb. 10-June 12	1,245	50	124	48
1995	Reno, Nev.	National Bowling Stadium	Feb. 4-July 1	1,625	50	158	78
1994	Mobile, Ala.	Mobile Convention Center	Feb. 5-June 12	1,256	50	128	40
1993	Tulsa, Okla.	Tulsa Convention Center	Feb. 13-June 6	1,165	50	114	40
1992	Corpus Christi, Texas	Bayfront Plaza Convention Center	Feb. 8-June 1	1,148	50	114	40
1991	Toledo, Ohio	Sea Gate Convention Center	Feb. 9-June 1	1,144	50	113	40
1990	Reno, Nev.	Reno-Sparks Convention Center	Feb. 3-June 5	1,229	50	123	40
1989	Wichita, Kan.	Century II Convention Center	Feb. 11-May 25	1,182	50	104	40
1988	Jacksonville, Fla.	Prime Osborn Convention Center	Feb. 13-May 25	1,101	50	103	40
1987	Niagara Falls, N.Y.	International Convention Center	Feb. 14-May 25	1,061	50	101	40
1986	Las Vegas	Cashman Field Center	Feb. 8-June 21	1,339	50	134	40
1985	Tulsa, Okla.	Tulsa Convention Center	Feb. 9-May 26	1,215	50	107	40
1984	Reno, Nev.	Reno-Sparks Convention Center	Feb. 4 May 25	1,123	50	112	40
1983	Niagara Falls, N.Y.	International Convention Center	Feb. 12-May 22	899	50	100	40
1982	Baltimore	Baltimore Convention Center	Feb. 6-May 16	889	50	100	40
1981	Memphis, Tenn.	Cook Convention Center	Feb. 28-May 25	935	50	87	40
1980	Louisville, Ky.	Commonwealth Convention Center	March 1-May 25	886	50	86	40
1979	Tampa, Fla.	Florida Expo Hall	March 22-June 12	857	50	83	40
1978	St. Louis	Cervantes Convention Center	Feb. 18-May 14	935	50	86	40
1977	Reno, Nev.	Centennial Coliseum	Feb. 5-May 4	957	50	89	42
1976	Oklahoma City	Oklahoma City Myriad	Feb. 14-May 2	902	49	79	40
1975	Dayton, Ohio	Dayton Convention Center	Feb. 15-May 4	1,685	50	79	40
1974	Indianapolis	Indiana Convention Center	Feb. 16-May 5	1,647	50	79	40
1973	Syracuse, N.Y.	Onondaga County War Memorial	March 3-May 20	1,560	50	79	36
1972	Long Beach, Calif.	Long Beach Arena	Feb. 26-April 30	1,250	50	65	40
1971	Detroit	Cobo Hall	March 6-May 23	1,459	50	79	40
1970	Knoxville, Tenn.	Civic Auditorium	March 7-May 25	1,268	50	80	32
1969	Madison, Wis.	Dane County Coliseum	Feb. 22-May 11	1,518	50	79	40
1968	Cincinnati	Convention/Expositon Center	Feb. 27-May 11	1,467	49	75	40
1967	Miami Beach, Fla.	Convention Hall	March 4-May 7	1,060	48	65	34
1966	Rochester, N.Y.	War Memorial Building	March 19-May 23	1,187	48	66	40
1965	St. Paul, Minn.	St. Paul Auditorium	March 25-May 31	1,380	46	68	40
1964	Oakland, Calif.	Oakland Auditorium	Feb. 22-April 26	830	46	65	32
1963	Buffalo	State Armory	Feb. 16-April 28	1,313	50	72	40
1962	Des Moines, Iowa	Veterans Memorial Auditorium	Feb. 17-April 26	1,353	45	69	40
1961	Detroit	Cobo Hall	March 4-May 21	1,262	48	79	40
1960	Toledo, Ohio	Sports Arena	March 5-May 22	1,197	46	79	36
1959	St. Louis	138th Infantry Armory	Feb. 14-April 26	1,112	46	72	38
1958	Syracuse, N.Y.	Onondaga County War Memorial	March 29-June 8	967	40	72	36
1957	Fort Worth, Texas	Will Rogers Memorial Coliseum	March 9-April 28	407	35	51	32
1956	Rochester, N.Y.	Rochester War Memorial Building	March 3-May 2	995	43	79	40
1955	Fort Wayne, Ind.	Allen County Memorial Coliseum	March 26-June 5	1,127	45	72	38
1954	Seattle, Wash.	Field Artillery Armory	March 20-May 3	638	46	45	32
1953	Chicago	Chicago Coliseum	Feb. 21-May 24	1,298	45	93	40
1952	Milwaukee	Milwaukee Arena	March 22-June 14	1,158	43	85	40
1951	St. Paul, Minn.	Municipal Auditorium	April 7-June 3	964	44	58	40
1950	Columbus, Ohio	Columbus Coliseum	April 15-June 13	968	43	60	36
1949	Atlantic City, N.J.	Convention Hall	Feb. 12-April 9	980	42	57	46
1948	Detroit	State Fair Coliseum	March 14-May 14	948	42	80	40
1947	Los Angeles	National Guard Armory	March 27-May 12	491	38	47	36
1946	Buffalo	74th Regiment Armory	March 14-May 14		37	62	40
1943-45	No Tournament	World War II					
1942	Columbus, Ohio	Columbus Coliseum	March 3-May 13	824	37	72	36
1941	St. Paul, Minn.	Municipal Auditorium	March 13-May 6	865	40	55	40
1940	Detroit	State Fair Coliseum	March 7-May 7	729	37	62	40
1939	Cleveland	Lakeside Hall	March 9-May 5	621	35	58	32
1938	Chicago	Chicago Coliseum	March 3-April 19	649	32	48	40
1937	New York	Coast Artillery Armory	March 10-May 4	527	32	56	28

Team Entry	Doubles Entry	Singles Entry	- Team -				- Doubles -		- Singles -		- All Events -			Prize Fund
			Above 3,200	3,100-3,199	3,000-3,099	2,900-2,999	Above 1,300	1,200-1,299	Above 700	600-699	Above 2,000	1,900-1,999	1,800-1,899	
9,480	23,700	47,400	21	49	120	335	202	1,283	235	5,407	107	554	2,028	$2,787,802
9,764	23,946	47,892	35	88	238	478	365	1,886	521	7,755	268	1,097	2,864	2,824,330
17,285	42,809	85,664	22	94	216	723	255	2,233	393	10,957	144	916	3,708	3,524,940
9,285	23,849	47,865	6	36	109	282	107	995	179	5,363	52	313	1,659	1,855,735
8,518	21,480	42,960	32	55	170	351	397	1,563	542	6,576	284	916	2,546	1,726,720
8,557	21,496	42,992	18	58	220	528	241	1,698	274	7,189	167	773	2,804	1,730,095
8,359	21,060	42,120	34	76	200	456	325	1,844	526	7,395	252	941	2,922	1,698,565
9,199	23,000	46,000	2	14	50	149	95	864	126	4,601	35	252	1,259	1,920,255
7,717	19,280	38,560	34	67	176	394	215	1,347	355	8,836	174	737	2,262	1,720,586
7,562	19,000	38,000	0	5	20	71	16	342	29	2,519	7	59	536	1,536,270
7,480	18,600	37,200	0	6	21	99	17	348	22	2,519	2	47	501	1,511,205
10,019	25,282	50,564	1	8	44	155	38	619	68	3,882	19	154	1,005	2,100,845
7,700	19,448	38,896	1	0	27	95	15	424	45	2,719	5	54	583	1,547,045
8,380	20,950	41,900	1	2	33	92	9	371	33	2,601	5	86	587	1,657,710
7,132	17,479	34,958	1	9	32	140	19	461	18	2,948	6	66	723	1,443,350
6,627	16,251	32,502	2	5	14	63	15	334	26	2,170	2	46	454	1,336,215
6,400	15,906	31,812	0	9	40	171	41	617	53	3,315	16	145	917	1,106,955
6,269	15,364	30,728	0	2	12	69	33	337	44	2,248	8	91	501	1,072,840
6,213	15,762	31,524	1	4	33	116	29	417	36	2,356	14	111	657	912,144
6,684	16,085	32,119	0	0	6	23	6	287	17	1,817	0	27	354	940,637
7,203	17,840	35,679	0	3	9	61	4	305	14	2,075	1	25	349	1,045,605
5,679	13,871	25,768	1	8	29	99	39	380	39	2,185	7	78	597	808,736
6,244	13,414	26,453	1	6	39	162	22	542	26	2,615	2	73	722	797,387
6,138	13,239	26,397	1	18	45	126	51	567	65	2,897	30	180	744	793,055
5,590	10,593	21,170	0	5	17	101	10	314	18	1,741	2	35	390	680,852
4,732	9,486	19,019	0	3	27	75	12	239	12	1,411	1	38	336	612,297
6,219	12,012	24,026	1	6	46	164	12	452	22	2,442	4	62	668	756,721
4,802	10,824	21,720	3	8	43	132	15	429	15	2,241	7	80	584	587,110
6,258	11,863	23,759	1	6	20	108	16	325	13	1,945	1	55	451	663,570
5,923	10,954	21,917	1	0	13	66	6	203	9	1,356	0	20	286	550,560
3,554	7,240	14,545	3	8	43	139	24	327	14	1,646	6	66	439	363,125
5,208	8,706	17,456	1	6	16	68	18	235	21	1,452	6	65	306	465,623
5,472	9,817	19,617	0	1	7	33	2	113	1	920	0	3	144	492,452
3,791	5,727	11,419	2	5	12	67	5	202	11	1,017	3	33	246	337,321
5,010	10,047	20,049	0	10	34	196	20	490	23	2,240	1	79	610	503,492
5,292	9,608	19,215	2	7	41	117	22	463	22	2,071	5	60	543	486,804
6,216	10,741	21,499	0	2	11	62	9	213	4	1,481	0	17	282	470,091
5,716	10,563	21,166	0	0	12	71	6	231	8	1,436	0	18	250	410,056
5,482	9,903	19,768	2	8	20	101	14	255	16	1,569	2	31	341	386,646
5,434	8,712	17,402	3	3	15	86	13	255	13	1,459	4	33	330	356,452
3,056	5,962	11,961	0	2	23	47	9	172	11	917	2	29	257	228,157
5,845	10,197	20,420	0	0	1	24	1	157	3	1,101	1	6	136	404,646
5,826	11,312	22,620	0	1	10	44	2	150	9	1,280	0	16	230	429,401
3,178	3,853	7,685	1	1	3	15	4	83	4	502	0	14	101	174,560
8,180	14,862	29,817	0	5	8	53	11	291	11	2,012	0	26	321	577,283
7,735	13,141	26,359	0	1	6	38	6	242	17	1,943	1	15	249	455,940
5,195	9,636	19,400	0	0	12	60	13	318	13	1,908	2	37	362	298,284
5,109	11,177	22,459	0	0	0	13	3	149	6	1,234	0	5	119	349,769
5,444	11,741	22,963	0	0	1	8	4	178	5	1,493	0	5	149	377,556
7,348	14,018	27,965	0	0	2	21	8	207	9	1,985	0	11	195	412,530
3,356	5,337	10,510	0	0	2	22	3	148	11	842	0	16	146	178,857
5,744	12,780	25,567	0	0	1	17	8	250	11	1,638	2	12	158	210,417
5,742	11,848	23,773	0	3	5	48	15	320	27	1,969	0	20	309	254,704
5,797	9,787	20,073	0	0	11	36	12	349	25	1,976	1	32	339	230,111
6,073	10,404	20,884	0	0	2	21	8	252	19	1,792	1	16	219	240,827
4,145	8,349	16,809	0	1	12	86	15	338	16	1,906	2	37	440	184,867
4,957	8,620	17,441	1	0	15	56	5	282	12	1,564	0	22	308	199,158
4,017	5,883	11,775	0	2	9	53	9	263	13	1,372	3	24	315	145,806

Year	City	Site	Dates	Entries Assns.	From States	Days	Lanes
1936	Indianapolis	Tomlinson Hall	March 9-April 14	393	32	37	32
1935	Syracuse, N.Y.	National Guard Armory	March 1-April 8	292	21	41	24
1934	Peoria, Ill.	Peoria Coliseum	March 8-April 9	257	20	33	24
1933	Columbus, Ohio	Columbus Coliseum	March 9-April 10	212	18	33	28
1932	Detroit	State Fair Coliseum	March 8-April 11	216	18	35	32
1931	Buffalo	Broadway Auditorium	Feb. 27-April 6	196	20	39	32
1930	Cleveland	Cleveland Public Auditorium	March 1-April 7	270	25	38	32
1929	Chicago	Dexter Park Pavilion	March 2-April 9	279	25	39	32
1928	Kansas City, Mo.	American Royal Building	March 5-April 2	159	25	29	28
1927	Peoria, Ill.	Peoria Armory	March 6-April 6	151	24	32	24
1926	Toledo, Ohio	Toledo Armory	March 6-April 6	134	16	32	28
1925	Buffalo	Broadway Auditorium	March 5-April 6	145	17	33	28
1924	Chicago	Chicago Armory	Feb. 23-March 26	183	18	33	28
1923	Milwaukee	Milwaukee Auditorium	March 10-April 10	168	17	31	28
1922	Toledo, Ohio	Terminal-Expo Building	Feb. 27-March 28	136	17	30	16
1921	Buffalo	Broadway Auditorium	Feb. 28-March 31	89	19	32	16
1920	Peoria, Ill.	Peoria Coliseum	March 10-April 16	129	20	28	14
1919	Toledo, Ohio	Terminal Building	March 8-29	74	19	23	16
1918	Cincinnati	Cincinnati Armory	Feb. 16-March 10	87	15	23	16
1917	Grand Rapids, Mich.	Grand Rapids Coliseum	March 3-25	71	15	23	16
1916	Toledo, Ohio	Terminal Building	March 4-25	97	24	22	16
1915	Peoria, Ill.	Peoria Coliseum	March 10-30	80	22	21	14
1914	Buffalo	Broadway Auditorium	March 8-25	79	16	18	16
1913	Toledo, Ohio	Terminal Building	Feb. 22-March 15	86	16	22	16
1912	Chicago	International Amphitheatre	March 2-24	66	16	23	18
1911	St. Louis	St. Louis Coliseum	Jan. 21-Feb. 1	76	15	17	16
1910	Detroit	Wayne Garden	Feb. 28-March 5	87	18	16	16
1909	Pittsburgh	Keystone Building	Feb. 27-March 15	87	16	15	16
1908	Cincinnati	Cincinnati Armory	Feb. 8-22	60	15	15	16
1907	St. Louis	West End Coliseum	March 16-31	46	13	16	12
1906	Louisville, Ky.	Louisville Armory	March 17-27	51	21	11	16
1905	Milwaukee	Exposition Building	Feb. 18-25	65	21	8	14
1904	Cleveland, Ohio	Central Armory	Feb. 8-23	33	13	6	10
1903	Indianapolis	Tomlinson Hall	Feb. 23-March 1	25	9	7	10
1902	Buffalo	Western NYAA Building	Jan. 20-24	20	9	5	8
1901	Chicago	Welsbach Building	Jan. 8-11	17	9	4	6
			Totals			5,738	3,010

Team Entry	Doubles Entry	Singles Entry	Above 3,200	3,100-3,199	3,000-3,099	2,900-2,999	Above 1,300	1,200-1,299	Above 700	600-699	Above 2,000	1,900-1,999	1,800-1,899	Prize Fund
					- Team -		- Doubles -		- Singles -		- All Events -			
2,853	4,571	9,181	0	0	6	26	4	190	10	1,026	1	11	219	108,928
2,837	3,429	6,889	0	0	2	20	4	113	3	678	1	5	129	92,927
1,329	2,601	5,231	0	0	4	23	2	147	5	682	0	13	137	57,212
1,597	2,329	4,687	0	0	2	17	7	141	9	704	2	13	190	60,655
2,336	3,582	7,177	0	2	4	24	5	158	11	880	0	13	170	86,737
2,639	3,649	7,305	0	0	1	12	1	98	4	693	0	5	118	92,660
2,443	4,503	9,021	0	1	1	30	7	181	13	1,082	0	16	221	100,807
2,523	4,917	9,888	0	0	9	51	8	233	12	1,166	0	16	273	107,790
2,251	2,280	4,571	0	0	4	29	4	150	2	591	0	7	151	67,953
1,452	3,243	6,498	0	1	10	33	3	168	4	856	1	12	205	67,480
1,876	3,790	7,626	0	0	4	27	7	135	15	931	0	12	192	81,953
2,200	3,441	6,817	0	0	1	13	1	78	4	546	0	2	89	82,331
2,132	4,702	9,451	0	0	2	24	8	177	15	924	0	23	198	98,383
1,956	3,794	7,666	0	2	1	16	5	174	11	961	3	17	117	83,446
1,126	2,411	4,838	0	0	0	11	3	81	1	464	0	5	80	50,967
940	2,133	4,229	0	0	2	5	1	45	1	306	0	1	45	43,984
900	1,977	3,994	0	0	2	15	1	53	2	381	0	1	65	41,493
796	1,727	3,504	0	0	0	7	1	50	2	290	0	5	45	36,460
654	1,494	3,033	0	0	1	2	1	40	1	277	0	3	40	30,970
714	1,534	3,099	0	0	2	6	3	55	0	234	0	3	48	32,460
756	1,566	3,178	0	0	0	1	0	28	0	185	0	1	28	33,633
513	1,139	2,327	0	0	0	1	0	22	1	125	0	0	8	23,900
450	953	1,926	0	0	0	2	0	14	0	113	0	0	6	20,273
502	1,166	2,369	0	0	1	6	0	41	0	200	0	1	30	24,037
596	1,415	2,894	0	0	0	1	0	13	0	115	0	0	8	29,013
414	851	1,711	0	0	0	1	0	15	0	87	0	2	9	21,932
401	986	2,007	0	0	0	0	0	5	1	104	0	1	14	25,432
374	799	1,551	0	0	0	1	1	5	0	68	0	0	10	21,331
362	763	1,469	0	0	0	1	0	12	0	92	0	1	5	20,400
244	512	1,026	0	0	0	0	0	0	0	14	0	0	0	13,897
221	460	897	0	0	0	0	0	2	0	34	0	0	0	12,418
217	435	813	0	0	0	0	0	1	0	18	0	0	0	11,610
112	224	452	0	0	0	0	0	0	0	0	0	0	1	6,395
78	152	247	0	0	0	0	0	4	0	26	0	0	3	4,137
61	104	219	0	0	0	0	0	2	0	8	0	0	1	2,600
41	78	115	0	0	0	0	0	1	0	4	0	0	0	1,592
16,236	888,470	1,774,016	235	722	2,460	8,132	2,975	31,591	4,247	171,881	1,365	8,968	44,720	53,573,268

ABC TOURNAMENT CHAMPIONS

(Tournament not held in 1943, 1944 and 1945 because of World War II)

SINGLES

Year	Winner	Games			Series
1997	John Socha, Milwaukee	278	290	279	847
1996	Don Scudder, Cincinnati	244	300	279	823
1995	Matt Surina, Mead, Wash.	268	258	300	826
1994	John Weltzien, Boca Raton, Fla.	287	277	246	810
1993	Dan Bock, Owatonna, Minn.	264	246	288	798
1992	Bob Youker Jr., Syracuse, N.Y.	246	288	267	801
	Gary Blatchford, Phoenix	243	279	279	801
1991	Ed Deines, LaPorte, Colo.	268	300	258	826
1990	Bob Hochrein, Dubuque, Iowa	278	255	258	791
1989	Paul Tetreault, Lebanon, N.H.	278	268	267	813
1988	Steve Hutkowski, Hershey, Pa.	223	287	264	774
1987	Terry Taylor, Nashville, Tenn.	226	268	255	749
1986	Jeff Mackey, Mexico, Mo.	216	279	279	774
1985	Glenn Harbison, Pittsburgh	263	236	275	774
1984	Bob Antczak, Chicago	208	298	258	764
	Neal Young, Louisville, Ky.	196	289	279	764
1983	Rickey Kendrick, Springfield, Ill.	257	221	257	735
1982	Bruce Bohm, Chicago	288	213	247	748
1981	Michael (Rob) Vital, Lancaster, Pa.	247	268	265	780
1980	Mike Eaton, Grand Rapids, Mich.	245	258	279	782
1979	Rick Peters, Franklin, Ohio	244	252	265	761
1978	Rich Mersek, Cleveland	239	256	244	739
1977	Frank Gadaleto, Lansing, Mich.	245	246	247	738
1976	Mike Putzer, Oshkosh, Wis.	279	258	221	758
1975	Jim Setser, Dayton, Ohio	219	279	258	756
1974	Gene Krause, Cleveland	247	257	269	773
1973	Ed Thompson, Denver	256	279	227	762
1972	Bill Pointer, Pontiac, Mich.	219	232	288	739
1971	Al Cohn, Chicago	226	245	267	738
1970	Jake Yoder, Ft. Wayne, Ind.	246	300	198	744
1969	Greg Campbell, St. Louis	259	238	254	751
1968	Wayne Kowalski, Revere, Mass.	279	241	218	738
1967	Frank Perry, Lorain, Ohio	265	227	231	723
1966	Don Chapman, Scranton, Pa.	268	226	267	761
1965	Kenneth Roeth, Dubuque, Iowa	224	257	219	700
1964	Jim Stefanich, Chicago	242	216	268	726
1963	Fred Delello, Oneonta, N.Y.	257	253	234	744
1962	Andrew Renaldy, Youngstown, Ohio	207	269	244	720
1961	Lyle Spooner, St. Cloud, Minn.	225	226	275	726
1960	Paul Kulbaga, Cleveland	256	202	268	726
1959	Ed Lubanski, Detroit	241	265	258	764
1958	Edward Shay, Chester, Pa.	210	223	300	733
1957	Bob Allen, Yonkers, N.Y.	235	196	298	729
1956	George Wade, Steubenville, Ohio	258	247	239	744
1955	Edward Gerzine, Milwaukee	225	235	278	738
1954	Tony Sparando, Rego Park, N.Y.	300	245	178	723
1953	Frank Santore, Long Island City, N.Y.	226	279	244	749
1952	Al Sharkey, Chicago	267	269	222	758
1951	Lee Jouglard, Detroit	242	255	278	775
1950	Everett Leins, Aurora, Ill.	228	266	263	757
1949	Bernard Rusche, Cincinnati	214	257	245	716
1948	Lincoln Protich, Akron, Ohio	256	233	232	721
1947	Junie McMahon, Chicago	247	248	245	740
1946	Leo Rollick, Santa Monica, Calif.	193	279	265	737
1942	John Stanley, Cleveland	258	253	245	756
1941	Fred Ruff Jr., Belleville, Ill.	258	258	229	745
1940	Ray Brown, Terre Haute, Ind.	231	278	233	742
1939	James Danek, Forest Park, Ill.	221	275	234	730
1938	Knute Anderson, Moline, Ill.	244	225	277	746
1937	Gene Gagliardi, Mt. Vernon, N.Y.	266	277	206	749
1936	Charles Warren, Springfield, Ill.	276	245	214	735
1935	Don Brokaw, Canton, Ohio	246	242	245	733
1934	Jerry Vidro, Grand Rapids, Mich.	243	277	201	721
1933	Earl Hewitt, Erie, Pa.	207	259	258	724
1932	Otto Nitschke, Cleveland	245	255	231	731
1931	Walter Lachowski, Erie, Pa.	243	267	202	712
1930	Larry Shotwell, Covington, Ky.	237	270	267	774
1929	Adolph Unke, Milwaukee	205	255	268	728
1928	Henry Summers, St. Louis	201	258	246	705
1927	William Eggars, Chicago	223	247	236	706
1926	Ed Votel, Braddock, Pa.	254	244	233	731
1925	Al Green, Chicago	205	244	257	706
1924	Harry Smyers, Pittsburgh	227	255	267	749
1923	Carl Baumgartner, Cincinnati	238	209	277	724
1922	Walter Lundgren, Chicago	234	232	263	729
1921	Fred Smith, Detroit	224	276	202	702
1920	Joe Shaw, Chicago	221	235	257	713
1919	Harry Cavan, Pittsburgh	279	215	224	718
1918	C. J. Styles, Detroit	247	233	222	702
1917	Otto Kallusch, Rochester, N.Y.	213	232	253	698
1916	Sam Schliman, Toronto, Ont.	239	256	190	685
	Bill Hueseman, Cincinnati	205	226	254	685
	F. Shaw, Chicago	205	257	223	685
1915	Wallace Pierce, Pueblo, Colo.	276	226	209	711
1914	William Miller, Detroit	248	204	223	675
1913	Frank Peterson, Columbus, Ohio	234	223	236	693
1912	Larry Sutton, Rochester, N.Y.	213	209	257	679
1911	James Blouin, Chicago	230	195	256	681
1910	Thomas Haley, Detroit	236	268	201	705
1909	Larry Sutton, Rochester, N.Y.	236	212	243	691
	Frank Bruggeman, Sioux City, Iowa	192	256	243	691
1908	Archie Wengler, Chicago	222	200	277	699
1907	Marshall Levey, Indianapolis	215	202	207	624
	R.T. Matak, St. Paul, Minn.	221	210	193	624
1906	Frank Favour, Oshkosh, Wis.	227	221	221	669
1905	C.M. Anderson, St. Paul, Minn.	230	216	205	651
1904	Martin Kern, St. Louis	221	194	232	647
1903	Dan Jones, Milwaukee	232	248	203	683
1902	Fred Strong, Chicago	214	209	226	649
1901	Frank Briell, Chicago	212	237	199	648

*Won rolloff

DOUBLES

Year	Winner	Series
1997	Paul Zuehlke, 761 Rob Stueber, 703, Oshkosh, Wis.	1,464
1996	Jamie Burke, 826, Loveland, Ohio Drew Hauck, 682, Finneytown, Ohio	1,508
1995	Michael Wambold, 763, Scott Kruppenbacher, 723, Rochester, N.Y.	1,486
1994	Dean Distin, 738, Mike Tryniski, 730, Fulton, N.Y.	1,468
1993	Rick Fangman, 750, Gilbertville, Iowa, Darrin Lindsey, 748, Vinton, Iowa	1,498

Dave Callery, 763, Terry Saccone, 735,
Cincinnati — 1,498

Ron Wilde, 810, Randy Wilde, 688,
Green Bay, Wis. — 1,498

1992 Dave Bernhardt, 771, Gene Stus, 716, Detroit — 1,487

1991 Jimmy Johnson, 784, Columbus, Ohio,
Dan Nadeau, 721, Las Vegas, Nev. — 1,505

1990 Bob Ujvari, 685, Mike Neumann, 763, Buffalo — 1,448

1989 Gary Daroszewski, 742,
Gus Yannaras, 757, Milwaukee — 1,499

1988 Mark Lewis, 713, Mark Jensen, 737,
Wichita, Kan. — 1,450

1987 Ray Betchkal, 751, Dennis Schlichting, 629,
Racine, Wis. — 1,380

1986 Don Cook, 762, Milwaukee, Bob Larson, 656,
Kenosha, Wis. — 1,418

1985 Howard Higby, 718, Clyde Gibson, 648,
Lake Jackson, Texas — 1,366

1984 Chris Cobus, 743, John Megna, 640,
Milwaukee — 1,383

1983 Rick McCardy, 731, Tony Loiacano, 651,
Detroit — 1,382

1982 Rich Wonders, 704, Racine Wis.,
Darold Meisel, 660, Milwaukee — 1,364

1981 Jim Kontos, 713, Munster, Ind.,
Al Bruder, 649, Chicago — 1,362

Ted Hannahs, 687, Zanesville, Ohio,
Bob Blaney, 675, Cambridge, Ohio — 1,362

1980 Ron Thacker, 617, Bob Bures, 761,
Cleveland, Ohio — 1,378

1979 Mike Turnbull, 767, Jack Wilson, 621,
Akron, Ohio — 1,388

1978 Bob Kulaszewicz, 644, Don Gazzana, 708,
Milwaukee — 1,352

1977 Bob Roy, Denver, 672, Walt Roy, 646,
Glenwood Springs, Colo. — 1,318

1976 Fred Willen Sr., 698,
Gary Voss, 658, St. Louis — 1,356

1975 Bob Metz, 746, Steve Partlow, 614,
Dayton, Ohio — 1,360

1974 Chuck Sunseri, 717, Bob Hart, 702, Detroit — 1,419

1973 Jamie Brooks, 651, Jim Paine, 686, Houston — 1,337

1972 Jerry Nutt, 664, Bill Stanfield, 686,
Grand Rapids, Mich. — 1,350

1971 Tony Maresca, 709, Bill Haley, 621, Phoenix — 1,330

1970 Dick Selgo, 686, Don Bredehoft, 685,
Toledo, Ohio — 1,371

1969 Robert Maschmeyer, 660,
Charles Guedel, 719, Indianapolis — 1,379

1968 Richard Stark, 712, Walt Roy, 613,
Glenwood Springs, Colo. — 1325

1967 Mark Kuglitsch, 694, Ron Wheeler, 663,
Milwaukee — 1,357

1966 Tony Loiacano, 658, Bob Kwiecien, 693,
Detroit — 1,351

1965 Buzz Bosler, 635, Dan Slak, 665, Milwaukee — 1,300

1964 Pat Russo, 691, Tony Russo, 652,
Teaneck, N.J. — 1,343

1963 Wilford (Bus) Oswalt, 677,
Gerry Schmidt, 660, Ft. Wayne, Ind. — 1,337

1962 John Gribin, 665, Gary Madison, 711,
Riverside, Calif. — 1,376

1961 Joseph Macaluso, 660, Eugene Hering, 682,
Irvington, N.J. — 1,342

1960 Andy Marzich, 706, Dick Jensen, 663,
Los Angeles — 1,369

1959 Barney Vehige, 691,
Gilbert (Gib) Fischbach, 681, St. Louis — 1,372

1958 John (Bill) Tucker, 731, Jim Vrenick, 683,
St. Louis — 1,414

1957 Ronald Jones, 726, Joe Meszaros, 643,
Sterling, Ohio — 1,369

1956 Bill Lillard, 674, Stan Gifford, 657, Chicago — 1,331

1955 Harry Zoeller, 666, George Pacropis, 699,
Wilkes-Barre, Pa — 1,365

1954 Don McClaren, 710, St. Louis, Mo.,
Billy Welu, 625, Houston — 1,335

1953 Edward Koepp, 624, Joe Kissoff, 715,
Cleveland — 1,339

1952 John Klares, 755, Steve Nagy, 698,
Cleveland — 1,453

1951 Bob Benson, 654, Eddie Marshall, 680,
Lansing, Mich. — 1,334

1950 Willis Ebosh, 696, Earl Linsz, 629, Cleveland — 1,325

1949 Donald Van Boxel, 688, Green Bay, Wis.,
Gene Bernhardt, 644, Sturgeon Bay, Wis. — 1,332

1948 James Towns, 732, William Sweeney, 629,
Chicago — 1,361

1947 Edward Doerr Jr., 707, Len Springmeyer, 649,
St. Louis — 1,356

1946 John Gworek, 662, Henry Kmidowski, 698,
Buffalo — 1,360

1942 Edward Nowicki, 682, George Baier, 695,
Milwaukee — 1,377

1941 William Lee, 579,
Ray Farness, 767, Madison, Wis. — 1,346

1940 Herbert Freitag, 642, Joe Sinke, 704, Chicago — 1,346

1939 Philip Icuss, 684, Murray Fowler, 721,
Steubenville, Ohio — 1,405

1938 Don Johnson, 649, Fonnie Snyder, 688,
Indianapolis — 1,337

1937 Virgil Gibbs, 665, Kansas City, Mo.,
Nelson Burton Sr., 694, Dallas — 1,359

1936 Anthony Slanina, 714, Mike Straka, 633,
Chicago — 1,347

1935 Clyde Sumerix, 662, Harry Souers, 686,
Akron, Ohio — 1,348

1934 George Rudolph, 692, John Ryan, 629,
Waukegan, Ill. — 1,321

1933 Gil Zunker, 750, Frank Benkovic, 665,
Milwaukee — 1,415

1932 Frank Benkovic, 690, Charley Daw, 668,
Milwaukee — 1,358

1931 Edward Rafferty, 638, Charles Reilly, 678,
Philadelphia — 1,316

1930 James Divine, 612, George Heup, 727,
Beloit, Wis. — 1,339

1929 Walter Klecz, 676, Peter Butler, 677,
Chicago — 1,353

1928 Henry Will, 686, Joe Hradek, 677,
Chicago — 1,363

1927 Michael Flick, 663, Frank Snyder, 654,
Erie, Pa. — 1,317

1926 Charles Aston, 650, Phil Young, 705,
Akron, Ohio — 1,355

Fred Gardella, 705, Fred Tocco, 650, Detroit — 1,355

1925 Ed Schupp, 702, Ed Karich, 616, Chicago — 1,318

1924 Harry Thoma, 655, Clarence Thoma, 725,
Chicago — 1,380

1923 Charley Daw, 727, Finnis Wilson, 631,
Milwaukee   1,358
1922 Chris Spinella, 622, Barney Spinella, 714,
New York   1,336
1921 Otto Kallusch, 627, Art Schieman, 687,
Rochester, N.Y.   1,314
1920 Marv Erickson, 635, Edward Krems, 666,
Chicago   1,301
1919 Otto Kallusch, 599, Ernie Barnes, 706,
Rochester, N.Y.   1,305
1918 Harry Steers, 715, Fred Thoma, 620, Chicago 1,335
1917 G. Satorius, 688, William Holzschuh, 648,
Peoria, Ill.   1,346
1916 Frank Thoma, 658, Hank Marino, 621,
Chicago   1,279
1915 Harold Allen, 656, Ray Allen, 641, Detroit 1,297
1914 John Negley, 615, D. H. Van Ness, 630,
Newark, N.J.   1,245
1913 Peter Schultz, 709, John Koster, 582,
Newark, N.Y.   1,291
1912 N. P. Owen, 615, Phil Sutton, 644,
Louisville, Ky.   1,259
1911 W. M. Hartley, 684, Louis Seiler, 562,
E. Liverpool, Ohio   1,246
1910 Al Daiker, 624, Ed Wetterman, 607,
Cincinnati   1,231
1909 Al Schwoegler, 628, Tony Schwoegler, 676,
Madison, Wis.   1,304
1908 James Chalmers, 655, Henry Kiene, 599,
Chicago   1,254
1907 E. G. Richter, 564, E. Bigley, 600,
Louisville, Ky.   1,164
1906 J. N. Reed, 660, Earl Dresbach, 587,
Columbus, Ohio   1,247
1905 Ed Stretch, 577, Robert Rolfe, 636, Chicago 1,213
1904 H. H. Krause, 562, C. H. Spies, 622,
Washington, D.C.   1,184
1903 Harry Collin, 604, Kip Selbach, 623,
Columbus, Ohio   1,227
1902 Jim McClean, 603, Harry Steers, 634,
Chicago   1,237
1901 John Voorhies, 633, Charles Starr, 570,
New York   1,203
*Won rolloff

ALL EVENTS

Year	Winner	T	D	S	Series
1997	Jeff Richgels, Oregon, Wis.	774	692	775	2,241
1996	Scott Kurtz, Somerset, N.J.	731	725	768	2,224
1995	Jeff Kwiatkowski, Maumee, Ohio	762	732	697	2,194
1994	Tom Holt, Lubbock, Texas	726	693	771	2,190
1993	Jeff Nimke, Oshkosh, Wis.	701	779	774	2,254
1992	Mike Tucker, Fountain Valley, Calif.	700	711	747	2,158
1991	Tom Howery, Madison, Wis.	782	662	772	2,216
1990	Mike Neumann, Buffalo	707	763	698	2,168
1989	George Hall, Mundelein, Ill.	747	747	733	2,227
1988	Rick Steelsmith, Wichita, Kan.	642	658	753	2,053
1987	Ryan Shafer, Elmira, N.Y.	798	635	611	2,044
1986	Ed Marzka, Detroit	685	740	691	2,116
1985	Barry Asher, Anaheim, Calif.	642	685	706	2,033
1984	Bob Goike, Detroit	672	710	760	2,142
1983	Tony Cariello, Chicago	661	677	721	2,059
1982	Rich Wonders, Racine, Wis.	641	704	731	2,076
1981	Rod Toft, St. Paul, Minn.	650	727	730	2,107
1980	Steve Fehr, Cincinnati	673	710	693	2,076
1979	Bob Basacchi, Detroit	681	709	707	2,097
1978	Chris Cobus, Milwaukee	646	663	685	1,994
1977	Bud Debenham, Los Angeles	716	748	653	2,117
1976	Jim Lindquist, Minneapolis	618	696	757	2,071
1975	Bobby Meadows, Dallas	636	701	696	2,033
1974	Bob Hart, Detroit	687	702	698	2,087
1973	Ron Woolet, Louisville, Ky.	760	669	675	2,104
1972	Mac Lowry, Seattle	691	669	666	2,026
1971	Al Cohn, Chicago	639	686	738	2,063
1970	Mike Berlin, Muscatine, Iowa	688	647	669	2,004
1969	Eddie Jackson, Cincinnati	649	685	654	1,988
1968	Vince Mazzanti, Philadelphia	732	600	639	1,971
1967	Gary Lewis, Chicago	620	719	671	2,010
1966	John Wilcox, Williamsport, Pa.	673	613	718	2,004
1965	Tom Hathaway, Los Angeles	589	694	639	1,922
1964	Les Zikes, Chicago	604	683	714	2,001
1963	Wilford (Bus) Oswalt, Ft. Wayne, Ind.	682	677	696	2,055
1962	Billy Young, Tulsa, Okla.	609	712	694	2,015
1961	Luke Karan, Detroit	579	750	631	1,960
1960	Vince Lucci, Trenton, N.J.	643	697	645	1,985
1959	Ed Lubanski, Detroit	700	652	764	2,116
1958	Al Faragalli, Paterson, N.J.	641	719	683	2,043
1957	Jim Spalding, Louisville, Ky.	706	720	662	2,088
1956	Bill Lillard, Chicago	683	674	661	2,018
1955	Fred Bujack, Detroit	627	631	735	1,993
1954	Brad Lewis, Ashland, Ohio	636	698	651	1,985
1953	Frank Santore, New York	600	645	749	1,994
1952	Steve Nagy, Cleveland	662	698	705	2,065
1951	Tony Lindemann, Detroit	656	663	686	2,005
1950	Frank Santore, New York	662	611	708	1,981
1949	John Small, Chicago	552	722	667	1,941
1948	Ned Day, Milwaukee	667	637	675	1,979
1947	Junie McMahon, Chicago	576	649	740	1,965
1946	Joe Wilman, Chicago	658	706	690	2,054
1942	Stanley Moskal, Saginaw, Mich.	599	711	663	1,973
1941	Harold Kelly, South Bend, Ind.	647	652	714	2,013
1940	Fred Fischer, Buffalo	688	667	646	2,001
1939	Joe Wilman, Chicago	627	693	708	2,028
1938	Donald Beatty, Jackson, Mich.	709	640	629	1,978
1937	Max Stein, Belleville, Ill.	658	707	705	2,070
1936	John Murphy, Indianapolis	685	682	639	2,006
1935	Ora Mayer, San Francisco	648	692	682	2,022
1934	Walter Reppenhagen, Detroit	634	702	636	1,972
1933	Gil Zunker, Milwaukee	598	750	712	2,060
1932	Hugh Stewart, Cincinnati	672	616	692	1,980
1931	Mike Mauser, Youngstown, Ohio	639	687	640	1,966
1930	George Morrison, Chicago	716	625	644	1,985
1929	Otto Stein Jr., St. Louis	637	691	646	1,974
1928	Phil Wolf, Chicago	657	650	630	1,937
1927	Barney Spinella, New York	595	732	687	2,014
1926	Harry Gerloski, Detroit	655	656	670	1,981
1925	Clarence Long, Buffalo	708	624	645	1,977
1924	A. F. Weber, Elizabeth, N.J.	683	638	654	1,975
1923	William Knox, Philadelphia	618	686	715	2,019
1922	Barney Spinella, New York	635	714	650	1,999
1921	Art Schieman, Rochester, N.Y.	658	687	564	1,909
1920	Jimmy Smith, Milwaukee	575	700	640	1,915
1919	Mort Lindsey, New Haven, Conn.	664	579	690	1,933

Year	Winner				
1918	Harry Steers, Chicago	569	715	675	1,959
1917	H. Miller, Detroit	693	649	603	1,945
1916	Frank Thoma, Chicago	628	658	633	1,919
1915	Matty Faetz, Chicago	646	624	606	1,876
1914	William Miller, Detroit	565	657	675	1,897
1913	Ed Hermann, Cleveland	723	634	615	1,972
1912	Phil Sutton, Louisville, Ky.	571	644	628	1,843
1911	Jimmy Smith, Buffalo	609	673	637	1,919
1910	Thomas Haley, Detroit	617	639	705	1,961
1909	James Blouin, Chicago	656	578	651	1,885
1908	Russ Crable, E. Liverpool, Ohio	648	653	623	1,924
1907	H. C. Ellis, Grand Rapids, Mich.	629	588	558	1,775
1906	J. T. Peacock, Indianapolis	585	591	618	1,794
1905	Jack Reilly, Chicago	609	605	577	1,791
1904	Martin Kern, St. Louis	536	621	647	1,804
1903	Fred Strong, Chicago	657	626	613	1,896
1902	John Koster, New York	639	555	647	1,841
1901	Frank Briell, Chicago	478	610	648	1,736

TEAM

Year	Winner	Games			Series
1997	Dan Ottman Enterprises, Troy, Mich.	1,078	1,065	1,236	3,379
1996	Trout's Minnows, Spokane, Wash.	1,191	1,138	1,144	3,473
1995	Arden Lanes, Seattle	1,139	1,145	1,103	3,387
1994	Bluemound Bowl, Milwaukee	1,113	1,155	1,037	3,305
1993	Bruegger's Bagels No. 1, Albany, N.Y.	1,185	1,189	1,163	3,537
1992	Coors Light, Reading, Pa.	1,065	1,161	1,118	3,344
1991	Tri-State Lanes, Chatanooga, Tenn.	1,167	1,195	1,048	3,410
1990	Brunswick Rhinos No. 1, Buffalo	1,042	1,077	1,082	3,201
	State Farm-Lou Magic Agency, Detroit	972	1,179	1,050	3,201
1989	Chilton Vending, Wichita, Kan.	1,232	1,155	1,094	3,481
1988	Minnesota Loons No. 1, St. Paul, Minn.	1,068	996	1,088	3,152
1987	Sound Track, Salamanca, N.Y.	1,037	1,057	1,103	3,197
1986	Faball Enterprises No. 2, Milwaukee	1134	1024	1095	3,253
1985	Terry's Pro Shop, Solon, Ohio	972	1,160	1,101	3,233
1984	Minnesota Loons No. 1, St. Paul, Minn.	1,121	1,095	1,012	3,228
1983	Doug Heim's Niagara Frontier Bowling Supply, Niagara Falls, N.Y.	1,036	1,123	1,127	3,286
1982	Carl's Bowlers Paddock, Cincinnati	1,107	1,096	1,065	3,268
1981	Strachota's Milshore Bowl, Milwaukee	1,049	1,089	1,050	3,188
1980	Stroh's Beer, Detroit	981	1,175	963	3,119
1979	Hal Lieber Trophies, Gary, Ind.	1,041	1,075	1,086	3,202
1978	Berlin's Pro Shop, Muscatine, Iowa	1,004	1,045	1,028	3,077
1977	Rendel's GMC, Joliet, Ill.	1,022	1,061	992	3,075
1976	Andy's Pro Shop, Tucson, Ariz.	1,071	1,041	1,075	3,187
1975	Roy Black Chrysler, Cleveland	1,119	1,053	1,062	3,234
1974	Olympia Beer, Omaha, Neb.	868	1,147	1,171	3,186
1973	Thelmal Masters, Louisville, Ky.	1,033	943	1,142	3,118
1972	Hamm's Beer, Minneapolis	1,057	1,050	994	3,101
1971	Carter Tool & Die, Rochester, N.Y.	1,069	1,037	1,132	3,238
1970	Hamm's Beer, Minneapolis	1,108	1,091	1,044	3,243
1969	PAC Advertising, Lansing, Mich.	1,043	1,005	1,117	3,165
1968	Dave's Auto Supply, Philadelphia	1,024	1,005	1,055	3,084
1967	Pinky's Bowl, Milwaukee	1,098	1,136	1,093	3,327
1966	Plaza Lanes, Sault Ste. Marie, Ont.	928	1,077	1,061	3,066
1965	G & C McDermitt, Pittsburgh	977	1,064	1,033	3,074
1964	300 Bowl, Pontiac, Mich.	1,030	1,075	1,012	3,117
1963	Old Fitzgerald, Chicago	1,053	1,053	1,074	3,180
1962	Strike 'n Spare, Chicago	1,044	1,013	1,071	3,128
1961	Meyerland Builders, Houston	1,068	970	1,096	3,134
1960	A & A Asphalt, Detroit	1,060	1,056	980	3,096
1959	Pfeiffer Beer, Detroit	992	1075	1176	3,243
1958	Falstaff Beer, St. Louis	1,060	1,034	1,116	3,210
1957	Peter Hand Beer, Chicago	1,044	1,112	970	3,126
1956	Falstaff Beer, Chicago	1,017	1,083	992	3,092
1955	Pfeiffer Beer, Detroit	1,068	994	1,074	3,136
1954	Tri-Par Radio Co., Chicago	1,115	1,051	1,060	3,226
1953	Pfeiffer Beer, Detroit	1,048	1,089	1,044	3,181
1952	E & B Beer, Detroit	1,037	1,050	1,028	3,115
1951	C. B. O'Malley Inc., Chicago	1,043	983	1,044	3,070
1950	Pepsi-Cola, Detroit	987	976	989	2,952
1949	Jimmie Smith's, South Bend, Ind.	1,061	987	979	3,027
1948	Washington Shirts, Chicago	1,056	994	957	3,007
1947	Eddie & Earl Linsz, Cleveland	1,050	987	995	3,032
1946	Llo-Da-Mar Bowl, Santa Monica, Calif.	944	1,093	986	3,023
1942	Budweiser, Chicago	1,049	1,050	1,032	3,131
1941	Vogel Brothers, Chicago	931	1,058	1,076	3,065
1940	Monarch Beer, Chicago	996	1,089	962	3,047
1939	Fife Electric Supply, Detroit	992	1,122	1,037	3,151
1938	Birk Bros., Chicago	1,129	970	1,135	3,234
1937	Krakow Furniture Co., Detroit	929	1,109	1,080	3,118
1936	Falls City Hi-Bru, Indianapolis	1,033	1,008	1,048	3,089
1935	Wolfe Tire Service, Niagara Falls, N.Y.	994	980	1,055	3,029
1934	Stroh's Bohemian Beer, Detroit	920	1,101	1,068	3,089
1933	Flaig's Opticians, Covington, Ky.	1,023	968	1,030	3,021
1932	Jefferson Clothiers, Dayton, Ohio	957	1,028	1,123	3,108
1931	S. & L. Motors, Chicago	992	1,080	941	3,013

1930 Graff & Sons, Kalamazoo, Mich. 1,009 1,013 1,078 3,100
1929 Hub Recreation, Joliet, Ill. 1,102 984 1,077 3,063
1928 Oh Henry Candy, Chicago 1,030 987 1,040 3,057
1927 Tea Shops, Milwaukee 990 1,023 1,186 3,199
1926 Castany, Chicago 1,025 937 1,101 3,063
1925 Weisser Blue Ribbons, Buffalo 959 1,006 1,058 3,023
1924 Herb's Indians, Cleveland 972 972 1,100 3,044
1923 Nelson Mitchells, Milwaukee 991 1,055 1,093 3,139
1922 Lincoln Life Insurance, Ft. Wayne, Ind. 1,067 940 991 2,998
1921 Saunders, Toronto, Ont. 977 1,040 1,049 3,066
1920 Brucks No. 1, Chicago 1,042 1,028 1,026 3,096
1919 Athearn Hotel, Oshkosh, Wis. 965 999 1,028 2,992
1918 Aquilas Cigars, St. Paul, Minn. 1,003 1,003 1,016 3,022
1917 Birk Bros., Chicago 1,015 944 1,102 3,061
1916 Commodore Barry, Chicago 936 960 1,009 2,905
1915 Barry-Ketteler, Chicago 908 1,014 985 2,907
1914 New Haven, New Haven, Conn. 900 1,044 1,000 2,944
1913 Flor de Knispel, St. Paul, Minn. 1,066 937 1,003 3,006
1912 Brunswick All Stars, New York 931 1,020 953 2,904
1911 Flenners, Chicago 1,040 903 981 2,924
1910 Cosmos, Chicago 893 955 1032 2,880
1909 Lipman, Chicago 985 979 998 2,962
1908 Bond, Columbus, Ohio 945 916 1066 2,927
1907 Furniture City, Grand Rapids, Mich. 903 883 989 2,775
1906 Century, Chicago 934 997 863 2,794
1905 Gunther No. 2, Chicago 980 884 931 2,795
1904 Anson's, Chicago 960 896 881 2,737
1903 O'Leary, Chicago 903 881 1,035 2,819
1902 Fidelia, New York 947 960 885 2,792
1901 Standard, Chicago 879 896 945 2,720

TEAM ALL EVENTS

(The championship began in 1947. It is designed to honor a five man team for its individual all events totals. The winner receives the Frank L. Pasdeloup trophy. There is no cash prize in the division.)

Year Winner	T	D	S	AE
1997 Lodge Lanes, Belleville, Mich.	3,349	3,282	3,662	10,293
1996 Pollard's Bowl, Versailles, Ind.	3,222	3,594	3,609	10,425
1995 J.W.'s All-Stars, Boca Raton, Fla.	3,333	3,265	3,295	9,893
1994 National Clean Way, Syracuse, N.Y.	2,970	3,508	3,330	9,808
1993 Sam's Town No. 1, Las Vegas	3,308	3,505	3,540	10,353
1992 Reeb's Funeral Home, Toledo, Ohio	3,231	3,414	3,294	9,939
1991 Nadeau's Pro Shop, Las Vegas	3,318	3,378	3,403	10,099
1990 Brunswick Rhinos No. 2, Buffalo	3,201	3,411	3,413	10,025
1989 Browning Pontiac No. 2, Cincinnati	3,166	3,444	3,497	10,107
1988 Chilton Vending, Wichita, Kan.	2,986	3,374	3,328	9,688
1987 Murdock Machine No. 1, Detroit	3,043	3,231	2,911	9,185
1986 Faball Enterprises No. 1, Milwaukee	3,132	3,251	3,231	9,614
1985 Minnesota Loons No. 1, St. Paul, Minn.	3,038	3,138	3,169	9,343
1985 Pony Express Lanes, St. Joseph, Mo.	2,954	3,195	3,194	9,343
1984 Minnesota Loons No. 1, St. Paul, Minn.	3,228	3,190	3,144	9,562
1983 Kendor Corp. No. 1, Milwaukee	3,039	3,134	3,185	9,358
1982 Kendor Corp. No. 1, Milwaukee	3,138	3,247	3,113	9,498
1981 Cook County Tobacco No. 2, Chicago	3,108	3,260	3,327	9,695
1980 Chadwick Studio, Houston	2,999	3,256	3,373	9,628
1979 Hal Lieber Trophies, Gary, Ind.	3,202	3,112	3,239	9,553
1978 ABC Lanes-West, Mechanicsburg, Pa.	2,949	2,987	3,113	9,049
1977 Tournament Bowler's Ledger, Ft. Wayne, Ind.	3,129	2,924	2,964	9,017
1976 Rusty Nail, Minneapolis	3,115	3,151	3,009	9,375
1975 Bison Sausage, Buffalo	3,110	3,114	3,058	9,282
1974 Goebel Beer, Detroit	3,053	3,379	3,142	9,574
1973 Skyway Lanes, Chicago	3,075	3,156	3,185	9,316
1972 Kenmore & Village Lanes, Seattle	3,026	3,124	3,025	9,175
1971 Hilton Shirts, Chicago	3,163	3,035	2959	9157
1970 ABC Lanes-East, Harrisburg, Pa.	3,048	3,058	3,158	9,264
1969 L & L Motor Supply, Sioux Falls, S.D.	3,021	3,021	3,130	9,172
1968 Cascade Natural Gas, Seattle	3,039	3,118	2,994	9,151
1967 Alexander & Hornung, Detroit	2,941	3,152	3,235	9,328
1966 Dr. E. Weinberg, Chicago	2,951	3,098	3,082	9,131
1965 Hamm's Beer, Minneapolis	3,029	2,809	3,215	9,053
1964 Old Fitzgerald, Chicago	2,988	3,081	3,282	9,351
1963 First Federal, Ft. Wayne, Ind.	3,090	3,127	3,118	9,335
1962 Jones Dairy, Kingston, N.Y.	3,076	3,124	2,955	9,155
1961 Adjust-A-Grip, Toledo, Ohio	3,013	3,082	2,967	9,062
1960 Buddy Simon Sign Co., Cleveland	3,060	3,143	3,095	9,298
1959 Pfeiffer Beer, Detroit	3,243	3,173	3,145	9,561
1958 Falstaff Beer, St. Louis	3,210	3,166	3,232	9,608
1957 Mando Photo, St. Paul, Minn.	3,032	3,158	3,261	9,451
1956 Falstaff Beer, Chicago	3,092	3,025	3,059	9,176
1955 Pfeiffer Beer, Detroit	3,136	2,979	3,334	9,449
1954 Tri-Par Radio, Chicago	3,226	3,073	2,925	9,224

Year	Winner	Games			Series
1953	Pfeiffer Beer, Detroit	3,181	3,132	3,166	9,479
1952	Radiart Corp., Cleveland	2,914	3,171	3,258	9,343
1951	Stroh's Beer, Detroit	3,045	3,117	3,344	9,506
1950	E & B Beer, Detroit	2,763	3,136	3,079	8,978
1949	E & B Beer, Detroit	2,984	2,954	3,103	9,041
1948	Knudten Paint, Milwaukee	2,910	3,100	3,171	9,181
1947	Monarch Beer, Chicago	2,853	3,030	3,322	9,205

BOOSTER DIVISION

(The Booster division began in 1916. Until 1936 teams in the division were confined to the host city area. In 1937 the division opened to nationwide teams, and champions formally were declared.)

Year	Winner	Games			Series
1997	Pinsetter Lanes No. 1, Columbus, Miss.	920	930	1,033	2,883
1996	Canterbury Lanes No. 4, Grove, Okla.	898	974	957	2,829
1995	First Texas Bank, Killeen, Texas	933	1,019	897	2,849
1994	Canterbury Lanes No. 1, Grove, Okla.	866	970	963	2,799
1993	Sooner Lanes, Norman, Okla.	924	973	994	2,891
1992	Suburban Lanes, Meade, Kan.	905	969	1,014	2,888
1991	Lewis Marine Supply, Ft. Lauderdale, Fla.	854	928	1,092	2,974
1990	Pro World Pro Shop, Milwaukee	1,049	968	917	2,934
1989	National By-Products, Wichita, Kan.	881	900	1,032	2,813
1988	Prudential Insurance, Newark, N.J.	854	898	997	2,749
1987	DeFazio's Stadium Grill No. 2, Niagara Falls, N.Y.	905	953	936	2,794
1986	The Breakers, Vancouver, B.C.	952	977	899	2,828
1985	Dr. Baur's No. 6, Milwaukee	930	937	935	2,802
1984	J&D Lawn Service, Lincoln, Neb.	986	884	950	2,820
1983	Good Sports, Greenville, N.C.	940	963	921	2,824
1982	Charlotte B.A. No. 1, Charlotte, N.C.	869	922	943	2,734
1981	Robey Tire, Ann Arbor, Mich.	986	891	956	2,833
1980	Aqua Lanes, Edgerton, Minn.	938	996	903	2,837
1979	Swisher's Painting Service No. 2, Urbana, Ohio	885	956	986	2,827
1978	Bush Pest Control, Austin, Texas	964	867	910	2,741
1977	Greater Richmond B.A. Capitals, Richmond, Va.	978	883	935	2,846
1976	T's Truckers, League City, Texas	942	899	965	2,806
1975	Leisure Lanes, Kankakee, Ill.	975	964	990	2,929
1974	Elliott's Jesters, Peoria, Ill.	959	945	935	2,839
1973	Comcrudeslant, Newport, R.I.	993	971	890	2,854
1972	North Ave. Furniture, Grand Junction, Colo.	961	896	967	2,824
1971	Bay Jewelers, Norfolk, Va.	943	1,005	908	2,856
1970	Family Lanes, Butler, Pa.	933	974	970	2,877
1969	Colman Florist, Rock Island, Ill.	971	880	991	2,842
1968	Powell's Restaurant No. 1, Frankfort, Ky.	903	882	983	2,768
1967	Klutzes, Miami	958	967	925	2,850
1966	Pat's Dairy, Rochester, N.Y.	966	922	946	2,834
1965	Ridge Bowl No. 1, Chicago	944	834	1,017	2,795
1964	State Market, Hanford, Calif.	964	931	962	2,857
1963	New London Recreation, New London, Ohio	1032	922	964	2,918
1962	Carroll Lanes, Mt. Carroll, Ill.	977	929	955	2,861
1961	Sylvania Electric, Ottawa, Ohio	950	887	975	2,812
1960	Brannan Boosters No. 2, McKees Rocks, Pa.	934	839	1,049	2,822
1959	Miami Lanes, Troy, Ohio	970	918	960	2,822
1958	Gleason Truers, Rochester, N.Y.	881	993	1,007	2,881
1957	Rea Cress, Junction City, Kan.	882	934	980	2,796
1956	Washington Grill, Rochester, N.Y.	903	944	944	2,791
1955	Fighting Irish, Dayton, Ohio	924	952	919	2,795
1954	Washington Boat Center, Seattle	891	994	962	2,847
1953	Frank's Jewelry, Chicago	891	1,025	936	2,852
1952	Northern Trust Securities, Chicago	905	928	957	2,790
1951	Mason City Tile & Marble Co., Mason City, Iowa	936	928	966	2,830
1950	Ternstedt, Columbus, Ohio	929	944	871	2,744
1949	Brincko Bowling Lanes, New Castle, Pa.	856	984	959	2,799
1948	Grand Central Recreation, Detroit	951	941	952	2,844
1947	Eastside Beer, Ventura, Calif.	907	872	930	2,709
1946	Hooker, Niagara Falls, N.Y.	944	938	892	2,774
1942	Skylight, Syracuse, N.Y.	862	938	941	2,741
1941	P.V. Fuel & Ice, Minneapolis	938	924	938	2,800
1940	Barnes Scale, Detroit	858	928	1,022	2,808
1939	Firestone Tires, Columbiana, Ohio	875	978	943	2,796
1938	Dressler's Market, Chicago	936	909	929	2,774
1937	Capitol Health Center, New York	959	916	891	2,766
1936	Ready Mix Concrete, Indianapolis	1,000	882	1,001	2,883
1935	Hamill Gruens, Lockport, N.Y.	911	901	904	2,716
1934	Kupper Cabs, Peoria, Ill.	964	824	901	2,689
1933	Independent Supply Co., Columbus, Ohio	911	988	866	2,765
1932	P.M. Freight Traffic, Detroit	921	894	1,046	2,861
1931	Courier-Express, Buffalo	932	912	976	2,820
1930	Cleveland Hardware Co., Cleveland	828	893	1,008	2,729
1929	Geo. J. Fee Co., Chicago	874	962	1,007	2,843
1928	Eagle Bottling Works, Kansas City	882	928	810	2,620
1927	Tazewell Club, Pekin, Ill.	833	887	847	2,617
1926	Gasiorowski Brothers, Toledo, Ohio	946	925	1009	2,880

Year	Team				
1925	Bison Ice & Coal, Buffalo	880	956	959	2,795
1924	Samuelson No. 4, Chicago	866	990	967	2,823
1923	Plankinton Globe, Milwaukee	878	916	966	2,760
1922	Hamilton Club Reds, Chicago	969	897	1,036	2,902
1921	Rose & Gregoire, Buffalo	946	891	950	2,787
1920	Carpenter's Union Local 183, Peoria, Ill.	847	843	834	2,524
1919	Waldorf Hotel, Toledo, Ohio	955	896	972	2,823
1918	Cabanne, St. Louis	974	969	887	2,830
1917	Centrals, Chicago	819	928	946	2,693
1916	Green Seal, Toledo, Ohio	909	1,009	859	2,777

CLASSIC DIVISION

(The Classic division began in 1961 to separate the professional and nonprofessional entrants in the tournament. It was discontinued after 1979.)

SINGLES

Year	Winner	Games			Series
1979	Ed Biro, Kingston, N.Y.	226	246	267	739
1978	Bill Beach, Sharon, Pa.	245	237	219	701
1977	Mickey Higham, Kansas City	279	266	256	801
1976	Jim Schroeder, Buffalo	258	247	245	750
1975	Les Zikes, Chicago	224	217	269	710
1974	Ed DiTolla, Maywood, N.J.	266	269	212	747
1973	Nelson Burton Jr., St. Louis	289	212	223	724
1972	Teata Semiz, River Edge, N.J.	254	233	267	754
1971	Victor Iwlew, Kalamazoo, Mich.	240	276	234	750
1970	Glenn Allison, Whittier, Calif.	258	258	214	730
1969	Nelson Burton Jr., St. Louis	207	267	258	732
1968	Dave Davis, Phoenix	275	235	231	741
1967	Lou Mandragona, Miami	255	234	247	736
1966	Les Schissler, Denver	249	255	256	760
1965	Bob Kennicutt, Norwalk, Calif.	246	243	208	697
1964	Billy Hardwick, San Mateo, Calif.	216	258	223	730
1963	Tom Hennessey, St. Louis	278	221	233	732
1962	Bob Poole, Pueblo, Colo.	257	258	244	759
1961	Earl Johnson, Chicago	255	256	222	733

DOUBLES

Year	Winner	Series
1979	Neil Burton, 641, Nelson Burton Jr., 772, St. Louis	1,413
1978	Steve Fehr, 614, Dave Newrath, 686, Cincinnati	1,300
1977	Frank Werman, 748, Randy Neal, 589, Los Angeles	1,337
	Don Bell, 655, Santa Maria, Calif., Kevin Gannon, 682, Long Beach, Calif.	1,337
1976	Don Johnson, 771, Las Vegas, Paul Colwell, 671, Tucson, Ariz.	1,442
1975	Marty Piraino, 772, Syracuse, N.Y., Bill Bunetta, 620, Fresno, Calif.	1,392
1974	Tye Critchlow, 693, Claremont, Calif., Bob Perry, 666, Paterson, N.J.	1,359
1973	Bobby Cooper, 661, Houston, George Pappas, 678, Charlotte, N.C.	1,339
1972	Carmen Salvino, 647, Chicago, Barry Asher, 719, Costa Mesa, Calif.	1,366
1971	Barry Warshafsky, 635, Bill Zuben, 722, Boston	1,357
1970	Dave Soutar, 747, Gilroy, Calif., Nelson Burton Jr., 684, St. Louis	1,431
1969	Don McCune, 734, Munster, Ind., Jim Stefanich, 621, Joliet, Ill.	1,355

Year	Winner	Series
1968	Bill Tucker, 697, Los Angeles, Don Johnson, 632, Kokomo, Ind.	1,329
1967	Norm Meyers, 757, Los Angeles Harry Smith, 665, Redwood City, Calif.	1,422
1966	Jim Stefanich, 753, Andy Rogoznica, 608, Chicago, Ill.	1,361
1965	Larry Oakar, 667, Cleveland, Ohio, Bill Beach, 688, Sharon, Pa.	1,355
1964	Hal Jolley, 627, Bob Strampe, 728, Detroit	1,355
1963	Joe Joseph, 728, Billy Golembiewski, 650, Detroit	1,378
1962	Glenn Allison, 780, Dick Hoover, 651, St. Louis	1,431
1961	Don Ellis, 678, Houston, Texas, Joe Kristof, 653, Chicago	1,331

ALL EVENTS

Year	Winner	T	D	S	AE
1979	Nelson Burton Jr., St. Louis	591	772	716	2,079
1978	Bill Beach, Sharon, Pa.	666	574	701	1,941
1977	Dick Ritger, River Falls, Wis.	593	646	725	1,964
1976	Gary Fust, Des Moines, Iowa	622	685	743	2,050
1975	Bill Beach, Sharon, Pa.	602	685	706	1,993
1974	Jim Godman, Lorain, Ohio	731	749	704	2,184
1973	Jimmy Mack, Hackettstown, N.J.	625	657	712	1,994
1972	Teata Semiz, River Edge, N.J.	609	631	754	1,994
1971	Gary Dickinson, Ft. Worth, Texas	655	635	710	2,000
1970	Bob Strampe, Detroit	687	686	670	2,043
1969	Larry Lichstein, Hartford, Conn.	618	716	726	2,060
1968	Jim Stefanich, Joliet, Ill.	664	652	667	1,983
1967	Bob Strampe, Detroit	667	699	726	2,092
1966	Les Schissler, Denver	665	687	760	2,112
1965	Tom Hennessey, St. Louis	577-611	668	693	2,549
1964	Billy Hardwick, San Mateo, Calif.	694	664	730	2,088
1963	Tom Hennessey, St. Louis	615	651	732	1,998
1962	Jack Winters, Philadelphia	679	792	676	2,147
1961	Bob Brayman, Detroit	646	680	637	1,963

TEAM

Year	Winner	Games			Series
1979	Robby's Automatic Positioner No. 1, Glendale, Calif.	1,030	1,019	1,061	3,110
1978	The Untouchable Lounge, Kirksville, Mo.	946	951	1,014	2,911
1977	Columbia 300 Bowling Balls, San Antonio	1,116	1,020	986	3,122
1976	Munsingwear No. 2, Minneapolis	1,052	1,086	1,143	3,281
1975	Munsingwear No. 2, Minneapolis	910	1,146	924	2,980
1974	Ebonite Corp., Hopkinsville, Ky.	999	1,057	1,061	3,117
1973	Stroh's Beer, Detroit	977	1,114	959	3,050
1972	Basch Advertising, New York	1,053	1,033	1,013	3,099
1971	Chester Iio Investments, Houston	1,138	977	966	3,081
1970*	Merchant Enterprises, New York	1,035	1,052	1,067	3,154
1969	Dick Weber Wrist Masters, Santa Ana, Calif.		3,132	3,281	6,413
1968	Bowl-Rite Supply, Joliet, Ill.		3,059	3,226	6,285

1967	Balancer Glove,				1964	Falstaff Beer, St. Louis	3,207 3,210 6,417

1967 Balancer Glove,
      Ft. Worth, Texas   3,235 3,063 6,298
1966 Ace Mitchell Shur-Hooks,
      Akron, Ohio   3,179 3,357 6,536
1965 Thelmal Lanes, Louisville, Ky.   3,073 3,078 6,151

1964 Falstaff Beer, St. Louis   3,207 3,210 6,417
1963 California Bombers,
      Los Angeles   3,141 3,092 6,233
1962 Don Carter Gloves, St. Louis   3,052 3,196 6,248
1961 Brentwood Bowl, San Francisco   2,996 2,987 5,983
*Format changed to six team rolloff.

ABC CHAMPIONS, ALPHABETICAL LISTING

Legend: Age when first became champion in parenthesis; T, team; D, doubles; S, singles; A, all events; C, Classic; TA, team all events; BT, Booster team; BD, Booster doubles; BS, Booster singles; M, Masters.

A

Abel, Dick, Milwaukee BT90
Adams, Brad, Las Vegas TA93
Abrams, Norm, St. Paul, Minn. (36) TA57
Adair, Robert, Rochester, N.Y. (43) BT58
Adam, Kevin, Reading, Pa. (33) T92
Adrian, Fred, Buffalo (23) T25
Aquilario, Arnold, Vancouver, B.C. (27) BT86
Ahman, Frank, Ottawa, Ohio (37) BT61
Albrecht, Dave, Milwaukee (33) T94
Almisegger, Curt, Detroit T90
Alexander, Pat, Ft. Wayne, Ind. (34) TA77
Allen, Bob, New York City (28) S57
Allen, Harold, Detroit (18) D15
Allen, Ray, Detroit (20) D15
Allison, Glenn, Los Angeles (31)...CD62, CT64, CT66,CS70
Aloi, Frank, Richmond, Va. (37) BT77
Alten, Harry, Chicago (23) T06
Alvarez, Joseph, Hanford, Calif. BT64
Amann, William, New York City (38)............T02
Andersen, Lloyd, Mason City, Iowa (31).........BT51
Anderson, C.M., St. Paul, Minn. (40)............S05
Anderson, Danny, Sioux Falls, S.D. (25) TA69
Anderson, Gene, Seattle BT54
Anderson, Knute, Moline, Ill. (47)..............S38
Anderson, Terrin, League City, Texas (35) BT76
Andolina, Jack, Los Angeles (35) CT79
Andrew, L.B., Joliet, Ill. (33).....................T29
Angel, Harry, Chicago (33)........................T40
Anson, Adrian (Cap), Chicago (43)...............T04
Anthony, Earl, Dublin, Calif. (30) TA68, M77,M84
Antonucci, Al, Niagara Falls, N.Y. (31)..........T35
Antczak, Bob, Chicago (25)......................S84
Ardillo, Sam, Rochester, N.Y. (31).................T71
Asher, Barry, Costa Mesa, Calif. (24)..........CD72,
                                     CT75, CT76, A85
Aston, Chick, Akron, Ohio (32) D26
Aulby, Mike, Indianapolis (29) M89
Ayers, Wallace, Hanford, Calif. BT64

B

Baden, Bill, Minneapolis (40)..............T70, T72
Badger, John, Ventura, Calif. (40)...............BT47
Baer, Gordy, Chicago (34) TA73, T79, TA79
Baier, George, Milwaukee (20).....................D42
Bakatselos, Ted, Detroit (26) TA67
Baker, John, Chicago (36) T17
Balding, Charles, Toronto (32) T21
Ballard, Del Jr., Richardson, Texas (24) M88
Ballard, Thomas, Charlotte, N.C. (33) BT82
Ballenger, Butch, Muscatine, Iowa (39)...........T78
Balz, Christian, Columbus, Ohio (27)..............T08

Barbera, Francis Jr., Hanford, Calif. BT64
Barclay, C.K., Joliet, Ill. (50) T29
Barkow, Bert, Milwaukee (44) TA48
Barnes, Chris, Wichita, Kan. (27) TA97
Barnes, Ernie, Rochester, N.Y. (39) D19
Barney, Ron, Cleveland (32) T75
Bartsch, Frank, Chicago (28).......................T09
Bartula, John, Houston (35).......................TA80
Basacchi, Bob, Detroit (21) A79, T80
Battista, Dick, New York City (40)...............CT72
Baudendistek, Elmer, Dayton, Ohio BT55
Bauman, Phil, Detroit (29) T34
Baumann, Larry, Milwaukee BT90
Baumgartner, Carl, Cincinnati (21) S23
Baur, Ed, Milwaukee (35) BT85
Bax, Fran, Niagara Falls, N.Y. (25) T83
Beach, Bill, Sharon, Pa. (35) CD65, CA75, CS78, CA78,
                                        M72
Beatty, Don, Jackson, Mich. (26) A38
Beck, Dave, Lansing, Mich. (26) T69
Becker, Irvin, Chicago BT38
Bell, Don, Santa Maria, Calif. (34) CD77
Bemis, William, Killeen, Texas (57) B95
Bennett, Mike, Ft. Lauderdale, Fla BT91
Benkovic, Frank, Milwaukee (28)...........D32, D33
Benson, Bob, Lansing, Mich. (57)..................D51
Berardi, Joe, Brooklyn, N.Y. (27).................M82
Berlin, Mike, Muscatine, Iowa (26)...............A70
Bernhardt, Gene, Sturgeon Bay, Wis. (39)........D49
Bernhardt, Dave, Detroit (45).....................D92
Betchkal, Ray, Racine, Wis. D87
Bigley, E., Louisville, Ky. (25) D07
Biro, Ed, Kingston, N.Y. (31).......................CS79
Bishop, Jack, Chicago (46)..........................T48
Bisset, James, Dayton, Ohio BT55
Blaney, Bob, Cambridge, Ohio (25) D81
Blatchford, Gary, Phoenix (35) S92
Blickle, George, Grand Rapids, Mich. (42) T07
Bliek, Edgar, Rochester, N.Y. (45)................BT58
Bliss, Dick, Gary, Ind. (35) T79, TA79
Blough, Henry, Mechanicsburg, Pa. (35)..........TA78
Blouin, Jim, Chicago (23) A09, S11
Bluth, Ray, St. Louis (34) ....CT62, CT74 ,M59
Bock, Dan, Owatonna, Minn. (23) S93
Bodis, Joe, Cleveland (27) T24
Bohm, Bruce, Chicago (29) S82
Boksza, Joseph, Dayton, Ohio BT55
Bolony, Mike, St. Joseph, Mo. TA85
Bomar, Buddy, Chicago (41)...............T56, TA56
Bonacci, George, Rochester, N.Y. (34) T71
Born, Jack, Detroit (36) T60
Bosler, Buzz, Milwaukee (50)......................D65
Bourdase, Ed, Hayward, Calif. (32)...............CT61

Bower, Bruce, Grand Junction, Colo. (47)....................BT72
Bower, Darryl, Mechanicsburg, Pa. (22)......................TA78
Bower, Gary, Mechanicsburg, Pa. (19) TA70, TA78
Bowling, Cliff, Columbiana, Ohio BT39
Braff, Henry, Detroit BT40
Brandtner, Allan, Newport, R.I. (34)..........................BT73
Brayman, Bob, Detroit (24)..............................T60, CA61
Breckle, Fred, Detroit..T39
Bredehoft, Don, Toledo, Ohio (47) TA61, D70
Brennan, William, Chicago (36) T20
Bridges, Bill, League City, Texas (35) BT76
Briell, Frank, Chicago (37) A01, S01
Brincko, John, New Castle, Pa. BT49
Brinkman, Steve, Milwaukee (29) T94
Broadwell, Clint, Houston (35)....................................TA80
Broadwell, Wayne, Houston (37)................................TA80
Brokaw, Don, Canton, Ohio (30)................................S35
Brooks, Jamie, Houston (38) D73
Brown, Charles, Junction City, Kan. (54) BT57
Brown, Ray, Terre Haute, Ind. (34)..............................S40
Browning, Terry, Wichita, Kan. BT89
Bruck, Nick, Chicago T03
Bruder, Al, Chicago (39) D81, TA81
Bruens, Anthony, McKees Rocks, Pa. (47)..................BT60
Bruggeman, Frank, Sioux City, Iowa S09
Brunette, Jerry, Rochester, N.Y. (29) T71
Bryan, Edward, Frankfort, Ky. (43) BT68
Bryant, Leroy, St. Paul, Minn. (37)....................T70, T72
Buckley, Roy, Columbus, Ohio (31)..................CT75, CT76
Buell, Steve, Salt Lake City, Utah (25)........................CT68
Bujack, Fred, Detroit (40) TA49, TA50, T52,
                              T53, TA53, TA55, T55, A55
Bukowski, Alex, Syracuse, N.Y.....................................BT42
Bukowski, Chet, Detroit (35) T50
Bunetta, Bill, Fresno, Calif. (30)TA50, T52,CT63, CT67, CD75
Burke, Jamie, Loveland, Ohio (33)..............................D96
Bures, Bob, Cleveland (23) D80
Burr, Louis, Detroit..T39
Burton, Neil, St. Louis (33) CD79, M80
Burton, Nelson Jr., St. Louis (22) CT65, CS69,
         CD70, CS73, CT75, CT76, M76, CD79, CA79
Burton, Nelson Sr., St. Louis (31)................................D37
Busateri, Sal, Austin, Texas BT78
Butler, Art, Chicago (45) T48
Butler, Peter, Chicago (33) D29
Butt, Steve, Mobile, Ala. BD94
Buzzell, Lee, Rock Island, Ill. (44) BT69

C

Callery, Dave, Cincinnati (31) T82, D93
Cambio, Pete, Buffalo (35) TA75
Campbell, Greg, St. Louis (28) S69
Campbell, Harry, Detroit (37) CT73, T80
Campbell, John, Niagara Falls, N.Y. (33)....................BT46
Campbell, Peter, Niagara Falls, N.Y.............................BT87
Cangey, Sam, New Castle, Pa. BT49
Cantwell, Dan, Columbus, Ohio BT50
Capshaw, Dave, Davenport, Iowa (27) T78
Capshaw, Sam, Louisville, Ky. (24) T73
Carey, William, Chicago (25)......................................T16
Cariello, Tony, Chicago (28) A83
Carlson, Bruce, Minneapolis (22)................................TA76
Carmichal, Oscar, Chicago (22) T10
Carteaux, Bob, Ft. Wayne, Ind. (29)............................TA63
Carter, Don, Miami (26)........T53, TA53, CT62, CT74, M61

Carter, Pete, Fallbrook, Calif. (39) TA51
Caso, William, Niagara Falls, N.Y.................................BT87
Cavan, Harry, Pittsburgh (38)......................................S19
Chalmers, Jim, Chicago T05, D08
Chamberlain, Bob, Detroit (31) T80
Chandler, Fred, St. Paul, Minn. (31)............................T18
Chapman, Don, Scranton, Pa. (22) S66
Chappell, Bob, Wichita, Kan. T89
Chapple, Roy, Columbus, Ohio. BT50
Cherup, John, Columbus, Ohio. BT50
Chesbro, Roy, Cincinnati TA89
Chestney, Jim, Denver (21) CT69, M69
Chewning, John, Peoria, Ill. (29)..................................BT74
Chiaro, Sonny, Grand Junction, Colo. (28) BT72
Chicovsky, George, Pontiac, Mich. (40)........................T64
Chilcott, David, Butler, Pa. (17) BT70
Chilcott, Maurice, Butler, Pa. (40)..............................BT70
Childress, Curtis, Cleveland T85
Chismudy, Andy, Gary, Ind. (37) T79, TA79
Christopher, Anthony, Rochester, N.Y. (42) BT56
Christopher, John, Rochester, N.Y. (26) BT56
Christopher, Leonard, Rochester, N.Y. (31) BT56
Cielepak, Stan, Niagara Falls, N.Y. (28) T83
Cieslik, Fritz, Cleveland (28)......................................TA60
Cimbalo, Sal, Rochester, N.Y. (36) BT66
Clark, Dewey, Milwaukee (28)....................................T23
Clawson, Larry, Peoria, Ill. (36)..................................BT74
Clemence, Mike, Detroit T90
Clinch, Fred, Chicago T04
Close, John, Detroit BT40
Cloud, Bob, Richmond, Va. (52) BT77
Cobus, Chris, Milwaukee (21) A78, D84
Cohn, Al, Chicago (38)................TA66, S71, A71, TA73
Colby, Gary, Ann Arbor, Mich. (30)............................BT81
Colby, James, Ann Arbor, Mich. (38) BT81
Collin, Herman, Columbus, Ohio (31) D03, T08
Collins, David, Miami (50) BT67
Colosi, Nicholas Jr., Niagara Falls, N.Y. BT87
Colosi, Nicholas Sr., Niagara Falls, N.Y.......................BT87
Colwell, Paul, Tucson, Ariz. (26)............CD76, CT77, M74
Comito, Robert, Boca Raton, Fla. (30)........................TA95
Conner, Fred, Los Angeles (31) CT79
Cooper, Bobby, Dallas (26) CT71, CD73
Cook, Don, Milwaukee (37)..............................D86, TA86
Cook, Robert, Norman, Okla. BT93
Cooke, Robert, New London, Ohio (18) BT63
Corbett, Gil, Junction City, Kan. (48)..........................BT57
Corey, Edgar, Chicago BT52
Coustenis, Steve, Salamanca, N.Y.................................T87
Cox, Rusty, Chatanooga, Tenn. T91
Cox, William, Troy, Ohio..BT59
Crable, Russell, Liverpool, Ohio (19) A08
Crake, Larry, Pontiac, Mich. (22) T64
Cray, Charles, Indianapolis (50) T36
Creamer, Russ, Chicago (35)..T48
Crimmins, John, Detroit (44)..T39
Critchlow, Tye, Claremont, Calif. (25)........................CD74
Croy, Kenneth, Ottawa, Ohio (24)..............................BT61
Curry, Jack, Lansing, Mich. (52) T69
Cummings, Norm, Milwaukee (52) BT90
Cuthbert, Frank, Detroit T37
Czigany, Joe, South Bend, Ind. (51)............................T49

D

Dahl, Gordy, Minneapolis (26) TA65, T70, T72

Daiker, Al, Cincinnati (38) D10
Daizovi, John, Ft. Lauderdale, Fla. BT91
Danek, Jim, Chicago (54) S39
Daniello, Terry, Newark, N.J. (42) BT88
Daniels, Michael, Newport, R.I. (25) BT73
Daroszewski, Gary, Milwaukee (23)........TA82, TA83, D89
Darwin, Ken, Seattle (41) T95
Davis, Dave, Atlanta (25) CS68
Davis, George, Milwaukee (35) T27
Davis, Therm, Chicago (30) CT68
Daw, Charley, Milwaukee (29) T23, D23, D32
Day, Ned, Milwaukee (38)...................A48, T56, TA56
Dean, Albert Jr., Frankfort, Ky. (53) BT68
Debenham, Bud, Los Angeles (55) A77
Deboer, Clyde, Edgerton, Minn. (30) BT80
DeGuchi, Yoneo, Chicago BT53
Deines, Ed, LaPorte, Colo. (57)................................S91
Delello, Fred, Oneonta, N.Y. (28) S63
DeLorme, Harry, Chicago T05
Denbo, George, Chicago BT38
DeRosa, Fred, Chicago T51
Detloff, Joe, Chicago (72).......................................BT65
Detloff, Len, Detroit T39
DeVincent, Storm, Ft. Lauderdale, Fla. (40) TA95
DiBlatto, Nick, Cleveland (27) T85
Dicken, Rusty, Killeen, Texas (45) B95
Dickinson, Gary, Ft. Worth, Texas (28) CA71
Dilly, Ed, Covington, Ky. (19)....................................T33
Distin, Dean, Fulton, N.Y. (27) D94, TA94
DiTolla, Ed, Maywood, N.J. (29) CS74
Divine, James, Beloit, Wis. (37) D30
Dixon, Gordon, Newport, R.I. (25) BT73
Dodd, Robert, Junction City, Kan. (28) BT57
Doehrman, Bill, Ft. Wayne, Ind. (34)..........................T22
Doerr, Ed Jr., St. Louis (29) D47
Dominguez, Gary, Grove, Okla. (41).........................BT94
Dominguez, Rayetta, Grove, Okla. (31) BT94
Domzalski, Larry, Cleveland (24) T85
Donabauer, Johnnie, Chicago..................................BT38
Donohoe, Harvey, Urbana, Ohio (44)........................BT79
Dorencamp, Ken, Pittsburgh (36) T65
Dornfeld, Herb, St. Paul, Minn. (23)...........................T13
Doss, Terry, St. Joseph, Mo.....................................TA85
Down, Alan, Cincinnati TA89
Downing, Vern, San Francisco (30) CT61
Dresbach, Earl, Columbus, Ohio...............................D06
Drury, Fred, Cleveland (42) T47
Drusbacky, Joe, Toledo, Ohio (21) TA61
Duke, Norm, Edmond, Okla. (29) M93
Dunbar, Alex, New York City (40) T12
Dunn, Larry, Chicago (35) T31
Durbin, Mike, Chagrin Falls, Ohio (28) CT69
Dutler, Jerry, Mankato, Minn. (36) CT65

E

Easter, Sarge, Winston-Salem, N.C. (67) T50
Easter, Theron, Grove, Okla. BT94
Eaton, Mike, Grand Rapids, Mich. (25) S80
Ebosh, Willis, Cleveland (36)....................................D50
Eckert, Norm, Harrisburg, Pa. (41) TA70, TA78
Ecoff, Art, Miami (36)..BT67
Edmonson, Randall, Columbus, Miss. BT97
Edwards, Henry, Buffalo (50) T25
Edwards Jr., James, Columbus, Miss. BT97
Eggars, William, Chicago (36) T20, S27
Eicke, Harry, Chicago T26

Elkins, Eugene, San Carlos, Calif.............................M54
Ellenburg, Frank, Chandler, Ariz. (26) M78
Ellis, Don, Houston (32) CD61
Ellis, Harry, Grand Rapids, Mich...................... A07, T07
Engan, Ralph, Monsey, N.Y. (41) CT69
English, Herbert, Joliet, Ill. (26) T29
Entrop, Elmer, Austin, Texas (39)...........................BT78
Erben, John, Chicago (46) T41
Erickson, Marv, Chicago (31)...........................D20, T28
Euwer, Dale, St. Joseph, Mo. (36)..........................TA85
Evers, Elmer, Dayton, Ohio.....................................BT55

F

Faetz, Leo, Chicago (25) T28, T40
Faetz, Matt Jr., Chicago (25) T40
Faetz, Matt Sr., Chicago (41)...................................A15
Fahy, Mark, Chicago (28).......................................M86
Faino, Charles, Philadelphia (27)..............................T68
Fangman, Rick, Gilbertsville, Iowa (33) D93
Faragalli, Al (Lindy), Paterson, N.J. (46).....................A58
Farnan, Frank, Chicago (38) T22
Farness, Ray, Madison, Wis. (50) D41
Faulkner, Bret, Milwaukee (27) T86
Favour, Frank, Oshkosh, Wis. (33) S06
Fazio, Buzz, Detroit (43) TA51, M55, T58, TA58
Feese, Jack, Houston (39)...T61
Fehr, Steve, Cincinnati (23) CD78, A80, T82, M94
Fenstermaker, Andy, Kalamazoo, Mich. (53) T30
Ferguson, Terry, Toledo, Ohio.................................TA92
Fernandez, Ken, Sacramento, Calif. (19) CT78
Ferraro, Buster, Kingston, N.Y. (39)..........................TA62
Ferraro, Jack, Kingston, N.Y. (31).............................TA62
Ferrias, Joe, Mason City, Iowa (48)..........................BT51
Fey, Rick, Edgerton, Minn. (26).................................BT80
Fischbach, Gib, St. Louis (46) D59
Fischer, Fred, Buffalo (51)...A40
Fisher, Glen, Chicago..T03
Fleischhacker, George, St. Paul, Minn. (21) TA57
Flesch, William, Chicago (33) T40
Flick, Michael, Erie, Pa. (32)....................................D27
Flowerday, Roy, Rochester, N.Y. (62) BT58
Foego, Otto, New York City (48) T02
Fondino, Angie, Kingston, N.Y. (32).........................TA62
Fontana, Frank, Killeen, Texas (69)...........................B95
Ford, James, Dayton, Ohio.....................................BT55
Foremsky, Skee, Houston (34) CT71
Forster, Ivan, Kalamazoo, Mich. (26) T30
Foster, Joseph, Pontiac, Mich. (35)...........................T64
Fowler, Murray, Steubenville, Ohio (51) D39
Fox, Benjamin, Milwaukee (39) T27
Fox, Don, Joliet, Ill. (39)...T77
Frantz, Lou Sr., Houston (47)...................................CT65
Freitag, Herb, Chicago (36).....................................D40
Frana, Jim, Chicago (52) T41
Fuggiasco, Jeff, Milwaukee (27) BT85
Fulton, Joe, Indianapolis (44)....................................T36
Fust, Gary, Des Moines, Iowa (20) CA76

G

Gabriel, Gary, Las Vegas..TA91
Gadaleto, Frank, Lansing, Mich. (26) S77
Gage, Dennis, Lincoln, Neb....................................BT84
Gagliardi, Gene, Los Angeles. (37) S37
Gaines, John, Davidsonville, Md. (30) TA97
Gallo, Chris, Kingston, N.Y. (30) TA62
Gannon, Kevin, Long Beach, Calif. (29) CD77
Gardella, Fred, Detroit (40) D26, T34

Garner, Travis, Chattanooga, Tenn..................T91
Garris, Grady, Detroit.....................................BT48
Gaston, Charles, Mobile, Ala.........................BD94
Gavie, Hank, Detroit (43).................................T50
Gaylor, Lou, Dayton, Ohio (38).......................T32
Gazzana, Don, Milwaukee (36).............D78, T81
Gearhart, Butch, Miami (25)...............CT70, CT72
Gehringer, Steve, Reading, Pa. (35)................T92
Geiger, Paul, Salamanca, N.Y. T87
Geiser, George, Chicago (30)...............T17, T38
Genal, Joseph, Oshkosh, Wis. (37)..................T19
Genal, Robert, Oshkosh, Wis. (34)...................T19
Gerloski, Harry, Detroit (36)............................A26
Gersonde, Russ, Milwaukee (41)....................TA48
Gerzine, Ed, Milwaukee (36) S55
Gibbs, Virgil, Kansas City (31) D37
Giblin, James, Cleveland (28).........................T24
Gibson, Clyde, Lake Jackson, Texas D85
Gibson, Therm, Detroit (31)..............TA49, TA50, T52,
T53, TA53, TA55, T55
Gifford, Stan, Ft. Worth, Texas (24)........T56, D56, TA56
Gilbertson, Ben, St. Paul, Minn. (37)................T18
Gilbertson, Dick, Minneapolis (21) TA65
Gillis, Herbert, Toronto (47).............................T21
Gilles, Paul, Milwaukee (31) TA48
Ginger, Arky, Chicago (30) T57
Girrins, Leo, Wichita, Kan..............................BT89
Glasco, George, Detroit.................................TA67
Glover, Don, Show Low, Ariz. (23)........CT69, M70
Glus, Dan, Pittsburgh (26) T65
Gniewek, Hank, Detroit (34) T60
Godfrey, Mike, Meade, Kan..........................BT92
Godman, Jim, Lorain, Ohio (28) CT74, CA74
Goike, Bob, Detroit (30) A84; TA97
Goldhoff, Irwin, Miami (37)...........................BT67
Golebiewski, Joe, Buffalo (33)........................TA75
Golembiewski, Billy, Detroit (29) T59, TA59, M60,
M63, CD63
Gordon, Jeff, Oswego, N.Y. (35).....................TA94
Gordon, Neil T., Chicago (37).........................BT65
Gorman, Paul, Chicago TA71
Graham, Luther, Grove, Okla. (58) BT96
Graves, Herbert, Newark, N.J. (37) BT88
Graziani, Dennis, Detroit (34) T80
Green, Al, Chicago S25
Green, Art, Kalamazoo, Mich. (50) T30
Greenfield, Bob, Milwaukee (34) T94
Greenwald, Mike, Cleveland T85
Greim, Al, Ft. Wayne, Ind. (30) T22
Greiner, G., Chicago T01
Gribin, John, Riverside, Calif. (20) D62
Grieshaber, Benjamin, Chicago T01
Gruber, Doug, Lincoln, Neb...........................BT84
Grygier, Cass, Detroit (25) T34
Guedel, Charles, Indianapolis (32)..................D69
Guenther, John, Seattle (31) CT67, CT74
Guston, Ed, Chicago (28)...............................T11
Gworek, John, Buffalo (43)..............................D46

H

Habetler, Rudy, Chicago M53
Hagemeier, Alan, Grove, Okla. (49)...............BT96
Hagen, Gordy, Minneapolis (18)....................TA65
Hale, David, Columbus, Miss.........................BT97
Haley, Tom, Detroit (27)........................S10, A10

Haley, William, Phoenix (24) D71
Hall, Andy, Chicago T11
Hall, George, Mundelein, Ill. A89
Hall, Ken, Albany, N.Y...................................T93
Hamilton, John, Newark, N.J. (57) BT88
Hammel, Mark, Detroit..................................T90
Hanke, Jim, Milwaukee (38)..........................T81
Hannahs, Ted, Zanesville, Ohio (23) D81
Hansen, Ed, Seattle (28)....................TA68, TA72
Hanson, Bob, Minneapolis (38)........TA65, T70, T72
Harahan, Tim, Encino, Calif. (22) CT68, CT78
Harbison, Glenn, Pittsburgh S85
Hardin, Carl, Indianapolis(43)........................T36
Hardin, Charlie, Seattle (41)..........................T95
Hardwick, Billy, Memphis, Tenn. (21)......CS64, CA64
Hargadon, William, Chicago T42
Harris, James, Richmond, Va. (52)..................BT77
Hart, Bob, Columbus, Ohio (36)........D74, A74, TA74
Hartley, W.M., Liverpool, Ohio (20) D11
Hartman, Adolph, Toronto (46).......................T21
Hartman, Don, Mt. Carroll, Ill. (48) BT62
Hartman, Harry, Philadelphia (32) T68, TA70
Hatch, Jerry, Hanford, Calif..........................BT64
Hathaway, Tom, Los Angeles (32) A65
Hauck, Drew, Finneytown, Ohio (35) D96
Hayden, Boyd, Omaha, Neb. (34) T74
Hayes, James, Richmond, Va. (44)..................BT77
Hazelhuhn, Henry, Chicago T05
Healey Jr., Pat, Niagara Falls, N.Y. (28) TA97
Hedenstrom, Eric, St. Paul, Minn. (30) T13
Heffron, Lew, Seattle BT54
Heil, William, Covington, Ky. (42) T33
Heim, Doug, Niagara Falls, N.Y. (30) T83
Heim, Henry, Milwaukee (30)..........................T27
Helle, Roger, Detroit (39)..............................TA74
Hemingway, Ed, Chicago (34)........................T11
Hennessey, Tom, St. Louis (36) CT62, CS63,
CA63, CA65, M58
Henry, Jeff, Milwaukee (29)............................T86
Hering, Eugene, Irvington, N.J. (29)..................D61
Hermann, Ed, Cleveland (25) A13
Hetzler, Harold Jr., Muscatine, Iowa (37).........T78
Heup, Garry, Beloit, Wis. (34) D30
Hewitt, Earl, Erie, Pa. (34).............................S33
Higby, Howard, Lake Jackson, Texas D85
Higham, Mickey, Kansas City (30) CS77
Hiles, Paul, Frankfort, Ky. (44) BT68
Hilton, Mark, Albany, N.Y..............................T93
Hinzman, Robert, Charlotte, N.C. (32) BT82
Hirner, Brian, Joliet, Ill. (36)...........................T77
Hiteshaw, Warren, Norfolk, Va. (31).................BT71
Hitt, Bob, Detroit (37).........................T59, TA59
Hochrein, Bob, Dubuque, Iowa (22) S90
Hoefer, Bob, Oswego, N.Y. (32).....................TA94
Hoffman, Les, Chicago (27)............................T57
Hoffman, William, Chicago (43) TA71
Holderman, Tom, Kankakee, Ill. (22) BT75
Hollenbeck, Bert, Buffalo (39) T25
Holloway, Ricky, Chattanooga, Tenn...............T91
Holstrom, Charles, Niagara Falls, N.Y. (30) BT46
Holt, Thomas, Lubbock, Texas (27) A94
Holzschuh, William, Peoria, Ill. (32)..................D17
Hood, Bob, San Francisco (24) CT72
Hoover, Dick, Akron, Ohio (32)..........CD62, CT64, CT66,
M56, M57

Meli, Ron, Kankakee, Ill. (28) BT75
Meredith, Glenn, Wichita, Kan. BT89
Merrill, Larry, New London, Ohio (20) BT63
Mersek, Rich, Cleveland (33).........................T75, S78
Mertens, Herb, Detroit...T37
Meszaros, Joe, Sterling, Ohio (44)...........................D57
Metz, Bob, Dayton, Ohio (47) D75
Meyer, Charles, Ottawa, Ohio (31)...........................BT61
Meyers, Norm, St. Louis (29).......CT63, CD67, CT75, CT76
Middleton, Jack, San Francisco (40) CT61
Mikolajczyk, Henry, Chicago (35) TA71
Milburn, Robert, McKees Rocks, Pa. (50)..............BT60
Miller, Andy, Chicago (42) BT65
Miller, Dana, Butler, Pa. (53)..................................BT70
Miller, H., Detroit (35) A17
Miller, John, St. Paul, Minn. (37)..............................T18
Miller, John, Chicago (20) T62
Miller, Pete, Kalamazoo, Mich. (41)..........................T30
Miller, Robert, Troy, Ohio BT59
Miller, Stan, Ottawa, Ohio (40) BT61
Miller, Ted, Cleveland (47) T47
Miller, Walter, Sioux Falls, S.D. (30) TA69
Miller, William, Detroit (29) S14, A14
Minaglia, Donald, Seattle.......................................BT54
Miner, William, Chicago (40) T11, T20
Minor, Tim, Spokane, Wash. (28) T96
Mistretta, Sam, Rochester, N.Y. (36) BT66
Moeck, Al, Toledo, Ohio TA92
Moffat, Dave, Chicago (28)......................................T57
Monroe, George, Grand Rapids, Mich. T07
Montgomery, Monty, Grand Junction, Colo. (65) BT72
Mooradian, Arnold, Niagara Falls, N.Y......................T35
Moore, John, Niagara Falls, N.Y. (32) BT46
Moore, Mickey, McKees Rocks, Pa. (45) BT60
Moore, Ronnie, Louisville, Ky. (24) T73
Morris, Ben, Norman, Okla.....................................BT93
Morris, Steve, Detroit (43) T50
Morrisette, Fran, St. Paul, Minn. (36) TA57
Morrison, George, Chicago (29)......................A30, T31
Moskal, Stanley, Saginaw, Mich. (29) A42
Mountain, Charley, Chicago.....................................T06
Mounts, Fred, Indianapolis (44) T36
Muehlstredt, Frank, Mason City, Iowa (44) BT51
Mueller, Glenn, Milwaukee (30)...............................T81
Muggley, Harry, St. Paul, Minn. (28).................T13, T18
Murphy, Johnny, Indianapolis (21)...........................A36
Murphy, Robert, Pontiac, Mich. (25) T64
Murray, Sam, Chicago (35)..............................T15, T16
Muscarello, Angelo, Niagara Falls, N.Y. (31)................T35
Musialowski, Rick, Buffalo (29)..............................TA75
Myers, Doug, El Toro, Calif. M79

N

Nadeau, Dan, Las Vegas, Nev. (25).................D91, TA91
Nagy, Steve, Cleveland (38)....D52, TA52, A52, T58, TA58
Natavio, Gerardo, Vancouver, B.C. (27) BT86
Neal, Randy, Los Angeles (26) CD77
Neelan, Dave, Kankakee, Ill. (35)............................BT75
Negley, John, Newark, N.J. (32) D14
Neiberding, Howie, Cleveland (58) T75
Nelson, Robert, Peoria, Ill. (27)..............................BT74
Nemeth, John, South Bend, Ind. (48) T49
Nesbit, Greg, Pittsburgh (19)....................................T82
Neujahr, Don Jr., Lincoln, Neb.................................BT84
Neujahr, Don Sr., Lincoln, Neb. BT84

Neumann, Mike, Buffalo (23) D90, A90, T90, TA90
Newrath, Dave, Cincinnati (26) CD78
Nicholas, Eddie, Austin, Texas (70)..........................BT78
Nickell, John, Detroit (27)...T60
Nicol, Ralph, Lansing, Mich. (43) T69
Niehaus, Otto, Chicago (43) T63, TA64
Nimke, Jeff, Oshkosh, Wis. (30) A93
Nitschke, Otto, Cleveland (53) S32
Nocera, Anthony, New Castle, Pa............................BT49
Noniman, Gus, Grand Rapids, Mich. (33) T07
Norris, Joe, San Diego (26)...............T34, T54, TA54
Norton, Dave, Chicago (33)....................................TA73
Notz, George, Chicago..T38
Nowicki, Ed, Milwaukee (29)..................................D42
Nusbaum, Keith, Toledo, Ohio TA92
Nutt, Jerry, Grand Rapids, Mich. (37) D72
Nystrom, Al, St. Paul, Minn. T13

O

Oakar, Larry, Cleveland (27)..................................CD65
Ober, Melby, Urbana, Ohio (47) BT79
O'Connor, Ed, Columbus, Ohio BT50
O'Connor, Mike, Salamanca, N.Y. T87
Odekirk, Gary, Milwaukee (32)................................T81
O'Donnell, Chuck, St. Louis (36)...................TA49. TA50
Ohmie, Robert, Wichita, Kan. BT89
O'Hop, Joe, Norfolk, Va. (54) BT71
Oishi, Fred, Chicago...BT53
Oliver, Ted, Seattle BT54
Olm, David, Jonesboro, Ga. (39) TA95
Olsheski, Ed, Rochester, N.Y. (36) BT66
Olson, Glen, Boulder City, Nev. (38) TA65, T70, T72
Oryhon, Paul, Chicago...TA66
Oswalt, Wilford (Bus), Ft. Wayne, Ind. (27) D63 A63, TA63
Ottman, Dan, Troy, Mich. (40).................................T97
Owan, N.P., Louisville, Ky. (41)...............................D12

P

Pacropis, George, Wilkes-Barre, Pa. (41) D55
Palko, John, Tucson, Ariz. (40) T76
Palumbo, Frank, Rochester, N.Y. (33) BT66
Palumbo, Lou, Sault Ste. Marie, Ont. (29) T66
Paine, Jim, Houston (35)..D73
Paine, William, Rochester, N.Y. (39) T71
Pantelione, Sam, Cleveland (38) T47
Pappas, George, Charlotte, N.C. (24) CT71, CD73
Parigian, Al, Detroit (42) T60
Partlow, Steve, Dayton, Ohio (42) D75
Paschen, George, St. Paul, Minn. (48) T18
Patterson, Earl, Columbiana, Ohio BT39
Patterson, Gary, St. Louis (29).................................CT78
Patterson, Pat, St. Louis (36)...................................CT62
Patton, Arvil, Ann Arbor, Mich. (47) BT81
Payne, Carl, Detroit..BT40
Peacock, J.T., Indianapolis (30)................................A06
Pearce, Durell, Rock Island, Ill. (45) BT69
Peart, Ed, Detroit (22) T80
Pecht, Brendan, Seattle (29) T95
Peek, Doug, Seattle (43)..TA72
Pencak, Jim, Cleveland (26) T85
Penoyer, Herbert, Norton (35)..................................T21
Perry, Bob, Paterson, N.J. (22) CD74
Perry, Frank, Lorain, Ohio (50) S67
Peters, Don, Chicago TA66
Peters, Raymond, Chicago......................................BT52

Peters, Rick, Middleton, Ohio (23) S79
Petersen, Larry, Kingston, N.Y. (44) TA62
Peterson, Frank, Columbus, Ohio (27) S13
Peterson, George, St. Paul, Minn. (33) T84, TA84,
                                        TA85, T88
Peterson, John, Milwaukee T86
Petraglia, John, Staten Island, N.Y. (23)...........CT70, CT72
Petro, John, Cleveland (42) TA52
Phillips, Robert, Hanford, Calif....................................BT64
Pierce, Randy, Detroit TA87
Pierce, Wally, Oshkosh, Wis. (37) S15
Pilon, Kurt, Clinton, Mich (24) T97
Pinkalla, Bob, Milwaukee (38) T67
Pinkalla, Wayne, Milwaukee (34) T67
Piraino, Marty, Syracuse, N.Y. (52)............................CD75
Piscalko, Steve, Cleveland (38) T47
Pointer, Bill, Pontiac, Mich. (24).................................S72
Polixa, David, Newark, N.J. (31)..................................BT88
Pollard, Rick, Versailles, Ind. (36) TA96
Pollard, Ron Sr., Versailles, Ind. (34)..........................TA96
Poole, Bob, Pueblo, Colo. (35) CS62
Poole, Walt, Ventura, Calif. (40) BT47
Popp, George, Chicago BT52
Porto, Joe, New Haven, Conn. (25) T14
Posnanski, Hank Jr., Milwaukee (31) T94
Post, Don, Edgerton, Minn. (51)..................................BT80
Powell, Cecil, Frankfort, Ky. (50) BT68
Priester, Ron, Albany, N.Y...T93
Procunier, Merritt, Chicago T51
Protich, Lincoln, Akron, Ohio (32) S48
Puccinelli, Joe, Chicago TA47
Puglie, Frank, Detroit TA67
Pusateri, Salvatore, Austin, Texas (43) BT78
Putzer, Mike, Oshkosh, Wis. (27) S76

R

Raffel, Gene, Milwaukee (36) T67
Rafferty, Edward, Philadelphia (25) D31
Raquet, Morris, Ft. Wayne, Ind. (27) TA77
Rea, Terry, Seattle (29)...TA68
Reaume, Tom, St. Clair Shores, Mich. (40) T97
Reckase, Jack, Chicago (48)...T57
Redman, Allen, Frankfort, Ky. (41) BT68
Reed, Jack, Columbus, Ohio...D06
Reilly, Charles, Philadelphia (40) D31
Reilly, Jack, Chicago (23) A05
Renaldy, Andrew, Youngstown, Ohio (42)......................S62
Reppenhagen, Walter, Detroit (36) T34, A34
Ressler, Ed Jr, Allentown, Pa..M75
Rice, Craig, Niagara Falls, N.Y. (28) T83
Rice, Oscar, Detroit BT40
Richard, Carl, Joplin, Mo. (34) T58, TA58
Richgels, Jeff, Madison, Wis. (23) T86, A97
Richter, E.G., Louisville, Ky. (45) D07
Riddle, Glenn, New York City (22) T12
Riethmiller, Dan, Salamanca, N.Y. T87
Risinger, Berry, Houston (39) T61
Ritger, Dick, River Falls, Wis. (28) CT67, CA77
Rittberg, Ross, Milwaukee (35) T81
Roberson, Larry, Muscatine, Iowa (31) T78
Roberson, Ray, Indianapolis (43) T36
Roediger, Fred, Chicago..T26
Roeth, Kenneth, Dubuque, Iowa (28) S65
Rogers, Lee, Minneapolis (30) TA76
Rogoznica, Andy, Chicago (39)...................................CD66
Rolfe, Robert, Chicago (24) D05

Rollick, Leo, Los Angeles (34) T46, S46
Rood, Jim, Omaha, Neb. (23) T74
Rosendal, John, Chicago..T06
Rosenkranz, Harry, Dayton, Ohio (34).............................T32
Rosser, Edward, Lansing, Mich. (44) T69
Rossi, Mike, Cleveland (43) T75
Rothbarth, Les, Pontiac, Mich. (42) T64
Rothermel, William, New York City (37)..........................T02
Rountree, Dave, Houston (35).....................................TA80
Roy, Bob, Denver (26) D77
Roy, Walt, Glenwood Springs, Colo. (45) D68, D77
Rudolph, George, Waukegan, Ill. (31)...........................D34
Ruff, Fred, Belleville, Ill. (28).......................................S41
Rusche, Bernard, Cincinnati (32) S49
Russell, Joe, Chicago (27)..................................T15, T16
Russo, Pat, Teaneck, N.J. (36) D64
Russo, Tony, Teaneck, N.J. (41) D64
Ryan, John, Waukegan, Ill. (34)....................................D34

S

Sabo, John, Detroit BT48
Saccone, Terry, Cincinnati (28)...........................T82, D93
Sajek, Rick, Chicago (21)...TA81
Sakamoto, Frank, Chicago...BT53
Salata, Joe, Chicago (25)..BT65
Saliba, Cliff, Niagara Falls, N.Y. (29) T83
Salvino, Carmen, Chicago (20)................T54, TA54, CD72
Sanders, Howard, Dayton, Ohio (38) T32
Santore, Frank, New York City (32).............A50, S53, A53
Sargeant, George, New Castle, Pa. BT49
Satorius, G., Peoria, Ill. (35) D17
Saul, Roy, Troy, Ohio BT59
Savas, Al, Milwaukee (41) T67
Savoy, Todd, St. Paul, Minn. (24) T84, TA84, TA85, T88
Scalia, Lou, Miami...M67
Schacht, Denny, St. Paul, Minn. (32) T84, TA84, TA85,
                                            T88
Schacht, Terry, St. Paul, Minn. (34)....T84, TA84, TA85, T88
Schafer, Henry, Rock Island, Ill. (61)............................BT69
Schanen, Ray, Milwaukee (36) TA48
Schanz, Ernest, Chicago (26) T28
Schecher, Charles, New Haven, Conn. (25)....................T14
Schieman, Art, Rochester, N.Y. (33)......................A21, D21
Schissler, Les, Denver (36)..................CT66, CS66, CA66
Schlaff, Cass, Detroit (47)..T50
Schlegel, Ernie, Vancouver, Wash. (26) CT70
Schlichting, Dennis, Racine, Wis. D87
Schliman, Sam, Toronto (37) S16, T21
Schmidt, Curt, Ft. Wayne, Ind. (31) TA63
Schmidt, Doug, Peoria, Ill. (23) BT74
Schmidt, Gene, Chicago (53) BT65
Schmidt, Gerry, Ft. Wayne, Ind. (33)...................D63, TA63
Schroeder, Jim, Toledo, Ohio (46) TA61
Schroeder, Jim, Buffalo (47)..CS76
Schuerman, Wayne, Cincinnati TA89
Schuld, George, Cleveland (34)...................................TA60
Schuldt, Clyde, Rock Island, Ill. (56) BT69
Schultz, Peter, Newark, N.J. (26)........................T02, D13
Schupp, Ed, Chicago (25) D25
Schwabl, Bud, Buffalo (49)..TA75
Schwessler, A., Joliet, Ill..T29
Schwoegler, Al, Madison, Wis. (31)..............................D09
Schwoegler, Tony, Madison, Wis. (24)...........................D09
Sciscioli, Nunzio, Rochester, N.Y. (59)..........................BT66
Scotland, Fred, Niagara Falls, N.Y. (37) T35
Scudder, Don, Cincinnati (30)..................T82, TA96, S96

Taylor, Terry, Nashville, Tenn. (33) S87
Taylor, Tim, Muscatine, Iowa (28)...............................T78
Taylor, Willard, Charleston, W.Va. M52
Tedford, Chris, Columbus, Miss....................................BT97
Teela, Richard, Oshkosh, Wis. (43) T19
Tetreault, Paul, Lebanon, N.H. (27) S89
Thacker, Ron, Cleveland (28) D80
Theel, George, Chicago (36)...............................T42
Thill, Phillip, Columbus, Ohio (37) T08
Thoma, Clarence, Chicago (31) D24
Thoma, Frank, Chicago (27) D16, A16
Thoma, Fred, Chicago (27)...............................D18
Thoma, Harry, Chicago (19) D24
Thomas, Jim, Toledo, Ohio (30) TA61, TA77
Thompson, David, Greenville, N.C. BT83
Thompson, Ed, Denver (27)...............................S73
Tocco, Fred, Detroit D26
Todd, Jim, Seattle TA68
Todd, Joe, Greenville, N.C. BT83
Toft, Rod, St. Paul, Minn. (36) A81, T84, TA84, TA85
Tordsen, John, Sioux Falls, S.D. (20) TA69
Toronski, Dan Sr., Cleveland (44)...............................T75
Totsky, Mike, Detroit (44)...............................CT73
Tountas, Pete, Tucson, Ariz. (37) T76, M68
Towns, James, Chicago (23) D48
Trader, Otto, Chicago (33) T17
Traficante, Joe, Pittsburgh (36)...............................T65
Trapp, August, Chicago. T17
Traubenik, Joe, Chicago (45) T38, T42, T48
Treloar, Jack, Detroit (32) TA74
Treloar, Norris, Mason City, Iowa (31) BT51
Treloar, Ralph, Mason City, Iowa (37) BT51
Trenton, Stephen, Peoria, Ill. (27) BT74
Tripp, Lyle, Mt. Carroll, Ill. (27) BT62
Trombetta, Joe, Chicago...............................TA66, TA73
Trudeau, Mark, Spokane, Wash. (37) T96
Tucker, John (Bill), Detroit (31) D58, CD68
Tryniski, Mike, Fulton, N.Y. (33) D94, TA94
Tucker, Mike, Fountain Valley, Calif. (25) A92
Tuliano, Danilo, Vancouver, B.C. BT86
Tuliano, Rodolfo, Vancouver, B.C. (27) BT86
Turnbull, Mike, Akron, Ohio (27) D79
Tuttle, Tommy, King, N.C. (35)...............................CT65

U

Ujvari, Bob, Buffalo (26) T90, D90, TA90
Unke, Adolph, Milwaukee (32)...............................S29
Urban, Robert, Wichita, Kan. BT89
Utt, Jeff, Spokane, Wash. (27)...............................T96

V

Vadakin, Gordon, Wichita, Kan. (34) TA88, T89
Van Boxel, Donald, Green Bay, Wis. (25) D49
Van Dalen, Frank, Niagara Falls, N.Y. (33)...............................T35
Vanderpool, Dale, Meade, Kan. BT92
Vanderpool, Scott, Meade, Kan. BT92
Van Hulzen, Virg, Edgerton, Minn. (37) BT80
Van Ness, D.H., Newark, N.J. (33)...............................D14
Van Stelten, Dave, Edgerton, Minn. (24) BT80
Vaughn, Bob, Tucson, Ariz. (44) T76
Vehige, Barney, St. Louis (32) D59
Verlo, Albert, Minneapolis (51)...............................BT41
Verlo, Arne, Minneapolis (56) BT41
Verlo, Arnold, Minneapolis (22)...............................BT41
Verlo, Peder, Minneapolis (32)...............................BT41
Veverka, James, Chicago (45) T41

Vidro, Jerry, Grand Rapids, Mich. (23)...............................S34
Vital, Rob, Lancaster, Pa. (26) S81
Vitali, Fred, Detroit (35) CT73
Vogel, George, Chicago (51) T41
Voorhees, L.O., Chicago T01
Voorhies, John, New York City (23)...............................D01
Vornhagen, Bernie, Erie, Pa. (27) T33
Voss, Gary, St. Louis (34) D76
Votel, Ed, Braddock, Pa. (35) S26
Votel, Frank, Covington, Ky. (24) T33
Vowels, Dwight, Grove, Okla. (53) BT96
Vrenick, Jim, St. Louis (47)...............................D58

W

Wachhaus, Dan, Harrisburg, Pa. (20)...............................TA70
Wade, George, Steubenville, Ohio (33)...............................S56
Wagner, Chuck, Chicago (27) T54, TA54
Wagner, Henry, Chicago...............................T26
Wagner, Scott, Ft. Lauderdale, Fla. BT91
Walewski, Henry, Syracuse, N.Y. BT42
Waliczek, Paul, Wichita, Kan. (39) TA88, T89
Wallace, Ben, Chicago (22) T10
Walters, Cecil, Sioux Falls, S.D. (35) TA69
Wambold, Michael, Rochester, N.Y. (27) D95
Ward, Dan, Chicago (27) T09
Ward, Tom, Columbus, Ohio BT50
Ward, W.E. Jr., Norfolk, Va. BT71
Warren, Charles, Springfield, Ill. (20)S 36
Warren, Chris, Dallas (26) M90
Warshafsky, Barry, Boston (22)...............................CD71
Watson, George, Greenville, N.C. BT83
Weber, A.F., Elizabeth, N.J. (39) A24
Weber, Dick, St. Louis (32) CT62
Wegerski, Theodore, Syracuse, N.Y. BT42
Wegley, Rob, Chicago (28) TA81
Weiske, Arnold, Joliet, Ill. (51) T77
Weisser, Michael, Buffalo (55) T25
Welu, Billy, Houston (22) D54, T58, TA58, CT64, CT66
                                                  M64, M65
Weltzien, John, Boca Raton, Fla. (42) S94, TA95
Wengler, Arch, Chicago (27) S08
Wenz, George, Niagara Falls, N.Y................................BT87
Werman, Frank, Los Angeles (24)...............................CD77
Wetterman, Ed, Cincinnati (32)...............................D10
Wheeler, Dave, Kirksville, Mo. (25) CT78
Wheeler, Ron, Delavan, Wis. (30)...............................D67
Whitehead, Dave, Las Vegas...............................TA93
Whiteman, Charles, Cleveland (48) T47
Wilcox, John, Williamsport, Pa. (19) A66, CT77
Wild, Bob, San Francisco (51) CT61
Wilde, Randy, Green Bay, Wis. D93
Wilde, Ron, Green Bay, Wis. 93
Will, Hank, Chicago (36) D28
Willen, Fred Sr., St. Louis (62) D76
Williams, Billy, Chicago (36) T11
Williams, Dick, League City, Texas (30) BT76
Wilman, Joe, Chicago (33)...............................A39, T42, A46
                                         TA47, T54, TA54
Wilson, Bob, Gary, Ind. (43) T79, TA79
Wilson, Finnus, Milwaukee (35) T23, D23
Wilson, Gary, Omaha, Neb. (26)...............................T74
Wilson, Jack, Akron, Ohio (24) D79
Wilson, Rick, St. Joseph, Mo. (31) TA85
Wilson, Robert, Cleveland (27)...............................T24
Winsberg, Dexter, Chicago (38) T40, TA47
Winters, Jack, Philadelphia (32) CA62, T68

Wintersteen, Chuck, Chicago (40) TA66
Wirth, Chester, Chicago BT38
Wittkowske, John, Milwaukee....................................T86
Wolf, Dean, Reading, Pa. (29) T92
Wolf, Phil, Chicago (41) T09, T20, A28
Wolfe, Dave, Albany, N.Y. T93
Wolfe, Harry, Chicago T03
Wolfe, Sam, Chicago..T03
Wonders, Rich, Racine, Wis. (35)..............D82, A82,
TA82, TA83, TA86
Wong, Tony, Vancouver, B.C.....................................BT86
Wood, Charley, Chicago...T05
Woodbury, Dave, Chicago..T04
Woodman, Leon, Chicago (38) T62
Woolet, Ron, Louisville, Ky. (21)...................T73, A73
Wright, Dennis, Milwaukee (38) T67
Wright, Frank, Chicago (35) T31
Wright, Les, Grand Junction, Colo. (55) BT72
Wright, Tom, Millbrae, Calif. (25)............................CT78
Wunderlich, Steve, St. Louis (27) M85, TA95

Y

Yannaras, Gus, Milwaukee D89
Yocum, Ray, Scottsburg, Ind. (33) T73
Yoder, Jake, Ft. Wayne, Ind. (37) S70
Yoho, Dewey, Tucson, Ariz. (45) T76
Yost, Frank, Detroit..T37

Youker, Bob Jr., Syracuse, N.Y. (23)..........................S92
Young, Billy, Tulsa, Okla. (26) A62
Young, Franklin, Chicago (39)...................................T48
Young, George, Detroit (39)............TA49, T52, T53, TA53,
T55, TA55
Young, Neal, Louisville, Ky. (33) S84
Young, Phil, Akron, Ohio (29) D26
Youngblood, Dewey, Seattle (37) TA72

Z

Zahn, Doug, Milwaukee (36).....................................BT85
Zahn, Wayne, Tempe, Ariz. (26) CT67
Zappa, Nick, Covington, Ky. (29) T33
Zavakos, Tom, Dayton, Ohio (31) T32
Zichterman, John, Chicago (35)................................T20
Zikes, Les, Chicago (27)...................T62, T63, A64, TA64,
CS75, CT77
Zimmerman, Jerry, Milwaukee BT90
Zimmerman, Richard, Tucson, Ariz. (41) T76
Zoeller, Harry, Wilkes-Barre, Pa. (40)........................D55
Zuben, William, Boston (24).....................................CD71
Zuehlke, Paul, Oshkosh, Wis. (36) D97
Zunker, Gil, Milwaukee (32)............................D33, A33
Zurcher, Fred, Ft. Wayne, Ind. (29)...........................T22
Zurchin, John Jr., McKees Rocks, Pa. (21)...................BT60
Zylstra, Cliff, Chicago BT52

ABC TOURNAMENT RECORDS

Legend: T, team; D, doubles; S, singles; CD, Classic doubles; CS, Classic singles, SR, seniors

300 GAMES (317)
1997
David Olynyk, Rosemont, Minn., T
Dave Theis, Chaska, Minn., T
Scot Keith, Addison, Ill., T
Merv Nelson, Modesto, Calif., D
Todd Rodgers, Lees Summit, Mo., S
Rainer Evans, College Park, Ga., S
Garry Green, Indianapolis, S
James Rober, Toledo, Ohio, S
Wyiatt Kosier, Toledo, Ohio, S
Rob Bailey, Sun Prairie, Wis., D
Jeffrey Bonnin, Kenosha, Wis., S
El Drye, Rockford, Ill., D
Mike Quinn, Fairbury, Neb., T
Rick Starbuck, Beavercreek, Ohio, S
David Murto, Sebring, Fla., D
Todd Minotti, Orlando, Fla., T
Stephen Krywy, Roseville, Mich., D
Chad Neff, Dublin, Ohio, S
Larry McDowell, Madison, Wis., D
Ralph DiDomenico, Whitby, Ontario, T
Chris Kishbaugh, East Stroudsburg, Pa., T
James Shifflett, Harrisonburg, Va., D
John Lieber, Omaha, Neb., S
Robert Chapman, Minneola, Texas, S
1996
Ronald Young, Lakewood, Colo., S
Michael Nape, Blue Island, Ill., D
Timothy Sepich, Portland, Ore., S
Troy Cox, Madison, Wis., D
Joe Cecil, Lexington, N.C., S
Thomas Howison, Chillicothe, Ohio, D
Alan Esperson, Williamsville, N.Y., S
Dave Oulman, Owatonna, Minn., S

Ken Alexander, Toledo, Ohio, S
Carlos Hernandez, Laredo, Texas, S
Gary Brown, Bloomington, Ind., D
Mike Marks, Kentwood, Mich., D
Tod Grams, Holland, Mich., S
John Hackett, Belleair Beach, Fla., S
Lynn Staude, Fort Atkinson, Wis., T
Ralph Krueger, Menomonee Falls, Wis., T
Dan Cabrera, Galesburg, Ill., D
Mike Medlen, Lawrence, Kan., D
Joseph Bertolone, Wickliffe, Ohio, S
Marvin Hittle, Jamestown, Colo., S
Bruce Ogata, Las Vegas, S
William Madden, Hastings, Mich., S
Jerry Kennedy, Walnut Creek, Calif., T
Don Scudder Jr., Cincinnati, S
Mike Dray, Felton, Calif., T
Dan McElligot, Portland, Ore., T
Mike Bouvia, Gresham, Ore., D
Tim Steckman, Colorado Springs, Colo., S
Tal Kennedy, Lake Oswego, Ore., S
James Davis, Lenexa, Kan., S
Danny Janssens, Anaheim, Calif., S
Tim Jeffries, Wooster, Ohio, T
Kenneth Shaw, Hales Corners, Wis., T
Eddy Kelley, Amarillo, Texas, S
Dan Guest, Angola, N.Y., D
Tim Jones, Hurricane, Utah, D
Lou Trunk, Castro Valley, Calif., D
Darrell Shoemaker, Kennewick, Wash., S
Steve Black, Denton, Texas, S
Craig Szplett, Burbank, Ill., D
1995
John Gualtieri, Edison, N.J., T
Todd Thompson, Reno, Nev., S

Robert Cathey, Duncanville, Texas, S
Bob Palinski, Bourbonnais, Ill., T
Matt Surina, Mead, Wash., S
James Carl, Richmond, Mich., S
Mike Jones, Chicago, T
Dale Price, Grand Island, Neb., S
Lynn Staude, Waterloo, Wis., T
Jeffery Magas, Willoughby, Ohio, D
Michael Procaccino, Henderson, Nev., D
Richard Smith, Melbourne, Fla., S
Gary Mills, Bowie, Md., D
Scot Mitamura, Kaneohe, Hawaii, S
Rick Moore, Roy, Utah, D
Clay Rivette, Missouri City, Texas, T
Rodney Lane, Los Angeles, S
George Randles, Louisville, Ky., T
Ray Candelaria, Rio Rancho, N.M., D
Steve Staton, Lynchburg, Va., S
Charles Avant, Ft. Worth, Texas, S
Gerald Eddings, Thousand Oaks, Calif., S
Scott Greene, Greenville, N.C., S
Terry Heffernan, Spokane, Wash., S
Roy Green, El Cajon, Calif., D
Alexander Lee III, Spokane, Wash., S
Arlond Frazier, Huntington, Calif., D
1994
Brad Reeves, Waterloo, Iowa, T
Bob Ujvari, Buffalo, S
Mike Neumann, Buffalo, S
Gregory Anderson, Ocala, Fla., S
Dan McNally, Waukesha, Wis., D
Kyle Yarter, Albany, N.Y., S
Charlie McLemore, Pensacola, Fla., T
Steve DuVall, Chamberlain, S.D., T
Craig Packer, Idaho Falls, Idaho, D

Tony Lindemann, Detroit, D
Robert Plaza Jr., Montgomery, Ill., D
Larry Pelfree, Layfayette, Ind., D
Eddie Kesler, Salt Lake City, S
Eddie Graham Jr., Midland, Texas, S
1993
Larry Delozier, Tulsa, Okla., S
Arnie Goldman, Roseville, Mich., D
Doug Killebrew, Las Vegas,
Richard Anderson, Canyon, Texas, T
Kirk Pierson, Denver, D
Kevin Williams, Springfield, Mo., D
Robert Castle, East Point, Mich., S
Don Davis, Houston, S
Chris Barnes, Wichita, Kan., T
Willard Lewis Sr., Nothingham, Pa., D
Ray Cyr, Utica, N.Y., S
Curt Oller, Rapid City, S.D., D
Wayne Nosse, Villa Park, Ill., S
Kevin McGerr, Lincoln, Neb., T
Gary Minatel, Indianapolis, T
John Bauerle, Indianapolis, S
Jay DeJaynes, Fayetteville, N.C., T
Clyde Fravel, Tomball, Texas, S
Dwight Albrecht, Milwaukee, S
James Scott, Audubon, Pa., S
Michael Tryniski, Fulton, N.Y., D
Chris Forry, Fairfield, Conn., D
Robert Ciambriello, Trumbull, Conn., S
Jimmy Nelson, Irving, Texas, D
Barry Mefford, Caledonia, Mich., T
Craig Conley, Baton Rouge, La., D
Keith Bennet, Baton Rouge, La., S
Stephen Donahue, Auburn, N.Y., D
Louis Wroblewski, Liverpool, N.Y., D
Ron Johnson, Griffith, Ind., S
Paul Klempa, Lincoln, Neb., S
Dave Ford, Indianapolis, S
Bob Fry, Loves Park, Ill., D
Royd Fettig, Killdeer, N.D., T
Jim Jundt, Minot, N.D., T
Brian Dexter, Holland, Mich., D
Ed Jackson, Charlotte, N.C., D
John Busley, Holt, Mich., S
Walt Cummings, Geneva, N.Y., S
Roy Kellow, Louisville, Ky., S
Dave LaBar, Green Bay, Wis., D
Ronald Wilde, Green Bay, Wis., D
Dick Jones, Wayne, Pa., D
Marc Lineberry, Clinton, Iowa, S
John Eiss, Brooklyn Park, Minn., D
Mike White, Battle Creek, Mich., S
Dennis Kreamer, Middleburg, Pa., D
Tony Gonzales, Irving, Texas, S
Hal Champenois, Irving, Texas, T
Richard Dooley, Granite City, Ill., D
Mark Spencer, Bloomington, Ind., S
1992
Dan Ash, Oregon, Ohio, D
Mark Cwiertniak, Lockport, Ill., D
Ken Siarkiewicz, Fort Atkinson, Wis., D
Michael Faliero, Buffalo, S
Nunzio Marino, Livonia, Mich., S
Kevin Mullins, Florissant, Mo., S
Brian Csipkes, Omaha, Neb., S

Robert Wagener, Holly, Mich., S
Leonard Kaleta, Warner Robins, Ga., D
Frank Endres, Akron, Ohio, D
Grover Bowman, Eureka, Calif., D
Derwin Pitre, Baton Rouge, La., T
Alan Spike, Mount Prospect, Ill., S
Don Nelson, Justice, Ill., D
1991
Keith Ehman, Cranford, N.J., D
John Brader, Lebanon, N.J., S
Michael Peters, Silvis, Ill., S
Mike Bodnariuk, El Segundo, Calif., S
Kenneth Eddinger, Sandusky, Ohio, T
Chris Gibbons, Madison, Wis., D
John Forst, Woodridge, Ill. D
Dan Nadeau, Las Vegas, D
David Roundtree, Houston, S
Bob Wronski, Tinley Park, Ill., D
Keith Perry, North Windham, Conn., S
Russell Huse, Lafayette, Ind., S
Brendan Komenda, Hamburg, Ill., D
Gail Myers, Monroe, Wis., T
Rod Jacobson, Duncan, Okla., S
Kurt Moshy, Phoenix, 1991D
Tracy Lamberth, Hendersonville, Tenn., S
Jeffrey Mraz, Akron, Ohio, S
John Hostetler, Middlefield, Ohio, S
Jim Albrecht, West Bend, Wis., S
Jamie Duke, Mt. Juliet, Tenn., D
Kevin Taber, Toledo, Ohio, S
David Freeman, Ft. Worth, Texas, S
Michael Lucich, Ferndale, Mich., S
Terry Taylor, Nashville, Tenn., S
Todd Stockton, South Bend, Ind., S
Dave Bohlin, Lansing, Ill., T
Jamie Gregory, Dayton, Ohio, S
Keith Muskiewicz, Huron, Ohio, D
Donald Burdick, DeKalb, Ill., S
Gary Cooper, Jackson, Mich., D
Tom Kelly, Omaha, Neb., S
Ted Bertrand, Billings, Mont., T
Derron Lax, Austin, Texas, S
Lonnie Sharkey, Bremerton, Wash., D
Ed Deines, LaPorte, Colo., S
Fred Carroll, Newport News, Va., T
Steve Erickson, Tempe, Ariz., S
Robert Wegley, Chicago Heights, Ill., D
Rich Avery, LaPorte, Ind., S
Gerard Conrad, Chalmette, La., S
Bill Hare, New Port Richey, Fla., D
Dennis Libby, Forty Fort, Pa., T
Brian Keller, Bellevue, Wash., S
Mark Hugo, Wallingford, Conn., S
Ryan Erickson, Davenport, Iowa, D
Richard Johnson, Rockford, Ill., S
Ed Jackson, Charlotte, Mich., D
1990
Fred Borden, Akron, Ohio, S
Jason Couch, Winter Garden, Fla., S
Craig Goodwin, Idaho Falls, Idaho, S
Rick Rhyno, Aurora, Ont., Canada, S
1989
William Anderson, Lansing, Mich., D
David Beck, Lansing, Mich., D
Lennie Boresch, Kenosha, Wis., D
Steve Brown, Norristown, Pa., T

Edward Cetwinski, Hammond, Ind., S
Joe Claypool, Prattville, Ala., D
Michael Clemence, Warren, Mich., D
Mathew Dalke, Valparaiso, Ind., D
August Dieckhoner, Fairfield, Ohio, S
Bill Essman, Bryan, Ohio, T
Bob Fleetwood, Trumbull, Conn., S
Charles Frank, Jacksonville, Fla., D
Gordy Fransen, Wyoming, Mich., T
Mike Friedrichs, Glendale, Ariz., S
Paul Grauzer, Westland, Mich., T
Dave Hammel, Cleveland, D
Russ Howell, Semmes, Ala., T
Mark Jensen, Wichita, Kan., S
Jim Johnson, Manhattan, Kan., D
Terry Kandes, Woodhaven, Mich., S
Barry Kleweno, Hays, Kan., D
Terry Kulibert, Oshkosh, Wis., T
Paul Kwiecien, Lansing, Mich., S
Steve Lang, Indianapolis, S
Mike Lebarre, Battle Creek, Mich., S
Michael Long, Topeka, Ind., D
Ronald Majeske Jr., San Diego, S
Robert Martin, Wichita, Kan., D
Norman Meyers, Bensalem, Pa., S
Bob Mills, Arlington Heights, Ill., T
Patrick Moffe III, Elmira, N.Y., S
Steve O'Malley, Rapid City, S.D., T
Floyd Piepenburg, Chilton, Wis., S
William Preckel, Florissant, Mo., S
Roy Rider, Medford, Ore., T
Scott Schlei, Menomonee Falls, Wis., S
Brian Schwanke, Michigan City, Ind., S
Keith Selment, Yukon, Okla., S
Al Shaner, North Olstead, Ohio, T
James Stiglich, West Allis, Wis., S
Jack Treloar, Redford, Mich., D
Michael Turnbull, Tallmadge, Ohio, S
Garl Walsh, Alamogordo, N.M., D
Tim Wilson, West Allis, Wis., D
1988
David Bernhardt, Detroit, T
David DeLorenzo, Milwaukee, S
David Slyne, Hartford, Conn., S
1987
Larry Carmack, Bolingbrook, Ill., T
1986
Keith Loran, Billings, Mont., T
Glenn Purpura, Lombard, Ill., S
Ron Wilde, Green Bay, Wis., S
William Block, Miami, D
1984
Doug Hayes, Kirksville, Mo., T
Joe Rock, Colorado Springs, Colo., S
Jamie Thomas, Kansas City, D
1983
Joe Natoli, Milwaukee, D
1981
Gary Engelby, Albert Lea, Minn., T
1979
Dave Norton, Hammond, Ind., D
Mike Hagan, Louisville, Ky., S
Nelson Burton Jr., St. Louis, CD
1978
Loren Kaiser, Albert Lea, Minn., S
Lloyd Furr, Wichita, Kan., T

1977
Don Bell, Santa Maria, Calif., CD
1976
Jimmy Doolen, Wichita Falls, Texas, S
Bud Horn, Los Angeles, CS
1975
Asa Morris, St. Louis, S
Marty Piraino, Syracuse, N.Y., CD
1974
Beryl Henshaw, Connoquenessing, Pa., D
Kiyoshi Kato, Honolulu, Hawaii, D
Gill Johansson, Naperville, Ill., S
Ray Williams, Detroit, T
1971
Eddy Patterson, Dallas, CS
1970
Jake Yoder, Ft. Wayne, Ind., S
1968
John Caras, Philadelphia, S
Bill Tucker, Los Angeles, CD
1967
Les Schissler, Denver, CT
Lou Cioffi, Chicago, CS
1961
Robert DeGraff, Grand Rapids, Mich., CD
1960
Louis Facsko, Lorain, Ohio, S
1958
Edward Shay, Chester, Pa., S
1955
Myron Ericksen, Racine, Wis., S
1954
Tony Sparando, New York, S
1953
Ray Mihm, Green Bay, Wis., S
1951
Vince Lucci, Trenton, N.J., D
1946
Leo Rollick, Los Angeles, D
1941
William Hoar, Cicero, Ill., D
1940
George Pallage, Akron, Ohio, S
Michael Domenico, Canton, Ohio, D
1939
William McGeorge, Kent, Ohio, S
1938
Michael Blasek, Conneaut, Ohio, S
1935
Carl Mensenberg, Scranton, Pa., S
1933
Jack Karstens, Fort Sheridan, Ill., D
1926
Charles Reinlie, Racine, Wis., D
1913
William Knox, Philadelphia, S

299 GAMES (153)
1997
Andrew Melnyk, Syracuse, N.Y., D
Chad Tisdale, Fayetteville, Ark., S
Richard Shawver, Amherst, Ohio, S
Ronald Buxbaum, Milwaukee, D
Tony Mithelavage, Grandview, Mo., S
Carey Hofmann, Glendale, Ariz., T

Vince Honeycutt, Charlotte, N.C., D
Floyd Harrison, Tulsa, Okla., D
Chuck Gollnick, Jamestown, N
1996
Pat Johns, Seatac, Wash., D
Jim Grigsby, Helena, Mont., T
Keith Proehl, Chillicothe, Ohio, S
Scott Salbeck, Chicago, S
Michael Wambold, Rochester, N.Y., D
Mike Abele, Mentor, Ohio, S
Bill Anderson, Millington, Tenn., T
Robert Burdick, Assumption, Ill., T
Frank Pavone, Baltic, Conn., T
Randy Wilson, Lincoln, Neb., D
Dennis Burns, Joliet, Ill., S
Jake Green, Chicago, D
Butch Krueger, Austin, Texas, S
Nick DiBlatto, Cleveland, S
Danny Inocencio, Humble, Texas, D
Ted Staikoff, Black Hawk, S.D., T
Joe Merrill, Ventura, Calif., D
Bob Maki, Muskego, Wis., S
Jerry Buchholz, Monterey, Calif., D
Richard Mariani, Philadelphia, S
1995
Keith Holland, Fleetwood, Pa., S
Jeff Kwiatkowski, Maumee, Ohio, T
Corby Larson, Grand Forks, Mich., S
David Williams Jr., Papillion, Neb., D
Kevin Stewart, Cape Coral, Fla., T
Barry Gulden, Hanover, Pa., D
Ron Unser, Albany, N.Y., D
Marc Bowman, Keokuk, Iowa, S
1994
Corbett Austin, Ogden, Utah, T
Jon McKeever, Davenport, Iowa, D
Doug Krueger, Milwaukee, T
Tom Glowicki, Palos Hills, Ill., S
Brian Allie, Cleveland, Ohio, D
Dean Distin, Oswego, N.Y., D
Mark Wukoman, Franklin, Wis., S
Barry McIllhaney, Allentown, Pa., T
George Hummell, Willingboro, N.J., S
Randy Alford, Tyler, Texas, T
Fernando Victorio, Athens, Ga., D
Larry Pelfree, Lafayette, Ind., S
Robert Stolp, Phoenix, S
John Scott, Westfield, Mass., T
1993
Mark Smith, Grosse Point, Mich., T
Gail Myers, Madison, Wis., D
Lonny DiRusso, Cleveland, D
Frank Tavella, Denver, D
Scott Livesay, Ann Arbor, Mich., S
Jeff Richgels, Madison, Wis., D
Johnny Lay, St. Charles, Mo., T
Robert Albrecht, Sandusky, Ohio, S
Brett Locher, Sheffield Lake, Ohio, D
Dave Addington, Tyler, Texas, S
Sam Anderson, Lansing, Mich., S
Robert Bonebrake, Hagerstown, Md., D
Robert Genz Jr., Moline, Ill., S
Bob Barnowski, Las Vegas, S
Rickey Kendrick, Monticello, Ill., T
Marvin Easter, Grove, Okla., S

Erv Lauterbach, North Riverside, Ill., S
1992
Jon Sisk, Seattle, D
Jim Von Holten, Broken Arrow, Okla., D
Larry Spetoskey, Grand Rapids, Mich., D
Bruce Torbeck, Milwaukee, D
Bret Bohnert, York, Pa., S
Joe Garza, Highspire, Pa., S
Ralph Slaber, Highland, Ind., S
Fred Mattson, Fircrest, Wash., S
1991
Terry Norton, Omaha, Neb., T
Walter Stopke Jr., St. Peters, Mo., S
Jimmy Johnson, Columbus, Ohio, D
Jim Hurl, Galloway, Ohio, S
Kevin Audritsh, Manchester, Mich., S
Luis Benavides, Lancaster, Texas, T
Bret Faulkner, Milwaukee, S
Jamie Burke, Loveland, Ohio, D
Jim Ewald Jr., Louisville, Ky., S
Tim Barth, Bartlett, Ill., T
Ron Vokes, Milwaukee, D
Terry Roberts, Aurora, Ill., S
Tom Martelli Sr., Palos Hills, Ill., S
Charley Endres, Portage, Mich., T
1990
Tom Fitzgerald III, St. Louis, D
Randy Holt, Panama City, Fla., D
Rodney Jones, Whitehall, Pa., D
Bill Orlikowski, Grand Rapids, Mich., S
Tim Struffolino, Woodville, Ohio, S
1989
Dennis Albers, Luzerne, Iowa, T
Michael Berry, St. Johns, Mich., D
Daniel Carpenter, Council Bluffs, Iowa, D
Ed Farley, Cincinnati, T
Larry Harris, Rochelle, Ill., D
Perry Keplinger, Amherst, Ohio, S
Dan Krzak, Justice, Ill., D
Larry Kubiak, Franklin, Tenn., S
Paul Lewis, Salt Lake City, D
Gus Marsala, Maryland Heights, Mo., D
Richard McCardy, Dearborn Heights, Mich., D
Bus Oswalt, Fort Wayne, Ind., T
Kevin Peachey, Virginia Beach, Va., S
Jeff Sabella, Canton, Ohio, D
Greg Sternberg, Creve Coeur, Mo., S
Mike Welter, Racine, Wis., D
Peter Wolfschaffner, Hanau, Germany, D
Ronald Wymen, Midland, Mich., D
1988
Chris Shinabarker, Lakeland, Fla., T
Jack Harmon, Aurora, Ill., S
1987
Mel Allen, Utica, N.Y., S
Ryan Erickson, Bettendorf, Iowa, S
1986
Tom Maczka, Franksville, Wis., S
1985
Kingston Gee, San Francisco, S
Jerry Dunlap, Detroit, D
1984
Bob Ferguson, Porterville, Calif., D

1982
Butch Krueger, Austin, Texas, D
Jeff Mraz, Akron, Ohio, S
1980
Pete Hainline, Wichita, Kan., T
Dave Peneguy, New Orleans, D
1979
Dave Bond, Brandon, Fla., T
1975
Bill Diedrich, Detroit, S
Dave Applegate, Janesville, Wis., D
1974
Leo Elliott, Detroit, T
James Johnson, Champaign, Ill., S
Dennis Campbell, Chicago., D
Jim Godman, Lorain, Ohio, CD
1970
Glenn (Pete) LaCell, Sylvan Beach, N.Y., D
William Sawon, Steubenville, Ohio, D
1969
Charles Guedel, Indianapolis, D
1965
Willie Clark, San Antonio, Texas, D
1963
Tony Baldwin, Tulsa, Okla., D
1958
Dick Karas, Chicago, D
1957
Stan Williams, Dayton, Ohio, S
1954
Dale Carter, Bremerton, Wash., S
1951
Howard Rommel, Sturgis, Mich., D
1948
William Brooks, Detroit, T
Samuel Dempsey, St. Louis, S
1942
Joe Heinreich, Chicago, S
1941
William Caskey, Canton, Ohio, T
1940
Lowell Jackson, St. Louis, D
1939
Henry Fischer, Houston, S
1932
J.L. Winko, Columbus, Ohio, D
1930
Sidney Baker, Peru, Ind., S
1929
Frank Fabing, Gary, Ind., D
Edward Judy, Chicago, S
1924
Joe Summermatter, Rochester, N.Y., T
1922
Frank Degen, Buffalo, D
1921
James Gilligan, Rochester, N.Y., S

298 GAMES (86)
1997
Bob Wolfe, Altoona, Wis., S
Pete Constantine, Oak Lawn, Ill., S
1996
Kurt Hanke, Altoona, Wis., D
Kevin Gmach, Sheboygan, Wis., T
Darrin Lindsey, Vinton, Iowa, D
Mark Cooney, Indianapolis, D
Timothy Hagar, Coldwater, Ohio, S
Jeffrey Couch, Lawndale, Ind., T
Gary Bower, Camp Hill, Pa., T
Dennis Bruder, Hellertown, Pa., D
Dave Roy, Glenwood Springs, Colo., S
Chris Griffin, Gainesville, Fla., T
Jeffrey Phillips, Huntsville, Ala., D
Kevin Million, Lincoln, Neb., T
Kenney Allen, Abilene, Texas, S
Tray Nelson, Round Rock, Texas, S
1995
Domenic Fantilli, Reading, Pa., D
Steve Badovinac, Denver, D
Robert Wagener, Davison, Mich., T
Kenneth Pfeiler, Dubuque, Iowa, D
Timm Cordes, Muskegon, Mich., T
Bill Torkelson, Sioux Falls, S.D., D
Mike Gilbert, Spring, Texas, D
1994
Al Bruder, Chicago, S
Scott Critchfield, Granada Hills, Calif., T
1993
Raymond Lee, Gaitherburg, Md., T
Jesse Burgher, Ft. Madison, Iowa, T
Les Zikes, Palatine, Ill., D
Gary Haynes, Springfield, Ill., D
Tim Kobs, Milwaukee, D
Mike Williams, Tulsa, Okla., D
Stan Peterson, St. Joseph, Mo., T
Willie Atwood, Scottsburg, Ind., D
Claude Neely Jr., Estes Park, Colo., SR
Marvin Kipp, Waterford, Mich., D
1992
David Mankey, Geneva, Ind., D
Gary Niemczyk, St. Paul, Minn., D
Jimmie Bradley, Alma, Mich., D
Wayne Brint, Orange, Texas, S
Clarence Birks, Eureka, Calif., D
John Nolterieke, Boca Raton, Fla., S
Randy Gregg, Guntersville, Ala., D
1991
Othel Smith, Springfield, Mo., S
Michael Christenson, Pensacola, Fla., D
Robert Daugherty, Duluth, Ga., S
Mike Beltz, Austin, Texas, D
Charles Majeski, Muskegon, Mich., T
Jon Walters, Shelby, Ohio, T
Derek Lee, Los Angeles, S

1990
Carlton Nogle, Okemos, Mich., S
Terry Magoon, Grand Rapids, Mich., S
Ron Chader, Tonawanda, N.Y., S
1989
Dale Diamond, Springfield, Ill., D
Richard Downer, Wood River, Ill., D
Jimbo Evans, Jamaica Beach, Texas, S
Stephen Foley, Mesa, Ariz., S
Tim Gall, Britton, Mich., D
Walter Lane, Saukville, Wis., S
Bob Powell, Wichita, Kan., D
Jeff Rampart, Kenosha, Wis., S
Craig Trapp, Topeka, Kan., T
Ken Warwick, Hoisington, Kan., S
1988
Darryl Davis, Des Moines, Iowa, D
1987
Rick Wright, Lansing, Mich., S
Gene Schaetter, O'Fallon, Mo., D
1986
Darrell Umbarger, Tujanga, Calif., T
1985
Art Bryer, Providence, R.I., D
John Nofziger, Toledo, Ohio, T
Roger Frank, Norfolk, Neb., S
Gary Mage, Spokane, Wash., T
Doug Webber, Jasper, N.Y., S
1984
Mitch Jabczenski, Detroit, T
Bob Antczak, Chicago, S
1983
Fran Bax, Niagara Falls, N.Y., T
1981
John Turner, Evansville, Ind., T
1979
Art Love, Toledo, Ohio, S
1978
Jim Ewald, Louisville, Ky., T
Ed Altenburg, Flint, Mich., D
1976
Marlyn Browning, Louisville, Ky., D
1957
Bob Allen, Yonkers, N.Y., S
1951
Joe Walsh, St. Louis, S
1948
Arthur Behrns, N. Tonawanda, N.Y., D
1934
Fred Weber, Milwaukee, T
1920
Louis Mertz, Fond du Lac, Wis., S
1919
James Wolfe, Chicago, T
Walter Pieper, Milwaukee, D

SCORING RECORDS

INDIVIDUAL, series, regular events

847	John Socha, Milwaukee, 1997 Singles
833	Fran Bax, Niagara Falls, N.Y., 1983 Team
826	Ed Deines, LaPorte, Colo., 1991 Singles
	Matt Surina, Mead, Wash., 1995 Singles

INDIVIDUAL, series, singles

847	John Socha, Milwaukee, 1996 (278 290 279)
826	Ed Deines, LaPorte, Colo., 1991 (268 300 258)

	Matt Surina, Mead, Wash., 1995 (268 258 300)
822	Mark Graczyk, Chicago, 1991 (289 276 257)

INDIVIDUAL, all events

2,254	Jeff Nimke, Oshkosh, Wis. 1993 (701 779 774)
2,241	Jeff Richgels, Oregon, Wis., 1997 (774 692 775)
2,231	Dave Theis, Chaska, Minn. 1997 (789 754 688)

DOUBLES, game

580   Ron Pollard (290)-Rick Pollard (290), Versailles, Ind., 1996

578   Gail Myers Jr. (299)-Jeff Barseness (279), Madison, Wis., 1993

       Mike Procaccino (300)-Mike Friedrichs (278), Glendale, Ariz., 1995

DOUBLES, series

1,508   Jamie Burke (826), Loveland, Ohio-Drew Hauck (682), Finneytown, Ohio, 1996

1,505   Jimmy Johnson (784), Columbus, Ohio-Dan Nadeau (721), Las Vegas, 1991

1,499   Gus Yannaras (757)-Gary Daroszewski (742), Milwaukee, 1989

BOOSTER TEAM, individual, series

716   Bud Debenham, Los Angeles, 1977 (267 216 233)

708   Dennis Gage, Lincoln, Neb., 1984 (257 193 258)

BOOSTER TEAM, game

1,092   Lewis Marine Supply, Ft. Lauderdale, Fla., 1991

1,075   Rochester (N.Y.) Sundries, 1958

1,054   Walton Radiators, Gary, Ind., 1963

BOOSTER TEAM, series

2,974   Lewis Marine Supply, Ft. Lauderdale, Fla., 1991

2,934   Pro World Pro Shop, Milwaukee, 1990

2,929   Leisure Lanes, Kankakee, Ill., 1975

REGULAR TEAM, game

1,255   Lake St. Louis Shell, O'Fallon, Mo., 1991

1,250   The Directors, Windsor, Ontario, 1995

1,247   Faball No. 1, Milwaukee, 1989

REGULAR TEAM, series

3,537   Bruegger's Bagels, Albany, N.Y., 1993

3,481   Chilton Vending, Wichita, Kan., 1989

3,473   Trout's Minnows, Spokane, Wash., 1996

TEAM ALL EVENTS

10,425   Pollard's Bowl, Versailles, Ind., 1996

10,353   Sam's Town No. 1, Las Vegas, 1993

10,107   Browning Pontiac No. 2, Cincinnati, 1989

ABC TOURNAMENT MISCELLANEOUS RECORDS

AGE, performance by Oldest Champion
75   Glenn Smith, Grove, Okla., 1996 Booster Team

AGE, oldest 300 Shooter
74   Tony Lindemann, Detroit, 1994 Doubles

AGE, doubles team
165   Jerry Ameling (83)-Joseph Lehnbeutter (82), St. Louis, 1955

AGE, highest score
736   Don Schmidt, Lansdale, Pa., 1959 Singles, age 18

AGE, champion
16   Ronnie Knapp, New London, Ohio, 1963 Booster Team.

ATTENDANCE, one tournament
201,175   Las Vegas, 1986 (134 days-1,501 daily average).
175,370   Reno, Nev., 1984 (112 days-1,566 daily average).
174,953   Reno, Nev., 1977 (89 days-1,966 daily average).

CHAMPIONSHIPS, brothers
11   Nelson Jr. and Neil Burton, St. Louis

CHAMPIONSHIPS, father and son
   Matt Faetz Sr. (AE15), Matt Jr. (T40) and Leo (T40),Chicago, Ill. were the first. Since then, five others have achieved this feat.

CHAMPIONSHIPS, individual, consecutive
3   Les Zikes, Chicago, T 1962, T 1963, AE 1964.

CHAMPIONSHIPS, individual, one tournament
4   Bill Lillard, Houston, 1956 (T, D, AE, TAE).
    Ed Lubanski, Detroit, 1959 (T, S, AE, TAE).
    Mike Neumann, Buffalo, 1990 (T, D, AE, TAE).

CHAMPIONSHIPS, individual, career
9   Nelson Burton Jr., St. Louis, CT 1965, CS 1969, CD 1970, CS 1973, CT 1975, CT 1976, M 1976 CD 1979, CAE 1979.

8   Fred Bujack, Detroit, TAE 1949, TAE 1950, T 1952, T 1953, TAE 1953, TAE 1955, T 1955, AE 1955.
    Bill Lillard, Houston, T 1955, TAE 1955, T 1956, TAE 1956, D 1956, AE 1956, CT 1962, CT 1971.

CHAMPIONSHIPS, individual in singles event
2   Larry Sutton, Rochester, N.Y., 1909, 1912
    Nelson Burton, Jr., St. Louis, C 1969, C 1973

CHAMPIONSHIPS, individual in doubles event
2   Frank Benkovic, Milwaukee, 1932, 1933 was the first. Since then, nine others have achieved this feat.

CHAMPIONSHIPS, individual in all events
2   Jimmy Smith, Buffalo, N.Y., 1911, 1920 was the first. Since then, six others have achieved this feat.

CHAMPIONSHIPS, individual in team event
4   Bill Lillard, Houston, 1955, 1956, C 1962, C 1971
    Bud Horn, Los Angeles, C 1963, C 1967, C 1975, C 1976

CHAMPIONSHIPS, individual in team all events
4   Fred Bujack, Detroit, 1949, 1950, 1953, 1955
    Therman Gibson, Detroit, 1949, 1950, 1953, 1955
    Lou Sielaff, Detroit, 1949, 1950, 1953, 1955

CHAMPIONSHIPS, individual in first tournament (Boosters not included)
Singles
   Carl Baumgartner, Cincinnati, 1923 (724) was the first. Since then, 11 others have achieved this feat.
Doubles
   Henry Kmidowski, Buffalo, 1946 (698) was the first. Since then, three others have achieved this feat.
All Events
   Ora Mayer, San Francisco, 1935 (2022) was the first. Since then three others have achieved this feat.
Team
   Don Glover, Show Low, Ariz., C 1969 (611-623-1234) was the first. Since then, seven others have achieved this feat.

CHAMPIONSHIPS, longest span between first and last title

21   George Geiser, Chicago, (T1917, T1938)
      Jule Lellinger, Chicago, (T1917, T1938)
20   Joe Norris, San Diego, (T1934, T1954)

CHAMPIONSHIPS, team, consecutive

2   Commodore Barry, Chicago, 1915, 1916. (Sponsor
      in 1915 was Barry-Ketteler but four of five men in
      lineups were the same)
      Pfeiffer Beer, Detroit, 1952, 1953. (Sponsor in 1952
      was E&B Beer, but four of five men in lineups were
      the same)
      Munsingwear No. 2, Minneapolis, Classic 1975,
      1976 (same lineup)
      Minnesota Loons No. 1, St. Paul, Minn., Team All
      Events 1984, 1985 (same lineup)

CHAMPIONSHIPS, team with at least the same three men in all lineups

7   Pfeiffer Beer, Detroit, T 1952, 1953, 1955; TAE
      1949, 1950, 1953, 1955. (Sponsor in 1949, 1950
      and 1952 was E&B Beer, but same three men were
      in lineup each year-Lou Sielaff, Fred Bujack,
      Therman Gibson.)
4   Minnesota Loons, St. Paul, Minn., T 1984, 1988;
      TAE 1984, 1985
3   Hamm's Beer, Minneapolis, T 1970, 1972;
      TAE 1965.
      Kendor Corp. No. 1-Faball Enterprises, Milwaukee,
      TAE 1982,1983, 1986

DECREASE, game to game, individual series

167 pins   Al LaBelle, Milwaukee, 1938 (266-99)
            Rusty Sutphin, Radford, Va., 1982 (288-121)

DECREASE, game to game, team series

271   Federal Market, Chicago, 1922 (1101-830)
268   Lieber Bowlers Shops, Gary, Ind., 1962 (1134-866)
243   Jalovec Dodge, Cleveland, 1952 (1162-919)

DUPLICATE GAMES, individual, consecutive

6   Lawrence Buller, Lincoln, Neb., 1992 (180)

DUPLICATE SCORES, team game

192   Moffat's Ale, Syracuse, N.Y., 1936 (all five had
      same score)

ENTRIES, all events

91,059   Reno, Nev., 1995
48,443   Las Vegas, 1986
45,030   Salt Lake City, 1996

ENTRIES, Booster division teams

4,020   Milwaukee, 1952
3,936   Chicago, 1953
3,060   Rochester, N.Y., 1956

ENTRIES, Regular division teams

15,325   Reno, Nev., 1995
9,009   Salt Lake City, 1996
8,416   Mobile, Ala., 1994

ENTRIES, teams in one tournament

17,185   Reno, Nev., 1995
10,019   Las Vegas, 1986
9,746   Salt Lake City, 1996

ENTRY, teams from Canada

195   Reno, Nev., 1995
161   Reno, Nev., 1990
153   Niagara Falls, N.Y., 1983

ERRORS, fewest by championship team

1   Pfeiffer Beer, Detroit, 1955
      Brunswick Rhinos, Buffalo, 1990
2   A & A Asphalt, Detroit, 1960
      Ace Mitchell Shur-Hooks, Akron, Ohio, 1966
      (Note-accomplished in second three game Classic
      team block during record 3,357)

FIRST GAME, individual in first ABC

299   Willie Clark, San Antonio, 1965
299   Dave Bond, Brandon, Fla., 1979

FIRST GAME, team

1,232   Chilton Vending, Wichita, Kan., 1989
1,185   Bruegger's Bagels No. 1, Albany, N.Y., 1993
1,168   Stroh's Beer, Detroit, 1981

INCREASE, individual series

358   Mike Williams, Lions, Ill., 1990, 350 T to 708 D
324   Russell Hicks, Vinton, Va., 449 T to 773 D
310   Dick Ciprich, Buffalo, N.Y., 1972, 469 CT to 779 CD

INCREASE, team series, game to game

332   Northridge Lanes, Springfield, Ohio, 1969
      Regular (762-1,094)
309   Sundries, Rochester, N.Y., 1958 Booster (766-1,075)
      Pacific Properties, Sequim, Wash, 1984 Regular
      (881-1,190)

LEFTHANDERS, highest series in singles

784   Rob Spivey, Taylor Mill, Ky., 1991 (247, 248, 289)
774   Frank Huspen, Chicago, 1981 (269, 269, 236)
760   Gary Mage, Tacoma, Wash., 1984 (243, 258, 259)

LEFTHANDERS, highest series in doubles

792   Ted Bertrand, Billings, Mont., 1995
793   Jason Couch, Windermere, Fla., 1990
783   Garl Walsh, Alanogordo, N.M., 1989

LEFTHANDERS, highest all events total

2,153   Ted Bertrand, Billings, Mont., 1989
          (687 791 675)
2,134   Jason Couch, Windermere, Fla., 1990
          (605 793 736)
2,132   Steve Brichta, Reading, Pa., 1990 (728 752 652)

LEFTHANDERS, highest series in team

786   Paul Grauzer, Westland, Mich., 1989
761   Jim Byrnes Sr., Wolcott, Conn., 1977 (Classic)
760   Ron Woolet, Louisville, Ky., 1973

LEFTHANDERS, highest doubles series

1,412   Ted Bertrand (791)-Alan Bredy (621),
          Billings, Mont., 1989
1,372   Dave Howlett (673)-Jim Kirchner (699),
          Louisville, Ky., 1980 (2nd place)
1,365   Mike Lay (694)-Paul Gage (676), Millstadt, Ill., 1995

LEFTHANDERS, highest team series

3,099   Basch Advertising, New York City, 1972
          (Classic rolloff)
          Basch Advertising, New York City, 1975
          (Classic qualifying)
3,068   Lefties, Richmond, Va., 1971 (Classic qualifying)
*Won Titles

PARTICIPATION, most tournaments

71   Bill Doehrman, Ft. Wayne, Ind. (consecutive through
      1981-deceased)

68   Joe Norris, San Diego (active)
62   Frank Carr, Ft. Wayne, Ind. (consecutive through
     1976-deceased)
NOTE: 41 have participated in at least 50 Tournaments.

PINS, individual, career
119,181   Joe Norris, San Diego, Calif. (active)
109,398   Bill Doehrman, Ft. Wayne, Ind. (deceased)
102,651   Frank Carr, Fort Wayne, Ind. (deceased)

PRIZE FUND, one tournament (including Masters and interest)
$3,524,940   Reno, Nev., 1995
$2,787,802   Huntsville, Ala., 1997
$2,100,845   Las Vegas, 1986

PRIZE WINNINGS, individual, one tournament (other than Masters)
$7,350   Rich Wonders, Racine, Wis., 1982
$7,002   Mike Neumann, Buffalo, N.Y., 1990
$5,975   Jim Kontos, Munster, Ind., 1981

PRIZE WINNINGS, team, one tournament
$21,402   Brunswick Rhinos No. 1, Buffalo, 1990
$19,279   Kendor Corp. No. 1, Milwaukee, 1982
$15,805   Minnesota Loons No. 1, St. Paul, Minn, 1984

SPARES, 10 in row with nine pin counts
190   Bernard Van Sice, Rochester, N.Y., 1956
     Jim Rutkowski, Detroit, 1953
     William Dougherty, Newark, N.J., 1963

SPLITS, fewest by championship team
4   Fife Electric, Detroit, 1939
     Eddie & Earl Linsz, Cleveland, 1947
     Meyerland Builders, Houston, 1961
     Rendel's GMC, Joliet, Ill., 1977

SPREAD, pins in doubles series
284   Henry Bruss (711), Dave Gallovich (427), St. Paul, Minn., 1970
273   Hank DeGraff (641), Ralph Heinzelman (368), Grand Rapids, Mich., 1962
270   Jerry Tucciarone (672), Jim Elliot (402), Sarasota, Fla., 1980

STRIKES, individual, consecutive
22   John Bauerle, Indianapolis, 1993
20   Lou Veit, Milwaukee, 1977
     Chris Barnes, Wichita, Kan., 1993
     Wayne Nosse, Villa Park, Ill., 1993
     Arnie Diaz, Missoula, Mont., 1993

STRIKES, individual, one event
32   Fran Bax, Niagara Falls, N.Y., 1983 Team
31   John Forst, Naperville, Ill., 1991 Doubles
30   Jack Winters, Philadelphia, 1962 Classic Doubles
     Glenn Allison, Los Angeles, 1962 Classic Doubles
     Mickey Higham, Kansas City, 1977 Classic Singles
     Craig Goodwin, Idaho Falls, Idaho, 1990 Singles
     Jamie Burke, Loveland, Ohio, 1996 Doubles

STRIKES, individual, one tournament
80   George Hall, Mundelein, Ill., 1989   T27 D26 S27
78   Jamie Burke, Loveland, Ohio, 1996   T24 D30 S24
76   Jeff Nimke, Oshkosh, Wis., 1993   T21 D27 S28

STRIKES, most by championship team
118   Chilton Vending, Wichita, Kan., 1989

100   Ace Mitchell Shur-Hooks, Akron, Ohio, 1966
     (Note-achieved in second three game Classic team
     block during record 3357)
99   Pinky's Bowl, Milwaukee, 1967

TRIPLICATES, consecutive
     Bob Szink, Ft. Wayne, Ind., 1955, had 178 in doubles,
     169 in singles
     Lawrence Buller, Lincoln, Neb., 1992, had 180 in
     doubles, 180 in singles

TRIPLICATES, highest score
247   Alan Hardesty, Chicago, 1993 Singles
246   Bill Beach, Sharon, Pa., 1966 Classic Team
     Karl Chorney, Pine Plains, N.Y., 1979 Team

200 GAMES
INDIVIDUAL, consecutive
27   Bob Goike, Belleville, Mich. (1989-92)
18   Clark Poelzer, St. Paul, Minn., (1991-92)
     Paul Banovic, LaGrange Park, Ill., (1996-97)

700 SERIES
INDIVIDUAL, consecutive
4   Mike Neumann, Buffalo, 705 (D), 794 (S), 1989;
     707 (T), 763 (D), 1990
     George Hall, Chicago, 747 (T) 747 (D) 733 (S), 1989;
     701 (T), 1990
3   Jim Godman, Lorain, Ohio 731 (CT), 749 (CD), 704
     (CS), 1974
     John O'Keefe, Chicago 719 (T), 737 (D), 711 (S),
     1989

INDIVIDUAL, lifetime
11   Jeff Richgels, Madison, Wis., 709 (S 1985), 706
     (T 1986), 706 (T 1992), 742 (D 1993), 747
     (S 1993), 726 (D 1995), 736 (S 1995), 723
     (D 1996), 704 (S 1996), 774 (T 1997), 775
     (S 1997)
8   Rich Wonders, Racine, Wis., 723 (D 1981), 711
     (S 1981), 704 (D 1982), 731 (S 1982), 704
     (T 1986), 706 (D 1991), 716 (S 1991), 719 (S 1992)

1,000 GAMES
TEAM, consecutive with same basic lineup
7   Ace Mitchell Shu-Hooks, Akron, Ohio. (one as Falstaff
     Beer, St. Louis, in 1965 Classic, six as Ace Mitchell
     in 1966 Classic.)
6   Achieved by many other teams

TEAM, highest three in one series
3,537   Bruegger's Bagels No. 1, Albany, N.Y., 1993
     (1,185 1,189 1,163)
3,481   Chilton Vending, Wichita, Kan., 1989 (1,232 1,155
     1,094)
3,357   Ace Mitchell Shur-Hooks, Akron, Ohio, 1966 Classic
     (1,138 1,087 1,132)

1,800 ALL EVENTS
INDIVIDUAL, consecutive
11   Bud Horn, Los Angeles, 1966-76
     Jim Godman, Lorain, Ohio, 1968-78
     Don Cook, Milwaukee, 1981-91

1,900 ALL EVENTS
INDIVIDUAL, consecutive
9   George Kontos, Joliet, Ill., 1989-97
7   Mike Tryniski, Fulton, N.Y., 1991-97
6   Tony Cariello, Chicago, 1989-94

INDIVIDUAL, lifetime

11	Ed Lubanski, Detroit, 1951-1981
10	Frank Tavella Jr., Denver, 1976-93
8	Dick Ritger, River Falls, Wis., 1962-1979

2,000 ALL EVENTS
INDIVIDUAL, lifetime
4   Bob Goike, Canton, Mich., 2,003 in 1980, 2,142 in
     1984, 2,096 in 1990, 2,120 in 1991
     Jim Ewald, Louisville, Ky., 2,003 in 1981, 2,088 in
     1989, 2,080 in 1991, 2,044 in 1992
     Kevin Dornberger, Sioux Falls, S.D., 2,051 in 1989,
     2,007 in 1990, 2,090 in 1993, 2,004 in 1994

INDIVIDUAL, Consecutive
3   Curt Guinn, Greenwood, S.C., 2,008 in1993,
     2,022 in1994, 2.003 in1995
     Arnie Diaz, Missoula, Mont., 2,026 in 1992,
     2,089 in 1993, 2,021 in 1995 (didn't bowl in 1994)

CAREER PINFALL LEADERS (Through 1997)

Joe Norris, San Diego	119,181
Bill Doehrman, Ft. Wayne, Ind.	109,358+
Frank Carr, Ft. Wayne, Ind.	102,651+
Greg Griffo, Syracuse, N.Y.	102,110
Frank Benkovic, Milwaukee	99,797+
Dick Weber, St. Louis	95,344
Bill Lillard, Houston	94,051
Thomas Carr, Ft. Wayne, Ind.	92,433+
Jim Schroeder, Buffalo, N.Y.	90,533
Vince Lucci Sr., Leviitown, Pa.	90,033
+ deceased	

AVERAGE LEADERS LIFETIME
(Active in 1997, minimum of 20 years)

George Pappas, Charlotte, N.C.	209.67
Steve Fehr, Cincinnati	208.86
Bob Goike, Belleville, Mich.	207.32
Frank Tavella Jr., Denver	206.50
Rick Minier, Garland, Texas	206.48
Frank Ellenberg, Chandler, Ariz.	206.48
Jim Ewald Jr., Louisville, Ky.	205.34
Gordon Vadakin, Wichita, Kan.	205.32
Doug Hayes, Clarksville, Tenn.	205.06
Mike Fiedler, Lockport, N.Y.	204.91

10 YEAR (Beginning 1988)

Kevin Dornberger, Sioux Falls, S.D.	218.93
Rick Minier, Garland, Texas	218.56
Mike Marks, Grand Rapids, Mich.	218.27
Steve Fehr, Cincinnati	217.86
Harry Sullins, Detroit	217.63
Sam Lantto, Minneapolis	217.37
Jim Pencak, Cleveland	216.72
Mike Nape, Chicago	216.62
Kevin Taber, Sylvania, Ohio	216.42

5 YEAR (Beginning 1993)

Mike Aulby, Indianapolis	227.59
Pat Healey Jr., Niagara Falls, N.Y.	226.42
Jeff Richgels, Oregon, Wis.	224.87
Kevin Dornberger, Sioux Falls, S.D.	223.82
Craig Harrington, Kearns, Utah	223.56
Steve Brinkman, Milwaukee	223.22
Ryan Shafer, Elmira, N.Y.	223.18

Steve Fehr, Cincinnati	222.60
Greg Shields, Springfield, Mo.	222.00
Mike Tryniski, Oswego, N.Y.	221.93

4 YEAR (Beginning 1994)

Mike Aulby, Indianapolis	232.00
Pat Healey Jr., Niagara Falls, N.Y.	224.64
Steve Brinkman, Milwaukee	224.56
John Socha, Milwaukee	224.36
Ryan Shafer, Elmira, N.Y.	224.20
Jeff Richgels, Oregon, Wis.	224.11
Steve Fehr, Cincinnati	222.58
Lonnie Waliczek, Wichita, Kan.	222.30
Kevin Dornberger, Sioux Falls, S.D.	221.72
Jerry Miller, Twin Falls, S.D.	221.36

3 YEAR (Beginning 1995)

Mike Aulby, Indianapolis	238.59
John Socha, Milwaukee	234.15
Jeff Richgels, Oregon, Wis.	233.78
Jerry Kessler, Englewood, Ohio	230.74
Steve Fehr, Cincinnati	228.41
Jerry Miller, Twin Falls, Idaho	226.67
Mark Munsch, Oshkosh, Wis.	225.96
Scott Kurtz, Somerset, N.J.	225.93
Dennis Horan, San Diego	224.87
Pat Healey Jr., Niagara Falls, N.Y.	224.78

2 YEAR (Beginning 1996)

Jeff Richgels, Oregon, Wis.	240.00
Mike Aulby, Indianapolis	238.74
John Socha, Milwaukee	237.11
Lennie Boresch, Kenosha, Wis.	236.11
Scott Kurtz, Somerset, N.J.	235.50
Steve Fehr, Cincinnati	235.17
Jerry Kessler, Englewood, Ohio	232.67
Mark Munsch, Oshkosh, Wis.	230.94
Don Scudder, Cincinnati	230.89
Jeremy Sonnenfeld, Sioux Falls, S.D.	230.56

ALL-TIME ABC
TOURNAMENT AVERAGE RECORDS
(Note—Only the highest average of each man is listed although he might have had several that would qualify for this section.)

	Starting Year	Avg.
10 YEAR		
Kevin Dornberger, Sioux Falls, S.D.	1988	218.93
Bob Goike, Belleville, Mich.	1984	218.56
Rick Minier, Garland, Texas	1988	218.56
Mike Marks, Grand Rapids, Mich.	1988	218.27
Jim Pencak, Cleveland	1987	218.26
Steve Fehr, Cincinnati	1988	217.86
Harry Sullins, Detroit	1988	217.63
Sam Lantto, Eden Prairie, Minn.	1988	217.37
Norm Duke, Edmond, Okla.	1987	216.92
Jim Ewald Jr., Louisville, Ky.	1987	216.82
5 YEAR		
Jim Pencak, Mayfield Heights, Ohio	1989	230.28
Mike Aulby, Indianapolis	1992	228.73

Mark Bowers, Baltimore	1991	226.88
Pat Healey Jr., Niagara Falls, N.Y.	1993	226.42
Harry Sullins, Detroit	1989	226.16
Mike Nape, Chicago	1992	225.47
Norm Duke, Edmond, Okla.	1991	225.24
Pete Weber, St. Ann, Mo.	1989	225.18
Gordon Vadakin, Wichita, Kan.	1989	225.17
John Forst, LaGrange, Ill.	1989	225.00

4 YEAR

Jim Pencak, Mayfield Heights, Ohio	1989	232.40
Harry Sullins, Detroit	1989	232.05
Mike Aulby, Indianapolis	1994	232.00
Mark Bowers, Baltimore	1991	228.83
Norm Duke, Edmond, Okla.	1991	228.18
Mike Neumann, Buffalo	1989	227.55
Dave D'Entremont, Cleveland	1992	227.53
Pete Weber, St. Ann, Mo.	1991	227.08
Jeff Lowe, Indianapolis	1991	226.47
Kevin Taber, Sylvania, Ohio	1991	225.92

3 YEAR

Mike Aulby, Indianapolis	1995	238.99
Jim Pencak, Mayfield Heights, Ohio	1991	235.40
Mark Bowers, Baltimore	1991	235.00
Harry Sullins, Detroit	1989	234.17
John Socha, Milwaukee	1995	234.15
Kevin Taber, Toledo, Ohio	1991	233.88
Jeff Richgels, Oregon, Wis.	1995	233.78
Brian Kretzer, West Carrollton, Ohio	1989	232.44
Mike Neumann, Buffalo	1989	231.96
Gail Myers Jr., Monroe, Wis.	1991	231.55

2 YEAR

Mike Aulby, Indianapolis	1995	242.53
Jim Pencak, Mayfield Heights, Ohio	1991	242.20
Mike Neumann, Buffalo	1989	240.61
Jeff Richgels, Oregon, Wis.	1996	240.00
Harry Sullins, Detroit	1990	237.85
Mark Bowers, Baltimore	1991	237.65
John Socha, Milwaukee	1996	237.11
Parker Bohn III, Freehold, N.J.	1991	236.85
Kevin Taber, Toledo, Ohio	1992	236.83
Jerry Miller, Twin Falls, Idaho	1995	236.17

YEARLY LIFETIME AVERAGE LEADERS

Year	Name	Tournaments	Avg.
1997	George Pappas, Charlotte, N.C.	29	209.67
1996	George Pappas, Charlotte, N.C.	28	209.88
1995	George Pappas, Charlotte, N.C.	27	210.03
1994	George Pappas, Charlotte, N.C.	26	209.41
1993	George Pappas, Charlotte, N.C.	25	209.41
1992	George Pappas, Charlotte, N.C.	24	209.59
1991	George Pappas, Charlotte, N.C.	23	209.36
1990	George Pappas, Charlotte, N.C.	22	208.78
1989	George Pappas, Charlotte, N.C.	21	208.70
1988	George Pappas, Charlotte, N.C	20	207.65
1987	Earl Anthony, Dublin, Calif.	23	206.26
1986	Earl Anthony, Dublin, Calif.	22	206.80
1985	Earl Anthony, Dublin, Calif.	21	206.64
1984	Earl Anthony, Dublin, Calif.	20	206.64
1983	Nelson Burton Jr., St. Louis	23	206.66
1982	Nelson Burton Jr., St. Louis	22	206.84

1981	Nelson Burton Jr., St. Louis	21	207.51
1980	Nelson Burton Jr., St. Louis	21	207.51
1979	Nelson Burton Jr., St. Louis	20	206.61
1978	Bill Beach, Sharon, Pa.	21	203.47
1977	Ed Lubanski, Detroit	28	203.01
1976	Bob Strampe, Detroit	22	203.96
1975	Bob Strampe, Detroit	21	204.84
1974	Bob Strampe, Detroit	20	205.45
1973	Ed Lubanski, Detroit	26	204.26
1972	Ed Lubanski, Detroit	25	204.96
1971	Ed Lubanski, Detroit	25	204.96
1970	Ed Lubanski, Detroit	24	204.72
1969	Ed Lubanski, Detroit	23	204.22
1968	Ed Lubanski, Detroit	22	203.93
1967	Ed Lubanski, Detroit	21	204.14
1966	Ed Lubanski, Detroit	20	204.47
1965	Lindy Faragalli, Wayne, N.J.	20	199.21
1964	*George Young, Detroit	20	202.62

*The first year lifetime averages were computed, all ABC performers were listed, which included deceased bowlers. Young was deceased at the time of the listing. Since 1965, all lifetime leaders must be living.

YEARLY 10 YEAR AVERAGE LEADERS

Year		Avg.
1997	Kevin Dornberger, Sioux Falls, S.D.	218.93
1996	Jim Pencak, Mayfield Heights, Ohio	218.26
1995	Jim Pencak, Mayfield Heights, Ohio	218.03
1994	Jim Pencak, Mayfield Heights, Ohio	215.68
1993	Bob Goike, Belleville, Mich.	218.56
1992	Bob Goike, Belleville, Mich.	215.44
1991	Bob Goike, Belleville, Mich.	213.82
1990	Don Cook, Milwaukee	212.19
1989	Mike Fiedler, Lockport, N.Y.	210.30
1988	Mike Fiedler, Lockport, N.Y.	210.69
1987	Mike Fiedler, Lockport, N.Y.	209.60
1986	Gordy Baer, Chicago	210.04
1985	George Pappas, Charlotte, N.C.	209.62
1984	Earl Anthony, Dublin, Calif.	209.25
1983	Earl Anthony, Dublin, Calif.	210.57
1982	Earl Anthony, Dublin, Calif.	208.94
1981	George Pappas, Charlotte, N.C.	210.15
1980	Nelson Burton Jr., St. Louis	210.33
1979	Dick Ritger, River Falls, Wis.	210.91
1978	Dick Ritger, River Falls, Wis.	210.32
1977	Jim Godman, Waukegan, Ill.	209.38
1976	Dick Ritger, River Falls, Wis.	209.03
1975	Dick Ritger, River Falls, Wis.	208.98
1974	Bob Strampe, Detroit	208.20
1973	Bob Strampe, Detroit	211.13
1972	Bob Strampe, Detroit	209.89
1971	Bob Strampe, Detroit	211.07
1970	Bob Strampe, Detroit	211.93
1969	Bob Strampe, Detroit	209.47
1968	Bob Strampe, Detroit	208.25
1967	Dick Weber, St. Louis	207.65
1966	Dick Weber, St. Louis	207.98
1965	Dick Weber, St. Louis	206.52
1964	Dick Weber, St. Louis	206.63
1963	Ed Lubanski, Detroit	207.06
1962	Ed Lubanski, Detroit	205.58
1961	Ed Lubanski, Detroit	205.43
1960	Steve Nagy, St. Louis	208.24

1959	Steve Nagy, St. Louis	206.98		1947	Andy Varipapa, New York	204.72
1958	George Young, Detroit	206.83		1946	Marty Cassio, Rahway, N.J.	203.74
1957	George Young, Detroit	205.67		1942	John Crimmins, Detroit	203.42
1956	George Young, Detroit	204.81		1941	Ned Day, Milwaukee	204.26
1955	Junie McMahon, Lodi, N.J.	204.77		1940	Ned Day, Milwaukee	202.94
1954	George Young, Detroit	205.58		1939	Hank Marino, Milwaukee	201.80
1953	Junie McMahon, Lodi, N.J.	205.42		1938	Gil Zunker, Milwaukee	201.94
1952	Junie McMahon, Lodi, N.J.	206.84		1937	Joe Bodis, Cleveland	204.02
1951	Junie McMahon, Chicago	201.01		1936	Joe Bodis, Cleveland	204.94
1950	Joe Wilman, Chicago	206.69		1935	Joe Bodis, Cleveland	205.84
1949	Junie McMahon, Chicago	206.77		1934	Joe Bodis, Cleveland	205.22
1948	Joe Wilman, Chicago	205.30				

LOW TO CASH IN ABC TOURNAMENTS, 1901-1997

Year	Team	Doubles	Singles	All Events	Year	Team	Doubles	Singles	All Events
1997	2,708	1,099	560	1,757	1950	2,633	1,086	554	1,681
1996	2,764	1,116	573	1,779	1949	2,667	1,092	559	1,688
1995	2,730	1,099	566	1,760	1948	2,660	1,096	561	1,697
1994	2,708	1,093	561	1,742	1947	2,686	1,102	562	1,737
1993	2,749	1,112	571	1,790	1946	2,649	1,108	568	1,759
1992	2,802	1,123	576	1,791	1942	2,656	1,113	571	1,785
1991	2,784	1,125	578	1,801	1941	2,671	1,127	577	1,796
1990	2,700	1,095	565	1,740	1940	2,638	1,113	572	1,776
1989	2,783	1,110	570	1,787	1939	2,717	1,129	579	1,809
1988	2,653	1,068	547	1,694	1938	2,694	1,125	575	1,797
1987	2,670	1,072	547	1,695	1937	2,708	1,133	582	1,814
1986	2,701	1,082	553	1,712	1936	2,703	1,135	582	1,811
1985	2,680	1,075	549	1,703	1935	2,678	1,121	578	1,809
1984	2,661	1,067	546	1,691	1934	2,775	1,148	574	1,819
1983	2,721	1,091	556	1,720	1933	2,753	1,157	587	1,817
1982	2,664	1,075	549	1,699	1932	2,723	1,137	586	1,810
1981	2,735	1,101	561	1,739	1931	2,672	1,123	576	1,790
1980	2,681	1,076	551	1,700	1930	2,709	1,131	583	1,810
1979	2,715	1,078	551	1,708	1929	2,736	1,139	582	1,815
1978	2,631	1,066	543	1,677	1928	2,659	1,144	584	1,821
1977	2,681	1,071	547	1,685	1927	2,753	1,140	586	1,829
1976	2,713	1,084	553	1,714	1926	2,709	1,134	584	1,821
1975	2,760	1,111	565	1,739	1925	2,621	1,112	571	1,787
1974	2,738	1,105	563	1,737	1924	2,691	1,126	576	1,813
1973	2,749	1,101	561	1,726	1923	2,682	1,135	584	1,813
1972	2,714	1,084	552	1,709	1922	2,700	1,127	576	1,798
1971	2,767	1,108	565	1,739	1921	2,689	1,121	575	1,777
1970	2,771	1,110	565	1,740	1920	2,700	1,120	577	1,797
1969	2,737	1,096	558	1,724	1919	2,686	1,119	574	1,794
1968	2,704	1,085	553	1,703	1918	2,700	1,119	575	1,795
1967	2,799	1,115	568	1,735	1917	2,687	1,124	572	1,801
1966	2,734	1,097	560	1,722	1916	2,628	1,103	561	1,778
1965	2,695	1,074	546	1,688	1915	2,662	1,109	565	1,768
1964	2,753	1,098	558	1,722	1914	2,658	1,107	564	1,765
1963	2,797	1,113	566	1,747	1913	2,716	1,128	575	1,819
1962	2,783	1,110	564	1,744	1912	2,635	1,091	555	1,761
1961	2,730	1,090	555	1,706	1911	2,625	1,103	557	1,769
1960	2,732	1,092	555	1,712	1910	2,645	1,107	561	1,785
1959	2,746	1,092	556	1,721	1909	2,685	1,101	563	1,789
1958	2,742	1,099	559	1,725	1908	2,629	1,105	565	1,778
1957	2,752	1,095	557	1,725	1907	2,537	1,066	540	1,699
1956	2,697	1,086	552	1,694	1906	2,604	1,079	554	1,736
1955	2,690	1,084	550	1,697	1905	2,616	1,089	555	
1954	2,734	1,094	556	1,710	1904	2,648	1,099	570	
1953	2,709	1,082	550	1,701	1903	2,709	1,124	590	
1952	2,686	1,085	554	1,703	1902	2,567	1,088	565	
1951	2,742	1,110	568	1,731	1901	2,608	1,076	564	

LOW TO CASH RECORDS

Event	High	Low
Singles —	590 (1903)	540 (1907)
Doubles —	1,157 (1933)	1,066 (1907, 1978)
All Events —	1,829 (1927)	1,677 (1978)
Team —	2,802 (1992)	2,537 (1907)

ABC BUD LIGHT MASTERS

MASTERS TOURNAMENT (The ABC Masters was a special event conducted on ABC Tournament lanes from 1951-79. It became part of the ABC Tournament in 1980.)

15 Game Qualifying

Year	City	Dates	Entries*	Low Score	High Score	Above 3,399	3,300-3,399	3,200-3,299	Prize Fund**
1997	Huntsville, Ala.	April 29-May 3	550	2,906	3,503	3	6	37	$250,000
1996	Salt Lake City	April 30-May 4	533	3,036	3,626	6	18	56	$250,000
1995	Reno, Nev.	May 2-6	608	2,969	3,547	5	17	48	$250,000
1994	Mobile, Ala.	May 3-7	481	2,945	3,442	1	2	25	$235,000
1993	Tulsa, Okla.	May 4- 8	481	3,278	3,509	12	39	46	$235,000
1992	Corpus Christi, Texas	April 28-May 2	481	3,323	3,625	30	46	39	$235,000
1991	Toledo, Ohio	April 30-May 4	481	3,318	3,625	30	39	49	$235,000
1990	Reno, Nev.	May 1-5	481	3,119	3,416	1	2	18	$235,000
1989	Wichita, Kan.	May 2-6	481	3,273	3,500	16	29	53	$235,000

10 Game Qualifying

Year	City	Dates	Entries*	Low Score	High Score	Above 2,299	2,200-2,299	2,100-2,199	Prize Fund**
1988	Jacksonville, Fla.	May 3-7	481	1,966	2,303	1	1	12	$215,000
1987	Niagara Falls, N.Y.	May 5-9	481	2,028	2,303	1	1	12	$215,000
1986	Las Vegas	May 6-10	481	2,023	2,229	0	1	17	$215,000
1985	Tulsa, Okla.	May 7-11	481	2,018	2,211	0	1	11	$200,000
1984	Reno, Nev.	May 8-12	481	2,036	2,300	1	0	17	$200,000
1983	Niagara Falls, N.Y.	May 10-14	481	2,033	2,229	0	0	14	$200,000
1982	Baltimore	May 11-15	481	2,011	2,169	0	0	11	$200,000
1981	Memphis, Tenn.	May 13-17	481	2,043	2,217	0	1	22	$141,000
1980	Louisville, Ky.	May 21-25	481	2,068	2,332	1	4	31	$116,000

*Includes defending champion **Does not include Pro-Am prize fund

WINNERS, RUNNERSUP

	WINNER	W-L	Avg.	RUNNERUP	W-L	Avg.
1997	**Jason Queen, Decatur, Ill.+	9-1	225.50	xEric Forkel, Tucson, Ariz.	6-1	234.10
1996	Ernie Schlegel, Vancouver, Wash.	7-0	221.20	xMike Aulby, Indianapolis	11-2	244.80
1995	Mike Aulby, Indianapolis	8-1	230.07	xMark Williams, Beaumont, Texas	6-1	230.00
1994	Steve Fehr, Cincinnati+	9-1	213.09	xSteve Anderson, Colorado Springs, Colo.	6-1	214.05
1993	Norm Duke, Edmond, Okla.	7-0	245.68	xPatrick Allen, Katonah, N.Y.	7-2	215.86
1992	Ken Johnson, North Richland Hills, Texas+	8-1	221.83	xDave D'Entremont, Parma, Ohio	6-1	230.00
1991	Doug Kent, Canandaigua, N.Y.	5-1	226.80	xGeorge Branham III, Indianapolis	6-1	225.60
1990	Chris Warren, Dallas	6-0	231.61	xDavid Ozio, Vidor, Texas	6-2	220.63
1989	**Mike Aulby, Indianapolis	6-0	218.84	** xMike Edwards, Tulsa, Okla.	6-1	237.00
1988	Del Ballard Jr., Richardson, Texas	7-0	219.12	xKeith Smith, Fremont, Neb.	6-2	221.38

1987	Rick Steelsmith, Wichita, Kan.+	7-1	210.69
1986	Mark Fahy, Chicago	7-0	206.48
1985	Steve Wunderlich, St. Louis	7-0	210.40
1984	Earl Anthony, Dublin, Calif.	7-0	212.52
1983	Mike Lastowski, Havre de Grace, Md.+	7-1	212.65
1982	Joe Berardi, Brooklyn, N.Y.	7-0	207.12
1981	Randy Lightfoot, St. Louis	7-1	218.34
1980	Neil Burton, St. Louis	7-1	206.69
1979	**Doug Myers, El Toro, Calif.	7-1	202.90
1978	*Frank Ellenburg, Mesa, Ariz.	8-1	200.61
1977	Earl Anthony, Tacoma, Wash.	7-0	218.21
1976	Nelson Burton Jr., St. Louis	7-0	220.79
1975	*Ed Ressler Jr., Allentown, Pa.	9-1	213.57
1974	Paul Colwell, Tucson, Ariz.	7-0	234.17
1973	Dave Soutar, Kansas City	7-0	218.61
1972	*Bill Beach, Sharon, Pa.	8-1	220.75
1971	*Jim Godman, Lorain, Ohio	9-1	229.20
1970	*Don Glover, Bakersfield, Calif.	9-1	215.25
1969	*Jim Chestney, Denver	10-1	223.05
1968	*Pete Tountas, Tucson, Ariz.	9-1	220.28
1967	Lou Scalia, Miami	7-0	216.32
1966	Bob Strampe, Detroit	7-0	219.29
1965	*Billy Welu, St. Louis	9-1	202.30
1964	Billy Welu, St. Louis	7-0	227.00
1963	Harry Smith, St. Louis	7-0	219.12
1962	Billy Golembiewski, Detroit	7-0	223.43
1961	*Don Carter, St. Louis	8-1	211.50
1960	Billy Golembiewski, Detroit	7-0	206.46
1959	Ray Bluth, St. Louis	7-0	214.93
1958	Tom Hennessey, St. Louis	7-0	209.54
1957	*Dick Hoover, Akron, Ohio	9-1	216.98
1956	Dick Hoover, Akron, Ohio	7-1	209.28
1955	Buzz Fazio, Detroit	7-0	204.46
1954	Eugene Elkins, San Carlos, Calif.	7-0	205.68
1953	*Rudy Habetler, Chicago	10-1	200.30
1952	*Willard Taylor, Charleston, W.Va.	8-1	200.89
1951	Lee Jouglard, Detroit	6-1	201.29

xBrad Snell, Chicago		6-1	207.92
xDel Ballard Jr., Richardson, Texas		5-2	211.00
xTommy Kress, Rochester, N.Y.		8-2	205.92
xGil Sliker, Washington, N.J.		6-2	212.26
xPete Weber, St. Louis		6-1	203.22
xTed Hannahs, Zanesville, Ohio		7-2	203.52
xSkip Tucker, Merritt Island, Fla.		6-1	220.50
xMark Roth, N. Arlington, N.J.		6-1	212.60
**Bill Spigner, Hamden, Conn.		9-2	206.56
Earl Anthony, Tacoma, Wash.		6-2	211.68
Jim Godman, Waukegan, Ill.		6-2	204.06
Steve Carson, Oklahoma City		6-2	213.35
Sam Flanagan, Parkersburg, W.Va.		6-2	206.93
Steve Neff, Sarasota, Fla.		8-2	232.27
Dick Ritger, Hartford, Wis.		10-2	211.04
Jim Godman, Lorain, Ohio		6-2	216.22
Don Johnson, Akron, Ohio		6-2	219.10
Bob Strampe, Detroit		6-2	212.26
Barry Asher, Costa Mesa, Calif.		6-2	212.50
**Buzz Fazio, Detroit		6-2	215.11
Bill Johnson, New Orleans		6-2	209.23
Al Thompson, Cleveland		6-2	209.30
Don Ellis, Houston		6-2	204.27
Harry Smith, Baltimore		6-2	214.60
Bobby Meadows, Dallas		7-2	203.29
Ron Winger, Los Angeles		10-2	207.32
Dick Hoover, Akron, Ohio		6-2	205.50
Steve Nagy, St. Louis		10-2	201.21
Billy Golembiewski, Detroit		6-2	201.27
Lou Frantz, Louisville, Ky.		6-2	199.27
Bill Lillard, Dallas		6-2	198.12
Ray Bluth, St. Louis		9-2	211.30
Joe Kristof, Chicago		6-2	202.40
Willard Taylor, Charleston, W.Va.		6-2	201.10
Ed Brosius, Chicago		6-2	199.50
Andy Varipapa, Hempstead, N.Y.		6-2	198.80
Joe Wilman, Chicago		6-2	202.23

*   From losers bracket, won both matches in finals
**   State Representative
x   Championship decided in one game stepladder final
+   Amateur

QUALIFYING LEADERS

YEAR PINS

(15 games)

1997	3,503	Brian Boghosian, Middletown, Conn.
1996	3,626	Charlie Bruno, Sewell, N.J.
1995	3,547	Eric Forkel, Porter Beach, Calif.
1994	3,442	Mike Miller, Albuquerque, N.M.
1993	3,509	Frank Ellenburg, Chandler, Ariz.
1992	3,635*	Jim Pencak, Mayfield Heights, Ohio
1991	3,625	Harry Sullins, Detroit
1990	3,416	Harry Sullins, Detroit
1989	3,500	Del Warren, Lake Worth, Fla.

(10 games)

1988	2,223	Curtis Odom (SR), Winston-Salem, N.C.
1987	2,303	Joe Vito Buenrostro, San Antonio
1986	2,229	John Wilcox, Mifflinburg, Pa.
1985	2,211	Mike Edwards, Tulsa, Okla.
1984	2,300	Tommy Hudson, Akron, Ohio
1983	2,229	Earl Anthony, Dublin, Calif.
1982	2,169	Dave Husted, Milwaukie, Ore.
1981	2,217	George Pappas (SR), Charlotte, N.C.
1980	2,332*	Sam Zurich, Centerport, N.Y.

(8 games)

1979	1,751	Terry Schacht, St. Paul, Minn.
1978	1,742	Paul Moser, Somerset, Mass.
1977	1,736	Mark Van Meter, Albuquerque, N.M.
1976	1,836	Nelson Burton Jr., St. Louis**
1975	1,790	Pete Tountas, Tucson, Ariz.
1974	1,904*	Mike Limongello, St. Paul, Minn.
1973	1,792	Gerald Loveless (SR), Moses Lake, Wash.
1972	1,841	Bill Lillard, Houston
1971	1,854	Mike Orlovsky, Endicott, N.Y.
1970	1,793	Jim Ewald, Louisville, Ky.
1969	1,783	Don Johnson, Kokomo, Ind.
1968	1,771	Al Thompson, Cleveland
1967	1,786	Allie Clarke, Cleveland
1966	1,853	Wayne Zahn, Atlanta
1965	1,723	Robbie Robinson, Wilmington, Del.
1964	1,822	Tommy Tuttle (SR), Rural Hall, N.C.
1963	1,776	Tony Politi, Buffalo
1962	1,849	Don Ellis, Houston
1961	1,771	Wayne Pinkalla, Milwaukee

1960   1,757   Ben Becker, Los Angeles
1959   1,733   Fred Riccilli, Detroit
1958   1,769   Marty Piraino, Syracuse, N.Y.
1957   1,748   Jim Carman, Dallas
1956   1,701   Stan Gifford, Chicago
1955   1,749   Fred Fikes, Chicago
        1,749   Bill Lillard, Dallas
1954   1,726   Eugene Elkins, San Carlos, Calif.**
1953   1,666   John Klares, Cleveland
*Format Record (SR) State Representative
**Won Championship

QUALIFYING RECORDS
15 game format
3,635   Jim Pencak, Mayfield Heights, Ohio, 1992
3,626   Charlie Bruno, Sewell, N.J., 1996
3,625   Harold Sullins, Detroit, 1991

10 game format
2,479   Jim Pencak, Mayfield Heights, Ohio, 1992

2,460   Harold Sullins, Detroit, 1991
2,442   Sean Swanson, Springfield, Mo., 1992

5 game block format
1,307   Robert Lawrence, Del Valle, Texas, 1991
         Michael Karch, Spanaway, Wash., 1996
1,288   Jim Pencak, Richmond Heights, Ohio, 1989

HIGHEST LOW SCORE TO QUALIFY–15 games
3,323   Jimmy Johnson, Columbus, Ohio, 1992

HIGHEST LOW SCORE TO QUALIFY–10 games
2,149   Don Moser, San Jose, Calif., 1993

LOWEST QUALIFYING SCORE–15 games
2,906   Thomas Campagni, Syracuse, N.Y., 1997

LOWEST QUALIFYING SCORE–10 games
2,010   Steve Wunderlich, St. Louis, 1982

MISCELLANEOUS RECORDS

CHAMPIONSHIPS, lifetime
2   Dick Hoover, Akron, Ohio (1956, 1957)
     Billy Golembiewski, Detroit (1960, 1962)
     Billy Welu, St. Louis (1964, 1965)
     Earl Anthony, Dublin, Calif. (1977, 1984)
     Mike Aulby, Indianapolis (1989, 1995)

HIGH MATCH PLAY AVERAGE, one year
(15 game minimum)
245.6   Norm Duke, Edmond, Okla., 1993, 19 games
244.8   Mike Aulby, Indianapolis, 1996, 35 games
239.7   Walter Ray Williams, Stockton, Calif.,
         1991, 27 games

HIGHEST SCORING MATCHES (three games)
1,601   Justin Hromek, Wichita, Kan. (822) vs. Bryan
         Alpert, Las Vegas (779), 1989
1,579   Del Ballard Jr., Richardson, Texas (796) vs. Tsuguo
         Tsukahara, Tokyo, Japan (783), 1989
1,576   Mike Edwards, Tulsa, Okla. (791) vs. Del Ballard
         Jr., Richardson, Texas (785), 1989

LOSING TOTAl, highest (three games)
785   Del Ballard Jr., Richardson, Texas, 1989

MATCH, longest
1954   Carroll (Red) Russell, Yakima, Wash., and Harry
        Livesy Jr., Missoula, Mont., tied at 746. They tied in
        the rolloff at 213. Russell won in second frame of
        second rolloff.
1983   Hirashi Nagatani, Tokyo, Japan and Bob
        Chamberlain, Detroit, Mich., tied at 768. They tied
        in the rolloff at 216. Nagatani won the two frame
        rolloff.

MATCHES, one tournament
13   Bobby Fleetwood, Milford, Ontario, 1997 (won 10)
12   Steve Nagy, St. Louis, 1960 (won 10)
      Ron Winger, Los Angeles, 1962 (won 10)
      Dick Ritger, Hartford, Wis., 1973 (won 10)
      Tom Baker, Buffalo, 1981 (won 9)

MATCHES, lifetime
101   Dick Weber, St. Louis (won 64)
 95   Earl Anthony, Dublin, Calif. (won 63)
 84   Don Carter, Miami (won 52)

TRIPLICATE (first three games)
213   Luke Karan, Detroit, 1962

VICTORIES, consecutive
13   Earl Anthony, Tacoma, Wash. (7 in 1977, 6 in
      1978)
12   Harry Smith, Baltimore (7 in 1963, 5 in 1964)
      Billy Welu, St. Louis (1 in 1963. 7 in 1964. 4 in
      1965)

WINNING MARGIN, pins one match (three games)
239   Mike Aulby, Indianapolis (730) defeated Danny
       Saunders, Hialeah, Fla. (491), 1996
231   David Billings, Beaverton, Ore. (813) defeated
       Mark Bradley, Cleveland (582), 1989
       Tom Crites, Tampa, Fla. (838) defeated John
       Petraglia, Manalpan, N.J. (607), 1991

300 GAMES, lifetime
3   Justin Hromlek, Andover, Kan.
     Mark Bowers, Aberdeen, Md.
2   Achieved by six players

300 GAMES (81)
1961: Bud Horn, Los Angeles; 1962: Don Carter, St. Louis
and Ray Bluth, St. Louis; 1967: Bob Hart, Erie, Pa.; 1969:
Bob Poole, Denver; 1971: Earl Anthony, Tacoma, Wash.;
Bill Tucker, Detroit and Jim Godman, Lorain, Ohio; 1972:
Don Robinson Jr., Denver and Larry Brott, Denver; 1974:
Steve Neff, Sarasota, Fla.; 1980: Dave Husted, Milwaukee,
Ore.; 1981: Jeff Valentine, Somerset, Mass. and Dave
Soutar, Kansas City, Kan.; 1983: Teata Semiz, Fairfield,
N.J.; 1986: Rey Perez, Cincinnati and Pete Couture,
Windsor Locks, Conn.; 1987: Tony Marrese, Cocoa, Fla.;
1988: John Brodersen, Helena, Mont. (cont. next page)

1989: Michael Karch, Tacoma, Wash.; Brian Brazeau, Milwaukee; Glenn Evans, Vacaville, Calif.; Gordon Vadakin, Wichita, Kan.; Terry Engel, Walnut Creek, Calif.; Billy Young, Oklahoma City; Pat Healey Jr., Niagara Falls, N.Y.; Paul Busch, Dover, Del.; Jim Pencak, Mayfield Heights, Ohio; Bob Handley, Pompano Beach, Fla.; Pat Danforth, Anaheim, Calif.; Bobby Moore, Columbus, Ohio; Joe Firpo, Lake Worth, Fla.; Dave Billings, Beaverton, Ore.; Mark Baker, Garden Grove, Calif.; Tsuguo Tsukahara, Tokyo, Japan, and Norm Duke, Ft. Worth, Texas; 1990: Bryan Alpert, Las Vegas; 1991: Stanley Geist, Dayton, Ohio; Mark Bowers, Aberdeen, Md.; Justin Hromek, Andover, Kan. (3, 2 consecutive); Brian Brazeau, Milwaukee; Jim Pencak, Mayfield Heights, Ohio; Doug Kent, Canandaigua, N.Y.; Parker Bohn III, Freehold, N.J.; John Petraglia, Manalapan, N.J.; Frank Edwards, Moscow, Pa.; Dennis Rakauskas, Centreville, Va.; Del Ballard Jr., Richardson, Texas (2, consecutive); Michael Tucker, Huntington Beach, Calif.; Amleto Monacelli, Barquisimeto, Venezuela (2); Richard Cheney, Miami; Ron Williams, North Richland Hills, Texas; Gary Kinyon, Lockport, N.Y.; Tom Crites, Tampa, Fla.; John Eiss, Brooklyn Park, Minn.; Harry Sullins, Detroit and Tom Baker, Buffalo; 1992: Skip Tucker, Merritt Island, Fla.; Curtis Messer, Aberdeen, Md.; Wayne Halliburton, Sun Valley, Nev.; Donald Hochstein, Garden City, Mich.; Steve Wunderlich, St. Charles; John Mazza, Mt. Clemens, Mich.; Kevin Gawelko, Las Vegas; Dean Wolf, West Reading, Pa. (2); George Branham III, Indianapolis; Robert Buckery, McAdoo, Pa.; Paul Fleming, Lincoln, Neb.; Orlando DeArmas, Miami; Gary Smith, East Peoria, Ill.; Rudy Kasimakis, Levittown, N.Y.; Michael Christenson, Pensacola, Fla.; Bill Oakes, Lawton, Okla.; Robert Brust, Bellmore, N.Y., and Bob Benoit, Topeka, Kan. 1993: John Forst, West Valley City, Utah; Richard Smock, Huntsville, Ala.; Kenneth Nix, St. Louis; Stephen Hardy, Metheun, Mass.; Daniel Saile, Winter Springs, Fla.; Timothy Weisbrod, Cincinnati; Rick Miller, Lincoln, Neb.; Fred Mattson, Tacoma, Wash.; Robert Lawrence, Del Valle, Texas; Kelly Urrea, Mesa, Ariz.; Mark Bowers, Aberdeen, Md.; Jason Couch, Winter Garden, Fla.; Mike Cordiero, Westport, Mass.; 1995: Mike Aulby, Indianapolis (2); Jon Murph, Dayton, Ohio; Robert Faragon, Albany, N.Y.; Ryan Shafer, Elmira, N.Y.; 1996: Mark Bowers, Aberdeen, Md.; Rick Steelsmith, Wichita, Kan.; Jim Daugherty, Bethany,

Okla.; Carl Chavez, Albuquerque, N.M.; Eddie Graham, Midland, Texas; Tony Gonzales, Grand Prairie, Texas; Tom Shucart, Florissant, Mo.; 1997: Jason Queen, Decatur, Ill.; Eric Forkel, Tucson, Ariz.

299 GAMES (26)

1952: Steve Nagy, Cleveland; 1970: Don Lemon, Rochester, N.Y.; 1971: Skee Foremsky, Houston; 1972: Dave Soutar, Tarzana, Calif.; 1973: Dick Ritger, Hartford, Wis.; 1976: Fred Conner, Los Angeles; 1980: Bill Spigner, Hamden, Conn.; 1981: Frank Ellenburg, Mesa, Ariz.; 1982: Joe Vito Buenrostro, San Antonio; 1983: Joe Hutchinson, Scranton, Pa. and Bob Roy, Denver; 1985: Tsuguo Tsukahara, Tokyo, Japan; 1986: Tom Bates, Sand City, Calif.; 1989: Del Warren, Lake Worth, Fla. and David Rosenburg, Rolla, Mo.; 1990: Rick Jones, Spokane, Wash. and Mike Fairchild, Nicholasville, Ky.; 1991: Ricky Corona, Orange, Calif. and Brian Brazeau; 1992: Michael Bernier, Ft. Wayne, Ind.; Jim Pencak, Mayfield Heights, Ohio, and Ray Edwards, Coram, N.Y.; 1993: Marlyn Browning, Eminence, Ky.; Brian Berg, Edmond, Okla.; Jim Pencak, Mayfield Heights, Ohio; Joe Firpo, Lake Worth, Fla.

298 GAMES (9)

1962: J.D. Myres, Casper, Wyo. and Bob Christensen, Phoenix; 1963: Therman Gibson, Detroit; 1974: Nelson Burton Jr., St. Louis; 1989: Bobby Moore, Columbus, Ohio; 1991: Gary Patterson, Warson Woods, Md. and John Eiss, Brooklyn Park, Minn.; 1993: Jay Estes, Tulsa, Okla.; 1994: Brian LeClair, Hudson, N.Y.

HIGH SERIES, three games

874	Eric Forkel, Tucson, Ariz., 1997
857	Norm Duke, Albuquerque, N.M., 1989
840	Mike Aulby, Indianapolis, 1996

PRIZE WINNINGS, lifetime

$127,625	Mike Aulby, Indianapolis
$87,325	Del Ballard Jr., Richardson, Texas
$85,725	Earl Anthony, Dublin, Calif.

YOUNGEST, qualifier

| 15 | Ron Pollard, Versailles, Ind., 1977 |

LIFETIME MATCH PLAY AVERAGE LEADERS
(Active bowlers with minimum of 60 games – averages do not include qualifying totals. Eligibility based on making finals within last five years.)

	Earnings	Matches	Games	Pins	Average
1. Joe Firpo, Lake Worth, Fla.	$ 44,125	29-17	136	30,901	227.2
2. Mike Aulby, Indianapolis	127,625	31-13	131	29,490	225.1
3. Mark Bowers, Aberdeen, Md.	20,550	14-9	67	15,064	224.8
4. Ryan Shafer, Elmira, N.Y.	26,775	15-12	77	17,025	221.1
5. Doug Kent, Canandaiga, N.Y.	48,390	12-9	65	14,366	221.0
6. Billy Myers Jr., Temple City, Calif.	9,550	14-6	60	13,181	219.7
7. Norm Duke, Clermont, Fla.	82,675	29-17	155	33,817	218.2
Walter Ray Williams Jr., Stockton, Calif.	15,400	21-17	135	29,455	218.2
9. Parker Bohn III, Freehold, N.J.	27,925	17-13	88	19,168	217.8
10. Del Ballard Jr., Richardson, Texas	87,325	25-14	127	27,591	217.2

All Events: Competition using individual bowlers' scores from more than one event in a single tournament (e.g. singles, doubles and team events).

All-Spare Game: Game in which bowler executes 10 consecutive spares from the first frame.

Anchor Bowler: Last bowler in team lineup.

Approach: Fifteen foot or more area where bowlers walk toward the foul line, or bowlers' bodily movements while walking toward the foul line.

Average: Bowler's total pins in one sanctioned league divided by number of games bowled in the same league. Decimals and fractions are not included.

Baby Split: 2-7 or 3-10 splits.

Ball: Required to meet several specifications. Generally must be 16 pounds or less and 27 inches or less in circumference. For more information, see WIBC Bylaws Book or contact ABC/WIBC equipment specifications department at (414) 423-3400.

Bed Posts: 7-10 split.

Big Four: 4-6-7-10 split.

Brooklyn: Hit to the left of a headpin for right-handed bowlers (1-2 pocket), or a hit to the right of a headpin for left-handed bowlers (1-3 pocket).

Bucket: 2-4-5-8 or 3-5-6-9 leaves.

Center: Preferred word for bowling establishment.

Channel: Preferred word for gutter.

Channel Ball: Preferred term for gutter ball.

Cherry: Knocking down a front pin, which fails to knock down pins standing directly behind or next to it.

Clean Game: Game where bowler executes spares or strikes in all 10 frames.

Count: Number of pins knocked down in one frame.

Delivery: Bowler's act of pushing away, swinging and releasing ball.

Dressing: Oil or conditioner applied on lanes.

Double: Two consecutive strikes.

Foul: When part of bowler's body touches any part of the lane, equipment or building beyond the foul line during or after delivering a ball.

Foul Line: Line separating approach area and lane. Although not marked, foul line also extends vertically up and encloses lane on all sides.

Frame: One-tenth of game. Each square on scoresheet or television monitor indicates one frame.

Greek Church: 4-6-7-8-10 or 4-6-7-9-10 leaves.

Headpin: First pin in the rack, also called 1 pin.

League: Group of four or more teams or individuals who bowl under a board of directors management, execute a pre-arranged schedule, and accept rules and a prize list (if any).

Pin: Required to meet several specifications. Must weigh between 3 pounds 6 ounces and 3 pounds 10 ounces, and stand 15 inches (plus or minus 1/32 of an inch). Must also be approved by ABC/WIBC equipment specifications department. For more information, see WIBC Bylaws Book or contact ABC/WIBC equipment specifications department at (414) 423-3400.

Pin Formation: Approved pin position. Distances from the center of one pin to the center(s) of its immediately adjacent pin(s) is (are) 12 inches.

Pocket: Area between 1-3 pins for right-handed bowlers and 1-2 pins for left-handed bowlers.

Proprietor: Person who owns or operates a bowling center.

Sanctioned Competition: Organized league and tournament competition in which bowling is played in accordance with WIBC, ABC and/or YABA rules and regulations. Events are scheduled on lanes currently certified and using ABC/WIBC approved equipment.

Scoring: Bowlers receive actual pinfall count, unless they bowl a strike or spare. If a strike, bowlers receive 10 pins or points plus the total of their next two deliveries. If they bowl a spare, bowlers receive 10 pins or points plus the total of their next delivery.

Spare: Knocking down all 10 pins in two deliveries in the same frame.

Split: Two or more pins standing after first delivery. Headpin must not be standing; and standing pins must be spaced without others standing directly in front or behind.

Stepladder: Series in which scores improve one pin each game.

Strike: Knocking down all 10 pins in first delivery in a frame.

Track: Path on lanes caused by numerous balls traveling in same line.

Triplicate: Three identical game scores in a three-game series or three identical three-game series scores (nine-game total).

Turkey: Three consecutive strikes.

Washout: 1-2-10, 1-2-4-10, 1-3-7, or 1-3-6-7 leaves. Not considered a split as headpin is standing.

Year	City	Site	Lanes	Dates
1997	Reno, Nev.	National Bowling Stadium	76	March 1-July 14
1996	Buffalo, N.Y.	Thruway Lanes, Transit Lanes	60-52	April 4-June 2
1995	Tucson, Ariz.	Golden Pin Lanes, Brunswick Camino Seco	48-32	March 30-June 12
1994	Salt Lake City	Fairmont Bowl, Ritz Classic Bowl	32-54	March 31-May 3
1993	Baton Rouge, La.	Metro Bowl, Don Carter's All Star Lanes	40-64	April 1-May 31
1992	Lansing, Mich.	Holiday Lane Pro Bowl	40-58	April 2-June 2
1991	Cedar Rapids, Iowa	Cedar Rapids Bowl, Westdale Bowl	32-48	April 4-June 20
1990	Tampa, Fla.	Oakfield Lanes, Regal Bowling Lanes	32-50	April 5-July 4
1989	Bismarck-Mandan, N.D.	Midway Lanes, Capitol Lanes	36-50	April 6-June 12
1988	Reno/Carson City, Nev.	Carson Lanes, Bally's Grand Lanes	36-48	March 31-July 31
1987	Hartford, Conn.	Vernon Lanes, Bloomfield Bowling Center	32-48	April 2-June 3
1986	Orange County, Calif.	Tustin Lanes, Kona Lanes	30 40	April 3-July 1
1985	Toledo, Ohio	Imperial Lanes, Southwyck Lanes	48-64	April 4-May 27
1984	Niagara Falls, N.Y.	Thunder Bowl, Beverly Lanes	32-64	April 5-June 9
1983*	Las Vegas	Showboat Lanes	106	April 7-July 1
1982	St Louis	Concord Bowl, Brunswick Four Seasons Bowl	32-40	April 1-June 18
1981	Baltimore	Bowl America Odenton, Brunswick Perry Hall Lanes	34-48	April 2-May 26
1980	Seattle	Leilani Lanes, Kenmore Lanes	36-50	April 3-June 11
1979	Tucson, Ariz.	Golden Pin Lanes, Cactus Bowl	48-60	April 5-June 1
1978	Miami	Palm Springs Lanes, Brunswick Congress Bowl	40-52	April 6-June 6
1977	Milwaukee	Red Carpet Celebrity	72	March 31-June 9
1976	Denver	Celebrity Sports Center	80	April 8-June 8
1975	Indianapolis	Meadows Bowl	64	April 3-May 22
1974	Houston	Stadium Bowl	72	April 4-May 18
1973	Las Vegas	Showboat Lanes	48	April 5-July 20
1972	Kansas City, Mo.	NKC Pro Bowl, King Louie East Lanes	32-40	April 6-May 27
1971	Atlanta	Brunswick Suburban, Atlanta Bowling Center	32-40	April 8-May 23
1970	Tulsa, Okla.	Yale Bowl	60	April 9-May 26
1969	San Diego	University Lanes	64	April 3-May 26
1968	San Antonio	Wonder Bowl	40	April 4-June 2
1967	Rochester, N.Y.	Gates, Olympic Bowl	48-64	April 13-May 28
1966	New Orleans	Pelican Lanes	48	April 14-May 30
1965	Portland, Ore.	20th Century	50	April 8-May 19
1964	Minneapolis	Southdale Bowl, New Hope	32-32	April 9-May 24
1963	Memphis, Tenn.	Imperial Lanes	48	April 4-May 20
1962	Phoenix.	Squaw Peak Lanes	40	April 5-May 16
1961	Fort Wayne, Ind.	Northcrest Bowling Lanes	40	April 6-May 29
1960	Denver	Belleview Bowl	48	April 21-May 25
1959	Buffalo	Southside Bowling Center	48	April 16-May 31
1958	San Francisco	Downtown Bowl	40	April 17-May 20
1957	Dayton, Ohio	McCook Bowl	44	April 11-May 26
1956	Miami	Bowlerama	32	April 19-May 20
1955	Omaha, Neb.	Music Box	22	April 14-June 12
1954	Syracuse, N.Y.	Jefferson Bowling Academy	40	April 8-May 31
1953	Detroit	Detroit Recreation	22-22	April 9-June 8
1952	St. Louis	Sports Bowl	24	April 24-June 12
1951	Seattle	Ideal Recreation	18	May 17-June 24
1950	St. Paul, Minn.	Harkins Bowling Palace	24	April 20-June 2
1949	Columbus, Ohio	Riverview Recreation	30	April 21-May 31
1948	Dallas	Hap Morse Bowling Alley	26	April 8-May 10
1947	Grand Rapids, Mich.	Fanatorium Recreation	18	April 10-June 8
1946	Kansas City, Mo.	Pla Mor	20	May 2-June 7
1942	Milwaukee	Bensinger Recreation	30	May 7-June 8
1941	Los Angeles	Vogue Bowl	24	May 15-June 9
1940	Syracuse, N.Y.	Jefferson Bowling Academy	20	April 25-May 24
1939	Oklahoma City	Jenks Bowling Palace	14	April 13-May 8

Days	Total Participants	Team Event	Doubles Event	Singles Event	Host City	Host State	Traveling	Prize Fund
136	88,279	14,872	42,252	84,504	123	281	14,749	$2,209,748
60	37,500	7,423	18,557	37,114	140	1,063	7,283	983,111
75	43,367	8,420	21,166	42,332	327	516	8,093	1,063,413
62	40,388	7,637	19,046	38,092	444	769	7,193	928,825
61	47,300	9,360	23,503	47,006	297	498	9,063	1,142,767
62	44,398	8,207	20,788	41,576	249	2,105	7,958	1,001,675
78	44,660	8,892	22,243	44,486	363	2,246	8,529	932,525
91	52,920	10,544	26,648	53,296	219	1,553	10,325	1,121,143
68	41,865	7,799	19,596	39,192	291	1,334	7,508	824,507
123	78,462	14,872	33,181	66,362	233	105	14,649	1,559,074
63	37,983	7,147	17,437	34,874	299	209	6,848	804,807
90	51,216	9,840	22,473	44,946	503	2,231	9,337	1,058,540
54	44,201	8,491	20,817	41,754	482	2,266	8,009	833,171
66	45,000 &	9,074	22,252	44,504	265	1,740	8,809	882,118
83	75,480	14,430	35,882	71,764	227	320	14,110	1,627,815
79	40,000 &	8,038	19,438	38,876	475	703	6,860	769,988
55	33,000 &	6,532	15,807	31,614	459	255	5,818	537,636
70	43,000 &	8,429	20,624	41,248	822	1,492	6,115	687,830
58	44,000 &	8,733	21,962	43,924	524	837	7,372	726,893
62	40,010	7,957	19,460	38,920	557	986	6,414	650,676
71	49,000 &	9,688	21,626	43,252	1,467	2,569	5,652	668,462
62	46,185 &	9,237	22,026	44,052	1,402	970	6,865	667,862
50	30,000 &	5,720	13,497	26,994	615	1,286	3,819	413,949
45	28,970 &	5,734	13,831	27,662	764	1,461	3,509	419,922
107	48,220	9,644	23,450	46,900	284	181	9,179	709,370
52	30,000 &	5,898	12,361	24,722	1,021	854	4,023	352,666
46	25,000 &	4,928	10,810	21,620	705	392	3,831	285,564
48	24,670 &	4,894	10,753	21,506	701	783	3,410	283,005
54	22,585 &	4,477	9,481	18,962	910	1,685	1,882	254,041
60	21,845 &	4,329	9,789	19,578	759	1,592	1,978	244,067
46	30,470 &	6,094	10,930	21,860	1,351	2,514	2,229	297,930
47	20,615 &	4,083	8,323	16,646	973	1,318	1,792	215,203
42	25,129	4,068	7,625	15,250	1,138	670	2,260	204,063
46	25,555 &	5,071	9,219	18,438	1,123	1,309	2,639	249,411
47	16,990 &	3,358	6,576	13,152	764	300	2,294	172,777
42	13,410 &	2,642	5,650	11,301	550	378	1,714	143,641
54	16,850 &	3,330	5,877	11,754	486	1,230	1,614	160,632
35	15,640 &	3,068	5,228	10,456	1,168	211	1,689	144,856
46	22,655 &	4,491	6,116	12,232	1,513	1,585	1,393	139,557
34	13,135 &	2,587	4,043	8,086	455	1,279	853	87,321
46	15,690 &	3,098	5,259	10,518	788	737	1,573	109,995
32	9,790 &	1,918	3,031	6,062	578	280	1,070	65,399
60	13,620 &	2,684	3,788	7,576	958	324	1,402	85,521
54	22,890 &	4,538	4,335	8,670	1,933	1,648	957	118,939
61	25,200 &	5,000	5,261	10,522	2,843	664	1,493	138,155
50	15,425 &	3,045	3,266	6,532	1,810	78	1,157	85,066
39	8,770 &	1,714	1,978	3,956	842	294	578	49,546
44	11,240 &	2,208	3,295	6,590	880	311	1,017	72,834
41	13,200 &	2,600	3,732	7,464	1,067	497	1,036	89,940
33	7,500 &	1,460	2,560	5,091	442	204	814	52,581
60	8,675 &	1,695	3,054	6,091	411	320	964	62,195
37	7,915 &	1,543	2,227	4,354	723	NR	NR	49,569
33	9,700 &	1,900	2,250	4,399	676	389	835	55,196
26	5,075 &	1,015	1,318	2,568	491	115	524	30,836
30	5,925 &	1,185	1,286	2,572	510	NR	675	32,963
26	2,740 &	548	787	1,583	NR	NR	333	17,691

Year	City	Site	Lanes	Dates
1938	Cincinnati	Cressler Bowling Palace	12	April 21-May 15
1937	Rochester, N.Y.	Buonomo Bowling Hall	10	April 15-May 11
1936	Omaha, Neb.	Ak-Sar Ben Recreation	12	April 23-May 11
1935	Chicago	Congress Recreation Center	12	April 25-May 15
1934	Indianapolis	Pritchett's Recreation	12	April 19-May 6
1933	Peoria, Ill.	Thoma Bowling Alleys	12	April 20-May 1
1932	St. Louis	Rogers Recreation	12	April 7-April 19
1931	New York City	Dwyer's Bowling Alleys	14	April 9-April 20
1930	Louisville, Ky.	Kosair Bowling Alleys	12	April 24-May 8
1929	Buffalo	Genesee Arcade	12	April 25-May 7
1928	Detroit	Garden Bowling Alleys	12	April 26-May 7
1927	Columbus, Ohio	Gettrost Recreation	8	April 21-May 4
1926	Milwaukee	Plankinton Arcade	6	April 21-May 10
1925	Cleveland	F.G. Smith Recreation	6	April 25-May 10
1924	Indianapolis	Central Lanes	12	April 19-April 28
1923	St. Louis	Washington Recreation	6	April 14-April 23
1922	Toledo, Ohio	Hagerty's Interurban Alleys	16	April 29-May
1921	Cleveland	Alhambra Bowling Alleys	12	April 30-May 6
1920	Chicago	Bensinger's Wabash Alleys	16	April 24-May 2
1919	Toledo, Ohio	Terminal Building	16	April 1-April 3
1918	Cincinnati	Cincinnati Armory	16	March 11-March 12
1916	St. Louis	Washington Recreation Parlor	6	Nov. 27-Nov. 28

& Estimate.

Days	Total Participants	Team Event	Doubles Event	Singles Event	Host City	Host State	Traveling	Prize Fund
25	3,705 &	741	1,010	2,008	307	NR	NR	23,198
27	2,655 &	531	691	1,359	250	NR	281	16,187
19	1,865 &	373	518	1,024	NR	NR	243	11,774
21	2,350 &	470	667	1,399	228	NR	242	15,249
18	1,265 &	253	405	824	81	NR	NR	8,697
12	885 &	177	280	553	62	NR	NR	5,993,
13	1,505 &	301	379	745	174	NR	NR	9,023
12	1,210 &	242	341	684	111	NR	NR	7,727
15	1,770 &	354	500	998	160	NR	194	11,328
13	1,535 &	307	421	824	150	NR	NR	9,590
12	1,100 &	220	437	857	NR	NR	NR	8,458
14	1,200 &	224	369	716	NR	NR	NR	7,722
20	1,370 &	274	414	819	124	165	NR	12,068
14	765 &	153	268	521	NR	NR	NR	5,466
10	630 &	126	225	443	NR	NR	NR	3,351
10	530 &	106	175	343	46	4	56	4,892
7	425 &	85	168	336	NR	NR	NR	4,388
7	330 &	66	132	260	NR	NR	NR	2,562
9	420 &	84	177	343	NR	NR	NR	2,234
3	200 &	40	103	202	10	18	22	1,216
2	160 &	32	72	145	10	18	14	1,347
2	40 &	8	16	24	7	7	1	225
		323,648	716,500	1,432,632				$25,676,135

The annual WIBC Championship Tournament provides competition for 40,000 or more women of all ages and bowling averages. Participants are classified into four average-based divisions: Classic Division, 180 average and above; Division I, 165-179 average; Division II, 145-164 average; and Division III, 144 average and below. WIBC distributes awards and prizes in all four divisions. Most entrants bowl a three-game series in the singles, doubles and five-woman team events. WIBC uses bowlers' nine-game cumulative totals (from these three events) for the all events competition. WIBC conducts the singles and doubles events in one bowling center, and the five-woman team event in a second center except during events at the National Bowling Stadium in Reno, Nev. Individuals usually bowl their three events on two consecutive days, and the tournament is held in a different city each year.

WIBC Championship Tournament Records

All Events, highest by individual in nine-game series

2,039	Kendra Cameron, Gambills, Md., 1997.
2,036	Debbie Kuhn, Baltimore, 1991.
2,032	Carolyn Dorin-Ballard, North Richland Hills, Texas, 1997.
2,011	Kim Adler, Las Vegas, 1997.
1,990	Anne Marie Duggan, Edmond, Okla., 1993.

Championships, most years between titles

25	Lorrie Nichols, Algonquin, Ill., 1971 to 1996.
23	LaVerne Carter, Las Vegas, 1951 to 1974.
19	Betty Maw, Buffalo, N.Y., 1956 to 1975.
18	Connie Powers, Fraser, Mich., 1939 to 1957.
17	Joan Karge, Chicago, 1961 to 1978.

Days, longest tournament in days

136	Reno, Nev., 1997.
123	Reno/Carson City, Nev., 1988.
107	Las Vegas, 1973.
91	Tampa, Fla., 1990.
90	Orange County Calif., 1986.
83	Las Vegas 1983.

Games, highest Team

1,159	Contour Power Grips, Detroit, 1996.
1,150	The Naccarato Group, Tacoma, Wash., 1996.
1,133	Robby's Glendale, Calif., (Linda Goodling, Donna Zuniga, Patty Ellenburg, Diana Davenport and Betty Morris), 1989.
1,119	Contour Power Grips, Detroit, 1995.
1,113	Strike Zone Pro Shop, Rolling Meadows, Ill., 1994.
1,109	Sims, Chicago,1956.
1,106	Wonder Women No. 1, Islip, N.Y., 1978.

Doubles

558	Linda Kelly-Mandy Wilson; Dayton, Ohio, 1996.
514	Sharon Powers-Lorrie Nichols; Wheat Ridge, Colo., and Algonquin, Ill., 1983.
512	Karen Collura-Gloria Collura, Toronto, 1993.
505	Jeanne Naccarato - Cheryl Shininger; Tacoma, Wash.-Solon, Ohio; 1987.
504	Marge Merrick-Elizabeth Miller; Columbus, Ohio,1962.

Individual

300	Lori Gensch, Milwaukee, 1979.
	Rose Walsh, Pomona, Calif., 1986.
	Linda Kelly, Huber Heights, Ohio, 1987.
299	Nikki Gianulias, Vallejo, Calif., 1982.
	Michele Meyer-Welty, Vacaville, Calif., 1988.
	Sharon Wanczyk, Ogden, Utah, 1997
	Leslie Jackson, Daytona Beach, Fla., 1997

Participation Attendance, most tournaments

61	Mary Covell, Chicago, through 1992.
60	Nancy R. Hampton, Carol Stream, Ill., through 1993.
57	Ethel Ann Constantine, Westland, Mich., through 1992.
	Helen Bassett, Peoria, Ill., through 1993.
56	Florence Seeds, Columbus, Ohio, through 1992.
51	Nellie Pestinger, Wichita, Kan., through 1991.

Prize Fund, largest in individual tournaments

$2,209,748	Reno, Nev., 1997.
1,627,815	Las Vegas, 1983.
1,559,073	Reno/Carson City, Nev. 1988.
1,121,143	Tampa, Fla., 1990.
1,142,767	Baton Rouge, La., 1993.

Prize Winnings, most won in same tournament

$6,900	Aleta Sill, Dearborn, Mich., 1983.
5,000	Virginia Norton, Cypress, Calif., 1983.
4,280	Dana Miller-Mackie, Fort Worth, Texas, 1990.
4,000	Beth Owen, Dallas, 1995.
3,900	Debbie Kuhn, Baltimore, 1991.

Three-Game Series, highest by event

Team

3,184	The Naccarato Group, Tacoma, Wash., 1996.
3,142	Contour Power Grips, Detroit, 1996.
3,125	Contour Power Grips, Detroit, 1995.
3,102	Midwest Connection, North Richland Hills, Texas, 1996.
3,096	Alpine Lanes, Euless, Texas, 1979.

Doubles

1,410	Linda Kelly-Mandy Wilson, Dayton, Hoio, 1996.
1,354	Jennifer Klekamp-Regina Snodgrass, Cleves, Ohio and Versailles, Ind, 1996.
1,345	Jennifer Klekamp-Regina Snodgrass, Cleves, Ohio and Versailles, Ind, 1997.
1,328	Laura Grant-Robin Romeo, Norwood, Conn., and Newhall, Calif., 1987.
1,325	Nancy Fehr-Lisa Wagner; Cincinnati, and Palmetto, Fla.; 1992.

Singles

773	Debbie Kuhn, Baltimore, 1991.
765	Jan Schmidt, Rochelle, Ill., 1997.
751	Anne Marie Duggan, Edmond, Okla., 1993.
749	Beth Owen, Dallas, 1995.
741	Joanne Harris, Occoquan, Va., 1995.

Three-Game Series, highest by individual in any event

773	Debbie Kuhn, Baltimore, 1991.
765	Jan Schmidt, Rochelle, Ill., 1997.
756	Anne Marie Duggan, Edmond, Okla., 1993.
749	Beth Owen, Dallas, 1995.
746	Linda Kelly, Huber Heights, Ohio, 1987.

WIBC Championship Tournament Champions

Beginning with the 1994 tournament and again in 1997, WIBC implemented new, average-based divisions in response to bowler requests. The new divisions further segment low, medium and high-average bowlers to meet WIBC's goal of providing tournament competition and prize-winning opportunities to bowlers of all skill levels.

The average breakdown for individual bowlers is:

Classic Division — 180 average and higher
Division I — 165-179 average

Division II — 145-164 average
Division III — 144 average and below

Tournament Champions are overall high scores in each event, regardless of division.

Year	Champion and City	Score
Team Event		
1997	Here 4 Beer II, Glendale, Ariz.	3,017
	Contour Power Grips, Vallejo, Calif.	3,017
1996	The Naccarato Group, Tacoma, Wash.	*3,185
1995	Contour Power Grips, Detroit	*3,125
1994	Strike Zone Pro Shop, Rolling Meadows, Ill.	3,027
1993	Strike Zone Pro Shop, Rolling Meadows, Ill.	2,978
1992	Hoinke Classic, Cincinnati	2,983
1991	Clear-Vu Window Cleaning, Inc., Milwaukee	2,984
1990	R.A.T.'s Team, Lakeland, Fla.	2,985
1989	Robby's, Glendale, Calif.	3,000
1988	Cook County Sales, Chicago	3,027
1987	Tool Warehouse, Hollywood, Fla.	3,033
1986	Silla's Custom Fit Pro Shop, Cleveland	2,891
1985	Don Redman Insurance, Toledo, Ohio	2,934
1984	All Japan, Tokyo	3,019
1983	Telectronic Systems, Inc., Manila, Philippines	2,868
1982	Zavakos Realtors, Dayton, Ohio	2,961
1981	Earl Anthony's Dublin Bowl, Dublin, Calif.	2,963
1980	All Japan, Tokyo	3,014
1979	Alpine Lanes, Euless, Texas	3,096
1978	Cook County Vending, Chicago	2,956
1977	Allgauer Restaurant, Chicago	2,818
1976	PWBA No. 1, Oklahoma City	2,839
1975	Atlanta Bowling Center (Ga.) No. 1, Buffalo, N.Y.	2,836
1974	Kalicak International Construction, St. Louis	2,973
1973	Fitzpatrick Chevrolet, Concord, Calif.	2,897
1972	Angeltown Creations, Placentia, Calif.	2,838
1971	Koenig Strey Real Estate, Wilmette, Ill.	2,891
1970	Parker-Fothergill Pro Shop, Cranston, R.I.	3,034
1969	Fitzpatrick Chevrolet, Concord, Calif.	2,986
1968	Hudepohl Beer, Cincinnati	2,923
1967	The Orphans, Los Angeles	2,970
1966	Gossard Girls, Chicago	2,755
1965	Belmont Bowl Pro Shop, Chicago	2,929
1964	Allgauer Restaurant, Chicago	2,920
1963	Linbrook Bowl, Los Angeles	2,841
1962	Linbrook Bowl, Los Angeles	3,061
1961	Allgauer Restaurant, Chicago	2,919
1960	Spare-Time Games, Cincinnati	2,876
1959	Bill Snethkamp Chrysler, Detroit	3,030
1958	Allgauer Restaurant, Chicago	2,972
1957	Colonial Broach Co., Detroit	2,881
1956	Daniel Ryan, Chicago	2,880
1955	Falstaff, Chicago	2,991
1954	Marheofer Wieners, Chicago	2,734
1953	B & B Chevrolet, Detroit	2,931
1952	Cole Furniture, Cleveland	2,854
1951	Hickman Oldsmobile Whirlaway, Indianapolis	2,705
1950	Fanatorium Majors, Grand Rapids, Mich.	2,903
1949	Gears by Enterprise, Detroit	2,786
1948	Kathryn Creme Pact, Chicago	2,812
1947	Kornitz Pure Oil, Milwaukee	2,987
1946	Silver Seal Soda, St. Louis	2,721
1942	Logan Square Buicks, Chicago	2,815
1941	Rovick Bowling Shoes, Chicago	2,661
1940	Logan Square Buicks, Chicago	2,689
1939	Kornitz Pure Oil, Milwaukee	2,618
1938	Heil Uniform Heat, Milwaukee	2,706
1937	Heil Uniform Heat, Milwaukee	2,685
1936	Easty Five, Cleveland	2,617
1935	Alberti Jewelers, Chicago	2,765
1934	Tommy Doll's Five, Cincinnati	2,616
1933	Alberti Jewelers, Chicago	2,867
1932	Martin Breitt Realtors, St. Louis	2,664
1931	Alberti Jewelers, Chicago	2,748
1930	Finucane Ladies, Chicago	2,784
1929	Harvey's Market Square Rec., Kansas City, Mo.	2,538
1928	Alberti Jewelers, Chicago	2,682
1927	Boyle Valves, Chicago	2,515
1926	Taylor Trunks, Chicago	2,525
1925	Estes Alibis, Chicago	2,518
1924	Albert Pick Co., Chicago	2,477
1923	Paige Dairy (also known as Page Dairy), Toledo, Ohio	2,348
1922	Birk Cola Girls, Chicago	2,531
1921	Grand B. and B. Co., Rockford, Ill.	2,482
1920	Stein's Jr., St. Louis	2,454
1919	Minor Butler, Toledo, Ohio	2,436
1918	Leffingwell, Chicago	2,479
1916	Progress, St. Louis	2,082

* Record

Year	Champion and City	Score
Doubles Event		
1997	Jennifer Klekamp-Regina Snodgrass, Cleves, Ohio and Versailles, Ind.	1,345
1996	Mandy Wilson-Linda Kelly, Dayton, Ohio	*1,410
1995	Carol Harsh-Debbie Villani, Las Vegas	1,299
1994	Lucy Giovinco-Cindy Coburn-Carroll, Norcross, Ga., and Tonawanda, N.Y. and Rachel Perez-Kim Straub, San Antonio, and Beatrice, Neb.	1,307
1993	Gloria Collura-Karen Collura, Toronto	1,304
1992	Nancy Fehr-Lisa Wagner, Cincinnati, and Palmetto, Fla.	1,325
1991	Lucy Giovinco-Cindy Coburn-Carroll, Norcross, Ga., and Tonawanda, N.Y.	1,318
1990	Margi Melvin-Ann Meconnahey, Newark, Del., and Bear, Del.	1,323
1989	Diana Goodman-Rene Fleming, Chino Hill, Calif., and Oklahoma City	1,283
1988	Dee Alvarez-Pat Costello, Tampa, Fla., and Orlando, Fla.	1,216

1987 Laura Grant-Robin Romeo, Norwalk, Conn.,
and Newhall, Calif. *1,328
1986 Sally Gates-Marilyn Frazier, Palmdale and
Lancaster, Calif. 1,260
1985 Linda Graham-Melody Philippson, Des Moines
and Colfax, Iowa 1,246
1984 Bea Hoffman-Sue Reese, Novato, Calif. 1,292
1983 Jeanne Maiden-Naccarato - Sue Robb,
Tacoma, Wash., and Euclid, Ohio 1,312
1982 Shirley Hintz-Lisa Wagner, Lantana and
Palmetto, Fla. 1,264
Pat Costello-Donna Adamek, Orlando,
Fla., and Apple Valley, Calif.....................1,264
1981 Nikki Gianulias-Donna Adamek, Vallejo and
Apple Valley, Calif. 1,305
1980 Carole Lee-Dawn Raddatz, Hempstead and
E. Northport, N.Y. 1,247
1979 Mary Ann Deptula-Geri Beattie, Warren and
Dearborn, Mich. 1,314
1978 Annese Kelly-Barbara Shelton, Las Vegas,
and Jamaica, N.Y. 1,211
1977 Ozella Houston-Dorothy Jackson, Detroit 1,234
1976 Georgene Cordes-Shirley Sjostrom,
Bloomington, Minn. 1,232
Debbie Rainone-Eloise Vacco, Cleveland.......1,232
1975 Jennette James-Dawn Raddatz, Oyster Bay and
E. Northport, N.Y. 1,234
1974 Carol Miller-Jane Leszczynski,
Waukesha, Wis., and Milwaukee 1,313
1973 Mildred Ignizio-Dorothy Fothergill, Rochester,
N.Y., and Center Ossippee, N.H. 1,238
1972 Judy Roberts-Betty Remmick, Denver, and
Lakewood, Colo. 1,247
1971 Dorothy Fothergill-Mildred Ignizio, Center
Ossippee, N.H., and Rochester, N.Y. 1,263
1970 Gloria Bouvia-Judy Soutar, Gresham, Ore.,
and Leawood, Kan. 1,256
1969 Gloria Bouvia-Judy Soutar, Gresham, Ore.,
and Leawood, Kan. 1,315
1968 Pauline Stickler-Mary Lou Graham, Miami.....1,250
1967 Elaine Liburdi-Joan Oleske, Union City and
Lyndhurst, N.J. 1,252
1966 Martha Morgan-Pat Spence, Hampton, Va. 1,231
1965 Betty Remmick-Mary Ann White, Denver 1,263
1964 Shirley Garms-Grace Werkmeister, Chicago..1,248
1963 Ann Heyman-Ruth Redfox, Toledo, Ohio........1,260
1962 Sandy Galvin-Jean Stevens, Oklahoma City ..1,238
1961 Betty Salvato-Georgiana Eakins,
Youngstown, Ohio 1,239
1960 Jette Mooney-Freda Laiber, South Bend, Ind. ..1,221
1959 Sylvia Martin-Adele Isphording, Philadelphia.1,263
1958 Jean Schultz-Tess Johns, Cleveland................1,173
1957 Nellie Vella-Jeanette Grzelak, Rockford, Ill.....1,218
1956 Betty Maw-Mary Quinn, Buffalo, N.Y...........1,242
1955 Wyllis Ryskamp-Marion Ladewig,
Grand Rapids, Mich. 1,264
1954 Frances Stennett-Rose Gacioch, Rockford, Ill..1,244
1953 Jane Grudzien-Doris Knechtges, Detroit..........1,211
1952 Loraine Quam-Martha Hoffman,
Madison, Wis. 1,206
1951 Esther Cooke-Alma Denini, Seattle................1,179
1950 Shirley Gantenbein-Flo Schick, Dallas 1,216
1949 Ann Elyasevich-Estelle Svoboda, Chicago 1,229
1948 Margaret Franklin-Merle Matthews,

Alhambra and Long Beach, Calif. 1,188
1947 Candace Fleet-Emma Beard,
Fort Wayne, Ind. 1,245
1946 Virginia Forster-Prudence Dusher,
Niagara Falls, N.Y. 1,251
1942 Stella Hartrick-Clara Allen, Detroit 1,204
1941 Jo Ettien-Mary Hogan, Los Angeles...............1,155
1940 Tess Small-Dorothy Miller, Chicago 1,181
1939 Connie Powers-Betty Reus,
Grand Rapids, Mich. 1,130
1938 Florence Probert-Ethel Sablatnik, St. Louis......1,215
1937 Loranne Frank-Garnette Weber,
Fort Wayne, Ind. 1,230
1936 Adelaide Lindemann-Loraine Baldy,
Milwaukee 1,116
1935 Erna Haufler-Violet Simon,
San Antonio, Texas....................................1,219
1934 Fritzie Rahn-Dorothy Miller, Chicago.............1,190
1933 Veronica Peters-Mary Kite, Syracuse, N.Y......1,135
1932 Edith Kirg-Margaret Frank, Chicago 1,218
1931 Zetta Baker-Gertrude Pomeroy, Detroit 1,145
1930 Fritzie Rahn-Marie Warmbier, Chicago..........1,173
1929 Mary Smith-Dorothy Miller, Chicago..............1,123
1928 Ann Weiller-Edna Estes, Chicago 1,155
1927 Alma Burke-Edith Kirg, Chicago 1,100
1926 Jennie Laib-Agnes Higgins, Chicago.............1,086
1925 Myrtle Baker-Mae Ebert, Chicago 1,119
1924 Jean Acker-Grace Smith, Chicago 1,124
1923 Zoe Quin-Agnes Higgins, Chicago 1,038
1922 Louise Stockdale-Helen Sneider, Detroit 1,094
1921 Pearl Ley-Grace Smith, Chicago 1,079
1920 Erna Willig-Jean Walz, Chicago 1,043
1919 Mae Butterworth-Frances Steib,
Columbus, Ohio, and Chicago...................1,042
1918 Jean Acker-Lita Reilly, Chicago....................1,012
1916 Jean Acker-Lita Reilly, Chicago 1,011
* Record

Singles Event
1997 Jan Schmidt, Rochelle, Ill. 748
1996 Cindy Berlanga, San Antonio, Texas 723
1995 Beth Owen, Dallas.....................................749
1994 Vicki Fifield, El Paso, Texas.........................716
1993 Karen Collura, Toronto 747
Kari Murph, Dayton, Ohio..........................747
1992 Patty Ann, Arlington Heights, Ill..................... 680
1991 Debbie Kuhn, Baltimore...........................*773
1990 Dana Miller-Mackie, Fort Worth, Texas 705
Paula Carter, ...705
1989 Sandy Flint, Sioux Falls, S.D. 694
1988 Michelle Meyer-Welty, Vacaville, Calif. 690
1987 Regi Jonak, St. Peters, Mo. 728
1986 Dana Stewart, Morgan Hill, Calif. 698
1985 Polly Schwarzel, Cheswick, Pa.....................694
1984 Freida Gates, N. Syracuse, N.Y. 712
1983 Aleta Sill, Dearborn, Mich. 726
1982 Gracie Freeman, Alexandria, Va. 652
1981 Virginia Norton, Cypress, Calif. 672
1980 Betty Morris, Stockton, Calif.........................674
1979 Betty Morris, Stockton, Calif.........................699
1978 Mae Bolt, Berwyn, Ill. 709
1977 Akiko Yamaga, Tokyo 714
1976 Beverly Shonk, Canton, Ohio.......................686

1975	Barbara Leicht, Water Vilet, N.Y.	689
1974	Shirley Garms, Island Lake, Ill.	702
1973	Bobbie Soldan, Costa Mesa, Calif.	706
1972	D.D. Jacobson, Playa Del Rey, Calif.	737
1971	Mary Scruggs, Richmond, Va.	698
1970	Dorothy Fothergill, Center Ossippee, N.H.	695
1969	Joan Bender, Arvada, Colo.	690
1968	Norma Parks, Raytown, Mo.	691
1967	Glorian Griffith, Port Huron, Mich.	652
1966	Gloria Bouvia, Gresham, Ore.	675
1965	Doris Rudell, Whittier, Calif.	659
1964	Jean Havlish, St. Paul, Minn.	690
1963	Dorothy Wilkinson, Phoenix	653
1962	Martha Hoffman, Madison, Wis.	693
1961	Elaine Newton, Park Forest, Ill.	661
1960	Marge McDaniels, Mountain View, Calif.	649
1959	Mae Bolt, Berwyn, Ill.	664
1958	Ruth Hertel, Lexington, Tenn.	622
1957	Eleanor Towles, Peoria, Ill.	664
1956	Lucille Noe, Columbus, Ohio	708
1955	Nellie Vella, Rockford, Ill.	695
1954	Helen Bassett, Peoria, Ill.	668
1953	Marge Baginski, Berwyn, Ill.	637
1952	Lorene Craig, Kansas City, Mo.	672
1951	Ida Simpson, Buffalo, N.Y.	639
1950	Cleo McGovern, Newport, Ky.	669
1949	Clara Mataya, St. Louis	658
1948	Shirlee Wernecke, Chicago	696
1947	Agnes Junker, Indianapolis	650
1946	Val Mikiel, Detroit	682
1942	Tillie Taylor, Newark, N.J.	659
1941	Nancy Huff, Los Angeles	662
1940	Sally Twyford, Aurora, Ill.	626
1939	Helen Hengstier, Detroit	626
1938	Rose Warner, Waukegan, Ill.	622
1937	Ann Gottstine, Buffalo, N.Y.	647
1936	Ella Mankie, Madison, Wis.	612
1935	Marie Warmbier, Chicago	652
1934	Marie Clemensen, Chicago	712
1933	Sally Twyford, Aurora, Ill.	628
1932	Audrey McVay, Kansas City, Mo.	668
1931	Myrtle Schulte, St. Louis	650
1930	Anita Rump, Fort Wayne, Ind.	613
1929	Agnes Higgins, Chicago	637
1928	Anita Rump, Fort Wayne, Ind.	622
1927	Florence Amrein, Akron, Ohio	577
1926	Evelyn Weisman, Indianapolis	579
1925	Eliza Reich, Chicago	622
1924	Alice Feeney, Indianapolis	593
1923	Emma Jaeger, Toledo, Ohio	594
1922	Emma Jaeger, Toledo, Ohio	603
1921	Emma Jaeger, Toledo, Ohio	579
1920	Birdie Humphreys, St. Louis	559
1919	Elizabeth Husk, Newark, N.J.	594
1918	Frances Steib, Detroit	537
1916	Agnes Koester, Detroit	486
*Record.		

All Events

1997	Kendra Cameron, Gambrills, Md.	*2,039
1996	Lorrie Nichols, Algonquin, Ill.	1,985
1995	Beth Owen, Dallas	1,983
1994	Wendy Macpherson-Papanos, Henderson, Nev.	1,940

1993	Anne Marie Duggan, Edmond, Okla.,	1,990
1992	Mitsuko Tokimoto, Tokyo	1,928
1991	Debbie Kuhn, Baltimore	2,036
1990	Carol Norman, Ardmore, Okla.	1,984
1989	Nancy Fehr, Cincinnati	1,911
1988	Lisa Wagner, Palmetto, Fla.	1,871
1987	Leanne Barrette, Yukon, Okla.	1,972
1986	Robin Romeo, Newhall, Calif.	1,877
	Maria Lewis, Manteca, Calif.	1,877
1985	Aleta Sill, Dearborn, Mich.	1,900
1984	Shinobu Saitoh, Tokyo	1,922
1983	Virginia Norton, Cypress, Calif.	1,922
1982	Aleta Sill, Dearborn, Mich.	1,905
1981	Virginia Norton, Cypress, Calif.	1,905
1980	Cheryl Robinson, Destrehan, La.	1,848
1979	Betty Morris, Stockton, Calif.	1,945
1978	Annese Kelly, Las Vegas	1,896
1977	Akiko Yamaga, Tokyo	1,895
1976	Betty Morris, Stockton, Calif.	1,866
1975	Virginia Norton, Cypress, Calif.	1,821
1974	Judy Soutar, Leawood, Kan.	1,944
1973	Toni Starin, Midwest City, Okla.	1,910
1972	Mildred Ignizio, Rochester, N.Y.	1,877
1971	Lorrie Nichols, Algonquin, Ill.	1,840
1970	Dorothy Fothergill, Center Ossippee, N.H.	1,984
1969	Helen Duval, Berkeley, Calif.	1,927
1968	Susie Reichley, Dallas	1,889
1967	Carol Miller, Waukesha, Wis.	1,862
1966	Kate Helbig, Mohnton, Pa.	1,835
1965	Donna Zimmerman, Thousand Palms, Calif.	1,833
1964	Jean Havlish, St. Paul, Minn.	1,980
1963	Helen Shablis, Detroit	1,849
1962	Flossie Argent, St. Louis	1,808
1961	Evelyn Teal, Miami	1,848
1960	Judy Roberts, Angola, N.Y.	1,836
1959	Pat McCormick, Grand Rapids, Mich.	1,927
1958	Mae Bolt, Berwyn, Ill.	1,828
1957	Anita Cantaline, Detroit	1,859
1956	Doris Knechtges, Detroit	1,867
1955	Marion Ladewig, Grand Rapids, Mich.	1,890
1954	Anne Johnson, Berwick, Pa.	1,880
1953	Doris Knechtges, Detroit	1,886
1952	Virginia Turner, Gardena, Calif.	1,854
1951	LaVerne Carter, Las Vegas	1,788
1950	Marion Ladewig, Grand Rapids, Mich.	1,796
1949	Cecilia Winandy, Chicago	1,840
1948	Virgie Hupfer, Burlington, Iowa	1,850
1947	Marge Dardeen, Cincinnati	1,826
1946	Catherine Fellmeth, Chicago	1,835
1942	Nina Burns, Chicago	1,888
1941	Sally Twyford, Aurora, Ill.	1,799
1940	Tess Small, Chicago	1,777
1939	Ruth Troy, Dayton, Ohio	1,724
1938	Dorothy Miller, Chicago	1,843
1937	Louise Stockdale, Detroit	1,761
1936	Ella Mankie, Madison, Wis.	1,683
1935	Marie Warmbier, Chicago	1,911
1934	Esther Ryan, Milwaukee	1,763
1933	Sally Twyford, Aurora, Ill.	1,765
1932	Marie Warmbier, Chicago	1,807
1931	Myrtle Schulte, St. Louis	1,742
1930	Sally Twyford, Aurora, Ill.	1,727
1929	Emma Jaeger, Toledo, Ohio	1,700
1928	Emma Jaeger, Toledo, Ohio	1,713

1927	Grayce Hatch, Cleveland	1,644	1921	Emma Jaeger, Toledo, Ohio ... 1,557
1926	Ermil Lackey, Fort Wayne, Ind.	1,641	1920	Mae Leibrich, Chicago ... 1,606
1925	Grayce Hatch, Cleveland	1,703	1919	Elizabeth Husk, Newark, N.J. ... 1,580
1924	Rose Steger, Chicago	1,647	1918	Emma Jaeger, Toledo, Ohio ... 1,552
1923	Deane Fritz, Toledo, Ohio	1,582	1916	Agnes Koester, Detroit ... 1,423
1922	Hattie Abraham, Milwaukee	1,659	* Record.	

Divisional Winners

**Prior to 1994, the divisional structure was: Open — 171 average and higher;
Division I — 151-170 average; Division II — 150 and under average**

Open Division Winners

(If Different from WIBC Champions)

Singles Event

1989 Lorraine Anderson, Northville, Mich. ... 683
1971 Ginny Younginer, Winnsboro, S.C. ... 667

Division I Winners

(Until 1969, Division I winners were also WIBC
Championship Tournament Champions)

Team Event

1997 Penalty Box Too, Windsor, Ontario ... 2,825
1996 Penalty Box Too, Windsor, Ontario ... 2,833
1995 Minier Lanes, Minier, Ill. ... *2,856
1994 Concordia Lanes, Belvidere, Ill. ... 2,688
1993 California Dreamin' III, Ventura, Calif. ... 2,842
1992 Rubber Mill, Medford, Ore. ... 2,716
1991 Jolly Ladies, Philadelphia ... 2,751
1990 Just Them, Hampton, Va. ... 2,697
       Lucky Strikes, Savannah, Ga.
1989 Wheaton Lanes, Wheaton, Minn. ... 2,768
1988 Blue Shield of California, San Francisco ... 2,773
1987 Classy Ladies, Hartford, Conn. ... 2,754
1986 Royal Buick, Tucson, Ariz. ... 2,676
1985 Taylor Chiropractic Life Center,
       Howell, Mich. ... 2,834
1984 Dave Diomedi's Washtenaw Lanes &
       Pro Shop, Ann Arbor, Mich. ... 2,721
1983 Production Plating, Lexington, Ky. ... 2,814
1982 Century Lanes, Hampton, Va. ... *2,856
1981 Gibson Specialty Co., Waterloo, Iowa ... 2,796
1980 Walkers Body Shop, Aurora, Ill. ... 2,703
1979 Don Smith's Classics, Milbrae, Calif. ... 2,862
1978 Joyner Garden Center, Alexandria, Minn. ... 2,706
1977 Sunbeam Girls, Birmingham, Ala. ... 2,670
1976 Famous Brand Shoes, St. Louis ... 2,753
1975 Channel Chargers, Robinson, Ill. ... 2,667
1974 Whitaker Trucking Inc., Roswell, N.M. ... 2,622
1973 Cacco's Hawaii, Honolulu ... 2,708
1972 Donson Inc., General Contractors, Alsip, Ill. ... 2,707
1971 Pepples Beauty Salon, Detroit ... 2,659
1970 Gene Hammon Ford Thunderbirds,
       Texas City, Texas ... 2,748
1969 Bowlorado Lanes, Fort Collins, Colo. ... 2,719
* Record.

Doubles Event

1997 Robynn Terry-Cindy McIntosh, Basin, Wyo.-
       Greybull, Wyo. ... 1,258
1996 Carlotta Piper-Merva Brison, Brooklyn, N.Y. ... 1,244
1995 Sande Crawford, Columbia Heights, Minn.-Cheryl
       Rasmussen, Osseo, Minn. ... 1,217
1994 Leslie Pappan-Debby Johns,
       Tulsa, Okla. and Broken Arrow, Okla. ... 1,225
1993 Mary Garrett-Rhondrea Simmons,
       Muskogee, Okla. ... *1,267

1992 Mary Piche-Karen Nicol, Burlington,
       Ontario, and Hamilton, Ontario ... 1,200
1991 Lina Rincon-Bonnie Van Steenburg,
       San Antonio and Universal City, Texas ... 1,227
1990 Joann Anastasio-Cathie Cross,
       Augusta, Maine ... 1,204
1989 Carol Feurerborn-Leeta Sweet, Olathe and
       Garnett, Kan. ... 1,208
1988 Judy Eldredge-Patricia Taum, Ridge Crest and
       Beale Air Force Base, Calif. ... 1,184
1987 Gloria Penn-Ruth Jensen, Plainfield and
       South Bound Brook, N.J. ... 1,232
1986 Cindy Brennan-Joy Eckley, Missoula and
       Roman, Mont. ... 1,188
1985 Sara Hennessey-Laura Lyons, Piqua, Ohio ... 1,232
1984 Shirley Heppner-Diane Wilde, Oshkosh and
       Waupaca, Wis. ... 1,255
1983 Bea Hatfield-Rose Swain, Shawnee and
       Lenexa, Kan. ... 1,233
1982 Bridgett Basiak-Donna Oldaker, Chesterton
       and Lake Station, Ind. ... 1,211
1981 Jeri Gue-Jo Ann Scott, New Castle and
       Wilmington, Del. ... 1,181
1980 Marie Fouche-Katherine Alexander,
       Los Angeles ... 1,176
1979 Vi Walde-Bernell Preul, Denison, Iowa ... 1,175
1978 Jean Hand-Judy Hart, Fairview and
       Canton, Ill. ... 1,201
1977 Viola Coombs-Jackie Hedrick, Mesa and
       Tempe, Ariz. ... 1,175
1976 Shirley Mansfield-Barbara Siemrzuch,
       North Glenn, Ohio ... 1,198
1975 Josie Freeman-Patsey Plumley,
       West Helena, Ark. ... 1,194
1974 Rachel Rookstool-Ruble Sizemore,
       Fort Walton Beach, Fla. ... 1,209
1973 Carol Sheppard-Laura Black, Phoenix, Ariz. ... 1,203
1972 Evelyn Porter-Billie Caldwell, Chicago ... 1,215
1971 Judy Bell-Daisy Trout, Lithonia and
       Marietta, Ga. ... 1,194
1970 Lorraine Petersen-Peggy Runyon,
       Garden Grove, Calif. ... 1,231
1969 Bertha Keeney-Joyce Georgeson,
       Wheat Ridge, Colo., and Denver ... 1,205
* Record.

Singles Event

1997 Donna Barnes, Perryton, Texas ... 687
1996 Jacqueline Pawlak, Wappingers Falls, N.Y. ... 660
1995 Linda Estep, Waldorf, Md. ... 683
1994 Michele Davis, Baytown, Texas ... 686
1993 Belle Turner, Paducah, Ky. ... 679
1992 Linda Lesniak, Evergreen Park, Ill. ... 669
1991 Kelly Smith, Faribault, Minn. ... 660
1990 Nancy Jones, Oklahoma City ... 682
1989 See champions list.

1988	Hazel Ivy, Omaha, Neb.	662
1987	Kathleen Lovett, Arthurdale, W.Va.	656
	Schanda Plank, Grand Rapids, Mich.	656
1986	Diane Smith, Lake Cowichan, British Columbia.	688
1985	Vicki Baker, St. Paris, Ohio	656
1984	Cathy Sartwell, Morgan City, La.	*690
1983	Doylie Seibel, Angleton, Texas	652
1982	Jan Sammon, Davenport, Iowa	650
1981	Dorothy Batey, East Orange, N.J.	651
1980	Cheri Mason, Lansing, Ill.	651
1979	Jean Carbone, Kenosha, Wis.	632
1978	Norma Walker, Tacoma, Wash.	659
1977	Edna Ruth, Belpre, Ohio	644
1976	Vanda Philson, Sidney, Neb.	666
1975	Beatrice Orendorf, Bridgeville, Del.	664
1974	Barbara Davis, Sterling Heights, Mich.	658
1973	Barbara Jacques, San Diego	680
1972	Shirley Frank, Woodside, N.Y.	657
1971	See champions list.	
1970	Jelemia Sanders, Richmond, Ky.	654
1969	Ann Keerbs, Churdan, Iowa	649

* Record.

All Events

1997	Theresa Adams, Pocomoke City, Md.	1,863
1996	Charlotte Chocrane, DeKalb, Ill.	1,818
1995	Kelly Seabloom, Scottsdale, Ariz.	1,807
1994	Michele Davis, Baytown, Texas	1,809
1993	Bertha Blacksher, Uriah, Ala.	1,807
	Sharon Davis, Orange, Texas	1,807
1992	Shari Ellison, Columbus, Ga.	1,848
1991	Chris Crowe, Prospect, Ky.	1,803
1990	Bonnie Piszczek, Wauwatosa, Wis.	1,791
1989	Sandy Flint, Sioux Falls, S.D.	1,801
1988	Karen Terry, Inglewood, Calif.	1,746
1987	Arlene Army, Millbury, Mass.	1,767
1986	Nancy Schubert-Balcer, Baltimore	1,780
1985	Barbara Hansen, Hyannis, Mass.	1,800
1984	Verona Gloudemans, Kimberly, Wis.	1,749
1983	Michelle Casella, Sun Valley, Calif.	1,827
1982	Elmere Harrison, Chalmette, La.	1,770
1981	Ferol Streib, Leavenworth, Wash.	1,738
1980	Velda Morris, Del City, Okla.	1,711
1979	Karen Russell, Bethany, Okla.	1,788
1978	Sandy Gazell, Boca Raton, Fla.	1,852
1977	Pat Booth, Memphis, Tenn.	1,739
	Marlene Willett, Marietta, Ga.	1,739
1976	Ethel Coverdell, Orlando, Fla.	1,748
1975	Jeanette Pease, Richmond, Va.	1,749
1974	JoAnne Rogalski, Buffalo, N.Y.	*1,907
1973	Reta Richardson, Boise City, Iowa	1,769
1972	Janice Denning, Wilmington, Del.	1,827
1971	Joyce Mooney, Pittsburgh	1,721
1970	Leah Ackerman, Sheldon, Iowa	1,796
1969	Janice Pickle, Tucson, Ariz.	1,743

* Record.

Division II Winners

Team Event

1997	Mill 3, Shelton, Wash.	*2,816
1996	Motor Electric, Elkhart, Ind.	2,693
1995	Southern Sights Landscape, Pascagoula, Miss.	2,757
1994	Ottawa Squaws, Toledo, Ohio	2,547
1993	Untouchables, Mobile, Ala.	2,495
1992	Put Together's, Muncie, Ind.	2,568
1991	Lindberg Shelter Insurance, Albia, Iowa	2,598
1990	Bristol Five, Bristol, Va.	2,492
1989	The Crickets, Minneapolis	2,627

1988	Dot's Trophy House, Lakeview, Ore.	2,531
1987	Miller's Chihuahua's, Plain City, Ohio	2,521
1986	Caffee Trucking, Wessington Springs, S.D.	2,530
1985	Fantastics Inc. *1, Detroit	2,532
1984	Spirit of Ely II, Ely, Nev.	2,511
1983	Scat's Brats No. 1, Simi Valley, Calif.	2,523
1982	Baldwin State Bank, Baldwin City, Kan.	2,526
1981	Matinee Five, Severna Park, Md.	2,631
1980	Erie Jr., Detroit Lakes, Minn.	2,414
1979	Silver Spur, Gallup, N.M.	2,475
1978	Dixie Doodles, Guntersville, Ala.	2,462
1977	Charlie Brown's, Superior, Wis.	2,535
1976	Partain Mechanical Contractor, Texarkana, Ark.	2,532
1975	Bowl-O-Mat Lounge, Muncie, Ind.	2,407
1974	Par-Matt Lanes, Oakland, Md.	2,479
1973	Killeen Merchants, Killeen, Texas	2,550
1972	Krolczyk's Plaza, Rosenberg, Texas	2,398
1971	Lady Bugs, Marietta, Ga.	2,366
1970	Sabre Lounge, Sierra Vista, Ariz.	2,646
1969	Five Pins, Fullerton, Calif.	2,416
1968	Just Made It, Westport, Conn.	2,448
1967	English's Windy Hill, Ithaca, N.Y.	2,569
1966	Jasperettes, Jasper, Texas	2,446
1965	Don's Medical Pharmacy, Havre, Mont.	2,480
1964	Miller Transporters, Ltd., Jackson, Miss.	2,635
1963	Embassy Bowl, Arcola, Ill.	2,436
1962	Reid Enterprises, Long Beach, Calif.	2,502
1961	Santelli Lumber Co., Lyons, N.Y.	2,478
1960	All Star Restaurant, Salina, Kan.	2,476
1959	Double J Tasty Freeze, Erie Co., N.Y.	2,488
1958	Manhattenite No. 2, New York	2,353
	Manx Hotel No. 3, San Francisco	2,353
1957	Johnnies Flower Shop, Van Wert, Ohio	2,408
1956	Sitnek Fuel, Clarksburg, W.Va.	2,455

* Record.

Doubles Event

1997	Tawnia Bryant-Londa Stout, Filer, Idaho and Kimberly, Idaho	*1,207
1996	Linda Chapman-Linda Hollins, Fort Worth, Texas	1,150
1995	Billie Baria, Mobile, Ala.-Jannice Petty, Saraland, Ala.	1,156
1994	Mary Ann Robinson-LaDora McPeters, Moorcraft, Wyo. and Casper, Wyo.	1,164
1993	Helen Self-Debbie Tesch, Monroe, La.	1,134
1992	Janelle Paksi-Jo Wendling, St. Johns, Mich.	1,110
1991	Shirley Piper-Rhonda Custer, Waynesboro, Pa.	1,150
1990	Anna Adams-Theresa Hruskocy, Whiting, Ind.	1,164
1989	Marianna Verdugo-Wanda Lundy, Tucson, Ariz.	1,123
1988	Shirley Stephan-Dianna Amos, Casa Grande, Ariz.	1,068
1987	Ann Wilson-Frances Scarborough, Ashdown and Texarkana, Ark.	1,130
1986	Kitty Eland-Arlene Magana, Ontario, and St. Chino, Calif.	1,110
1985	Peggy O'Neal-Carole Fischer, Catlettsburg, Ky. and Wayne, W.Va.	1,094
1984	Janice Daniels-Ursula Schroeder, Elizabethtown, Ky.	1,125
1983	Dorothy Croxton-Elizabeth Richardson, Philadelphia and Richmond, Va.	1,153
1982	Gloria Tayek-Gayle Comerer, Crystal Lake and Elgin, Ill.	1,067

1981 Constance Calveric-Barbara White,
      Sayre and Athens, Pa. 1,050
1980 Cindy Ortiz-Pauline Gullion, San Jose, Calif.
      and Toledo, Ohio.....................................1,070
1979 Frances Unruh-Diane Watts, Garden
      Grove and Cypress, Calif. 1,067
1978 Kris Ihlenfeldt-Margaret Thelander,
      Arlington Heights and Mount Prospect Ill. ..1,049
1977 Betty Jo Schilling-Coralee Yeager,
      Lockwood, Mo. 1,088
1976 Kay Larison-Margaret Bolyard, Hansen,
      Idaho 1,098
1975 Betty Cornelius-Opal Baker, Prescott and
      Blevins, Ark. 1,060
1974 Marie Smothermon-Doris Shaw, Tyro
      Coffeyville, Kan. 1,109
1973 Judy Hiler-Jerry Thompson, Springfield, Ill. 1,109
1972 Jerry Wise-Sue Minks, Higginsville, Mo. 1,109
1971 June Durham-Sharon Chambers,
      Jacksonville, Fla. 1,088
1970 Fern Clampitt-Marge Porter,
      Neodesha, Kan. 1,098
1969 Patricia Rose-Mary Redman,
      Sierra Madre, Calif. 1,047
1968 Lamar Wars-Betty Beamon, Alice, Texas........1,105
1967 Ann Schauer-Julia Nungesser,
      College Point, N.Y. 1,108
1966 Sally Riggin-Margie Porter, W. Monroe and
      Monroe, La. 1,100
1965 Nona Yaeger-Starr Cotton, Coos Bay and
      Empire, Ore. 1,135
1964 Dona Clapsaddle-Shirley Willis, Mason
      City, Iowa 1,129
1963 Ruby Williams-Bernice Hotchkins, Gary, Ind. 1,062
* Record.

Singles Event
1997 Roxanna Henson, Leavenowrth, Kan...............*695
1996 Janet Burrone, North Branford, Conn...............612
1995 Peg Childers, Compton, Ill. 628
1994 Shirley Coleman, Tucson, Ariz. 644
1993 Cynthia Hedge, Branford, Conn......................637
1992 Barb Davis, Mt. Morris, Ill. 655
1991 Darlene Schoon, Freeman, S.D. 656
1990 Denise Brockman, Cincinnati 642
1989 Beverly Tays, Crawfordsville, Ind. 689
1988 Pat Albert, Withee, Wis. 579
1987 Luann Stavola, Atlantic Highlands, N.J. 608
1986 Kitty Eland, Ontario, Calif. 656
1985 Bobbi Conkin, Kingsport, Tenn. 620
1984 Lorraine Hands, Lucan, Ontario 635
1983 Linda Anderson, Spanish Forks, Utah 631
1982 Sammie Gray, Martin, Tenn. 582
1981 Bonnie Bowley, Savage, Md. 594
1980 Connie Deasy, Ephrata, Wash. 583
1979 Connie Pelloni, Louisville, Colo. 593
1978 Faydra Austin, Miami 618
1977 Mary Ann Jocius, Riverdale, Md. 667
1976 Pat Wahner, Stanfield, Ore. 647
1975 Helen Jacobs, Valley, Neb. 609
1974 Patti Perkins, Tacoma, Wash. 635
1973 Marijoye Williams, San Marcos, Texas.............620
1972 Elvadeen Parris, Edina, Mo. 587
1971 Shyrlye White, Kansas City, Mo. 583
1970 Mae Rose Knauf, Mason, Mich. 602
1969 Marcia White, Rowland Heights, Calif. 607
1968 Beatrice Harm, Enola, Pa. 610
1967 Lillian Royer, Woodlyn, Pa. 613
1966 Kay Riddell, New Orleans...............................598

1965 Shirley Banks, El Cerrito, Calif. 604
1964 El Ferguson, Lansing, Mich. 650
1963 Vivian Strout, Nashville, Tenn. 586
* Record.

All Events
1997 Shirley Petty, Pocahontas, Ark. 1,804
1996 Linda Boeheme, Milwaukee 1,708
1995 Lisa Rascon, Augusta, Ga...............................1,711
1994 Peggy Bush, Idaho Falls, Idaho 1,727
1993 Judy Guitreau, Geismar, La. 1,713
1992 Sandy Woelk, Kingsville, Ontario...................1,651
1991 Ruth Reimer, St. Catharine, Ontario 1,661
1990 Pamela Schmal, Winston-Salem, N.C. 1,664
1989 Del Tkach, Bismarck, N.D. 1,671
1988 Linda Veatch, Madera, Calif. 1,608
1987 Kathy Burley, Bethlehem, Pa. 1,610
1986 Kitty Eland, Ontario, Calif. *1,819
1985 Bobbi Conkin, Kingsport, Tenn. 1,679
1984 Janet Marsteller, Sandy Lake, Pa. 1,711
1983 Peg Borer, Albion, Neb. 1,689
1982 Brenda Draper, Auburn, Neb. 1,672
1981 Doris Fletcher, Chestertown, Md. 1,618
1980 Nadine Collins, Peotone, Ill. 1,592
1979 Robyn Bodin, Norman, Okla. 1,611
1978 Faydra Austin, Miami 1,798
1977 Mary Ann Jocius, Riverdale, Md. 1,672
1976 Beverly Morgan, Long Beach, Calif. 1,678
1975 Barbara Perkins, Waynesville, Mo. 1,637
1974 Patti Perkins, Tacoma, Wash. 1,612
1973 Bernadine Sobotta, Lansing, Ill. 1,660
1972 Elvadeen Parris, Edina, Mo. 1,587
1971 Kathleen Morgan, Devonshire, Bermuda 1,624
1970 Mary Dixon, Abilene, Texas 1,668
1969 Beverly Pluhowsky, Phoenix 1,668
1968 May Monroe, Childress, Texas 1,626
1967 Pat Beasley, Lansing, Mich. 1,653
1966 Gail Arce, Tampa, Fla. 1,644
1965 Trudy Hatton, N. Vancouver, British Columbia1,631
1964 Emma Randolph, Memphis, Tenn. 1,772
* Record.

Division III Winners

Team Event
1997 Plum Loco, Longmont, Colo.......................*2,482
1996 Lee'z Restaurant, Shawano, Wis. 2,438
1995 Z-92 Zeesters, Holbrook, Ariz. 2,380
1994 Arch of Wyoming, Hanna, Wyo..................2,266

Doubles Event
1997 Virginia Davis-Sandra Hudnall, ...*1,106
      Des Moines, Iowa
1996 Roxanne Lynds-Suzanne Fisher 1,043
      Broad Brook, Conn., Hummelstown, Pa.
1995 Michelle Smith-Gloria Gillespie,
      Seaford, Del. 1,102
1994 Lindy Whillock-Amy Dubberly,
      Lubbock, Texas......................................1,085

Singles Event
1997 Michelle Ferguson, Tacoma, Was. *625
1996 Sue Tschcepe, Cypress, Texas 574
1995 Mary F. Jones, Henderson, Nev. 582
1994 Mary Dale, Santa Monica, Calif. 616

All Events
1997 Thelma Ugay, Jeddah, Saudi Arabia *1,656
1996 Danyele Ely, Gautier, Miss.............................1,564
1995 Stephanie Pulda, Yuma, Ariz. 1,554
1994 Natalie Chopey, Alameda, Calif.....................1,568
* Record.

WIBC Championship Tournament and Queens Winners

Alphabetical listing and year won. Women with hyphenated names are listed under their maiden name. (T-team event, A-all events, D-doubles events, S-singles, Q-Queens Tournament, C-Classic Division, O-Open Division, I-Division I, II-Division II, III-Division III.)

A

Abbott, JoAnn, Texas City, Texas . . . . .T (I) 70
Abel, Joy, Lansing, Ill. .T (I) 66
Abernathy, Margaret, Marietta, Ga. . . . . .T (II) 71
Abraham, Hattie, Milwaukee . . . . .A (I) 22
Acker, Jean, Chicago . . . . . .D (I) 16, 18, 24; T (I) 24, 25
Ackerman, Leah, Sheldon, Iowa . . . . .A (I) 70
Adamek, Donna, Apple Valley, Calif. . . . . .Q 79, 80;
                        D (O) 81, 82; T (O) 81, 87, 92
Adams, Anna, Whiting, Ind. . . . . .D (II) 90
Adams, Cindy, Camarillo, Calif. . . . . .T (I) 93
Adams, Ginny, Norwalk, Calif . . . . .T (O) 83
Adams, Teresa, Pocomoke City, Md. . . . . .A (I) 97
Adamson, R., Kansas City, Mo . . . . .T (I) 29
Albarello, Dolly, Chicago Ridge, Ill. . . . . .T(O) 88
Albert, Pat, Withee, Wis. . . . . .S (II) 88
Alexander, Katherine, Los Angeles . . . . .T (I) 80
Allen, Clara, Detroit . . . . .D (I) 42
Allen, Rose, Chicago . . . . .T (I) 48
Almeida, Cathy, Pennsauken, N.J. . . . . .Q 87
Alongi, Sarah, Chicago . . . . .T (I) 54
Alsip, Linda, Aurora, Ill .T (I) 80
Altman, Bea, Chicago . . . . .T (I) 64
Alva, Olivia, Moorpark, Calif. . . . . .T (II) 83
Alvarez, Dee, Tampa, Fla. . . . . .D (O) 88
Alwes, M., Kansas City, Mo. . . . . .T (I) 29
Amos, Dianna, Casa Grande, Ariz. . . . . .D (II) 88
Amrein, Florence, Akron, Ohio . . . . .S (I) 27
Anastasio, Joann, Augusta, Maine . . . . .D (I) 90
Anderson, Geri, Waukesha, Wis. . . . . .T (O) 91
Anderson, Linda, Spanish Fork, Utah . . . . .S (II) 83
Anderson, Lorraine, Northville, Mich. . . . . .S (O) 89
Anderson, Merilee, Minier, Ill. . . . . .T (1) 95
Anderson, Wilma, Los Angeles . . . . .T (I) 62, 63
Ann, Patiy, Arlington Heights, Ill. . . . . .T (O) 86;
                                            S (O) 92; Q 90
Arce, Gail, Tampa, Fla. . . . . .A (II) 66
Argent, Flossie, Florissant, Mo. . . . . .A (I) 62
Armstrong, Billie, Lakeview, Ore. . . . . .T (II) 88
Army, Arlene, Millbury, Mass. . . . . .A (I) 87
Asher, Christy, Anaheim, Calif. . . . . .T (O) 93; T(C) 94
Austin, Faydra, Miami . . . . .A, S (II) 78

B

Boginski, Marge, Berwyn, Ill. . . . . .S (I) 53
Bagley, LaVerne, Marietta, Ga. . . . . .T (II) 71
Baird, Mary Lou, Harvey, Ill. . . . . .T (O) 71, 77
Baker, Myrtle, Chicago .D (I) 25
Baker, Opal, Blevins, Ark. . . . . .D (I) 75
Baker, Vicki, St. Paris, Ohio. . . . . .S (I) 85
Baker, Zetta, Detroit . . . . .D (I) 31
Baldy, Loraine, Milwaukee . . . . .T (I) 37, 38; D (I) 36
Ball, Helen, Marietta, Ga. . . . . .T (II) 71
Banks, Shirley, El Cerrito, Calif. . . . . .S (II) 65
Baria, Billie, Mobile, Ala. . . . . .D (II) 95
Barnes, Donna, Perryton, Texas . . . . .S (I) 97
Barnes, Margaret, Shelton, Wash. . . . . .T (II) 97
Barnett, Arlene, Jasper, Texas . . . . .T (II) 66
Barrette, Leanne, Yukon, Okla. . . . . .A (O) 87
Basiak, Bridgett, Chesterton, Ind. . . . . .D (I) 82
Basile, Dolores, Alsip, Ill. . . . . .T (I) 72

Bassett, Helen, Peoria, Ill. . . . . .S (I) 54
Bates, Maryann, Severna Park, Md. . . . . .T (II) 66
Batey, Dorothy, East Orange, N.J. . . . . .S (I) 81
Baude, Elizabeth, Springboro, Ohio. . . . . .T (O) 82
Beamon, Betty, Alice, Texas . . . . .D (II) 68
Beard, Emma, Fort Wayne, Ind. . . . . .D (I) 47
Beasley, Pat, Lansing, Mich. . . . . .A (II) 67
Beasley, Teresa, Richmond Hills, Ga. . . . . .T (I) 90
Beattie, Geri, Dearborn Heights, Mich . . . . .D (O) 79
Beck, Lorraine, St. Louis .T (I) 76
Belcher, Janie, Savannah, Ga. . . . . .T (I) 90
Bell, Deanne, Baldwin City, Kan. . . . . .T (II) 82
Bell, Judy, Lithonia, Ga. .D (I) 17
Bell, Susan, Baldwin City, Kan. . . . . .T (II) 82
Bender, Joan, Arvada, Colo . . . . .S (O) 69
Berghaus, Cornella, St. Louis . . . . .T (I) 20
Berlanger, Cindy, San Antonio, Texas . . . . .S (C) 96
Billing, Gertha, Hartford, Conn. . . . . .T (I) 87
Binggeli, Kay, St. Louis . . . . .T (I) 76
Bishop, Lisa, Belleville, Mich. . . . . .T (O) 95
Black, Janet, Fort Huachuca, Ariz. . . . . .T (II) 70
Blacksher, Bertha, Uriah, Ala. . . . . .A (I) 93
Blackwell, Judy, Marietta, Ga. . . . . .T (II) 71
Blake, Laura, Phoenix . . . . .D (I) 73
Blomenberg, Alayne, Cranston, R.I. . . . . .T (C) 97
Bodin, Robyn, Norman, Okla. . . . . .A (I) 79
Boehme, Linda, Milwaukee . . . . .A (II) 96
Bolden, Mamie, Detroit .T (I) 71
Bolden, Viola, Detroit . . . . .T (i) 71
Bolt, Mae, Berwyn, Ill. . . . . .T (O) 58, 61, 64, 77;
                        A (O) 58; S (O) 59, 78
Boluyt, Marie, Grand Rapids, Mich. . . . . .T 50
Bolyard, Margaret, Hansen, Idaho . . . . .D (II) 76
Booth, Pat, Memphis, Tenn . . . . .A (I) 77
Bopp, Jeonette, Milwaukee . . . . .T (O) 91
Borer, Peg, Albion, Neb. .A (II) 83
Borgmann, Darlene, Longmont, Colo. . . . . .T(III)97
Bostelman, Phyllis, St. Louis . . . . .T (II) 32
Boundy, G., St. Louis . . . . .T (I) 16, 17
Bourbon, Neil, Jasper, Texas . . . . .T (II) 66
Bouvia, Gloria, Gresham, Ore . . . . . .S 66; D (O) 69, 70;
                                            T (O) 74
Bowhall, Ruth, Howell, Mich. . . . . .T (I) 85
Bowley, Bonnie, Savage, Md . . . . .S (II) 81
Bowman, Helen, Champlin, Minn . . . . .T (II) 89
Boyle, Valves, Chicago . . . . .T (I) 27
Boxberger, Loa, Russell, Kan . . . . . . .T (O) 69, 73; Q 78
Brandon, Madlyn, Philadelphia . . . . .T (I) 91
Brands, Delphene, Alsip, Ill . . . . .T (I) 72
Brazeal, Blanche, Kansas City, Mo. . . . . .T (I) 29
Breault, Vivian, Westport, Conn . . . . .T (II) 68
Brede, Susan, Alexandria, Minn. . . . . .T (II) 78
Brennan, Cindy, Missoula, Mont. . . . . .D (I) 86
Brewer, Joan, Tucson, Ariz . . . . .T (I) 86
Brichta, Dorothy, Detroit . . . . .T (I) 49
Bridgmon, Tami, Lakeview, Ore. . . . . .T (II) 88
Bridgmon, Virginia, Lakeview, Ore. . . . . .T (II) 88
Briggs, Mary, Lakewood Calif. . . . . .T (I) 67
Brignall, Mamie, Chicago . . . . .T (I) 22
Brison, Mena, Brooklyn, N.Y. . . . . .D (I) 96
Britton, Wilma, Plain City, Ohio . . . . .T (II) 87

Brockman, Denise, Cincinnati . . . . .S (II) 90
Brooks, Juanita, Robinson, Ill. . . . . .T (I) 75
Brower, Verna, Texarkana, Texas . . . . .T (II) 76
Brown, Rita, Minier, Ill. .T (I) 95
Bryant, Tawnia, Filer, Idaho . . . . .D (II) 97
Buckner, Pam, Reno, Nev. . . . . .Q 76
Buge, Rita, Glenview, Ill. . . . . .T (O) 71
Bundrick, Mary, Chicago . . . . .T (I) 56
Burby, Theresa, Hartford, Conn. . . . . .T (I) 87
Burcham, Pat, Arcola, Ill. . . . . .T (I) 63
Burke, Alma, Chicago . . . . .D (I) 27; T (I) 30
Burke, Geri, Westport, Conn. . . . . .T (II) 68
Burley, Kathy, Bethlehem, Pa. . . . . .A (II) 87
Burling, Catherine, Cincinnati . . . . .T (I) 34
Burmeister, Barb, Elkhart, Ind. . . . . .T (II) 96
Burney, Mary Ann, Lakeland, Fla. . . . . .T (O) 90
Burns, Nina, Chicago . . . . .A, T (I) 42
Burrone, Janet, North Branford, Conn. . . . . .S (II) 96
Burton, Doris, Birmingham, Ala. . . . . .T (I) 77
Bush, Peggy, Idaho Falls, Idaho . . . . .A (II) 94
Butterworth, Mae, Columbus, Ohio . . . . .D (I) 19

C

Caffee, Ada, Wessington Springs, S.D. . . . . . . .T (II) 63
Caldwell, Billie, Chicago . . . . .D (I) 72
Callaway, Helen, Jackson, Miss. . . . . .T (II) 64
Calveric, Constance, Sayre, Pa. . . . . .D (II) 81
Calzone, Ellen, Westport, Conn. . . . . .T (II) 64
Cameron, Evelyn, Howell, Mich. . . . . .T (I) 85
Cameron, Kendra, Gambrills, Md. . . . . .A (C) 97
Cantaline, Anita, Detroit . . . . .A (I) 57; T (I) 57, 59
Carbone, Jean, Kenosha, Wis. . . . . .S (I) 79
Carlon, Martha, Buffalo, N.Y. . . . . .T (O) 75
Carmeon, Toni, Elkhart, Ind. . . . . .T (II) 96
Carroll, Jacqueline, Philadelphia . . . . .T (I) 91
Carter, LaVerne, Las Vegas . . . . .A (I) 51; T (O) 74
Carter, Paula, Miami . . . . .S (O) 90
Cartier, Marg, Windsor, Ontario . . . .T (I) 96; T (I) 97
Casepo, Ruth, Honolulu . . . . .T (I) 73
Casey, Mildred, Chicago . . . . .T (I) 26
Cassidy, Sharon, Son Mateo, Calif. . . . . .T (I) 88
Caulum, Anita, Indianapolis . . . . .T (I) 51
Cavalini, Edith, Riverdale, Ill. . . . . .T (O) 71
Ceberano, Myrtle, Honolulu . . . . .T (I) 73
Cetinsky, Sophie, Cleveland . . . . .T (I) 52
Chadbourne, Virginia, Detroit Lokes, Minn. . . . . . .T (II) 80
Chambers, Sharon, Jacksonville, Fla. . . . . .D (II) 71
Chaplin, Clara, Chicago . . . . .T (I) 31
Chapman, Emily, Chicago . . . . .T (I) 26
Champman, Joanne, Blencoe, Iowa . . . . .T (O) 69, 73
Chatman, Linda, Fort Worth, Texas . . . . .D (II) 96
Cheney, Debra, Minneapolis . . . . .T (II) 89
Childers, Peg, Compton, Ill. . . . . .S (II) 95
Ching, Edith, Honolulu .T (I) 73
Choat, Cora, Lyndenhurst,Ill. . . . . .T (I) 84
Chong, Kahili, Honolulu . . . . .T (I) 73
Chopey, Natalie, Almeda, Calif. . . . . .A (III) 94
Christensen, Wilda, Fort Collins, Colo. . . . . .T (I) 69
Clampit, Fern, Neodesha, Kan. . . . . .D (II) 70
Clapsaddle, Dona, Mason City, Iowa . . . . .D (II) 64
Clatterbuck, Corann, Deer Park, Md. . . . . .T (II) 74
Clay, Brenda, Philadelphia . . . . .T (I) 91
Clegg, Kelly, Burbank, Ill. . . . . .T (O) 88
Clegg, Sheila, Burbank, Ill. . . . . .T (O) 78,88
Clemensen, Marie, Chicago . . . . .S (I) 34
Clifford, Hattie, Kansas City, Mo. . . . . .T (I) 29
Coburn, Doris, Buffalo . . . . .T (O) 70, 72

Coburn-Carroll, Cindy, Tonawanda, N.Y . . . .D (O) 91;
Q 92, D (C) 94
Cochrane, Charlotte, DeKalb, Ill. . . . . .A (II) 96
Codera, Bea, Fort Huachuca, Ariz. . . . . .T (II) 70
Coffman, Lois, Fort Collins, Colo . . . . .T (I) 69
Collins, Nadine, Peotone, Ill. . . . . .A (II) 80
Collura, Gloria, Toronto . . . . .D (O) 93
Collura, Karen, Toronto . . . . .S (O) 93; D (O) 93
Coleman, Shirley, Tucson, Ariz. . . . . .S (II) 94
Combs, Linda, Shelton, Wash. . . . . .T (I) 97
Comerer, Gayle, Elgin, Ill. . . . . .D (II) 82
Compton, Jill, Minier, Ill. . . . . .T (I) 95
Conkin, Bobbi, Kingsport, Tenn. . . . . .A (II) 85; S (II) 85
Cook, Esther, Seattle . . . . .D (I) 51
Coombs, Viola, Mesa, Ariz. . . . . .D (I) 77
Cooper, Vicki, Columbio City, Ind. . . . . .T (II) 92
Copeland, Rochell, Detroit . . . . .T (II) 85
Corbell, Karen, Newport News, Va. . . . . .T (I) 90
Cordes, Georgene, Bloomington, Minn. . . . . .D (O) 76
Cornelius, Betty, Prescott, Ark. . . . . .D (I) 75
Costello, Pat, Orlando, Fla . . . . .T (O) 69, 73, 81;
D (O) 82, 88
Costello, Patty, Scranton, Pa. . . . . .T (O) 70, 72
Cotton, Starr, Empire, Ore. . . . . .D (II) 65
Cousino, Denise, Erie, Mich. . . . . .T (II) 94
Coverdell, Ethel, Orlando, Fla. . . . . .A (I) 76
Coward, Shelby, Fort Huochuca, Ariz. . . . . .T (II) 70
Cowger, A.E., St. Louis .T (I) 16
Cox, Linda, Rosenberg, Texas . . . . .T (II) 72
Craig, Lorene, Kansas City, Mo. . . . . .S (I) 52
Cranson, Bonnie, Milan, Mich. . . . . .T (I) 84
Crawford, Sande, Columbia Heights, Minn. . . . . .D (I) 95
Cravens, Linda, Oblong, Ill. . . . . .T (I) 75
Cross, Cathie, Brooks, Maine . . . . .D (I) 90
Cross, Evelyn, Robinson, Ill. . . . . .T (I) 75
Crowe, Chris, Prospect, Ky. . . . . .A (I) 91
Crowley, Margaret, Lyons, N.Y . . . . .T (II) 61
Crowther, Karen, Canogo Park, Calif. . . . . .T (O) 81
Croxton, Dorothy, Philadelphia . . . . .D (II) 83
Cruchon, Maxine, Detroit . . . . .T (I) 57, 59
Crull, Ann, Indianapolis . . . . .T (I) 51
Culpepper, Pat, Lakelond, Flo. . . . . .T (O) 90
Custer, Rhonda, Waynesboro, Pa. . . . . .D (II) 91

D

Dale, Mary, Santa Monica, Calif. . . . . .S (III) 94
Dalbec, Ruth, Superior, Wis. . . . . .T (II) 77
Dane, Pamela, Monticello, Minn. . . . . .T (I) 78
Daniels, Cheryl, Detroit . . . . .T (O) 95
Daniels, Janice, Elizabethtown, Ky. . . . . .D (II) 84
Dardeen, Marge, Cincinnati . . . . .A (I) 47
Davenport, Diana, Shreveport, La. . . . . .T (O) 89
David, Kitty, Jackson, Miss. . . . . .T (II) 64
Davidson, Dede, San Jose, Calif. . . . . .Q 91
Davis, Barb, Mt. Morris, Ill. . . . . .S (II) 92
Davis, Barbara, Sterling Heights, Mich. . . . . .S (I) 47
Davis, Faye, Bristol, Va. . . . . .T (II) 90
Davis, Michelle, Baytown, Texas . . . . . .D (I) 94; A (I) 94
Davis, Patsy, Longmont, Colo. . . . . .T (III) 97
Davis, Virginia, Des Moines, Iowa . . . . .D (III) 97
Davison, Morge, Grand Ropids, Mich . . . . .T (I) 50
Dawson, Edna, Killeen, Texas . . . . .T (II) 73
Deal, Joanne, Wheaton, Minn. . . . . .T (I) 89
Deasy, Connie, Ephrata, Wash. . . . . .S (II) 80
DeCaire, Marily, Superior, Wis. . . . . .T (II) 77
Deering, Emily, Chicago . . . . .T (I) 42
Deighton, Diana, Toledo, Ohio . . . . .T (II) 94

J

K

L

M

Manguso, Beverly, Phoenix . . . . .A (II) 69
Mankie, Ella, Madison, Wis. . . . . .S, A (I) 36
Manning, Kathy, Wessington Springs, S.D. . . . . . .T (II) 86
Mansfield, LeeAnne, Muncie, Ind. . . . . .T (II) 75
Mansfield, Shirley, North Glenn, Colo. . . . . .D (I) 76
Marsteller, Janet, Sandy Lake, Pa. . . . . .A (II) 84
Martin, Faye, Marietta, Ga. . . . . .T (II) 71
Martin, Helen, Cleveland . . . . .T (I) 36
Martin, Jane, Long Beach, Calif. . . . . .T (II) 62
Martin, Lillian, Bristol, Va. . . . . .T (II) 90
Martin, Sylvia, Philadelphia . . . . .D (I) 59
Mason, Cheri, Lansing, Ill. . . . . .S (I) 80
Mason, Cindy, Sunnyvale, Calif. . . . . .T (O) 81
Massey, Phyllis, Alameda, Calif. . . . . .Q 68
Mataya, Clara, St. Louis . . . . .S (I) 49
Matsuzaki, Fujio, Tokyo . . . . .T (O) 84
Matthews, Merle, Los Angeles . . . . . .T (I) 62, 63; D (I) 48
Mattingly, Betty, Oakland, Md. . . . . .T (II) 74
Mattingly, Dixie Lee, Lexington, Ky. . . . . .T (I) 83
Maw, Betty, Buffalo, N.Y. . . . . .D 56; T (O) 75
Mayer, Alice, Erie City, N.Y. . . . . .T (II) 59
Mayer, Isabella, Erie City, N.Y. . . . . .S (I) 59
McAllister, Lois, Detroit . . . . .T (I) 49
McCormick, Pat, Grand Rapids, Mich. . . .A (I) 59; T (I) 67
McCoy, Cris, Guntersville, Ala. . . . . .T (II) 78
McCurley, Jenny, Rosenberg, Texas . . . . .T (II) 78
McDaniels, Marge, Mountain View, Calif. . . . . . .S (I) 60
McDonald, Kathy, Buffalo, N.Y. . . . . .T (O) 72
McFall, Eunice, Ithaca N.Y. . . . . .T (II) 67
McGinnis, Brenda, Laguna Hills, Calif. . . . . .T (I) 86
McGovern, Cleo, Silver Grove, Ky . . . . .S (I) 50
McIntosh, Cindy, Greybull, Wyo. . . . . .D (I) 97
McKee, Carol, Salina, Kan. . . . . .T (I) 60
McKeller, Harriet, Chicago . . . . .T (I) 18
McLaughlin, Nellie, Detroit . . . . .T (I) 49, 53
McManigal, Vi, Fullerton, Calif. . . . . .T (II) 69
McPeters, LaDora, Casper, Wyo. . . . . .D (II) 94
McVay, Audrey, Kansas City, Mo. . . . . .S (I) 32
Meconnahey, Ann, Bear, Del. . . . . .D (O) 90
Meinholz, Marilyn, Madison, Wis. . . . . .T (II) 94
Melcher, Darlen, Salina, Kan. . . . . .T (II) 60
Melvin, Margi, Newark, Del. . . . . .D (O) 90
Mentzer, Vonna, Wessington Springs, S.D. . . . .T (II) 86
Merlo, Janet, Roswell, N.M. . . . . .T (I) 74
Merrigan, Rita, New York . . . . .T (II) 58
Meyer, Doris, San Francisco . . . . .T (II) 58
Meyer-Welty, Michelle, Vacaville, Calif. . . . . . . .S (O) 88
Meyer, Vicki, Alexandria, Minn. . . . . .T (I) 78
Meyers, Faye, Lexington, Ky. . . . . .T (I) 83
Mica, Angela, St. Louis . . . . .T (I) 46
Michal, Shirlee, Chicago . . . . .T (I) 54
Mielke, Shirley, Oconomowoc, Wis. . . . . .T (O) 91
Mikiel, Val, Detroit . . . . .S (I) 46
Miller, Carol, Waukesha, Wis. . . . . . .A (I) 67; D (O) 74
Miller-Mackie, Dana, Fort Worth, Texas . . . . . . .S (O) 90
Miller, Debbie, Muncie, Ind. . . . . .T (II) 92
Miller, Dorothy, Chicago . . . . . .D (I) 29, 34, 40; A (I) 38;
 T (1) 28, 31, 33, 35, 40, 48
Miller, Joan, Roswell, N.M. . . . . .T (I) 74
Miller, Norma, Plain City, Ohio . . . . .T (II) 87
Miller, Pat, Bristol, Tenn. . . . . .T (II) 90
Mills, Boots, Cincinnati . . . . .T (I) 60
Mills (Jocius), Mary Ann, Riverdale, Md. . . . . .A S (II) 77
Mine, Estelle, Rockford, Ill. . . . . .T (I) 21
Minning, Lynne, Aurora, Ill. . . . . .T (I) 80
Minks, Sue, Higginsville, Mo. . . . . .D (II) 72
Mitchell, Ella, Oxnard, Calif. . . . . .T (I) 93
Mitchell, Jane, Birmingham, Ala. . . . . .T (I) 77

Mitchell, Joyce, Baldwin City, Kan. . . . . .T (II) 82
Mivelaz, Betty, Tujunga, Calif. . . . . .T (I) 67
Mizobuchi, Hidemi, Tokyo . . . . .T (O) 80
Mochienkamp, Ruth, St. Louis . . . . .T (I) 46
Mokier, Mary, Los Angeles . . . . .T (I) 62 63
Monroe, Margaret, Fowlerville, Mich. . . . . .T (I) 85
Monroe, May, Childress, Texas . . . . .A (II) 68
Monroe, Minnie, Lyons, N.Y. . . . . .T (II) 61
Monterosso, Irene, Flushing, N.Y. . . . . .Q 63
Mooney, Jette, South Bend, Ind. . . . . .D (I) 60
Mooney, Joyce, Pittsburgh . . . . .A (I) 71
Moore, Edith, Detroit . . . . .T (I) 71
Moore, Patricia, Killeen, Texas . . . . .T (II) 73
Morehouse, Artel, San Francisco . . . . .T (II) 58
Morgan, Beverly, Long Beach, Calif. . . . . .A (I) 76
Morgan, Kathleen, Devonshire, Bermuda . . . . .A (II) 71
Morris, Betty, Stockton, Calif. . . . .T (O) 74, 89; A (O) 76,
 79; S (O) 79, 80
Morris, Velda, Del City, Okla. . . . . .A (I) 80
Morton, Deborah, Hampton, Va. . . . . .T (I) 82
Morton, Jean, Hampton, Va. . . . . .T (I) 82
Muhly, Kathy, Severna Park, Md. . . . . .T (II) 81
Mullins, Lois, Lexington, Ky. . . . . .T (I) 83
Murney, Mary Lou, Chicago . . . . .T (I) 61
Murph, Kari, Dayton, Ohio . . . . .S (O) 93
Mustari, Dorothy, Chicago . . . . .T (I) 65

N

Naccarato, Jeanne, Tacoma, Wash. D (O) 83, T (O) 86; (C) 96
Nagi, Massayo, Tokyo . . . .(O) 80
Nelson, Ada, Rockford, Ill. . . . . .T (I) 21
Nelson, Carol, Simi Valley, Calif. . . . . .T (II) 83
Nelson, Debbie, Capron, Ill. . . . . .T (I) 94
Newman, Joyce, Texas City, Texas . . . . .T (I) 70
Newlin, Barbara, Robinson, Ill. . . . . .T (I) 75
Newton, Elaine, Park Forest, Ill. . . . . .S (I) 61
Niblock, Mary, Howell, Mich. . . . . .T (I) 85
Nichols, Lorrie, Algonquin, Ill. . . . . .A (O) 71; A (C) 96
Nicol, Koren, Hamilton, Ont. . . . . .D (I) 92
Noe, Lucille, Columbus, Ohio . . . . .S (I) 56
Nordman, Corine, Cincinnati . . . . .T (I) 34
Norman, Carol, Ardmore, Okla. . . . . .A (O) 90; T (C) 96
Norman, Edie Jo, Miami . . . . .T (O) 76
Norton, Virginia, Cypress, Calif. . . . . .T (O) 74, 83;
 A (O) 75, 81, 83; S (O) 81
Notaro, Phyllis, Brant, N.Y. . . . . .T (O) 75
Nungesser, Julia, College Point, N.Y. . . . . .D (II) 67

O

Obermeier, Lorrie, St. Helens, Ore. . . . . .T (I) 92
Oldaker, Donna, Lake Station, Ind. . . . . .D (I) 82
O'Leary, Elizabeth, Wheaton, Minn. . . . . .T (I) 89
Oleske, Joan, Lyndhurst, N.J. . . . . .D (I) 67
Olive, Iva, Ciollup, N.M. . . . . .T (II) 79
Olszewski, PaHi, Toledo, Ohio . . . . .T (O) 85
O'Neal, Tia, Aurora, Ill. . . . . .T (1) 80
Opicka, Joann, Milwaukee . . . . .T (O) 91
Orendorf, Beatrice, Bridgeville, Del. . . . . .S (I) 79
Ortiz, Cindy, San Jose, Calif. . . . . .D (II) 80
Ortner, Beverly, Tucson, Ariz. . . . . .T (O) 69
Osaki, Alieen, Honolulu . . . . .T (I) 73
Owen, Beth, Dallas . . . . .S (O) 95; A (O) 95

P

Padden, Gerry, St. Louis . . . . .T (I) 76
Paksi, Janelle, St. Johns, Mich. . . . . .D (II) 92
Pappan, Leslie, Tulsa, Okla. . . . . .D (I) 94
Parks, Norma, Raytown, Mo. . . . . .S (I) 68

Parr, Phoebe, Ithaca, N.Y. . . . . .T (II) 67
Parrish, Elvadean, Edina, Mo. . . . . .S (II) 72
Patterson, Rene, Tucson, Ariz. . . . . .T (I) 86
Pawlak, Jacqueline, Wappingers Falls, N.Y. . . . . . .S (I) 96
Pearson, Barb, Shelton, Wash. . . . . .T (II) 97
Pease, Jeanette, Richmond, Va. . . . . .A (I) 75
Pelloni, Connie, Louisville, Colo. . . . . .S (II) 79
Penn, Gloria, Plainfield, N.J. . . . . .D (I) 87
Penn, Virginia, St. Louis . . . . .T (I) 46
Perdue, Tillie, Gallup, N.M. . . . . .T (II) 79
Perez, Rachel, San Antonio . . . . .D (C) 94
Perkins, Barbara, Fort Leonard Wood, Mo. . . . . . .A (II) 75
Perkins, Patti, Tacoma, Wash. . . . . .S, A (II) 74
Peters, Veronica, Syracuse, N.Y. . . . . .D (I) 35
Petersen, Lorraine, Garden Grove, Calif. . . . . .D (I) 70
Petty, Jannice, Saraland, Ala. . . . . .D (II) 95
Petty, Shirley, Pocahontas, Ark. . . . . .A (II) 97
Phemester, Jan, Daly City, Calif. . . . . .T (I) 79
Philippson, Melody, Colfax, Iowa . . . . .D (O) 85
Phillips, Betty, Los Angeles . . . . .T (I) 62, 63
Philson, Vanda, Sidney, Neb. . . . . .S (I) 76
Piche, Mary, Burlington, Ontario . . . . .D (I) 92
Pichinino, Gloria, San Francisco . . . . .T (II) 58
Pickle, Janice, Tucson, Ariz. . . . . .A (I) 69
Piper, Carlotta, Brooklyn, N.Y. . . . . .D (I) 96
Piper, Myrtle, Chicago . . . . .T (I) 55
Piper, Shirley, Waynesboro, Pa. . . . . .D (II) 91
Pipher, Donna, Hanaa, Wyo. . . . . .T (III) 94
Piscovich, Ann, Ely, Nev. . . . . .T (II) 84
Piszczek, Bonnie, Wauwatosa, Wis. . . . . .A (I) 90
Plank, Schanda, Grand Rapids, Mich. . . . . .S (I) 87
Plumley, Patsy, West Helena, Ark. . . . . .D (I) 75
Pomeroy, Gertrude, Detroit . . . . .D (I) 31
Porter, Evelyn, Chicago . . . . .D (II) 72
Porter, Marge, Neodesha, Kan. . . . . .D (II) 70
Porter, Margie, Monroe, La. . . . . .D (II) 66
Postma, Sandra, Lansing, Ill. Q95
Powell, Cindy, Navarre, Ohio Q75
Powell, June, Toledo, Ohio . . . . .T (I) 55
Powers, Connie, Detroit . . . . .D (I) 39; T (I) 57,59
Pratt, Blanche, Chicago . . . . .T (I) 27
Preul, Bernell, Denison, Iowa . . . . .D (I) 79
Priest, Jackie, Severna Park, Md. . . . . .T (II) 81
Primosch, Mary, Cleveland . . . . .T (I) 52
Prince, Florence, Ithaca, N.Y. . . . . .T (II) 67
Probert, Florence, St. Louis . . . . .D (I) 38
Pucel, Pam, Joliet, Ill. .T (O) 86
Pulda, Stephanie, Yuma, Ariz. . . . . .A (III) 95

Q

Quin, Zoe, Chicago . . . . .T (I) 18; D (I) 23
Quinn, Mary, Buffalo .D (I) 56

R

Raber, Ann, St. Louis .T (I) 46
Raddatz, Dawn, E. Northport, N.Y. . . . . . . .D (O) 75, 80
Rader, Angie, Pascagoula, Miss. . . . . .T (II) 95
Rohn, Fritzie, Chicago . . . . .T (I) 27, 28, 31, 33, 35, 40;
                                          D (I) 30, 34
Rainone, Debbie, Cleveland . . . . .D (O) 76
Ramsey, Bernice, Salina, Kan. . . . . .T (II) 60
Randolph, Emma, Memphis, Tenn. . . . . .A (II) 64
Rascon, Lisa, Augusta, Ga. . . . . .A (II) 95
Rasmussen, Cheryl, Osseo, Minn. . . . . .D (I) 95
Rearick, Ann, Pooler, Ga. . . . . .T (I) 90
Redel, Marcella, Sierra Vista, Ariz . . . . .T (II) 70
Redfox, Ruth, Toledo, Ohio . . . . .D (I) 63

Redman, Rose, Sierra Madre, Calif. . . . . .D (II) 69
Reece, Ethel, Wilson, N.C. . . . . .T (O) 70
Reeder, Rose, Van Wert, Ohio . . . . .T (II) 57
Reese, Jane, Wilmington, Del. . . . . .T (O) 87
Reese, Sue, Novato, Calif. . . . . .D (O) 84
Reich, Eliza, Chicago . . . . .S (I) 25
Reichley, Susie, Waco, Texas . . . . .A (I) 68
Reid, Darleen, Long Beach, Calif. . . . . .T (II) 62
Reilly, Lita, Chicago . . . . .D (I) 16, 18; T (I) 21
Reimer, Ruth, St. Catharines, Ontario . . . . .A (II) 91
Remmick, Betty, Denver . . . . .D (O) 65, 72
Repking, Bernette, St. Louis . . . . .T (II) 66
Resk, Gertrude, Chicago . . . . .T (I) 24, 25
Reus, Betty, Grand Rapids, Mich. . . . . .D (I) 39
Rice, Gloria, Mobile, Ala. . . . . .T (II) 93
Richardson, Elizabeth, Richmond, Va. . . . . .D (II) 83
Richardson, Reta, Boise City, Okla. . . . . .A (I) 73
Richter, Elsie, Long Beach, Calif. . . . . .T (II) 62
Rickard, Robbie, Los Angeles . . . . .T (I) 62, 63
Riddell, Kay, New Orleans . . . . .S (II) 66
Riggin, Sally, W. Monroe, La. . . . . .D (I) 69
Rincon, Lina, San Antonio, Texas . . . . .D (I) 91
Rinehart, Mary Lou, Albia, Iowa . . . . .T (II) 91
Rinella, Debbie, Akron, Ohio . . . . .T (O) 87
Ritchison, Bonita, Muncie, Ind. . . . . .T (II) 75
Robb, Sue, Euclid, Ohio . . . . .D (O) 83
Robbins, Betty, Lyons, N.Y. . . . . .T (II) 61
Roberts, Alma, Erie City, N.Y. . . . . .T (II) 59
Roberts, Judy, Angola, N.Y. . . . . .A (I) 60
Roberts, Judy, Denver . . . . .D (O) 72
Robinson, Cheryl, Destrehan, La. . . . . .A (O) 80
Robinson, Leona, Santa Susana, Calif. . . . . .T (I) 29
Robinson, Mary Ann, Long Beach, Calif. . . . . . . .T (II) 62
Robinson, Mary Ann, Moorcroft, Wyo. . . . . .D (II) 94
Rogalski, JoAnne, Buffalo, N.Y. . . . . .A 74; T (O) 75
Romeo, Robin, Newhall, Calif. . . . . A (O) 86; D (O) 87
Rookstool, Rachel, Fort Walton Beach, Fla. . . . . . . .D (I) 74
Roop, Pat, Severna Park, Md. . . . . .T (II) 81
Rose, Patricia, Sierra Madre, Calif. . . . . .D (II) 69
Rosecrans, Celia, Chicago . . . . .T (I) 41
Roush, Eva, Indianapolis . . . . .T (I) 51
Rowan, Nancy, Tucson, Ariz. . . . . .T (O) 76
Rowe, Annie, New York . . . . .T (II) 58
Royer, Lillian, Woodlyn, Pa. . . . . .S (I) 67
Rubino, Morie, Westport, Conn. . . . . .T (II) 68
Rudell, Doris, Whittler, Calif. . . . . .S (I) 65
Rump, Anita, Fort Wayne, Ind. . . . . .S (I) 28, 30
Running Wolf, Neva, Baltimore . . . . .T (I) 79
Runyon, Peggy, Garden Grove, Calif. . . . . .D (I) 70
Russell, Estelle, St. Louis . . . . .T (I) 76
Russell, Karen, Bethany, Okla. . . . . .A (I) 79
Ruth, Edna, Belpre, Ohio . . . . .S (I) 77
Ryan, Esther, Milwaukee . . . . .T (I) 39, 47; A (I) 34
Ryskamp, Wyllis, Grand Rapids, Mich. . . .T (I) 50; D (I) 55

S

Sabine, Jackie, Windsor, Ontario . . . . . . .T (I) 96; T (I) 97
Sabine, Marilyn, Windosr, Ontario . . . . . .T (I) 96; T (I) 97
Sablatnik, Ethel, W Palm Beach, Fla. . . . . .D (I) 38
Sadowski, Helen, Chicago . . . . .T (I) 56
Saitoh, Shinobu, Tokyo . . . . .A (O) 84; T (O) 84
Salata, Irene, Waukegan, Ill. . . . . .T (I) 65
Salvato, Betty, Youngstown, Ohio . . . . .D (I) 61
Salvino, Evelyn, Clarksburg, W.Va. . . . . .T (II) 56
Salzman, Michelle (Casella), Sun Valley, Calif. . . . .A (I) 83
Sammon, Jan, Davenport, Iowa . . . . .S (I) 82
Sanders, Bertha, Oakland, Md. . . . . .T (II) 74

Sanders, Jelemia, Richmond, Ky. . . . . .S (I) 70
Santiago, Claudette, Huntington Beach, Calif. . . . .T (O) 83
Sarbenoff, Marilyn, Roswell, N.M. . . . . .T (I) 74
Sorlwell, Cathy, Morgan City, La. . . . . .S (I) 84
Scanlon, Karen, Toledo, Ohio . . . . .T (O) 85
Scarborough, Frances, Texarkana, Ark. . . . . .D (I) 87
Scarrareggia, Jan, Simi, Calif. . . . . .T (II) 83
Schaflein, Beverly, Chicago . . . . .T (I) 56
Schauer, Ann, College Point, N.Y. . . . . .D (II) 67
Scherer, Charlotte, Paden City, W.Va. . . . . .T (I) 34
                                                         D (I) 50
Schick, Flo, Dallas . . . . .D (I) 50
Schilling, Betty Jo, Lockwood, Mo. . . . . .D (II) 77
Schienk, Flora, St. Louis . . . . .T (I) 32
Schmal, Pamela, Winston-Salem, N.C. . . . . .A (II) 90
Schmidt, Ann, Rockford, Ill. . . . . .T (I) 21
Schmidt, Jan, Rochelle, Ill. . . . . .Q 93; S (C) 97
Schmitz, Paulette, Wheaton, Minn. . . . . .T (I) 89
Schoon, Darlene, Freeman, S.D. . . . . .S (II) 91
Schroder, Shirley, Cincinnati . . . . .T (I) 60, 68
Schroeder, Margaret, Chicago . . . . .T (I) 22
Schroeder, Ursula, Elizabethtown, Ky. . . . . .P (II) 84
Schoon, Dorlene, Freeman, S.D. . . . . .S (II) 91
Schubert-Balcer, Nancy, Baltimore . . . . .A (I) 86
Schulte, Myrtle, St. Louis . . . . .S, A (I) 31; T (I)32
Schultz, Jean, Cleveland . . . . T (I) 52; D (I) 58
Schultz, Shirley, Fox River Grove, Ill. . . . . .T (O) 71
Schumacher, Ruth, Cincinnati . . . . .T (I) 60
Schwarzel, Polly, Cheswick, Pa. . . . . .S (O) 85
Schwindt, Jo, Fort Collins, Colo. . . . . .T (I) 69
Scoles, Karen, Shelton, Wash. . . . . .T (II) 97
Scott, Jo Ann, Wilmington, Del. . . . . .D (I) 81
Scruggs, Mary, Richmond, Va. . . . . .S (I) 71
Seabloom, Kelly, Scottsdale, Ariz. . . . . .A (I) 95
Seavers, Nancy, Shawano, Wis. . . . . .T (III) 96
Seibel, Doylie, Angleton, Texas . . . . .S (I) 83
Self, Helen, Monroe, La. . . . . .D (II) 93
Setlock, Ann, Detroit . . . . .T (I) 57, 59
Shablis, Helen, Detroit . . . . .A (I) 63
Shamlock, Marie, Detroit . . . . .T (I) 49, 53
Sharp, Louise, Clarksburg, W.Va. . . . . .T (II) 56
Shaw, Dorris, Coffeyville, Kan. . . . . .D (II) 74
Shelton, Barbara, Hempstead, N.Y. . . . . .D (O) 78
Shelton, Edythe, Salina, Kan. . . . . .T (II) 60
Sheppard, Carol, Phoenix . . . . .D (I) 73
Sherman, Ann, Chicago . . . . .T (I) 61, 64
Shiery-Odom, Sandra Jo, Coldwater, Mich. . . . . . .Q 97
Shininger, Cheryl, Solon, Ohio . . . . .T (O) 86
Shonk, Beverly, Canton, Ohio . . . . .S (O) 76
Shono, Michiko, Tokyo . . . . .T (O) 84
Sibley, Marie, Chicago . . . . .T (I) 58
Siemrzuch, Barbara, North Glenn, Ohio . . . . . . .D (I) 76
Sill, Aleta, Dearborn, Mich. . . . . .A (O) 82, 85; S (O) 83;
                                                     Q 83, 85; T (O) 95
Simmons, Rhondrea, Muskogee, Okla. . . . . .D (I) 93
Simon, Violet, San Antonio, Texas . . . . .D (I) 35
Simms, Helen, Waterloo, Iowa . . . . .T (I) 81
Simpson, Ida, Buffalo, N.Y. . . . . .S (I) 51
Simpson, Penny, Windsor, Ontario . . . . . .T (I) 96; T (I) 97
Sipniewski, Donna, Dayton, Ohio . . . . .T (O) 82
Sipos, Dee, Frankfort, Ill. . . . . .T (O) 78
Sirman, Cassandra, Texarkana, Ark. . . . . .T (I) 76
Sittason, Hattie, Cincinnati . . . . .T (I) 34
Sizemore, Ruble, Fort Walton Beach, Fla. . . . . . .D (I) 74
Sjostrom, Shirley, Bloomington, Minn. . . . . .D (O) 76
Skeries, Wanda, Waterloo, Iowa . . . . .T (I) 81
Slaughter, Sherrie, Hurst, Texas . . . . .T (O) 79

Slewinski, Connie, Shawano, Wis. . . . . .T (III) 96
Small, Tess, Chicago . . . . .D, A (I) 40; T (I) 40, 42
Smith, Brenda, Albertville, Ala. . . . . .T (II) 78
Smith, Diane, Lake Cowichan, British Columbia . . .S (I) 86
Smith, Donna, Hillsborough, Calif. . . . . .T (I) 79
Smith, Grace, Chicago . . . . .D (I) 21, 24; T (I) 24, 25
Smith, Kelly, Faribault, Minn. . . . . .S (I) 91
Smith, Mary, Chicago . . . . .D (I) 29; T (I) 28, 31
Smith, Michelle, Seaford, Del. . . . . .D (III) 95
Smotherman, Marie, Tyro, Kan. . . . . .D (I) 74
Smut, Jean, Erie City, N.Y. . . . . .T (I) 74
Sneider, Helen, Detroit . . . . .D (I) 22
Snider, Bernette, Cleveland . . . . .T (I) 36
Snider, Linda, Albertville, Ala. . . . . .T (II) 78
Snodgrass, Regina, Versailles, Ind.   .T (O) 87, 92; D (C) 97
Sobota, Bernadine, Lansing, Ill. . . . . .A (II) 73
Soldan, Bobbie, Costa Mesa, Calif. . . . . .T (I) 67, S (O) 73
Sopchak, Bessie, Rosenberg, Texas . . . . .S (I) 72
Soutar, Judy, Leawood, Kan . . . . . .D (O) 69, 70; Q 74;
                                                         A, T (O) 74
Sparano, Kelly, Vancouver, Wash. . . . . .T (C) 96
Spence, Pat, Hampton, Va. . . . . .D (I) 66
Spinelli, Ruby, Gallup, N.M. . . . . .T (II) 79
Spiva, Darlene, Glendale, Ariz. . . . . .T (C) 97
Springs, Cristie, Lakeview, Ore. . . . . .T (II) 88
Sprow, Pam, Lakeland, Fla. . . . . .T (O) 90
Srnecz, Beverly, Westport, Conn. . . . . .T (II) 68
Stanish, Bea, New York . . . . .T (II) 58
Stansell, Dot, Birmingham, Ala. . . . . .T (I) 77
Stanton, Realene, Holbrook, Ariz. . . . . .T (III) 95
Starin, Toni, Midwest City, Okla. . . . . .A (O) 73; T (O) 76
Stavola, Luanne, Atlantic Heights, N.J. . . . . .S (II) 87
Steadman, Florence, Toledo, Ohio . . . . . . .T (I) 19, 23
Steger, Rose, Chicago . . . . .A (I) 24
Steib, Frances, Detroit . . . . .S (I) 18
Stennett, Frances, Rockford, Ill. . . . . .D (I) 54
Stephan, Shirley, Casa Grande, Ariz. . . . . .D (II) 88
Sterling, Terri, Shelton, Wash. . . . . .T (II) 97
Stevens, Jean, Oklahoma City . . . . .D (I) 62
Stevens, Patricia, Texarkana, Ark. . . . . .T (I) 76
Stewart, Dana, Mountain View, Calif. . . . .Q 77, S (O) 88
Stewart, Donna, Grant, Ala. . . . . .T (II) 78
Stickler, Pauline, Miami . . . . .D (I) 68
Stidham, Jerry, Muncie, Ind. . . . . .T (II) 75
Stille, Dolores, Chicago . . . . .T (I) 65
Stinn, Margaret, Longmont, Colo. . . . . .T (III) 97
Stockdale, Louise, Detroit . . . . .D (I) 22; A (I) 37
Stockmar, Ida, Chicago . . . . .T (I) 22
Strouse, Barbara, Muncie, Ind. . . . . .T (II) 92
Strouse, Cindy, Muncie, Ind. . . . . .T (II) 92
Stout, Londa, Kimberly, Idaho . . . . .D (II) 97
Stout, Vivian, Nashville, Tenn. . . . . .S (II) 63
Straub, Kim, Beatrice, Neb. . . . . .D (C) 94
Streib, Ferol, Leavenworth, Wash. . . . . .A (I) 81
Sugimoto, Katsuko, Tokyo . . . . .Q 81, 82
Sullivan, Missy, Coon Rapids, Minn. . . . . .T (C) 97
Summers, Marge, St. Louis . . . . .T (I) 32
Sutor, Billie, Havre, Mont. . . . . .T (II) 65
Sutton, Charlene, Toledo, Ohio . . . . .T (III) 94
Svoboda, Estelle, Chicago . . . . .D (I) 49
Swain, Rose, Lenexa, Kan. . . . . .D (I) 83
Sweet, Leeta, Garnett, Kan. . . . . .D (I) 89

T

Taleton, Susie, Mobile, Ala. . . . . .T (II) 93
Tapp, Marliss, Portage, Mich. . . . . .T (C) 97
Tate, Catherine, Mobile, Ala. . . . . .T (II) 93

Taum, Patricia, Beale Air Force Base, Calif. . . . . . .D (I) 88
Tayek, Gloria, Crystal Lake, Ill. . . . . .D (II) 82
Taylor, Hazel, Texas City, Texas . . . . .T (I) 70
Taylor, Tillie, Newark, N.J. . . . . .S (I) 42
Taylor, Velma, Van Wert, Ohio . . . . .T (II) 57
Tays, Beverly, Crawfordsville, Ind. . . . . .S (II) 89
Teal, Evelyn, Miami . . . . .A (I) 61
Terry, Karen, Inglewood, Calif. . . . . .A (I) 88
Terry, Lois, Van Wert, Ohio . . . . .T (II) 57
Terry, Robin, Basin, Wyo. . . . . .D (I) 97
Terzan, Charlene, Milwaukee . . . . .T (I) 37, 38
Tesch, Debbie, Monroe, La. . . . . .D (II) 93
Thayer, Carol, Clare, Mich. . . . . .T (II) 82
Thawley, Nancy, Pascagoula, Miss. . . . . .T (II) 95
Thelander, Margaret, Arlington Heights, Ill. . . . . . .D (II) 78
Thiel, Jill, Shawano, Wis. . . . . .T (III) 96
Thomas, Gloria, Detroit . . . . .T (II) 85
Thomas, Linda, Detroit . . . . .T (O) 88
Thompson, Jerry, Springfield, Ill. . . . . .D (II) 73
Thorberg, Barbara, Florissant, Mo. . . . . .T (O) 76
Tkach, Del, Bismarck, N.D. . . . . .A (II) 89
Toepfer, Elvira, Detroit . . . . .T (I) 57, 58
Tokimoto, Mitsuko, Tokyo . . . . .A (O) 92
Towler, Ruth, Ypsilanti, Mich. . . . . .T (I) 84
Towles, Eleanor, Peoria, Ill. . . . . .S (I) 57
Toyer, Pat, Long Beach, Calif. . . . . .T (II) 62
Trout, Daisy, Marietta, Ga. . . . . .D (I) 71
Troy, Ruth, Dayton, Ohio . . . . .A (I) 39
Tschoepe, Sue, Cypress, Texas . . . . .S (III) 96
Turner, Belle, Paducah, Ky. . . . . .S (I) 93
Turner, Virginia, Gardena, Calif. . . . . .A (I) 52
Twyford, Sally, Aurora, Ill. . . . . .S (I) 33, 40; T (I) 30;
                                                   A (I) 30, 33, 41

U

Ugay, Thelma, Jeddah, Saudi Arabia . . . . .A (III) 97
Underwood, Pat, Ithaca, N.Y. . . . . .T (II) 67
Unruh, Frances, Garden Grove, Calif. . . . . .D (II) 79

V

Vacco, Eloise, Cleveland Heights, Ohio . . . . .D (O) 76
Van Otten, Elaine, Pacifica, Calif. . . . . .T (I) 88
Van Steenburg, Bonnie, Universal City, Texas . . . . .D (I) 91
Varnado, Glenda, Jackson, Miss. . . . . .T (II) 64
Veatch, Linda, Madera, Calif. . . . . .A (II) 88
Vella, Nellie, Rockford, Ill. . . . . .S (II) 55, D (I) 57
Verdugo, Marianna, Tucson, Ariz. . . . . .D (II) 89
Villani, Debbie, Las Vegas . . . . .D (O) 95
Visnyel, Dawn, Ithaca, N.Y. . . . . .T (II) 67
Vollmer, Anita, Cincinnati . . . . .T (I) 68

W

Wadley, Mary Ellen, Winter Haven, Fla. . . . . . . .T (O) 90
Wagner, Leila, Annapolis, Md. . . . . .T (O) 79
Wagner, Lisa, Palmetto, Fla. D (O) 82, 92; A (O) 88; Q 96
Wahner, Pat, Stanfield, Ore. . . . . .S (II) 76
Walde, Vi, Denison, Iowa . . . . .D (I) 79
Walz, Jean, Chicago .D (I) 20
Walker, Anne, Killeen, Texas . . . . .T (II) 73
Walker, Norma, Tacoma, Wash. . . . . .S (I) 78
Walters, Joy, Hood River, Ore. . . . . .T (I) 92
Warburton, Barbara, Lexington, Ky. . . . . .T (I) 83
Warder, A., St. Louis .T (I) 20
Warmbier, Marie, Chicago . . . . .T (I) 28, 31, 33; D (I) 30;
                                                   A (I) 32, 35; S (I) 35
Warner, Rose, Waukegan, Ill. . . . . .S (I) 38
Warring, Mary, Superior, Wis. . . . . .T (II) 77
Wars, Lamar, Alice, Texas . . . . .D (II) 68
Watkins, Lila, Baldwin City, Kan. . . . . .T (II) 82

Wattam, Lorna, Havre, Mont. . . . . .T (II) 65
Watts, Diane, Cypress, Calif. . . . . .D (II) 79
Watts, Maxine, Lyon, N.Y. . . . . .T (II) 61
Webber, Corliss, Fullerton, Calif. . . . . .T (II) 69
Weber, GarneHe, Fort Wayne, Ind. . . . . .D (I) 37
Weber, Ruth, Cleveland . . . . .T (I) 52
Weiler, Ann, Chicago . . .D (I) 28; T (I) 24, 25, 26, 35, 40
Wejner, Bertha, Chicago . . . . .T (I) 27
Wellman, Laurie, Longmont, Colo. . . . . .T (III) 97
Wendling, JoLynn, St. Johns, Mich. . . . . .D (II) 92
Werkmeister, Grace, Chicago . . . . . .D (I) 64, T (I) 65
Wernecke, Shirlee, Chicago . . . . .S (I) 48- T (I) 54
Whillock, Lindy, Lubbock, Texas . . . . .D (III) 94
White, Barbara, Athens, Pa. . . . . .D (I) 81
White, Marcia, Rowland Heights, Calif. . . . . .S (II) 69
White, Marilyn, Ely, Nev. . . . . .T (I) 84
White, Mary Ann, Denver . . . . .D (I) 65
White, Shyrlye, Kansas City, Mo. . . . . .S (II) 71
Widman, Dottie, Chicago . . . . .T (O) 77
Wiesmann, Evelyn, Indianapolis . . . . .S (I) 26
Wilcox, Yvonne, Shreveport, La. . . . . .A (II) 72
Wilde, Diane, Waupaca, Wis. . . . . .D (II) 84
Wilkinson, Dorothy, Phoenix, Ariz. . . . .Q 62; S (O) 63
Williams, Diana, Everett, Wash. . . . . .T (C) 96
Williams, Gertrude, Chicago . . . . .T (I) 24, 25
Williams, Jean, San Francisco . . . . .T (II) 58
Williams, Marijoye, San Marcos. Texas . . . . .S (II) 73
Williams, Ruby, Gary, Ind. . . . . .D (II) 63
Williams, Suzie, Killeen, Texas . . . . .T (II) 73
Willig, Erna, Chicago .D (I) 20
Willis, Shirley, Mason City, Iowa . . . . .D (II) 64
Wilman, Henrietta, Chicago . . . . .T (I) 30
Wilson, Ann, Ashdown, Ark. . . . . .D (II) 87
Wilson, Elaine, Eagle Point, Ore. . . . . .T (I) 92
Wilson, Mandy, Dayton, Ohio . . . . . .T (O) 92; D (C) 96
Wilson, Tammy, Red Oak, Iowa . . . . .T (II) 84
Winandy, Cecilia, Chicago . . . . .A (I) 49; T (I) 58
Winegar, Judy, Wessington Springs, S.D. . . . . . . .T (II) 86
Wise, Jamie, Savannah, Ga. . . . . .T (I) 90
Wise, Jerry, Higginsville, Mo. . . . . .D (II) 72
Wittnebel, Pinky, Detroit Lakes, Minn. . . . . .T (II) 80
Wodka, Kathy, Las Vegas . . . . .T (O) 79
Wolf, Anna, Chicago .T (I) 18
Wood, Jessie, Jasper, Texas . . . . .T (II) 66
Wood, Marie, Arcola, Ill. . . . . .T (II) 63
Wright, Connie, Howell, Mich. . . . . .T (II) 85
Wright, Elaine, Guntersville, Ala. . . . . .T (II) 78
Wright, Lyn, Decatur, Ala. . . . . .T (I) 92
Wynn, Rita, Winter Haven, Fla. . . . . .T (O) 90
Wynn, Kim, Albia, Iowa . . . . .T (II) 91

Y

Yaeger, Corolee, Lockwood, Mo. . . . . .D (II) 77
Yamaga, Akiko, Tokyo . . . . .S, A (O) 77
Yon, Mary, Bristol, Va. . . . . .T (II) 90
Young, Carolyn, Jackson, Miss. . . . . .T (II) 64
Young, Edna, Plain City, Ohio . . . . .T (II) 87
Younginer, Ginny, Winnsboro, S.C. . . . . .S (O) 71
Yurcic, Josephine, Gallup, N.M. . . . . .T (II) 79

Z

Zalinski, Linda, Holbrook, Ariz. . . . . .T (III) 95
Zaph, Clara, Cincinnati . . . . .T (I) 60, 68
Zimmerman, Donna, Thousand Palms, Calif. . . . . .A (I) 65
Zimmerman, Eleanor, Chicago . . . . .T (I) 56
Zimmerman, Ollie, Chicago . . . . .T (I) 26
Zuniga, Donna, Tulsa, Okla. . . . . .T (O) 89
Zygmond, Zonie, Havre, Mont. . . . . .T (II) 65

WIBC Championship Tournament Statistics

Ages, oldest doubles teams in years
178 Ethel Brunnick (96) and Elsie Spicer (82),
Santa Monica, Calif., 1984.
176 Ethel Brunnick (98) and Elsie Mueller (78),
Santa Monica and N. Hollywood, Calif., 1986.
165 Ethel Brunnick (94) and Juanita Chalmer (71),
Santa Monica, Calif., and Los Angeles, 1982.
159 Stella Hartrick (81) and Clara Allen (78),
Detroit, 1977.
158 Dorothy Keeler (71) and Margaret Joslyn (87),
Berlin Center, Ohio, 1985.

Ages, oldest teams in years
395 Detroit Lakes Traveling Team, Minnesota, 1986.
382 Wallace Floors, Columbus, Ohio, 1985.

Ages, oldest tournament participants in years
99 Ethel Brunnick, Santa Monica, Calif., 1987
(born Aug. 30, 1887).
98 Ethel Brunnick, Santa Monica, Calif., 1986
(born Aug. 30, 1887).
96 Ethel Brunnick, Santa Monica, Calif., 1984
(born Aug. 30, 1887).
95 Clara Wise, Las Vegas, 1983 (born March 7,
1888).
94 Ethel Brunnick, Santa Monica, Calif., 1982
(born Aug. 30, 1887).

Ages, youngest champions in years
18 years, 10 months, 21 days
Leila Wagner, Annapolis, Md., team event, 1979.
19 years, 2 months, 4 days
Dee Sipos, Frankfort, Ill., team event, 1978.
19 years, 5 months, 11 days
Lorrie Nichols, Algonquin, Ill., all events, 1971.
19 years, 8 months, 11 days
Cindy Mason, Sunnyvale, Calif., team event, 1981.
19 years, 9 months, 10 days
Aleta Sill, Dearborn, Mich., all events, 1982.
19 years, 9 months, 17 days
Leanne Barrette, Yukon, Okla., all events, 1987.

Ages, youngest teams in total years*
33 Stein Starlettes, St. Louis: Mary Ann Keiper, 5;
Jane Steger, 6; Kathy Justi, 6; Carol Radaelli, 7;
Carol Steger 9; 1952.
51 E.B. Shields, St. Louis: Jackie Shields, 9;
Joy Repetto 10; Theresa Kinney, 10; Barbara
Wulkoff, 10; Becky McKane, 12, 1952.

* Students less than 18 years of age may compete in the
WIBC Championship Tournament with written parental
consent.

Ages, youngest participants
5 Mary Ann Keiper, St. Louis, 1952.
6 Jane Steger, St. Louis, 1952.
Kathy Justi, St. Louis, 1952.
7 Carol Radaelli, St. Louis, 1952.
9 Judy Soutar, Leawood, Kan., 1954.
Jackie Shields, St. Louis, 1952.
Carol Steger, St. Louis, 1952.

All-Events Totals, most 1800-plus totals
9 Pat Costello, Orlando, Fla., 1,852, 1,802,
1,810, 1,812, 1,818, 1,828, 1,843, 1,846,
1,864.
8 Betty Morris, Stockton, Calif., 1,817, 1,866,
1,810, 1,803, 1,945, 1,821, 1,930, 1,808
6 Dorothy Fothergill, Center Ossippee, N.H., 1,816,
1,885 (2), 1,984, 1,812, 1,839.
Lorrie Nichols, Algonquin, Ill., 1,840, 1,872,
1,846, 1,831, 1,948, 1,825.
Nikki Gianulias, Vallejo, Calif., 1,833, 1,832,
1,890, 1,822, 1,897, 1,826.

All-Events Totals, most 1900-plus totals
3 Aleta Sill, Dearborn, Mich., 1,921, 1,905, 1,900.
Cindy Coburn-Carroll, Tonawanda, N.Y., 1,927,
1,914, 1,902.
Carol Norman, Ardmore, Okla., 1,923, 1,925,
1,984.
2 Virginia Norton, Cypress, Calif., 1,922, 1,905.
Leanne Barrette, Yukon, Okla., 1,972, 1,935.
Dana Miller-Mackie, Fort Worth, Texas, 1,947,
1,900.
Betty Morris, Stockton, Calif., 1,945, 1,930.
Robin Romeo, Newhall, Calif., 1,904, 1,943.
Judy Soutar, Leawood, Kan., 1,944, 1,953.
Lisa Wagner, Palmetto, Fla., 1,944, 1,944.

Automatic Pinsetters, first used
1957 McCook Bowl, Dayton, Ohio, AMF.

Automatic Scorers, first used
1972 King Louie East, Kansas City, Mo., doubles and
singles events, Brunswick.
1978 Palm Springs Lanes, Miami, team event, Brunswick.
1983 Showboat Lanes, Las Vegas, doubles, singles and
team events, Brunswick.

Averages, five-year tournament leaders by years
1994 Dana Miller-Mackie, Fort Worth, Texas, 205.
1993 Dana Miller-Mackie, Fort Worth, Texas, 207.
1992 Dana Miller-Mackie, Fort Worth, Texas, 202.
1991 Nellie Glandon, Columbus, Ohio, 201.
1990 Nellie Glandon, Columbus, Ohio, 201.
1989 Robin Romeo, Newhall, Calif., 200.
1988 Lorrie Nichols, Algonquin, Ill., 201.
1987 Lorrie Nichols, Algonquin, Ill., 206.
1986 Lorrie Nichols, Algonquin, Ill., 202.
1985 Aleta Sill, Dearborn, Mich., 202.
1984 Virginia Norton, Cypress, Calif., 197.
1983 Virginia Norton, Cypress, Calif., 203.
1982 Betty Morris, Stockton, Calif., 200.

1981   Betty Morris, Stockton, Calif., 203.
1980   Betty Morris, Stockton, Calif., 205.
1979   Betty Morris, Stockton, Calif., 202.
1978   Betty Morris, Stockton, Calif., 195.

Averages, 10-year tournament leaders by years
1994   Robin Romeo, Newhall, Calif., 199.
1993   Robin Romeo, Newhall, Calif., 200.
1992   Lorrie Nichols, Algonquin, Ill., 199.
1991   Lorrie Nichols, Algonquin, Ill., 199.
1990   Lorrie Nichols, Algonquin, Ill., 199.
1989   Lorrie Nichols, Algonquin, Ill., 198.
1988   Lorrie Nichols, Algonquin, Ill., 199.
1987   Lorrie Nichols, Algonquin, Ill., 199.
1986   Lorrie Nichols, Algonquin, Ill., 196.
1985   Betty Morris, Stockton, Calif., 197.
1984   Betty Morris, Stockton, Calif., 197.
1983   Virginia Norton, Cypress, Calif., 198.
1982   Betty Morris, Stockton, Calif., 195.
1981   Betty Morris, Stockton, Calif., 194.
1980   Lorrie Nichols, Algonquin, Ill., 190.
1979   Lorrie Nichols, Algonquin, Ill., 192.
1978   Judy Soutar, Leawood, Kan., 195.

Champions, mothers and daughters in same events
Ruth Hartmann and Nell Hartmann, Chicago, team event, 1941.
Doris Coburn and Kathy McDonald, Buffalo, N.Y., team event, 1972.
Eloise Vacco and Debbie Rainone, Cleveland Heights, Ohio, doubles event, 1976.
Sheila Clegg and Kelly Clegg, Burbank, Ill., team event, 1988.
Gloria Collura and Karen Collura, Toronto, doubles event, 1993.

Championship Ties, by events
Singles Event
612   Ella Mankie, Madison, Wis., won rolloff over Marge Slogar, Cleveland, 1936.

(WIBC changed rolloff rule in the 1950s. Since the 1950s, co-champions are allowed.)

705   Dana Miller-Mackie, Fort Worth, Texas, and Paula Carter, Miami, 1990.
747   Karen Collura, Toronto, and Kari Murph, Dayton, Ohio, 1993.

Doubles Event
1,188   Margaret Franklin, Alhambra, Calif., and Merle Matthews, Long Beach, Calif., won rolloff to defeat Edna Harold and Marge Slogar, Cleveland, 1948.
1,232   Georgene Cordes and Shirley Sjostrom, Bloomington, Minn.; and Debbie Rainone and Eloise Vacco, Cleveland Heights, Ohio; 1979.
1,264   Shirley Hintz and Lisa Wagner, Merritt Island and Palmetto, Fla.; and Pat Costello and Donna Adamek, Orlando, Fla., and Apple Valley, Calif.; 1982.

1,307   Lucy Giovinco and Cindy Coburn-Carroll, Norcross, Ga. and Tonawanda, N.Y., and Rachel Perez and Kim Straub, San Antonio and Beatrice, Neb., 1994.

All Events
1,877   Robin Romeo, Newhall, Calif. and Maria Lewis, Manteca, Calif., 1986.
1,807   Bertha Blacksher, Uriah, Ala., and Sharon Davis, Orange, Texas, 1993.
Team
3,017   Contour Power Grips, Vallejo, Calif., and Here 4 Beer II, Glendale, Ariz., 1997

Championships, in first tournaments
Mary Scruggs, Richmond, Va., singles event, 1971.
Leila Wagner, Annapolis, Md., team event, 1979.
Elizabeth Baude, Dayton, Ohio, team event, 1982.
Sharon Davis. Orange, Texas, all events (tie), 1993.
Cynthia Hedge, Branford, Conn., singles event, 1993.
Jody Fritschle, Dayton, Ohio, team event, 1982.
Donna Sipniewski, Dayton, Ohio, team event, 1982.
Janine Ditch, San Pedro, Calif., team event, 1983.
Ginny Adams, Norwalk, Calif., team event, 1983.
Maria Lewis, Manteca, Calif., all events (tie), 1986.
Michelle Meyer-Welty, Vacaville, Calif., singles event, 1988.

Championships, by foreign participants
Mitsuko Tokimoto, Tokyo, all events, 1992.
Shinobu Saitoh, Tokyo, all events, 1984.
All Japan, Tokyo, team event (Satoko Imaizuma, Michiko Shono, Kazue Inahashi, Shinobu Saitoh and Fujio Matsuzaki), 1984.
All Japan, Tokyo, team event (Hidemi Mizobuchi, Masayo Nagai, Kazue Inahashi, Kazuko Inouye and Kazumi Kimura), 1980.
Akiko Yamaga, Tokyo, singles event, 1977.
Akiko Yamaga, Tokyo, all events, 1977.

Championships, longest title winning spans in years (three or more titles)
20   Dorothy Miller, Chicago, 10 titles, 1928 to 1948.
     Connie Powers, Fraser, Mich., three titles, 1939 to 1959.
     Mae Bolt, Berwyn, Ill., seven titles, 1958 to 1978.
19   Shirley Garms, Island Lake, Ill., four titles, 1955 to 1974.
16   Ann Weiler, Chicago, five titles, 1924 to 1940.
15   Agnes Higgins, Chicago, seven titles, 1918 to 1933.
     Merle Matthews, Los Angeles, three titles, 1948 to 1963.

Championships, most all events titles by individuals
4   Emma Jaeger, Toledo, Ohio, 1918, 1921, 1928, 1929.
3   Sally Twyford, Aurora, Ill., 1930, 1933, 1941.
    Virginia Norton, Cypress, Calif., 1975, 1981, 1983.
2   Grace Hatch, Cleveland, 1925, 1927.
    Marie Warmbier, Chicago, 1932, 1935.
    Marion Ladewig, Grand Rapids, Mich., 1950, 1955.
    Doris Knechtges, Detroit, 1953, 1956.
    Betty Morris, Stockton, Calif., 1976, 1979.
    Aleta Sill, Dearborn, Mich., 1982, 1985.

Championships, most consecutive
4   Agnes Higgins, Chicago, D 26, T 27-28, S 29.
      Dorothy Fothergill, Lincoln, R.I., T-S-A 70, D 71,
      T 72, D 73.
      Mildred Ignizio, Rochester, N.Y., T 70, D 71, T 72,
      D 73.
      Marie Warmbier, Chicago, D 30, T 31, A 32,
      T 33.
3   Emma Jaeger, Toledo, Ohio, A-S 21, S 22, T-S 23.
      Loraine Baldy, Milwaukee, D 36, T 37-38.

Championships, most consecutive all events titles
2   Emma Jaeger, Toledo, Ohio, 1928-1929.

Championships, most consecutive doubles event titles
2   Jean Acker-Lita Reilly, Chicago, 1916 and 1918.
      (No event in 1917.)
      Gloria Bouvia-Judy Soutar, Gresham, Ore., and
      Leawood, Kan., 1969 and 1970.
      Donna Adamek, Apple Valley, Calif., 1981 and
      1982. (With Nikki Gianulias, Vallejo, Calif.,
      1981; and Pat Costello, Orlando, Fla.,
      1982.)

Championships, most consecutive team event titles
2   Albert Pick & Co. and Estes Alibis, Chicago (Jean
      Acker, Gertrude Resk, Grace Smith, Ann Weiller
      and Gertrude Williams), 1924-1925.
      Heil Uniform Heat of Milwaukee, Milwaukee
      (Loraine Baldy, Emma Dobrient, Irma Jones,
      Gladys Light and Charlene Terzan), 1937-1938.
      Linbrook Bowl, Los Angeles (Wilma Anderson,
      Mary Hoyt, Merle Matthews, Betty Phillips and
      Robbie Rickard), 1962-1963.
      Strike Zone Pro Shop, Rolling Meadows, Ill. (Lana
      Larvis, Christy Asher, Shirley Hintz, Karen
      Ellingsworth and Anne Marie Duggan), 1993 and
      1994.

**Championships, most doubles event titles by
individuals**
3   Jean Acker, Chicago, 1916, 1918, 1924.
      Dorothy Miller, Chicago 1929 1934 1940.

Championships, most by individuals
10   Dorothy Miller, Chicago, T 28-31-33-35-40-48;
      D 29-34-40; A 38.
9   Emma Jaeger, Toledo, Ohio, T 19-23; S 21-22-23;
      A 18-21-28-29.
8   Fritzie Rahn, Chicago, T 27-28-31-33-35-40;
      D 30-34.
7   Marie Warmbier, Chicago, T 28-31-33; D 30;
      S 35; A 32-35.
      Mae Bolt, Berwyn, Ill., T 58-61-64-77; S 59-78;
      A 58.

**Championships, most singles event titles by
individuals**
3   Emma Jaeger, Toledo, Ohio, 1921, 1922, 1923.
2   Anita Rump, Fort Wayne, Ind., 1928, 1930.
      Sally Twyford, Aurora, Ill., 1933, 1940.
      Mae Bolt, Berwyn, Ill., 1959, 1978.
      Betty Morris, Stockton, Calif., 1979, 1980.

Championships, most team event titles by individuals
6   Fritzie Rahn, Chicago, 1927, 1928, 1931, 1933,
      1935, 1940.
      Dorothy Miller, Chicago, 1928, 1931, 1933,
      1935, 1940, 1948.
4   Ann Weiler, Chicago, 1924, 1925, 1935, 1940.
      Mae Bolt, Berwyn, Ill., 1958, 1961, 1964, 1977.
3   Agnes Higgins, Chicago, 1927, 1928, 1933.
      Marie Warmbier, Chicago, 1928, 1931, 1933.
      Edith Kirg, Chicago, 1930, 1933, 1935.
      Kay Freitag, Chicago, 1955, 1958, 1961.
      Pat Costello, Orlando, Fla., 1969, 1973,
      1981.
      Donna Adamek, Apple Valley, Calif., 1981, 1987,
      1992.
      Linda Kelly, Huber Heights, Ohio, 1982, 1987,
      1992.

**Championships, most team event titles with same
sponsors**
4   Alberti Jewelers, Chicago, 1928, 1931, 1933,
      1935.
      Allgauer Restaurant, Chicago, 1958, 1961, 1964,
      1977.

Championships, most titles in same tournaments
3   Mrs. A.J. Koester, St. Louis, T-S-A, 1916.
      Tess Small, Chicago, T-D-A, 1940.
      Doris Knechtges, Detroit, T-D-A, 1953.
      Dorothy Fothergill, Lincoln, R.I., T-S-A, 1970.

**Championships, won all four events
(not same tournaments)**
Marie Warmbier; Chicago; T 1928, 1931, 1933; D 1930;
S 1935; A 1932, 1935
Dorothy Fothergill; Lincoln, R.I.; T 1970, 1972; D 1971;
S 1970; A 1970.

**Chartered Groups, most teams by one organizer
(in teams)**
389   Gertrude Finke, Minneapolis to Reno, Nev., 1997.
263   Gertrude Finke, Minneapolis to Las Vegas, 1983.
253   Gertrude Finke, Minneapolis to Orange County,
      Calif., 1986.
241   Gertrude Finke, Minneapolis to Baton Rouge, La.,
      1991.
219   Gertrude Finke, Minneapolis to Tucson, Ariz.,
      1995.

Entries, by division by year

Year	Classic Division	Division I	Division II	Division III
1997	542	3,253	10,302	2,557
1996	316	2,528	4,059	466
1995	300	2,849	4,742	531
1994	254	2,453	4,309	621

Year	Open Division	Division I	Division II
1993	8,162	21,925	17,069
1992	6,426	18,777	16,337
1991	5,913	19,998	18,575
1990	7,831	24,892	20,011

Entries, most by events
All Events
88,279   Reno, Nev., 1997.
68,686   Las Vegas, 1983.
62,949   Reno/Carson City, Nev., 1988.
49,923   Tampa, Fla., 1990.
44,827   Baton Rouge, La., 1993.

Doubles Event
42,252   Reno, Nev., 1997.
35,882   Las Vegas, 1983.
33,181   Reno/Carson City, Nev., 1988.
26,648   Tampa, Fla., 1990.
23,503   Baton Rouge, La., 1993.

Singles Event
84,504   Reno, Nev., 1997.
71,764   Las Vegas, 1983.
66,362   Reno/Carson City, Nev., 1988.
53,296   Tampa, Fla., 1990.
47,006   Baton Rouge, La., 1993.

Team Event
16,704   Reno, Nev., 1997.
14,872   Reno/Carson City, Nev., 1988.
14,430   Las Vegas, 1983.
10,519   Tampa, Fla., 1990.
9,840   Orange County, Calif., 1986.

Entries, most teams from Host Cities
2,843   Detroit, 1953.
1,933   Syracuse, N.Y., 1954.
1,810   St. Louis, 1952.
1,513   Buffalo, N.Y., 1959.
1,467   Milwaukee, 1977.

Host Cities and States
4,036   Wisconsin to Milwaukee, 1977.
3,865   New York to Rochester, N.Y., 1967.

3,581   New York to Syracuse, N.Y., 1954.
3,507   Michigan to Detroit, 1953.
3,098   New York to Buffalo, N.Y., 1959.

Host States (excluding host cities)
2,569   Wisconsin to Milwaukee, 1977.
2,514   New York to Rochester, N.Y., 1967.
2,231   California to Orange County, Calif., 1986.
1,784   Ohio to Toledo, Ohio, 1985.

Non-Host States
2,441   California to Reno/Carson City, Nev., 1988.
2,155   California to Las Vegas, 1983.
2,006   California to Las Vegas, 1973.
1,006   Texas to Las Vegas, 1983.
936   Michigan to Toledo, Ohio, 1985.

Entries, most traveling teams (excluding host cities)
14,749   Reno, Nev., 1997.
14,649   Reno/Carson City, Nev., 1988.
14,110   Las Vegas, 1983.
10,325   Tampa, Fla., 1990.
9,337   Orange County, Calif., 1986

Tournaments, largest for a state association in teams
5,411   Wisconsin WBA, 1984.
5,089   Wisconsin WBA, 1985.
5,048   Wisconsin WBA, 1983.
4,880   Wisconsin WBA, 1982.
4,853   Wisconsin WBA, 1987.

Lanes, most used in individual host centers
106   Las Vegas, Showboat Lanes, 1983.
80   Denver, Celebrity Sports Center, 1976.
76   National Bowling Stadium, Reno, Nev. 1997.
72   Houston, Stadium Bowl, 1974.
      Milwaukee, Red Carpet Celebrity Lanes, 1977.

Prize Winnings, lowest scores to cash by divisions, years and events

Year	Team Event	Doubles Event	Singles Event	All Events	Year	Team Event	Doubles Event	Singles Event	All Events
Classic Division					1984	2,631	1,083	553	1,632
1997	2,758	1,131	578	1,702	1983	2,616	1,079	553	1,631
1996	2,780	1,107	569	1,695	1982	2,636	1,036	532	1,593
1995	2,775	1,124	578	1,708	1981	2,721	1,066	546	1,634
1994	2,689	1,120	573	1,677	1980	2,582	1,058	539	1,597
					1979	2,675	1,072	544	1,622
Open Division					1978	2,640	1,067	543	1,606
1993	2,606	1,107	563	1,650	1977	2,633	1,082	552	1,621
1992	2,629	1,095	561	1,649	1976	2,654	1,091	557	1,603
1991	2,710	1,104	565	1,674	1975	2,580	1,085	550	1,622
1990	2,628	1,105	565	1,652	1974	2,626	1,102	563	1,642
1989	2,670	1,089	556	1,648	1973	2,643	1,086	557	1,634
1988	2,649	1,025	527	1,580	1972	2,626	1,110	562	1,643
1987	2,614	1,100	560	1,648	1971	2,592	1,091	555	No Cash
1986	2,544	1,081	555	1,624	1970	2,736	1,126	575	No Cash
1985	2,629	1,068	548	1,623	1969	2,695	1,123	575	1,827

Year	Team Event	Doubles Event	Singles Event	All Events	Year	Team Event	Doubles Event	Singles Event	All Events
Division I*					**Division II**				
1997	2,510	1,035	530	1,599	1997	2,343	971	497	1,498
1996	2,524	997	508	1,560	1996	2,365	920	470	1,442
1995	2,485	1,019	521	1,576	1995	2,334	945	484	1,459
1994	2,389	1,022	525	1,561	1994				
1993	2,362	1007	515	1,534	1993	2,182	922	469	1,404
1992	2,403	995	509	1,530	1992	2,222	910	463	1,397
1991	2,448	1,014	518	1,553	1991	2,261	933	474	1,426
1990	2,376	1,001	513	1,530	1990	2,193	921	468	1,404
1989	2,437	988	506	1,531	1989	2,256	902	459	1,397
1988	2,396	934	478	1,464	1988	2,212	856	436	1,339
1987	2,407	990	504	1,515	1987	2,231	895	457	1,383
1986	2,351	998	509	1,523	1986	2,171	913	463	1,389
1985	2,417	983	504	1,518	1985	2,230	900	457	1,387
1984	2,384	986	503	1,511	1984	2,193	896	456	1,376
1983	2,384	992	507	1,517	1983	2,186	905	460	1,380
1982	2,419	948	501	1,486	1982	2,214	862	437	1,344
1981	2,493	979	483	1,528	1981	2,267	884	452	1,381
1980	2,327	954	487	1,475	1980	2,114	861	439	1,323
1979	2,401	958	489	1,493	1979	2,163	864	439	1,337
1978	2,305	939	472	1,487	1978	2,094	843	423	1,338
1977	2,303	955	484	1,504	1977	2,088	859	433	1,357
1976	2,311	965	491	1,523	1976	2,127	877	443	1,385
1975	2,297	951	479	1,500	1975	2,085	854	432	1,354
1974	2,249	948	481	1,500	1974	2,042	852	429	1,342
1973	2,329	959	485	1,514	1973	2,117	866	436	1,370
1972	2,302	967	491	1,518	1972	2,085	873	439	1,367
1971	2,277	955	483	No Cash	1971	2,047	863	433	No Cash
1970	2,339	973	492	No Cash	1970	2,096	872	441	No Cash
1969	2,325	958	484	1,635	1969	2,083	861	434	1,463
1968	2,368	984	500	1,684	1968	2,127	883	445	1,461
1967	2,430	989	503	1,674	1967	2,143	875	442	1,478
1966	2,317	975	497	1,654	1966	2,081	877	444	1,476
1965	2,387	987	501	1,675	1965	2,157	894	450	1,481
1964	2,473	1,026	517	1,740	1964	2,174	916	462	1,527
1963	2,324	965	490	1,634	1963	2,056	864	434	
1962	2,333	847	460	1,639	1962	1,965			
1961	2,335	870	456	1,614	1961	2,046			
1960	2,298	845	439	1,597	1960	1,986			
1959	2,314	831	433	1,584	1959	2,034		(Booster Division)	
1958	2,155	801	403	1,547	1958	1,956			
1957	2,224	820	403	1,579	1957	2,071			
1956	2,239	849	432	1,582	1956	2,035			
1955	2,190	846	424	1,618	1955	1,900			
1954	2,094	808	420	1,566	**Division III**				
1953	2,129	814	399	1,550	1997	2,159	886	450	1,360
					1996	2,179	836	426	1,311
					1995	2,135	859	438	1,328
					1994	2,035	871	444	1,323

Series Margins, widest from events to events

263   Barb Moesch, Menomonee Falls, Wis., 383 doubles event to 646 team event, 1977.

261   Kathryn Hegge, Whitehall, Wis., 297 team event to 558 doubles event, 1983.

258   D.D. Jacobson, Playa Del Rey, Calif., 479 doubles event to 737 singles event, 1972.

252   Mary Scruggs, Richmond, Va., 446 doubles event to 698 singles event, 1971.

232   Barbara McCaskill, Nashville, Tenn., 409 team event to 641 doubles event, 1978.

Three game series, highest by youth bowlers

697   Sandra Lee Weiss, St. Louis, 17, singles event, 1978.

Triplicate, highest in any event

212   Gale Woodin, Deer Park, Texas, singles event, 1974.

203   Stasia Peters, North Attleboro, Mass., singles event, 1988.

201   Susan Teater, Lincoln, Neb., doubles event, 1978.

200   Chie Endoh, Tokyo, team event, 1976.

193   Janice Sartain, Spokane, Wash., singles event, 1978.

* Because of a change in division structure, Division I and II scores prior to 1994 are not reflective of the revised Division structure.

The prestigious WIBC Queens Tournament attracts 481 high-average amateur and professional bowlers for five days of bowling competition. The tournament is held in the WIBC Championship Tournament host city during the WIBC Championship Tournament.

The competition begins with bowlers bowling two, five-game qualifying blocks. The field is cut to the top-63 scorers and the defending Queens champion, who is seeded into the competition. These 64 women advance to the double-elimination, match-play round.

Effective with the 1994 tournament, match-play blocks consist of three games. The double-elimination format places a bowler in the contenders' bracket after one loss. A second match-play loss eliminates her from the event.

The undefeated match-play survivor and the last four contenders' bracket survivors advance to the stepladder finals round. The five finalists meet in four head-to-head games in position order.

The WIBC Queens Tournament champion receives a prize check, tiara, diamond pendant necklace and seeding into the next WIBC Queens Tournament.

WIBC Queens Tournament Champions and Runner-Ups

(Numbers in ( ) are finals scores)

Matches

Match-Play	Won-Loss		Average
1997 Sandra Jo Shiery-Odom, Coldwater, Mich (209-185) 7	0		217
Runner-up - Audray Mullan, Richmond, Va. 6	2		205
1996 Lisa Wagner, Bradenton, Fla. (231-226) 9	2		207
Runner-up - Tammy Turner, West Palm Beach, Fla. 6	1		220
1995 Sandra Postma, Lansing, Ill. (226-187) 5	1		205
Runner-up - Carolyn Dorin, North Richland Hills, Texas 6	0		231
1994 Anne Marie Duggan, Edmond, Okla. (238-218) .6	2		203
Runner-up - Aleta Sill, Dearborn, Mich. 6	0		212
1993 Jan Schmidt, Rochelle,Ill. (201-163) 7	0		212
Runner-up - Pat Costello, Orlando, Fla. 9	3		210
1992 Cindy Coburn-Carroll, Tonawanda, N.Y. (184-170) 7	**1		216
Runner-up - Dana Miller-Mackie, Fort Worth, Texas 6	0		200
1991 Dede Davidson, San Jose, Calif. (231-159) 7	**1		188
Runner-up - Jeanne Maiden-Naccarato, Tacoma, Wash. 6	0		205
1990 Patty Ann, Arlington Heights, Ill. (207-173) 9	**1		202
Runner-up - Vesma Grinfelds, San Francisco 6	0		197
1989 Carol Gianotti, Perth, Australia (207-177) 7	**1		202
Runner-up - Sandra Jo Shiery, Bronson, Mich. 6	1		202
1988 Wendy Macpherson, Henderson, Nev. (213-199) 7	1		191
Runner-up - Leanne Barrette, Yukon, Okla. 6	1		202
1987 Cathy Almeida, Pennsauken, N.J. (850-817) 7	0		214
Runner-up - Lorrie Nichols, Algonquin, Ill. 9	1		218
1986 Cora Fiebig, Madison Heights, Mich. (223-177) 9	2		191
Runner-up - Barbara Thorberg, Florissant, Mo. 6	1		194
1985 Aleta Sill, Dearborn, Mich. (279-192) 7	1		212
Runner-up - Linda Graham, Des Moines, Iowa 6	1		203
1984 Kazue Inahashi, Tokyo (248-222) 7	1		202
Runner-up - Aleta Sill, Dearborn, Mich. 6	1		200
1983 Aleta Sill, Dearborn, Mich. (214- 188) 6	1		205
Runner-up - Dana Miller, Fort Worth, Texas 10	1		211
1982 Katsuko Sugimoto, Tokyo (160-137) 10	1		189
Runner-up - Nikki Gianulias, Vallejo, Calif. 7	1		192
1981 Katsuko Sugimoto, Tokyo (166-158) 6	0		192
Runner-up - Virginia Norton, Cypress, Calif. 7	3		198
1980 Donna Adamek, Apple Valley, Calif. (213-165) 7	0		205
Runner-up - Cheryl Robinson, Destrehan, La. 6	2		197
1979 Donna Adamek, Apple Valley, Calif. (216-181) 7	0		218
Runner-up - Shinobu Saitoh, Tokyo 9	2		205
1978 Loa Boxberger, Russell, Kan. (197-176) 7	**1		196
Runner-up - Cora Fiebig, Madison Heights, Mich. 6	1		198
1977 Dana Stewart, Morgan Hill, Calif. (175-167) 7	0		197
Runner-up - Vesma Grinfelds, San Francisco 6	2		200
1976 Pam Buckner, Reno, Nev. (214-178) 7	1		200
Runner-up - Shirley Sjostrom, Bloomington, Minn. 6	1		193

Year	Player			
1975	Cindy Powell, Navarre, Ohio (758-674)	.8	**1	190
	Runner-up - Pat Costello, Orlando, Fla.	.6	2	185
1974	Judy Soutar, Leawood, Kan. (939-705)	.7	0	211
	Runner-up - Betty Morris, Stockton, Calif.	.9	2	201
1973	Dorothy Fothergill, Center Ossippee, N.H. (804-791)	.7	0	211
	Runner-up - Judy Soutar, Leawood Kan.	.6	2	203
1972	Dorothy Fothergill, North Attleboro, Mass. (890-841)	.7	0	210
	Runner-up - Maureen Harris, Irving, Texas	.8	**1	202
1971	Mildred Ignizio, Rochester, N.Y. (809-778)	.6	2	191
	Runner-up - Katherine Brown, Columbus, Ohio	.6	2	215
1970	Mildred Ignizio, Rochester, N.Y. (807-797)	.7	0	216
	Runner-up - Joan Holm, Chicago	.8	2	201
1969	Ann Feigel, Tucson, Ariz. (832-765)	.7	0	213
	Runner-up - Mildred Ignizio, Rochester, N.Y.	.6	2	200
1968	Phyllis Massey, Alameda, Calif. (884-853)	.9	**1	200
	Runner-up - Marian Spencer, Oklahoma City	.6	2	197
1967	Mildred Ignizio, Rochester, N.Y. (840-809)	.7	0	215
	Runner-up - Phyllis Massey, Alameda, Calif.	.9	2	208
1966	Judy Lee, Lakewood, Calif. (771-742)	.8	**1	188
	Runner-up - Jancy Peterson, Phoenix, Ariz.	.6	2	190
1965	Betty Kuczynski, Cicero, Ill. (772-739)	.7	0	190
	Runner-up - LaVerne Carter, St. Louis	.6	2	196
1964	D.D. Jacobson, Playa Del Rey, Calif. (740-682)	.7	0	199
	Runner-up - Shirley Garms, Island Lake, Ill.	.6	2	198
1963	Irene Monterosso, E. Rutherford, N.J. (852-803)	.7	**1	194
	Runner-up - Georgette DeRosa, Hillside, Ill.	.6	2	192
1962	Dorothy Wilkinson, Phoenix, Ariz. (799-794)	.6	0	195
	Runner-up - Marion Ladewig, Grand Rapids, Mich.	.5	2	195
1961	Janet Harman, Cerritos, Calif. (794-776)	.6	0	199
	Runner-up - Eula Touchette, E. St. Louis, Ill.	.5	2	188

**Advanced from losers' bracket.

WIBC Queens Tournament Records

AVERAGES, highest
Qualifying Competition (10 games)
227.9 Aleta Sill, Dearborn, Mich., 1995.
224.8 Carol Norman, Ardmore, Okla., 1995.
223.7 Carol Gianotti, Perth, Australia, 1997.
221.8 Dona Adamek, Stevenson Ranch, Calif., 1995.
221.0 Jackie Rowe, Englewood, Colo., 1996.

Match-Play Competition
231 Carolyn Dorin, North Richland Hills, Texas, 1995.
226 Tish Johnson, Northridge, Calif., 30 games, 1995.
225 Pat Costello, Orlando, Fla., 25 games, 1979.
Kim Canady, San Francisco, 21 games, 1995.
Liz Johnson, Niagra Falls, N.Y., 15 games, 1997.

AVERAGES, highest lifetime in match play
(60 match-game minimum)
206.7 Tish Johnson, Panorama City, Calif., 168 games.
203.0 Dana Miller-Mackie, Forth Worth, Texas, 165 games.
201.6 Lorrie Nichols, Algonquin, Ill., 349 games.
201.4 Donna Adamek, Apple Valley, Calif., 311 games.
200.1 Pat Costello, Orlando, Fla., 271 games.

GAMES, highest
300 Sharon Todd, Ashland, Ky., 1993.
Karen Wakefield, Elmira, N.Y., 1993.
Carol Norman, Ardmore, Okla., 1995.
Tish Johnson, Northridge, Calif. (2), 1995.

GAMES, lowest
34 Joan Gutchen, Royersford, Pa., 1993.
82 Linda Dombrowski, Blue Springs, Mo., 1982.
85 Judy Wellman, Gerber, Calif., 1988.
87 Doris Obrinski, Roseville, Mich., 1966.
Jennifer Jaslyn, Horseheads, N.Y., 1996.

GAMES, number of 275 and higher

Games	Total	Games	Total	Games	Total
300	5	290	1	278	23
299	2	289	5	277	15
298	2	288	1	276	8
297	3	287	3	275	6
295	1	279	28		

FIVE-GAME Series, highest

1,199	Chele Rutherford, Bel Air, Md., 1995
1,181	Donna Adamek, Stevenson Ranch, Calif., 1995
1,143	Aleta Sill, Dearborn, Mich., 1995
1,142	Leann Butts, Verona, Wis., 1995
	Carol Gianotti, Perth, Australia, 1997

FOUR-GAME Series, highest

1,015	Wendy Macpherson-Papanos, Henderson, Nev., 1993.
1,011	Robin Romeo, Newhall, Calif., 1990.
997	Carol Norman, Ardmore, Okla.,1993
995	Cheryl Robinson, Destrehan, La., 1972.
988	Donna Adamek, Apple Valley Calif., 1979.

FOUR-GAME Series, highest in finals (four-game format)

939	Judy Soutar, Leawood, Kan., 1974.
890	Dorothy Fothergill, North Attleboro, Mass., 1972.
884	Phyllis Massey, Alameda, Calif., 1968.
853	Marian Spencer, Oklahoma City, 1968.
852	Irene Monterosso, East Rutherford, J.J., 1963.
850	Cathy Almeida, Blackwood, N.J. 1987.

GAME, highest in finals

Stepladder Finals Format

299	Shinobu Saitoh, Tokyo, 1979.
279	Aleta Sill, Dearborn, Mich., 1985.
267	Patty Ann, Arlington Heights, Ill., 1990.
265	Loa Boxberger, Russell, Kan., 1978.
248	Kazue Inahashi, Tokyo, 1984.

Four-Game Format

277	Phyllis Massey, Alameda, Calif., 1968.
258	Dorothy Fothergill, North Attleboro, Mass., 1972.
	Phyllis Massey, Alameda, Calif., 1968.
	Judy Soutar, Leawood, Kan., 1974.

MATCH Totals, highest in four-game finals formats

1,737	Phyllis Massey, Alameda, Calif. (884), defeated Marian Spencer, Oklahoma City (853), 1968.
1,731	Dorothy Fothergill, Center Ossippee, N.H. (890), defeated Maureen Harris, Irving, Texas (841), 1972.
1,667	Cathy Almeida, Blackwood, N.J. (850), defeated Lorrie Nichols, Algonquin, Ill. (817), 1987.
1,655	Irene Monterosso, East Rutherford, N.J. (852), defeated Georgette DeRosa, Hillside, Ill. (803), 1963.
1,649	Mildred Ignizio, Rochester, N.Y. (840), defeated Phyllis Massey, Alameda, Calif. (809), 1967.

PARTICIPATION, most years

37	Joan Bender, Arvada, Colo.

	Helen Duval, Berkeley, Calif.
28	Barbara Thorberg, Florissant, Mo.
27	Judy Soutar, Bradenton, Fla.
26	Phyllis Notaro, Brant, N.Y.

QUALIFYING Scores, highest and lowest by years

Year	Highest	Lowest
10 Games		
1997	2,237	1,193
1996	2,210	1,936
1995	2,279	2,004
1994	2,177	1,936
8 Games		
1993	1,786	1,559
1992	1,803	1,574
1991	1,724	1,560
1990	1,709	1,576
1989	1,722	1,529
1988	1,636	1,445
1987	1,832	1,606
1986	1,715	1,512
1985	1,685	1,520
1984	1,682	1,512
1983	1,725	1,518
1982	1,701	1,467
1981	1,673	1,487
1980	1,672	1,480
1979	1,742	1,555
1978	1,738	1,490
1977	1,725	1,493

TITLES, most

3	Millie Ignizio, Rochester, N.Y., 1971, 1970 1967.
2	Donna Adamek, Apple Valley, Calif., 1980, 1979.
	Dorothy Fothergill, North Attleboro, Mass., 1973, 1972.
	Aleta Sill, Dearborn, Mich., 1985, 1983.
	Katsuko Sugimoto, Tokyo, 1982, 1981.

TITLES, most consecutive

2	Donna Adamek, Apple Valley, Calif., 1980, 1979.
	Dorothy Fothergill, Lincoln, R.I., 1973, 1972.
	Millie Ignizio, Rochester, N.Y., 1971, 1970.
	Katsuko Sugimoto, Tokyo, 1982, 1981.

TITLES, most runner-up finishes

2	Vesma Grinfelds, San Francisco, 1990, 1977.
	Dana Miller-Mackie, Forth Worth, Texas, 1993, 1992.
	Pat Costello, Orlando, Fla., 1993, 1975.

VICTORY Margins, narrowest in finals (in pins)

Stepladder Format

1	Alayne Blomenberg, Cranston, R.I. (184), defeated Phyllis Notaro, Brant, N.Y. (183), 1984.

2   Lorene Woods, North Chicago, Ill. (163), defeated Robin Romeo, Newhall, Calif. (161) 1982.
Cora Fiebig, Madison heights, Mich. (191), defeated Cindy Schuble, Louisville, Ky. (189), 1986.

3   Edie Jo Norman, Miami (234), defeated Vesma Grinfelds, San Francisco (231) (including frames to rolloff tie), 1976.

5   Carol Gianotti, Perth, Australia (185), defeated Donna Adamek, Apple Valley, Calif. (180), 1992.
Lisa Wagner, Bradenton, Fla. (231), defeated Tammy Turner, West Palm Beach, Fla. (226), 1996.

Four-Game Format

5   Dorothy Wilkinson, Phoenix, Ariz. (799), defeated Marion Ladewig, Grand Rapids, Mich. (794), 1962.

10   Mildred Ignizio, Rochester, N.Y. (807), defeated Joan Holm, Chicago (797), 1970.

13   Dorothy Fothergill, North Attleboro, Mass. (804), defeated Judy Soutar, Leawood, Kan. (791), 1973.

18   Janet Harman, Cerritos, Calif. (794), defeated Eula Touchette, E. St. Louis, Ill. (776), 1961.

VICTORY Margins, widest in finals (in pins)
Stepladder Format

109   Shinobu Saitoh, Tokyo (299), defeated Pat Costello, Orlando, Fla. (190), 1979.

98   Patty Ann, Arlington Heights, Ill. (267), defeated Pat Costello, Orlando, Fla. (169), 1990.

91   Laurie Soto, Canyon Country, Calif. (245), defeated Lynda Norry, Concord, Calif. (154), 1991.

87   Aleta Sill, Dearborn, Mich. (279), defeated Linda Graham, Des Moines, Iowa (192), 1985.

72   Dede Davidson, San Jose, Calif. (231), defeated Jeanne Maiden-Naccarato, Tacoma, Wash. (159), 1991.

Four-Game Format

234   Judy Soutar, Leawood, Kan. (939), defeated

Betty Morris, Stockton, Calif. (705), 1974.

84   Cindy Powell, Navarre, Ohio (758), defeated Pat Costello, Orlando, Fla. (674), 1975.

67   Ann Feigel, Tucson, Ariz. (832), defeated Mildred Ignizio, Rochester, N.Y. (765), 1969.

58   D.D. Jacobson, Playa Del Rey, Calif. (740), defeated Shirley Garms, Island Lake, Ill. (682), 1964.

900 Series, most in same tournament
(includes qualifying)

2   Marianne Dirupo, Succasunna, N.J., 1993.
Wendy Macpherson-Papanos, Henderson, Nev., 1993.
Sue Neidig, Miami, 1993.
Robin Romeo, Newhall, Calif, 1993.
Jan Schmidt, Rochelle, Ill., 1993.
Tish Johnson, Panorama City, Calif., 1990.

800 Series, most in same tournament
(includes qualifying)

13   Lorrie Nichols, Algonquin, Ill., 1987.

11   Phyllis Massey, Alameda, Calif., 1967.

10   Kim Kinyon-Sutton, Buffalo, N.Y., 1987.
Aleta Sill, Dearborn, Mich., 1989.

9   Mildred Ignizio, Rochester, N.Y., 1970.
Betty Mivelaz, Tujunga, Calif., 1969.
Pat Costello, Orlando, Fla., 1987.

200 Games, most in same tournament in games
and total games (includes qualifying)

Games	Total Games	
40	48	Wendy Macpherson-Papanos, Henderson, Nev., 1993.
36	52	Lorrie Nichols, Algonquin, Ill, 1987.
35	52	Phyllis Massey, Alameda, Calif., 1967.
32	48	Kim Kinyon-Sutton, Buffalo, N.Y., 1987.
29	40	Pat Costello, Orlando, Fla., 1987.
29	44	Bev Ortner, Tucson, Ariz., 1967.

Money Winners, Top 10 leaders

Rank	Total	Tournament	Cashed
1. Aleta Sill, Dearborn, Mich.	$77,170	18	12
2. Donna Adamek, Apple Valley, Calif.	42,010	18	14
3. Katsuko Sugimoto, Tokyo	37,420	7	4
4. Sandra Jo Shiery-Odom, Coldwater, Mich.	31,530	9	6
5. Pat Costello, Orlando, Fla.	31,225	21	16
6. Dana Miller-Mackie, Fort Worth, Texas	29,115	17	11
7. Kazue Inahashi, Tokyo	28,120	7	5
8. Jeanne Naccarato, Tacoma, Wash.	26,650	18	14
9. Cindy Coburn-Carroll, Tonawanda, N.Y.	23,870	16	14
10. Carol Gianotti, Perth, Australia	23,650	9	5

The WIBC/ABC Mixed Championships is the only national mixed bowling tournament conducted by WIBC and ABC.

Tournament participants using handicaps of 90 percent of 220 compete in the tournament's mixed doubles event, mixed four-player team event and optional all events.

Four-player teams are comprised of two women and two men, and doubles teams are comprised of one woman and one man. Tournament rules do not allow more than one professional bowler on each mixed doubles or four-player team.

Effective with the 1993 event, men and women will compete in separate optional all-event categories. WIBC and ABC conduct the tournament, which runs daily, in a different U.S. city each year. A special WIBC/ABC committee selects the tournament location at least one year in advance.

WIBC/ABC Mixed Championships Champions

Four-Player Team Event

1997 Coosa Body Shop, Talladega, Ala., 2,077 actual, 2,833 with handicap.

1996 Lang Exploritory Drilling, Elko Nev., 2,106 actual, 2,793 with handicap.

1995 Rolling Thunder, Lawrenceville, Ga., 2,025 actual, 2,880 with handicap.

1994 Dick's Sandbaggers, Coeur d'Alene, Idaho, 2,224 actual, 2,847 with handicap.

1993 Ranch West Bowl 2, Kansas City, Kan., 2,348 actual, 2,869 with handicap.

1992 Ord Bowl, Ericson, Neb., 2,352 actual, 2,954 with handicap.

1991 Ypsilanti Seafood, Ypsilanti, Mich., 2,009 actual, 2,795 with handicap.

Doubles Event

1997 Karen Riley-Mark Riley, Normandy, Tenn., 1,226 actual, 1,523 with handicap.

1996 Mary Marks-Ron Marks, Cudahy, Wis., 1,153 actual, 1,514 with handicap.

1995 Debbie Corvo-Chuck Corvo, Lawrenceville, Ga., 1,100 actual, 1,526 with handicap.

1994 Cindy Harker-Roy Harker, Portland, Ore., 1,232 actual, 1,480 with handicap.

1993 Paula Sheraon-Glenn Leonard, Greenville, N.C. 1,018 actual, 1,531 with handicap.

1992 Helen Tomczuk-John Kettering, Chicago, 1,329 actual, 1,536 with handicap.

1991 Brenda Thomas-Gary Thomas, Ennis, Texas, 1,202 actual, 1,456 with handicap.

Men's All Events

1997 Mario Escamillia, Monahans, Texas, 1,542 actual, 2,220 with handicap.

1996 Larry Gallegos, Mesa, Ariz., 1,735 actual, 2,260 with handicap.

1995 Robert Lunny, Lawrenceville, Ga., 1,642 actual, 2,245 with handicap.

1994 John Mottern, Coeur d'Alene, Idaho, 1,805 actual, 2,192 with handicap.

Women's All Events

1997 Juanita Rogers-Joe, Detroit, Mich., 1,757 actual, 2,177 with handicap

1996 Paula Miller, Dallas, Ore., 1,518 actual, 2,220 wtih handicap

1995 Debbie Corvo, Lawrenceville, Ga., 1,496 actual, 2,231 with handicap.

1994 Erma Garvey, Austin, Texas, 1,367 actual, 2,159 with handicap.

Overall All Events

1993 Glenn Leonard, Greenville, N.C., 1,219 actual, 1,591 with handicap.

1992 Mike Lent, Coeur d'Alene, Idaho, 1,112 actual, 1,538 with handicap.

1991 Tommy Harbarth, New Braunfels, Texas, 1,151 actual, 1,491 with handicap.

Men's Singles

1997 Richard Minogue, Anaheim, Calif., 729 actual, 812 with handicap.

1996 Dale Eaton, Seward, Alaska, 668 actual, 805 with handicap.

1995 Robert Lunny, Lawrenceville, Ga., 575 actual, 766 with handicap.

1994 Joe Jefferson, Orangeburg, S.C., 668 actual, 765 with handicap.

Women's Singles

1997 Tera Durham, Prospect, Ky. 689 actual, 805 with handicap.

1996 Tracy Kwon, Berkeley, Calif., 548 actual, 782 with handicap.

1995 Cindy Burks, Sherman, Texas, 549 actual, 770 with handicap.

1994 Bee Garrett, Quincy, Wash., 565 actual, 745 with handicap.

WIBC/ABC Mixed Championships Records

Games, highest

Handicapped

336 Dale Kay, Riverton, Wyo., 1992.

328 Norman Parton, Talladega, Ala., 1992.

324 Daniel Chambers, Ft. Riley, Kan., 1993.
Andy Collinson, Normal, Ill., 1996.

322 John Russell, Camden, Ark., 1996.

Scratch

300 Dale Kay, Riverton, Wyo., 1992.
Todd Thompson, Reno, Nev., 1992.
John Russell, Camden, Ark., 1996.
Andy Collinson, Normal, Ill., 1996.
Herman Roark, Calhan, Ga., 1997.

Games, highest
Four-Player Team Event

Handicapped

1,090 Ord Bowl, Ericson, Neb., 1992.

1,039 Georgia Strait Penguins, Campbell, B.C., 1994.

1,022 Fishin' 4 Strikes, Houston, 1993.

1,020 TPA/Rolling Thunder, Lawrenceville, Ga., 1992.

1,015 A Family Affair, Chula Vista, Calif., 1997.

Scratch

975 Taz Pin Pals, Dayton, Ohio, 1997.

933 Holiday Lanes II, Lansing, Mich., 1997.

908 Lefty's Rights, Louisville, Ky., 1997.

906 Two Wrongs & Two Rights, Stockton, Calif., 1992.

903 Brackman By Integreat, Lyndon, Ky., 1997.

Doubles Event
Handicapped
582 Andy Magerle and Desiree Magerle, Central Point, Ore., 1996
572 Darlene Williams and Kevin Williams, Nyssa, Ore., 1996
571 Millie Gilliland and Craig Chang, San Francisco and Petaluma, Calif., 1992
569 Jonnie Parton and Norman Parton; Talladega, Ala., 1992
562 Betty Jo Hampton and Bill Reeves; Prescott, Ark., and Nashville, Ark.; 1992

Scratch
496 Sandy Sanderson and Shawn Minke; Miamisburg and Westerville, Ohio, 1993
495 Bob Bolander and Doreen Koos, Mesa, Ariz., 1997
493 Cathy Martinich and Tim Minor; Spokane, Wash., 1992
490 Helen Tomczuk and John Kettering, Crestwood, Ill., 1992
Andy Magerle and Desilee Magerle, Central Point, Ore., 1996

Singles Event
Handicapped
322 John Russell, Camden, Ark., 1996
317 Tera Durham, Prospect, Ky., 1997
315 Marjorie Williams, 1996
Pamela Carda, Rapid City, S.D., 1997
309 Dick Cowley, Olympia, Wash., 1994

Scratch
300 John Russell, Camden, Ark., 1996
289 Lennie Hall, Las Vegas, 1996
288 Lowell Lougren, Wyoming, Wash., 1994
279 Alex Arizala, Tualatin, Ore., 1994
James Cermin, Deer Park, Texas, 1996
Mike Burke, Columbus, Ohio, 1997

Three-Game Series, highest by individual
Handicapped
832 Percy Jackson, Hawthorne, Calif., 1992
828 Sidney Golding, Apple Valley, Calif., 1993
827 Craig Chang, Petaluma, Calif., 1992
825 Glenn Leonard, Greenville, N.C., 1993
Robert Lunny, Lawrenceville, Ga., 1993

Scratch
776 Todd Thompson, Reno, Nev., 1992

760 Ron Smith, Lowell, Ind., 1997
759 Aaron Ellingsworth, Louisville, Ky., 1997
757 Sean Heath, Spokane, Wash., 1992
748 Richard Flores, Stockton, Calif., 1992

Three-Game Series, highest by teams
Four-Player Teams
Handicapped
2,954 Ord Bowl, Ericson, Neb., 2,352 scratch, 1992
2,947 Rolling Thunder, Lawrenceville, Ga., 2,175 scratch, 1992
2,901 Two Wrongs & Two Rights, Stockton, Calif., 2,629 scratch, 1992
2,877 Shasta Lanes, Old Shasta, Calif., 2,391 scratch, 1992
2,869 Ranch West Bowl 2, Kansas City, Kan., 2,348 scratch, 1993

Scratch
2,629 Two Wrongs & Two Rights, Stockton, Calif., 1992
2,564 Brackman By Integreat, Lyndon, Ky., 1997
2,540 Taz Pin Pals, Dayton, Ohio, 1997
2,535 Holiday Lanes II, Lansing, Mich., 1997
2,507 Lefty's Rights, Louisville, Ky., 1997

Doubles Event Teams
Handicap
1,531 Helen Tomczuk and John Kettering; Crestwood, Ill. and Chicago; 202 handicap; 1992
Paula Sheraon and Glenn Leonard; Greenville, N.C., 513 handicap; 1993
Karen Riley and Mark Riley, Normany, Tenn., 305 handicap, 1997
1,526 Debbie Corvo and Chuck Corvo; Lawrenceville, Ga., 426 handicap, 1995
1,514 Mary Marks and Ronald Marks, Cudahy, Wis., 361 handicap, 1996

Scratch
1,359 Debra Sinek and Michael Sinek, Odenton, Md., 1997
1,329 Helen Tomczuk and John Kettering; Crestwood, Ill., and Chicago; 1992
Bob Bolander and Doreen Koos, Mesa, Ariz., 1997
1,325 Michelle Boomershine and Josh Hale, Wichita, Kan., 1996
1,305 Ron Pollard and Regina Snodgrass, Versailles, Ind., 1997

SENIOR CHAMPIONSHIPS

WIBC and ABC Senior Championships

The National Seniors Tournament had its origin in 1960 when the United States Seniors Bowling Assn. conducted an event in Skokie, Ill. just outside of Chicago. It continued to hold national events until 1963.

In 1964, ABC took over sponsorship of the event, keeping the event in Skokie for four more years before moving it to Milwaukee.

For the first 22 years, the Seniors was basically a regional event, drawing participants mainly from the Midwest.

The Seniors tournament became a truly national event in 1982 when the finals were held on the ABC Tournament lanes in the Baltimore Convention Center in Baltimore, Md. The WIBC was invited to initiate a Seniors event and conduct it on the ABC Tournament lanes. Since 1994, WIBC and ABC have held their events on each organization's Tournament lanes.

When the Tournament was held in Milwaukee and Skokie, any senior bowler who wanted to enter could participate. Now, seniors must qualify through state and provincial competitions to earn the right to compete in the finals.

Tournament participants compete in four age-based categories: Class A (70 years or more); Class B (65 to 69 years); Class C (60 to 64 years); and Class D (55 to 59 years).

Seniors bowl six qualifying games. The top-four scorers in each class advance to match-play competition. Since 1987, seniors' qualifying scores are not carried over to match-play competition.

In match play, bowlers face their class's other three match-play finalists. Match-play winners receive 30 bonus points per win and 15 points per tie, in addition to their actual and handicap scores. After three match-play games, the highest scorer in each class is named the class's WIBC or ABC Senior Champion.

WIBC/ABC Senior Championships Class Champions
Women's Champions

Class A

1997	Rose Aitken, Sechelt, British Columbia
1996	Jeanne Stear, Winnipeg, Manitoba
1995	Darlene Nelson, Maryville, Mo.
1994	Madge Roberts, Pulaski, N.Y.
1993	Maurine Dempsey, West Chicago, Ill.
1992	Frances O'Hop, Norfolk, Va.
1991	Clara Gamble, Charleston, S.C.
1990	Margaret Hunter, South Ogden, Utah
1989	Reta Waterman, Surrey, British Columbia
1988	Trudy Todd, Denver
1987	Helen Wold, Shelton, Wash.
1986	Muriel Tacy, Hampton, Va.
1985	Leona Seele, Belvue, Kan.
1984	Roberta Koon, Charleston Heights, S.C.
1983	Betty Bushee, Bennington, Vt.
1982	Hazel Houchard, Plain City, Ohio

Class B

1997	Anna Lou Thompson, Lander, Wyo.
1996	Sara Bottorff, Feds, Colo.
1995	Polly McQueen, Barstow, Texas
1994	Nellie Danis, Braymer, Md.
1993	Anita Hoscher, Point Pleasant, W. Va.
1992	Helen Ward, Lincoln, Neb.
1991	Connie Peterson, N. Kingston, R.I.
1990	Faye Kessel, Marion, Ill.
1989	Maudie Siler, Beaver Dam, Ky.
1988	Gladys White, Newark, N.J.
1987	Lula Dodson, Orlando, Fla.
1986	Marjorie Schreiner, Hays, Kan.
1985	Jean Tolle, Joliet, Ill.
1984	Edith naile, Elaine, Ark.
1983	Theda Ryan, Richland Center, Wis.
1982	Priscilla Marshall, Minn.

Class C

1997	Hazel Montgomery, Bowling Green, Ky.
1996	Lillian Hayes, Louisville, Ky.
1995	Katherine Hubert, Union Grove, Ala.
1994	Darlene Shepard, New Bedford, Ill.
1993	Betty Fuqua, Wilmar, Ark.
1992	Dixie Pence, Braymer, Mo.
1991	Virginia Malson, Neptune, N.J.
1990	June Leslie, Madoc, Ontario
1989	Betty June Thomas, Pahrump, Nev.
1988	Betty Crane, Chicago
1987	Marcy Bayne, Calais, Vt.
1986	Agnes Kochin, Sayre, Pa.
1985	Georgia East, Fort Cobb, Okla.
1984	Gerry Cutler, Claremont, S.D.
1983	Loree Taylor, Lexington, Texas
1982	Velma Storey, Kingsport, Tenn.

Class D

1997	Jeannette DeLoach, Reidsville, Ga.
1996	Patricia Galla, Reynoldsville, W. Va.
1995	Lois Tillotson, London, Ontario, Canada
1994	Rose Rogers, Atlanta
1993	Ruby Dill, Lincoln, Neb.
1992	Irene Schriner, Blue Hill, Neb.
1991	June Kochis, Pueblo, Colo.
1990	Lorie Perry, Tucson, Ariz.
1989	Vivian Breier, Fairfield, N.J.
1988	Chris Cornes, Joppa, Md.
1987	Betty Moore, Romney, W. Va.
1986	Mertie Siders, Little Rock, Ark.
1985	Jan Fay, Blackfoot, Idaho
1984	Estelle Sinclair, Sublette, Kan.
1983	Frances Wallis, Imlay City, Mich.
1982	Eileen Ennis, Crofton, Md.

Men's Champions

Class A		Class C	
1997	Donald Andrew, Sierra Vista, Ariz.	1997	Donald Smith, Aiken, S.C.
1996	Donald Andrew, Sierra Vista, Ariz.	1996	Jerry Zabriskie, Murray, Utah
1995	Harry Upton, Leon, W. Va	1995	Richard Legg, Chugiak, Alaska
1994	Marvin Soliday, Piqua, Ohio	1994	Bob Hubbard, Pahrump, Nev.
1993	Hal Ogata Sr., Honolulu	1993	Norman Heywood, Winnipeg, Manitoba
1992	Dick Branson, Tulsa, Okla.	1992	Bob Gunner, Decatur, Ala.
1991	Jonnie Collins, San Diego	1991	Louis Fisher, Manville, N.J.
1990	Vincente Berdeguer, Caparra Height, Puerto Rico	1990	Harold Zorning, Hull, Ga.
1989	Dan Chovan, Grants Pass, Ore.	1989	Ernie Hiser, Roseville, Calif.
1988	George Ruschak, Warren, Ohio	1988	Roland Forcier, Manchester, N.H.
1987	Peter Kavalski, Fond du Lac, Wis.	1987	Fred Pope, Concord, N.H.
1986	Idus Abney, Penticon, British Columbia	1986	Harold Clevenger, Kennewick, Wash.
1985	Ted Geiser, Louisville, Ky.	1985	Art Prather, Natchez, Miss.
1984	Bill Andberg, Anoka, Minn.	1984	Walter Brooks, Philipsburg, Mont.
1983	Bill Perham, Tucson, Ariz.	1983	J.C. Jensen, Lavina, Mont.
1982	John Taylor, Hockessin, Del.	1982	Ralph Lloyd, Denver

Class B		Class D	
1997	Richard Davies, Pocahontas, Ark.	1997	Arthur Gallegos, Cottonwood, Ariz.
1996	Willie Locke, Ely, Nev.	1996	Joe Wiedmier, Braymer, Mo.
1995	Bill Burnett, Greer, S.C.	1995	F. Gordy Bittner, McCleary, Wash.
1994	Robert Bennett, Paola, Kan.	1994	Ron Spilman, Manassas, Va.
1993	David Childers, Caddo, Okla.	1993	Clarence Woolums, Frankfort, Ky.
1992	Warren Watson, Truth or Consequences, N.M.	1992	Tony Frigon, Port Coquitlam, British Columbia
1991	Jess Marshall, Frankfort, Ky.	1991	Guillermo Sotomayor, Arlington Heights, Ill.
1990	Glen Thruston, Cascade, Idaho	1990	Floyd Boss, Osage City, Kan.
1989	Reinold Krause, Walnut, Calif.	1989	Rich Peters, Forsyth, Mo.
1988	Lee Rodawalt, Enterprise, Ala.	1988	Robert Gantenbien, Gaffney, S.C.
1987	Floyd Lansdale, Fordyce, Ark.	1987	Edgar Galloway, Dillsburg, Pa.
1986	Warren Adams, Columbia, Miss.	1986	Leonard Wiedmier, Braymer, Mo.
1985	John Erska, Denver	1985	Anthony Quaranto, Niagara Falls, N.Y.
1984	Bill Gilmore, Eureka, Kan.	1984	Harold Clore, Cameron, Texas
1983	Charles Reed, Omaha, Neb.	1983	George Haushahn, Kansas City, Mo.
1982	Floyd Smith, Auburn, Ala.	1982	John Turick, Leesville, La.

WIBC Senior Championships
Women's Records

Games, highest match-play by class
Handicapped

Class A	271	Catherine Spence, New York, 1982
Class B	256	Lorraine Revell, Fox Lake, Ill., 1992
Class C	279	Darlene Shepard, New Bedford, Ill., 1994
Class D	245	Irene Schriner, Blue Hill, Neb., 1992

Scratch

Class A	235	Catherine Spence, New York, 1982
Class B	224	Lorraine Revell, Fox Lake, Ill., 1992
Class C	234	Darlene Shepard, New Bedford, Ill., 1994
Class D	214	Alice Linebarger, The Dalles, Ore., 1992
		Irene Schriner, Blue Hill, Neb., 1992

Three-Game Series, highest match-play by class
Handicapped

Class A	678	Clara Gamble, Charleston, S.C., 1991
Class B	663	Mary Ann Hamer, Rensselaer, Ind., 1996
Class C	702	Katherine Hubert, Union Grove, Ala., 1995
Class D	658	Barbara Montey, Wisconsin, 1983

Scratch

Class A	594	Clara Gamble, Charleston, S.C., 1991
Class B	565	Velma Springer, Artesia, N.M., 1995
Class C	585	Connie Tichgelaar, Montclair, Calif., 1992
Class D	570	Eleanore Libby, Oregon City, Ore., 1986

Games, highest qualifying by class
Handicapped

Class A	273	Jeanne Stear, Winnipeg, Manitoba, 1996
Class B	283	Marcy Bayne, Calais, Vt., 1992
Class C	270	Ruth Weisenbach, Maynard, Ark., 1996
Class D	265	Wilene Barnes, Bethany, Okla., 1992

Scratch

Class A	234	Jeanne Stear, Winnipeg, Manitoba, 1995
Class B	257	Helen Duval, Berkeley, Calif., 1985
Class C	235	Willa Houston, Los Angeles, 1995
Class D	235	Carol Morris, Brady, Mont., 1992

Three-Game Series, highest qualifying by class
Handicapped

Class A	685	Mary Jane Meyer, Louisville, Ky., 1994
Class B	712	Virginia Willie, Fridley, Minn., 1990
Class C	740	Ruth Weissenbach, Maynard, Ark. 1996
Class D	696	Irene Schriner, Blue Hill, Neb., 1992

Scratch

Class A	596	Jeanne Stear, Winnipeg, Manitoba, 1996
Class B	643	Helen Duval, Berkeley, Calif., 1985
Class C	630	Connie Tichgelaar, Montclair, Calif., 1992
Class D	603	Irene Schriner, Blue Hill, Neb., 1992

The original dream of a bowling hall of fame and museum came in the minds of former ABC Executive Secretary Frank Baker and former ABC Public Relations Manager Bruce Pluckhahn. Land was purchased at ABC's former headquarters in the Milwaukee suburb of Shorewood for an appropriate shrine.

When ABC moved to its present headquarters in the Milwaukee suburb of Greendale to where WIBC moved from Columbus, Ohio, two floors were set aside in the building for a hall of fame. That compact area served nearly 10 years as a small tribute to the sport.

Then came the notion that a separate, special place should be designed and built. After much consideration from many cities, downtown St. Louis was selected and the International Bowling Museum and Hall of Fame was opened in 1984. Today it contains old and new artifacts of the sport, tributes to the greats of the game, even lanes where people still set the pins. It truly is the sport's ultimate shrine.

Salute to Champions

Jim Bennett, a career Brunswick employee and dedicated bowling official, determined bowling needed something special to honor those who had helped the sport. So was born the Salute to Champions.

Since 1990, the event has drawn everyone from corporate presidents to association officers, bowling suppliers to league bowlers, professional and amateur sports stars to writers. All have helped pay tribute to the sport while raisingfunds for the International Bowling Museum and Hall of Fame. Honorees include individuals and corporations.

Salute to Champions Honorees

1997	1996	1995	1994
Carter Burgess	Joe Norris	Frank Baker	Earl Anthony
Keijuro Nakano		Don Carter	Jack Reichert
AC Delco		Showboat Hotel	Nick Mormando

1993	1992	1991	1990
Helen Duval	Dick Weber	Marion Ladewig	Michael Roarty
ESPN	Bridgestone/Firestone Inc.	Dennis Swanson	Chris Schenkel
Coca-Cola Co.	Knight/Ridder Newspapers		

Bud Light Hall of Fame Tournament

From 1982-96, the Bud Light Hall of Fame Tournament was a handicap competition for six ABC members, six ABC Hall of Famers, six WIBC members and six WIBC Hall of Famers. The 24 bowlers were divided into two divisions. Division I included six ABC members and six WIBC Hall of Famers and Division II includes six WIBC members and Six ABC Hall of Famers. ABC and WIBC members enter when they pay $1 at their local bowling center and bowl a three-game series in league or tournament competition. High scorers advance to one of four regional competitions, with the regional competitions selecting the 12 bowlers who will advance to the national competition. Tournament champions share a $15,000 first-place payoff, second place is worth $10,000.

The tournament has undergone several name and format changes in its history. The Bud Light Hall of Fame Tournament — the event's original name — returned in 1991. No tournament was held in 1993. Beginning in February 1994, the tournament was held annually in conjunction with the International Bowling Museum and Hall of Fame Salute to Champions. In 1997 it was renamed the Bud Light Hall of Fame Challenge and changed to a national pins over average format.

Bud Light Hall of Fame Tournament Winners

1997	Bob Gray, Lexington, Ky. and Alice Flanders, Palmyra, Va.
1996	LeVett Martin, Newark, N.J. and Steve Fehr, Cincinnati
1995	Martine Miller, Miami and Don Johnson, Las Vegas
1994	Pat Costello, Orlando, Fla. and William Bell, Stone Mountain, Ga.
1992	Pat Costello, Orlando, Fla. and Johnny Weber, Southhaven, Miss.
1991	George Pappas, Charlotte, N.C. and Mary Kolb, Burnside, Ill.
1990	Betty Morris, Stockton, Calif. and Stewart Sisler, Grimsby, Ont.
1989	Judy Soutar, Leawood, Kan. and Tom Dorsey, Tulsa, Okla.
1988	Betty Morris, Stockton, Calif. and Doug Hawkins, Lancaster, Calif.
1987	Dick Weber, St. Louis and Lynn Pitts Thomas, Carrolton, Ga.
1986	Dick Weber, St. Louis and Linda Rankin, Pahrump, Nev.
1985	Dick Weber, St. Louis and Esther Finney, Guthrie, Okla.
1984	Judy Soutar, Leawood, Kan. and Bill Vanderpool, Meade, Kan.
1983	Nelson Burton Jr., St. Louis and Sandi Simmons, Overland Park, Kan.
1982	Shirley Garms, Chicago and John Kisler, Twin Falls, Idaho

BOWLING HALL OF FAME AND MUSEUM

The International Bowling Museum and Hall of Fame in St. Louis communicates, celebrates and preserves the history of the sport and its athletes. Since its June 2, 1984 opening, more than 200,000 bowling enthusiasts have studied the shrine's 3,500-plus artifacts. The first Bowling Hall of Fame was located at Bowling Headquarters in Greendale, Wis. The creation of the Young American Bowling Alliance, and the continued growth of WIBC and soon required the Hall's Bowling Headquarters space. As a result, the museum was constructed in St. Louis.

WIBC HALL OF FAME

The WIBC Hall of Fame recognizes members in two categories: Superior Performance, which recognizes remarkable bowling achievements, or Meritorious Service, which recognizes dedicated service to WIBC on the local, state and national levels. Superior Performance candidates must hold a WIBC Championship Tournament, WIBC Queens Tournament, national professional title, or international competition title; and have bowled in 15 or more WIBC Championship Tournaments (unless injury or illness have shortened their careers).

WIBC HALL OF FAME SUPERIOR PERFORMANCE
Total Number Inducted - 80

JOY ABEL
Lansing, Ill.
Inducted 1984

Joy Abel emerged into the forefront of women's bowling in the early 1960s. She won five titles, headed by the WIBC Championship Tournament team championship. In addition, she won the BPAA All-Star Tournament and National Team Tournament.

MAE BOLT
Berwyn, Ill.
Inducted 1978

Mae Bolt began her career in some of the best 1950s leagues. She won seven WIBC Tournament Championship titles in a 20-year span from 1958-1978 and has bowled four 1,800s in WIBC events. In addition, she has earned numerous local and state titles.

DONNA ADAMEK
Stevenson Ranch, Calif.
Inducted 1996

Adamek was Bowler of the Year from 1979-82 after winning the 1975 Alberta E. Crowe Star of Tomorrow. She went on to win 19 pro titles including five major championships. She also won four WIBC Tournament titles in the 1980s.

GLORIA BOUVIA
Gresham, Ore.
Inducted 1987

Gloria Bouvia has achieved recognition on local, state and national levels. Teamed with another WIBC Hall of Fame member, Judy Soutar, Bouvia won consecutive WIBC Championship Tournament doubles event titles in 1969 and 1970.

PATTY ANN
Kernersville, N.C.
Inducted 1995

Ann, an Illinois native, won the 1992 WIBC Tournament singles title, the 1990 WIBC Queens Tournament and 1989 AMF World Cup as a TEAM USA member. She has three of WIBC's four all-time high season averages (232, 231 and 230) among her numerous records.

LOA BOXBERGER
Russell, Kan.
Inducted 1984

Loa Boxberger earned major titles in two decades, the 1960s and 1970s. In addition to winning the prestigious WIBC Queens Tournament, she won two WIBC Championship Tournament team event titles, two professional bowling titles, two Japan Pearl Cup events and the Brunswick Red Crown Classic.

* Deceased   + Star of Yesteryear

PAM BUCKNER
Reno, Nev.
Inducted 1990

Pam Buckner has many national, state and local bowling honors to her credit. She has won 22 professional titles and 14 local WBA titles. Buckner's most prestigious accomplishment came in 1976 when she won the WIBC Queens Tournament.

CATHERINE BURLING
Cincinnati
Inducted 1958

Catherine Burling competed in 50 WIBC Championship Tournaments. In 1934 her Tommy Dall's Five won the WIBC team event title. She also won the grand slam of the Cincinnati Women's Bowling Association Tournament four times.

NINA BURNS*
Pompano Beach, Fla.
Inducted 1977

Nina Burns, a self-taught bowler, gained fame in 1942 at the WIBC Championship Tournament. In addition, to winning the all-events title, Burns, a member of the Logan Square Buicks Team, anchored the team to a 2,815 tally and a championship title.

ANITA CANTALINE
Warren, Mich.
Inducted 1979

Three WIBC Championship Tournament crowns are held by Anita Cantaline. She won the WIBC all-events title in 1957. Additionally, in 1957 and 1959, Canataline was a member of the WIBC team champions.

LA VERNE CARTER
Las Vegas
Inducted 1977

LaVerne Carter is a two-time winner in the WIBC Championship Tournament, claiming an all— events championship in 1951 and a team title in 1974. In addition, she won the BPAA doubles tournament in 1958 and 1959 and the 1964 BPAA U.S. Open All-Star tournament.

PAULA CARTER
Miami
Inducted 1994

Paula Carter's outstanding professional career includes a tie with pro bowler Dana Miller-Mackie for the 1990 WIBC Championship Tournament singles event with a 705 three game series. Carter was also named Bowler of the Year in 1971 and has won two first place BPAA finishes in 1971 and 1975.

DORIS COBURN
Buffalo, N.Y.
Inducted 1976

Doris Coburn has won team, doubles, singles and all events titles on both state and local levels. She earned WIBC Championship Tournament titles in 1970 and 1972. Another career highlight came in 1975 when she won the Brunswick Red Crown Classic.

CINDY COBURN-CARROLL
Buffalo, N.Y.
Inducted 1998

Coburn-Carroll joins Doris Coburn as the first mother-daughter combination in the WIBC Hall of Fame. She became the youngest bowler ever to lead the WIBC membership in average with 211 during the 1976-77 season. That same year, she teamed with her mother to set a then-WIBC doubles record with a 1,444 total. She has gone on to win 15 professional titles including the 1992 WIBC Queens. She won the 1991 and 1994 WIBC Classic Division doubles titles with Lucy Giovinco-Sandelin.

PAT COSTELLO
Orlando, Fla.
Inducted 1986

Pat Costello distinguished herself in both the WIBC Championship Tournament and the Queens Tournament. She has also won numerous professional titles. Costello won WIBC team event titles in 1969, 1973 and 1981 and is only one of nine women to earn three or more WIBC team titles. Costello's fourth WIBC title came in 1982 when she tied for doubles event honors. She won a fifth title in doubles in 1988.

* Deceased   + Star of Yesteryear

PATTY COSTELLO
Scranton, Pa.
Inducted 1989

Patty Costello holds two team titles from the WIBC Championship Tournament, winning honors in 1970 and 1972. She also holds 25 professional titles and 29 regional titles, 20 of which were earned since 1980.

PAT DRYER
Indianapolis
Inducted 1978

Pat Dryer is noted as one of the premier exhibition and tournament performers. Dryer was a member of the 1951 WIBC Championship Tournament team event champions. On the state level, she has captured 20 titles in singles, doubles team and all-events competition. She holds 27 city crowns.

HELEN DUVAL
Berkeley, Calif.
Inducted 1970

Helen Duval won both the WIBC Championship Tournament team event and all events titles in 1969. She also captured two professional bowling titles and in 1961 she won the BPAA national doubles title with Nobu Asami.

CATHERINE FELLMETH**⁺
Lake Geneva, Wis.
Inducted 1970

One of Chicago's best women bowlers and athletes, Catherine Fellmeth was a member of the 1942 WIBC Championship Tournament team event champion, the Logan Square Buicks. She also won the all events title in 1946.

DOROTHY FOTHERGILL
Center Ossippee, N.H.
Inducted 1980

Dorothy Fothergill won eight WIBC titles from 1970 to 1973. She won back-to-back Queens Tournament titles in 1972 and 1973. Fothergill also won the BPAA All-Star crown in 1968 and 1969.

DEANE FRITZ**⁺
Toledo, Ohio
Inducted 1966

Deane Fritz bowled in 45 WIBC Championship Tournaments, winning three titles. In 1919 and 1923 she was a member of the team event champions. Additionally, in 1923 she also won the all events title. In 1966, Fritz was named "Star of Yesteryear."

SHIRLEY GARMS
Island Lake, Ill.
Inducted 1971

Shirley Garms holds four WIBC Championship Tournament titles. In addition to being Chicago's 1960s Bowler of the Decade, Garms won the BPAA All-Star event in 1962 and was named Woman Bowler of the Year in 1961 and 1962.

NIKKI GIANULIAS
Valejo, Calif.
Inducted 1997

Gianulias began earning national attention in 1977 when she won the first of six collegiate championships while attending the University of Santa Clara. She was selected the Alberta E. Crowe Star of Tomorrow in 1978, Ladies Pro Bowlers Tour Rookie of the Year in 1979 and has won 18 professional titles. She was the WIBC Open Doubles champ with Donna Adamek in 1981, a member of the 1986 championship team and runnerup in the 1982 Queens tournament. She is a six-time WIBC All-American and the 1982 Bowling Writers Association of America Bowler of the Year.

OLGA GLOOR⁺
Vista, Calif.
Inducted 1976

Olga Gloor has the distinction of achieving great success in professional, amateur and international levels of competition. She was a member of the 1954 WIBC Championship Tournament team event champions, the Marhoefer Weiners. She captured the World's Invitational title in 1959 and on the international level won the women's all events title at the 1974 FIQ American Zone Championships.

* Deceased   + Star of Yesteryear

ALDA (ASHIE) GONZALEZ
San Juan, Puerto Rico
Inducted 1998

Ashie Gonzalez became the first WIBC Hall member from outside the territorial United States. She made her debut as a Puerto Rican national team member in the 1966 FIQ American Zone Championships where she earned a bronze medal in the team event. Since then, she has represented Puerto Rico in eight FIQ American Zone championships, four FIQ world Championships, two Pan American Games and six World Cups.

LINDA GRAHAM
Des Moines, Iowa
Inducted 1992

Linda Graham won a WIBC Championship Tournament doubles event title in 1985. In addition, Graham has represented the United States as a TEAM USA member, and as the 1989 U.S. Amateur Champion.

MARY LOU GRAHAM
Chiefland, Fla.
Inducted 1989

Mary Lou Graham won a WIBC Championship Tournament doubles event title in 1986. During her bowling career, Graham earned 17 Florida Championships and 14 Miami WBA Titles.

GOLDIE GREENWALD*
Cleveland
Inducted 1953

In 1918, Goldie Greenwald bowled a world record series for women, 732, while competing in a men's league. She accumulated more than 50 medals during her outstanding, but brief career.

VESMA GRINFELDS
San Francisco
Inducted 1991

Vesma Grinfelds has 10 professional and 13 regional titles to her credit. She participated in 15 WIBC Championship Tournaments and 18 Queens Tournaments. She was a member of the 1983 WIBC team event champions, Telectronic Systems.

JANET HARMAN*
Cerritos, Calif.
Inducted 1985

Janet Harman amassed more than 20 titles in national, state and local competition during her 30-year career. Her most memorable triumph came in 1961 when she won the inaugural WIBC Queens Tournament in Fort Wayne, Ind.

STELLA HARTRICK*+
Detroit
Inducted 1972

Stella Hartrick captured the WIBC Championship Tournament doubles event title, along with partner Clara Allen in 1941. Her awards on the local and state level earned her inclusion the Michigan Amateur Sports Hall of Fame.

GRAYCE HATCH*+
Cleveland
Inducted 1953

Grayce Hatch was WIBC Championship Tournament all events champion in both 1925 and 1927. During her career she pursued three levels in the sport of bowling— administration, instruction and competition. Hatch reached the top of each level before her death in 1965.

JEAN HAVLISH
St Paul, Minn.
Inducted 1987

Jean Havlish's career includes bowling accomplishments on the amateur, international and professional levels. In 1964 she won the WIBC Championship Tournament singles event championship and the all events in 1980.

MARTHA HOFFMAN*
Madison, Wis.
Inducted 1979

Martha Hoffman won the 1952 WIBC Championship Tournament doubles event title and in 1962 captured the tournament singles crown. In addition to the national titles, Hoffman won six local titles and one state title.

* Deceased   + Star of Yesteryear

JOAN HOLM
Chicago
Inducted 1974

Joan Holm, a standout in league bowling, was a member of the 1966 WIBC Championship Tournament team, the Gossard Girls. In addition, she also captained the U.S. women's team to two gold medals in the five-woman and four-woman events at the 1971 FIQ World Bowling Championships.

BIRDIE HUMPHREYS**＋**
St. Louis
Inducted 1979

Many of Birdie Humphreys' accomplishments were recorded before WIBC was organized in 1916. She won titles in singles competition and as a member of the Stein's Junior Team at the 1920 WIBC Championship Tournament.

MILDRED IGNIZIO
Rochester, N.Y.
Inducted 1975

Mildred Ignizio is the only woman to have won three WIBC Queens Tournament titles, in 1967, 1970 and 1971. In addition, she captured the WIBC Championship Tournament doubles event title in 1971 and 1973, team event titles in 1970 and 1972 and all events in 1972.

D.D. JACOBSON
Playa Del Rey, Calif.
Inducted 1981

D.D. Jacobson won the WIBC Queens Tournament crown in 1963. She was a member of the 1967 WIBC Championship Tournament team event champions. She also rolled a 737 championship singles record three-game series in 1972. In addition, Jacobson has six local and state titles to her credit.

EMMA JAEGER**＋**
Toledo, Ohio
Inducted 1953

Emma Jaeger's nine WIBC Championship Tournament titles rank her second in most titles won in WIBC history. Jaeger also holds the WIBC record for consecutive championships in both singles (three) and all events (four).

ANNESE KELLY
Las Vegas
Inducted 1985

Although Annese Kelly is a two-time WIBC Championship Tournament winner, she earned her greatest fame as a member of the U.S. women's teams competing in FIQ events. Six gold medals and one silver medal adorn Kelly's record from three FIQ tournaments.

DORIS KNECHTGES*
Ferndale, Mich.
Inducted 1983

Known as "The Bolt," Doris Knechtges won three titles; team, doubles, and all events, in the 1953 WIBC Championship Tournament. She added another all events title in 1956.

BETTY KUCZYNSKI
Cicero, Ill.
Inducted 1981

Betty Kuczynski won the 19th WIBC Queens Tournament title and was named bowler of the year in 1965. In 1966, she was a member of the WIBC Championship Tournament team champions. On the women's professional tour, she won the 1964 National Pro Championship.

MARION LADEWIG
Grand Rapids, Mich.
Inducted 1964

Recognized as the greatest woman bowler of all time, Marion Ladewig compiled a list of achievements that includes the 1950 and 1955 WIBC Championship Tournament all events crowns. In the 1950-51 season, Ladewig became the only bowler in history to win all events titles on the city, state and national levels in one season.

SYLVIA MARTIN
Philadelphia
Inducted 1966

Sylvia Martin won the 1959 WIBC Championship Tournament doubles event crown with Adele Isphording. She also recorded major wins in the BPAA All-Star Tournament in 1955 and 1960. Martin was awarded Woman Bowler of the Year honors in 1955 and 1960.

MERLE MATTHEWS**

Huntington Beach, Calif.

Inducted 1974

Merle Matthews has an impressive WIBC Championship Tournament record. She captained the Linbrook Bowl team to back-to-back titles in 1962 and 1963 and teamed with Margaret Franklin in 1948 for the doubles event title. She also has several local and state titles to her name.

FLORETTA MCCUTCHEON**

Pasadena, Calif.

Inducted 1956

Floretta McCutcheon is the most widely known woman bowler of the pre-1940s. McCutcheon averaged 206 in WIBC league play in 1938-39, a record that stood until 1952-53. Her victory in a match against ABC Hall of Famer Jimmy Smith was recognized by Ripley's "Believe It or Not."

MARGE MERRICK

Columbus, Ohio

Inducted 1980

Marge Merrick and her sister set a WIBC Championship Tournament record in 1962; the two combined for a 504 doubles games. Merrick was an eight-time finalist in the BPAA All-Star Tournament and a four-time finalist in the World's Invitational. She defeated fellow hall of famer Marion Ladewig in 1961 to win that event.

VAL MIKIEL*

Detroit

Inducted 1979

Val Mikiel won the 1946 WIBC Championship Tournament singles event title. She was named the first Woman Bowler of the Year in 1948 and again received the honor in 1949.

CAROL MILLER

Milwaukee

Inducted 1997

Miller became one of Wisconsin's most dominant bowlers, capturing 15 state and 16 local association championships to earn induction into the Milwaukee WBA and Wisconsin WBA Halls of Fame in 1971 and 1989, respectively. She won two WIBC Tournament titles, the 1967 all events and doubles crown

with Jane Leszczynski in 1974. Her 1967 victory earned her a berth on the national team where she won a silver medal in the 1967 Federation Internationale des Quilleurs World team competition. She also served as a TEAM USA assistant coach for many years.

DOROTHY MILLER**

Chicago

Inducted 1954

Dorothy Miller earned 10 WIBC Championship Tournament titles during a 20-year span between 1928-1948. She bowled on six championship teams, won three doubles event titles and won one all events title. In 1961 she was honored as Quarter Century Bowler of the Year.

BETTY MIVELAZ

Tujunga, Calif.

Inducted 1991

Betty Mivelaz has earned national, regional, state and local titles in more than two decades of competitive bowling. She was a member of the 1967 WIBC Championship Tournament team event champions.

MARY MOHACSI

Livonia, Mich.

Inducted 1994

Mary Mohacsi has achieved success as an amateur bowler in international, national, state and local competitions. At the pinnacle of her sport, she was invited to the Oval Office to visit with then President Ronald Reagan and Vice President George Bush. In 1984, she was named the U.S. Olympic Committee's Bowling Athlete of the Year.

BETTY MORRIS

Stockton, Calif.

Inducted 1983

Betty Morris has won five WIBC Championship Tournament titles in seven years. She was a member of the 1974 team event champions and won all events titles in 1976 and 1979. She won the singles crown in 1979 and 1980. Morris was named Bowler of the Decade in the 1970s.

LORRIE NICHOLS
Algonquin, Ill.
Inducted 1989

Lorrie Nichols made her mark on all levels of the sport, capturing a WIBC Championship Tournament title, a Federation Internationale des Quilleurs (FIQ) title and 13 professional titles.

EDIE JO NORMAN
Miami
Inducted 1993

Edie Jo Norman has achieved success in the WIBC Championship Tournament and WIBC Queens Tournament. She was a member of the winning 1976 WIBC Championship Tournament Open Division Team, PWPA No. 1. In 1977, Norman led the WIBC Championship Tournament Average List with a 196.17 average.

VIRGINIA NORTON
Cypress, Calif.
Inducted 1988

Virginia Norton holds three WIBC Championship Tournament all-events titles, two team crowns and a singles event championship. On the professional circuit she has nine titles.

PHYLLIS NOTARO
Brant, N.Y.
Inducted 1979

Phyllis Notaro has enjoyed a three-decade career in bowling. In 1961 she won the BPAA Tournament followed in 1966 by the BPAA national doubles event with partner Jessie Miller. In 1975 Notaro notched a WIBC Championship Tournament title in the team event.

BEVERLY ORTNER
Tucson, Ariz.
Inducted 1972

Beverly Ortner was the first WIBC member to roll a three-game series over 800. She was a member of the 1969 WIBC Championship Tournament team event champions. Ortner is also the holder of numerous local and state women's bowling association titles.

CONNIE POWERS*
Grand Rapids, Mich.
Inducted 1973

Connie Powers and partner Betty Rews won the WIBC Championship Tournament doubles event title in 1939. Powers also bowled on WIBC championship teams in 1957 and 1959. She bowled in her 50th WIBC Championship Tournament in 1987.

ALETA RZEPECKI SILL
Dearborn, Mich.
Inducted 1996

Sill owns four WIBC titles in addition to capturing the Queens in 1983 and 1985. Winner of 28 pro titles, she was Bowler of the Year in 1984 and 1985. She set an all-time pro earnings record in 1994 with $126,325 and leads the all-time LPBT earnings list.

ROBBIE RICKARD
San Antonio
Inducted 1994

Robbie Rickard earned national recoginition during her bowling career that includes back-to-back WIBC Championship Tournament team event titles in 1962 and 1963 as a member of the Linbrook Bowl Team. Between 1962 and 1974, Rickard earned 10 top-three finishes in national and regional professional tournaments and holds 31 state and local bowling titles.

LEONA ROBINSON*
Phoenix
Inducted 1969

Leona Robinson, known as "Johnnie," was Kansas City's highest average bowler. Once, she rolled 33 games without an error. Bowling in 25 WIBC Championship Tournaments, Robinson was a member of the team event champions in 1929.

ROBIN ROMEO
Van Nuys, Calif.
Inducted 1995

Robin Romeo, 37, is a six-time WIBC All-American, the 1986 WIBC doubles and all events champion and owns 16 professional titles including the 1989 U.S. Open. She was named 1989 Bowler of the Year by the Bowling Writers Association of America.

* Deceased   + Star of Yesteryear

ADDIE RUSCHMEYER*+
White Plains, N.Y.
Inducted 1961

Addie Ruschmeyer's bowling career lasted more than 60 years. In 1933 Ruschmeyer was invited to compete in the first-ever International Bowling Championships in Frankfurt, West Germany where she won the women's title and was crowned "Bowler of the Year."

ANITA RUMP*+
Fort Wayne, Ind.
Inducted 1962

Anita Rump won the WIBC Championship Tournament singles event title in 1928 and 1930. Rump served as a league officer and was a charter member of the Les Dames de 700 Club.

ESTHER RYAN*+
Milwaukee
Inducted 1963

Esther Ryan was a member of the Kornitz Pure Oil team for 23 years. Ryan shared two WIBC Championship Tournament titles (1939 and 1947), nine state and 13 local championships. She won the WIBC all events title in 1934, her first individual title.

ETHEL SABLATNIK*
W. Palm Beach, Fla.
Inducted 1979

Ethel Sablatnik bowled in 47 WIBC Championship Tournaments. In 1938 she combined with Florence Probert to win the doubles event.

MYRTLE SCHULTE*+
St Louis
Inducted 1965

Myrtle Schulte won the WIBC Championship Tournament singles event and all events titles in 1931. In 1933, she was a member of the championship team. Schulte earned WIBC's first 50-year participation award. Before her death, Schulte competed in 54 WIBC Tournaments.

HELEN SHABLIS*+
Brooklyn, Mich.
Inducted 1977

Helen Shablis won the all events title at the 1963 WIBC Championship Tournament. In addition, she was captain of the U.S. women's team to the FIQ which won the European-style team titles. Paired with Dorothy Wilkinson, she won the doubles medal and won the all events title.

VIOLET SIMON*+
San Antonio
Inducted 1960

Violet Simon teamed with Erna Hautler to win the 1935 WIBC Championship Tournament doubles event title. Simon is credited with introducing bowling to the San Antonio area and was instrumental in organizing local associations as well as the Texas Women's Bowling Associaion.

TESS SMALL*+
Wisconsin Rapids, Wis.
Inducted 1971

Tess Small captured the team, doubles and all events titles at the 1940 WIBC Championship Tournament. In 1942, she captained the team champion Logan Square Buicks.

GRACE SMITH*+
Albuquerque, N.M.
Inducted 1968

Grace Smith won the WIBC Championship Tournament doubles event titles in 1921 and 1924, bowling with Pearl Ley and Jean Acker. She was also a member of the first team to win back-to-back team titles in 1924 and 1925.

JUDY SOUTAR
Bradenton, Fla.
Inducted 1976

Judy Soutar first competed in a WIBC Championship Tournament in 1954 at the age of nine. She earned doubles event titles in 1969 and 1970, teaming both times with Gloria Bouvia. In 1974 she earned all events and team event titles in the Tournament. Additionally, in 1974 she won the WIBC Queens Tournament title.

* Deceased   + Star of Yesteryear

LOUISE STOCKDALE*+
Buena Park, Calif.
Inducted 1953

Louise Stockdale and her sister, Helen Sneider, won the 1922 WIBC Championship Tournament doubles event title. Stockdale also won the all events title in the 1937 Tournament. She was a member of Detroit's first women's league and captured countless league titles in addition to numerous state and city titles.

ELVIRA TOEPFER+
East Detroit, Mich.
Inducted 1976

Elvira Toepfer holds two WIBC Championship Tournament titles as a member of the 1957 Colonial Broach team champions and the 1959 Bill Snethkamp Chrysler team event champions. In all, Toepfer has competed in 53 tournaments.

SALLY TWYFORD*+
Nashville, Ind.
Inducted 1964

Sally Twyford was a six-time WIBC Tournament Champion, winning her first two titles in 1930 for all events and team event. She also won the all events competition in 1933 and 1941 and garnered singles event championships in 1933 and 1940.

MARIE WARMBIER*+
Chicago
Inducted 1953

Marie Warmbier won seven WIBC Championship Tournament titles including a record four consecutive titles. She won the doubles event in 1930, team event in 1931, all events in 1932 and team event in 1933. She also was on the winning team in 1928 and won the singles event and all events in 1935.

DOROTHY WILKINSON
Phoenix
Inducted 1990

Dorothy "Dot" Wilkinson was a multiple-medal winner in the 1963 Federation Internationale des Quilleurs World Championships. She secured her berth on the U.S. bowling team by winning the singles event title at the 1963 WIBC Championship Tournament. She gained national recognition in 1962 when she won the WIBC Queens Tournament by defeating Marion Ladewig.

CECELIA WINANDY*+
Chicago
Inducted 1975

Cecelia Winandy's first WIBC Championship Tournament title came in 1949 when she won all events. She was also a member of Allgauer's Restaurant the championship team in 1958.

DONNA ZIMMERMAN
Thousand Palms, Calif.
Inducted 1982

Donna Zimmerman dominated the headlines in 1965 when she recorded two major wins, the WIBC Championship Tournament all events title and the Bowling Proprietors Association Award doubles crown with Janet Harmon. In addition, she has 25 major titles to her credit.

MERITORIOUS SERVICE
Total Number Inducted - 43

HELEN BAETZ
San Antonio
Inducted 1977

Helen Baetz was elected to the WIBC Board of Directors in 1952, in 1962 she was appointed fifth vice president and in 1974 became third vice president. In addition, Baetz spearheaded the formation of the Texas Women's Bowling Association.

HELEN BAKER*
Cocoa Beach, Fla.
Inducted 1989

Helen Baker was the fifth woman in WIBC history to hold the office of president, serving from 1981 to 1988. Baker served on virtually every WIBC committee and received many awards, including WIBC life membership.

GLADYS M. BANKER*
Charles Town, W.Va.
Inducted 1994

Gladys M. Banker served as WIBC president from July 1, 1988 to July 31, 1993. Banker aggressively worked to establish grass-roots programs to strengthen WIBC's membership ranks and implemented the WIBC Future Leaders Program. In addition to the WIBC presidency, Banker also held several other national and international bowling positions. She was a life member of WIBC.

CLOVER BAYLEY*
Watertown, N.Y.
Inducted 1992

Clover Bayley was elected to the WIBC Board of Directors in 1963 and served as a WIBC director for four years. She was a member of several Committees, including Legislative, Championship Tournament and 50th Anniversary.

WINIFRED BERGER*
Sonoma, Calif.
Inducted 1976

Winifred Berger was elected to the WIBC Board of Directors in 1946 and served for 24 years. During her chairmanship of the WIBC Championship Tournament committee, Berger saw the event grow into the largest sporting event in the world for women.

PHILENA BOHLEN*+
Los Angeles
Inducted 1955

Philena Bohlen was WIBC's fifth vice president from 1944 through 1949. She previously served five years as a member of the Executive Board. Bohlen is best remembered for designing the WIBC flag, which was first presented to the delegates at the 1940 convention.

LO BORSCHUK
Sioux City, Iowa
Inducted 1988

Lo Borschuk was an administrator with WIBC for 20 years including six years as the third vice president. During her tenure, Borschuk particpated on 15 WIBC Committees which included Advisory and Planning, Finance and Budget, Site Inspection and Equipment Specifications.

FREDA BOTKIN*
Tucson, Ariz.
Inducted 1986

Freda Botkin succeeded Emma Phaler as the executive secretary-treasurer of WIBC and served the Congress from 1965 to 1975. In her position, Botkin directed the day-to-day operations of the WIBC staff.

EMILY CHAPMAN*+
Long Island, N.Y
Inducted 1957

Emily Champman was a member of the 1926 Championship Tournament team event champions, the Taylor Trunks. Chapman helped organize the Poughkeepsie (N.Y.) and New York State WBAs. Throughout her career, Chapman taught thousands of people to bowl and served as teacher and organizer in many bowling establishments.

* Deceased   + Star of Yesteryear

ALBERTA E. CROWE*
Liverpool, N.Y.
Inducted 1982

Alberta E. Crowe was elected to the WIBC Board of Directors in 1939 and was named president in 1960. She served seven three-year terms as the chief-executive-officer of the world's largest sports organization for women. During her tenure, WIBC membership grew to more than 4.2 million.

GERTRUDE DORNBLASER*
Chicago
Inducted 1979

One of women's bowling pioneers, Gertrude Dornblaser won the first recorded "national tournament" in 1905, 11 years before WIBC was organized. She competed in 20 WIBC Championship Tournaments and was a member of the team event champions in 1918 and 1920.

AGNES DUFFY
Richmond, Calif.
Inducted 1987

Agnes Duffy served as a member of the WIBC Board of Directors for 18 years. During her tenure, she served on 19 committees including Finance and Budget.

GERTRUDE FINKE
Minneapolis
Inducted 1990

Gertrude Finke has served bowling's administrative side on the local, state and national levels. Finke also served as local association chairman of the 1964 WIBC Championship Tournament which was the largest Championship Tournament, at the time.

RAE FISK*
Houston
Inducted 1983

Rae Fisk served on the WIBC Board of Directors for 20 years. During her tenure, Fisk was a member of several WIBC committees, including Advisory and Planning, Legal, Finance and Budget and Unification.

DOROTHY HAAS*
Perth Amboy, N.J.
Inducted 1977

Dorothy Haas was appointed to the WIBC Board of Directors in 1962. She served on the board for 14 years, nine of those as sergeant-at-arms. She also served as chairman of the Hall of Fame Committee.

MITZI HEROLD
Aiken, S.C.
Inducted 1998

Mitzi Herold has devoted countless hours promoting youth and women's bowling during her more than 30 years of leadership as a South Carolina Women's Bowling Association and WIBC officer. After 15 years as a WIBC Board member, where she served on a variety of committees, Herold was named seventh vice president in 1989 and advanced to fifth vice president in 1992. She was elected Member Emeritae upon her retirement from the WIBC Board in 1996.

MARGARET HIGLEY*
Orange, Calif.
Inducted 1969

Marge Higley was a member of the WIBC Board of Directors for 22 years, including 12 as sergeant-at-arms. She is one of the few women to compete in 50 WIBC Championship Tournaments.

MADALENE (BEE) HOCHSTADTER*+
Chicago
Inducted 1967

Madalene (Bee) Hochstadter helped promote the image of bowling in many ways, including working with the blind association to develop and conduct its national tournament. She was a delegate to the WIBC Annual Meeting for over 20 years and captained the Boyle Valves to the team event title at the 1927 WIBC Championship Tournament.

* Deceased   + Star of Yesteryear

NORA KAY*
Toledo, Ohio
Inducted 1964

Nora Kay was elected to the WIBC Board of Directors in 1932. She became sergeant-at-arms the following year and served in that office until 1955. A dedicated leader, Kay served as president, vice president and director of the Wisconsin Women's Bowling Assocation.

ELLEN KELLY*
St. Louis
Inducted 1979

Ellen Kelly was one of the early promoters of women's bowling. She served as the first secretary to the organization which became WIBC. Kelly was also a member of Progress of St. Louis, which captured the first WIBC Championship Tournament team event title in 1916.

THERESA KELONE
Little Rock, Ark.
Inducted 1978

Theresa Kelone served on the WIBC Board of Directors for 18 years. She was a member of the Finance and Budget Committee, including eight years as chairman. She retired from her post as WIBC first vice president in 1977.

JEANNETTE KNEPPRATH*
Milwaukee
Inducted 1963

Jeannette Knepprath was the first woman inducted into the WIBC Hall of Fame for Meritorious Service. Knepprath was known as a pioneer of women's bowling and served a 36-year term as WIBC president (1924-1960). Under her leadership, membership grew from 2,885 members to more than 1.5 million.

IOLIA LASHER*
Albany, N.Y.
Inducted 1967

Iolia Lasher was elected WIBC second vice president in 1934 and retired from the Board of Directors in 1963. Lasher was also instrumental in organizing the Albany and New York State Women's Bowling Associations.

MABEL MARRS*
Vancouver, Wash.
Inducted 1979

Mabel Marrs was elected to the WIBC Board of Directors in 1960. She held the offices of fourth, sixth and seventh vice president. During her tenure, she served on several committees, including Finance and Budget and the President's Advisory Council. She served as president of the National Bowling Council during the 1971-72 season.

BERTHA McBRIDE*
St. Paul, Minn.
Inducted 1968

Bertha McBride served on the WIBC Board of Directors for 19 years, the last six as third vice president. In 1961, she was appointed chairman of the WIBC Legal Committee, serving in that position until her retirement in 1967.

CATHERINE MENNE*
St. Louis
Inducted 1979

Catherine Menne was the first president of WIBC, serving from 1916 to 1919. She was instrumental in laying the groundwork for what would become the world's largest sports organization for women.

FLORA MITCHELL
Springfield, Mo.
Inducted 1996

Flora Mitchell served as WIBC's seventh Executive Secretary-Treasurer from 1975 until her retirement in 1991. She started her bowling career at the grassroots level as Springfield WBA Secretary in 1960. She became a Missouri WBA Director in 1961, president in 1966 and a member of the WIBC Board of Directors in 1971. She joined WIBC full-time in 1973 as Assistant Secretary-Treasurer before taking over the top spot two years later upon the retirement of Freda Botkin.

JO MRAZ*+
Cleveland
Inducted 1959

Jo Mraz was a member of the WIBC Board of Directors for seven years, including three as treasurer and one as

* Deceased   + Star of Yesteryear

second vice president. Mraz helped organize the National 600 Bowling Club and was a charter member of the Pioneer Club.

BILLIE O'CONNOR
Chehalis, Wash.
Inducted 1992

Billie O'Connor served as a WIBC director from 1970 to 1983. She was appointed sixth vice president in 1977, and fifth and fourth vice presidents in 1981. She was chairman and committee member of the WIBC Legislative Committee and committee member on Advisory and Planning, Nominating, Industry Relations and Lane Certification Committees.

EMMA PHALER*
Columbus, Ohio
Inducted 1965

Emma Phaler served as WIBC executive secretary for 38 years. During Phaler's tenure (1927-1965), WIBC membership grew from 5,537 members to nearly 2.7 million. She was accorded life membership in 1965 and was the recipient of the Flowers for the Living Award in 1965.

CORA PORTER*
Franklin, Tenn.
Inducted 1986

Cora Porter served on the WIBC Board of Directors for 14 years. During that time, she served on a variety of WIBC Committees including Hall of Fame—which she chaired for seven years, Site Inspection, Legislative and Championship Tournament.

ZOE QUIN*
Chicago
Inducted 1979

Zoe Quin served as WIBC's second vice president, from 1919 to 1924. She is credited with initiating policies that still serve as WIBC's guidelines. In addition, Quin captured two WIBC Championship Tournament titles, the 1918 championship team event and the 1923 doubles event title.

GERTRUDE RISHLING*
Omaha, Neb.
Inducted 1972

Gertrude Rishling served on the WIBC Board of Directors for 17 years and was involved with the Insurance,

Building and Budget and Finance Committees. In addition, she represented WIBC on the National Bowling Council.

ANNE SIMONE
Ware, Mass.
Inducted 1991

Anne Simone was appointed to the WIBC Board of Directors in 1965. Eleven years later, she was named sergeant-at-arms. Simone resigned her position from the board to accept a WIBC staff position. Simone was elected a WIBC member emerita in 1985.

CATHERINE SLOAN
Alexandria, La.
Inducted 1985

Catherine Sloan served on the WIBC Board of Directors for 12 years. She held a director's post from 1966 to 1978 and was a member of several committees, including Legal, Championship Tournament and Secretary's Report.

BERDIE SPECK*
St Louis
Inducted 1966

Berdie Speck was elected first vice president of the WIBC Board of Directors in 1932 and served in that position for 30 years.

MILDRED SPITALNICK
Toms River, N.J.
Inducted 1994

Mildred Spitalnick was instrumental in organizing numerous local women's bowling associations in New Jersey and throughout the eastern United States from 1938 to 1960. She is also credited with coining the image-enhancing bowling term "channel" to replace "gutter".

ALMA SPRING*
Grand Rapids, Mich.
Inducted 1979

Alma Spring served as a WIBC director from 1936 to 1958 and served on the WIBC Rules Committee. In 1939, she was appointed WIBC historian and compiled the organization's early history from the years 1916 until 1942.

* Deceased   + Star of Yesteryear

PEARL SWITZER*
South Bend, Ind.
Inducted 1973

Pearl Switzer became a WIBC member in the organization's inaugural year, 1916. Switzer was elected to the WIBC Board of Directors in 1934. In addition to being a tournament worker, Switzer bowled in 42 WIBC Championship Tournaments.

TRUDY TODD
Denver
Inducted 1993

Trudy Todd was a member of the WIBC Board of Directors from 1962 to 1987. Todd also served as a board member of other national bowling organizations including the National Women Bowling Writers and National 600 Club. In 1987 she was elected a member emerita.

GEORGIA E. VEATCH*
Morton Grove, Ill.
Inducted 1974

Georgia E. Veatch served on the WIBC Board of Directors for 26 years, 12 as first vice president. Additionally, she served as editor of *The Women Bowler*

magazine from 1947-1959. Veatch founded the Professional Women Bowlers Association and served as its executive director for nine years.

MILDRED WHITE*
Rockford, Ill.
Inducted 1975

Mildred White served on the WIBC Board of Directors for 28 years. During that time she rose to the position of second vice president and served numerous committees.

ANN WOOD*
Cincinnati
Inducted 1970

Ann Wood was a member of the WIBC Board of Directors from 1945 until 1968, serving as fourth vice president for 18 years. Wood was well-known for her involvement in the development of the WIBC Queens Tournament, which began in 1961.

WIBC LIFE MEMBERS

WIBC Life Members are past WIBC presidents, executive secretary-treasurers or executive directors. The WIBC Board of Directors nominates the candidates for the honor and the WIBC Annual Meeting delegates approve the candidates at the WIBC Annual Meeting. WIBC Life Members may participate in meeting deliberations of the WIBC Board of Directors and WIBC delegates, though only vote at the WIBC Annual Meeting. WIBC's most recent Life Member was Gladys M. Banker of Charles Town, W.Va., who served as WIBC president from 1988 to 1993.

WIBC MEMBERS EMERITA

WIBC Members Emeritus are WIBC members who have been honored for their dedicated service. The WIBC Board of Directors nominates candidates and the WIBC Annual Meeting delegates approve the candidates. WIBC Members Emeritus may participate and vote in WIBC Annual Meeting deliberations. The WIBC Members Emeritus are: Helen Baetz, San Antonio; Bernice Bennie, Forest Heights, Md.; Winifred Berger, Sonoma, Calif.; Lo Borschuk, Sioux City, Iowa; Freda Botkin, Tucson, Ariz.; Betty Butler, Douglas, Ariz.; Ila Callaway, Marietta, Ga.; Agnes Duffy, Richmond, Calif.; Bonnie Hodgson, Salinas, Kan.; Margaret Howell, Rome, Ga.; Theresa Kelone, Little Rock, Ark.; Jane Lamb, Durham-Edina, Minn.; Beatrice Lane, Lansing, Mich.; Maud McGrainer, Pompano Beach, Fla.; Eleanor Meeks, Fort Benton, Mont.; Flora Mitchell, Springfield, Mo.; Clara Morton, Powell, Tenn.; Billie O'Connor, Chehalis, Wash.; C. Jean Shonka, Brigham City, Utah; Anne Simone, Ware, Mass.; Catherine Sloan, Alexandria, La.; Ruth Smith, Findlay, Ohio; Mary Jane Sporar, Joliet, Ill.; Nancy Tatum, Greenfield, Wis.; Trudy Todd, Aurora, Colo; Martha Burton, Washington, D.C., Shirlee Kutzner; Nutley, N.J.; Virginia Craig, Tucson, Ariz.

WIBC HELEN BAKER AWARD AND RECIPIENTS

The WIBC Helen Baker Award annually recognizes the outstanding leadership of a WIBC member who promotes and supports bowling on the local or state levels. The award's namesake-the late Helen Baker of Cocoa Beach, Fla.-served as WIBC president from 1981 to 1988. On behalf of WIBC, Baker presented the first award in 1990. Award candidates must currently serve as an officer, director or committee chairman of a local or state women's bowling association. Candidates are nominated by either their local or state association board of directors.

1997	Jo Leibrock, Columbus, Ohio	1993	Gennelle Pecoraro, Conyers, Ga.
1996	Marie Hisel, St. Louis	1992	Kathryn Hotzel, Anderson, Ind.
1995	Viola Brannen, Omaha, Neb.	1991	Marilyn Hensley, Tucson, Ariz.
1994	Margaret Sue Moore, Vicksburg, Miss.	1990	Marcy Bayne, Calias, Vt.

* Deceased   + Star of Yesteryear

The American Bowling Congress Hall of Fame was founded in 1941 as the third oldest sports shrine in the United States after baseball (1936) and golf (1940).

The Hall was the brainchild of Eli Whitney, ABC's first public relations director. He was inducted into the ABC Hall's Meritorious Service Section in 1975.

Eleven men entered the Hall in the first induction ceremonies in 1941.

The Hall is governed by a Board of Directors equally made up by representatives of the Hall, ABC and the Bowling Writers Association of America. The Hall has three committees that meet annually — Veterans, Meritorious Service and Ballot. The Veterans committee studies the records of older bowlers who might have been passed over for various reasons. The Meritorious Service committee studies the records of non-bowlers who made tremendous contributions that had national impact. The committee elects those people with 70% required for election.

The Ballot committee studies the records of current bowlers and forwards those who qualify to either the regular or nonpro national ballot. The first requirement is 20 years of participation in the ABC National Championships Tournament. To be elected, the bowler must receive 70% of the votes cast. A second ballot among the highest three votegetters can be held with specific requirements to be elected.

A special Pioneer committee was formed in 1990 to elect people who were at the foundation of bowling history including some who excelled before the beginning of ABC in 1895. The committee does not meet annually.

PERFORMANCE BIOGRAPHIES

GLENN ALLISON
Los Angeles
Born: May 22, 1930
Inducted 1979

Allison's 42-year ABC Tournament career has included four titles and 10 other top 10 finishes. Allison, known as "Mr. 900" for an unapproved 900 series in 1982, went to Chicago from California to bowl with the Pabst team, then shifted to St. Louis and joined the Falstaffs. While on the PBA tour, he often assisted announcers Chris Schenkel and Billy Welu with statistics and color information on the ABC-TV telecasts. He owns six PBA titles and currently serves as an ABC Ambassador.

HAROLD ASPLUND
Los Angeles
Born: Nov. 29, 1905
Died: April 20, 1982
Inducted 1978

Asplund did not start bowling until age 21 after watching pot games in a Denver bowling center. But he soon carried a 200 average and owned nearly every tournament title in the Northwest. His ABC Tournament debut in 1930 resulted in two top 10 finishes, and his record for winning big money in the Petersen Classic was unparalleled. He cashed 11 times in 16 tries, claiming more than $11,000, big money at that time. Asplund accumulated 15 other tournament titles.

EARL ANTHONY
Cornelius, Ore.
Born: April 27, 1938
Inducted 1986

The 1970s Bowler of the Decade was the sport's first millionaire and owns more professional championships than anyone else with 45. His ABC Tournament record also is outstanding with two Masters titles, a team all events championship and 13 other top 10 finishes. Retired from competition after earning nearly every accolade the sport affords, Anthony more recently has served as color commentator on ABC's Brunswick World Team Bowling Challenge and other television shows.

GORDY BAER
Chicago
Born: Aug. 20, 1939
Inducted 1987

Baer was selected the top non-professional in the world for his 1980 achievements by the Bowler's Journal. That same year he became the second player in ABC Tournament history to roll consecutive 2,000 nine game all events totals, the latter helping Hal Lieber Trophies to the team and team all events titles. He also won a team all events title in 1973 with Skyway Lanes.

BILL BEACH
Sharon, Pa.
Born: Sept. 12, 1929
Inducted 1991

The former Sharon, Pa. barber provided some of the most exciting moments in ABC Masters history to win the 1972 title when he came from the losers' bracket to defeat defending champion Jim Godman with clutch strikes in the final frames of both matches. He won five ABC titles including the Masters crown. In 1981, Beach captured his second PBA title by winning the first PBA seniors tournament in New Orleans.

FRANK BENKOVIC
Milwaukee
Born: Oct. 7, 1904
Died: March 8, 1995
Inducted 1958

Benkovic is the only bowler to win successive doubles championships in the ABC Tournament. He bowled on several prominent teams in Milwaukee and also bowled with leading teams in Cincinnati and Kansas City when his sales position with Brunswick took him to those cities.

MIKE BERLIN
Muscatine, Iowa
Born: Dec. 24, 1943
Inducted 1994

Berlin became the first Iowa-based bowler to be elected to the ABC Hall of Fame. He has won several big titles including the 1970 ABC Tournament all events and the 1977 Tournament of Champions. The 1976 PBA Rookie of the Year also won the 1968 Petersen Classic in Chicago. He was the first bowler inducted into Quad Cities Hall of Fame.

GEORGE BILLICK
Old Forge, Pa.
Born: April 13, 1910
Died: Sept. 8, 1992
Inducted 1982

Billick was the first bowler to roll more than 15 perfect games in ABC sanctioned competition. His total of 17 was the top ABC total for many years and was compiled over a 25-year span in 10 different establishments. His best ABC Tournament series came in 1978 with a 664 in singles at age 68. In the 1949-50 season, he bowled in eight leagues a week in Wilkes-Barre, Old Forge and Scranton.

JAMES BLOUIN
Blue Island, Ill.
Born: Dec. 1, 1886
Died: April 6, 1947
Inducted 1953

Blouin made his mark on the lanes in the days when challenge matches were the determining factor for the stamp of greatness. Blouin possessed steely nerves and a strong, slow curve ball he seemed to push rather than roll. For many years he took on all comers in the Chicago area and around the nation. Blouin won the ABC Tournament all events title in 1909 and captured the singles title two years later.

RAY BLUTH
St. Louis
Born: Dec. 31, 1927
Inducted 1973

Bluth's intense concentration, especially in developing a delivery of near mathematical perfection, made him one of the most consistent top performers for more than 15 years. Bluth, who owns two ABC Tournament titles, rolled the first 300 game in the ABC Masters finals in 1962. His 806 for the first three games of that series was a Masters record for 24 years and came three years after winning the event. Bluth bowled 267, 267, 300 in the St. Louis Budweisers' longtime record three-game 3,858 total.

JOSEPH BODIS
Cleveland
Born: Jan. 16, 1897
Died: April 26, 1970
Inducted 1941

Bodis came to national attention when he set a then ABC Tournament record eight consecutive all events totals above 1,800 in the 1925-32 period. Included was a team title in 1924. Bodis was an outstanding team bowler for many years in the Cleveland area and was particularly noted for bowling in street shoes to which he added a rubber heel for sliding. He was the first man to head the ABC Tournament 10-year average listings, starting with a 205.20 figure in 1934.

BUDDY BOMAR
Chicago
Born: Sept. 27, 1916
Died: Nov. 17, 1989
Inducted 1966

In addition to his 1956 team and team all events ABC Tournament championships and three BPAA titles, including the 1944 All-Star, Bomar accumulated no less than 38 other tournament titles. Those included three

Petersen Classic crowns, the Texas B.A. all events twice and all events titles in three Texas local associations — Wichita Falls, Ft. Worth and Dallas. Bomar was one of bowling's most articulate and prominent instructors. For many years while on the Brunswick exhibition staff, he conducted clinics around the nation.

ALLLIE BRANDT
Lockport, N.Y.
Born: Dec. 14, 1902
Died: April 17, 1982
Inducted 1960

One of bowling's feisty little men, Brandt was a battler to his final days. Best known for holding the record for highest three game series in ABC sanctioned competition for 49 years — 297-289-300 — 886 in 1939 — Brandt was well known and respected in the Western New York area for his prowess on the lanes and his fierce determination. Despite his 5'5", 130-pound stature, Brandt proved he had the stamina to handle pressure over the long haul, finally finishing second to Andy Varipapa in the final contest of the 100 game 1946 All-Star.

ED BROSIUS
Chicago
Born: May 30, 1920
Died: Aug. 16, 1981
Inducted 1976

Brosius was one of the top stars of several Chicago teams and joined his old captain and teammate Paul Krumske of Chicago in the Hall of Fame. He was a member of four BPAA championship teams. Brosius owned 13 other tournament titles.

FRED BUJACK
Detroit
Born: Jan. 23, 1912
Died: Jan. 2, 1971
Inducted 1967

Bujack won more ABC Tournament championships (eight) than any other bowler until fellow Hall of Famers Bill Lillard and Nelson Burton Jr. tied his mark. He and three other Hall of Fame members, Therm Gibson, Lou Sielaff and George Young, were the nucleus of the E&B/Pfeiffer team formed in 1944. It won three ABC Tournament titles and four team all events titles (two of each as Pfeiffer Beer) between 1949-55, constantly battling the great Stroh's teams for the supremacy of Detroit and the nation. Among Bujack's 14 other tournament championships were five more team titles in BPAA events.

BILL BUNETTA
Fresno, Calif.
Born: Oct. 20, 1919
Inducted 1968

Bunetta, in addition to top-flight individual performances for two decades, gained great respect as one of the game's finest instructors. Many young professionals came to Bunetta for advice in the early stages of their careers. He was a member of several famous teams, among them E&B and Pfeiffers of Detroit and Munsingwear of Chicago. He owns five ABC Tournament titles and in 1960 won a PBA title in Fairless Hills, Pa.

NELSON BURTON SR.
St. Louis
Born: Nov. 25, 1906
Died: May 13, 1994
Inducted 1964

Burton spent most of his early years in Dallas, moving to St. Louis in 1938. In addition to his brilliant ABC Tournament career which included a doubles title in 1937, he was considered one of the top head-to-head match game stars in the 1930s and 1940s. A fearless competitor, Burton was particularly noted for risking his own money in these matches instead of depending on sponsors.

NELSON BURTON JR. (Bo)
St. Louis
Born: June 5, 1942
Inducted 1981

In 1981, Burton was elected his first year on the ballot. He joined his father Nelson Sr. as the first father-son combination inducted into the performance section. Burton highlighted his professional career by winning the 1976 ABC Masters. His record eight ABC titles ties him with fellow Hall of Famers Fred Bujack and Bill Lillard. For many years, he handled the color commentary on ABC-TV's PBA telecasts. He was nominated for an Emmy in the sports analyst category in 1982, 1983, 1985 and 1987.

LOU CAMPI
Dumont, N.J.
Born: March 23, 1905
Died: Aug. 31, 1989
Inducted 1968

Campi, a righthander, ended his slide at the foul line on his right foot. That unorthodox finish stemmed from his having played Italian bocci as a youth. Campi won the first PBA tournament, the Empire Open in Albany, N.Y. in 1959. He and fellow Hall of Famer Al (Lindy) Faragalli were stars of the fabled Faber Cement Block that was the highest scoring team in the East in the 1950s and early '60s. In 1947, he won the BPAA Doubles with Hall of Famer Andy Varipapa and again in 1957 with Faragalli.

ADOLPH CARLSON
Chicago
Born: June 23, 1897
Died: Jan. 16, 1967
Inducted 1941

Carlson bowled with such famous Chicago teams as Pabst, Birk Bros., Joseph L. Gill and St. Paul Federal Savings. He was noted for the way in which he whipped the ball off a 2 1/2 step delivery. Carlson came to the United States in 1912 and started bowling a year later. In 1928, he defeated Charley Daw for the match game championship and defended successfully against fellow ABC Hall of Famer Walter (Skang) Mercurio before losing in 1929 to Joe Scribner.

DON CARTER
Miami
Born: July 29, 1926
Inducted 1970

Voted the greatest bowler in history in a 1971 Bowling Magazine poll, Carter was the first star to score a "grand slam" of bowling's match game titles. He won the All-Star, World's Invitational, PBA National and the ABC Masters. He also owns four ABC titles. Carter started as a youth with the veteran Hermann Undertakers of St. Louis, then went to the Ziern Antiques whose lineup included Ray Bluth, Pat Patterson and Tom Hennessey. After two years with the Pfeiffers of Detroit, he returned to St. Louis when the Budweiser team was organized in 1954. He bowled 266, 253, 235 in the Buds' longtime record 3,858 series in 1958.

FRANK CARUANA
Buffalo
Born: 1897
Died: Jan. 9, 1967
Inducted 1977

Caruana was the first to roll consecutive 300 games. His 1,115 four game record, which included the back-to-back 300s, stood for 50 years before being tied in 1974. Caruana followed the perfect games with 247 and 268. He also had a successful ABC Tournament career, including three finishes in the top 10 of all events.

MARTIN CASSIO
Rahway, N.J.
Born: Aug. 15, 1904
Died: Dec. 20, 1972
Inducted 1972

Cassio was brought to this country at age 5 in 1909. He took up bowling in 1930 and, despite a partially crippled right hand suffered in a work accident, he mastered the game quickly. He bowled with leading Eastern teams, among them Bowlers Journal and Wagner & Adler, and his teammates included Hall of Famers Tony Sparando, Lou Campi and Al (Lindy) Faragalli. In 1946, he led the ABC Tournament 10-year average list with 203. That same year he starred in AMF's first bowling film, "Ten Pin Magic" His impressive tournament record included 15 titles.

GRAZIO CASTELLANO
New York
Born: July 2, 1917
Died: Aug. 29, 1964
Inducted 1976

Castellano was the first to roll a 300 game on live television — during an Eastern All-Star league session at Newark (N.J.) Recreation on Oct. 4, 1953. His five victories in major match game competition — The World-Telegram and Newsday Eastern Open, each of 96 to 124 games in length - is an achievement never equalled by an East Coast bowler. He was a star with the Faber Cement Blocks, whose lineups included fellow ABC Hall members Lou Campi, Al (Lindy) Faragalli, Tony Sparando and Chuck Pezzano.

FRANK CLAUSE
Old Forge, Pa.
Born: March 29, 1913
Died: Nov. 26, 1977
Inducted 1980

Clause won $67,000 on two televised bowling shows. The former high school English and history teacher caught the attention of AMF in 1957 and eventually traveled the world for the company instructing men, women and children in the tenpin sport. He authored two books on bowling and had a syndicated bowling column which was carried by hundreds of newspapers. He earned seven tournament titles in the East.

ALFIE COHN
Chicago
Born: Nov. 1, 1927
Inducted 1985

Cohn long has been one of Chicago's leading bowlers. He reached his national peak in the 1971 ABC when he won both the singles and all events titles. He later added two more ABC titles. He won gold medals in the five and eight man team events in the 1977 FIQ American Zone tournament.

JOHN CRIMMINS
Detroit
Born: May 2, 1895
Died: Jan. 30, 1992
Inducted 1962

Crimmins was a controversial person from whose fiery temperament stemmed his nickname "The General." One story was that he toured as "The Masked Marvel," but few were the bowling followers in the Detroit area who did not readily recognize Crimmins in his heyday. The one-time ABC titlist was the first bowler elected to the Polish-American Sports Hall of Fame. In the 1937 Elks national tournament, he shared in all four titles - team, doubles, singles, all events.

DAVE DAVIS
West Palm Beach, Fla.
Born: April 28, 1942
Inducted 1990

Davis was a top contender through the 1960s and '70s on the PBA tour. He was the first lefthander to win a major match game championship when he captured the PBA National crown in 1965 at age 23. After suffering through some non-winning years, he returned to form in 1975 by winning three titles and being elected to *Bowling Magazine's* All-America first team for the fourth time. He won the ABC Tournament Classic singles title in 1968, the same year he won the Tournament of Champions. He won consecutive ABC Senior Masters titles in 1995 and 1996.

CHARLIE DAW
Milwaukee
Born: April 12, 1894
Died: Jan. 18, 1947
Inducted 1941

Daw was a mainstay of the Heil Products team that included four other future Hall of Famers - Hank Marino, Ned Day, Billy Sixty and Gil Zunker. He was a soft-spoken person still remembered for rolling one of the greatest hook balls, a noteworthy feat in an era when the widesweeping curve ball was the vogue. In 1936, he was on the team that bowled special matches in Germany before the Olympics. His tournament titles include three in the ABC Tournament.

NED DAY
Milwaukee
Born: Nov. 11, 1911
Died: Nov. 26, 1971
Inducted 1952

A three-time ABC champion, Day was one of the first to make extensive exhibition and match game tours. He was one of the game's great stylists, who excelled in speaking, instructing and promotion work, and he performed in film shorts produced in Hollywood by Pete Smith. He won the All-Star title in 1943, and his 23 other titles include nine championships in BPAA national events. Day was named BWAA Bowler of the Year in 1943 and 1944, and he was selected to *Bowling Magazine's* Pre-1950 All-America team.

GARY DICKINSON
Edmond, Okla.
Born: March 26, 1943
Inducted 1992

Dickinson long was among the steadiest performers on the pro tour. His breakthrough came in 1971 when he won the ABC Tournament Classic all events title and finished third in two other events. Dickinson had one of his best years in 1983 when he won the U.S. Open and earned $60,000. He continued strong in 1997, winning the ABC Senior Masters. He was the recipient of the PBA's Steve Nagy Sportsmanship Award in 1972, 1973 and 1974 and was 1993 PBA Senior Player of the Year.

EBBER (SARGE) EASTER
Cana, Va.
Born: Nov. 20, 1882
Died: Aug. 14, 1961
Inducted 1963

Truly one of bowling's nomads, Easter spent the majority of his life between military assignments and bowling centers. In fact in 1938, bowling in his first ABC Tournament came at the same time as his Army re-enlistment, and he chose to bowl and his rank dropped from first sergeant to private. He won his only ABC title in 1950 at age 67 and teamed with then 21 year old Ed Lubanski, another eventual Hall of Famer, to capture the BPAA National Doubles title in 1950. In 1953, at age 70, Easter bowled a 300 game, then repeated the feat two years later when he posted his fourth perfect game.

DON ELLIS
Houston
Born: Sept. 4, 1928
Inducted 1981

Ellis teamed with fellow Hall of Famer Joe Kristof to win the 1961 ABC Classic doubles title and was runnerup to Billy Welu in the 1965 ABC Masters. He re-emerged into the spotlight through the Great and the Greatest competition. He teamed with Mark Roth to win the 1979 championship and made the TV finals again in 1980. He has won several association titles in Texas and Illinois, including three Houston B.A. titles, two Texas B.A. and two Illinois B.A. titles. He also won the 1955 Petersen Classic.

JOSEPH FALCARO
Lawrence, N.Y.
Born: Jan. 3, 1896
Died: Sept. 6, 1951
Inducted 1975

Falcaro was one of bowling's most controversial and highly publicized figures. He gained fame throughout the country in his early years as a trick bowler and gave many benefit bowling exhibitions under the sponsorship of the Coca Cola Co. His greatest accomplishment among five tournament titles was winning the National Match Game championship from Joe Scribner in 1929. He later defended the title against Scribner but forfeited it in 1933.

ALFRED (LINDY) FARAGALLI
Wayne, N.J.
Born: Dec. 12, 1911
Died: Jan. 1997
Inducted 1968

Faragalli starred with leading Eastern teams, particularly the high-scoring Faber Cement Blocks. He was a teammate of and often a doubles partner with fellow Hall of Famers such as Lou Campi, Chuck Pezzano, Tony Sparando and Graz Castellano. He hit a television jackpot on June 18, 1957 when he rolled a 300 game worth $10,000 on a film series in Chicago. He had an 835 series on that show and had total earnings of $17,000. One year later he won his only ABC title.

BASIL (BUZZ) FAZIO
Delton, Mich.
Born: Feb. 7, 1908
Died: Feb. 16, 1993
Inducted 1963

Fazio captained the Stroh's Beer team for nine seasons, then moved to St. Louis in 1957 to form the Falstaff Beer team. The three-time ABC champion had been a star in Akron, Ohio before joining Stroh's in 1947. In the fall of 1955, he won seven straight live television matches in Chicago. He also had an 802 in Detroit, the first live 800 ever televised. He won the 1955 Masters before losing the 1968 title to Pete Tountas, 29, who came out of the losers' bracket to win both matches in the double elimination finals.

STEVE FEHR
Cincinnati
Born: Nov. 14, 1954
Inducted 1993

The youngest person to be elected to the ABC Hall of Fame, Fehr had a successful career in amateur, international and professional competition until wrist surgery in June 1986 ended his touring pro career. Fehr's success in international competition came during the 1981 FIQ American Zone Tournament in Winnipeg, Canada, winning two golds and a silver medal. He showed in 1989, however, that he can still fare well as he and wife Nancy captured the Brunswick Gold Rush National Mixed Doubles event in Las Vegas. He also won the 1994 ABC Bud Light Masters. Fehr, the 1981 *Bowlers Journal* Amateur Bowler of the Year, has captured three ABC Tournament titles and has nine top 10 finishes.

RUSS GERSONDE
Ft. Atkinson, Wis.
Born: Sept. 15, 1907
Died: March 14, 1989
Inducted 1968

A one-time ABC champion, Gersonde was one of the tallest of the leading bowlers at 6-4 1/2. He bowled on Milwaukee's best teams for many years. Gersonde won 12 major doubles titles, seven with Bert Barkow, four with fellow Hall of Famer Frank Benkovic and one with Ernie Imse. His five Wisconsin B.A. all events titles is an all-time record.

THERMAN GIBSON
Detroit
Born: Jan. 30, 1917
Died: March 28, 1969
Inducted 1965

He won seven ABC championships as a member of the fabled E&B/Pfeiffer lineup that included George Young, Fred Bujack and Lou Sielaff, all deceased, and Chuck O'Donnell, Don Carter and Bill Bunetta. All are in the ABC Hall of Fame. He once bowled a 268 triplicate. Gibson won $75,000 for rolling six straight strikes on the Jackpot Bowling TV show on Jan. 2, 1961. He also was a member of five BPAA team champions under the E&B banner and his other tournament titles number 18.

JIM GODMAN
Melbourne, Fla.
Born: Jan. 5, 1946
Inducted 1987

Godman was one of the ABC Tournament's most prolific bowlers during the 1970s. He thrilled the crowd at the 1974 ABC Tournament by unleashing 67 strikes and a 2,184 all events total. He was the first man in ABC Tournament history to record three 700 series in one Tournament. Godman's performance in the 1974 ABC Tournament resulted in his two ABC championships, but he had success on ABC Tournament lanes before that.

He also rolled 11 consecutive 1,800 all events totals from 1968-78 and shot a 299 game in Classic doubles in 1974. He reached another personal high in 1969 when he won the Tournament of Champions, a title he won again in 1973.

BOB GOIKE
Belleville, Mich.
Born: Dec. 6, 1953
Inducted 1996

Goike won the 1984 ABC all events title with a then record 2,142 and established a 10-year average record in 1993 with 218. Since his title he has accumulated six other ABC Tournament top 10 finishes including the 1997 team all events title. A first alternate for TEAM USA 1995, he earned a silver medal in the team event of the 1995 U.S. Olympic Festival.

BILLY GOLEMBIEWSKI
Detroit
Born: July 31, 1929
Inducted 1979

Sportswriters tagged Golembiewski with the name "Billy G" early in his career, and that was the way he was known to thousands who watched him perform. Billy was a great example of how little men can do big things in the bowling game. He won the ABC Masters championship for the first time in 1960, then won it again in 1962, a feat only three other men— Hall of Famers Billy Welu, Dick Hoover and Earl Anthony—have been able to accomplish. He also won three other ABC titles.

GREG GRIFFO
Syracuse, N.Y.
Born: Feb. 23, 1910
Inducted 1995

Griffo competed in his 60th ABC Tournament in 1996 one year after his induction to the ABC Hall of Fame. The next day, he became only the fourth player in Tournament history to surpass 100,000 pins. The 5'2" righthander carried the highest average in Syracuse for 30 years. Nationally, he won the 1957 Petersen Classic and 1961 Vargo Classic and was winner of the Bowling Writers Association of America's 1985 Rip Van Winkle Award for accomplishments 20 or more years previous.

JOHN GUENTHER
Edmonds, Wash.
Born: Jan. 19, 1936
Inducted 1988

Still an active bowler in the Seattle area, Guenther owns two ABC Tournament Classic championships and gained national acclaim when he rolled a 300

game on television during a PBA tournament in San Jose, Calif. in 1969. He rolled an 809 league series at age 18 and continued to develop into one of the Northwest's top stars. He earned PBA's Steve Nagy Sportmanship award in 1966 and 1967 and shared it in 1970.

BILLY HARDWICK
Memphis, Tenn.
Born: July 25, 1941
Inducted 1985

Hardwick was voted to *Bowling Magazine's* Post-1950 All-America team. He literally burst into national bowling prominence when he won seven PBA titles and two ABC Tournament crowns within three years after entering the pro ranks in 1963-64. All of this came after failing to cash in a single PBA tournament in 1962.

BOB HART
Norcross, Ga.
Born: Aug. 14, 1937
Inducted 1994

Hart was a standout with Detroit's Stroh's and Goebel Beer teams and won three ABC Tournament titles in 1974. The 1954 National Junior Singles champion won five titles as U.S. representative in the 1974 Tournament of the Americas.

TOM HENNESSEY
St. Louis
Born: May 11, 1925
Inducted 1976

Hennessey was a member of the Ziern Antiques of St. Louis, whose lineup included fellow Hall of Famers Ray Bluth, Pat Patterson and Don Carter in the beginning stages of their careers. He left St. Louis to bowl with the Stroh's in Detroit and later returned to join the great Budweisers. He shot 759, including a 300 game, when the Buds bowled the record 3,858 series in 1958. He won four ABC Tournament titles in four years between 1962-65.

DICK HOOVER
Akron, Ohio
Born: Dec. 15, 1929
Inducted 1974

Hoover made his ability apparent at an early age, having an 847 at age 16, the highest series ever rolled in ABC league play by a teenager. In 1950, he became the youngest to win the All-Star tournament, capturing the title the day after his 21st birthday. He was one of only two men to capture two consecutive ABC Masters titles, winning the crown in 1956 and 1957. He also won three titles in ABC Tournament Classic division play.

ALVIN (BUD) HORN
Las Vegas
Born: Aug. 15, 1937
Inducted 1992

Horn won four ABC Tournament titles and two PBA crowns in his career. Much of his success has been in the ABC Tournament where he has nine other top 10 finishes, shares the record with 11 consecutive 1,800-plus all events totals, has a 202 average for 21 years and rolled 300 games in the Masters and Classic singles. Horn rolled the first 300 game in Masters history in the 1961 qualifying. He shot another 300 in the 1976 Classic singles.

GEORGE HOWARD
Kalamazoo, Mich.
Born: Feb. 1, 1930
Inducted 1986

Howard was a steady performer in local competition as well as the ABC Tournament. While not winning an ABC title, he owns three seconds and seven other finishes in the top 10. He went to Detroit from Kalamazoo to join the Stroh's team early in his career, then returned to work in a bowling establishment in Kalamazoo.

EDDIE JACKSON
Cincinnati
Born: March 21, 1926
Inducted 1988

Jackson is highly recognized around the world for his coaching abilities as the man who directed U.S. teams in international competition from 1971-79. An international star himself, he won a gold medal in team, silver in doubles and bronze in all events in the 1969 FIQ American Zone tournament in Puerto Rico. The same year, he won three championships in the Tournament of the Americas in Miami. He won the 1969 ABC Tournament all events championship and was eligible for the 1971 U.S. Team Trials until he was forced to withdraw for health reasons. He was then appointed coach.

DON JOHNSON
Las Vegas
Born: May 19, 1940
Inducted 1982

Johnson established a record of winning a PBA title in 12 straight years and is one of only a handful of performers to capture more than 20 titles. His most famous moment came in 1970 when he sprawled on the approach during the finals of the Tournament of Champions after a 10 pin kept him from bowling a perfect game on national television. A two-time BWAA Bowler of the Year, he owns three ABC Tournament Classic titles and three runnerup finishes.

EARL JOHNSON
Minneapolis
Born: Nov. 28, 1928
Inducted 1987

Johnson has been an outstanding bowler over four decades, first in his native Tacoma, Wash., later in Chicago and then in Minneapolis where he has been since the early 1960s. Johnson was recruited by Buddy Bomar to move from Tacoma to Chicago and bowl with Bomar's Falstaff Beer team. Later, he performed with other great Chicago teams before moving to the Twin Cities for a stint in the National Bowling League. Johnson owns three ABC Tournament titles and four other top 10 ABC finishes.

JOE JOSEPH
Lansing, Mich.
Born: April 11, 1918
Died: June 10, 1988
Inducted 1969

Joseph, noted for one of the smoothest deliveries in the bowling game, was an outstanding semipro football player and fastpitch softball pitcher in his younger days. However, he made bowling his major sport and went on to win three ABC titles plus eight other finishes in the top 10. He won the first Tournament of Champions in 1962 after winning his first pro tournament in St. Louis that same year. He also teamed with Tommy Hudson to win the initial Great and Greatest tournament in 1978.

LEE JOUGLARD
Detroit
Born: Jan. 12, 1921
Died: Nov. 18, 1978
Inducted 1979

Jouglard won the first ABC Masters Tournament in 1951. He also captured the ABC Tournament singles and team all events titles that year en route to earning BWAA Bowler of the Year honors. He was one of the few stars who stayed with the three-step approach. While an outstanding individual performer, he always was considered one of the best team players in the country.

FRANK KARTHEISER
Chicago
Born: Nov. 14, 1888
Died: Dec. 19, 1968
Inducted 1967

Kartheiser began a brilliant career in 1899 when he was 11 years old. He became interested in the sport and began to earn money by setting pins. Within a few years his skill improved, and he was sought by top-flight Chicago teams, including the famous Brunswick

Mineralites. He was a top star on that club for 10 years. In addition to his league performances, Kartheiser was considered one of the nation's top head-to-head competitors. He held the national match game championship in 1926 and among his seven other tournament titles was the Petersen Classic in 1924.

ED KAWOLICS
Chicago
Born: Nov. 15, 1907
Died: Dec. 4, 1976
Inducted 1968

Kawolics gained his early fame in Cleveland and then bowled with several outstanding Chicago teams, including those captained by Buddy Bomar and Paul Krumske, who also are in the Hall of Fame. In addition to his two ABC championships, he won 20 other tournament titles. As a professional, Kawolics was ineligible to compete in the 5th FIQ World Tournament in Mexico City in 1963. However, he was named coach of both the men's and women's teams, the first ever to represent the U.S. in world competition.

JOSEPH KISSOFF
Cleveland
Born: March 21, 1901
Died: July 18, 1976
Inducted 1976

Kissoff won the 1953 ABC Tournament doubles championship with Eddie Koepp and captured eight other tournament titles. He was a billiards expert in his youth, adept at the "kiss shot." His real name was Zelinsky, but he finally adopted Kissoff as a reflection of his billiards skill. He was equally adept on the bowling lanes.

JOHN KLARES
Las Vegas
Born: July 13, 1910
Died: Jan. 31, 1997
Inducted 1982

The 1952 ABC Tournament was a memorable one for Klares as he captured two titles, establishing one record in the process. He teamed with fellow Hall of Famer Steve Nagy to win the doubles championship with a then-record 1,453 series, Klares contributing 755. The record stood until 1989. He also captained Radiart Corp. of Cleveland and led it to the team all events title. After later moving to California, he served as technical adviser on Milton Berle's Jackpot Bowling television show and became nationally recognized for being the umpire on that show.

WILLIAM KNOX
Philadelphia
Born: April 21, 1887
Died: May 16, 1944
Inducted 1954

In 1913 in Toledo, Knox rolled the first 300 game in ABC Tournament history. He won the ABC all events title 10 years later with 2,019, the first total above 2,000 and the record until 1933. Knox built a great reputation for match game and league bowling in the East. He once rolled a 300 game while a screen was suspended at the foul line so he couldn't see the pins.

JOHN KOSTER
East Nyack, N.Y.
Born: Jan. 21, 1872
Died: Aug. 14, 1945
Inducted 1941

Koster was the first to win four ABC Tournament titles, a record unmatched until Joe Wilman won his fourth in 1954. Only 27 pins kept Koster from winning the singles title in the first ABC Tournament in 1901.

EDWARD KREMS
Chicago
Born: Feb. 2, 1893
Died: June 9, 1978
Inducted 1973

Krems was regarded as the best all-around bowler in Chicago in the 1920s. He was captain of the strong Pabst team for many years. From 1926 through 1935, he had a 200 ABC Tournament average. He won an ABC championship in 1920 and nine other tournament titles.

JOSEPH KRISTOF
Columbus, Ohio
Born: Dec. 8, 1920
Inducted 1968

Kristof made his name in Chicago as a member of the Kathryns and Tavern Pales teams that won the BPAA team championships in 1947, 1948 and 1949. He was also captain of the famed Pabst team from 1955-59. Known as one of the game's great stylists, Kristof later moved to Columbus to open his own pro shop. He finished second to Hall member Buzz Fazio in the 1955 Masters. He won his only ABC title six years later, teaming with Hall member Don Ellis for the Classic doubles crown.

PAUL KRUMSKE
Chicago
Born: July 25, 1912
Died: July 23, 1979
Inducted 1968

Krumske captained numerous great Chicago teams, among them King Louie and Meister Brau. He also developed many young stars. He was voted Chicago's bowler of the half-century in a 1951 *Chicago Bowler* newspaper poll. Krumske won the National Match Game title in 1944 from Ned Day, but lost the title a month later in the All-Star Tournament. He was one of the few to have won three national match play titles in individual, doubles and team play.

HERBERT LANGE
Lake Mills, Wis.
Born: June 20, 1901
Died: Oct. 8, 1982
Inducted 1941

Lange rose to early stardom as an undergraduate at the University of Wisconsin, paying his way through school with money won in tournaments. He was the first to roll nine 200 games in one ABC Tournament, doing it in 1922. Six years later, he won his only ABC title. He also was the first to have five all events totals above 1,900. Lange bowled with such famous Chicago teams as the 1928 ABC champion Oh Henry's, Monarch Beer, Quaker Oats and Chapin & Gore.

HANK LAUMAN
Los Angeles
Born: Feb. 16, 1916
Died: Aug. 2, 1993
Inducted 1976

Lauman bowled with the Hermann Undertakers of St. Louis for several years. The sponsor, the late Cone Hermann, is believed to be the first to pay a bowler a yearly salary. This was his arrangement with Lauman for nearly three years after Lauman's discharge from the service and until he moved to California in 1949. He was second in doubles and all events in the 1947 ABC Tournament and earned $1,531, the most of any individual that year.

BILL LILLARD
Houston
Born: Oct. 13, 1927
Inducted 1972

After winning his first two ABC Tournament titles in 1955 with the Detroit Pfeiffers, Lillard made bowling history on March 24-25, 1956 when he became the first man to win four titles in one ABC Tournament, bowling with the team and team all events

champion Falstaffs, pairing with Stan Gifford for the doubles crown and capturing the individual all events as well. He gained his seventh title in 1962, then tied Hall of Famer Fred Bujack for the most lifetime ABC championships when he notched his eighth in 1971.

TONY LINDEMANN
Detroit
Born: May 23, 1919
Inducted 1979

Lindemann became active in bowling after moving to Detroit in 1942 and soon developed enough talent to join some of the strongest teams in that city. He became a member of the Stroh's in 1950 and succeeded Buzz Fazio, also an ABC Hall of Famer, as captain of that crew in 1957. He was a double winner in the 1951 ABC as a member of the team all events champion while also winning the all events. Lindemann also won the BPAA National Doubles in 1951, 1952 and 1954 with Fazio and won the team championship with Stroh's in 1952, 1953 and 1954.

MORT LINDSEY
Stamford, Conn.
Born: Dec. 20, 1888
Died: May 16, 1959
Inducted 1941

Lindsey was one of the first of the game's colorful performers, a delightful storyteller, an admirer of good food and a fearless competitor under any conditions. The three-time ABC Tournament champion started bowling in 1902 but leaned toward semipro baseball as a catcher and also was proficient at billiards. At age 64, he finished fourth in the *Bowlers Journal* tournament and until age slowed him a few years later, he entered many events where most of the competitors were less than half his age.

HARRY LIPPE
Chicago
Born: Nov. 8, 1911
Died: Oct. 1, 1995
Inducted 1989

Regarded as one of the finest team bowlers in the Chicago area for many years, Lippe was one of the unsung stars of a bygone era. His 36-year ABC Tournament average was 193 and he was a member of the Old Fitzgerald fivesome that captured the 1963 team title and 1964 team all events crown. He also captured two gold medals in the 1963 FIQ World Championships in Mexico City when ABC made its official debut in international events.

ED LUBANSKI
Detroit
Born: Sept. 3, 1929
Inducted 1971

In 1959, Lubanski became the second man to win four ABC titles in one Tournament, after earning one crown in 1951. He quit baseball at the age of 21 to join Ed (Sarge) Easter (67 years old) as the youngest-oldest duo ever crowned BPAA National Doubles champions. Lubanski was one of the last of the top stars to use a two-finger ball. He also was a member of BPAA championship teams in 1952, 1953, 1954 and 1964.

VINCE LUCCI SR.
Morrisville, Pa.
Born: Oct. 6, 1912
Inducted 1978

Lucci rolled his first 300 game in the doubles of the 1951 ABC Tournament in St. Paul, Minn. By winning the all events title in 1960, Lucci became the second person in history to roll a perfect game in one ABC Tournament and win a championship in another. Fellow Hall member Billy Knox was the first. Lucci won three events in the 1978 ABC National Seniors Tournament and rolled a 300 game at age 80 in 1993.

HANK MARINO
Milwaukee
Born: Nov. 27, 1889
Died: July 12, 1976
Inducted 1941

Marino came to Chicago when he was 11 years old and it was there he began his career and became a star. He moved to Milwaukee in 1930 where he operated a bowling establishment until retiring in 1965. He was the only bowler of prominence to spin the ball while it was hanging on the thumb. The one-time ABC champion was elected Bowler of the Half Century in 1951 and later named to the Bowling Magazine's Pre-1950 All-America team. He won three championships in the Berlin international competition held before the 1936 Olympics.

JOHN MARTINO
Syracuse, N.Y.
Born: July 8, 1897
Died: Sept. 2, 1985
Inducted 1969

Martino made his mark in three levels of the game. He was an outstanding bowler, holding a 190 average after 41 ABC Tournaments. In 1929, he won the all events title in an international event in Stockholm, Sweden, the first gold medal won by an American in international play.

He also was active in administrative positions, serving as ABC President (1947-48) and also president of the New York and Syracuse associations and served as the first president of the Bowling Writers Association of America.

ANDY MARZICH
Torrance, Calif.
Born: July 3, 1935
Inducted 1993

A three-time ABC Tournament champion, Marzich owns three other top 10 finishes and a 25-year career Tournament average of 195. He captured doubles with Dick Jensen in 1960 and earned team titles with the Falstaffs in 1964 and Shur-Hooks in 1966. Marzich won the first of his six PBA titles in St. Paul in 1962 and the last in San Diego in 1964. He was a member of the Falstaffs when they captured the 1963 National Team Match Game event and joined Ed Hardnett in winning the 1962 Bowlers Journal doubles.

MIKE McGRATH
Anaheim, Calif.
Born: May 13, 1946
Inducted 1993

McGrath made a sensational professional debut, winning the first PBA tournament he entered in 1965 at Portland, Ore. at age 19. He also was the hero in the first ABC Tournament Classic division team rolloff series in 1970 at Knoxville, Tenn. when he converted the difficult 1-3-6-9 spare that brought his Merchant Enterprises the title by eight pins. He later added two other ABC titles. In 1970, he became the first bowler to win consecutive PBA National Tournament titles. He retired from the tour with 10 titles.

JAMES (JUNIE) McMAHON
River Edge, N.J.
Born: Jan. 3, 1912
Died: Nov. 1, 1974
Inducted 1955

McMahon was one of the great ABC Tournament bowlers of all time. Starting with his first Tournament in 1937, he rolled four straight 1,800s, missed by 21 pins in 1941 and then had seven more 1,800s on his way to two titles. He bowled with leading New York area teams until 1945 when he moved to Chicago, where he competed with the Monarch and Meister Brau teams. He moved to Fair Lawn, N.J. shortly after winning the 1951 All-Star tournament. McMahon was named to the *Bowling Magazine* Pre-1950 All-America second team, and was voted BWAA Bowler of the Year in 1950.

DAROLD MEISEL
Muskego, Wis.
Born: Nov. 7, 1947
Died: May 13, 1994
Inducted 1998

Meisel constructed a brilliant career on the national and international levels. He captured the Federation Internationale des Quilleurs American Zone Masters title in 1989 to cap a career that included 24 medals in international competition for TEAM USA. Meisel was the National Amateur Champion in 1988 and had four ABC Tournament Championships. He also won numerous state and local titles.

WALTER (SKANG) MERCURIO
Cleveland
Born: July 24, 1896
Died: Jan. 25, 1972
Inducted 1967

Mercurio was an outstanding Cleveland tenpin star for almost three decades. Skang, a nickname picked up from a baseball catcher of a bygone era, Wally Schang, turned in one of bowling's greatest performances when he averaged 238 for an entire season in the Tomasch All-Star league in 1934-35. In 1929, Mercurio lost a 60-game match against Ad Carlson by 240 pins, but completed the 60 games without a miss. He stretched that mark to 65 games before missing a 10 pin.

NORM MEYERS
St. Louis
Born: Dec. 30, 1933
Died: June 26, 1981
Inducted 1984

If ever anyone "came to bowl" in the annual ABC Tournament, Meyers was the man. He won four Classic Division championships in the 1960s and '70s and finished in the top 10 another 16 times, including the runnerup position on four occasions. In 1971, he bowled series of 847, 816 and 806 in a four hour span in a doubles tournament. He is the only man named Southern California Bowler of the Year three times and was the brother-in-law of Hall of Famer Dick Weber.

STEVE NAGY
Cleveland
Born: Aug. 10, 1913
Died: Nov. 10, 1966
Inducted 1963

Nagy bowled in his first ABC Tournament in 1939 as a Booster division entrant and 13 years later set an ABC doubles record 1,453 with fellow Hall of Famer Johnny Klares that stood until 1989. Nagy compiled an outstanding record during the 1950s, including five ABC

championships and selection to *Bowling Magazine's* All-America first team twice (1956, 1958) and the second team in 1957. He was named BWAA Bowler of the Year in 1952 and 1955, and he earned a first-team berth on Bowling Magazine's Post-1950 All-America.

JOE NORRIS
San Diego
Born: Feb. 10, 1908
Inducted 1954

Norris, still an active bowler at 89, became the third person in ABC Tournament history to knock down 100,000 pins on March 12, 1986. He set the record for all-time pinfall on March 10, 1992 and entered 1998 with 119,181 pins, a 195 average for 65 ABCs, the second-longest participation in Tournament history. On Dec. 14, 1994, he became the oldest person with a 300 game. Norris, who had become well known through his bowling feats in Detroit, started on the road to superstardom when he organized the Stroh's Beer team in 1933. Under his captaincy the Stroh's won the 1934 ABC Tournament championship (he won two other ABC titles) and also won the National Match Game championship five times between 1934 and 1945. He also competed in the international exhibition before the 1936 Olympics in Berlin, Germany.

CHUCK O'DONNELL
St. Louis
Born: Oct. 12, 1913
Inducted 1968

O'Donnell learned his bowling in St. Louis and soon developed enough skill to join the then famous Hermann Undertakers. He then moved to Detroit and was a standout on the E&B and Pfeiffers teams before returning to St. Louis to open a bowling supply store. The two-time ABC champion was a member of the Budweiser lineup of Pat Patterson, Don Carter, Bill Lillard, Dick Weber, Ray Bluth and Tom Hennessey, all of whom are in the Hall. Ironically, when the Buds bowled the record 3,858 series, O'Donnell was captain of the opposing Pulaski Savings team which had a 3,494 total.

GEORGE PAPPAS
Charlotte, N.C.
Born: March 1, 1947
Inducted 1989

Pappas extended his excellent ABC Tournament consistency record in 1988 when he took over the lead for lifetime average with his 209.67 mark for 20 years, continuing in the top spot through 1997 at 209.67. Pappas' victory in the 1979 Tournament of Champions capped a fine decade for the former PBA President. In the 1970s, Pappas won six PBA titles, 10 PBA regionals, two ABC Tournament championships and had 12 other top 10 ABC finishes. In recognition of his accomplishments he was named four times to *Bowling Magazine's* All-America second team in the '70s before making it to the first team in 1979.

PAT PATTERSON
St. Louis
Born: Oct. 30, 1925
Died: May 9, 1972
Inducted 1974

Patterson was "low man" with 736 when the St. Louis Budweisers bowled the record 3,858 series in 1958. Earlier, he was a member of the Ziern Antiques, a great St. Louis team that included Tom Hennessey, Ray Bluth and Don Carter at the beginning of their careers. Patterson was a member of the Budweiser team when it was organized and succeeded Whitey Harris as captain, continuing in that role when the team later became Don Carter Gloves. The team, under the two names, won six BPAA team championships, and Carter Gloves captured the 1962 ABC Classic team title.

DICK RITGER
River Falls, Wis.
Born: Nov. 3, 1938
Inducted 1984

Ritger, once a top-flight professional, now devotes full time to his career as an instructor worldwide. Ritger became the fourth man to win 20 PBA titles and the first bowler to be elected to a college or university hall of fame. That honor came in 1979 when his alma mater, the University of Wisconsin-La Crosse, inducted him to the "Wall of Fame." The two-time ABC titlist has authored several bowling instructional books including the ABC instruction book, "Bowlers Guide."

ANDY ROGOZNICA
Chicago
Born: Nov. 20, 1926
Died: June 1990
Inducted 1993

Rogoznica was born in Yugoslavia but nurtured his bowling career in Chicago. He won the 1966 ABC Classic doubles with Jim Stefanich, finished second in team twice. He also finished third, fourth, eighth and 10th in other ABC Tournament appearances and averaged 196 for 37 years. He won the 1962 PBA Birmingham Open and was first in the 1965 BPAA Team Match Game championships.

CARMEN SALVINO
Chicago
Born: Nov. 23, 1933
Inducted 1979

Salvino first burst onto the national scene when helped Tri-Par Radio to the 1954 ABC title. He later won another ABC title when he teamed with Barry Asher for the 1972 Classic doubles crown. His PBA career was going smoothly until he began a slump in 1969 that lasted until 1973 when he and engineer Hank Lahr devised the "Equation" which turned his game around. He now is very much involved with new developments in bowling balls. But he has continued to show his prowess on the lanes with a Senior tour win in 1984 and a Senior/Touring Pro title with Randy Pedersen in 1988.

LES SCHISSLER
Denver
Born: May 12, 1930
Inducted 1991

Schissler rolled one of bowling's most dramatic games when he strung 12 strikes for a 300 in the Classic event in the 1967 ABC Tournament. It was the first 300 in team play in ABC Tournament history. In 1966, he also had a brilliant ABC performance, taking three titles. Schissler returned to the pro spotlight when he finished fourth in the 1983 ABC Masters.

ERNIE SCHLEGEL
Vancouver, Wash.
Born: April 11, 1943
Inducted 1997

Schlegel, a steady and controversial performer on the pro tour, once was known for his flamboyant antics and attire on the lanes. The 1996 ABC Bud Light Masters champion has won six PBA tour titles. He also has had success in ABC Tournament competition as a member of the 1970 Classic team champion Merchants, finishing third with Basch Advertising in Classic team in 1976 and fifth in Classic doubles with Joe Nuzzo in 1978. The PBA Hall of Famer served as PBA president in 1987 and 1988,

JIM SCHROEDER
Buffalo
Born: May 31, 1929
Inducted 1990

Schroeder's bowling talents, developed in Buffalo, were good enough to earn him spots on outstanding teams in St. Louis (Falstaffs) and Detroit (Stroh's). The 1976 ABC Classic singles champ is a charter member of the PBA and has been a member of the AMF Staff of Champions for 30 years. He also is bowling director for Special Olympics International.

CONNIE SCHWOEGLER
Madison, Wis.
Born: Jan. 2, 1917
Died: Aug. 3, 1982
Inducted 1968

Schwoegler became a bowling sensation when he won the 1942 All-Star at age 24 and repeated as champion in 1948. He was named BWAA Bowler of the Year in 1949. Schwoegler won 15 other tournament titles. In 1948, Schwoegler pioneered an extended ball grip which was copyrighted under his name and led to the popularity of what is now known as the fingertip grip.

TEATA SEMIZ
River Edge, N.J.
Born: April 16, 1934
Inducted 1991

Semiz has been one of the nation's best bowlers, although he continues to divide his time between the Senior pro tour and his pro shop. He won the ABC Tournament Classic singles and all events titles in 1972. Semiz has won 10 PBA titles and has also done well in ABC Masters play, finishing fourth in 1973, seventh in 1983 and 11th in 1987. Semiz also rolled a 300 in match play of the 1983 Masters and finished fifth in the 1997 Masters

LOUIS SIELAFF
Detroit
Born: Dec. 10, 1915
Died: May 1, 1964
Inducted 1968

Sielaff captained the Pfeiffers team from its organization as E&B in 1944 until 1958 when he turned over the reins to Ed Lubanski. He was part of seven of E&B/Pfeiffers's unprecedented four ABC Tournament team titles and five team all events championships. Sielaff, who captured 13 other tournament titles, remained the seventh man in the Pfeiffer lineup after stepping down as captain.

JOSEPH SINKE
Chicago
Born: Jan. 28, 1909
Died: June 26, 1981
Inducted 1977

Sinke teamed with Herb Freitag to win the 1940 ABC Tournament doubles title, and he won the BPAA doubles crown with fellow Hall of Famer Paul Krumske in 1945. His list of other tournament titles numbered 19. Sinke also was a standout for several years in the Chicago Classic league. He used a two-finger ball and a three-step approach.

BILLY SIXTY
Milwaukee
Born: Nov. 30, 1899
Died: Nov. 1, 1983
Inducted 1961

Sixty wrote for the *Milwaukee Journal* sports staff from 1914- 74. He was noted nationally for both golf and bowling writing, plus being highly proficient at both sports. He captained several outstanding Milwaukee teams including the match game champion Heil Products. He won the Wisconsin Match Game championship in 1931, 1932, 1937 and 1944. He won one ABC title.

HARRY SMITH
Akron, Ohio
Born: April 29, 1930
Inducted 1978

Smith gained a reputation as an outstanding bowler while still in his teens in the Cleveland area. He moved to Detroit in 1955 and performed with the great Pfeiffers team, then moved to St. Louis to compete with the Falstaffs. Called Tiger by his bowling rivals because of his fierce competitive spirit, He has won four ABC Tournament titles and owns an outstanding ABC Masters record, winning the 1963 title and having five other finishes in the top eight.

JIMMY SMITH
Buffalo
Born: Sept. 19, 1885
Died: April 21, 1946
Inducted 1941

Smith was principally an exhibition bowler, although he won two ABC Tournament all events titles. He was named to the first team of *Bowling Magazine's* Pre-1950 All-America squad. He twice won the Petersen Classic in Chicago. In 1928, in one of the few "arranged" matches of his career, he defeated John (Count) Gengler to send that fabled gentleman into retirement.

DAVE SOUTAR
Bradenton, Fla.
Born: March 7, 1940
Inducted 1985

Soutar still is active on the Senior pro tour, where he won the 1990 Senior/Touring Pro Doubles event. In 1973, he became the first undefeated ABC Masters champion in six years. He owns one other ABC Tournament crown plus many other high finishes. Dave and his wife Judy are one of the few successful husband-wife pro bowling teams. Judy is a member of the WIBC Hall of Fame.

TONY SPARANDO
Rego Park, N.Y.
Born: Jan. 18, 1906
Died: Sept. 22, 1989
Elected 1968

Impaired vision failed to keep Sparando from becoming one of the East's all-time great stars. Tony was one of the few remaining top stars who "pin" bowled rather than spot bowled. Among famous Eastern teams he bowled with were Ronson Lighters and Faber Cement Block. Teammates on the Faber's included fellow Hall of Famers Lou Campi, Lindy Faragalli, Chuck Pezzano and Graz Castellano.

BARNEY SPINELLA
San Bernardino, Calif.
Born: Feb. 1, 1893
Died: Nov 28, 1991
Inducted 1968

Spinella was nicknamed "Jumping Jack" during his heyday as one of the greatest bowlers in the New York area because of his leaping antics on the approach after delivering his ball. He was regarded as one of the greatest 1-3 pocket shooters in the sport's history. He was famous in the hardwood duckpin circles and once held the world's record average for five games—145. He was a three-time ABC Tournament champion, taking the all events title in 1922 and 1927 and sharing the doubles with brother Chris in 1922.

HARRY STEERS
Chicago
Born: Oct. 3, 1880
Died: Feb. 13, 1963
Inducted 1941

On April 18, 1955, Steers was presented with a diamond lapel pin for being the first man to bowl in 50 ABC Tournaments. Steers did not participate in the first ABC Tournament in 1901, but was a scoremarker. The next year he participated and won the doubles event. He missed again in 1903, then bowled in every one from 1904 until 1962. Steers won the first Petersen Classic in 1921 in Chicago.

JIM STEFANICH
Joliet, Ill.
Born: Nov. 1, 1941
Inducted 1983

An outstanding ABC Tournament competitor, Stefanich has won seven titles, one short of the record. In ABC Masters play, he has finished in third place three times and fifth once. Stefanich also had a fine international career as a non-professional, being a member of the U.S. teams in the 1963 and 1964 FIQ competitions and winning four gold medals. As a professional he has won 13 PBA titles, including the 1967 Tournament of Champions.

OTTO STEIN JR.
St. Louis
Born: Jan. 20, 1893
Died: March 16, 1949
Inducted 1971

Stein compiled an outstanding record in St. Louis, where few challenged his supremacy as a match game bowler in the 1920s and '30s. He was one of the first to roll three 1,900 all events totals in the ABC Tournament, winning the 1929 crown with 1,974. Stein won the National Match Game title in 1934 by defeating Joe Miller of Buffalo, then lost it the following year to Hank Marino.

MARVIN (BUD) STOUDT
Lebanon, Pa.
Born: Oct. 17, 1931
Inducted 1991

Stoudt's career reached its zenith in 1975 when he became the second straight American to win the coveted FIQ World individual championship in London. Two years later, he earned a title in the mixed foursomes event of the Tournament of the Americas. His clutch 10th frame strike, in the 14th and final game, gave him the all events title at the Canada-U.S.A. Friendship matches. That reputation became further embellished at the ABC Tournament where the veteran garnered ABC championships in 1968, 1970 and 1978.

BOB STRAMPE
Detroit
Born: April 14, 1931
Inducted 1977

Strampe gained his early fame as a member of leading teams in the Minneapolis area, then joined the Stroh's of Detroit. The four-time ABC champion returned to the Twin Cities for a year to bowl with the Minnesota entry in the National Bowling League in 1960-61. When the league folded, he rejoined the Stroh's before eventually heading out for the pro tournament trail. He followed Don Carter as the second person to win the BPAA All-Star in 1963, PBA National in 1964 and ABC Masters in 1966. He is one of the few bowlers with 300 games in five different decades.

FRANK THOMA
Chicago
Born: Jan. 29, 1896
Died: Feb. 19, 1980
Inducted 1971

He was one of four Thoma brothers who earned five ABC Tournament championships during a nine-year period. Thoma, one of the top bowlers during the World War I era, had two of those and also recorded many top finishes in Illinois B.A. tournaments and won the Petersen Fall Classic in 1916.

ROD TOFT
Lake Elmo, Minn.
Born: April 30, 1945
Inducted 1991

Toft became a four-time ABC Tournament champion in 1985 as a member of the Minnesota Loons No. 1 team which successfully defended its 1984 team all events crown. Toft also found success in international play, winning three titles in the 1979 Tournament of the Americas and two in the 1984 event. Toft won a silver medal in the five player event of the 1983 FIQ World Tournament in Caracas, Venezuela. He also earned one gold and two silver medals in the 1983 Pan-Am Games.

MIKE TOTSKY
Detroit
Born: Aug. 31, 1928
Died: March 25, 1990
Inducted 1996

One one of Detroit's all-time greats, Totsky was named King of Detroit bowlers five times, a feat unequaled in what is regarded as the nation's strongest bowling community. While he won one ABC title, the 1973 Classic Team crown with the famous Stroh's, he had 12 other top 10 finishes and had a 26-year average of 197.

PETE TOUNTAS
Tucson, Ariz.
Born: Aug. 8, 1938
Inducted 1989

Tountas has a share of one of bowling's greatest records with a string of 21 four-game series above 800 in ABC Masters competition, ending with a 794 block of the 1968 finals. The one-time ABC champion went on to win the title that year. However, perhaps his proudest moment came in the 1988 ABC Tournament when he and son Michael finished ninth in doubles.

BILL TUCKER
Detroit
Born: Oct. 10, 1926
Inducted 1988

Tucker came to bowling stardom in St. Louis where he was in the shadow of the top stars with the Budweiser and Falstaff teams of the 1950s. In 1958, he won the ABC doubles with Jim Vrenick, then a decade later rolled a 300 game as he and Don Johnson won the Classic doubles. In 1971, he became the first to roll two 300s on ABC Tournament lanes when he had a perfect game in the Masters. Tucker won the 1961 BPAA All-Star tournament, the first year in which he qualified for the 16-man, round-robin finals.

TOMMY TUTTLE
King, N.C.
Born: May 12, 1929
Inducted 1995

Tuttle was a stellar competitor in the ABC Tournament and on the professional tour in the 1960s. His ABC title was in 1965 as a member of the Thelmal Lanes fivesome that captured the Classic team event. Two second-place and two third-place Classic division finishes plus six other top 10 places helped Tuttle to a 201 average for 25 ABCs. He also won three PBA national titles and continues to compete in PBA senior events.

ANDY VARIPAPA
Hempstead, N.Y.
Born: March 31, 1891
Died: Aug. 25, 1984
Inducted 1957

Varipapa developed trick shot bowling to its peak and through that ability starred in the first bowling film short, "Strikes and Spares", in 1934. He made more such films than any bowler. He was a leading instructor and exhibition bowler, one of the first to make nationwide tours. Varipapa's bowling ability often was overshadowed by his trick shooting, but his achievements on the lanes have been almost legendary. At age 55, he won the 1946 All-Star tournament and the following year became the first to repeat as All-Star champion. He also won BPAA doubles in 1947 and 1948 with fellow Hall of Famer Lou Campi.

WALTER WARD
Scottsdale, Ariz.
Born: Nov. 29, 1897
Died: Feb. 8, 1984
Elected 1959

During World War II, Ward gave exhibitions at 263 military bases. He had series scores of at least 700 an amazing 317 times. Ward holds six Cleveland B.A. titles and three Ohio B.A. titles.

DICK WEBER
St. Louis
Born: Dec. 23, 1929
Inducted 1970

No bowler has spanned decades of superior performance better than this Indianapolis native who has won pro tournaments in five decades. Weber came on the scene in the 1950s with the fabled Budweisers of St. Louis and has won major titles in nearly every portion of the United States. The three-time Bowler of the Year won one ABC Tournament title, is a four-time All-Star champion, and teamed with Ray Bluth to win four BPAA doubles crowns and was a member of six BPAA national team champions. Weber was voted to the Bowling Magazine All-America first team 11 times. He was edged by teammate Don Carter in 1970 voting for the honor of Greatest Bowler of All-Time. As a member of the Buds, Weber bowled 258, 258, 259 when the team posted the longtime record 3,858 in 1958.

BILLY WELU
Houston
Born: July 30, 1932
Died: May 16, 1974
Inducted 1975

After serving a stint with the Budweisers, Welu became captain of the Falstaffs and led them to national honors in ABC and BPAA team action. He also was a great individual performer, scoring back-to-back victories in the 1964-65 ABC Masters and winning the 1959 All-Star. At 6'4 1/2" and 230 pounds, he was proof that big men can be stars in bowling. For many years, he was the color commentator on PBA telecasts with broadcaster Chris Schenkel.

JOE WILMAN
Chicago
Born: Dec. 20, 1905
Died: Oct. 22, 1969
Inducted 1951

Wilman was the second man to win four ABC Tournament championships and the first with two 2,000 all events totals. Wilman was one of the game's leading instructors and analysts. He was an excellent radio and television commentator on bowling. Noted for his ability to "play" lanes, he also was famous for his ready grin and rapid gum chewing. He was named to Bowling Magazine's first-team All-America Pre-1950 team.

PHIL WOLF
Chicago
Born: Oct. 7, 1869
Died: June 16, 1936
Inducted 1961

Wolf came to Chicago in 1899, where he soon gained a reputation as a rough and ready competitor who gave no quarter in a match. He won his third ABC Tournament title in 1928 at age 58. Included in his other tournament triumphs was a pair of Illinois B.A. championships.

RICH WONDERS
Racine, Wis.
Born: Dec. 29, 1946
Inducted 1990

Wonders has had a splendid career on all levels. In international competition, Wonders won a gold in team and bronze in singles in the 1981 FIQ Zone Tournament and in the 1983 FIQ World won a silver in five player, bronze in trios and another bronze in all events. He earned three silver medals in the 1983 Pan-Am Games and also placed fourth in the International Amateur Tournament in 1984. In the U.S., he owns five ABC Tournament titles including three in 1982. In the process, he earned $7,350 to set a single Tournament record and also was the first to post 700-plus series in singles and doubles for two consecutive years.

GEORGE YOUNG
Detroit
Born: Oct. 3, 1909
Died: Aug. 30, 1959
Inducted 1959

Young was a member of the four-time ABC Tournament champion E&B/Pfeiffer team and won two other ABC titles. He had one of the most glittering ABC Tournament records with an unparalleled string of nine consecutive all events totals above 1,800. Between 1942 and 1958 (with three years out for World War II when there was no Tournament), his only total below 1800 was 1778 in 1949. His 202 lifetime average was the highest in history for 20 or more tournaments at that time.

WAYNE ZAHN
Tempe, Ariz.
Born: Jan. 20, 1941
Inducted 1980

Zahn became the youngest bowler ever to be inducted into the ABC Hall of Fame until Nelson Burton Jr.'s induction in 1981. A one-time ABC champion, he was a teenage sensation in

Milwaukee, reaching a 222 league average in 1960-61. At age 19, he finished ninth in the All-Star tournament, the youngest ever to finish that high. He later moved to Tempe where he operates a 24-lane center. The 14-time PBA titlist and PBA Hall of Famer rolled the first 300 game ever in the Hall of Fame Tournament in 1989.

LES ZIKES
Chicago
Born: Oct. 15, 1934
Inducted 1983

Zikes is the only man to win ABC Tournament titles in three successive years. He was a member of the winning teams in 1962 and 1963 and took the all events and team all events titles in 1964 in addition to two other championships. His 1963 win qualified him for the United States team in the 1963 FIQ World Tournament, thereby launching him on what was to become the most decorated nonprofessional, international career in bowling history. He collected no less than eight gold medals during two FIQ World and one American Zone championships. He was the all events champion in both the 1963 World and 1964 American Zone.

GILBERT ZUNKER
Milwaukee
Born: March 14, 1901
Died: Dec. 19, 1938
Inducted 1941

Zunker was a strong team bowler who helped make the Heil Products team consisting of Hall of Fame members Hank Marino, Charley Daw, Ned Day and Billy Sixty a feared club in the middle 1930s. He died at age 37 after suffering a cold for a brief time. He was the first to roll two 700s in one ABC Tournament, posting 750 and 712 while winning the 1933 all events.

MERITORIOUS SERVICE BIOGRAPHIES

HAROLD ALLEN
Detroit
Born: Jan. 6, 1897
Died: Nov. 15, 1964
Inducted 1966

Allen was active in tenpins both on and off the lanes. Allen became the youngest bowler to win an ABC championship when at the age of 18 he combined with his brother, Ray, for the doubles title in 1915. That record stood for 48 years. In 1950 he served as president of the Bowling Proprietors Association of America which he helped found and also was active in Detroit B.A. and proprietor projects.

JOHN ARCHIBALD
St. Louis
Born: Feb. 17, 1925
Inducted 1996

As a respected bowling columnist and reporter with the St. Louis Post-Dispatch, Archibald traveled the country covering such tournaments as the All-Star, World's Invitational, ABC Masters and Firestone Tournament of Champions. He served as Bowling Writers Association of America President in 1970. When he retired in 1989, he had completed 39 years as a bowling writer. The PBA Hall of Famer has won 50 Bowling Magazine writing awards and six in the Professional Bowlers Assn. writing competition. For 25 years he has written the yearly bowling summary for the Encyclopedia Britannica Book of the Year.

FRANK BAKER
Milwaukee
Born: June 14, 1907
Died: July 28, 1995
Inducted 1975

During Baker's 1951-72 tenure as only ABC's fourth top leader, the Congress enjoyed a massive growth in membership, jumping from 1.3 million to more than four million. His media background, calling for careful attention to detail, plus his foresight in keeping ABC in pace with fast-moving technological advances, kept the organization in tune with the times. He also gave unselfishly of his time and talent to the National Bowling Council and became active in the international world of tenpins serving as Federation Internationale des Quilleurs President from 1977-83.

ELMER BAUMGARTEN
Milwaukee
Born: April 26, 1881
Died: March 26, 1961
Inducted 1951

Baumgarten served as ABC secretary from 1933 to 1951, directing the Congress through turbulent times and on into the beginning of the boom. While serving as secretary, he was known as a tower of strength for the game through the Depression years and World War II. He was a rugged individualist who believed in action and complete authority. His rigid demands for honesty, fair play and strict adherence to rules and regulations stamped him "Mr. ABC" in the eyes of Congress members.

LOU BELLISIMO
Eugene, Ore.
Born: Aug. 8, 1906
Died: Oct. 3, 1987
Inducted 1986

A pioneer bowling teacher, Bellisimo was senior instructor at the University of Oregon from 1949 to 1972 where he established one of the nation's most popular bowling programs. Lou earned the nickname "Mr. Scientific" because of constant analyzing and discussions of bowling form, action of the ball, etc. He wrote one of the most popular bowling instruction books in history (The Bowlers Manual) that sold more than 200,000 copies its first three editions.

ROBERT BENSINGER
Chicago
Born: Feb. 10, 1898
Died: March 5, 1988
Inducted 1969

Bensinger served as chairman of the board of the Brunswick Corp. from 1950 until his retirement in 1963. His support of bowling went far beyond the role of manufacturing firm executive. Under his guidance, the company built a large staff of star players for exhibition work and personal appearances which helped popularize the sport.

LEROY CHASE
Peoria, Ill.
Born: July 31, 1908
Died: Nov. 20, 1971
Inducted 1972

Chase devoted his life to bowling, writing about the game for 40 years as a member of the Peoria Journal-Star sports staff and serving in such executive capacities as president of the Illinois B.A. and the Bowling Writers Association of America. He was ABC's third vice president at the time of his death. He was elected to the Board of Directors in 1959 and became a vice president in 1965.

JOHN COKER
San Diego
Born: Feb. 24, 1892
Died: Aug. 31, 1967
Inducted 1980

An electronics whiz from his early working days, "J.B." turned his talents to bowling inventions such as the Tel-E-Score overhead projector and the electronic foul detector. Coker invented the foul detector in 1937, not only because a human judge was needed for every league session, but because bowlers were sliding past the foul line and ruining the lane finish. During the same period, a proprietor suggested Coker develop something to project scores so bowlers and fans could see what was taking place. Coker drafted basic plans, then sought out scientists at Cal Tech who helped him design what was to become the Tel-E-Score.

CHARLES COLLIER
Chicago
Born: Dec. 31, 1877
Died: Oct. 11, 1957
Inducted 1963

Collier was a familiar and colorful personality at ABC Tournament installations from 1912 to 1951 when he supervised the construction and maintenance of the Tournament lanes for Brunswick. One of the top stars of his day, Collier rolled in 39 ABC Tournaments and compiled a 186 lifetime average. For more than three decades, he captained the famous Brunswick Mineralite team which included fellow Hall of Famer Harry Steers.

STEVE CRUCHON
Detroit
Born: June 13, 1914
Died: Nov. 22, 1986
Inducted 1983

Cruchon was one of bowling's most honored writers. His journalistic ability earned him 21 awards in Bowling Magazine's writing competition including a record seven first places. From 1945-76 he served as editor of the Modern Bowler. He then started his own publication, Bowler's Digest, and continued as its editor-publisher until his death.

WALT DITZEN
Phoenix
Born: June 18, 1914
Died: March 4, 1973
Inducted 1973

Ditzen created the popular "Fan Fare" cartoon which appeared in more than 200 newspapers in the United States and foreign countries. The three panel strip covered all sports, and two of his best known characters were "Gutter Gus" and "Gutter Gussie," whose humorous and sometimes irreverent remarks about bowling gave Ditzen a wide following. He created a series of posters in 1957 for the National Bowling Council to fight a plague of slow bowling. The posters still are seen occasionally in bowling establishments.

WILLIAM DOEHRMAN
Ft. Wayne, Ind.
Born: Feb. 7, 1888
Died: Sept. 11, 1984
Inducted 1968

Doehrman compiled one of sports' most impressive longevity records, competing in an unprecedented 71 consecutive ABC Tournaments. He competed in every Tournament from 1908 to 1981. He is one of only three bowlers (along with the late Chick Carr of Ft. Wayne and Joe Norris of San Diego) ever to participate in more than 60 ABCs and knock down more than 100,000 pins.

EDDIE ELIAS
Akron, Ohio
Born: Dec. 12, 1928
Inducted 1985

Elias gathered 33 top bowlers for a meeting in 1958 at the ABC Tournament in Syracuse, N.Y., convinced them to put up $50 each and the Professional Bowlers Assn. was formed. The tour began in 1959 with a total prize fund of less than $50,000. By the early 1980s, the prize fund for national and regional events exceeded $7 million. He was also instrumental in helping bowling gain national exposure by convincing ABC-TV to telecast the winter tour.

FRANK ESPOSITO
Deerfield Beach, Fla.
Born: April 28, 1920
Inducted 1997

Esposito, the longtime owner of the famed Paramus Bowl in New Jersey, has contributed to the sport in many ways during his career. His contributions to the sport are far-reaching, being regarded as a pioneer for ideas and innovations over 50 years of involvement in the sport. Many of the bowling TV show formats were Esposito brainchilds. While he became best known for his role as TV coordinator for PBA Tour events on ABC-TV, he also hosted PBA events and was the first to award merchandise to pro-am entrants.

DICK EVANS
Daytona Beach, Fla.
Born: Sept. 20, 1931
Inducted 1992

Evans' contributions to the sport have come as a bowling columnist for the *Miami Herald* and through his affiliation with the Bowling Writers Association of America. He joined the *Miami Herald* in 1949 and began his bowling coverage in 1957. Since then he has covered nearly every major national event along with the Miami bowling scene and has earned more awards for his work than anyone else.

BILL FRANKLIN
Lake San Marcos, Calif.
Born: July 1, 1913
Inducted 1992

Franklin has been a bowling writer, editor, researcher, innovator, speaker, publicist, historian, tournament official, promoter, member of the ABC Board of Directors and Hall of Fame worker. He helped research the records and oddities section for the original ABC Yearbook. He came up with the idea for on-site awards at the ABC Tournament, a program adopted in 1950 that has been copied in other competitions and continues at the annual ABC Tournament.

JACK HAGERTY
Toledo, Ohio
Born: Sept. 8, 1876
Died: July 31, 1955
Inducted 1963

Hagerty spent nearly 60 years as a Toledo bowling proprietor and played a prominent role in obtaining and helping stage five ABC Tournaments in that city between 1913 and 1926. He was a charter member and president of the Bowling Proprietors Association of America, and also presided over the Ohio BPA. He was a prime organizer of the Central States tournament, once the most important of all regional events.

DR. HILDING HATTSTROM
Evanston, Ill.
Born: Feb. 6, 1896
Died: Jan. 3, 1980
Inducted 1980

Dr. Hattstrom was the champion of bowling promotion for men and women 55 and older, and today's ABC National Seniors Tournament is a result of his dedication. In his heyday, he was a good bowler who hovered around the 200 average mark and he won a national seniors' title in 1961 in actual singles. Besides writing technical articles for the National *Bowlers Journal*, Hattstrom was a top instructor.

CONE HERMANN
St. Louis
Born: April 9, 1903
Died: April 26, 1957
Inducted 1968

Hermann's name was synonymous with the great Hermann Undertakers teams (named after the family funeral business) of the late 1930s and early '40s. Hermann was one of the most dynamic influences of his time on the formation of all-star teams of national repute. He began organizing such teams in 1931 and later his teams included Hall of Famers Don Carter and Chuck O'Donnell.

PETER HOWLEY
Chicago
Born: May 30, 1881
Died: Jan. 31, 1958
Inducted 1941

Howley was the only man to bowl in the first 46 ABC Tournaments (1901-49), averaging 178, finally retiring because of illness. He was a charter member of the ABC Hall of Fame in 1941 and was moved into the Meritorious Service section in 1963. He was general manager of several bowling and billiard establishments in the Windy City.

ROBERT KENNEDY
Detroit
Born: Sept. 6, 1895
Died: Dec. 26, 1955
Inducted 1981

Kennedy was the driving force in the development of the automatic pinsetter which freed bowling from the bondage of the pinboy and lifted the sport to its present eminence. As vice president of the Brunswick Corp. in the 1930s, Kennedy saw the need for modernization of the bowling game and made recommendations embodied in a report which led to the introduction of Brunswick's 20th Century line of bowling equipment. Lanes were streamlined; colorful semi-circle leatherette seats were created, and the introduction of the forerunner to the masking unit to hide the pinboy from view were just a few improvements he instituted that led to the revitalization of the sport.

ABRAHAM LANGTRY
Milwaukee
Born: Aug. 1, 1873
Died: July 30, 1942
Inducted 1963

Langtry served for 25 years as ABC secretary. Upon taking office in 1907 as the Congress' second administrative leader, he moved ABC headquarters from Dayton, Ohio to Milwaukee. He administered Congress business through the first stages of growth and widespread public respect. It was his vision and determination during a period when ABC needed an uncompromising leader that helped build its sturdy foundation on which the game rests.

SAM LEVINE
Cleveland
Born: April 20, 1913
Died: July 22, 1982
Inducted 1971

Levine was a wearer of many hats. He founded the Cleveland Kegler bowling newspaper in 1937 and was its editor and publisher until his death. He helped raise thousands of dollars for charity with innovations that included a bowlers' picnic and sending children to summer camp through bowlers rolling 300 games. He broadcasted bowling for two decades, handled many live television programs and announced syndicated match game shows.

DAVID LUBY
Chicago
Born: April 7, 1870
Died: Nov. 27, 1925
Inducted 1969

Luby founded the *Bowlers Journal* in 1913. He was a traveling shoe salesman who scurried back to Chicago each week to bowl in the famed Randolph league. Out of this interest grew plans for the weekly newspaper, which later became a national monthly publication under the leadership of his son, Mort Sr., who also is in the Hall. His grandson, Mort Jr., another Hall member, is the present publisher.

MORT LUBY SR.
Chicago
Born: June 6, 1897
Died: Oct. 1, 1956
Inducted 1974

Luby first suggested the formation of a bowling Hall of Fame in 1937, an idea that was realized in 1941. He also was a founding father of the Bowling Writers Association of America. He served as publisher of the *Bowlers Journal* from 1925 until his death having taken over the publication upon the death of his father, Hall of Famer Dave Luby. The Lubys were the first father-son ABC Hall combination.

MORT LUBY JR.
Chicago
Born: July 14, 1931
Inducted 1988

As former publisher of the *Bowlers Journal*, Luby followed in the footsteps of father Mort Sr. and grandfather Dave Luby in the *Bowlers Journal*. The Lubys are believed to be the only family with three generations in a sports hall of fame. One of Luby's proudest achievements was the founding of the World Bowling Writers, a fraternity of writers, promoters and other bowling enthusiasts from 50 nations. He published a monthly "Worldletter" which provides bowling news on the world scene.

AL MATZELLE
Milwaukee
Born: April 11, 1917
Inducted 1995

Matzelle devoted most of his adult life to the administrative side of bowling. Besides his efforts on behalf of ABC, he was instrumental in the early years of the Bowling Hall of Fame and Museum. He joined ABC in 1938 as "official typist of rule book envelopes." After later serving as assistant to Hall of Famer Frank K. Baker for 19 years, he eventually was elected to the ABC Executive post in 1972. In 1980, he moved to St. Louis to plan and organize the Bowling Hall of Fame and Museum and was the person in charge of the shrine when it opened in 1984. He returned to Milwaukee the next year and has spent part of his time since volunteering his services at ABC Headquarters.

HOWARD MCCULLOUGH
Chicago
Born: July 25, 1899
Died: Feb. 15, 1974
Inducted 1971

McCullough was credited with creating the captain-sponsor dinner in 1941, still a popular activity for associations in many cities. He was instrumental in founding the Detroit Bowling Council, one of the first citywide bowling councils of its kind. He also was noted for his work with charity promotions, notably as chairman of the March of Dimes sports committee in the 1950s.

MOREHEAD PATTERSON
New York
Born: Oct. 9, 1897
Died: Aug. 5, 1962
Inducted 1985

Patterson was one of the prime forces behind development of the AMF pinspotter, a project which encountered a number of detours in the late 1940s. His hiring of fellow Hall member Robert Kennedy and insistence on continuing with the development despite rising costs and pessimism allowed AMF to become the first company to gain ABC approval of a pinsetting machine in 1951. Patterson also was instrumental in the beginning of the Association of College Unions-International tournament in 1959.

LOUIS PETERSEN
Chicago
Born: Sept. 23, 1883
Died: June 20, 1958
Inducted 1963

A scoring system and a bowling tournament have etched Petersen's name indelibly in the upper strata of bowling contributors. He started his famous Petersen Classic in 1921 and that event's popularity has grown each year. Petersen also originated the point system bearing his name. He also was a founder of the Bowling Proprietors Association of America in 1932 and a prime mover of high school bowling.

CHUCK PEZZANO
Clifton, N.J.
Born: Jan. 14, 1929
Inducted 1982

One of the sport's foremost authorities, Pezzano is considered bowling's most prolific author. He is active as a television, film and video bowling consultant, advisor, color man and coordinator. Pezzano also is closely involved with the Professional Bowlers Assn. A charter member as a top bowler and a PBA Hall of Famer, he was its secretary from 1971-90 and currently serves as historian and Eastern Regional Director. Pezzano bowled the first 800 series by a full-time collegian.

REMO PICCHIETTI
Bannockburn, Ill.
Born: Jan. 23, 1930
Inducted 1993

Currently chairman of the board and formerly president of DBA Products Inc., Picchietti long has been one of the most involved and visible personalities in bowling. He is considered among the sport's leading authorities on lane maintenance and procedures, conducting hundreds of seminars on the subjects worldwide. Picchietti has been recognized by his peers for the presidencies of the National Bowling Council, the Billiard & Bowling Institute of America and the National Association of Independent Resurfacers.

BRUCE PLUCKHAHN
St. Louis
Born: Oct. 10, 1924
Inducted 1989

Because of his knowledge of many areas of the sport, from the international aspect to such projects as the National Bowling League, Pluckhahn is regarded by many as one of the world's top experts on the sport. He also was in on the ground floor of the planning of the National Bowling Hall of Fame and Museum. Pluckhahn has been a vital force in various areas of bowling for nearly four decades, first as a newspaperman in Milwaukee, Wausau, Wis. and Dayton, Ohio, but more prominently with the ABC Public Relations Department for 23 years and the National Bowling Hall of Fame and Museum for 12 years. His dedication and research has been instrumental in the establishment of the ABC Hall of Fame Pioneer section.

MILTON RAYMER
Chicago
Born: Aug. 3, 1906
Died: Oct. 26, 1991
Inducted 1972

Raymer, founder of the American Junior Bowling Congress, spent almost endless days traveling to all corners of the country espousing junior bowling, teaching youngsters to bowl and training adults for teaching bowling and organizing leagues. In 1946, the AJBC was founded in Chicago with Raymer as its executive secretary. He held the post for 15 years. From a membership of 8,767 in 1946, he led the growth to 410,000 boys and girls of high school age and under. The program, now the Young American Bowling Alliance, has approximately 600,000 members.

J. ELMER REED
Cleveland
Born: May 6, 1903
Died: Dec. 27, 1983
Inducted 1978

Reed has the distinction of becoming the first black member of the ABC Hall of Fame. Perhaps that's fitting because in the 1940s he was instrumental in the fight against ABC's "caucasian only" membership rule which was rescinded at the 1950 ABC Convention. After learning blacks virtually were excluded from bowling because of race, Reed traveled to many cities at his own expense in the 1930s to organize black bowling leagues, usually in old, rundown centers. In 1941, he and two partners built the first black bowling center in the U.S. (United Recreation in Cleveland).

JACK REICHERT
Chicago
Born: Sept. 27, 1930
Inducted 1998

Reichert retired as Brunswick's chairman of the board and president and chief executive officer in 1995. Tireless in his commitment to promote bowling as a medal sport in the Olympics, he led his company's efforts in the Olympic quest. He provided the leadership to guide Brunswick's growth into a leader in the bowling and recreation industry. He remains a member of the Strike Ten Entertainment, Inc. and Professional Bowlers Association boards of directors. Reichert has been a driving force behind bowling since his early days as a pinsetter for Hall of Famer Ned Day in his hometown of Milwaukee.

MILT RUDO
Chicago
Born: Jan. 17, 1919
Inducted 1984

Rudo earned his niche in bowling's history by always endeavoring to better the sport, a dedication that reached far beyond four decades of business commitment to the Brunswick Corp. He was a creative executive who developed ideas that benefited the industry. He fought for product improvement, including removal of the hand towel and unsightly chalk, without which old-timers insisted they couldn't bowl. Such innovations helped attract the family to bowling.

CHRIS SCHENKEL
Leesburg, Ind.
Born: Aug. 21, 1923
Inducted 1988

One of the most popular and widely honored sports announcers in the United States, Schenkel became known as the "voice" of the Professional Bowlers Assn. tour as host of ABC-TV's PBA telecasts from 1962 to 1997. Schenkel has covered virtually every major sporting event in his more than 45 years as a broadcaster. But he is best known and most respected for his commentary on bowling. He also donated much of time as honorary chairman of the National Bowling Hall of Fame and Museum.

DENNIS SWEENEY
St. Louis
Born: Oct. 3, 1873
Died: July 23, 1965
Inducted 1974

Sweeney founded the Women's International Bowling Congress and was one of the first to campaign the cause of women in bowling. In 1907, he received permission to hold a national women's tournament on the ABC Tournament lanes and encouraged women's bowling at every turn. Finally in 1916, a group of representatives met in St. Louis and organized the WIBC.

ROGER TESSMAN
Homosassa, Fla.
Born: April 5, 1927
Inducted 1994

As Federation Internationale des Quilleurs President since 1984, Tessman has strived to gain bowling Olympic recognition for the sport. He led the movement to have bowling gain membership in the United States Olympic Committee in 1984 and two years later he was instrumental in gaining recognition for the sport in the Pan American Games. But his original legacy began with ABC from association official all the way to the post of Executive Secretary-Treasurer for seven years.

JOSEPH THUM
New York
Born: Jan. 24, 1858
Died: Jan. 9, 1937
Inducted 1980

Heralded as the father of international bowling, "Uncle Joe" also was a driving force in the organization of ABC. His creative ventures took many of the best U.S. bowlers to Stockholm, Sweden in 1923, two other European trips in 1926 and 1929 and his last visit, to Berlin in 1936, where the bowlers competed in a special event held in conjunction before the Olympic Games. He was elected president of the International Bowling Assn. when it was founded in Stockholm in 1926.

SAM WEINSTEIN
Chicago
Born: Aug. 7, 1914
Inducted 1970

Weinstein's love affair with bowling began in 1931 when, at age 17, he became a secretary-writer for *Bowlers Journal*. In 1935, he originated the "Tenpin Tattler" radio program, today the longest-running show in history. For years, he helped other cities start bowling broadcasts. He also was a driving force behind Chicago's famous *Sun-Times* Charity tournament "Beat the Champs" television series and has helped hundreds of humanitarian causes with contributions of bowling promotions and private donations.

ELI WHITNEY
Milwaukee
Born: Sept. 16, 1893
Died: Dec. 11, 1957
Inducted 1975

Whitney founded the ABC Hall of Fame in 1941, a year after he had joined the Congress staff as its first public relations manager. Whitney was an idea man. Among his innovations were the ABC Newsletter, which for a time included a special report to the hundreds of radio stations that carried bowling news in those days; the bowling writing competition sponsored by *Bowling Magazine*, the official publication for which he served as executive editor, and the Rip Van Winkle Award of the Bowling Writers Association of America, which he had helped organize in 1934.

FRED WOLF
Detroit
Born: May 26, 1911
Inducted 1976

Wolf was an outstanding bowler and a member of the powerful Stroh's Beer team for seven years. But his greatest mark was made in radio and television as a bowling commentator in Detroit. He covered the 1948 ABC Tournament from a booth behind the score-markers for 80 consecutive nights. He moved into television the next year and had a succession of popular local shows which led to a network opportunity with the Championship Bowling series.

PIONEER BIOGRAPHIES

LAFAYETTE ALLEN JR.
Detroit
Born: Oct. 21, 1921
Died: Feb. 2, 1992
Inducted 1994

Known as "the voice of the Black bowling community" of the Greater Detroit area, Allen devoted a lifetime to service in his community in a multitude of ways. An outstanding bowler, he became one of the great sponsors of individuals, teams and leagues. His sponsorship fame became national in 1951 when he entered his Allen Supermarket team in the ABC Tournament in St. Paul. It was the first Black team to bowl in the ABC following the rescinding of the "caucasian only" clause in 1950.

FRANK BRIELL
New York City
Born: March 28, 1864
Died: Nov. 19, 1944
Inducted 1996

Briell was the first national champion as he won the 1901 ABC Tournament singles and all events in Chicago. He was a member of the first team to tour the country, the Linden Groves, which was organized by ABC Secretary Samuel Karpf. He averaged a then astounding 196 for 10 games to win the New York Herald Tournament.

REV. CHARLES CAROW
Brooklyn, N.Y.
Born: Jan. 2, 1908
Died: Sept. 20, 1970
Inducted 1995

Father Carow was heavily involved in conducting a bowling program for the Catholic Youth Organization in the New York City area. He became a New York City Bowling Assn. Director and later an ABC Convention delegate where he pleaded with ABC to open its membership to minorities in the late 1940s. The "Caucasian-Only" rule was changed in 1950.

SYDNEY CELESTINE
Chicago
Born: Nov. 11, 1900
Died: March 1, 1983
Inducted 1993

Celestine helped lead the fight to force the ABC to eliminate the rule that had been adopted in 1915-16 limiting membership in the organization to members of the Caucasian race. Although noted for his calm, sensible, diplomatic approach to the membership problem, he never wavered in his determination that the rule had to be removed from the books. Many honors came to Celestine in recogni-

tion of his role in obtaining eradication of the rule. The one he most treasured was his being the first electee in 1980 to the National Bowling Assn. Hall of Fame.

THOMAS CURTIS
New York
Born: Jan. 3, 1827
Died: Aug. 21, 1905
Inducted 1993

Generally regarded as the "Father of Bowling," Curtis was elected as the first ABC President in 1895. He was hailed as the originator of the tournament concept in the 1880s and was involved in center management and ownership. Even before ABC was organized, Curtis was credited with writing the first set of bowling rules in 1875.

ERIC DEFREITAS
New York
Born: Aug. 5, 1908
Inducted 1994

deFreitas was the first black bowler to become a member of the AMF Staff of Champions, and one of the first black members of the Professional Bowlers Association. He has been deeply involved in all phases of bowling, as a bowler, pioneer organizer and instructor, public relations man, fighter for fairness in bowling and elsewhere, and has been a student, teacher and historian. He was instrumental in the formation of numerous junior leagues and tournaments, guided many young black bowlers into better competition and the pros and was an outstanding role model because of his many charitable, civic and church involvements.

WILLIAM HALL SR.
Omaha, Neb.
Born: March 2, 1910
Inducted 1994

Hall made his mark on the sport through his constant search for Black bowling history. In 1970 Hall earned the honor of which he is most proud, election as the first Black to the ABC Board of Directors. He served for 16 active years, then became an Honorary member in 1986. He was one of the leaders in the fight to force the ABC to rescind its limiting of membership to members of the "Caucasian race."

HIROTO HIRASHIMA
Kaneohe, Hawaii
Born: July 11, 1910
Inducted 1995

Hirashima led the sport through difficult times in Hawaii and eventually became the first minority ABC Director in 1963. He organized nine teams for the 1954 ABC Tournament in Seattle, the first Japanese-Americans to compete in the event. ABC invited him to become more involved in activites and eventually he was elected an ABC Director.

SAMUEL KARPF
Dayton, Ohio
Born: April 23, 1986
Died: Nov. 9, 1923
Inducted 1993

As ABC's first Secretary, Karpf added credibility and direction to that position, even challenging the rights of ABC President Thomas Curtis to unilaterally rule on the eligibility of players during the first season of the Congress. While not being in total agreement on all matters, he helped find compromise to overcome many challenges to the rules, such as the number of pins, how many players on a team, how many balls per frame and lane measurements.

HENRY MOORE
Dunning, Neb.
Born: 1908
Died: February 1966
Inducted 1996

Moore was the inventor of the plastic coated bowling pin. He once was a Nebraska chicken farmer who went into bowling pin restoration in the days of wooden pins. The automatic pinsetter cut their life to a maximum of 500 lines, and along with the scarcity of maple for the pins after World War II, necessitated a substitute.   After lengthy tests of more than one million games, his plastic coated pin was approved by ABC in 1962.

FRANK PASDELOUP
Chicago
Born: 1866
Died: Jan. 15, 1938
Inducted 1993

Pasdeloup was credited with cementing the "East vs. West" battle within the ABC by giving up the Presidency three hours after being elected in 1902. His contribution at that time was recognized the following year when he was elected ABC Treasurer, a position he held until he died in 1938. His name still is honored by the ABC Tournament with the team all events trophy named in his honor.

BILL RHODMAN
Detroit
Born: April 6, 1914
Died: 1961
Inducted 1997

Rhodman was perhaps the top black competitor in the Detroit area and the nation at a time when he and fellow blacks could not join ABC. The Congress' Constitution

was amended in 1951 removing "white" from its membership requirements. Two years later, Rhodman was a member of the first all-black team to participate in the ABC Tournament. He was elected to the Hall for his efforts in expanding the interest in bowling within his ethnic group as well as youngsters. He also was an accomplished instructor, promoter and competitor.

MASAO SATOW
Los Angeles
Born: 1908
Died: March 3, 1976
Inducted 1994

Satow is regarded by his peers as the individual who worked the hardest and accomplished the most for Japanese American bowling in the U.S. He overcame World War II internment and played a major role in establishing the national championship for Nisei bowlers in 1947. When interest in the event waned when non-whites were admitted to ABC membership in 1950, Satow led the drive to save it and helped guide it for 25 years. Now the event is under the direction of the Japanese American Bowling Assn.

LOUIS SCHUTTE
New York
Born: Not Available
Died: Aug. 12, 1916
Inducted 1993

As the publisher of The (New York) *Bowlers Journal,* Schutte played a strong role in the sport in the late 1800s covering all aspects of the sport. Through editorials he continuously urged the formation of a national membership and rules making organization. This helped prompt ABC's founding, and Schutte continued his support of the organization, offsetting opposition from other sources.

ROKURO (FUZZY) SHIMADA
Mountain View, Calif.
Born: Oct. 26, 1971
Inducted 1997

Shimada devoted his career to leadership of the sport within his ethnic group. A strong bowler who was barred from ABC membership because of the caucasian rule, Shimada was instrumental in promoting the sport to Japanese-Americans. He shared his knowledge as an instructor and promoter throughout California and helped organize the National Japanese-American tournament where he won 13 titles in 43 years of participation. He has five top 10 ABC Tournament finishes and three times won the Northern California BPAA match play crown.

LOUIS STEIN
New York City
Born: Sept. 4, 1858
Died: Oct. 3, 1949
Inducted 1997

Stein far outlived his fellow ABC founding fathers, but is best known for waging a tough battle in that first ABC meeting in 1895 to make 12 consecutive strikes a 300 game, rather than continuing with 200 as the maximum Stein himself eventually achieved perfection seven times. For many years he operated a six-lane center near Times Square.

WILLIAM THOMPSON
Chicago
Born: April 25, 1863
Died: Sept. 30, 1938
Inducted 1993

A top bowler and premier organizer in his native Chicago, Thompson was best known as a bowling official, promoter, innovator, writer and visionary. In 1904 the Bowling Encyclopedia said: "Few in tenpin history have equaled Mr. Thompson's combination of skills as a bowler, leader and administrator." A bowling equipment expert familiar with fair playing rules, he called for uniformity. He built the first regulation alleys in Chicago's Plaza Hotel in 1893.

DR. HENRY TIMM
New York
Born: Oct. 21, 1851
Died: Aug. 12, 1923
Inducted 1993

As ABC's second President, Timm was as instrumental in establishing the fledgling organization's acceptance and stability as anyone. He strongly supported the rules and specifications approved at the first ABC Convention, having helped frame them during his association (from 1875-1915) with the United Bowling Clubs, an important New York City group.

HONORS

Bowlers of the Year

Members of the Bowling Writers Association of America vote to determine the Woman and Male Bowlers of the Year. A special committee representing bowling industry groups selects the leading female and male Bowler-of-the-Year candidates for each group and compiles the candidates' bowling-achievement resumes. These ballots and resumes are distributed to BWAA members.

BWAA members choose five candidates and rank them. The BWAA committee awards 10 points for first-place votes, five points for second-place votes, three points for third-place votes, two points for fourth-place votes and one point for fifth-place votes. The BWAA names the candidate with the most points in each group the Bowler of the Year.

Woman Bowler of the Year

1996	Wendy Macpherson, Henderson, Nev.
1995	Tish Johnson, Northridge, Calif.
1994	Anne Marie Duggan, Edmond, Okla.
1993	Lisa Wagner, Palmetto, Fla.
1992	Tish Johnson, Panorama City, Calif.
1991	Leanne Barrette, Yukon, Okla.
1990	Tish Johnson, Panorama City, Calif.
1989	Robin Romeo, Newhall, Calif.
1988	Lisa Wagner, Palmetto, Fla.
1987	Betty Morris, Stockton, Calif.
1986	Lisa Wagner, Palmetto, Fla.
1985	Aleta Sill, Dearborn, Mich.
1984	Aleta Sill, Dearborn, Mich.
1983	Lisa Wagner, Palmetto, Fla.
1982	Nikki Gianulias, Vallejo, Calif.
1981	Donna Adamek, Apple Valley, Calif.
1980	Donna Adamek, Apple Valley, Calif.
1979	Donna Adamek, Apple Valley, Calif.
1978	Donna Adamek, Apple Valley, Calif.
1977	Betty Morris, Stockton, Calif.
1976	Patty Costello, Scranton, Pa.
1975	Judy Soutar, Leawood, Kan.
1974	Betty Morris, Stockton, Calif.
1973	Judy Soutar, Leawood, Kan.
1972	Patty Costello, Scranton, Pa.
1971	Paula Carter, Miami
1970	Mary Baker Harris, Central Islip, N.Y.
1969	Dorothy Fothergill, Center Ossippee, N.H.
1968	Dorothy Fothergill, Center Ossippee, N.H.
1967	Mildred Ignizio, Rochester, N.Y.
1966	Joy Abel, Lansing, Ill.
1965	Betty Kuczynski, Cicero, Ill.
1964	LaVerne Carter, Las Vegas
1963	Marion Ladewig, Grand Rapids, Mich.
1962	Shirley Garms, Island Lake, Ill.
1961	Shirley Garms, Island Lake, Ill.
1960	Sylvia Martin, Philadelphia
1959	Marion Ladewig, Grand Rapids, Mich.
1958	Marion Ladewig, Grand Rapids, Mich.
1957	Marion Ladewig, Grand Rapids, Mich.
1956	Anita Cantaline, Detroit
1955	Sylvia Martin, Philadelphia
1954	Marion Ladewig, Grand Rapids, Mich.
1953	Marion Ladewig, Grand Rapids, Mich.
1952	Marion Ladewig, Grand Rapids, Mich.
1951	Marion Ladewig, Grand Rapids, Mich.
1950	Marion Ladewig, Grand Rapids, Mich.
1949	Val Mikiel, Detroit
1948	Val Mikiel, Detroit

Male Bowler of the Year

1996	Walter Ray Williams Jr., Stockton, Calif.
1995	Mike Aulby, Indianapolis
1994	Norm Duke, Edmond, Okla.
1993	Walter Ray Williams Jr., Stockton, Calif.
1992	Marc McDowell, Madison, Wis.
1991	David Ozio, Vidor, Texas
1990	Amleto Monacelli, Barquisimeto, Venezuela
1989	Mike Aulby, Indianapolis
1988	Brian Voss, Tacoma, Wash.
1987	Marshall Holman, Medford, Ore.
1986	Walter Ray Williams, Stockton, Calif.
1985	Mike Aulby, Indianapolis
1984	Mark Roth, Spring Lake Heights, N.J.
1983	Earl Anthony, Dublin, Calif.
1982	Earl Anthony, Dublin, Calif.
1981	Earl Anthony, Dublin, Calif.
1980	Wayne Webb, Reheboth, Mass.
1979	Mark Roth, North Arlington, N.J.
1978	Mark Roth, North Arlington, N.J.
1977	Mark Roth, North Arlington, N.J.
1976	Earl Anthony, Dublin, Calif.
1975	Earl Anthony, Dublin, Calif.
1974	Earl Anthony, Dublin, Calif.
1973	Don McCune, Munster, Ind.
1972	Don Johnson, Akron, Ohio
1971	Don Johnson, Akron, Ohio
1970	Nelson Burton Jr., St. Louis
1969	Billy Hardwick, Louisville, Ky.
1968	Jim Stefanich, Joliet, Ill.
1967	Dave Davis, Phoenix
1966	Wayne Zahn, Atlanta
1965	Dick Weber, St. Louis
1964	Billy Hardwick, San Mateo, Calif.
1963	Dick Weber, St. Louis
1962	Don Carter, St. Louis
1961	Dick Weber, St. Louis
1960	Don Carter, St. Louis
1959	Ed Lubanski, Detroit
1958	Don Carter, St. Louis
1957	Don Carter, St. Louis
1956	Bill Lillard, Chicago
1955	Steve Nagy, Detroit
1954	Don Carter, St. Louis
1953	Don Carter, St. Louis
1952	Steve Nagy, Cleveland
1951	Lee Jouglard, Detroit
1950	Junie McMahon, Fair Lawn, N.J.
1949	Connie Schwoegler, Madison, Wis.
1948	Andy Varipapa, Brooklyn, N.Y.
1947	Buddy Bomar, Chicago
1946	Joe Wilman, Chicago
1945	Buddy Bomar, Chicago
1944	Ned Day, Milwaukee
1943	Ned Day, Milwaukee
1942	Johnny Crimmins, Detroit

Canadian Bowler of the Year

Since the 1988-89 season, the Canadian Tenpin Federation has annually selected a Canadian Bowler of the Year. The federation's 16-member board of directors bases its selection on a bowler's success on the lanes and representation of his or her country.

Canadian Woman Bowler of the Year

1996-97	Jane Amlinger, Kitchener, Ontario
1995-96	Catharine Willis, Ladysmith, British Columbia
1994-95	Debby Ship, Montreal
1993-94	Catharine Willis, Ladysmith, British Columbia
1992-93	Sandy Lowe, Oshawa, Ontario
1991-92	Miriam Reid, Richmond, British Columbia
1990-91	Catharine Willis, Duncan, British Columbia
1989-90	Jane Amlinger, Kitchener, Ontario
1988-89	Jane Amlinger, Kitchener, Ontario

Canadian Male Bowler of the Year

1996-97	Bill Rowe, Hamilton, Ontario
1995-96	Bill Rowe, Hamilton, Ontario
1994-95	Bill Rowe, Hamilton, Ontario
1993-94	Bill Rowe, Hamilton, Ontario
1992-93	Warren Rennox, Ajax, Ontario
1991-92	Howard Kotchie, Barrie, Ontario
1990-91	Earl Demmery, Toronto
1989-90	Al Tone, Hamilton, Ontario
1988-89	Craig Woodhouse, St. Catherine, Ontario

Bowlers of the Decade
1980s Bowlers of the Decade

Lisa Wagner, Palmetto, Fla.

Both *Woman Bowler* Magazine and *Bowling Magazine* named Lisa Wagner of Palmetto, Fla., the 1980s Bowler of the Decade. *Woman Bowler* Magazine readers selected Wagner by a special Bowler-of-the-Decade ballot. Veteran bowling writers, members of the American Bowling Congress and Women's International Bowling Congress halls of fame and selected ABC officials took part in the *Bowling Magazine* balloting.

Wagner, a professional bowler for 15 years, has earned 30 professional titles (as of Nov. 11, 1997). She has also earned WIBC Championship Tournament titles in the doubles event (1982) and all events (1988). Throughout the decade, *Woman Bowler* magazine named Wagner an All-America Team member seven times, and the Bowling Writers Association of America named her Woman Bowler of the Year three times.

In 1988, Wagner became the first woman to earn $100,000 in a single year. Today, she leads the career earnings list for women's bowling. Wagner's winnings total $543,277 (as of Feb. 1, 1994). In 1991, she earned her record-setting 26th title, teaming with Carolyn Dorin of Linden, N.J., to win the LPBT National Doubles in Las Vegas, Nev. *Bowlers Journal* and *Bowling Magazine* also named Wagner the 1980s Bowler of the Decade.

Mike Aulby, Indianapolis

Aulby, who burst on the national scene as the Professional Bowlers Assn. Rookie of the Year in 1979, indeed had a stellar 1980s. In addition to 18 titles, he earned $1,036,000 for the decade. He capped off the period with major titles at the ABC Bud Light Masters and the U.S. Open.

The 1985 PBA Player of the Year and BWAA Bowler of the Year, Aulby also was 1989 BWAA Bowler of the Year. He finished 1993 fourth on the all-time money earnings list with $1,404,710. He entered 1998 with 25 titles, fifth-best in PBA history.

1970s Bowlers of the Decade

Betty Morris, Stockton, Calif.

Bowler's Journal and *Bowling Illustrated* (a newsstand tenpin publication) named Betty Morris of Stockton, Calif., the 1970s Bowler of the Decade. After winning her first professional title in 1972, Morris earned 11 professional titles — at least one major title each year — and four WIBC Championship Tournament titles during the decade.

She bowled five nine-game sets of 1,800 or more; led the 300-game honor roll with five sanctioned perfect games; recorded the most 700 three-game series ever; headed the money winners' list with nearly $140,000 in prize money; and led the WIBC Championship Tournament five-year average list with 195. She was also named Bowler of the Year in 1974 and 1977.

Morris' most prosperous year was 1974. In only 15 professional events, she captured three titles, eight second-place finishes and one fourth-place finish.

In 1990, Morris teamed with amateur bowler Stuart Sisler of Grimsley, Ontario, to win the Budweiser Hall of Fame Tournament. The win gave Morris titles in four consecutive decades: the 1960s, 1970s, 1980s and 1990s.

Today, Morris ranks seventh in number of LPBT titles with 17; and 21st in LPBT career winnings with $335,417 (as of Nov. 11, 1997).

Earl Anthony, Dublin, Calif.

Ask today's casual bowler to name the sport's all-time great and one name likely will be heard. Earl Anthony.

His name has been synonomous with the sport for more than two decades. He won 46 professional titles and finished second 42 other times. He has won two prestigious American Bowling Congress Masters crowns and was a member of an ABC Tournament championship team.

Bowling Magazine listed him on its first All-America team a record 12 consecutive times starting in 1972. He was Bowler of the Year six times including 1976, 1977 and 1978. He became the sport's first person to earn $1 million in 1982.

Today, he is retired from the PBA Tour but continues his affiliation with the sport as color analyst on the American Bowling Congress' Brunswick World Team Challenge. He also owns two bowling centers.

All-America Teams

Bowling Magazine, the official publication of the American Bowling Congress, started its All-America team in 1956. In establishing the selections, the magazine's editors felt there was a definite need to make permanent the outstanding yearly accomplishments of the men who glamorize the sport.

The original poll featured ballots from more than 450 bowling writers, broadcasters, sports editors and publicity people. The tradition has continued every year since then.

Woman Bowler — the only magazine exclusively dedicated to women's bowling — began naming an All-America team in 1974. The team, comprised of five women, may include both professional and amateur bowlers. Beginning in 1996, WIBC took over the *Woman Bowler* voting.

Members of the Bowling Writers Association of America cast ballots to select the *Woman Bowler* All-America team.

Prior to 1990, voting for team members was based on bowlers' accomplishments during that particular bowling season. Beginning in 1990, the qualification was changed to include only the calendar year.

Both organizations name the leading votegetter as honorary All-America team captain.

1996
WIBC
Wendy Machperson, Henderson, Nev.
Kim Adler, Las Vegas, Nev.
Tammy Turner, Canyon, Texas
Aleta Sill, Dearborn, Mich.
Liz Johnson, Niagara Falls, N.Y.

Bowling Magazine
Walter Ray Williams Jr., Stockton, Calif.
Bob Learn Jr., Erie, Pa.
Parker Bohn III, Jackson, N.J.
Mike Aulby, Indianapolis
Dave Husted, Milwaukie, Ore.

1995
Woman Bowler
Anne Marie Duggan, Edmond, Okla.
Tish Johnson, Northridge, Calif.
Cheryl Daniels, Detroit
Aleta Sill, Dearborn, Mich.
Robin Romeo, Newhall, Calif.

Bowling Magazine
Mike Aulby, Indianapolis
Dave D'Entremont, Cleveland
Norm Duke, Edmond, Okla.
Walter Ray Williams, Stockton, Calif.
Parker Bohn III, Jackson, N.J.

1994
Woman Bowler
Anne Marie Duggan, Edmond, Okla.
Tish Johnson, Panorama City, Calif.
Marianne DiRupo, Succasunna, N.J.
Aleta Sill, Dearborn, Mich.
Carol Gianotti, Perth, Australia

Bowling Magazine
Norm Duke, Edmond, Okla.
Walter Ray Williams, Stockton, Calif.
Bryan Goebel, Merriam, Kan.
Amleto Moncelli, Venezuela
Eric Forkel, Chatsworth, Calif.

1993
Woman Bowler
Anne Marie Duggan, Edmond, Okla.
Lisa Wagner, Palmetto, Fla.
Wendy Macpherson, Henderson, Nev.
Dana Miller-Mackie, Fort Worth, Texas
Robin Romeo, Van Nuys, Calif.

Bowling Magazine
Walter Ray Williams, Stockton, Calif.
Brian Voss, Atlanta
Mike Aulby, Indianapolis
Parker Bohn III, Freehold, N.J.
Pete Weber, St. Ann, Mo.

1992
Woman Bowler
Tish Johnson, Panorama City, Calif.
Carol Gianotti, Perth, Australia
Anne Marie Duggan, Edmond, Okla.
Leanne Barrette, Yukon, Okla.
Robin Romeo, Van Nuys, Calif.

Bowling Magazine
Dave Ferraro, Kingston, N.Y.
Amleto Monacelli, Venezuela
Marc McDowell, Madison, Wis.
Parker Bohn III, Jackson, N.J.
Eric Forkel, Chatsworth, Calif.

1991
Woman Bowler
Leanne Barrette, Yukon, Okla.
Anne Marie Duggan, Edmond, Okla.
Tish Johnson, Panorama City, Calif.
Nikki Gianulias, Vallejo, Calif.
Donna Adamek, Apple Valley, Calif.

Bowling Magazine
David Ozio, Vidor, Texas
Del Ballard Jr., Richardson, Texas
Norm Duke, Albuquerque, N.M.
John Mazza, Mt. Clemens, Mich.
Pete Weber, St. Louis

1990
Woman Bowler
Tish Johnson, Panorama City, Calif.
Dana Miller-Mackie, Fort Worth, Texas
Leanne Barrette, Yukon, Okla.
Lisa Wagner, Palmetto, Fla.
Nikki Gianulias, Vallejo, Calif.

Bowling Magazine
Amleto Monacelli, Venezuela
Parker Bohn III, Freehold, N.J.
Chris Warren, Dallas
Robert Lawrence, Austin, Texas
Dave Husted, Milwaukie, Ore.

1989
Woman Bowler
Robin Romeo, Van Nuys, Calif.
Lisa Wagner, Palmetto, Fla.
Jeanne Maiden-Nacarrato, Tacoma, Wash.
Leanne Barrette, Yukon, Okla.
Cheryl Daniels, Detroit

Bowling Magazine
Amleto Monacelli, Venezuela
Mike Aulby, Indianapolis
Del Ballard Jr., Richardson, Texas
Pete Weber, St. Louis
Brian Voss, Boca Raton, Fla.

1988
Woman Bowler
Lisa Wagner, Palmetto, Fla.
Betty Morris, Stockton, Calif.
Lorrie Nichols, Algonquin, Ill.
Leanne Barrette, Yukon, Okla.
Tish Johnson, Panorama City, Calif.

Bowling Magazine
Brian Voss, Boca Raton, Fla.
Dave Ferraro, Kingston, N.Y.
Joe Berardi, Wellington, Fla.
Mark Roth, Spring Lake Heights, N.J.
Marshall Holman, Medford, Ore.

1987
Woman Bowler
Cindy Coburn-Carroll, Tonawanda, N.Y.
Jeanne Maiden-Nacarrato, Tacoma, Wash.
Lorrie Nichols, Algonquin, Ill.
Carol Norman, Ardmore, Okla.
Robin Romeo, Van Nuys, Calif.

Bowling Magazine
Marshall Holman, Medford, Ore.
Walter Ray Williams, Stockton, Calif.
Pete Weber, St. Louis
Rick Steelsmith, Wichita, Kan.
Mark Roth, Spring Lake Heights, N.J.

1986
Woman Bowler
Patty Costello, Scranton, Pa.
Aleta Sill, Dearborn, Mich.
Robin Romeo, Newhall, Calif.
Cindy Coburn-Carroll, Tonawanda, N.Y.
Lisa Wagner, Palmetto, Fla.

Bowling Magazine
Walter Ray Williams, Stockton, Calif.
Dave Husted, Milwaukie, Ore.
Steve Cook, Roseville, Calif.
Marshall Holman, Medford, Ore.
John Gant, Pittsburgh

1985
Woman Bowler
Aleta Sill, Dearborn, Mich.
Lisa Wagner, Palmetto, Fla.
Pat Mercatanti, Newtown, Pa.
Pat Costello, Orlando, Fla.
Dana Miller-Mackie, Fort Worth, Texas

Bowling Magazine
Mike Aulby, Indianapolis
Pete Weber, St. Louis
Marshall Holman, Medford, Ore.
Wayne Webb, Indianapolis
Mark Williams, Beaumont, Texas

1984
Woman Bowler
Aleta Sill, Dearborn, Mich.
Lorrie Nichols, Algonquin, Ill.
Lisa Wagner, Palmetto, Fla.
Kazue Inahashi, Tokyo
Dana Miller-Mackie, Fort Worth, Texas

Bowling Magazine
Mark Roth, Spring Lake Heights, N.J.
Pete Weber, St. Louis
Marshall Holman, Jacksonville, Ore.
Gary Skidmore, Albuquerque, N.M.
Mike Aulby, Indianapolis

1983
Woman Bowler
Nikki Gianulias, Vallejo, Calif.
Aleta Sill, Dearborn, Mich.
Dana Miller-Mackie, Fort Worth, Texas
Lisa Wagner, Palmetto, Fla.
Donna Adamek, Apple Valley, Calif.

Bowling Magazine
Earl Anthony, Dublin, Calif.
Marshall Holman, Medford, Ore.
Tom Milton, St. Petersburg, Fla.
Joe Berardi, Brooklyn, N.Y.
Mike Durbin, Chagrin Falls, Ohio

1982
Woman Bowler
Donna Adamek, Apple Valley, Calif.
Nikki Gianulias, Vallejo, Calif.
Cindy Coburn-Carroll, Tonawanda, N.Y.
Pat Costello, Orlando, Fla.
Robin Romeo, Newhall, Calif.

Bowling Magazine
Earl Anthony, Dublin, Calif.
Dave Husted, Milwaukie, Ore.
Mike Durbin, Chagrin Falls, Ohio
Wayne Webb, Indianapolis
Art Trask, Fresno, Calif.

1981
Woman Bowler
Donna Adamek, Apple Valley, Calif.
Virginia Norton, Cypress, Calif.
Nikki Gianulias, Vallejo, Calif.
Cindy Coburn-Carroll, Tonawanda, N.Y.
Pam Buckner, Reno, Nev.

Bowling Magazine
Earl Anthony, Dublin, Calif.
Mark Roth, Spring Lake Heights, N.J.
Marshall Holman, Medford, Ore.
Tom Baker, Buffalo
Wayne Webb, Tucson, Ariz.

1980
Woman Bowler
Donna Adamek, Apple Valley, Calif.
Pat Costello, Orlando, Fla.
Betty Morris, Stockton, Calif.
Cheryl Robinson, Destrehan, La.
Nikki Gianulias, Vallejo, Calif.

Bowling Magazine
Mark Roth, Spring Lake Heights, N.J.
Wayne Webb, Rehoboth, Mass.
Mike Aulby, Indianapolis
Nelson Burton Jr., St. Louis
Earl Anthony, Dublin, Calif.

1979
Woman Bowler
Donna Adamek, Apple Valley, Calif.
Betty Morris, Stockton, Calif.
Vesma Grinfelds, San Francisco
Virginia Norton, Cypress, Calif.
Pat Costello, Orlando, Fla.

Bowling Magazine
Earl Anthony, Tacoma, Wash.
Mark Roth, North Arlington, N.J.
Marshall Holman, Medford, Ore.
Joe Berardi, New York
George Pappas, Charlotte, N.C.

1978
Woman Bowler
Virginia Norton, Cypress, Calif.
Betty Morris, Stockton, Calif.
Vesma Grinfelds, San Francisco
Donna Adamek, Apple Valley, Calif.
Patty Costello, Scranton, Pa.

Bowling Magazine
Earl Anthony, Tacoma, Wash.
Mark Roth, North Arlington, N.J.
Marshall Holman, Medford, Ore.
Nelson Burton Jr., St. Louis
Tommy Hudson, Akron, Ohio

1977
Woman Bowler
Betty Morris, Stockton, Calif.
Patty Costello, Scranton, Pa.
Vesma Grinfelds, San Francisco
Pam Buckner, Reno, Nev.
Virginia Norton, Cypress, Calif.

Bowling Magazine
Mark Roth, Staten Island, N.Y.
Earl Anthony, Tacoma, Wash.
Tommy Hudson, Akron, Ohio
Marshall Holman, Medford, Ore.
Mike Berlin, Muscatine, Iowa

1976
Woman Bowler
Judy Soutar, Leawood, Kan.
Betty Morris, Stockton, Calif.
Patty Costello, Scranton, Pa.
Virginia Norton, Cypress, Calif.
Vesma Grinfelds, San Francisco

Bowling Magazine
Earl Anthony, Tacoma, Wash.
Mark Roth, Staten Island, N.Y.
Larry Laub, San Francisco
Roy Buckley, Akron, Ohio
Carmen Salvino, Chicago

1975
Woman Bowler
Betty Morris, Stockton, Calif.
Doris Coburn, Buffalo
Judy Soutar, Leawood, Kan.
Pat Costello, Orlando, Fla.
Lorrie Nichols, Algonquin, Ill.

Bowling Magazine
Earl Anthony, Tacoma, Wash.
Dave Davis, Atlanta
Carmen Salvino, Chicago
Ed Ressler, Allentown, Pa.
Roy Buckley, Akron, Ohio

1974
Woman Bowler
Judy Soutar, Leawood, Kan.
Betty Morris, Stockton, Calif.
Loa Boxberger, Russell, Kan.
Pat Costello, Orlando, Fla.
Cheryl Robinson, Destrehan, La.

Bowling Magazine
Earl Anthony, Tacoma, Wash.
Larry Laub, San Francisco
Johnny Petraglia, Brooklyn, N.Y.
Dick Ritger, Hartford, Wis.
Jim Stefanich, Joliet, Ill.

1973
Bowling Magazine
Don McCune, Munster, Ind.
Dick Ritger, Hartford, Wis.
Barry Asher, Costa Mesa, Calif.
Earl Anthony, Tacoma, Wash.
Jim Godman, Lorain, Ohio

1972
Bowling Magazine
Nelson Burton Jr., St. Louis
Don Johnson, Akron, Ohio
Earl Anthony, Tacoma, Wash.
Barry Asher, Costa Mesa, Calif.
Larry Laub, San Francisco

1971
Bowling Magazine
John Petraglia, Brooklyn, N.Y.
Don Johnson, Akron, Ohio
Dave Soutar, Gilroy, Calif.
Mike Limongello, N. Babylon, N.Y.
Dick Weber, St. Louis

1970
Bowling Magazine
Nelson Burton Jr., St. Louis
Dave Soutar, Gilroy, Calif.
Mike McGrath, El Cerrito, Calif.
Don Johnson, Akron, Ohio
Dave Davis, Miami

1969
Bowling Magazine
Billy Hardwick, Louisville, Ky.
Dick Weber, St. Louis
Jim Godman, Hayward, Calif.
Dick Ritger, Hartford, Wis.
Don Johnson, Kokomo, Ind.

1968
Bowling Magazine
Jim Stefanich, Joliet, Ill.
Dave Davis, Phoenix
Wayne Zahn, Atlanta
Bill Allen, Fresno, Calif.
Don Johnson, Kokomo, Ind.

1967
Bowling Magazine
Dave Davis, Phoenix
Les Schissler, Denver
Jim Stefanich, Joliet, Ill.
Wayne Zahn, Atlanta
Don Johnson, Kokomo, Ind.

1966
Bowling Magazine
Dick Weber, St. Louis
Wayne Zahn, Atlanta
Bob Strampe, Detroit
Les Schissler, Denver
Nelson Burton Jr., St. Louis

1965
Bowling Magazine
Dick Weber, St. Louis
Bob Strampe, Detroit
Billy Hardwick, Louisville, Ky.
Bill Allen, Orlando, Fla.
Jim St. John, San Clara, Calif.

1964
Bowling Magazine
Billy Hardwick, San Mateo, Calif.
Dick Weber, St. Louis
Billy Welu, St. Louis
Bob Strampe, Detroit
Jim St. John, San Jose, Calif.

1963
Bowling Magazine
Don Carter, St. Louis
Dick Weber, St. Louis
Billy Welu, St. Louis
Ray Bluth, St. Louis
Harry Smith, St. Louis

1962
Bowling Magazine
Don Carter, St. Louis
Dick Weber, St. Louis
Ray Bluth, St. Louis
Billy Golembiewski, Detroit
Dick Hoover, St. Louis

1961
Bowling Magazine
Don Carter, St. Louis
Dick Weber, St. Louis
Ray Bluth, St. Louis
Billy Welu, St. Louis
Joe Joseph, Detroit

1960
Bowling Magazine
Don Carter, St. Louis
Billy Golembiewski, Detroit
Ray Bluth, St. Louis
Dick Weber, St. Louis
Harry Smith, St. Louis

1959
Bowling Magazine
Ed Lubanski, Detroit
Don Carter, St. Louis
Ray Bluth, St. Louis
Billy Welu, St. Louis
Tom Hennessey, St. Louis

1958
Bowling Magazine
Don Carter, St. Louis
Tom Hennessey, St. Louis
Buzz Fazio, Detroit
Ed Lubanski, Detroit
Steve Nagy, Detroit

1957
Bowling Magazine
Don Carter, St. Louis
Dick Hoover, Akron, Ohio
Bill Lillard, Chicago
Dick Weber, St. Louis
Lou Campi, Dumont, N.J.

1956
Bowling Magazine
Bill Lillard, Chicago
Don Carter, St. Louis
Dick Hoover, Akron, Ohio
Dick Weber, St. Louis
Steve Nagy, Detroit

Collegiate Bowlers of the Year
(Selected by Bowling Writers Association of America)

1997
Kelly Kulick, Morehead State University
Joe Ciccone, Arizona State University
1996
Keli Rapp, Erie Community College
Bryan Manno, Indiana University
1995
Rosine Marsche, Wichita State University
Steve Kloempken, Wichita State University
1994
Stacy Manley, California State University-Sacramento
Joe Ciccone, Erie Community College
1993
Elizabeth Johnson, Morehead State University
William Hoffman, Ohio State University
1992
Kari Murph, Morehead State University
Chris Barnes, Wichita State University

1991
Kari Murph, Morehead University
Sanford Carvajal, San Diego State University
1990
Lynda Norry, San Jose State University
David Carter, William Paterson College
1989
Lynda Norry, San Jose State University
David Carter, William Paterson College
1988
Jackie Sellers, Penn State University
Chris Viale, William Paterson College
1987
Jackie Sellers, Penn State University
Rick Steelsmith, Wichita State University

Collegiate All-America Teams
(Selected by the National Collegiate Bowling Coaches Association)

1996-97
Men's First Team
Joe Ciccone, Arizona State University; Lee Johnson, Indiana University; Bryan Manno, Indiana University; Brett Wolfe, Arizona State University; Brian Waliczek, Saginaw Valley State University.
Women's First Team
Kelly Kulick, Morehead State University; Brenda Edwards, University of Nebraska; Jennifer Daugherty, University of Nebraska; Keli Rapp, Erie Community College; Janet Piesczynski, Erie Community College.

1995-96
Men's First Team
Bryan Manno, Indiana University; Bryan O'Keefe, University of Nebraska; Jeffrey Phillips, University of Alabama-Huntsville; Michael Mullin, St. John's University; Brett Wolfe, Arizona State University.
Women's First Team
Karen Stroud, West Texas A & M University; Keli Rapp, Erie Community College; Janette Piesczynski, Erie Community College; Jennifer Daugherty, University of Nebraska; Brenda Norman, University of Nebraska.

1994-95
Men's First Team
Steve Kloempken, Wichita State University; Charlie Esteban, San Jose State University; Brian Graham, University of Nebraska; Tony Reyes, San Jose State University; Jose Hale, Wichita State University.
Women's First Team
Estella Arteaga, Illinois State University; Vickie Salazar, San Jose State University; Vicki Ghrist, Morehead State University; Andrea Rigby, University of Nebraska; Jody Ellis, Erie Community College.

1993-94
Men's First Team
Joe Ciccone, Erie Community College; Robert Vance, Michigan State University; Dave Garber, Wichita State University; Tony Manna, University of Nebraska; Brian Ziesig, St. John's University.
Women's First Team
Karen Stroud, West Texas A&M University; Kristen McEntee, Ohio State University; Vicki Ghrist, Morehead State University; Allyson Allmang, Wichita State University; Kim Murakami, San Jose State University; Melinda Johnson, Morehead State University.

1992-93
Men's First Team
Sanford Carvajal, San Diego State University; Bill Hoffman, Ohio State University; Tony Reyes, San Jose State University; Robert Vance, Michigan State University; Brian Aldridge, University of Cincinnati.
Women's First Team
Elizabeth Johnson, Morehead State University; Carrie Machuga, University of Nebraska; Robin Ostro, West Texas State University; Sheri Pohlad, Morehead State University; Kristen McEntee, Ohio State University.

1991-92
Men's First Team
Chris Viale, William Paterson College; Chris Barnes, Wichita State University; Rob Schuh, Saginaw Valley State University; Chris Valdivia, Arizona State University; Jon Murph, Morehead State University.
Women's First Team
Kari Murph, Morehead State University; Tammy Turner, West Texas State University; Lisa Skibinski, Wichita State University; Kristen McEntee, Ohio State University; Cathy Dorin, West Texas State University.

1990-91

Men's First Team

Chris Sole, William Paterson College; Warren Guernsey, Erie Community College; Brandon Keister, Vincennes University; Dave Carter, William Paterson College; Steve Such, San Jose State University.

Women's First Team

Kari Murph, Morehead State University; Darla Martin, Temple University; Kim Berke, University of Nebraska; Brandi LaRoque, West Texas State University; Sandy Youker, Erie Community College.

1989-90

Men's First Team

Jeff Smith, Saint Peter's College; Donald Savant, University of Houston; Dave Carter, William Paterson College; Greg Derrick, University of Texas-Arlington; Chris Barnes, Wichita State University.

Women's First Team

Lynda Norry, San Jose State University; Robin Davis, West Texas State University; Tracie Harook, Indiana State University; Karen Postelwait, San Jose State University; Leslie Beamish, Wichita State University.

1988-89

Men's First Team

Chris Sole, William Paterson College; Chris Viale, William Paterson College; Sanford Carvajal, San Diego State University; Mike Bailey, San Jose State University; Justin Hromek, Wichita State University.

Women's First Team

Carolyn Dorin, West Texas State University; Sharon Owen Todd, Morehead State University; Lynda Norry, San Jose State University; Jackie Sellers, Pennsylvania State University; Maja Rode, San Jose State University.

1987-88

Men's First Team

Chris Viale, William Paterson College; Camp Goodlett, California State University-Fresno; Pat Healey, Wichita State University; Scott Johnson, Morehead State University; Mike Shady, University of Nebraska.

Women's First Team

Jackie Sellers, Penn State University; Carolyn Dorin, West Texas State University; Sharon Owen, Morehead State University; Kathy Edwards, Indiana State University; Sheila Allen, Pennsylvania State University.

1986-87

Men's First Team

Rick Steelsmith, Wichita State University; Tom Delutz Jr., William Paterson College; Ted Glattke, University of California; Mike Shady, University of Nebraska; Kevin Gray, San Jose State University.

Women's First Team

Jackie Sellers, Penn State University; Kim Terrell, San Jose State University; Sharon Owen, Morehead State University; Carolyn Dorin, West Texas State University; Maja Rode, San Jose State University.

1985-86

Men's First Team

Paul Brenner, University of California; Tom Delutz Jr., William Paterson College; Rick Steelsmith, Wichita State University; Ted Glattke, University of California; Eric Oglesby, Rutgers University.

Women's First Team

Vicki Parker, Indiana State University; Kim Terrell, San Jose State University; Debbie DiTrani, Wichita State University; Julie Bishop, West Texas State University; Lynn Pruitt, Indiana State University.

1984-85

Men's First Team

Phil Dlugo, Saint Peter's College; Jack Jurek, West Texas State University; Rick Steelsmith, Vincennes University Junior College; Scott Thomsen, Washington State University; Joseph Vicenzotti, William Paterson College.

Women's First Team

Donna DiTrani, Wichita State University; Laura Dulisse, Temple University; Heather Hohm, University of Illinois; Michelle Mullen, University of Illinois; Vickie Parker, Indiana State University.

1983-84

Men's First Team

Rick Corona, University of California; Mike Jasnau, Wichita State University; Jack Jurek, West Texas State University; Rick Steelsmith, Vincennes University; Chris Whitty, Wichita State University.

Women's First Team

Theresa Kolcz, Arizona State University; Michelle Mullen, University of Illinois; Vicki Parker, Indiana State University; Kristi Tite, Indiana State University; Janet Woolum, Boise State University.

1982-83

Men's First Team

Tim Baker, California State University-Los Angeles; Mike Betke, West Texas State University; Paul Fabianski, Erie Community College; Mike Jasnau, Wichita State University; Myrl Serra, Arizona State University.

Women's First Team

Sharon Bailey, California State University-Fresno; Patty Bowie, Arizona State University; Vicki Parker, Indiana State University; Barb Peltz, Wichita State University; Mary Wolfe, West Texas State University.

Alberta E. Crowe / Chuck Hall
Star of Tomorrow Awards

WIBC annually presents the Alberta E. Crowe Star of Tomorrow award to a female junior or collegiate bowler who demonstrates star qualities. These qualities include outstanding bowling achievement, bowling potential and sportswomanlike conduct.

The award is named for Alberta E. Crowe who served as WIBC president from 1960 to 1981. The award offers a $4,000 scholarship, $1,000 for each of a recipient's four years in college.

WIBC presents the award and scholarship at the WIBC Annual Meeting. Eligible candidates must be U.S. residents, hold a 175 or higher average and be amateur bowlers as defined by the Young American Bowling Alliance.

The ABC annually presents the Chuck Hall Star of Tomorrow award at its convention to an outstanding junior male bowler. The award is named in honor of the former YABA and American Junior Bowling Congress Executive Director. It is designed for an amateur male high school or college student who has compiled a strong YABA/ABC bowling record in addition to displaying solid scholastic aptitude and school involvement. The award offers a $4,000 scholarship, $1,000 for each of a recipient's four years in college.

Alberta E. Crowe
Award Recipients

Year	Recipient	Year	Recipient
1997	Kimberly Claus, Mesquite, Texas	1978	Nikki Gianulias, Vallejo, Calif.
1996	Michelle Ewald, St. Claire Shores, Mich.	1977	Kathy Kirst, San Antonio, Texas
1995	Kassy Hyman, Dyer, Ind.	1976	Regina Loveall, Amarillo, Texas
1994	Pamela Inloes, Modesto, Calif.	1975	Donna Adamek, Apple Valley, Calif.
1993	Elizabeth Johnson, Niagara Falls, N.Y.	1974	Pam Dusek, Ontario, Calif.
1992	Kari Murph, Dayton, Ohio	1973	Leslie Ferris, Arlington, Va.
1991	Laura Ross, Mahwah, N.J.	1972	Karen Gustafson, Sunland, Calif.
1990	Kelly Everding, Arvada, Colo.	1971	Rosalyn Raab, San Antonio, Texas
1989	Stefanie Marek, Wilmington, Del.	1970	Cheryl Robinson, Destrehan, La.
1988	Lynda Norry, Concord, Calif.	1969	Janice Sue Reichley, Dallas
1987	Dionne Lee, Modesto, Calif.	1968	Pamela Carver, Phoenix, Ariz.
1986	Lori Benge, Wichita, Kan.	1967	Mildred Ignizio, Rochester, N.Y.
1985	Becky Kregling, Stratford, Conn.	1966	Betty Jo Crow, Fairway, Kan.
1984	Kristine Gross, Citrus Heights, Calif.	1965	Karen Linton, El Paso, Texas
1983	Laura Dulisse, Blauvelt, N.Y.	1964	Ann Bosworth, Belleville, Ill.
1982	Vicki Parker, Pelham, N.H.	1963	Judy Soutar, Leawood, Kan.
1981	Shelley Johnson, Toledo, Ohio	1962	Joy Abel, Lansing, Ill.
1980	Tish Johnson, Panorama City, Calif.	1961	Betty Kuczynski, Cicero, Ill.
1979	Audrey Gable, Whitehall, Pa.		

Chuck Hall Award Recipients

Year	Recipient	Year	Recipient
1997	Todd Filter, Cedarburg, Wis.	1988	Bradley Joinetz, San Antonio, Texas
1996	David Eisenberg, Kendall Park, N.J.	1987	Mark Fisser, Buena Park, Calif.
1995	John Miller, Wichita, Kan.	1986	Pat Healey, Wichita, Kan.
1994	Michael Mullin, New City, N.Y.	1985	Justin Hromek, Andover, Kan.
1993	Vince Biondo, Hoffman Estates, Ill.	1984	Robert Beck, Houston
1992	Robert Smith, Moorpark, Calif.	1983	Dan Nadeau, Las Vegas
1991	Chris Williams, Anchorage, Alaska	1982	Ricky Corona, Oakland, Calif.
1990	Jason McCarty, Fultondale, Ala.	1981	Drew Barthle, Tampa, Fla.
1989	Lonnie Waliczek, Wichita, Kan.	1980	Chris Whitty, Simonton, Texas

Bowling Writers Association of America
Presidents

Year	President	Year	President
1997	Mike Hennessy, Centerville, Ohio	1979	Alex Simpson, Knoxville, Tenn.
1996	John Jowdy, El Cajon, Calif.	1978	Joe Antczak, Grand Rapids, Mich.
1995	Bob Cosgrove, Crofton, Md.	1977	John January, Nashville, Tenn.
1994	Jim Dressel, Chicago	1976	Jim Bradley, Lexington, Ky.
1993	Steve James, Milwaukee	1975	Ray Gray, Chicago
1992	Pearl Keller, Chappaqua, N.Y.	1974	Dave DeLorenzo, River Falls, Wis.
1991	Don Snyder, Los Angeles	1973	Ken Rush, Louisville, Ky.
1990	Jerry Levine, Hackensack, N.J.	1972	Seymour Shub, Chicago
1989	Bruce Pluckhahn, St. Louis	1971	Gayle Hayes, San Antonio, Texas
1988	Walt Steinsiek, Baltimore	1970	John Archibald, St. Louis
1987	Dick Evans, Miami	1969	Mort Luby Jr., Chicago
1986	Dick Evans, Miami	1968	Joe Kissel, Chicago
1985	Jim Fitzgerald, Chicago	1967	Chuck Pezzano, Clifton, N.J.
1984	Frank Kietz, Southgate, Fla.	1966	Frank Sczepanski, Flint, Mich.
1983	Bob Zellner, Uniondale, N.Y.	1965	Hank Sayrs, Milwaukee
1982	Jim Wyckoff, Little Rock, Ark.	1964	Ed Reddy, Syracuse, N.Y.
1981	Bob Weaver, Bellingham, Wash.	1963	Angelo Biondo, Chicago
1980	Ed Browalski, Detroit	1962	Bob Schabert, St. Paul, Minn.

1961	Sam Levine, Cleveland	1950	Jerry Hogan, Kalamazoo, Mich.
1960	Fred Wolf, Detroit	1949	Tom Bolger, Toledo, Ohio
1959	George Bell, York, Pa.	1948	Paul Walker, Columbus, Ohio
1958	Sam Weinstein, Chicago	1947	Dick McGeorge, Toledo, Ohio
1957	Steve Cruchon, Detroit	1946	Mike Devitt, Philadelphia
1956	Charlie Smith, Miami	1942	Harold Kahl, Detroit
1955	Elmer Fischer, Springfield, Ill.	1941	LeRoy Chase, Peoria, Ill.
1954	John Walter, Detroit	1939	Billy Sixty, Milwaukee
1953	Mort Luby Sr., Chicago	1935	Fred Turek, Peoria, Ill.
1952	Fritz Howell, Cleveland	1934	John Martino, Syracuse, N.Y.
1951	Bill Hengen, Minneapolis		

John O. Martino Award
Presented to an individual, organization or firm for its outstanding contributions to bowling.

1997	Fred Borden, Akron, Ohio	1985	Dick Weber, St. Louis
1996	Helen Duval, Berkeley, Calif.	1984	Albert Matzelle, St. Louis
1995	Jack Reichert, Chicago		Frank Esposito, Paramus, N.J.
1994	Joe Antenora, Akron, Ohio	1983	Joe Norris, San Diego
1993	Earl Anthony, Cornelius, Ore.	1982	Marion Ladewig, Grand Rapids, Mich.
1992	Chuck Pezzano, Clifton, N.J.	1981	Alberta Crowe, Syracuse, N.Y.
1991	Sam Weinstein, Chicago	1980	Bill Doehrman, Ft. Wayne, Ind.
1990	Chris Schenkel, Leesburg, Ind.	1979	Don Carter, Miami
1989	Harry Golden, Las Vegas	1978	Frank Baker, Milwaukee
1988	Bowlers Journal, Chicago	1977	Andy Varipapa, W. Hempstead, N.Y.
1987	Anheuser-Busch Inc., St. Louis	1976	Eddie Elias, Akron, Ohio
1986	Bruce Pluckhahn, St. Louis		

Mort Luby Distinguished Service Award
Presented for meritorious service to bowling journalism.

1997	Jim Dressel, Palatine, Ill.	1975	Bill McDonald, New York
1996	Joe Lyou, Gardena, Calif.	1974	Chuck Pezzano, Clifton, N.J.
1995	Joe Antczak, Grand Rapids, Mich.	1973	George Bell, York, Pa.
1994	Mike Hennessy, Dayton, Ohio	1972	Charlie Smith, Clearwater, Fla.
1993	Wayne Todd, Aurora, Colo.	1971	Ed Reddy, Syracuse, N.Y.
1992	Bob Zellner, Uniondale, N.Y.	1969	Frank Sczepanski, Flint, Mich.
1991	John Jowdy, El Cajon, Calif.	1968	Angelo Biondo, Chicago
1990	Pearl Keller, Chappaqua, N.Y.	1967	Hank Sayrs, Milwaukee
1989	Jerry Levine, Hackensack, N.Y.	1966	Sam Levine, Cleveland
1988	Don Snyder, Los Angeles	1965	Fred Wolf, Detroit
1987	Steve James, Milwaukee	1964	Sam Weinstein, Chicago
1986	Augie Karcher, Winona, Minn.	1963	Elmer Fischer, Springfield, Ill.
1985	Jim Fitzgerald, Chicago	1962	Jerry Hagan, Kalamazoo, Mich.
1984	Mort Luby Jr., Chicago	1961	Steve Cruchon, Detroit
1983	John Archibald, St. Louis	1960	Fritz Howell, Columbus, Ohio
1982	Dick Evans, Miami	1959	Bill Hengen, Minneapolis
1981	Bud Fisher, Akron, Ohio	1958	John Martino, Syracuse, N.Y.
1980	Ray Nelson, Milwaukee	1957	Tom Bolger, Toledo, Ohio
1979	Pat McDonough, Union City, N.J.	1956	LeRoy Chase, Peoria, Ill.
1978	Joe Kissel, Chicago	1955	Billy Sixty, Milwaukee
1977	Seymour Shub, Chicago	1953	Mort Luby Sr., Chicago
1976	Dave DeLorenzo, River Falls, Wis.	1952	Eli Whitney, Milwaukee

Rip Van Winkle Award
Presented for achievements and contributions to bowling 20 or more years ago.

1997	Tom Kouros, Palatine, Ill.	1977	Charles Mitchell, Akron, Ohio
1996	Chief Halftown, Philadelphia	1976	Dick Watson, Los Angeles
1995	Jeannette Robinson, Las Vegas	1975	Paul Marian, Chicago
1994	Bill Taylor, San Gabriel, Calif.	1974	Cecil Ward, Detroit
1993	Angelo Biondo, Chicago	1973-71	None Presented
1992	Wayne Todd, Wheat Ridge, Colo.	1970	Paul Cito, Detroit
1991	Pepper Martin, San Antonio, Texas	1969	Elmer Irwin, San Francisco
1990	Sandy Shub, Chicago	1968	Jerome Harris, St. Louis
1989	George Amato, Eugene, Ore.		Eli Maricich, Mattoon, Ill.
1988	Don Snyder, Los Angeles	1967	J.B. Coker, San Diego
1987	Bill Franklin, Marina Del Rey, Calif.		Arthur Johnson, Milwaukee
1986	Woody Woodruff, Westbury, N.Y.		Bill McDonald, New York
1985	Greg Griffo, Syracuse, N.Y.	1966	Peter Revelt, Detroit
1984	George Billick, Old Forge, Pa.		Ben Sands, Cleveland
1983	John Gavie, Detroit	1965	Lester Baston, Tulsa, Okla.
1982	Eddie Edgar, Detroit		John Canelli, Toledo, Ohio
1981	Gus Lombardi, New York		Ossie (Rags) Ragogna, St. Paul, Minn.
1980	Joe Wilson, Chicago	1964	Warren Sloan, Blackwood, N.J.
1979	Chuck Pezzano, Clifton, N.J.		Dennis Sweeney, St. Louis
1978	Arthur Engberg, Minneapolis		Sam Weinstein, Chicago

1963	Wilfred Albert, St. Petersburg, Fla.	1959	Allie Brandt, Lockport, N.Y.
	Fred Lipovetz, La Crosse, Wis.		Joe McCord, Santa Monica, Calif.
	George Obenauer, Buffalo, N.Y.		Rudy Matak, St. Paul, Minn.
	Milton Raymer, Chicago		Walter (Skang) Mercurio, Clefeland
1962	William Landgraf, Island Park, N.Y.	1958	Frank Caruana, Buffalo, N.Y.
	Walt Ditzen, Phoenix		Frank Snyder, Erie, Pa.
	John Martino, Syracuse, N.Y.		Harry Steers, Chicago
	Jim Tinney, Chicago		Fred Thoma, Peoria, Ill.
1961	Harold Lloyd, Los Angeles	1957	Cone Hermann, St. Louis
	Emory Krauthoefer, Milwaukee		Frank Benkovic, Milwaukee
	William Mattison, Toledo, Ohio	1956	Clarence Brayshaw, Omaha, Neb.
1960	Joe Fliger-Frank (Bud) Wight, Chicago		Larry Sutton, Rochester, N.Y.
	Sam Garofolo-Lowell Jackson, St. Louis		Frank Bruggeman, Burlington, Iowa
	Walter Ward, Cleveland		

National Women Bowling Writers Association
Presidents

1995-present	Rilla Yeater, Akron, Ohio	1966-71	Mary Jane Sporar, Joliet, Ill.
1989-95	Ann Adams, Las Vegas	1963-65	Mary Jannetto, Cleveland
1983-89	Shirlee Kutzner, Nutley, N.J.	1956-62	Georgia Veatch, Morton Grove, Ill.
1977-83	Pearl Keller, Chappaqua, N.Y.	1951-56	Alberta E. Crowe, Liverpool, N.Y.
1974-77	Kay Heggie, Deerfield, Ill.	1948-51	Lola Yoakem, Santa Monica, Calif.
1971-74	Winifred Ford, San Francisco		

Jo Ettien Lieber Award
Presented for distinguished service to the game of American tenpins.

1997	Trudy Todd, Aurora, Colo.	1972	Frank Baker, Milwaukee
1996	Nancy Chapman, Green Bay, Wis.	1971	Arville Ebersole, Washington, D.C.
1995	Joyce Deitch. Las Vegas	1970	Clover Bayley, Watertown, N.Y.
1994	Alice Meglemre, Long Beach, Calif.	1969	Lola Yoakem, Camarillo, Calif.
1993	Annis Niemier, South Bend, Ind.	1968	Mildred White, Rockford, Ill.
1992	Alpharetta Callaway, Pittsburgh	1967	Helen Baetz, San Antonio, Texas
1991	Mary Lynly, Roseville, Calif.	1966	Theresa Kelone, Little Rock, Ark.
1990	Shirlee Kutzner, Nutley, N.J.	1965	Mary Jannetto, Cleveland
1989	Billy Hughes, Springfield, Mo.	1964	Madelene Hochstadter, Chicago
1988	Elaine Hagin, Castro Valley, Calif.	1963	Martha Werner, Toledo, Ohio
1987	Lo Borschuk, Sioux City, Iowa	1962	Bertha McBride, St. Paul, Minn.
1986	Dorothy Mauldin, Marietta, Ga.	1961	Ann Wood, Cincinnati
1985	Dorothy Johnson, Lebanon, Mo.	1960	Marian Brister, Kenosha, Wis.
1984	Pearl Keller, Chappaqua, N.Y.	1959	Leone Cohen, Toledo, Ohio
1983	Not Presented	1958	Margaret Higley, San Jose, Calif.
1982	Kathryn Hotzel, Anderson, Ind.	1957	Jo Mraz, Cleveland
1981	Gladys M. Banker, Charles Town, W.Va.	1956	Sylvia Martin, Philadelphia
1980	Mary Jane Sporar, Joliet, Ill.	1955	Marion Ladewig, Grand Rapids, Mich.
1979	Pearl Switzer, South Bend, Ind.	1954	Berdie Speck, St. Louis
1978	Mabel Marrs, Vancouver, Wash.	1953	Georgia Veatch, Chicago
1977	Freda Botkin, Tucson, Ariz.	1952	Georgia Veatch, Chicago
1976	Myrtle Schulte, Jennings, Mo.	1951	Alberta E. Crowe, Liverpool, N.Y.
1975	Helen Baker, Cocoa Beach, Fla.	1950	Milton Raymer, Chicago
1974	Billy Simon, San Antonio, Texas	1949	Emma Phaler, Columbus, Ohio
1973	Winifred Berger, Sonoma, Calif.	1948	Jeanette Knepprath, Milwaukee

Alberta E. Crowe Award
Presented for distinguished service in the field of communications.

1997	No Winner	1989	Pearl Keller, Chappaqua, N.Y.
1996	Marie Hisel, Arnold, Mo.	1988	Sam Weinstein, Chicago
1995	Wayne Todd, Denver	1987	Kathryn Hotzel, Anderson, Ind.
1994	Shirlee Kutzner, Nutley, N.J.	1986	Dick Evans, Miami
1993	Billy Hughes, Springfield, Mo.	1985	Steve Cruchon, Harper Woods, Mich.
1992	Alice Meglemre, Long Beach, Calif.	1984	Chuck Pezzano, Clifton, N.J.
1991	Freda Botkin, Tucson, Ariz.	1983	Mary Jannetto, Cleveland
1990	Mary Jane Sporar, Joliet, Ill.		

Mary Jannetto Award
Presented to NWBW member for outstanding promotion of local bowling, exclusive of
WIBC Championship Tournament host city.

1997	Phillis Eager, Tucson, Ariz.	1988	Ann Adams, Las Vegas
1996	Helen Lash, Roseburg, Ore.	1987	Elaine Hagin, Castro Valley, Calif.
1995	Marilyn Smith, Lake Charles, La.	1986	Nancy Chapman, Green Bay, Wis.
1994	Sylvia Broyles, Spring Branch, Texas	1985	Millie Kraft, Tucson, Ariz.
1993	Marie Hisel, St. Louis.	1984	Alpharetta Callaway, Pittsburgh
1992	Beverly McLendon, Houston	1983	Billy Hughes, Springfield, Mo.
1991	Rilla Yeater, Akron, Ohio	1982	Mary Lynly, Sunnyvale, Calif.
1990	Lily May Hester, Scottsdale, Ariz.	1981	Carolyn Gilbert, Hannibal, Mo.
1989	Annis Niemier, South Bend, Ind.	1980	Shirlee Kutzner, Nutley, N.J.

1979	Dee Dee Grant, Big Fork, Mont.	1965	Ila Callaway, Miami
1978	Helen Baetz, San Antonio, Texas	1964	Margaret Higley, Orange, Calif.
1977	Alice Meglemre, Long Beach, Calif.	1963	Agnes Duffy, Richmond, Calif.
1976	Pearl Keller, Chappaqua, N.Y.	1962	Theresa Kelone, Little Rock, Ark.
1975	Mary Jane Sporar, Joliet, Ill.	1961	Pearl Switzer, South Bend, Ind.
1974	Kay Heggie, Deerfield, Ill.	1960	Arbutus Stigall, Rock Falls, Ill.
1973	Kathryn Hotzel, Anderson, Ind.	1959	Iolia Lasher, Albany, N.Y.
1972	Dorothy Mauldin, Marietta, Ga.	1958	Mildred White, Rockford, Ill.
1971	Betty Natale, Orlando, Fla.	1957	Lillian Jacob, Detroit
1970	Constance Bechtel, San Diego	1956	Loveica Hardy, Van Nuys, Calif.
1969	Lucelle Ware, Los Angeles	1955	Zelda Hardin, Joplin, Mo.
1968	Kay Donovan, Chicago	1954	Hazel Fischer, Syracuse, N.Y.
1967	Dorothy Wieser, Spenceport, N.Y.	1953	Erma Nelson, Detroit
1966	Leah Rohli, Metairie, La.		

Bev Ortner-AMF Award

Was Presented to WIBC member for outstanding promotion in WIBC Championship Tournament host city. Discontinued in 1997.

1996	Terry Sabia, Buffalo, N.Y.	1977	Emily McPherson, Milwaukee
1995	Marilyn Hensley, Tucson, Ariz.	1976	Ila Herrin, Denver
1994	Vi Bjorkman, Salt Lake City, Utah	1975	Pat Dryer, Indianapolis
1993	Lee Duszynski, Baton Rouge, La.	1974	Beverly McLendon, Houston
1992	Alberta Kuhn, Lansing, Mich.	1973	Maxine Ruggeroli, Las Vegas
1991	Phyllis Newhouse, Marion, Iowa	1972	Not Presented
	Jackie Mundorf, Swisher, Iowa	1971	Not Presented
1990	Pilar Cohalla, Tampa, Fla.	1970	Carol Higgins, Tulsa, Okla.
1989	Eunice Schneider, Bismarck, N.D.	1969	Betty Foster, San Diego
1988	Betty Barnes, Reno, Nev.	1968	Helen Baetz, San Antonio, Texas
	Karen Williford, Carson City, Nev.	1967	Martha Martell, Rochester, N.Y.
1987	Cathy DeVine, East Hartford, Conn.	1966	Merle Thomas, New Orleans
1986	Ramona Clark, Placentia, Calif.	1965	Eleanor Fisher, Portland, Ore.
1985	Carmen Walton, Toledo, Ohio	1964	Gertrude Finke, Minneapolis
1984	Marjorie Gerg, Youngstown, N.Y.	1963	Loyce Winfield, Memphis, Tenn.
1983	Ann Adams, Las Vegas	1962	Maxine Newman, Phoenix
1982	Carol Tillman, Berkeley, Mo.	1961	Martha Herrick, Fort Wayne, Ind.
1981	Vette Elkins, Baltimore	1960	Bebe Krueger, Denver
1980	Patricia Handel, Seattle	1959	Eleanor Debus, Buffalo, N.Y.
1979	Freda Botkin, Tucson, Ariz.	1958	Winifred Berger, San Rafael, Calif.
1978	Charlotte Wilkin, North Miami, Fla.		

AMF-Helen Duval Award

Presented for outstanding service to the Young American Bowling Alliance.

1997	Beth Ortner, Tucson, Ariz.	1976	Millie Kraft, Tucson, Ariz.
1996	Mary Jane Sporar, Joliet, Ill.	1975	Agnes Duffy, Richmond, Calif.
1995	Virginia Rummett, Tucson, Ariz.	1974	Lo Borschuk, Sioux City, Iowa
1994	Cathy Cooper, Anderson, Ind.	1973	Fay Browning, Garland, Texas
1993	Merrilyn Mallette, Baltimore	1972	Charles Hall, Milwaukee
1992	Elaine Hagin, Castro Valley, Calif.	1971	Marion McDaniel, Hutchinson, Kan.
1991	Shirlee Kutzner, Nutley, N.J.	1970	Maxine Pearl, Memphis, Tenn.
1990	Boots Rausch, Rock Falls, Ill.	1969	Jo Ettien, Santa Monica, Calif.
1989	Gertrude Finke, Minneapolis	1968	Hilda Schroeder, Peoria, Ill.
1988	Betty Butler, Douglas, Ariz.	1967	Mildred Wood, Abilene, Texas
1987	Joyce Deitch, Las Vegas	1966	May Bailey, Garden Grove, Calif.
1986	Vickie Campbell, Bend, Ore.	1965	Mildred White, Rockford, Ill.
1985	Carolyn Gilbert, Hannibal, Mo.	1964	Hazel Mooney, Memphis, Tenn.
1984	Martha Burton, Washington, D.C.	1963	Laura Albrecht, Davenport, Iowa
1983	Trudy Todd, Denver	1962	Audrey McCain, Long Beach, Calif.
1982	Gladys M. Banker, Charles Town, W.Va.	1961	Florence Klinecht, Elyria, Ohio
1981	Stevie Singletary, Wautoma, Wis.	1960	Theresa Reynolds, Endicott, N.Y.
1980	Zelda Hardin, Joplin, Mo.	1959	Edwardina Coy, Detroit
1979	Milton Raymer, Seminole, Fla.	1958	Carol Tito, West Palm Beach, Calif.
1978	Eleanor Rice, Port Arthur, Texas	1957	Helen Duval, Berkeley, Calif.
1977	Dorothy Kerley, Milwaukee		

Herta Kissell Memorial-Brunswick Award
NWBW Writer of the Year

1997	Diane Squires, Battle Creek, Mich.	1987	Rilla Yeater, Akron, Ohio
1996	Diane Squires, Battle Creek, Mich.	1986	Cindy Tunstall, Lecanto, Fla.
1995	Diane Squires, Battle Creek, Mich.	1985	Pearl Keller, Chappaqua, N.Y.
1994	Lisa Vint, East Troy, Wis.	1984	Bobbie Baker, McMinnville, Tenn.
1993	Lydia Rypcinski, Chicago	1983	Mary Lynly, Sunnyvale, Calif.
1992	Jeff Nowak, Milwaukee	1982	Joan Zinser, Hackettstown, N.J.
1991	Judith Becker, Livonia, Mich.	1981	Patty Webber, Colton, Calif.
1990	Victoria Hansen, Hazelwood, Mo.	1980	Dee Dee Grant, Big Fork, Mont.
1989	Maureen Baker, Valley Cottage, N.Y.	1979	Patty Webber, Colton, Calif.
1988	Mary Tumosa-Lawler, Lake Havasu City, Ariz.		

USA Bowling

USA Bowling is recognized by the United States Olympic Committee as the governing body for the sport of American tenpins. Its 12-member board of trustees is comprised of four WIBC appointees, four ABC appointees, one YABA appointee and three athlete representatives. Board members include:

Elaine Hagin, Castro Valley, Calif., president
Kevin Dornberger, Sioux Falls, S.D., first vice president
Cathy Cooper, Anderson, Ind., second vice president
Therese Abair-Wilson, West Palm Beach, Fla., secretary-treasurer
Linda Scott, Portland, Ore.
Paul Fleming, Bedford, Texas

Stacy Werth, Rocklin, Calif.
Max Skelton, Ada, Okla.
Mark Jensen, Wichita, Kan.
Sylvia Broyles, Spring Branch, Texas
Brian Fedrow, San Jose, Calif.

Four of the USA Bowling appointees, Werth, Lantto, Mickelson and Abair-Wilson are athletes who have competed in at least one major international competition in the past 10 years. Jerry Koenig of Colorado Springs, Colo., serves as USA Bowling's executive director and also Federation Internationale des Quilleurs President. Koenig is a former ABC group executive and works on a variety of special programs including international competition contracts. Prior to joining ABC staff, Koenig was an ABC director-at-large, an ABC jurisdictional director and a member of the ABC Legal Committee.

USA Bowling operates exclusively for the advancement of national and international amateur bowling competition. The USOC granted WIBC and ABC Group A membership February 1989, contingent on USA Bowling's formation. USA Bowling was officially formed in June 1989. WIBC and ABC held Group C membership since 1985.

TEAM USA

Since 1987, TEAM USA members represent the United States in most national and international amateur bowling competitions. Most bowlers begin their process of becoming a TEAM USA member on the local level. Local qualifiers, local-association-sponsored bowlers and other top bowlers advance to regional TEAM USA competition.

These selected athletes advance directly to the USA Bowling Championships. Among those joining these athletes are additional athletes seeded into the competition. These individuals include:

• Current TEAM USA members and alternates
• Intercollegiate Bowling Championships female and male most valuable players
• Association of College Unions-International Bowling Tournament champions
• Four female and four male military representatives who qualify through special tournaments conducted by the
     U.S. military's four branches
• Youth Bowling Championships female and male scratch champions.

In the USA Bowling Championships, bowlers roll three eight-game qualifying blocks. The top 24 scorers in both divisions (men's and women's) advance to match play. In match play, athletes bowl 24 match-play games, with the 24th game being a position-round game. Match-play winners earn 10 bonus points for each victory. The top-five scorers in each division are named the next year's TEAM USA members.

TEAM USA members must be U.S. citizens, amateur bowlers for at least three years before entering TEAM USA qualifying competition, and members of WIBC, the ABC or YABA. The USA Championships are under the auspices of USA Bowling.

1998 TEAM USA
Aug. 15-20, 1997 - Eden Prairie, Minn.
90 men, 86 women

Women

1. Janette Piesczynski, Cheektowaga, N.Y.*
2. Lisa Duenow, Orono, Minn.
3. Kelly Kulick, Union, N.J.
4. Lynda Norry, Wichita, Kan.
5. Missy Sullivan, Coon Rapids, Minn.
   Kendra Cameron, Gambrills, Md.**
6. Stacy Werth, Rocklin, Calif.
7. Debbie Kuhn, Baltimore
8. Lucy Giovinco-Sandelin, Norcross, Ga.

Men

1. John Gaines, Davidsonville, Md.*
2. Kurt Pilon, Clinton, Mich.
3. Michael Neumann, Buffalo, N.Y.
4. Tony Manna Jr., Omaha, Neb.
5. Chris Barnes, Wichita, Kan.
6. Carl Fietek, Eden Prairie, Minn.
7. Brad Angelo, Newfane, N.Y.
8. Shawn Evans, Satellite Beach, Fla.

*1997 National Amateur Champion
**Cameron resigned her 1998 TEAM USA postion to turn professional. Giovinco-Sandelin assumed Cameron's place.

1997 TEAM USA
Aug. 17-21, 1996 - St. Louis
88 men, 89 women

Women

1. Lucy Giovinco, Norcross, Ga.*
2. Kendra Cameron, Gambrills, Md.
3. Lynda Norry, Wichita, Kan.
4. Denise Kalaola, Waianae, Hawaii
5. Lesia Moos, Lancaster, Calif
6. Lisa Duenow, Orono, Minn.

Men

1. Vernon Peterson, Dearborn Heights, Mich.
2. Chris Barnes, Wichita, Kan.
3. Jerry Sikora, Southgate, Mich.
4. Bruce Steffani, Great Falls, Mont.
5. Brad Angelo, Newfane, N.Y.
6. Brian Graham, Kokomo, Ind.

*1996 National Amateur Champion

1996 TEAM USA
Aug. 27-Sept.1, 1995 - Reno, Nev.
91 men, 89 women

Women

1. Lynda Norry, Pleasant Hill, Calif.*
2. Kendra Cameron, Gambrills, Md.
3. Denise Kalaola, Waianae, Hawaii
   Liz Johnson, Niagara Falls, N.Y.**
   Lana Mink, San Antonio***
6. Lucy Giovinco, Norcross, Ga.
   Becky Kregling, Stratford, Conn.
   Stacy Werth, Rocklin, Calif.

Men

1. Drew Hylen, Denver*
2. Chris Barnes, Wichita, Kan.
3. Mike Faliero, Buffalo, N.Y.
4. David Berman, Pittsburgh
5. David Hurtt, Lafayette, Ind.
6. Jerry Sikora, Southgate, Mich.

*1995 National Amateur Champions.
**Johnson resigned her 1996 TEAM USA position to turn professional. Alternate Kregling assumed Johnson's place.
***Mink resigned her 1997 Team USA position for personal reasons. Alternate Werth assumed her place.

1995 TEAM USA
Aug. 21-25, 1994 - Bloomington, Minn.
90 men, 87 women

Women

1. Elizabeth Johnson, Niagara Falls, N.Y.*
2. Missy Howard, Coon Rapids, Minn.
3. Lesia Stark, Lancaster, Calif.
4. Lisa Bishop, Belleville, Mich.
5. Kendra Cameron, Gambrills, Md.
6. Janet Woolum, Tempe, Ariz.

Men

1. Pat Healey Jr., Niagara Falls, N.Y.*
2. Mark Van Meter, Albuquerque, N.M.
3. Chris Barnes, Wichita, Kan.
4. John Eiss, Brooklyn Park, Minn.
5. Brian Fedrow, San Jose, Calif.
6. Ed Roberts, Cambridge, Mass.

*1994 National Amateur Champions.

1994 TEAM USA
Aug. 8-13, 1993 - Akron, Ohio
88 men, 84 women

Women

1. Elizabeth Johnson, Niagara Falls, N.Y.*
   Tammy Turner, Canyon, Texas**
2. Mandy Wilson, Dayton, Ohio
3. Lisa Rothe, St. Louis
4. Pamela Inloes, Modesto, Calif.
5. Lisa Vint, East Troy, Wis.
6. Lucy Giovinco, Norcross, Ga.

*1993 National Amateur Champions.

**Turner resigned her 1994 TEAM USA position to turn professional. Alternate Giovinco assumed Turner's place.

Men

1. Robert Smith, Moor Park, Calif.*
2. Chris Barnes, Wichita, Kan.
3. Pete Partridge, Phoenix
4. Samuel Lantto, Maple Grove, Minn.
5. Steve Kloempken, Las Vegas
6. David Garber, Bedford, Texas

1993 TEAM USA
Aug. 2-8, 1992 - San Diego
87 men, 84 women

Women

1. Joey Simpson, Lexington, Ky.*
2. Diana Williams, Raymond, Wash.
3. Tammy Turner, Canyon, Texas
4. Stacy Robards, Carmichael, Calif.
5. Ann Johnson, Hinesville, Ga.
6. Nancy Ennis, Clyde, Calif.

*1992 National Amateur Champions.

Men

1. Anthony Chapman, Landover, Md.*
2. Vince Biondo, Hoffman Estates, Ill.
3. David Garber, Bedford, Texas
4. Samuel Lantto, Maple Grove, Minn.
5. Dan Nadeau, Las Vegas
6. Dave Berman, Pittsburgh

1992 TEAM USA
July 22-27, 1991 - Atlanta
49 men, 44 women

Women

1. Julie Gardner, Huntington Beach, Calif.*
2. Mary Betke, Waco, Texas
3. Lucy Giovinco, Norcross, Ga.
4. Lynda Norry, Concord, Calif.
5. Mandy Wilson, Dayton, Ohio
6. Nancy Ennis, Clyde, Calif.

*1991 National Amateur Champions.

Men

1. Paul Fleming, Lincoln, Neb.*
2. John Eiss, Brooklyn Park, Minn.
3. Vince Biondo, Hoffman Estates, Ill.
4. Mike Terrell, Ocean Springs, Miss.
5. Pat Healey Jr., Wichita, Kan.
6. Larry Walker, Garden City, Mich.

1991 TEAM USA
Aug. 20-25 - Chicago
35 men, 39 women

Women

1. Julie Gardner, Huntington Beach, Calif.*
2. Lynda Norry, Concord, Calif.
3. Maureen Webb, North Andover, Mass.
4. Mandy Wilson, Dayton, Ohio
5. Linda Woods, Hudson, Fla.
6. Mary Betke, Waco, Texas

*1990 National Amateur Champions.

Men

1. Jon Juneau, Baton Rouge, La.*
2. Ralph Solan, St. Louis
3. Steve Kloempken, Las Vegas
4. Pat Healey Jr., Wichita, Kan.
5. Vince Biondo, Hoffman Estates, Ill.
6. Ron Mohr, Eagle River, Alaska

1990 TEAM USA
Aug. 15-19, 1989 - Milwaukee
36 men, 38 women

Women

1. Linda Graham, Des Moines, Iowa*
2. Cathy Almeida, Blackwood, N.J.
3. Maureen Webb, North Andover, Mass.
4. Lynda Norry, Concord, Calif.
5. Mandy Wilson, Dayton, Ohio
   Linda Kelly, Huber Heights, Ohio @
6. Lucy Giovinco, Norcross, Ga.

Men

1. Adam Apo, Mililani, Hawaii*
2. Tony Stipcak Jr., Redford, Mich.
3. Marc Skier, Denver
4. Rod McLean, Las Vegas
5. Jon Juneau, Baton Rouge, La.
6. Darold Meisel, Muskego, Wis.

*1989 National Amateur Champions.
@ Kelly resigned her 1990 TEAM USA position to turn professional. Alternate Giovinco assumed Kelly's place.

1989 TEAM USA
Aug. 16-20, 1988 - Milwaukee
35 men, 38 women

Women

1. Patty Ann, Arlington Heights, Ill.*
2. Debbie McMullen, Denver
3. Linda Graham, Des Moines, Iowa
4. Therese Abair, Hales Corners, Wis.
5. Lynda Norry, Concord, Calif.
6. Maureen Webb, North Andover, Mass.

Men

1. Darold Meisel, Muskego, Wis.*
2. Brad Briggs, West Palm Beach, Fla.
3. Mark Lewis, Wichita, Kan.
4. Ron Mohr, Eagle River, Alaska
5. Gordon Vadakin, Wichita, Kan.
6. Butch Cullum, Hollister, Calif.

*1988 National Amateur Champions.

1988 TEAM USA
Aug. 16-22, 1987 - Detroit
35 men, 34 women

Women

Heather Nelson, West Brattleboro, Vt.*@
1. Linda Kelly, Huber Heights, Ohio
2. Linda Graham, Des Moines, Iowa
3. Maureen Webb, North Andover, Mass.
4. Therese Abair, Hales Corners, Wis.
5. Kim Terrell-Canady, San Francisco
6. Debbie McMullen, Denver

Men

1. Mark Lewis, Wichita, Kan.*
2. Kevin Doane, Owosso, Mich.
3. Harry Mickelson, Kodiak, Alaska
4. Jack Nelson, Mandan, N.D.
5. Bob Daugherty, Dayton, Ohio
6. Michael Landrith, Phoenix

*1987 National Amateur Champions.
@Nelson resigned her 1988 TEAM USA position due to personal commitments. Alternate McMullen assumed Nelson's place.

1987 TEAM USA
Aug. 25-30, 1986 - Milwaukee
29 men, 61 women

Women

1. Cora Fiebig, Madison Heights, Mich.*
2. Sandra Jo Shiery, Bronson, Mich.
3. M. Sue Holton, Orlando, Fla.
4. Nellie Glandon, Columbus, Ohio
5. Kathy Wodka, Las Vegas
6. Karen Bender, Lansing, Ill.

Men

1. Dan Nadeau, Las Vegas*
2. Rick Steelsmith, Wichita, Kan.
3. Duane Sandvick, Bismarck, N.D.
4. Rod McLean, Las Vegas
5. Jerry Ledbetter, Puyallup, Wash.
6. Rick Graham, Lancaster, Pa.

*1986 National Amateur Champions.

U.S. National Amateur Bowling Championships Records

Averages, highest in qualifying
Women
215	Lucy Giovinco, Norcross, Ga., 1996
211	Kelly Kulick, Union, N.J., 1997
208	Mary Betke, Waco, Texas, 1991
	Kendra Cameron, Gambrills, Md., 1996
	Lisa Duenow, Orono, Minn., 1997

Men
227	Kurt Pilon, Clinton, Mich., 1997
224	Vince Biondo, Hoffman Estates, Ill., 1991
	John Eiss, Brooklyn Park, Minn., 1991

Games, highest
Women
300	Elizabeth Johnson, Niagara Falls, N.Y., 1993
	Tammy Turner, Canyon, Texas, 1993
	Mandy Wilson, Dayton, Ohio, 1992
	Jackie Sellers, DuBois, Pa., 1988
	Lynda Norry, Concord, Calif., 1988

Men
300	Mike Bronsart, Lake Havasu City, Ariz., 1997
	Chad Murphy, Wichita, Kan., 1997
	Dale Constance, Miami, 1991
	Ricky Beck, McClellan AFB, Calif., 1991

Records, best in match play
Women
19-4-1	Sandy Jo Shiery, Bronson, Mich., 1986
	Julie Gardner, Huntington Beach, Calif., 1991
18-6-0	Missy Howard, Coon Rapids, Minn., 1994
	Lesia Stark, Lancaster, Calif., 1994
	Lana Mink, San Antonio, 1995
	Kendra Cameron, Gambrills, Md., 1997

Men
20-4-0	Robert Smith, Moorpark, Calif., 1993
19-5-0	Pat Healey Jr., Niagra Falls, N.Y., 1994
	Marc Skier, Dillon, Colo., 1989

Six-Game Blocks, highest match play
Women
1,399	Julie Gardner, Huntington Beach, Calif., 1990
1,353	Linda Kelly, Huber Heights, Ohio, 1987
1,339	Mary Betke, Waco, Texas, 1991

Men
1,478	Vince Biondo, Hoffman Estates, Ill., 1991
1,453	Paul Fleming, Lincoln, Neb., 1991
1,439	Steve Kloempken, Las Vegas, 1990

Six-Game Blocks, highest qualifying
Women
1,427	Lynda Norry, Concord, Calif., 1988
1,345	Patty Ann, Arlington Heights, Ill., 1987
	Maureen Webb, North Andover, Mass., 1988

Men
1,486	Robert Smith, Simi Valley, Calif., 1991
1,437	Brad Briggs, West Palm Beach, Fla., 1988
1,406	Chris Barnes, Wichita, Kan., 1991
	Duane Mellinger, Aurora, Colo., 1991

Eight-Game Blocks, highest match play
Women
1,749	Lesia Stark, Lancaster, Calif., 1994
1,742	Lisa Duenow, Orono, Minn., 1997
1,735	Missy Sullivan, Coon Rapids, Minn., 1997

Men
1,875	Chris Barnes, Wichita, Kan., 1997
1,870	John Gaines, Davidsonville, Md., 1997
1,811	Kurt Pilon, Clinton, Mich., 1997

Eight-Game Blocks, highest qualifying
Women
1,869	Missy Sullivan, Coon Rapids, Minn., 1996
1,798	Stacy Werth, Rocklin, Calif., 1997
1,775	Lucy Giovinco, Norcross, Ga., 1996

Men
1,894	Kurt Pilon, Clinton, Mich., 1997
1,872	Carl Fietek, Eden Prairie, Minn., 1997
1,830	Nick Wissinger IV, Sterling Heights, Mich., 1997

24-Game Blocks, highest match play
Women
5,012	Joey Simpson, Lexington, Ky., 1992
5,009	Mart Betke, Waco, Texas, 1991
4,933	Lynda Norry, Concord, Calif., 1989

Men
5,415	John Eiss, Brooklyn Park, Minn., 1991
5,393	Mike Terrell, Ocean Springs, Miss., 1991
5,385	Mike Terrell, Ocean Springs, Miss., 1991

24-Game Blocks, highest qualifying
Women
5,172	Lucy Giovinco, Norcross, Ga., 1996
5,086	Kelly Kulick, Union, N.J., 1997
5,055	Lesia Moos, Lancaster, Calif., 1997

Men
5,468	Kurt Pilon, Clinton, Mich., 1997
5,399	Vince Biondo, Hoffman Estates, Ill., 1991
5,380	John Eiss, Brooklyn Park, Minn., 1991

48-Game Totals, best (includes 10 bonus pins per win)
Women
10,177	Mary Betke, Waco, Texas, 1991
10,135	Tammy Turner, Canyon, Texas, 1993
9,983	Lisa Duenow, Orono, Minn., 1997

Men
10,965	John Eiss, Brooklyn Park, Minn., 1991
10,939	Vince Biondo, Hoffman Estates, Ill., 1991
10,789	Kurt Pilon, Clinton, Mich., 1997

United States Olympic Festival

From 1989-95, bowling was a full-medal sport in the U.S. Olympic Festival. The U.S. Olympic Committee conducted the multi-event festival every year, with the exception of years the International Olympic Committee conducts the Olympics. The USOC decided in 1995 to no longer hold the competition because of financial considerations.

The U.S. Olympic Festival was held in a different U.S. city each session, with the bowling competitions being held in a local WIBC/ABC-certified bowling center. Today, 16 female and 16 male bowlers compete in four U.S. Olympic Festival bowling events. Events include: doubles, match play, singles, and four-player team which features regular and Baker System games.

In the team events, players are divided into teams based on the geographic location of their hometowns. The bowlers earn their U.S. Olympic Festival berths by virtue of their finishes in the U.S. National Amateur Bowling Championships. USA Bowling conducts the U.S. National Amateur Bowling Championships to select the 12 members of TEAM USA.

U.S. Olympic Festival - '95 Results
Denver

Women's Four Player

(Six regular, 24 Baker games) —

7,189   East (Joanne Harris, Jeanne Zappula, Lisa Bishop, Kendra Cameron)

6,962   South (Lana Mink, Lucy Giovinco, Leslie Beamish, Pat Costello)

6,725   West (Linda Petersdorf, Linda Lunsford, Janet Woolum, Stacy Manley-Werth)

Women's Doubles

4,828   Janet Woolum and Stacey Manley-Werth (West)

4,662   Lisa Bishop and Joanne Harris (East)

4,546   Timi McCorvey and Mandy Wilson (North)

Women's Singles

2,355   Joanne Harris (East)

2,342   Lucy Giovinco (South)

2,322   Linda Petersdorf (West)

Women's Match Play

3,307   Pat Costello (South)

3,280   Linda Petersdorf (West)

3,248   Kendra Cameron (East)

Men's Four Player

(6 regular, 24 Baker games) —

7,609   West (Pete Partridge, Robert Smith, Brian Fedrow, Andrew Udahl)

7,481   East (Ed Roberts, Scott Santos, Eric Cox, Chris Barnes)

7,473   North (John Eiss, Bob Goike, Sam Lantto, Nick Wissinger IV)

Men's Doubles

5,003   Pete Partridge and Robert Smith (West)

4,914   Eric Cox and Scott Santos (East)

4,914   John Eiss and Sam Lantto (North)

Men's Singles

2,564   Pete Partridge (West)

2,482   David Hurtt (South)

2,464   Robert Smith (West)

Men's Match Play

3,534   Brian Fedrow (West)

3,516   John Eiss (North)

3,439   Mark Van Meter (South)

U.S. Olympic Festival - '94 Results
St. Louis

Women's Four Player

(Six regular, 18 Baker match games, totals include 20 bonus pins for each match play victory) —

8,530   West (Pam Inloes, Karen Sookikian, Sharon Wanczyk, Kim Wong)

8,444   North (Shelly Machuga, Lisa Rothe, Lisa Vint, Stephanie Wiest)

8,413   South (Lucy Giovinco, Eleanore Korzec, Stacy Manley, Lana Mink)

Women's Doubles

5,010   Elizabeth Johnson and Mandy Wilson (East)

4,870   Lana Mink and Eleanore Korzec (South)

4,847   Lisa Rothe and Lisa Vint (North)

Women's Singles

2,726   Elizabeth Johnson (East)

2,601   Lana Mink (South)

2,523   Diane Lagravinese (East)

Men's Four Player

(Six regular, 18 Baker match games, totals include 20 bonus pins for each match play victory) —

8,915   South (Eric Cox, David Garber, Mike Nyitray, Pete Partridge)

8,880   North (Terry Clayton, Sam Lantto, Ron Mohr, Jeff Zink)

8,622   East (Anthony Chapman, Russell Rose, Scott Santos, Mike Terrell)

Men's Doubles

5,136   Eric Cox and Mike Nyitray (South)

5,096   Anthony Chapman and Mike Terrell (East)

5,038   Jim Wagner and Darren Wong (West)

Men's Singles

2,674   Jim Wagner (West)

2,642   Ron Mohr (West)

2,601   Terry Clayton (North)

Women's Match Play
3,507 Elizabeth Johnson (East)
3,248 Eleanore Korzec (South)
3,248 Lisa Vint (North)

Men's Match Play
3,717 Eric Cox (South)
3,554 Terry Clayton (North)
3,496 Gordon Kilpatrick (West)

U.S. Olympic Festival - '93 Results
San Antonio, Texas

Women's Four Player
6,056 South (Ann Johnson, Lori Leonard, Susie Minshew, Tammy Turner)
5,879 East (Leslie Beamish, Sharon Nipp, Linda Petersdorf, Stacy Robards)
5,800 North (Debbie Lantto, Lana Mink, Geri Anderson, Mandy Wilson)

Men's Four Player
6,320 North (Harry Mickelson, Steve Brinkman, Sam Lantto, Larry Walker)
6,110 East (Dave Berman, Brian Boghosian, Vince Biondo, Sam Ventura)
6,040 West (Derek Banks, Dave Symes, Ron Mohr, Dan Nadeau)

Women's Doubles
4,515 North (Geri Anderson and Mandy Wilson)
4,494 East (Sharon Nipp and Linda Petersdorf)
4,484 South (Susie Minshew and Tammy Turner)

Men's Doubles
5,064 West (Ron Mohr and Dan Nadeau)
5,029 North (Sam Lantto and Steve Brinkman)
4,942 East (Dave Berman and Brian Boghosian)

Women's Singles
2,374 Mandy Wilson (North)
2,324 Janice Cowell (West)
2,285 Tammy Turner (South)

Men's Singles
2,591 Rod McLean (South)
2,467 Dave Berman (East)
2,433 Harry Mickelson (North)

Women's Match Play
3,537 Mandy Wilson (North)
3,320 Geri Anderson (North)
3,213 Pamela Inloes (West)

Men's Match Play
3,589 Larry Walker (North)
3,552 Brian Boghosian (East)
3,551 Dave Berman (East)

U.S. Olympic Festival '91 Results
Los Angeles

Women's Four Player
4,603 West (Patty Ellenburg, Julie Gardner, Lynda Norry, Darlene Weekly)
4,561 South (Linda Woods, Dionne Lee, Lucy Giovinco, Robin Davis)
4,550 East (Maureen Webb, Terrie Brensinger, Jackie Williams, Mary Betke)

Men's Four Player
4,880 West (Steve Kloempken, Steve Smith, Rod McLean, Bill Anthony Jr.)
4,875 South (Jon Juneau, Brad Briggs, Pat Healey Jr., Greg Short)
4,873 North (Ron Mohr, Harry Mickelson, Joe Natoli, Vince Biondo)

Women's Doubles
4,700 East (Maureen Webb and Jackie Williams)
4,674 West (Julie Gardner and Darlene Weelky)
4,658 North (Mandy Wilson and Kathy Haislip)

Men's Doubles
5,207 West (Steve Smith and Steve Kloempken)
5,138 North (Joe Natoli and Ron Mohr)
4,900 North (Vince Biondo and Harry Mickelson)

Women's Singles
2,509 Judy Gurney (North)
2,489 Darlene Weekly (West)
2,456 Maureen Webb (East)

Men's Singles
2,635 Steve Smith (West)
2,568 Bill Anthony Jr. (West)
2,561 Vince Biondo (North)

Women's Match Play
3,495 Lynda Norry (West)
3,456 Dionne Lee (South)
3,302 Maureen Webb (East)

Men's Match Play
3,419 Pat Healey Jr. (North)
3,373 Bill Anthony Jr. (West)
3,369 Rod McLean (West)

Mixed Doubles
4,957 Maureen Webb and Ralph Solan (East)
4,879 Julie Gardner and Steve Kloempken (West)
4,855 Lucy Giovinco and Brad Briggs (South)

U.S. Olympic Festival-'90 Results
Minneapolis

Women's Six Player

5,928 West (Linda Graham, Judy Gurney, Lynda Norry, Julie Gardner, Dionne Lee, Linda Lunsford)

5,824 North (Patty Ann, Nellie Glandon, Dawn Thorkildson, Kathy Kaplan, Lisa Lungwitz, Kelly Sparano)

5,703 South (Wanda Chovanec, Linda Kelly, Mandy Wilson, Lucy Giovinco, Jan Sanders, Beverly Warner)

Women's Trios

3,751 East (Cathy Almeida, Donalle Effort, Maureen Webb)

3,716 North (Kathy Kaplan, Lisa Lungwitz, Kelly Sparano)

3,709 South (Wanda Chovanec, Linda Kelly, Mandy Wilson)

Women's Doubles

4,993 West (Lynda Norry and Judy Gurney)

4,885 South (Linda Kelly and Mandy Wilson)

4,837 West (Dionne Lee and Julie Gardner)

Women's Singles

2,482 Lynda Norry (West)

2,457 Nellie Glandon (North)

2,436 Judy Gurney (West)

Women's Match Play

2,553 Linda Kelly (South)

2,536 Mandy Wilson (South)

2,448 Judy Gurney (West)

Men's Six Player

6,484 East (Darold Meisel, Bob Ujvari, Bill Watson, James Servis, Tony Stipcak Jr., Stan Swanson)

6,286 West (Todd Adams, William Anthony, Adam Apo, Rod McLean, Marc Skier, Robbie Tanaka)

6,208 South (Jon Juneau, Mark Lewis, Jason McCarty, Brad Briggs, Graham Ready, John Ringer)

Men's Trios

3,923 East (Darold Meisel, Bob Ujvari, Bill Watson)

3,805 North (Harry Mickelson, Ron Mohr, Duane Sandvick)

3,781 South (Jon Juneau, Mark Lewis, Jason McCarty)

Men's Doubles

5,446 East (Bob Ujvari and Bill Watson)

5,378 South (Jon Juneau and Mark Lewis)

5,229 North (Harry Mickelson and Ron Mohr)

Men's Singles

2,847 Jon Juneau (South)

2,712 Bill Watson (East)

2,671 Bill Anthony Jr. (West)

Men's Match Play

2,790 Jon Juneau (South)

2,692 Stan Swanson (East)

2,687 Todd Adams (West)

U.S. Olympic Festival '89 Results
Oklahoma City

Women's Six Player

5,823 East (Maureen Webb, Linda Rose, Jacki Sellers, Linda Graham, Sue Schotke, Jackie Williams)

5,689 North (Donna DiTrani, Freida Gates, Lana Mink, Lynda Norry, Judy Gurney, Karen Hagen)

5,555 South (Nellie Glandon, Kim Terrell, Therese Abair, Lucy Giovinco, Carol Tomko, Lisa Barfield)

Women's Trios

3,654 West (Dawn Houghtling, Dionne Lee and Debbie McMullen)

3,640 East (Maureen Webb, Linda Rose and Jackie Sellers)

3,534 North (Lynda Norry, Debbie DiTrani and Frieda Gates)

Women's Doubles

4,739 North (Frieda Gates and Lana Mink)

4,718 North (Lynda Norry and Karen Hagan)

4,669 East (Maureen Webb and Linda Rose)

Women's Singles

2,600 Debbie McMullen (West)

2,384 Nellie Glandon (South)

2,378 Linda Rose (East)

Women's Match Play

2,722 Lynda Norry (North)

2,667 Maureen Webb (East)

2,594 Kim Terrell-Canady (South)

Men's Six Player

6.043 South (Brad Briggs, Mike Landrith, Mark Knight, Jon Juneau, David Garber, Steve Kiss)

5,952 North (Bob Daughtery, Gordon Vadakin, Kevin Doane, Jeff Henry, Harry Mickelson, Bob LaPorte)

5,802 West (David Biber, Don Freund, Butch Cullum, Bryan Russell, Stan Wright, Bill Poff)

Men's Trios

3,727 East (Mark Lewis, Alan Runkel and Bob Ujvari)

3,701 West (David Biber, Don Freund and Bill Poff)

3,685 South (Brad Briggs, Mark Knight and Mike Landrith)

Men's Doubles

5,133 West (Don Freund and Bill Poff)

5,071 South (Brad Briggs and Mike Landrith)

5,064 North (Bob Daugherty and Gordon Vadakin)

Men's Singles

2,660 Bill Poff (West)

2,621 Bob Ujvari (East)

2,592 Jon Juneau (South)

Men's Match Play

2,689 Don Breeden (East)

2,599 Mike Landrith (South)

2,591 Jon Juneau (South)

Olympic Bowling Exhibition

The Olympic Bowling Exhibition in the XXIV Summer Olympic Games was held Sept. 18, 1988, at Royal Bowling Center in Seoul, South Korea. Twelve women and 12 men competed for the three Federation Internationale des Quilleurs medals each. Eleven of the women and 11 of the men were selected through a FIQ Pre-Olympic Qualifier Tournament. The 12th woman and man, South Korean bowlers, were seeded into the competition.

The exhibition's format consisted of 11 head-to-head, one-game matches. In addition to their actual pinfall, match-play winners earned 10 bonus points per win. The top-three scorers advanced to the stepladder finals to determine medal positions.

Men's Division Standings

	Match-Play	Actual Avg. (11 Games)	Record Points	Bonus	Total
1. Jack Lake Chin, Singapore	2,345	213.18	9-2	90	2,435
2. Kwan Jong Yul, South Korea	2,263	205.78	7-4	70	2,333
3. Tapani Peltola, Finland	2,224	202.18	5-6	50	2,274
4. Philippe Dubois, France	2,206	200.55	5-5-1	55	2,261
5. Kanesumi Mori, Japan	2,163	196.64	8-2-1	85	2,248
6. Mark Lewis, United States	2,187	198.82	5-6	50	2,237
7. Luis Velez, Puerto Rico	2,159	196.27	5-6	50	2,209
8. T.C. Cheng, Taiwan	2,095	190.45	7-4	70	2,165
9. Walter Costa, Brazil	2,114	192.18	4-7	40	2,154
10. Wolfgang Strupf, Germany	2,071	188.27	3-8	30	2,101
11. Christer Danielsson, Sweden	2,054	186.73	3-8	30	2,084
12. Marco Brosens, Argentina	1,992	181.10	4-7	40	2,032

Medal-Round Standings

1. Kwon Jong Yul, South Korea, gold medal.
2. Jack Lake Chin, Singapore, silver medal.
3. Tapani Peltola, Finland, bronze medal.

Yul defeated Petola, 177-163; Yul defeated Chin, 236-194 and 254-223 (championship match).

Women's Division Standings

	Match-Play	Actual Avg. (11 Games)	Record Points	Bonus	Total
1. Arianne Cerdena, Philippines	2,294	208.55	6-5	60	2,354
2. Annikki Maattola, Finland	2,225	202.27	9-2	90	2,315
3. Atsuko Asai, Japan	2,191	199.18	9-2	90	2,281
4. Jane Amlinger, Canada	2,211	201.00	6-5	60	2,271
5. Mette Hermansen, Norway	2,178	198.00	8-3	80	2,258
6. Gabi Bagai, Venezuela	2,108	191.64	5-6	50	2,158
7. Debbie McMullen, United States	2,087	189.73	5-6	50	2,137
8. Kimberley Coote, Great Britain	2,085	189.55	4-7	40	2,125
9. Annemiek Dagelet, Netherlands	2,066	187.82	5-6	50	2,116
10. Edda Piccini, Mexico	2,075	188.64	3-8	30	2,105
11. Carol Gianotti, Australia	2,073	188.45	3-8	30	2,103
12. Kyung-Mi Song, South Korea	1,841	167.36	3-8	30	1,871

Medal-Round Standings

1. Arianne Cerdena, Philippines, gold medal.
2. Atsuko Asai, Japan, silver medal.
3. Annikki Maattola, Finland, bronze medal.

Asai defeated Maattola, 209-187; Cerdena defeated Asai, 249-211 (championship match).

Federation Internationale des Quilleurs World and Zone Tournaments

The Federation Internationale des Quilleurs is the world governing body for bowling. It divides its world constituency into three geographical zones: the American Zone, Asian Zone and European Zone.

The American Zone is comprised of North, South and Central American countries. The FIQ alternately holds world and zone tournaments in different locations. World and Zone tournaments are alternately held every two years, with both women and men competing.

Beginning in 1977, World and Zone tournament participants competed in singles, two-player, three-player and five-player events. The four-player team and European-style format were discontinued. In the European-style format, individuals bowl an entire game or one-half of a game on only one lane. The individuals then move to another lane to bowl an additional game or complete the previous one. In the American-style format, individuals alternate each frame between two lanes.

After four events, the field is cut to the top 16 scorers. The 16 men and women bowl 15, head-to-head, match-play games. Match-play winners earn 10 points per victory. After 15 games, the field is cut to the top three. These competitors compete in a stepladder final for the individual event title. The third-place bowler faces the second-place bowler. The winner of this one-game match faces the first-place bowler. The challenger and the first-place finisher then compete in a two-game match. The winner of the match (combined total pinfall) is declared the individual event champion.

U.S. women began competing in FIQ world and zone events in 1963, and U.S. men began competing in 1962.

FIQ World Championships Standings

13th World Championships
Reno, Nev. 1995
61 Nations, 280 men, 196 women

Women's Five-Player

1, Finland 5,974
Jaana Puhakka 1,306, Paulina Aalto 1,199, Anu Peltola 1,092, Leena Pulliainen 1,256, Heta Maija Allen 1,121
2. Sweden 5,914
Asa Larsson 1,221, Marie Holmqvist 1,268, Eva Hagggvist 1,172, Susanne Olsson 1,143, Eva Nordstrom 584, Eva Jonsson 526
3. 5,900
Isabelle Saldjian 1,224, Pascale Moynot 1,095, A. Loeb 1,279, Maryelle Pagola 1,206, Brigitte Fievet 1,096

Women's Trios

1. Australia 3,594
Cara Honeychurch 1,246, Sharon McLeish 1,198, Sue Cassell, 1,182
2. Malaysia 3,606
Shalin Zulkifli 1,158, Lisa Kwan 1,222, Shirley Chow 1,226
3. Chinese Taipei 3,594
Su-Fen Tseng 1,281, Su-Ling Tsai 1,135, Miao-Ling Chou 1,178

Women's Doubles

1. Thailand 2,489
Kanit Kitchatham 1,293, Phetchara Kaewsuk 1,196
2. Finland 2,450
Jaana Puhakka 1,205, Pauliina Aalto 1,245
3. Singapore 2,405
Katherine Lee 1,135, Jesmine Ho 1,270

Women's Singles

1. Debby Ship, Canada .1,318
2. Liz Johnson, United States 1,295
3. Catherine Che, Hong Kong 1,288

Women's All Events

1. Jaana Puhakka, Finland 4,916
2. Cara Honeychurch, Australia 4,908
3. Asa Larsson, Sweden 4,838

Women's Individual (Playoff Results)

1. Celia Flores, Mexico
2. Asa Larsson, Sweden
3. Luz Adriana Leal, Colombia
Larsson def. Leal 244-174 and Flores def. Larsson 472-453 in the two-game title match.

Men's Five Player

1. The Netherlands 6,282
Michael Sassen 1,326, Marcel van den Bosch 1,277, Niko Thienpondt 1,235, Geert Van Baest 1,214, Maarten Krull 577, Erwin Groen 653
2. Sweden 6,257
Tomas Leandersson 1,229, Patrik Eriksson 1,243, Ulf Haemnaes 544, Patrik Johansson 1,329, Raymond Jansson 1,264, Par Svensson, 648
3. France 6,177
Claude Giovannetti 1,186, Francois Sacco 1,296, Claude Bouchereau 1,233, Alain Laucris 1,224, Phillipe DuBois 1,238

Men's Trios

1. The Netherlands 3,954
Erwin Groen 1,231, Niko Thienpondt 1,273, Michael Sassen 1,450
2. The Netherlands 3,889
Geert Van Baest 1,310, Maarten Krull 1,216, Marcel van den Bosch 1,363
3. Sweden 3,852
Tomas Leandersson 1,369, Patrick Johansson 1,246, Raymond Jansson 1,236

Men's Doubles

1. Sweden 2,702
Tomas Leandersson 1,335, Raymond Jansson 1,367
2. Australia 2,627
Warren Stewart 1,328, Andrew Frawley 1,299
3. Venezuela 2,620
Agustin de Faria 1,335, Pedro Carreyo 1,287

Men's Singles

1. Marc Doi, Canada 1,364
2. Bill Rowe, Canada 1,356
3. Chen-Min Yang, Chinese Taipei 1,347

Men's All Events

1. Michael Sassen, The Netherlands 5,496
2. Tore Torgersen, Norway 5,237
3. Mohammed Kalifa, United Arab Emirates 5,218

Men's Individual (Playoff Results)

1. Chen-Min Yang, Chinese Taipei
2. Raymond Jansson, Sweden
3. Chris Barnes, United States
Jansson def. Barnes 247-215 and Yang def. Jansson 430-423 in the two-game title match.

12th World Championships
Singapore 1991
48 Nations, 280 men, 196 women

Women's Five Player
1. Korea 5,850
   Shin Sun 1,184, Lee Hyung 1,164, Kim Sim 1,132,
   Hong Suk 1,220, Cho Suk 532, Kim Young 618
2. Finland 5,784
   Sari Yrjola 1,178, Tytti Kujanen 1,228,
   Arja Itkonen 1,141, Annikki Maattola 1,121,
   Heidi Lind 1,116
3. Germany 5,731
   Ute Strauss 1,038, Gisela Wilde 1,109,
   Gertrud Bauer 1,329, Michaela Viol 1,179,
   Martina Beckel 1,076

Women's Trios
1. Canada 3,563
   Catharine Willis 1,230, Jane Amlinger 1,098,
   Anne Saasto 1,235
2. Sweden...3,531
   Asa Larsson 1,229, Carina Eriksson 1,188,
   Annette (Hagre) Johannesson 1,114
3. Sweden 3,495
   Monica Johansson 1,171, Marie Holmquist 1,233,
   Gerda Ohman 1,091

Women's Doubles
1. Japan 2,438
   Tomoko Hatanaka 1,144, Kumiko Inatsu 1,294
2. Canada 2,420
   Jane Amlinger 1,211, Catharine Willis 1,230
3. United States 2,392
   Lynda Norry 1,184, Maureen Webb 1,208

Women's Singles
1. Martina Beckel, Germany 1,272
2. Lynda Norry, United States.................1,243
3. Sari Yrjola, Finland.........................1,234

Women's All Events
1. Helle Andersen, Denmark 4,821
2. Catharine Willis, Canada 4,810
3. Kumiko Inatsu, Japan.......................4,782

Women's Individual (Playoff Results)
1. Catharine Willis, Canada
2. Lisa Kwan, Malaysia
3. Maria Ortiz, Puerto Rico
Kwan defeated Ortiz 206-167; and Willis defeated Kwan 420-382 (two games).

Men's Five Player
1. Taiwan..6,021
   Y.C. Ma 1,283, C.Y. Tang 1,200, Te-Lin Lai 1,176,
   Chao Lin 1,143, Cheng Yang 1,219
2. The Philippines 6,011
   Paeng Nepomuceno 1,271, Rudy Salazar 1,209,
   Paulo Valdez 1,206, Rene Reyes 1,139,
   Jing Sablan 536, Efren Guerrero 650
3. The Netherlands 5,968
   Erik Kok 1,102, Erwin Groen 1,237,
   Fedde deBoer 1,212, Marcel VandenBosch 1,252,
   Andre VanGurp 552, B.J. VandenBoogaart 613

Men's Trios
1. United States 3,880
   Pat Healey 1,322, Vince Biondo 1,252,
   Steve Kloempken 1,306
2. Taiwan...3,701
   Y. C. Ma 1,242, C.Y. Tang 1,203,
   Cheng Yang 1,256
3. Finland 3,689
   Mika Koivuniemi 1,308, Kai Virtanen 1,107,
   Tapani Peltola 1,274

Men's Doubles
1. United States 2,532
   Pat Healey 1,325, Steve Kloempken 1,207
2. Japan...2,526
   Kengo Tagata 1,271, Hiroshi Yamamoto 1,255
3. The Philippines 2,470
   Paeng Nepomuceno 1,223, Paulo Valdez 1,247

Men's Singles
1. Y. C. Ma, Taiwan................................1,327
2. Roberto Silva, Mexico 1,310
3. Bom Sok Suh, Korea...........................1,277

Men's All Events
1. Y.C. Ma, Taiwan.................................5,048
2. Mika Juhani Koivuniemi, Finland.........4,978
3. Bom Sok Suh, Korea...........................4,939

Men's Individual (Playoff Results)
1. Mika Koivuniemi, Finland
2. Teemu Raatikainen, Finland
3. Tomas Leandersson, Sweden
Raatikainen defeated Leandersson, 236-188; and Koivuniemi defeated Raatikainen. 436-405 (two games).

11th World Championships
Helsinki, Finland 1987
44 Nations, 230 men, 196 women

Women's Five Player
1. United States 6,011
   Nellie Glandon 1,198, Karen Bender 1,188,
   Sandra Jo Shiery 1,276, Kathy Wodka 1,170,
   Cora Fiebig 531, M. Sue Holton 648
2. Sweden..5,946
   Asa Larsson 1,291, Monica Johansson 1,171,
   Gerda Ohman 1,183, Annette Hagre 1,183,
   Lena Sulkanen 1,118
3. Australia 5,884
   Carol Gianotti 1,159, Jeanette Baker 1,187,
   JoEllen Day 1,213, Ruth Guerster 1,193,
   Barb Richmond 1,132

Men's Five Player
1. Sweden..6,272
   Raymond Jansson 1,236, Per Jonsson 1,167,
   Ulf Haemnaes 1,185, Ulf Bolleby 1,322,
   Tony Rosenquist 1,362
2. Finland 6,196
   Arvi Korhonen 1,220, Kari Jehkinen 1,151,
   Tom Hahl 1,374, Mikko Kaartinen 1,273,
   Olli Tiainen 592, Teemu Raatikainen 586
3. The Netherlands 6,055
   Erwin Groen 1,254, B.J. VandenBoogaart 1,363,
   Cyriel Winters 1,144, Andre Reyerse 1,144,
   Ton Plummen 1,150

Women's Trios

1. United States 3,603
   M. Sue Holton 1,183, Karen Bender 1,237,
   Nellie Glandon 1,183
2. Sweden...3,578
   Carina Eriksson 1,238, Monica Johansson 1,212,
   Gerda Ohman 1,128
3. United States 3,570
   Cora Fiebig 1,176, Sandra Jo Shiery 1,272,
   Kathy Wodka 1,122

Women's Doubles

1. United States 2,566
   Cora Fiebig 1,330, Kathy Wodka 1,236
2. Sweden...2,486
   Asa Larsson 1,247, Annette Hagre 1,239
3. Austria 2,414
   Christine Felcmann 1,224, Hilde Reitermaier 1,190

Women's Singles

1. Edda Piccini, Mexico...............................1,259
2. Ji-Yeon Lee, Korea 1,258
3. Nellie Glandon, United States.................1,247

Women's All Events

1. Sandra Jo Shiery, United States 4,894
2. Edda Piccini, Mexico...............................4,842
3. Asa Larsson, Sweden 4,809

Women's Individual (Playoff Results)

1. Annette Hagre, Sweden
2. Mayumi Hayashi, Japan
3 Carol Gianotti, Australia
Hayashi defeated M. Sue Holton, United States, 205-191;
   Hayashi defeated Gianotti, 226-170; and Hagre defeated
   Hayashi, 419-405 (two games).

Men's Trios

1. United States 3,873
   Dan Nadeau 1,188, Duane Sandvick 1,249,
   Rick Steelsmith 1,436
2. Finland...3,795
   Teemu Raatikainen 1,198, Tom Hahl 1,349,
   Mikko Kaartinen 1,248
3. The Netherlands 3,741
   B.J. vandenBoogaart 1,261, Cyriel Winters 1,226, Ton
   Plummen 1,254

Men's Doubles

1. Sweden...2,638
   Ulf Haemnaes 1,310, Ulf Bolleby 1,328
2. Singapore 2,529
   Patric Wee 1,267, Sam Goh 1,262
3. United States 2,523
   Dan Nadeau 1,147, Rick Steelsmith 1,376

Men's Singles

1. Patrick Rolland, France............................1,332
2. Paeng Nepomuceno, The Philippines 1,307
3. Rick Steelsmith, United States................1,301

Men's All Events

1. Rick Steelsmith, United States................5,261
2. Ulf Bolleby, Sweden 5,138
3. Tom Hahl, Finland.................................5,110

Men's Individual (Playoff Results)

1. Roger Pieters, Belgium
2. Rick Steelsmith, United States
3. Tom Hahl, Finland
Hahl defeated Raymond Jansson of Sweden, 221-182;
   Pieters defeated Hahl, 201-193; Pieters defeated
   Steelsmith, 451-367 (two games); and Pieters defeated
   Steelsmith, 232-197.

10th World Championships
Caracas, Venezuela 1983
37 Nations, 206 men, 175 women

Women's Five Player

1. Sweden...5,866
   Karin Glennert 1,111, Gerda Ohman 1,213,
   Asa Larsson 1,242, Lena Sulkanen 1,180,
   Yvonne Berndt 1,120
2. Japan 5,772
   Kumiko Inatsu 1,127, Kyoko Yamaguchi 1,131,
   Yoshiko Sakamaru 1,094, Mayumi Hayashi 1,207,
   Kazumi Koike 1,213
3. United States 5,649
   Mary Mohacsi 1,116, Marion Brisk 1,148,
   Cathy Almeida 1,199, Dixie Kirk 1,132,
   Janine Ditch 526, Yvonne Dowland 528

Women's Trios

1. Germany 3,532
   Hani Hoplitchek 1,212, Christel Huesler 1,162,
   Gisela Lins 1,158
2. United States 3,479
   Dixie Kirk 1,195, Yvonne Dowland 1,164,
   Janine Ditch 1,120
3. The Philippines 3,479
   Bong Coo 1,267, Arianne Cerdena 1,177,
   Lita de la Rosa 1,035

Men's Five Player

1. Finland...6,355
   Mikko Kaartinen 1,220, Sam Anker 1,388,
   Martti Koskela 1,269, Hannu Narhi 1,250,
   Simo Vahakorpela 615, Ailo Votila 613
2. United States 6,285
   Tony Cariello 1,249, Gordon Vadakin 1,351,
   Rod Toft 1,229, Darold Meisel 1,242,
   Rich Wonders 1,214
3. Sweden...6,235
   Kenneth Andersson 1,226, Lars Hedquist 1,285,
   Olle Svensson 1,087, Tony Rosenquist 1,257,
   Mats Karlsson 1,380

Men's Trios

1. Sweden 3,899
   Kenneth Andersson 1,333, Tony Rosenquist 1,205,
   Mats Karlsson 1,361
2. The Philippines 3,897
   Paeng Nepomuceno 1,305, Raul Reformado 1,396,
   Oliver Ongtawco 1,196
3. United States 3,879
   Tony Cariello 1,207, Darold Meisel 1,261,
   Rich Wonders 1,411

Women's Doubles

1. Denmark...2,409
   Birgitte Jensen 1,203, Jette Hansen 1,206
2. Finland...2,367
   Tuula Kaartinen 1,198, Airi Leppala 1,169
3. Great Britain....................................2,363
   Judy Robins 1,180, Jane Virot 1,183

Women's Singles

1. Lena Sulkanen, Sweden 1,293
2. Asa Larsson, Sweden..........................1,279
3. Karin Glennert, Sweden........................1,269

Women's All Events

1. Bong Coo, The Philippines 4,806
2. Lena Sulkanen, Sweden 4,791
3. Asa Larsson, Sweden..........................4,755

Women's Individual (Playoff Results)

1. Lena Sulkanen, Sweden
2. Cathy Almeida, United States
3. Kumiko Inatsu, Japan

Inatsu defeated Asa Larsson, Sweden, 210-203; Almeida defeated Inatsu, 205-182; Almeida defeated Sulkanen, 404-392 (two games); Sulkanen defeated Almeida, 213-200.

Men's Doubles

1. Great Britain 2,515
   Chris Buck 1,270, Alan Fawcett 1,245
2. Australia 2,515
   Ken Harding 1,268, John Sullivan 1,247
3. Germany 2,514
   Bernd Bauhofer 1,282, Norbert Griesert 1,232

Men's Singles

1. Armando Marino, Colombia....................1,357
2. Eddie Garofalo, Puerto Rico..................1,314
3. Takashi Shino, Japan...........................1,309

Men's All Events

1. Mats Karlsson, Sweden........................5,242
2. Erik Kok, The Netherlands.....................5,146
3. Rich Wonders, United States 5,142

Men's Individual (Playoff Results)

1. Tony Cariello, United States, 1,163.
2. Mats Karlsson, Sweden, 632.
3. Ron Allenby, Canada, 180.

Cariello defeated Ron Powell of Australia, 227-178; Cariello defeated Allenby, 229-180; Cariello defeated Karlsson, 482-436 (two games); and Cariello defeated Karlsson, 225-196.

9th World Championships
Manila, The Philippines 1979
30 Nations, 175 men, 146 women

Women's Five Player

1. United States 5,667
   Cindy Schuble 1,171, Sandi Tice 1,118,
   Betty Maw 1,064, Jackie Stormo 1,125,
   Annese Kelly 1,189
2. Germany 5,577
   Daniela Gruber 1,105, Elke Brosch 1,068,
   Dorothea Weiche 1,104, Marianne Schmelzle 1,142,
   Anne Haefker 1,148
3. Australia 5,487
   Ruth Guerster 1,059, Jeanette Baker 1,103,
   Lavina Pietens 1,069, Sharon Gowing 1,088,
   Del Da-Re 1,168

Women's Trios

1. United States.......................................3,419
   Annese Kelly 1,197, Cindy Schuble 1,152,
   Jackie Stormo 1,070
2. The Philippines 3,331
   Bong Coo 1,203, Nellie Castillo 1,020,
   Lita de la Rosa 1,108
3. Sweden 3,321
   Ingrid Sellgren 1,071, Annette Hagre 1,096,
   Yvonne Nilsson 1,154

Women's Doubles

1. The Philippines 2,348
   Lita de la Rosa 1,071, Bong Coo 1,277
2. Finland 2,334
   Eija Krogerus 1,082, Tuula Kaartinen 1,252
3. Japan 2,258
   Kyoko Yamaguchi 1,024, Harumi Morisaki 1,234

Women's Singles

1. Lita de la Rosa, The Philippines 1,220
2. Yvonne Nilsson, Sweden.......................1,198
3. Orawan Nithinakakorn, Thailand.............1,193

Men's Five Player

1. Australia 5,892
   Eric Thompson 1,206, Kevin Quinn 1,194,
   Gary Kee 1,184, John Sullivan 1,190, Ron Powell 1,118
2. Great Britain 5,793
   John Reeves 1,084, Gerry Bugden 1,160,
   Tom Marshall 1,181, Jez Darvill 1,123, Geoff Buck 1,245
3. The Netherlands 5,774
   Ruud VandenSchlude 1,190, Leen VanderZwan 1,070,
   Fon VanGulick 1,171, Erik Kok 1,174,
   Ton Plummen 1,169

Men's Trios

1. Malaysia..3,582
   Allan Hoo 1,139, Ed Lim 1,085, J.B. Koo 1,358
2. United States 3,564
   Terry Kulibert 1,147, Jack Wilson 1,245,
   Rich Supanich 1,143
3. France 3,561
   Jean Moulenac 1,184, Jacques Marengo 1,219,
   Albert Arama 1,158

Men's Doubles

1. Austalia 2,460
   Eric Thompson 1,244, Ron Powell 1,216
2. South Korea..2,432
   Byon Chul 1,267, Ahn Byung Ku 1,165
3. United States......................................2,421
   Jim Lindquist 1,278, Rich Supanich 1,143

Men's Singles

1. Ollie Ongtawco, The Philippines 1,278
2. Rogelio Felice, Venezuela 1,265
3. Michio Matsubara, Japan 1,263

Women's Individual (Playoff Results)
1. Lita de la Rosa, The Philippines
2. Daniela Gruber, Germany
3. Yvonne Nilsson, Sweden

Nilsson defeated Annese Kelly, United States, 171-169; de la Rosa defeated Nilsson, 224-200; de la Rosa defeated Gruber, 416-331.

Men's Individual (Playoff Results)
1. Gerry Bugden, Great Britain 775.
2. Philippe Dubois, France 372.
3. J.B. Koo, Malaysia 181.

Bugden defeated Mikko Kaartinen of Finland, 195-192; Bugden defeated Koo, 201-181; and Bugden defeated Dubois, 379-372 (two games).

8th World Championships
London, England 1975
32 Nations, 271 men, 152 women

Women's Four Player
1. Japan 4,551
   Yasuyo Ono 1,136, Miyoko Sakai 1,034,
   Fumiko Iwasaki 1,184, Miyuki Motoi 1,197
2. United States 4,486
   Mary Lou Graham 1,185, Olga Gloor 1,075,
   Carol Schemers 1,121, Janie Leszczynski 1,105
3. Australia 4,474
   Jeanette Baker 1,117, Trish Datson 1,118,
   Julie Delgano 1,070, Jean Soderlund 1,169

Men's Eight Player (8 games)
1. West Germany 12,406
   Bernd Baule 1,610, Hans Dreiss 1,521,
   Claus Hase 1,579, Dieter Henrichs 1,493,
   Bernd Kornak 1,489, Friedhelm Remmel 1,518,
   Friedhold Ritz 1,578, Ulrich Rohloff 1,618
2. Canada 12,266
   Sid Allen 1,532, Gerard Duranceau 1,592,
   Joe Lazzaro 1,489, Don Lutz 1,549,
   Gil Smallwood 1,424, Glen Watson 1,625,
   Joe Williams 1,519, Paul Yoshimasu 1,536
3. Great Britain 12,265
   Chris Buck 1,586, Geoff Buck 1,485,
   Gerry Bugden 1,507, Eric Butcher 1,517,
   Bernie Caterer 1,546, Cass Edwards 1,588,
   Brian Michael 1,472, Jon Reeves 1,564

Women's Five Player
1. Japan 5,461
   Miyuki Motoi 1,071, Fumiko Iwasaki 1,086,
   Miyoko Sakai 1,119, Keiko Kamo 1,115,
   Yasuyo Ono 1,070
2. Australia 5,455
   Dale Gray 976, Del Da-Re 1,129, Jeanette Baker 1,123,
   Julie Delgarno 1,136, Trish Datson 1,091
3. West Germany 5,438
   Siegunde Huser 973, Dorothea Weiche 1,090,
   Daniela Gruber 1,178, Anne Haefker 1,179,
   Margot Simon 441, Barbera Boy 577

Men's Five Player
1. Finland 5,769
   Leo Hilokoski 1,092, Reijo Rasijarvi 1,190,
   Kaj Sveholm 1,094, Matti Nieminen 1,187,
   Tapio Vuorinen 1,206
2. United States 5,752
   Bud Stoudt 1,284, Ron Woolet 1,107, Gary Beck 1,139,
   Chuck Sunseri 1,098, Bobby Meadows 1,124
3. Norway 5,720
   Svein Laregg 1,073, Gulbrand Gagnum 1,176,
   Marthon Vabo 1,077, Per Kittelsen 1,145,
   Arne Stroem 1,249

Women's Doubles
1. Sweden 2,334
   Britt Cederbrink 1,131, Svea Ljungkvist 1,203
2. United States..2,305
   Carol Gaddis 1,177, Carol Schemers 1,128
3. Australia...2,304
   Del Da-Re 1,174, Dale Gray 1,130

Men's Doubles
1. Great Britain 2,553
   Brian Michael 1,360, Bernie Caterer 1,193
2. Singapore...2,500
   Dennis Tay 1,215, Henry Tan 1,285
3. United States...2,440
   Bud Stoudt 1,308, Bobby Meadows 1,132

Women's All Events
1. Anne Haefker, Germany 4,615
2. Eija Krogerus, Finland 4,528
3. Carol Schemers, United States.............................4,523

Men's All Events
1. Bud Stoudt, United States...................................5,816
2. Arne Stroem, Norway 5,742
3. Matti Nieminen, Finland 5,634

7th World Championships
Milwaukee 1971
32 Nations, 268 men, 103 women

Women's Four Player
1. United States 4,656
   Penny McClain 1,173, Lorrie Koch 1,120
   Dixie Burmeister 1,197, Joan Holm 1,166
2. Australia 4,530
   Lillian Bruce 1,122, Shirley Ellis 1,131,
   Jean Soderlund 1,087, Ruth Guerster 1,190

Men's Eight Player (8 games)
1. United States 12,691
   Dom DiCicco 1,558, Bob Hanson 1,643,
   Fred Vitali 1,621, John Handegard 1,609,
   Bob Glaser 1,591, Russ London 1,551,
   Butch Luther 1,667, Larry Rabkin 1,451

3. Mexico..4,317
Maralla Arzate 1,191, Ann Luisa Moelett 1,117
Irma Urrea 989, Angie Nunez 1,020

2. Mexico..12,502
Victor Castillo 1,566, Rogelio Cardenas 1,539,
Alfredo Diaz 1,485, Fernando Barocia 1,577,
Bernardo Bravo 1,581, Miguel Estrada 1,638,
Miguel Anaya 1,577, Mario Boneta 1,577

3. Venezuela 12,470
Ricardo Alvizu 1,593, Luis Castellanos 1,574,
Vicente Piccari 1,652, Jose Flores 1,514,
Pablo Hernandez 1,503, Carlos Lovera 1,566,
Rafael Fernandez 1,535, Pedro Hernandez 1,513

Women's Five Player

1. United States 5,474
Penny McClain 1,059, Ranae Adams 1,106,
Dixie Burmeister 1,094, Jacquline Kott 1,083,
Joan Holm 1,132
2. Australia 5,322
Ruth Guerster 1,097, Lillian Bruce 1,024,
Del Da-Re 1,054, Shirley Ellis 1,066,
Jean Soderlund 1,081
3. Venezuela 5,283
Ivonne Mayorca 1,081, Carmen Marchandet 962,
Judith Wagner 1,064, Mary Carmen Farias 1,068,
Carmina Reiner 1,108

Men's Five Player

1. United States 6,194
Butch Luther 1,320, Bob Glaser 1,197, Fred Vitali 1,218,
Bob Hanson 1,228, Dom DiCicco 1,234
2. Belgium..5,980
Edmond Clauws 1,187, Hubert Bessemans 1,172,
Rik Clerckx 1,283, Frans Labordery 1,157,
Louis Wildemeersch 1,181
3. Italy 5,948
Luigino Cangemi 1,130, Lino Braghieri 1,208,
Nicola DiPinto 1,233, Dario Barbieri 1,183,
Vittorio Noveletto 1,194

Women's Doubles

1. Japan 2,302
Yoshimi Fukuda 1,213, Michiko Horooka 1,089
2. United States 2,215
Penny McClain 1,139, Dixie Burmeister 1,076
3. United States 2,194
Jacquline Kott 1,125, Ranae Adams 1,069

Men's Doubles

1. Puerto Rico 2,520
Rolando Sebelen 1,231, Carlos Diaz 1,289
2. United States 2,478
Bob Glaser 1,274, John Handegard 1,204
3. Australia 2,474
Victor Bubniw 1,175, Graham Smith 1,299

Women's All Events

1. Ashie Gonzalez, Puerto Rico.....................4,535
2. Dixie Burmeister, United States 4,514
3. Penny McClain, United States...................4,471

Men's All Events

1. Ed Luther, United States........................5,963
2. Edmond Clauws, Belgium 5,825
3. Bob Glaser, United States.......................5,779

6th World Championships
Malmo, Sweden 1967
21 Nations, 161 men, 84 women

Women's Four Player

1. Finland 4,455
Eija Krogerus 1,133, Gundborg Liljegren 1,113,
Maire Rautakoski 1,120, Lea Hilokoski 1,089
2. Germany 4,398
Hettie Papenhoff 1,043, Christine Penkwitz 1,049,
Marion Forster 1,182, Anne Haefker 1,124
3. Belgium...4,318
Jeannine Coudere 1,069, Lea Vertsappen 1,158,
Nadine Kindermans 993, Agnes VandenBerghe 1,098

Men's Eight Player (8 games)

1. United States 12,403
Gene Raffel 1,472, Dennis Wright 1,541,
Mark Kuglitsch 1,593, Ron Wheeler 1,679,
Bob Pinkalla 1,518, Wayne Pinkalla 1,604,
Frank Perry 1,386, Les Zikes 1,610
2. Japan 12,360
Jyunnosuke Yamanaka 1,683, Syuij Araki 1,574,
Osamu Sugamachi 1,499, Kazuo Hayashi 1,619,
Ryoji Taruya 1,501, Seiji Kaneko 1,484,
Masasuke Tanaka 1,581, Tadakazu Handa 1,419
3. Mexico...12,245
Roberto Ocampo 1,490, Jesus Lopez 1,679,
Miguel Estrada 1,398, Manual Azcona 1,528,
Ramino Munoz 1,479, Avelino Martinez 1,559,
Emilio Galindo 1,481, Miguel Anaya 1,631

Women's Five Player

1. Finland 5,417
Eija Krogerus 1,165, Katri Hoivassilta 1,009,
Gundborg Liljegren 1,146, Maire Rautakoski 1,048,
Karin Selenius 463, Lea Hilokoski 586
2. United States 5,392
Carol Miller 1,045, Vivian Trumper 1,065,
Helen Weston 1,126, Jean Stehle 1,096,
Eleanor Jones 1,060

Men's Five Player

1. Finland 5,700
Kalevi Ihalainen 1,245, Matti Nieminen 1,103,
Erkki Lax 1,145, Pentti Koivula 1,096,
Pentti Virtanen 1,111
2. Japan 5,679
Jyunnosuke Yamanaka 1,120, Syuij Araki 1,187,
Osamu Sugimachi 1,096, Ryoji Taruya 1,195,
Kazuo Hayaski 1,071

3. Mexico..5,368
  Tea Orozco 1,067, Christina Rosas 1,166,
  Vicky Alonso 992, Alicia Sarabia 1,078,
  Irma Urrea 1,065

Women's Doubles
1. Mexico..2,328
  Tea Orozco 1,158, Alicia Sarabia 1,170
2. United States 2,296
  Jean Stehle 1,104, Helen Weston 1,192
3. Mexico..2,285
  Christina Rosas 1,074, Irma Urrea 1,211

Women's All Events
1. Helen Weston, United States....................4,585
2. Eija Krogerus, Finland............................4,577
3. Jean Stehle, United States.......................4,509

3. Great Britain 5,676
  David Pond 1,223, Chris Buck 1,158, Tony King 1,047,
  Terry Sullivan 1,047, David Waugh 497, Steve
  Russell 569

Men's Doubles
1. Great Britain 2,433
  David Pond 1,264, Jeff Morley 1,169
2. Mexico..2,416
  Miguel Estrada 1,202, Manuel Azcona 1,214
3. United States 2,414
  Bob Pinkalla 1,155, Wayne Pinkalla 1,259

Men's All Events
1. David Pond, Great Britain 5,708
2. Jyunnosuke Yamanaka, Japan 5,649
3. Wayne Pinkalla, United States 5,627

5th World Championships
Cuernavaca-Mexico City, Mexico 1963
19 Nations, 132 men, 45 women

Women's Four Player, American Style
1. Mexico..4,237
  Irma Urrea 1,098, Gracelia Aguirre 1,109,
  Sody Iruretagoyena 992, Mele Anaya 1,038
2. United States 4,042
  Ruth Redfox 1,029, Ann Heyman 978,
  Helen Shablis 1,033, Dot Wilkinson 1,002
3. Finland 3,933
  Eija Krogerus 1,042, Maire Rautakoski 1,019,
  Kaarina Piira 892, Kirsti Lamberg 980

Men's Eight Player (8 games)
1. United States 12,617
  Harry Lippe 1,620, Otto Niehus 1,530,
  Jim Schroeder 1,575, Bus Oswalt 1,558,
  Pat Porrini 1,487, Andy Hudoba 1,598,
  Jim Stefanich 1,596, Les Zikes 1,653
2. Mexico..12,111
  Carlos Moles 1,504, Guillermo Trevino 1,453,
  Dan Fluchiere 1,486, Higinio Ortiz 1,457,
  Avelino Martinez 1,614, Jesus Lopez 1,557,
  Gus Valle 1,486, Tito Reynolds 1,554
3. Venezuela 11,882
  Antonio Marcano 1,575, Jesus Urbaez 1,491,
  Enrique Lara 1,563, Fred Mata 1,523,
  Vicente Hernandez 1,435, Luis Aulestia 1,364,
  Rafael Martinez 1,488, Humberto Gallego 1,443

Women's Four Player, European Style
1. United States 4,300
  Ruth Redfox 1,037, Ann Heyman 943,
  Helen Shablis 1,201, Dot Wilkinson 1,119
2. Mexico..4,240
  Irma Urrea 1,062, Mele Anaya 1,103,
  Sody Iruretagoyena 1,004, Gracelia Aguirre 1,071
3. Finland 4,189
  Maire Rautakoski 1,057, Kaarina Piira 995,
  Eija Krogerus 1,034, Kirsti Lamberg 1,103

Men's Five Player
1. United States 5,786
  Les Zikes 1,133, Harry Lippe 1,086, Otto Niehus 1,232,
  Jim Stefanich 1,190, Bus Oswalt 1,145
2. Mexico..5,661
  Avelino Martinez 1,137, Jesus Lopez 1,156,
  Higinio Ortiz 1,158, Tito Reynolds 1,138,
  Gus Valle 1,072
3. Venezuela 5,587
  Felipe Prieto 1,040, Rafael Martinez 1,053,
  Antonio Marcano 1,196, Jesus Urbaez 1,124,
  Fred Mata 1,174

Women's Doubles
1. United States 2,270
  Helen Shablis 1,151, Dorothy Wilkinson 1,119
2. United States 2,104
  Ruth Redfox 1,023, Ann Heyman 1,081
3. Mexico..2,064
  Irma Urrea 1,041, Mele Anaya 1,023

Men's Doubles
1. United States 2,449
  Jim Schroeder 1,217, Bus Oswalt 1,232
2. Finland..2,368
  Tauno Nieminen 1,191, Pontii Virtanen 1,177
3. Mexico..2,329
  Jesus Lopez 1,161, Avelino Martinez 1,168

Women's All Events
1. Helen Shablis, United States 4,535
2. Chela Aquirre, Mexico...........................4,380
3. Dorothy Wilkinson, United States............4,277

Men's All Events
1. Les Zikes, United States 5,519
2. Jim Stefanich, United States...................5,515
3. Avelino Martinez, Mexico 5,502

4th World Championships
Hamburg, Germany 1960
14 Nations, 102 men

Men's Eight Player (8 Games)

1. Mexico 11,992
   Miguel Anaya 1,611, Tito Reynolds 1,575, Jesus Lopez
   1,523, Gustavo Alanis 1,518, Avelino Martinez 1,508,
   Carlos Bustani 1,502, Guillamo Orozco 1,491,
   Jose Arberas 1,264
2. Finland 11,938
   Eero Walden 1,514, Kalle Asukas 1,448, Onni Kyto
   1,515, Pekka Juutilainen 1,561, Rauno Manni 1,439,
   Stig Lindfors 1,535, Pekka Jaakkola 1,443,
   Eino Lahti 1,485
3. Sweden 11,860
   Ake Andersson 1,541, Carl-Gustav Carjo 1,412, Berndt
   Hellstrom 1,446, Nils Stromstedt 1,509, Gosta Algeskog
   1,500, Gunnar Hall 1,575, Tosten Petterson 1,441,
   Sune Westlund 1,436

Men's Doubles

1. Mexico 2,377
   Tito Reynolds 1,268, Miguel Anaya 1,106
2. Finland 2,334
   Kalle Asukas 1,201, Rauno Manni 1,133
3. Sweden 2,302
   Sune Westkind 1,169, Gunnar Hall 1,133

Men's Five Player

1. Venezuela 2,919
   Miguel Correa 638, Luis Garcia 591, Pedro Diaz 565,
   Jesus Urbaez 569, Jose Villamizar 556
2. Sweden 2,810
   Aka Andersson 571, Gosta Akgeskog 533, Gunnar
   Hall 556, Berndt Hellstrom 615, Carl-Gustav Carjo 535
3. Mexico 2,665
   Tito Reynolds 594, Miguel Anaya 567, Gustavo Alanis
   477, Avelino Martinez 494, Jesus Lopez 533

Men's All Events

1. Tito Reynolds, Mexico 4,963
2. Miguel Correa, Venezuela 4,904
3. Miguel Anaya, Mexico 4,896

3rd World Championships
Halsingborg, Sweden 1958
10 Nations, 99 men

Men's Eight Player (8 Games)

1. Sweden 12,560
   Berndt Hellstrom 1,674, Carl-Gustav Carjo 1,656,
   Gosta Algeskog 1,609, Sven Kallfelt 1,570, Henrik Berg
   1,550, Arne Reinodt 1,517, Aka Andersson 1,508,
   Evert Lindbergh 1,476
2. West Germany 12,278
   Willi Schuler 1,634, Alfred Plechaty 1,625, Hans Riedel
   1,618, Karl Sendelbach 1,551, Hans Greepler 1,493,
   Franz Dombrowski 1,477, Willy Laun 1,457, Fritz
   Frolich 1,423
3. Venezuela 12,264
   Jesus Urbaez 1,622, Luis Garcia 1,596, Miguel Corre
   1,584, Antonio Romero 1,580, Luis Aulestia 1,519,
   Jose Medina 1,469, Oswaldo Este 1,457, Miguel
   Raimondi 1,437

Men's Doubles

1. Sweden 2,459
   Evert Lindbergh 1,300, Carl-Gustaf Carje 1,159
2. Venezuela 2,449
   Jose Medina 1,237, Miguel Correa 1,212
3. Venezuela 2,436
   Luis Garcia 1,237, Miguel Raimondi 1,199

Men's Five Player

1. Finland 2,877
   Pekka Pietila 638, Osmo Koivunen 565, Rauno Manni
   564, Kalle Asukas 561, Tauno Nieminen 549
2. Sweden 2,839
   Gosta Algeskog 618, Sven Kallfelt 605, Evert Lindbergh
   590, Arne Reinodt 535, Nils Stromstedt 491
3. Mexico 2,838
   Tito Reynolds 606, Miguel Anaya 594, Antonio
   Rodriguez 566, Luis Mateios 557, Ignacio Anaya 521

Men's All Events

1. Kalle Asukas, Finland 5,034
2. Gosta Algeskog, Sweden 5,023
3. Bernt Hellstrom, Sweden 5,007

2nd World Championships
Essen, Germany 1955
6 Nations, 64 men

Men's Eight Player (8 Games)

1. Finland 11,910
   Antti Jokinen 1,593, Pekka Pietila 1,543, Artturi
   Paldanius 1,524, Odin Koskinen 1,507, Lauri Alen
   1,485, Matti Nieminen 1,480, Kalle Asukas 1,469, Yrjo
   Ilvespalo 1,309

Men's Five Player (3 Games)

1. West Germany 2,735
   Willie Laun 591, Peter Winkler 574, Alfred Plechaty,
   534, Willi Laun 527, Walter Freese 509

2. Sweden..................................11,754
   Henry Gustafsson 1,527, Nisse Backstrom 1,499, Gote
   Andersson 1,471, Sven Kallfelt 1,467, Gosta Algeskog
   1,478, Pelle Pihl 1,456, Ake Andersson 1,443, Eric
   Ericsson 1,413
3. West Germany..........................11,753
   Karl Sendelbach 1,560, Hans Riedel 1,537, Willi Laun
   1,500, Peter Winkler 1,462, Alfred Plechaty 534, Hans
   Eberhardt 1,434, Walter Freese 1,431, Gerhardt
   Dannecker 1,394

2. Finland...................................2,684
   Odin Koskinen 568, Matti Nieminen 548, Osmo
   Virtanen 543, Kalle Asukas 528, Pekka Pietila 497
3. Sweden....................................2,677
   Sven Kallfelt 583, Henry Gustafsson 572, Walter
   Ohlsson 532, Folke Nilsson 501, Pelle Pihl 489

Men's Doubles

1. Sweden.....................................2,362
   Pele Pihli 1,195, Fritiof Soderberg 1,167
2. Finland....................................2,319
   Yrio Ilvespalo 1,218, Artturi Paldanlius 1,101
3. West Germany 2,302
   Willi Laun 1,197, Peter Winkler 1,105

Men's All Events

1. Nisse Backstrom, Sweden..................4,838
2. Matti Nieminen, Finland..................4,793
   Henry Gustafsson, Sweden.................4,793

1st World Championships
Helsinki, Finland 1954
7 Nations, 58 men

Men's Eight Player (8 Games)

1. Sweden....................................12,171
   Gosta Algeskog 1,674, Nils Backstrom 1,552, Ake
   Hansson 1,547, Eric Ericsson 1,538, Folke Nilsson
   1,503, Gunnar Karlbom 1,484, Gote Andersson 1,462,
   Erland Ottosson 1411
2. Finland...................................12,025
   Osmo Koivunen 1,568, Ossi Sandholm 1,544, Onni
   Kyto 1,540, Kalle Asukas 1,515, Kauko Ahlstrom
   1,513, Odin Koskinen 1,454, Matti Tarkiala 1,450,
   Jouko Toivo 1,441
3. West Germany 11,691
   Peter Winkler 1,568, Klaus Pesoldt 1,506, Hans Riedel
   1,472, Gerhardt Dannecker 1,490, Karl Hartmann
   1,471, Karl Schaller 1,437, Karl Nesper 1,401, Karl
   Sendelbach 1,334

Men's Five Player

1. Sweden II.................................2,892
   Eric Ericsson 573, Nils Backstrom 583, Henry
   Gustafsson 530, Folke Nilsson 617, Aka Hansson 592
2. Sweden I..................................2,865
   Gunnar Karlbom 538, Sven Carlsson 537, Gote
   Andersson 538, Gosta Algeskog 646, Erland Ottosson
   606
3. Finland I.................................2,794
   Kalle Asukas 597, Kauko Ahlstrom 527, Toivo Sillanpaa
   490, Osmo Koivunen 571, Onni Kyto 609

Men's Doubles

1. Finland...................................2,380
   Osmo Koivunen 1,216, Odin Koskinen 1,164
2. Sweden....................................2,295
   Gosta Algeskog 1,151, Erland Ottosson 1,144
3. Finland...................................2,291
   Kauko Ahlstrom 1,192, Onni Kyto 1,099

Men's All Events

1. Gosta Algeskog, Sweden 4,892
2. Osmo Koivunen, Finland..................4,847
3. Kauko Ahlstrom, Finland.................4,813

FIQ World Tournament Records

Individual
24-Game Qualifying Series

Women		Men	
4,916	Janna Puhakka, Finland, 1995	5,496	Michael Sassen, The Netherlands, 1995
4,908	Cara Honeychurch, Australia, 1995	5,261	Rick Steelsmith, United States, 1987
4,894	Sandra Jo Shiery, United States, 1987	5,242	Mats Karlsson, Sweden, 1983

16-Game Match Play Series

Women		Men	
3,391	Celia Flores, Mexico, 1995	3,427	Chris Barnes, United States, 1995
3,389	Luz Adriana Leal, Colombia, 1995	3,426	Chen-Min Yang, Chinese Taipei, 1995
3,374	Asa Larsson, Sweden, 1995	3,395	Raymond Jansson, Sweden, 1995

16-Game Match Play Series Total*

Women
3,461 Celia Flores, Mexico, 1995
3,439 Luz Adrianna Leal, Colombia, 1995
3,419 Asa Larsson, Sweden, 1995
*Includes 10 bonus points for each victory.

Men
3,476 Chen-Min Yang, Chinese Taipei, 1995
3,447 Chris Barnes, United States, 1995
3,445 Raymond Janssen, Sweden, 1995
*Includes 10 bonus points for each victory.

Six-Game Series

Women
1,330 Cora Fiebig, United States, doubles event, 1987.
1,318 Debby Ship, Canada, singles event, 1995.
1,313 Mariela Alarza, Venezuela, doubles event, 1987.

Men
1,450 Michael Sassen, The Netherlands, trios event, 1995.
1,436 Rick Steelsmith, United States, trios event, 1987.
1,411 Rich Wonders, United States, trios event, 1983.

Three-Game Series

Women
700 Delia Milne, Singapore, doubles event, 1983.
694 Lena Sulkanen, Sweden, singles event, 1983.
691 Asa Larsson, Sweden, team event, 1983.
    Janna Puhakka, Finland, team event, 1995.

Men
774 Lars Oager, Denmark, trios event, 1987.
768 Andre Reyerse, The Netherlands,
    doubles event, 1987.
765 Rich Wonders, United States, trios event, 1983.

One Game

Women
289 Dorette Boelens, Netherlands, doubles event, 1987.
284 Sara Varas, Colombia, doubles event, 1995.
280 Cora Fiebig, United States, doubles event, 1987.

Men
300 Rick Steelsmith, United States, trios event, 1987.
299 Rick Steelsmith, United States,
    individual event, 1987.
298 Henry Tan, Singapore, team event, 1975.

Team Series—Six Games

Women's Five Player
6,011 United States, 1987
    Cora Fiebig 531, Nellie Glandon 1,198, M. Sue
    Holton 648, Karen Bender 1,188, Sandra Jo
    Shiery 1,276, Kathy Wodka 1,170
5,974 Finland, 1995
    Janna Puhakka 1,306, Pauline Aalto 1,199,
    Anu Peltola 1,092, Leena Pulliainen 1,256,
    Heta Maija Allen, 1,121
5,946 Sweden, 1987
    Asa Larsson 1,291, Monica Johansson 1,171,
    Gerda Ohman 1,183, Anette Hagre 1,183,
    Lena Sulkanen 1,118

Men's Five Player
6,355 Finland, 1983
    Mikko Kaartinen 1,220, Sam Anker 1,388,
    Martti Koskela 1,269, Hannu Narhi 1,250,
    Simo Vahakorpela 615, Ailo Votila 613
6,285 United States, 1983
    Tony Cariello 1,249, Gordon Vadakin 1,351,
    Rod Toft 1,229, Darold Meisel 1,242,
    Rich Wonders 1,214
6,282 The Netherlands, 1995
    Michael Sassen 1,326, Marcel Van den Bosch
    1,277, Niko Thienpondt 1,235, Geert Van Baest
    1,214, Maarten Krull 577, Erwin Groen 653

Women's Trios
3,626 Australia, 1995
    Cara Honeychurch 1,246, Sharon McLeish
    1,198, Sue Cassell 1,182
3,606 Malaysia, 1995
    Shalin Zulkifi 1,158, Lisa Kwan 1,222,
    Shirley Chow 1,226
3,603 United States, 1987
    M. Sue Holton 1,183, Karen Bender 1,237,
    Nellie Glandon 1,183

Men's Trios
3,954 The Netherlands, 1995
    Erwin Groen 1,231, Niko Thienpondt 1,273,
    Michael Sassen 1,450
3,899 Sweden, 1983
    Kenneth Andersson 1,333, Tony Rosenquist
    1,205, Mats Karlsson 1,361
3,897 The Philippines, 1983
    Paeng Nepomuceno 1,305, Raul Reformado
    1,396, Ollie Ongtawco 1,196

Women's Doubles
2,566 United States, 1987
    Cora Fiebig 1,330, Kathy Wodka 1,236
2,489 Thailand, 1995
    Kanit Kitchatham 1,293,
    Pletchara Kaewsuk 1,196
2,486 Sweden, 1987
    Asa Larsson 1,247, Annette Hagre 1,239

Men's Doubles
2,702 Sweden, 1995
    Raymond Jansssen 1,367, Tomas Leandersson
    1,335
2,638 Sweden, 1987
    Ulf Haemnaes 1,310, Ulf Bolleby 1,328
2,627 Australia, 1995
    Warren Stewart 1,328, Andrew Frawley 1,299

Team Series—Three Games

Women's Five Player

3,066 Sweden, 1983
Karin Glennert 534, Gerda Ohman 628, Asa Larsson 661, Lena Sulkanen 630, Yvonne Berndt 613

3,065 United States, 1987
M. Sue Holton 648, Sandra Jo Shiery 624, Nellie Glandon 614, Karen Bender 601, Kathy Wodka 578

3,020 Sweden, 1987
Asa Larsson 691, Monica Johansson 581, Gerda Ohman 586, Annette Hagre 623, Lena Sulkanen 539

Men's Five Player

3,218 Sweden, 1983
Kenneth Andersson 649, Lars Hedquist 676, Olle Svensson 552, Tony Rosenquist 695, Mats Karlsson 638

3,207 Finland, 1983
Mikko Kaartinen 620, Ailo Votila 613, Sam Anker 690, Martti Koskela 687, Hannu Narhi 597

3,168 Finland, 1987
Arvi Korhonen 633, Kari Jehkinen 591, Tom Hahl 699, Olli Tiainen 592, Mikko Kaartinen 653

Women's Trios

1,946 United States, 1987
M. Sue Holton 621, Karen Bender 662, Nellie Glandon 663

1,838 Mexico, 1987
Edda Piccini 613, Alejandra Prado 651, Mary Carmen Parra 574

1,818 United States, 1987
Cora Fiebig 598, Sandra Jo Shiery 667, Kathy Wodka 553

Men's Trios

2,059 Sweden, 1983
Kenneth Andersson 698, Tony Rosenquist 601, Mats Karlsson 760

2,007 United States, 1983
Rich Wonders 765, Darold Meisel 624, Tony Cariello 618

1,998 United States, 1987
Rick Steelsmith 740, Dan Nadeau 613, Duane Sandvick 645

Women's Doubles

1,293 Cora Fiebig 680, Kathy Wodka 613, United States, 1987

1,279 Asa Larsson 677, Annette Hagre 616, Sweden, 1987

1,279 Jane Amlinger 657, Catharine Willis 622, Canada, 1991

Men's Doubles

1,423 Ulf Haemnaes (737)-Ulf Bolleby (686), Sweden, 1987

1,386 Peter Panas (718)-Bernd Kornak (668), West Germany, 1983

1,355 Patric Wee (680)-Sam Goh (675), Singapore, 1987

Team Games

Women's Five Player

1,092 Singapore, 1991
Catherine Kang 212, Vicky Teh 265, Katherine Lee 223, Grace Young 186, Alice Tay 206

1,063 United States, 1987
Sandra Jo Shiery 211, Karen Bender 234, Nellie Glandon 211, Kathy Wodka 183, M. Sue Holton 224

1,058 Venezuela, 1987
Carmen Aguilar 190, Mariela Alarza 222, Liliana Rodriguez 245, Gabi Bigai 199, Gladys Fernandez 202

Men's Five Player

1,158 Finland, 1987
Arvi Korhonen 222, Kari Jehkinen 209, Tom Hahl 275, Olli Tiainen 241, Mikko Kaartinen 211

1,118 The Philippines, 1983
Paeng Nepomuceno 243, Vicente Sotto 235, Raul Reformado 188, Arnaldo San Jose 248, Ollie Ongtawco 204

1,107 Venezuela, 1983
Ruben Olivares 220, Henry Fuenmayor 235, Zenon Piatek 184, Pedro Cardozo 253, Rogelio Felice 215

Women's Trios

709 Mexico, Minerva Amezcua 193, Yascara Cerda 237, Sayuri Yamada 279, 1995

686 Australia, Cara Honeychurch 235, Sharon McLeish 230, Sue Cassell 221, 1995

684 Australia, Ann Marie Putney 219, Kelly Warren 201, Maxine Nable 264, 1995

Men's Trios

756 United States, Rick Steelsmith 300, Dan Nadeau 233, Duane Sandvick 223, 1987

754 United States, Tony Cariello 212, Darold Meisel 263, Rich Wonders 279, 1983

734 The Philippines, Raul Reformado 269, Ollie Ongtawco 258, Paeng Nepomuceno 207, 1983

Women's Doubles

504 Sweden, Asa Larsson 269, Annette Hagre 235, 1987

489 Austria, Renate Pekarek 225, Christa Kirschbaum 264, 1995

476 Thailand, Kanit Kitchatham 233, Phetchara Kaewsuk 243, 1995

Men's Doubles

511 Sweden, Ulf Haemnaes 297, Ulf Bolleby 214, 1987

508 Italy, Lorenzo Monti 264, Bartolomeo Caffaratti 244, 1983

503 Sweden, Tomas Leandersson 236, Raymond Jansson 267, 1995

FIQ American Zone Tournament Standings

12th FIQ American Zone Championships
Santa Domingo, Dominican Republic, 1997
18 Nations, 108 men, 88 women

Women's Five Player

1. United States..5,965
   Lisa Duenow 1,122, Becky Kregling 1,168, Lucy Giovinco-Sandelin 1,195, Lesia Moos 1,180, Lynda Norry 1,300
2. Colombia..5,757
   Maria Clara Salazar 1,164, Paola Gomez 1,210, Sara Vargas 1,042, Clara Guerrero 1,172, Luz Leal 1,169
3. Canada..5,734
   Jane Amlinger 1,176, Jennifer Willis 1,160, Sharon Tataryn 1,117, Linda Cuartas 1,114, Catharine Willis 1,167.

Men's Five Player

1. United States..6,190
   Vernon Peterson 1,181 Bruce Steffani 1,207 Brad Angelo 1,143 Brian Graham 1,252 Chris Barnes 1,407
2. Canada..5,911
   Joe Ciach 1,119 Howard Kotchie 1,179 Danyck Briere 1,049 Warren Rennox 1,184 Bill Rowe Jr. 1,380
   Venezuela...5,911
   Agustin De Faria 1,154 Joseph Fuentes 1,274 Jose Lander 1,073 Arturo Hernandez 1,218 Pedro Carreyo 1,192

Women's Trios

1. United States..3,770
   Brecky Kregling 1,323, Lucy Giovinco-Sandelin 1,281, Lesia Moos 1,166
2. Venezuela..3,565
   Margalit Mizrachi 1,198, Mirella Trasolini 1,155, Marcano, Venezuela 1,212
3. United States..3,541
   Lisa Duenow 1,100, Kendra Cameron 1,191, Lynda Norry 1,250

Men's Trios

1. United States 4,006
   Brad Angelo 1,266 Vernon Peterson 1,384 Chris Barnes 1,356
2. Canada..3,921
   Warren Rennox 1,411 Danyck Briere 1,208 Bill Rowe Jr. 1,302
3. United States..3,694
   Jerry Sikora 1,140 Bruce Steffani 1,289 Brian Graham 1,265

Women's Doubles

1. United States..2,481
   Lucy Giovinco-Sandelin 1,210, Lesia Moos 1,271
2. Colombia..2,442
   Maria Clara Salazar 1,240, Luz Leal, Colombia 1,202.
3. Mexico 2,366
   Teresa Piccini 1,201, /Maria Del Mar Rodriguez 1,165.

Men's Doubles

1. Canada 2,616
   Danyck Briere 1,241, Warren Rennox 1,375
2. United States 2,519
   Brad Angelo 1,170, Chris Barnes 1,349
3. Venezuela..2,513
   Joseph Fuentes 1,291, Arturo Hernandez 1,222

Women's Singles

1. Alicia Marcano, Venezuela.....................................1,273
2. Lesia Moos, U.S. 1,272
3. Maria Salazar, Colombia 1,266

Men's Singles

1. Brian Graham, U.S., ...1,408
2. Bill Rowe Jr., Canada, ...1,403
3. Bruce Steffani, U.S., ...1,364
   Jaime Almendro, Puerto Rico.....................................1,364

Women's All Events

1. Becky Kregling, United States.................................4,960
2. Lesia Moos, United States 4,889
3. Maria Clara Salazar, Colombia 4,842

Men's All Events

1. Chris Barnes, U.S. 5,451
2. Bill Rowe Jr., Canada..5,286
3. Warren Rennox, Canada 5,216

Women's Individual

1. Lynda Norry, United States
2. Maria Clara Salazar, Colombia
3. Maria Del Mar Rodriguez, Mexico

Salazar def. Rodriguez 199-154 and Norry def. Salazar 434-398 (two-game final).

Men's Individual

1. Chris Barnes, United States
2. Bill Rowe Jr. , Canada
3. Warren Rennox, Canada

Barnes def. Rennox 230-196 and Barnes def. Rowe 444-411 (two-game final).

11th American Zone Championships
Guadalajara, Mexico 1993
18 Nations, 106 men, 86 women

Women's Five Player
1. United States 5,851
   Tammy Turner 1,186, Nancy Ennis 1,166,
   Diana Williams 1,179, Joey Simpson 1,183,
   Stacy Robards 1,137
2. Canada 5,482
   Sandy Lowe 1,236, Debbie Ship 1,087,
   Carol Mielczarek 1,099, Catharine Willis 1,001,
   Connie Ward 549, Miriam Reed 510
3. Mexico..5,383
   Teresa Piccini 1,078, Lupita Gongora 1,085,
   Angelica Wong 1,025, Gabriela Sandoval 1,052,
   Edda Piccini 1,143

Men's Five Player
1. United States..6,148
   Tony Chapman 1,294, David Garber 1,229,
   Dan Nadeau 1,179, Vince Biondo 1,269,
   Sam Lantto 1,177
2. Mexico..6,028
   Alfonso Rodriguez 1,309, Daniel Falconi 1,227,
   Jesus Gutierrez 1,164, Jorge Siegrist 1,191,
   Roberto Silva 1,137
3. Canada 5,685
   Warren Rennox 1,119, Craig Woodhouse 1,204,
   Bill Rowe 1,179, Howard Kotchie 1,145,
   John Pavicic 1,038

Women's Trios
1. Canada..3,583
   Sandy Lowe 1,185, Carol Mielczarek 1,177,
   Connie Ward 1,221
2. United States 3,524
   Tammy Turner 1,192, Joey Simpson 1,125,
   Stacy Robards 1,207
3. Venezuela 3,435
   Miralla Trasolini 1,124, Gisela Sanchez 1,149,
   Mirella Alarza 1,162

Men's Trios
1. United States 3,824
   Vince Biondo 1,293, Anthony Chapman 1,247,
   Dan Nadeau 1,284
2. Canada..3,681
   Howard Kotchie 1,260, Warren Rennox 1,159,
   Craig Woodhouse 1,262
3. Canada..3,679
   John Pavicic 1,184, Jack Brace 1,205, Bill Lowe 1,290

Women's Doubles
1. Mexico..2,458
   Lupita Gongora 1,258, Edda Piccini 1,200
2. Mexico..2,384
   Gaby Sandoval 1,199, Angelica DeWong 1,185
3. Canada..2,376
   Miriam Reid 1,218, Connie Ward 1,158

Men's Doubles
1. Puerto Rico..2,486
   Jim Porter 1,295, Jaime Almendro 1,191
2. Costa Rica...2,348
   Rolando Vargas 1,190, Marco Odio 1,274
3. Mexico..2,463
   Roberto Silva 1,238, Jorge Siegrist 1,225

Women's Singles
1. Carmina Aleman, Panama 1,243
2. Carol Mielczarek, Canada 1,195
3. Lety Ituarte, Mexico...1,186

Men's Singles
1. Anthony Chapman, United States 1,306
2. Roberto Silva, Mexico 1,297
3. Arturo Hernandez, Venezuela 1,279

Women's All Events
1. Sandy Lowe, Canada..4,790
2. Tammy Turner, United States 4,677
3. Stacy Robards, United States 4,640

Men's All Events
1. Anthony Chapman, United States 5,103
2. Alfonso Rodriguez, Mexico 5,028
3. Vince Biondo, United States.................................4,949

Women's Individual
1. Sandy Lowe, Canada
2. Marie Ramirez, Costa Rica
3. Debbie Ship, Canada

Ramirez def. Ship 245-232, Ramirez def. Lowe 204-181 and
Lowe def. Ramirez 173-170 (challenger was required to
defeat top qualifier twice for the gold medal).

Men's Individual
1. Warren Rennox, Canada
2. Alfonso Rodriguez, Mexico
3. Vince Biondo, United States

Rodriguez def. Biondo 168-161 and Rennox def. Rodriguez
200-184.

10th American Zone Championships
Wichita, Kansas 1989
15 Nations, 94 men, 69 women

Women's Five Player
1. United State *5,965
   Lisa Duenow 1,122, Becky Kregling 1,168,
   Lucy Giovinco-Sandelin 1,195, Lesia Moos 1,180,
   Lynda NOrry 1,300
2. Colombia..*5,757
   Maria Clara Salazar 1,164, Paola Gomez 1,210,
   Sara Vargas 1,042, Clara Guerrero 1,172,
   Lutz Leal 1,169
3. Canada 5,734
   Jane Amlinger 1,176, Jennifer Willis 1,160,
   Sharon Tataryn 1,117, Linda Cuartas 1,114,
   Catharine Willis 1,167

Men's Five Player
1. Dominican Republic..............................6,180
   Rolly Sebelen 1,331, Rolando Sebelen 1,227,
   Manuel Santo 1,272, R. Antonio Sebelen 1,153,
   Miguel Ventura 1,197
2. United States 6,131
   Harry Mickelson 1,153, Ron Mohr 1,201,
   Gordon Vadakin 1,330, Darold Meisel 1,277,
   Brad Briggs 622, Mark Lewis 548
3. Mexico...5,991
   Alfonso Rodriguez 1,251, Victor Mar 1,140,
   Vicente Mendez 1,094, Marco Zepeda 1,333,
   Mario Boneta 1,173

Women's Trios
1. United State *3,770
   Becky Kregling 1,323, Lucy Giovinco-Sandelin 1,281,
   Lesia Moos 1,166
2. Venezuela..*3,565
   Margalit Mizrachi 1,198 Mirella Trasolini 1,155,
   Marcano Venezuela 1,212
3. United States *3,541
   Lisa Duenow 1,100, Kendra Cameron 1,191,
   Lynda Norry 1,250

Men's Trios
1. United States 4,024
   Mark Lewis 1,209, Ron Mohr 1,396,
   Harry Mickelson 1,419
2. Canada..3,819
   Howard Kotchie 1,270, Al Tone 1,302,
   Craig Woodhouse 1,247
3. Venezuela...3,769
   Jaime Bracho 1,330, Eduardo Pena 1,123,
   Pedro Carreyo 1,316

Women's Doubles
1. United States.......................................*2,481
   Lucy Giovinco-Sandelin 1,210, Lesia Moos 1,271
2. Colombia...*2,442
   Maria clara Salazar 1,240, Luz Leal, Colombia, 1,202
3. Mexico *2,366
   Teresa Piccini 1,201, Maria Del Mar Rodriquez 1,165

Men's Doubles
1. Mexico..2,709
   Victor Mar 1,323, Vincente Mendez 1,386
2. United States 2,702
   Gordon Vadakin 1,370, Darold Meisel 1,332
3. Canada...2,640
   Howard Kotchie 1,412, Marc Doi 1,228

Women's Singles
1. Alicia Marcano, Venequela *1,273
2. Lesia Moos, U.S. *1,272
3. Maria Salazar, Colombia *1,266

Men's Singles
1. Craig Woodhouse, Canada 1,383
2. Alfonso Rodriquez, Mexico 1,359
3. Ed Maurer, Canada 1,338

Women's All Events
1. Becky Kregling, United States................*4,960
2. Lesia Moos, United States *4,889
3. Maria Clara Salazar, Colombia *4,842

Men's All Events
1. Gordon Vadakin, United States 5,217
2. Marco Zepeda, Mexico.........................5,117
3. Ron Mohr, United States.......................5,077

Women's Individual
1. Lynda Norry, United States
2. Maria Clara Salazar, Colombia
3. Maria Del Mar Rodriguez, Mexico
Salzar def. Rodriquez 199-154 and Norry def. Salazar 434-398 (two-game final).

Men's Individual
1. Darold Meisel, United States
2. Brad Briggs, United States
3. Alfonso Rodriquez, Mexico
Briggs def. Rodriquez 220-202 and Meisel def. Briggs 509-391 (two games).

9th American Zone Championships
Bogota, Colombia 1985
17 Nations, 95 men, 92 women

Women's Five Player

1. Mexico...5,618
   Betty Madrigal 1,259, Alexandra Prado 1,077,
   Mato Puente 1,048, Edda Piccini 1,099,
   Mary Carmen Parra 1,135
2. United States.......................................5,392
   Regi Jonak 1,020, Peggy Funk 1,156,
   Susan Schottke 1,075, Kathy Butler 1,026,
   Debbie Bennett 1,115
3. Canada 5,361
   Fran Sanderson 1,009, Miriam Reid 1,074,
   Candy Marshall 1,047, Jan Crock 1,097,
   Joyce Campbell 1,134

Women's Trios

1. Mexico...3,204
   Betty Madrigal 1,108, Cony Lugo 1,034,
   Alexandra Prado 1,062
2. Mexico...3,171
   Mago Puente 1,094, Edda Piccini 1,035,
   Mary Carmen Parra 1,042
3. Panama 3,159
   Julietta Gutierrez 1,089, Graciela Bemporad 1,069,
   Sara Tom 1,001

Women's Doubles

1. Puerto Rico...2,214
   Ashie Gonzalez 1,065, Algie Badovinac 1,149
2. Venezuela 2,208
   Gladys Fernandez 1,119, Carmen Aguilar 1,089
3. United States.......................................2,197
   Regi Jonak 1,094, Debbie Bennett 1,103

Women's Singles

1. Carmen Aguilar, Venezuela...................1,177
2. Ashie Gonzalez, Puerto Rico 1,116
3. Tereza Muelas, Brazil.............................1,064

Women's Individual

1. Edda Piccini, Mexico
2. Debbie Bennett, United States
3. Jan Crock, Canada
4. Joyce Campbell, Canada
Crock def. Campbell 182-164, Bennett def. Crock 253-190
and Piccini def. Bennett 363-354 (two games).

Men's Five Player

1. United States.......................................5,836
   Larry Jones 1,119, Jack Jurek 1,236, Jeff Richgels 1,145,
   Dan Nadeau 1,245, Todd Savoy 524, Scott Thomsen 567
2. Venezuela 5,700
   Luis Serfaty 1,254, Hector Pappe 1,177,
   Nicolas Massazri 1,091, Angel Zugarramundi 1,058,
   Daniel Bonell 1,120
3. Bermuda 5,407
   Dean Lightbourn 1,033, Chris Bardgett 1,048,
   Steve Riley 1,056, Victor Thompson 1,155,
   Roger Raynor 1,115

Men's Trios

1. United States.......................................3,453
   Larry Jones 1,131, Todd Savoy 1,150,
   Jeff Richgels 1,172
2. United States.......................................3,353
   Jack Jurek 1,113, Dan Nadeau 1,175,
   Scott Thomsen 1,065
3. Canada...3,297
   Randy Kostenuk 1,024, Al Dickinson 1,184,
   Robin Edge 1,089

Men's Doubles

1. United States.......................................2,303
   Dan Nadeau 1,188, Scott Thomsen 1,115
2. Bahamas..2,228
   Clarence Wallace 1,119, Ivan Bethel 1,109
3. United States.......................................2,225
   Todd Savoy 1,058, Jack Jurek 1,167

Men's Singles

1. Juan Roquebert, Panama 1,200
2. Jairo Ocampo, Colombia 1,191
3. Reynolds Ando, Argentina 1,173

Men's Individual

1. Enrique Sepulveda, Mexico
2. Larry Jones, United States
3. Jaime Almendro, Puerto Rico
4. Chris Bardgett, Bermuda
Jones def. Bardgett 220-147, Jones def. Almendro 189-178;
and Sepulveda def. Jones 383-331 (two games).

8th American Zone Championships
Winnipeg, Canada 1981
12 Nations, 69 men, 72 women

Women's Five Player

1. United States.......................................5,336
   Cora Fiebig 1,014, Barbara Walker 1,090,
   Mary Mohacsi 1,042, Annese Kelly 1,148,
   Jean Havlish 1,042
2. Venezuela 5,273
   Ana Viera 1,049, Leonor Castillo 1,005,
   Morelia Lopez 971, Gladys Fernandez 1,155,
   Gerardy Pappe 1,093

Men's Five Player

1. United States.......................................6,045
   Jerry Edwards 1,243, Steve Fehr 1,208, Bill Foster 1,165,
   Rich Wonders 1,262, Chris Neidert 1,167
2. Venezuela 6,003
   Pedro Carreyo 1,192, Gustavo Manrique 1,198,
   Amleto Monacelli 1,184, Hector Pappe 1,208,
   Ruben Ghiragossian 1,221

3. Canada 5,192
Joanne Walker 1,100, Cathy Townsend 1,028,
Lorna Pollock 1,050, Simone Hindmarsh 991,
Wendy Zielonka 1,023

Women's Trios

1. Canada...3,362
Lorna Pollock 1,080, Simone Hindmarsh 1,156,
Joanne Walker 1,126
2. Panama 3,246
Mary Acosta 1,062, Edissa Andrade 1,168,
Yvonne Champsaur 1,016
3. Venezuela 3,192
Morelia Lopez 1,066, Gladys Fernandez, 1,049
Gerardy Pappe 1,077
United States
Cora Fiebig 1,096, Donna Dillon 965,
Jean Havlish 1,131

Women's Doubles

1. United States 2,274
Barbara Walker 1,191, Annese Kelly 1,083
2. Panama 2,145
Rosemary Piper 1,014, Julietta Gutierrez 1,131
3. Venezuela No. 1 2,141
Ana Viera 1,006, Morelia Lopez 1,135
Venezuela No. 2
Gladys Fernandez 1,065, Gerardy Pappe 1,076

Women's Singles

1. Mary Mohacsi, United States.................1,265
2. Simone Hindmarsh, Canada 1,145
3. Cora Fiebig, United States....................1,143

Women's Individual Event

1. Barbara Walker, United States
2. Edda (Boneta) Piccini, Mexico
3. Gladys Fernandez, Venezuela
4. Annese Kelly, United States
(Boneta) Piccini def. Kelly 199-194, Piccini def. Fernandez
183-180 and Walker def. Piccini 356-348 (two games).

3. Canada 5,739
Steve Lee 1,160, Don Wira 1,217, Dan Russo 1,154,
Bob Puttick 1,186, Rick Hughes 470, Ed Maurer 552

Men's Trios

1. Mexico...3,555
Mario Boneta 1,169, Agustin Garzak 1,184,
Alfonso Rodriquez 1,202
2. Mexico 3,531
Roberto Lopez 1,179, Antonio Rivas 1,243,
Leon Perez 1,109
3. Puerto Rico.......................................3,524
Eddie Garofalo 1,188, Antonio Vidal 1,114,
Jaime Almendro 1,222

Men's Doubles

1. Canada...2,445
Bob Puttick 1,312, Don Wira 1,133
2. Mexico 2,392
Antonio Rivas 1,229, Alfonso Rodriguez 1,163
3. Panama 2,389
David Malca 1,061, Tito de la Guardia 1,328

Men's Singles

1. Steve Fehr, United States 1,385
2. Chris Neidert, United States 1,280
3. Rich Wonders, United States..................1,274

Men's Individual

1. Bob Puttick, Canada
2. Steve Fehr, United States
3. Pedro Carreyo, Venezuela
4. Jose Arzu, Guatemala
Carreyo def. Arzu 168-160, Puttick def. Carreyo 205-185
and Puttick def. Fehr 454-431 (two games).

7th American Zone Championships
Panama City, Panama 1977
17 Nations, 150 men, 106 women

Women's Six-Player

1. United States 6,527
Lauren LaCost 1,167, Betty Brennan 1,118,
Linda Hansen 1,086, Cindy Schuble 1,082,
Lucy Giovinco 1,077, Deborah Cook 997
2. Canada...6,404
Norah Lee 1,163, Lorna Pollock 1,071,
Marilyn Hayden 1,042, Adeline Armstrong 1,033,
Lillian Hilton 978, Shirley Mickoski 1,117
3. Mexico...6,176
Ana Sapina 1,125, Elena Solis 1,076,
Ana Angulo 1,062, Olga Flores 1,002,
Margarita Saaib 972, Refugio Escutia 939

Men's Eight Player (8 games)

1. United States 12,689
Bob Roy 1,645, Wade Smith 1,618, Dale Euwer 1,618,
Al Cohn 1,596, Frank Gadaleto 1,584,
Jim Lindquist 1,562, Mickey Spiezio 1,540,
Sam Ferrell 1,535
2. Mexico 12,542
Mario Boneta 1,647, Alfonso Rodriguez 1,629,
Jorge Figueroa 1,606, Rodolfo Leon 1,591,
Francisco Issa 1,582, Fernando Barocio 1,555,
Humberto Montemayor 1,475, Angel Makutonin 1,457
3. Panama 12,322
John Bates 1,631, Tito de la Guardia 1,627,
Roberto Malek 1,546, Octavio Chang 1,532,
Jaime Mendoza 1,507, Alberto Cruz 1,501,
Tomas Barria 1,490, Alfredo Boyd 1,488

Women's Five Player

1. United States 5,440
   Cindy Schuble 1,196, Betty Brennan 1,093,
   Lucy Giovinco 1,062, Linda Hansen 1,060,
   Lauren LaCost 1,029
2. Canada 5,371
   Norah Lee 1,125, Lillian Hilton 1,079,
   Shirley Mickoski 1,072, Adeline Armstrong 1,049,
   Marilyn Hayden 1,046
3. Puerto Rico...5,200
   Sylvia Reyna 1,066, Judy Perez 1,058,
   Aida Gonzalez 1,055, Maria LaSalle 1,049,
   Josefina Montero 972

Women's Doubles

1. United States 2,283
   Lucy Giovinco 1,104, Lauren LaCost 1,179
2. United States 2,245
   Betty Charles 1,176, Cindy Schuble 1,069
3. Canada..2,205
   Shirley Mickoski 1,088, Lillian Hilton 1,117

Women's All Events

1. Cindy Schuble, United States 4,512
2. Betty Charles, United States 4,497
3. Norah Lee, Canada 4,439

Men's Five Player

1. United States 6,102
   Dale Euwer 1,276, Jim Lindquist 1,257,
   Mickey Spiezio 1,200 Al Cohn 1,186, Bob Roy 579,
   John Corbin 604
2. Guatemala 5,647
   Jose Arzu 1,224, Miguel Aguilar 1,145,
   Hans Kissner 1,121, Roberto Alonso 1,117,
   Rolando Conde 1,040
3. Venezuela 5,628
   Fernando Chagin 1,260, Rogelio Felice 525,
   Jorge Gosset 1,123, Eduardo Pena 510,
   Luis Deadessis 548, Porfino Garcia 587, Vicente Picari
   1,075

Men's Doubles

1. United States 2,585
   Dale Euwer 1,316, Jim Lindquist 1,269
2. Venezuela 2,571
   Fernando Chagrin 1,208, Jorge Gossett 1,363
3. United States 2,551
   Frank Gadaleto 1,258, Mickey Spiezio 1,293

Men's All Events

1. Dale Euwer, United States.....................................5,921
2. Wade Smith, United States 5,788
3. Alan Tone, Canada..5,713

6th American Zone Championships
Caracas, Venezuela 1974
16 Nations, 129 men, 66 women

Women's Four Player

1. Venezuela 4,459
   Nancy Beherens 1,281, Carmen Marchandet 1,080,
   Gerardy Troconis 1,073, Edilia Martin 1,025
2. Canada 4,309
   Cathy Townsend 1,137, Joyce Stoddart 1,084,
   Lillian Hilton 1,066, Joanne Walker 1,022
3. United States 4,307
   Norma Rittelmeyer 1,104, Mary Mohacsi 1,090,
   Lila Lambert 1,060, Joan Holm 1,053

Men's Eight Player (8 games)

1. Venezuela 12,948
   Carlos Lovera 1,774, Ricardo Alvizu 1,696,
   Enrique Lander 1,673, Alvaro Galindo 1,613,
   Hector Pappe 1,595, Pedro Arandia 1,582,
   Enrique Fortoul 1,519, Andres Gimenez 1,496
2. United States 12,517
   Mac Lowry 1,613, Virg Enger 1,609, Jim Paine 1,600,
   Ron Woolet 1,570, Bob Mills 1,569, Roger Dalkin 1,541,
   Bob Hanson 1,525, Bud DeLuca 1,490
3. Puerto Rico...11,848
   Eddie Garofalo 1,565, Pepe Blanco 1,520,
   John Basaraba 1,517, Francisco Perez 1,494,
   Rolando Sebelen 1,487, Paco Rosa 1,477,
   Frank Betancourt 1,439, Tofito Iraola 1,349

Women's Five Player

1. United States 5,857
   Mary Mohacsi 1,193, Norma Rittelmeyer 1,087,
   Lila Lambert 1,216, Joan Holm 1,190,
   Olga Gloor 1,171
2. Venezuela 5,471
   Nancy Beherens 1,057, Carmen Marchandet 1,156,
   Gerardy Troconis 1,168, Edilia Martin 1,053,
   Omaira Leon 1,037
3. Canada 5,292
   Cathy Townsend 1,175, Joanne Walker 1,092,
   Lillian Hilton 1,005, Joyce Stoddart 991,
   Adelaide Armstrong 1,029

Men's Five Player

1. United States.......................................6,200
   Virg Enger 1,263, Ron Woolet 1,280, Jim Paine 1,197,
   Bob Mills 1,281, Mac Lowry 1,179
2. Venezuela 6,062
   Ricardo Alvizu 1,055, Pedro Arandia 1,313,
   Enrique Lander 1,348, Alvaro Galindo 1,153,
   Carlos Lovera 1,193
3. Mexico..5,932
   Javier Guitterez 1,258, Bernardo Bravo 1,118,
   Alfonso Rodriguez 1,232, Tomas Barria 1,169,
   Benny Corona 1,155

Women's Doubles
1. Canada..2,285
   Joanne Walker 1,182, Cathy Townsend 1,103
2. United States.....................................2,259
   Joan Holm 1,115, Olga Gloor 1,144
3. United States.....................................2,175
   Norma Rittelmeyer 979, Mary Mohacsi 1,196

Women's All Events
1. Olga Gloor, United States 4,679
2. Mary Mohacsi, United States................4,649
3. Lila Lambert, United States 4,535

Men's Doubles
1. United States 2,606
   Virg Enger 1,408, Jim Paine 1,198
2. United States 2,563
   Bob Mills 1,232, Mac Lowry 1,331
3. United States 2,445
   Ron Woolet 1,261, Bob Hanson 1,184

Men's All Events
1. Ron Woolet, United States 6,047
2. Virg Enger, United States.....................6,016
3. Enrique Lander, Venezuela 5,940

5th American Zone Championships
San Juan, Puerto Rico 1969
9 Nations, 85 men, 34 women

Women's Five Player
1. United States 5,272
   Annese Kelly 1,052, Rosemary Losee 1,073,
   Irene Monterosso 1,066, Neva Running Wolf 993,
   Grace Werkmeister 1,088
2. Puerto Rico.......................................5,087
   Nidia Resto 1,003, Fina Montero 971,
   Ashie Gonzalez 1,015, Marga Benitez 1,140,
   Silvia Reyna 958
3. Mexico...4,965
   Irma Urrea 1,034, Ana Luisa Morlett 985,
   Luz Torres 1,045, Machila Diaz 452, Alicia Sarabia 449,
   Marlla Arzate 1,000

Women's Four Player
1. United States 4,210
   Grace Werkmeister 1,061, Janie Leszczynski 1,045,
   Rosemary Losee 1,067, Irene Monterosso 1,037
2. Venezuela 4,075
   Hilda Moreno 1,055, Elizabeth Espinosa 1,072,
   Carmina Reiner 1,065, Rosa Angulo 883
3. Mexico...3,928
   Irma Urrea 1,121, Ana Luisa Morlett 970, Luz Torres 947,
   Alicia Sarabia 890

Women's Doubles
1. United States 2,170
   Irene Monterosso 1,074, Rosemary Losee 1,096
2. United States 2,151
   Annese (Dunleavy) Kelly 1,123, Neva Running Wolf
   1,028
3. Puerto Rico 2,112
   Marga Benitez 1,140, Ashie Gonzalez 972

Women's All Events
1. Annese Kelly, United States 4,387
2. Rosemary Losee, United States..................4,385
3. Irene Monterosso, United States...............4,353

Men's Eight Player (8 games)
1. United States 11,996
   Dave Beck 1,569, Greg Campbell 1,429,
   Jack Curry 1,639, Charles Guedel 1,343,
   Eddie Jackson 1,586, Ralph Nicol 1,466,
   Ed Rosser 1,348, Bruce Sherman 1,616
2. Venezuela 11,626
   Jose Espinoza 1,445, Jose Camargo 1,478,
   Carlos Lovera 1,452, Luis Mayaudon 1,498,
   Marcos Navas 1,344, Luis Graterol 1,460,
   Miguel Correa 1,526, Francisco Ferraro 1,423
3. Mexico...11,459
   Tito Reynolds 1,564, Enrique Nieto 1,446,
   Miguel Estrada 1,390, Carlos Villareal 1,490,
   Catarino Garza 1,348, Juventino Obezo 1,341,
   Rafael Vazquez 1,415, Gustavo Alanis 1,465

Men's Five Player
1. Mexico...5,528
   Tito Reynolds 1,107, Enrique Nieto 1,159,
   Carlos Villareal 1,052, Hector Tlapanco 1,178,
   Rafael Vazquez 528, Gustavo Alanis 504
2. Puerto Rico 5,493
   Eddie Garofalo 1,147, Carlos Diaz 1,155,
   Rolando Sebelen 1,076, Luis Velez 1,068,
   Tofito Iraola 1,047
3. United States 5,489
   Dave Beck 1,114, Jack Curry 986, Ralph Nicol 1,134,
   Ed Rosser 1,108, Bruce Sherman 1,147

Men's Doubles
1. Puerto Rico 2,356
   Luis Valez 1,210, Tofita Iraola 1,146
2. United States 2,298
   Jack Curry 1,155, Eddie Jackson 1,143
3. Colombia 2,297
   Juan Arengo 1,216, Javier Alvarez 1,081

Men's All Events
1. Dave Beck, United States 5,435
2. Bruce Sherman, United States...................5,415
3. Eddie Jackson, United States 5,358

4th American Zone Championships
Guatemala City, Guatemala 1966
9 Nations, 84 men, 33 women

Women's Five Player

1. United States 5,148
   Sue Riley 1,037, Ann Brown 1,018, Lois Yut 954,
   Mary Ann Chew 1,029, Laura Mead 1,110
2. Mexico...5,117
3. Puerto Rico..4,933

Women's Four Player

1. United States 4,320
   Betty Remmick 1,036, Laura Mead 1,013,
   Sue Riley 1,219, Ann Brown 1,052
2. Mexico...4,300
3. Venezuela...4,175

Women's Doubles

1. Mexico...2,237
   Irma Urrea 1,096, Tere Vargas 1,141
2. United States 2,185
   Betty Remmick 1,116, Lois Yut 1,069
3. United States 2,179
   Sue Riley 1,075, Laura Mead 1,104

Women's All Events

1. Irma Urrea, Mexico 4,569
2. Sue Riley, United States............................4,353
3. Betty Remmick, United States....................4,322

Men's Eight Player

1. United States 12,161
   Dan Glus 1,526, Ken Dorencamp 1,484,
   George Kopko 1,492, Tom Hathaway 1,627,
   Dan Slak 1,477, Buzz Bosler 1,570, Ken Roeth 1,510,
   Ray Mazzei 1,475
2. Mexico...11,864
3. Venezuela...11,773

Men's Five Player

1. Venezuela...5,668
   Miguel Correa 1,157, Pablo Hernandez 1,031,
   Luis Aulestia 1,088, Jesus Urbaez 1,320,
   Oswaldo Este 1,070
2. United States 5,604
   Ken Dorencamp 1,135, Dan Glus 1,181,
   Ray Mazzei 1,060, Joe Traficante 1,073,
   Tom Hathaway 1,155
3. Mexico...5,592

Men's Doubles

1. Mexico...2,471
   Manuel Guijarro 1,236, Roberto Ocampo 1,235
2. United States 2,404
   George Kopko 1,307, Joe Traficante 1,097
3. United States 2,329
   Ken Dorencamp 1,151, Dan Glus 1,178

Men's All Events

1. Avelino Martinez, Mexico 5,575
2. Tom Hathaway, United States 5,561
3. Manual Guijarro, Mexico 5,544

3rd American Zone Championships
Caracas, Venezuela 1964
14 Nations, 88 men, 31 women

Women's Five Player

1. Mexico...5,105
   Irma Urrea 1,017, Tere Vargas 1,072,
   Alicia Sarabia 1,036, Josefina Dominguez 979,
   Mele Anaya 1,001
2. Venezuela...4,923
   Leonor Fernandez 1,015, Enriqueta Sanchez 950,
   Clarysa Padron 960, Esther Dugarte 928,
   Araminta Camacho 1,070
3. United States 4,896
   Virginia Thoms 1,090, Ann Sherman 971,
   Mary Ann Mullen 902, Eileen Skidmore 960,
   Frances Colohan 973

Women's Four Player

1. Puerto Rico..4,081
   Fina Montero 1,031, Mayda Sacarello 1,003,
   Nydia Resto 956, Frances Perez 1,091
2. Mexico...4,041
   Alicia Sarabia 973, Irma Urrea 1,067, Tere Vargas 936,
   Mele Anaya 1,065

Men's Six Player

1. United States 7,012
   Les Zikes 1,235, Joe Foster 1,233, Jim Stefanich 1,101,
   Larry Crake 1,188, Bob Murphy 1,083,
   Les Rothbarth 1,172
2. Mexico...6,845
   Juan Castilleja 1,076, Carlos Moles 1,083,
   Manual Guijarro 1,103, Ramior Munoz 1,159,
   Gustavo Valle 1,188, Tito Reynolds 1,210
3. Venezuela...6,517
   Jorge Jimenez 1,091, Vincente Hernandez 1,016,
   Luis Pineda 1,117, Nicolas Espana 1,154,
   Miguel Correa 1,108, Jesus Urbaez 1,031

Men's Five Player

1. United States 5,620
   Joe Foster 1,187, Larry Crake 1,117,
   Les Rothbarth 1,107, Bob Murphy 464,
   Pat Russo 531, Les Zikes 1,214
2. Venezuela...5,508
   Miguel Correa 1,161, Luis Pineda 1,112,
   Nicolas Espana 1,150, Jesus Urbaez 1,048,
   Vincente Hernandez 1,037

3. Venezuela 3,975
Karelia Lozano 933, Enriqueta Sanchez 969,
Leonor Fernandez 1,054, Araminta Camacho 1,019

3. Mexico...5,490
Carlos Moles 1,093, Ramiro Munoz 1,111,
Manuel Guijarro 1,122, Gustavo Valle 1,053,
Tito Reynolds 1,097

Women's Doubles

1. Venezuela 2,135
Leonar Fernandez 1,085, Arminta Camacho 1,050
2. Peru 2,094
Mecha Arana 1,061, Joy Escobar 1,033
3. Mexico..2,091
Alicia Scarabia 988, Gloria Martinez 1,103

Men's Doubles

1. United States 2,453
Les Zikes 1,206, Jim Stefanich 1,247
2. Mexico..2,357
Tito Reynolds 1,176, Gustavo Valle 1,181
3. Venezuela 2,329
Miguel Correa 1,154, Jesus Urbanez 1,175

Women's All Events

1. Alicia Sarabia, Mexico 4,237
2. Mele Anaya, Mexico 4,208
3. Frances Perez, Puerto Rico 4,175

Men's All Events

1. Les Zikes, United States 5,217
2. Joe Foster, United States 5,146
3. Jim Stefanich, United States.................5,064

2nd American Zone Championships*
Lima, Peru 1962

Women's Four Player, American Style

1. Mexico...4,312
2. Puerto Rico.......................................3,966
3. Peru..3,717

Men's Six Player

1. Mexico...6,790
2. Venezuela 6,782
3. Puerto Rico.......................................6,614

Women's Four Player, European Style

1. Mexico...4,470
2. Puerto Rico.......................................3,976
3. Peru..3,828

Men's Five Player

1. Venezuela 5,534
2. Mexico...5,376
3. United States 5,200

Women's Doubles

1. Mexico..2,165
Josephina Dominguez, Irma Urrea
2. Mexico...2,119
Gracelia Aguirre, Maria Anaya
3. Puerto Rico.......................................2,026
J. Loughram, L. Corrfa

Men's Doubles

1. Mexico..2,463
Tito Reynolds, Gustavo Valle
2. Venezuela 2,435
Jesus Urbanez, Miguel Raimondi
3. Mexico..2,341
Avelino Martinez, Luis Christmann

Women's All Events

1. Maria Anaya, Mexico............................4,346
2. Irma Urrea, Mexico 4,254
3. Josefina Dominguez, Mexico 4,245

Men's All Events

1. Jesus Urbaez, Venezuela......................5,122
2. Avelino Martinez, Mexico 5,121
3. Gustavo Valle, Mexico 5,116

1st American Zone Championships*
Mexico City 1961

Men's Six Player

1. Venezuela 6,655
2. Puerto Rico.......................................6,621
3. Mexico..6,496

Men's Five Player

1. Mexico...5,563
2. Puerto Rico.......................................5,298
3. Venezuela 5,277

Women's Doubles

1. Mexico..2,134
Josephina Dominguez, Olivia Hernandez
2. Puerto Rico.......................................2,054
Nilda Terres, Frances Perez
3. Mexico..2,033
Gracelia Aguirre, Maria Anaya

Men's Doubles

1. Mexico..2,285
Avelino Martinez, Jaime Fuentes
2. Guatemala...2,282
Luis Echivarria, Miguel Brandenburg
3. Chile..2,240
T. Seagars, L. Franck

Women's All Events

1. Maria Anaya, Mexico............................4,559
2. Gracella Aguirre, Mexico......................4,541
3. Josefina Dominguez, Mexico 4,501

Men's All Events

1. Don Yandell, Puerto Rico 5,110
2. Tito Reynolds, Mexico 5,080
3. Jaime Fuentes, Mexico 4,922

*The United States was represented by U.S. military personnel on a guest basis.

FIQ American Zone Tournament Records

Individual
24-Game Series, highest by individuals

Women		Men	
4,968	Linda Graham, United States, 1989.	5,451	Chris Barnes, United States, 1997.
4,960	Becky Kregling, United States, 1997.	5,286	Bill Rowe Jr., Canada, 1997.
4,911	Maureen Webb, United States, 1989.	5,217	Gordon Vadakin, United States, 1989.

15-Game Match Play

Women		Men	
3,232	Patty Ann, United States, 1989	3,411	Darold Meisel, United States, 1989.
3,128	Linda Graham, United States, 1989	3,294	Brad Briggs, United States, 1989.
3,116	Debbie McMullen, United States, 1989	3,266	Alfonso Rodriquez, Mexico, 1989.

15-Game Match Play Total*

Women		Men	
3,429	Sandi Lowe, Canada, 1993.	3,536	Darold Meisel, United States, 1989.
3,332	Patty Ann, United States, 1989.	3,399	Brad Briggs, United States, 1989.
3,256	Maria La Paz, Costa Rica, 1993.	3,336	Alfonso Rodriguez, Mexico, 1989.
*10 bonus points for each victory.		*10 bonus points for each victory.	

Six-Game Series

Women		Men	
1,323	Becky Kregling, United States, three-woman team event, 1997.	1,419	Harry Mickelson, United States, three-man team event, 1989.
1,313	Patty Ann, United States, five-woman team event, 1989.	1,412	Howard Kotchie, Canada, singles event, 1989.
1,309	Sara Alonso, Mexico, two-woman team event, 1989.	1,411	Warren Rennox, Canada, trios event, 1997.

Three-Game Series

Women		Men	
704	Sandi Lowe, Canada, match play, 1993	772	Alfonso Rodriquez, Mexico, singles event, 1989.
682	Sara Alonso, Mexico, singles event, 1989.	770	Craig Woodhouse, Canada, singles event, 1989.
672	Maureen Webb, United States, two-woman team event, 1989.	762	Bill Rowe Jr., Canada, singles event, 1997.

One-Game

Women		Men	
297	Patty Ann, United States, match play, 1989.	300	Alfonso Rodriques, Mexico, singles event, 1989.
280	Jane Amlinger, Canada, match play, 1989.		Howard Kotchie, Canada, doubles event, 1989.
279	Zussette DeMachon, Guatemala, singles, 1997.		Chris Barnes, United States, team event, 1997.

Team Series—Six Games

Women's Five Player		Men's Five Player	
6,067	United States, 1989 Patty Ann 670, Debbie McMullen 1,181, Linda Graham 1,250, Therese Abair 511, Lynda Norry 1,204, Maureen Webb 1,251	6,200	United States, 1974 Ron Woolet 1,280, Jim Paine 1,197, Mac Lowry 1,179, Bob Mills 1,281, Virg Enger 1,263,
5,965	United States, 1997 Lisa Duenow 1,122, Becky Kregling 1,168 Lucy Giovinco-Sandelin 1,195, Lesia Moos 1,180, Lynda Norry 1,300	6,190	United States, 1997 Vernon Peterson 1,181, Bruce Steffani 1,207 Brad Angelo 1,143, Brian Graham 1,252 Chris Barnes 1,407
5,857	United States, 1974 Norma Rittelmeyer 1,087, Lila Lambert 1,216, Mary Mohacsi 1,193, Olga Gloor 1,171, Joan Holm 1,190	6,180	Dominican Republic, 1989 Rolly Sebelen 1,331, Rolando Sebelen 1,227, Manuel Santo 1,272, R. Antonio Sebelen 1,153, Miguel Ventura 1,197

Women's Trios

3,770 United States, Becky Kregling 1,323, Lucy Giovinco-Sandelin 1,281, Lesia Moos 1,166, 1997
3,671 United States, Linda Graham 1,298, Therese Abair 1,208, Patty Ann 1,165, 1989
3,583 Canada, Carol Meilczarek 1,177, Connie Ward

Women's Doubles

2,545 Mexico, Sara Alonso 1,309, Edda Piccini 1,236, 1989
2,504 United States, Debbie McMullen 1,224, Maureen Webb 1,280, 1989
2,481 United States, Lucy Giovinco-Sandelin 1,210, Lesia Moos 1,271

Men's Trios

4,024 United States, Mark Lewis 1,209, Ron Mohr 1,396, Harry Mickelson 1,419, 1989
4,006 United States, Brad Angelo 1,266, Vernon Peterson 1,384, Chris Barnes 1,356, 1997
3,921 Canada, Warren Rennox 1,411, Danyck Brieie 1,208, Bill Rowe Jr. 1,302, 1997

Men's Doubles

2,709 Mexico, Victor Mar 1,323, Vincente Mendez 1,386, 1989
2,702 United States, Gordon Vadakin 1,370, Darold Meisel 1,332, 1989
2,640 Canada, Howard Kotchie 1,412, Marc Doi 1,228, 1989

Team Series—Three Games

Women's Five Player

3,089 United States, Patty Ann 670, Debbie McMullen 559, Linda Graham 627, Lynda Norry 608, Maureen Webb 626, 1989
3,025 United States, Tammy Turner, Nancy Ennis, Diana Williams, Joey Simpson, Stacy Robards, 1993
2,988 United States, Norma Rittelmeyer 577, Lila Lambert 617, Mary Mohacsi 619, Olga Gloor 609, Joan Holm 566, 1974

Women's Trios

1,892 United States, Becky Kregling, 654, Lucy Giovinco-Sandelin 663, Lesia Moos, 575, 1997
1,889 United States, Linda Graham 661, Therese Abair 657, Patty Ann 571, 1989
1,878 United States, Becky Kregling 669, Lucy Giovinco-Sandelin 618, Lesia Moos 591, 1997

Women's Doubles

1,296 United States, Lucy Giovinco-Sandelin 608, Lesia Moos 688
1,290 Mexico, Sara Alonso 682, Edda Piccini 608, 1989
1,266 United States, Debbie McMullen 594, Maureen Webb 672, 1989

Men's Five Player

3,248 United States, Ron Woolet 694, Jim Paine 605, Mac Lowry 603, Bob Mills 690, Virg Enger 656, 1974
3,165 United States, Harry Mickelson 598, Brad Briggs 622, Darold Meisel 628, Ron Mohr 675, Gordon Vadakin 642, 1989
3,164 Dominican Republic, Rolly Sebelen 675, Rolando Sebelen 557, Manuel Santos 650, R. Antonio Sebelen 633, Miguel Ventura 649, 1989

Men's Trios

2,049 United States, Mark Lewis 632, Ron Mohr 687, Harry Mickelson 730, 1989
2,033 United States, Brad Angelo 644, Vernon Peterson 701, Chris Barnes 688
2,012 Canada, Howard Kotchie 712, Al Tone 645, Craig Woodhouse 655, 1989

Men's Doubles

1,456 Canada, Al Tone 750, Craig Woodhouse 706, 1989
1,442 Mexico, Victor Mar 694, Vincente Mendez 748, 1989
1,413 United States, Gordon Vadakin 760, Darold Meisel 653, 1989

Team Games

Women's Five Player

1,103 United States, Debbie McMullen 218, Linda Graham 244, Therese Abair 202, Lynda Norry 228, Maureen Webb 211, 1989
1,073 United States, Patty Ann, Debbie McMullen, Linda Graham, Lynda Norry, Maureen Webb, 1989
1,067 United States, Tammy Turner, Nancy Ennis, Diana Williams, Joey Simpson, Stacy Robards, 1993

Women's Trios

725 United States, Becky Kregling 235, Lucy Giovinco-Sandelin 266, Lesia Moos 224, 1997
685 Mexico, Sara Alonso 265, Celia Flores 215, Edda Piccini 205, 1989
672 United States, Linda Graham 242, Therese Abair 204, Patty Ann 226, 1989

Men's Five Player

1,176 United States, Vernon Peterson 177, Bruce Steffani 207, Brad Angelo 224, Brian Graham 268, Chris Barnes 300, 1997
1,146 United States, Ron Woolet 248, Jim Paine 242, Mac Lowry 232, Bob Mills 217, Virg Enger 207, 1974
1,126 Canada, Steve Lee 202, Don Wira 238, Ed Maurer 194, Dan Russo 238, Bob Puttick 254, 1981

Men's Trios

763 United States, Mark Lewis 217, Ron Mohr 257, Harry Mickelson 289, 1989
748 United States, Mark Lewis 210, Ron Mohr 241, Harry Mickelson 297, 1989
717 Canada, Howard Kotchie 267, Al Tone 227, Craig Woodhouse 223, 1989

Women's Doubles

479   United States, Debbie McMullen 213, Maureen Webb 266, 1989

473   United States, Becky Dregling 259, Lisa Duenow 214, 1997

469   Puerto Rico, Evelyn Ortiz 253, Ashie Gonzalez 216, 1989

Men's Doubles

525   United States, Gordon Vadakin 279, Darold Meisel 246, 1989

519   Puerto Rico, Jim Porter 288, Jaime Almendro 231, 1993

509   Mexico, Victor Mar 210, Vincente Mendez 299, 1989

U.S. FIQ MEDAL WINNERS

The United States has been participating in Federation Internationale des Quilleurs World and American Zone tournaments since 1962. Competitions are held every two years, alternating between World and Zone tournaments.

The men's division of each tournament through 1977 consisted of eight, five and two player and individual competition. The women's division was five, four, two and individual. In one instance, there was a six player women's event.

FIQ changed the tournament format for World and Zone events after 1977 and three new events were added, singles and trio competition as well as all events. The men's eight player and women's four player were eliminated. And all European style (an entire game on one lane or half a game on one lane, then the second half on the adjoining lane) was eliminated in favor of the American style of alternating lanes.

After singles, doubles, trios and five player events, the top 16 men and women begin round robin competition, with 10 bonus points for each victory. After 15 games, the top three men and three women enter the stepladder elimination. The championship is decided on a two game total pins match between the No. 1 qualifier and the opponent who won the first one game match.

Below is a listing of the U.S. men and women who have won medals in FIQ competition. FIQ awards gold, silver and bronze medals for first, second and third place finishes, respectively. Thus, G (for gold), S (silver) and B (bronze) indicate in which position the player finished.

The listing also shows where and when the bowler won his or her medal(s). Examples: W63 means 1963 World tournament; Z69 means 1969 Zone tournament.

Men

Aarestad, Paul, Minneapolis ....(5G)Z81

Angelo, Brad, Newfane, N.Y. ....(5G-3G-2S)Z97

Barnes, Chris, Wichita, Kan. ....(IB)W95, (5G-3G-2S-AG-IG)Z97

Beck, Dave, Lansing, Mich......................(8G-AG-5B)Z69

Beck, Gary, St. Louis..........................(5S)W75

Biondo, Vince, Hoffman Estates, Ill....................(3G)W91, (5G-3G-AB-IB)Z93

Bosler, Buzz, Milwaukee ....(8G)Z66

Briggs, Brad, North Palm Beach, Fla. ....(IS-5S)Z89

Campbell, Greg, St. Louis.......................(8G)Z69

Cariello, Tony, Chicago.........................(IG-5S-3B)W83

Chapman, Anthony, Landover, Md......(5G-3G-1G-AG)Z93

Cohn, Al, Chicago ....(8G-5G)Z77

Corbin, John, Springfield, W.Va. ....(5G)Z77

Crake, Larry, Pontiac, Mich.....................(5G-6G)Z64

Curry, Jack, Lansing, Mich......................(8G-2S-5B)Z69

Dalkin, Roger, Milwaukee ....(8S)Z74

DeLuca, Buddy, Pittsburgh......................(8S)Z74

DiCicco, Dom, Philadelphia.........................(8G-5G)W71

Dorencamp, Ken, Pittsburgh ....(8G-5S-2B)Z66

Edwards, Jerry, Chicago.........................(5G)Z81

Enger, Virg, Minneapolis.....................(5G-2G-8S-AS)Z74

Euwer, Dale, Topeka, Kan. ....(8G-5G-2G-1G)Z77

Fehr, Steve, Cincinnati.........................(5G-1G-AS)Z81

Ferrell, Sam, Star City, W.Va. ....(8G)Z77

Foster, Bill, Chicago............................(5G)Z81

Foster, Joe, Pontiac, Mich. ....(5G-6G-AS)Z64

Gadaleto, Frank, Lansing, Mich. ....(8G-2B)Z77

Garber, David, Bedford, Texas ....(5G)Z93

Glaser, Bob, Chicago ....(8G-5G-2S-AB)W71

Glus, Dan, Pittsburgh ....(8G-5S-2B)Z66

Graham, Brian, Kokomo, Ind. ....(5G-3B-1G)Z97

Guedel, Charles, Indianapolis ....(8G)Z69

Handegard, John, Reno, Nev. ....(8G-2S)W71

Hanson, Bob, Minneapolis ....(8G-5G)W71, (8S-2B)Z74

Hathaway, Tom, Los Angeles ....(8G-5S-AS)Z66

Healey Jr., Pat, Niagara Falls, N.Y.. ....(2G-3G)W91

Hudoba, Andy, Youngstown, Ohio ....(8G)W63

Jackson, Eddie, Cincinnati.........................(8G-2S-AB)Z69

Jones, Larry, Louisville, Ky. ....(5G-3G-1S)Z85

Jurek, Jack, Tonawanda, N.Y.................(5G-2B-3S-AB)Z85

Kloempken, Steve, Las Vegas.........................(2G-3G)W91

Kopko, George, Pittsburgh..........................(8G-2S)Z66

Kuglitsch, Mark, Milwaukee ....(8G)W67

Kulibert, Terry, Oshkosh, Wis. ....(3S)W79

Lantto, Sam, Maple Grove, Minn. ....(5G)Z93

Lewis, Mark, Wichita, Kan..........................(3G-5S)Z89

Lindquist, Jim, Minneapolis ....(8G-5G-2G), Z77, (2B)W79

Lippe, Harry, Chicago.........................(8G-5G)W63

London, Russ, Chicago..........................(8G)W71

Lowry, Mac, Seattle ....(5G-8S-2S)Z74

Luther, Ed, Racine, Wis. ....(8G-5G-AG)W71

Mazzei, Ray, Pittsburgh ....(8G-5S)Z66

McLean, Rod, Baltimore ....(5S)W83

Meadows, Bobby, Dallas ....(5S-2B)W75

Meisel, Darold, Milwaukee ....(5S-3B)W83, (IG-2S-5S)Z89

Mickelson, Harry, Kodiak, Alaska ....(3G-5S)Z89

Mills, Bob, Chicago ....(5G-8S-2S)Z74

Mohr, Ron, Fairbanks, Alaska ....(3G-5S-AB)Z89

Murphy, Bob, Pontiac, Mich.........................(5G-6G)Z64

Nadeau, Dan, Las Vegas...................(5G-2G-AG-3S)Z85, (3G-2B)W87, (5G-3G)Z93

Nicol, Ralph, Lansing, Mich. ....(8G-5B)Z69

Neidert, Chris, Akron, Ohio ....(5G-1S)Z81

Niehus, Otto, Chicago..........................(5G-8G)W63

Oswalt, Bus, Ft. Wayne, Ind. ....(5G-2G-8G)W63

Paine, Jim, Houston.........................(5G-2G-8S)Z74

Perry, Frank, Lorain, Ohio.........................(8G)W67

Peterson, Vernon, Dearborn Heights, Mich.......(5G-2G)Z97

Pinkalla, Bob, Milwaukee ....(8G-2B)W67

Pinkalla, Wayne, Milwaukee ....(8G-2B-AB)W67

Porrini, Pat, Philadelphia..........................(8G)W63

Rabkin, Larry, Buffalo ....(8G)W71

Raffel, Gene, Milwaukee..................................(8G)W67
Richgels, Jeff, Madison, Wis. ....(5G-3G)Z85
Roeth, Ken, Dubuque, Iowa ....(8G)Z66
Rosser, Ed, Lansing, Mich. ....(8G-5B)Z69
Rothbarth, Les, Pontiac, Mich. ....(5G-6G)Z64
Roy, Bob, Denver ....(8G-5G)Z77
Russo, Pat, Teaneck, N.J. ....(5G)Z64
Sandvick, Duane, Bismarck, N.D. ....(3G)W87
Savoy, Todd, Superior, Wis. ....(5G-2B-3G)Z85
Schroeder, Jim, Ottawa, Ohio ....(8G-2G)W63
Sherman, Bruce, Lansing, Mich. ....(8G-AS-5B)Z69
Sikora, Jerry, Southgate, Mich. ....(5G-3B)Z75
Slak, Dan, Milwaukee ....(8G)Z66
Smith, Wade, Springfield, Ill. ....(8G-AS)Z77
Spiezio, Mickey, Joliet, Ill. ....(8G-5G-2B)Z77
Steelsmith, Rick, Wichita, Kan. ....(AG-3G-IS-2B-1B)W87
Steffani, Bruce, Great Falls, Mont. ....(5G-3B-1B)Z97

Stefanich, Jim, Joliet, Ill. (8G-5G-AS)W63, (6G-2G-AB)Z64
Stoudt, Bud, Lebanon, Pa. ....(AG-5S-2B)W75
Sunseri, Chuck, Detroit ....(5S)W75
Supanich, Rich, Chicago...........................(3S-2B)W79
Thomsen, Scott, Pullman, Wash.................(5G-2G-3S)Z85
Toft, Rod, St. Paul, Minn. ....(5S)W83
Traficante, Joe, Pittsburgh ....(5S-2S)Z64
Vadakin, Gordon, Wichita, Kan. (5S)W83, (AG-2S-5S)Z89
Vitali, Fred, Detroit ....(8G-5G)W71
Wheeler, Ron, Delavan, Wis. ....(8G)W67
Wilson, Jack, Akron, Ohio.............................(3S)W79
Wonders, Rich, Racine, Wis. .(5G-1B)Z81, (5S-3B-AB)W83
Woolet, Ron, Louisville, Ky. ....(5G-AG-8S-2B)Z74, (5S)W75
Wright, Dennis, Milwaukee ....(8G)W67
Zikes, Les, Chicago...........................(8G-5G-AG)W63,
(6G-5G-2G-AG)Z64, (8G)W67

Women

Abair, Therese, Long Beach, Calif....................(3G-5G)Z89
Adams, Ranae, New York City ....(5G-2B)W71
Almeida, Cathy, New Bedford, Mass..............(1S-5B)W83
Ann, Patty, Kernersville, N.C. ....(IG-3G-5G)Z89
Behn, Penny (McClain), Detroit..........(4EG-5G-2S-AB)W71
Bender, Karen, Lansing, Ill...........................(3G)W87
Bennett, Debbie, Akron, Ohio ....(5S-2B-1S)Z85
Brennan, Betty, Elizabeth, N.J. ....(6EG-5G-2S-AS)Z77
Brisk, Marion, Bethpage, N.Y. ....(5B)W83
Brown, Ann, Rochester, N.Y. ....(5G-4EG)Z66
Broadwell, Dixie (Burmeister), Houston ....
(5G-4EG-AS2S)W71
Butler, Kathy, Garden Grove, Calif. ....(5S)Z85
Cameron, Kendra, Gambrills, Md. ....(5G-3B)Z97
Chew, Mary Ann, Redwood City, Calif. ....(5G)Z66
Colohan, Frances, Washington, D.C. ....(5B)Z64
Cook, Debbie, Mentor, Ohio ....(6EG)Z77
Dillon, Donna, Dallas ....(5G-3B)Z81
Ditch, Janine, San Pedro, Calif.....................(3S-5B)W83
Dowland, Yvonne, Los Angeles ....(3S-5B)W83
Duenow, Lisa, Orono, Minn. ....(5G-3B)Z97
Ennis, Nancy, Clyde, Calif. ....(5G)Z93
Fiebig, Cora, Detroit ....(5G-3B-1B)Z81,
(5G-2G-3B)W87
Funk, Peggy, Tonawanda, N.Y. ....(5S-AB)Z85
Gaddis, Carol, Detroit ....(2S)W75
Giovinco-Sandelin, Lucy, Norcross, Ga...(6EG-2G-5G)Z77,
(5G-3G-2G)Z97
Glandon, Nellie, Columbus, Ohio.............(5G-3G-SB)W87
Gloor, Olga, Vista, Calif. ....(5G-AG-2S)Z74, (4ES)W75
Graham, Linda, Des Moines, Iowa...(AG-3G-5G-IB-2B)Z89
Graham, Mary Lou, Miami ....(4ES)W75
Hansen, Linda, Waukesha, Wis. ....(6EG-5G)Z77
Havlish, Jean, St. Paul, Minn. ....(5G-3B)Z81
Helmer, Sandi (Tice), Buffalo, N.Y. ....(5G)W79
Heyman, Ann, Toledo, Ohio ....(4EG-4AS-2S)W63
Holm, Joan, Chicago ....(4EG-5G)W71, (5G-2S-4EB)Z74
Holton, M. Sue, Orlando, Fla. ....(5G-3G)W87
Johnson, Ann, Hinesville, Ga. ....(5G)Z93
Johnson, Liz, Niagara Falls, N.Y. ....(1S)W95
Jonak, Regi, St. Peters, Mo. ....(5S-2B)Z85
Jones, Eleanor, Williamstown, Mass. ....(5S)W67
Kelly, Annese (Dunleavy), Las Vegas ....(5G-AG-2S)Z69,
(5G-3G)W79, (2G-5G)Z81
Kirk, Dixie, Belvidere, Ill...........................(3S-5B)W83
Kott, Jacquline, Harrisonville, Mo. ....(5G-2B)W71
Kregling, Becky, Stratford, Conn. ....(5G-3G-AG)Z97

LaCost, Lauren, Fort Wayne, Ind. ....(6G-5G-2G)Z77
Lambert, Lila, Indianapolis.......................(5G-4EB-AB)Z74
Leszczynski, Jane, Milwaukee............(4EG)Z69, (4ES)W75
Losee, Rosmary, Poughkeepsie, N.Y. ..(5G-4EG-2G-AS)Z69
Loveall, Regina (Hillier), Amarillo, Texas ....(5G)W79
Maw, Betty, Buffalo ....(5G)W79
McMullen, Debbie, Denver ....(5G-1G-2S-3B-AB)Z89
Mead, Laura, Rochester, Mich. ....(5G-4EG-2B)Z66
Miller, Carol, Milwaukee ....(5S)W67
Mohacsi, Mary, Detroit ....(5G-AS-2B-4EB)Z74,
(5G-1G)Z81, (5B)W83
Monterosso, Irene, Flushing, N.Y. ....(5G-4EG-2G-AB)W71
Moos, Lesia, Lancaster, Calif...........(5G-3G-2G-AS-1S)Z97
Mullen, Mary Ann, Perry, Iowa ....(5B)Z64
Nichols, Lorrie (Koch), Chicago ....(4EG)W71
Norry, Lynda, Concord, Calif...............(5G-IS-3B-2B) Z89,
(1S-2B) W91, (5G-3B-IG)Z97
Redfox, Ruth, Toledo, Ohio ....(4EG-4AS-2S)W63
Remmick, Betty Jean, Denver ....(4EG-2S-AB)Z66
Riley, Sue, San Francisco ....(5G-4EG-AS-2B)Z66
Rittelmeyer, Norma, Dallas ....(5G-4EB-2B)Z74
Robards, Stacy, Sacramento, Calif. ....(5G-3S-AB)Z93
Running Wolf, Neva, San Francisco ....(5G-2S)Z69
Salzman, Michelle, Los Angeles ....(5S)Z85
Schemers, Carol, Detroit...................(2S-4ES-AB)W75
Schottke, Sue, Tonawanda, N.Y. ....(5S)Z85
Schuble, Cindy, Louisville, Ky. ....(6EG-5G-AG-2S)Z77,
(3G-5G)W79
Shablis, Helen, Detroit..................(4EG-2G-AG-4AS)W63
Sherman, Ann, Chicago ....(5B)Z64
Shiery, Sandra Jo, Coldwater, Mich. ....(5G-AG-3B)W87
Simpson, Joey, Lexington, Ky. ....(5G-3S-AB)Z93
Skidmore, Eileen, Washington, D.C......................(5B)Z74
Stehle, Jean, Sturgis, Mich. ....(5S-2S-AB)W67
Stormo, Jackie, Barstow, Calif. ....(3G-5G)W79
Thoms, Virginia, Washington, D.C....................(5AB)Z74
Trumper, Vivian, Greenwood Lake, N.Y..............(5AS)Z69
Turner, Tammy, Canyon, Texas ....(5G-3S-AS)Z93
Walker, Barbara, San Francisco...............(2G-5G-1G)Z81
Webb, Maureen, North Andover, Mass..........................
(5G-2S-IS-1S-3B)Z89, (2B)W91
Werkmeister, Grace, Chicago ....(5G-4EG)Z66
Weston, Helen, Detroit ....(AG-5S-2S)W67
Wilkinson, Dot, Phoenix, Ariz.........(2G-4EG-4AS-AB)W63
Williams, Diana, Raymond, Wash. ....(5G)Z93
Wodka, Kathy, Las Vegas ....(5G-2G-3B)W87
Yut, Lois Henrietta, San Francisco....................(5G-2S)Z66

FIQ World Tenpin Team Cup

The World Tenpin Team Cup was created in 1994 in answer to the International Olympic Committee's call for future team competitions that could not be dominated by any individual, nor be decided by the arbitrary decision of judges. Also, the event achieved an FIQ goal of creating at least one World Championship tournament each year.

Thus the World Tenpin Team Cup became an elite event for the top five men's and women's five-player teams from each of the FIQ's American, European and Asian Zone Championships, with Malaysia's men and women filling the 16th berths as "host country" entries.

The tournament was conducted exclusively using Baker Format competition. Each player bowled two frames to complete one game. Qualifying involved two-game matches with one point awarded for each game won and a third point for series total. Each team bowled three matches against each other team within the gender divisions with total pinfall determining the top three finalists. Those teams then bowled three-game, four-point matches to decide medal positions.

2nd FIQ World Tenpin Team Cup
Calgary, Alberta 1996
15 men's and 15 women's five-player teams

Men's Results
1. Finland (gold)
2. Sweden (silver)
3. Denmark (bronze)

Women's Results
1. Finland (gold)
2. TEAM USA, (silver)
3. Malaysia (bronze)

Playoff results:
Finland def. Denmark 3-1 (204-211, 243-200, 175-158, 622-569) and Finland def. Sweden 3-1 (191-154, 183-205, 194-149, 568-508).

Playoff results:
United States def. Malaysia 3-1 (197-191, 236-226, 207-215, 640-632) and Finland def. TEAM USA 2-2, 56-40 in two-frame playoff (224-159, 162-187, 182-219, 568-565)

1st FIQ World Tenpin Team Cup
Kuala Lumpur, Malaysia 1994
15 men's and 15 women's five-player teams

Men's Results
1. Sweden (gold)
2. Chinese Taipei (silver)
3. Finland (bronze)

Women's Results
1. United States (gold)
2. Korea (silver)
3. Denmark (bronze)

Playoff results:
Sweden def. Finland 3-1 (234- 199, 225-210, 170-226, 670-594) and Sweden def. Chinese Taipei 4-0 (219-192, 222-212, 207-201, 648-605).

Playoff results:
Korea def. Denmark 3-1 (213-155, 191-181, 180-221, 584-557) and United States def. Korea 3-1 (186-143, 225-146, 171-201, 582- 490).

FIQ World Tenpin Team Cup Records
Qualifying Points (42 matches)

Men
1. Sweden 86.0
2. Chinese Taipei 83.5
3. Sweden 83.0

Women
1. United States 15,751
2. Finland 15,749
3. The Netherlands 15,658

Women
1. Finland 90.5
2. United States 89.9
3. Malaysia 85.0

Baker Format Team High Game

Men	Women
279 - The Netherlands	266 - United States
277 - Malaysia	257 - Germany
- United States	256 - The Netherlands

Actual Pinfall, 84 Baker Format Games
Men
1. Sweden 17,253
2. Finland 16,953
3. Chinese Taipei 16,841

Baker Format Team 2-Game Series

Men	Women
502 - Finland	475 - United States
499 - Sweden	461 - Germany
- United States	460 - The Netherlands

Pan American Games

The Pan American Games are held in a different country every four years. Several years in advance, the host country for the Pan American Games selects at least 15 medal-status sports from an approved list of 28 medal-status sports. Bowling is included in the list of 28 medal sports.

By this selection, the host country has determined which sports will be included in that Pan American Games session. Bowling received medal status from the Pan American Sports Organization Council in November 1986.

12th Pan American Games
Buenos Aires, Argentina 1995

Four-Man Team Event
1. United States. 4,923
   (Pat Healey, Mark Van Meter, John Eiss, Chris Barnes), 4,923
2. Venezuela. 4,684
   (Agustin De Farias, Pedro Avendano, Arturo Hendandez, Pedro Carreyo)
3. Canada 4,677
   (Marc Doi, Doug Schatz, Paul Gyarnati, Bill Rowe)

Men's Doubles
1. Pat Healey/Chris Barnes, United States. 2,559
2. Samir Daou/Carlos Finx Jr., Netherland Antilles. . 2,545
3. Mark Doi/Bill Rowe, Canada. 2,463

Men's Singles
1. Bill Rowe, Canada 1,295
2. Pat Healey Jr., United States. 1,260
3. Marco Zepeda, Mexico. 1,237

Men's Individual
1. Pat Healey Jr., United States. 3,464
2. Pedro Carreyo, Venezuela. 3,410
3. Agustin De Farias, Venezuela 3,404

Four-Woman Team Event
1. Canada 4,676
   Sandy Lowe, Anne Saasto, Debbie Ship, Catharine Willis
2. United States 4,557
   Lisa Bishop, Lesia Stark, Missy Howard, Liz Johnson
3. Venezuela 4,547
   Margalit Mizrachi, Mariela Alarza, Marianela Lista, Mirella Trasolini

Women's Doubles
1. Missy Howard/Lesia Stark, United States 2,548
2. Georgina Serratos/Gabriela Sandoval, Mexico . .2,463
3. Margalit Mizrachi/Mariela Alarza, Venezuela . . .2,445

Women's Singles
1. Catharine Willis, Canada 1,305
2. Mariela Alarza, Venezuela 1,266
3. Lisa Bishop, United States 1,212

Women's Individual
1. Liz Johnson, United States 2,726
2. Edda Piccini, Mexico 2,590
3. Luz Leal, Colombia .2,485

11th Pan American Games
Havana, Cuba 1991

Four-Man Team Event
1. United States 7,442
   Steve Kloempken, Ralph Solan, Jon Juneau, Pat Healey Jr.
2. Venezuela 7,007
   Pedro Carreyo, Pedro Elias Cardozo, Luis Serfaty, Francisco Carabano
3. Mexico. 6,989
   Alfonso Rodriguez, Roberto Silva, Daniel Falconi, Luis Javier Iserte

Men's Individual Event
1. Pat Healey Jr., United States
2. Luis Serfaty, Venezuela
3. Jon Juneau, United States
4. Ray Vervynck, Canada

Double Elimination Finals
Round No. 1: Healey defeated Vervynck, 222-160; Juneau defeated Serfaty, 189-187.
Round No. 2: Healey defeated Juneau, 161-144; Serfaty defeated Vervynck (eliminated), 279-186.
Bronze Medal Round: Serfaty defeated Juneau (bronze), 193-152.
Gold Medal Round: Healey (gold) defeated Serfaty (silver), 237-201.

Four-Woman Team Event
1. United States. 6,733
   Maureen Webb, Julie Gardner, Mandy Wilson, Lynda Norry
2. Venezuela. 6,687
   Mirella DeTrasolini, Gabela Sanchez, Mariela Alarza, Gabi Bagai
3. Mexico. 6,627
   Edda Piccini, Anna Maria Avila, Letticia Rosas, Celia Flores

Women's Individual Event
1. Edda Piccini, Mexico
2. Julie Gardner, United States
3. Mandy Wilson, United States
4. Mari Ortiz, Puerto Rico

Double Elimination Finals
Round No. 1: Piccini defeated Wilson, 197-194; Gardner defeated Ortiz, 192-172.
Round No. 2: Piccini defeated Gardner, 221-201; Wilson defeated Ortiz (eliminated), 220-195.
Bronze Medal Round: Gardner defeated Wilson (bronze), 204-179.
Gold Medal Round: Piccini (gold) defeated Gardner (silver), 212-156.

1983 Pan American Games

Bowling was a demonstration sport in the 1983 Pan American Games in Caracas, Venezuela. In the demonstration, four-player teams from 12 nations competed in singles, doubles and mixed-foursome events. Athletes bowled six games in each event. The top-four scorers in total pinfall advanced to a stepladder final.

9th Pan American Games
Caracas, Venezuela 1983

Mixed-Foursomes Event
1. Puerto Rico 4,433
   Ashie Gonzalez, Esther Yordan, Francisco Perez, Felipe Blanco

2. United States.......................................4,312
   Jean Hammond, Mary Lou Vining, Rod Toft, Rich Wonders
3. Venezuela..4,262
   Selma Flores, Regina Penazloza, Pedro Carreyo, Luis Cedeno

Two-Man Team Event
1. Puerto Rico 2,338
   Francisco Perez, Felipe Blanco
2. United States.......................................2,248
   Rod Toft, Rich Wonders
3. Venezuela...2,231
   Pedro Carreyo, Luis Cedeno

Two-Woman Team Event
1. United States.......................................2,171
   Jean Hammond, Mary Lou Vining
2. Puerto Rico 2,030
   Esther Yordan, Ashie Gonzalez
3. Bahamas 2,029
   Sahara Johnson, Gerry Smith

Men's Singles Event
1. Luis Cedeno, Venezuela......................1,181
2. Francisco Perez, Puerto Rico 1,169
3. Rich Wonders, United States................1,165

Women's Singles Event
1. Isabel de Makino, Peru........................1,143
2. Jean Hammond, United States 1,129
3. Gloria Ramierz, Columbia....................1,107

Stepladder Final
1. Pedro Carreyo, Venezuela
2. Rich Wonders, United States
3. Miguel Almonte, Dominican Republic
4. Felipe Blanco, Puerto Rico

Stepladder Final
1. Jean Hammond, United States
2. Ashie Gonzales, Puerto Rico
3. Selma Flores, Venezuela
4. Mary Lou Vining, United States

Carreyo defeated Blanco, 172-170; Carreyo defeated Almonte, 170-160; Carreyo defeated Wonders, 407-368; Carreyo defeated Wonders, 213-170 (championship match).

Flores defeated Vining, 211-170; Hammond defeated Flores, 193-181; Hammond defeated Gonzales, 346 (175-171) to 302 (169-133); Hammond defeated Gonzales, 213-170 (championship match).

World Games

The World Games provide international competition for federated sports that have not been accorded full-medal status in the Olympic Games. The World Games are a quadrennial event.

5th World Games
Lahti Finland 1997

Men's Division Singles
1. Gery Verbruggen, Belgium
2. Vernon Peterson, United States
3. Paeng Nepomuceno, The Philippines

Women's Division Singles
1. Patricia Schwarz, Germany
2. Isabelle Saldjian, France
3. Mi Young Lee, Korea

Peterson def. Nepomuceno 217-173 and Verbruggen def. Peterson 463-430 (two games).

Mixed Doubles Event
1. Sharron Low/Daniel Lim, Malaysia
2. Cara Honeychurch/Andrew Frawley, Australia
3. Tomomi Shibata/Shiegeo Saito, Japan

Low/Lim def. Shibata/Saito 446-438 and Low/Lim def. Honeychurch/Frawley 838-816 (two games).

4th World Games
The Hague, Netherlands 1993

Men's Division Stepladder Results
1. Tomas Leandersson, Sweden
2. Yvan Augustin, France
3. Rafael Nepomuuceno, Philippines

Augustin defeated Nepomuceno, 218-245; and Leandersson defeated Augustin, 237-176.

Women's Division Stepladder Results
1. Pauline Smith, Great Britian
2. Lisa Kwan, Malaysia
3. Yuon Oh, Korea

Kwan defeated Oh, 168-215; and Smith defeated Kwan 365-374 (two games).

Mixed Doubles Event
1. Finland 2,350
   Pauliina Aalto, Mika Koivuniemi
2. Sweden..2,345
   Asa Larson, Tomas Leandersson
3. France 2,293
   Isabel Saldjian, Yvan Augustin

3rd World Games
Karlsruhe, Germany 1989

Men's Stepladder Results
1. Yingh Chieh Ma, Taiwan
2. Darold Meisel, United States
3. Hendro Pratono, Indonesia

Meisel defeated Pratono, 198-164; and Ma defeated Meisel, 424-380 (two games).

Women's Stepladder Results
1. Jane Amlinger, Canada
2. Arianne Cerdena, The Philippines
3. Patty Ann, United States

Amlinger defeated Ann, 40-38, in a two-frame rolloff (184-184); and Amlinger defeated Cerdena, 364-352 (two games).

Mixed Doubles
1. Taiwan..4,708
   Yuen Yue Huang, Ying Chieh Ma
2. The Philippines 4,646
   Arianne Cerdena, Jorge Fernandez
3. Germany 4,616
   Michaela Viol, Wolfgang Strupf

2nd World Games
London 1985

Men's All Events
1. Raymond Jansson, Sweden 6,093
2. Utz Dehler, Germany 6,053
3. Byun Yonghwan, Korea...5,742

Women's All Events
1. Gisela Lins, Germany 5,396
2. Josette Romon, Switzerland 5,358
3. Pamela Pope, Australia...5,225

Men's Singles
1. Raymond Jansson, Sweden 1,699
2. Arne Stroem, Norway 1,654
3. Utz Dehler, Germany 1,567

Women's Singles
1. Adelene Wee, Singapore.......................................1,601
2. Pamela Pope, Australia...1,531
3. Jette Hansen, Denmark 1,483

Mixed Doubles
1. Belgium..3,184
   Nora Haveneers, Dominique DeNolf
2. Germany 3,127
   Gisela Lins, Utz Dehler
3. The Philippines 3,072
   Bong Coo, Rene Reyes

1st World Games
Santa Clara, Calif. 1981

Men's Final Standings
1. Arne Stroem, Norway
2. Ernst Berndt, Austria
3. Chris Batson, Australia

Berndt defeated Baston, 382-376; Berndt defeated Stroem, 398-390; and Stroem defeated Berndt, 224-170.

Women's Final Standings
1. Lilane Gregori, France
2. Porntip Singha, Thailand
3. Mary Lou Vining, United States

Singha defeated Vining, 351-336; and Gregori defeated Singha, 349-341.

Mixed Doubles
1. Australia
   Ruth Guerster, Chris Batson
2. Finland
   Airi Leppala, Mikko Kaartinen
3. Austria
   Hilde Reitermaier, Ernst Berndt
   Guerster-Batson defeated Kaartinen-Leppala, 399-345.

AMF Bowling World Cup

The AMF Bowling World Cup is held in a different country each year. The tournament began in 1965, however, the women's competition was not included until 1972. Today, the AMF Bowling World Cup attracts approximately 90 women and men representing 50 countries.

The competitors start the four-stage tournament by rolling 18 qualifying games during a three-day period. With the exception of the stepladder finals, all scores are carried. In stage two, the field is cut to the top 24 men and women scorers. These 48 athletes bowl 16 games, in eight-game blocks, during a two-day period.

In stage three, the field is cut to the top eight scorers. The eight women and eight men bowl seven head-to-head matches and one head-to-head position match. Players earn their game score, 20 points per win, 10 points per tie, five points per 200-249 game, and 10 points per 250-300 game.

The top-five scorers advance to the scratch stepladder finals. All qualifying and match-play scores are dropped. In the first stepladder matches, the fifth-place qualifers bowl the fourth-place qualifiers. The winners of those matches bowl the third-place qualifiers. The order continues until match winners bowl the first-place qualifiers. The winners of this final match are declared the men's and women's tournament champions.

In the past and present, the U.S. was represented by TEAM USA members or intercollegiate champions. From 1992-94, the U.S. women and men were selected through a series of qualifying competitions conducted by AMF.

AMF Bowling World Cup Tournament Champions, Runnersup

1996
Belfast, Ireland

Men
1. Paeng Nepomuceno, The Philippines
2. Drew Hylen, United States

Women
1. Cara Honeychurch, Australia
2. Shalin Zulkifli, Malaysia

1995
Sao Paulo, Brazil

Men
1. Pat Healey Jr., United States
2. Nobuyuki Takahama, Japan

Women
1. Gemma Burden, Great Britain
2. Kendra Cameron, United States

1994
Hermosillo, Mexico

Men
1. Tore Torgensen, Norway
2. Mohamed Khalifa, United Arab Emirates

Women
1. Anne Jacobs, South Africa
2. Lucy Giovinco, United States

1993
Johannesburg, South Africa

Men
1. Rainer Puisis, Germany
2. Tomas Leandersson, Sweden

Women
1. Pauline Smith, Great Britain
2. Roslind Greiner, The Netherlands

1992
LeMans, France

Men
1. Paeng Nepomuceno, The Philippines
2. Achim Graboski, Germany

Women
1. Martina Beckel, Germany
2. Maria Lanzavecchia, Argentina

1991
Bejing, China

Men
1. Jon Juneau, United States
2. Ulf Hamnaes, Sweden

Women
1. Asa Larsson, Sweden
2. Pauline Smith, Great Britain

1990
Pattaya, Thailand
Men
1. Tom Hahl, Finland
2. Adam Apo, United States

Women
1. Linda Graham, United States
2. Marie Holmquist, Sweden

1989
Dublin, Ireland
Men
1. Salem Monsuri, Qatar
2. Kenneth Andersson, Sweden

Women
1. Patty Ann, United States
2. Martina Beckel, West Germany

1988
Guadalajara, Mexico
Men
1. Mohamed Khalifa, United Arab Emirates
2. Ian Bradford, Australia

Women
1. Linda Kelly, United States
2. Diana Tanlimco, The Philippines

1987
Kuala Lumpur, Malaysia
Men
1. Remo Fornasari, Italy
2. Shin-Bin Wu, Chinese Taipei

Women
1. Irene Gronert, Netherlands
2. Heidi Maarit Lind, Finland

1986
Copenhagen, Denmark
Men
1. Peter Ljung, Sweden
2. Paeng Nepomuceno, The Philippines

Women
1. Annette Hagre, Sweden
2. Bec Watanabe, The Philippines

1985
Seoul, South Korea
Men
1. Alfonso Rodriguez, Mexico
2. Eric Kok, Holland

Women
1. Marjorie McEntree, Ireland
2. Judy Howlett, Great Britain

1984
Sydney, Australia
Men
1. Jack Jurek, United States
2. Hakeesatit Katha, Thailand

Women
1. Eliana Rigato, Italy
2. Ursula Eckert, West Germany

1983
Mexico City
Men
1. You-Tien Chu, Taiwan
2. Michael Church, Malaysia

Women
1. Jeanette Baker, Australia
2. Gisela Lins, West Germany

1982
Scheveningen, Holland
Men
1. Arne Stroem, Norway
2. Krua Somsak, Thailand

Women
1. Jeanette Baker, Australia
2. Inger Levhorn, Sweden

1981
New York
Men
1. Robert Worrall, United States
2. Manny Magno, The Philippines

Women
1. Pauline Smith, Great Britain
2. Miyuki Motoi, Japan

1980
Jakarta, Indonesia
Men
1. Paeng Nepomuceno, The Philippines
2. Alfonso Rodriguez, Mexico

Women
1. Jean Gordon, Canada
2. Hannelore Hoplitschek, West Germany

1979
Bangkok, Thailand
Men
1. Philippe Dubois, France
2. Montree Vipitsini, Thailand

Women
1. Bong Coo, The Philippines
2. Hattieann Morrissette, Bermuda

1978
Bogota, Colombia
Men
1. Samran Banyen, Thailand
2. Philippe Dubois, France

Women
1. Lita de la Rosa, The Philippines
2. Pauline Caffola, Ireland

1977
London, England
Men
1. Arne Stroem, Norway
2. Philippe Dubois, France

Women
1. Rea Rennox, Canada
2. Lauren La Cost, United States

1976
Tehran, Iran

Men
1. Paeng Nepomuceno, The Philippines
2. Carlos Lovera, Venezuela

Women
1. Lucy Giovinco, United States
2. Doris Graden, Sweden

1975
Manila, The Philippines

Men
1. Lorenzo Monti, Italy
2. Carlos Lovera, Venezuela

Women
1. Cathy Townsend, Canada
2. Hattieann Morrissette, Bermuda

1974
Caracas, Venezuela

Men
1. Jairo Ocampo, Colombia
2. Louis Wildenmeersch, Belgium

Women
1. Birgette Lund, Denmark
2. Dale Gray, Australia

1973
Singapore

Men
1. Bernie Carterer, Great Britain
2. Glen Watson, Canada

Women
1. Kesinee Srivises, Thailand
2. Mele Anaya, Mexico

1972
Hamburg, West Germany

Men
1. Ray Mitchell, Canada
2. Loreto Maranan, The Philippines

Women
1. Irma Urrea, Mexico
2. Oy Sri-Saard, Thailand

1971
Hong Kong

Men
1. Roger Dalkin, United States
2. Benjamin Corona, Mexico

1970
Copenhagen, Denmark

Men
1. Klaus Mueller, Germany
2. Henry Tan, Singapore

1969
Tokyo, Japan

Men
1. Graydon Robinson, Canada
2. Ut Lenavat, Thailand

1968
Guadalajara, Mexico

Men
1. Fritz Blum, Germany
2. Jim Kramer, Canada

1967
Paris, France

Men
1. Jack Connaughton, United States
2. Kazuo Hayaski, Japan

1966
London, England

Men
1. John Wilcox, United States
2. Vittorio Noveletto, Italy

1965
Dublin, Ireland

Men
1. Lauri Ajanto, Finland
2. Tom Hathaway, United States

Lee Evans Bowling Tournament of the Americas

The Lee Evans Bowling Tournament of the Americas provides annual international competition for top male and female bowlers from North, Central and South America. The tournament, which has been held for three decades, is conducted at Cloverleaf Lanes in Miami.

Lee Evans, the late bowling writer for the Miami Herald, founded the tournament to bring together international athletes with dissimilar backgrounds and a similar love of bowling. Since its inception, the number of tournament entries continues to grow. Today, nearly 20 countries attend the week-long tournament.

1997 Tournament of the Americas Results

Men's Singles
1. Matt Ratliff, United States 2,613
2. Frankei Colon, Puerto Rico 2,483
3. Alex Frank, Guatemala 2,483

Women's Singles
1. Tammy Jordan, United States 2,438
2. Leslie Young, United States 2,394
3. Kerrie Ryan, Canada 2,349

Senior Men's Singles
1. Vinnie Atria, United States 2,678
2. Junior Perez, Puerto Rico 2,429
3. Julio Acosta, El Salvador 2,293

Senior Women's Singles
1. Carol Trump, United States 2,485
2. Linda Lunsford, United States 2,287
3. Maggie Lassale, Puerto Rico 2,032

Junior Boys' Singles
1. Juan Colon, Puerto Rico 2,384
2. Alejandro Reuna, Costa Rica 2,285
3. Juliano Oliverira, Brazil 2,261

Junior Girls Singles
1. Clara Guerrero, Colombia 2,375
2. Tennelle Grifalva, United States 2,332
3. Paola Gomz, Columbia 2,235

Men's Doubles
1. Mike Faliero/Ratliff, United States 2,602
2. Francisco Fonseca/Alvaro Castro, Costa Rica 2,391
3. Jaime Gomez/Carlos Acosta, Columbia 2,345

Women's Doubles
1. Aida Granillo/Lizzie Acosta, El Salvador 2,326
2. Maria Salazar/Sara VArgas, Colombia 2,318
3. Cathy Townsend/Kerrie Ryan, Canada 2,230

Senior Men's Doubles
1. Juan Bragadin/Pedro Izaguirre, Argentina 2,492
2. Atria/Henry Rodriguez, United States 2,293
3. Fernando Munoz/Perez, Puerto Rico 2,261

Senior Women's Doubles
1. Lunsford/Trump, United States 2,180
2. Milena Carvalho/Sonia Saldanha, Brazil 2,119
3. Glori Collura/Maddy Watson, Canada 2,090

Junior Boys' Doubles
1. Carlos Mejia/Celso Siado, Colombia 2,193
2. Mike Schmidt/Michael Tuomela, Canada 2,188
3. Travis Best/Jamie Flynn, United States 2,187

Junior Girls' Doubles
1. Anick Desjardins/Diana Dante, Canada 2,195
2. Laura Hinojosa/Marimar Rodriguez, Mexico 2,171
3. Staci Grisham/Kristi Ann Richards, U.S. 2,128

Adult Mixed Doubles
1. Granillo/Mauricio Galdamez, El Salvador 2,462
2. Salazar/Gomez, Colombia 2,449
3. Zussie Machon/Frank, Guatemala 2,425

Senior Mixed Doubles
1. Trump/Atria, U.S. 2,621
2. Collura/Frank Sobil, Canada 2,318
3. Lassalle/Perez, Puerto Rico 2,316

Junior Mixed Doubles
1. Hyman/Flynn, U.S. 2,513
2. Guerrero/Mejia, Colombia 2,329
3. Ursell Arends/Maroushka Tromp, Aruba 2,221

Adult Mixed Foursomes
1. U.S. 10,043
2. Colombia 9,541
3. Guatemala 9,185

Senior Mixed Foursomes
1. U.S. 9,394
2. Canada 8,737
3. Puerto Rico 8,563

Junior Mixed Foursomes
1. U.S. 9,462
2. Colombia 9,067
3. Puerto Rico 8,551

Men's All Events
1. Ratliff, U.S. 7,754
2. Faliero, U.S. 7,437
3. Gomez, Colombia 7,343

Women's All Events
1. Young, U.S. 7,197
2. Salazar, Colombia 7,118
3. Granillo 7,030

Senior Men's All Events
1. Atria, U.S. 7,845
2. Perez, Puerto Rico 7,156
3. Sobil, Canada 7,026

Senior Women's All Events
1. Trump, U.S. 7,378
2. Lunsford, U.S. 6,943
3. Lassalle, Puerto Rico   .6,193

Junior Boys' All Events
1. Flynn, U.S. 6,830
2. Mejia, Colombia 6,827
3. Jimmy Ortelli, Argentina 6,816

Senior National All Events
1. U.S. 28,172
2. Puerto Rico 25,888
3. Canada 25,689

Adult National All Events
1. U.S. 29,325
2. Colombia 28,103
3. Guatemala 27,598

Junior National All Events
1. U.S. 27,509
2. Colombia 26,814
3. Puerto Rico .25,538

FIQ World Youth Championships
Hong Kong, 1996

Girls' Team
1. Taipei 4,702
2. Norway 4,643
3. Korea 4,602

Girls' Doubles
1. Tomie Kawaguchi/Tomomi Shibata, Japan 2,411
2. Miyuki Yamamoto/Shima Washizuki, Japan 2,407
3. Sarah Yap/Shalin Zulkifli, Malaysia 2,378

Girls' All Events
1. Yu-Ling Wang, Taipei 3,642
2. Verhoeven, The Netherlands 3,639
3. Yeau-Jin Kim, Korea 3,622

Girls' Singles
1. Sara Vargas, Colombia 1,289
2. Sarah Yap, Malaysia 1,263
3. Wendy Verhoeven, The Netherlands 1,249

Girls' Masters
1. Yu-Ling Wang, Taipei 3,417
2. Yeau-Jin Kim, Korea 3,356
3. Jennifer Swanson, U.S. 3,328

Boys' Singles
1. Masaru Ito, Japan 1,313
2. Sang-Hun Lee, Korea 1,302
3. Robert Smith, United States 1,300

Boys' Team
1. Taipei 4,842
2. Malaysia 4,778
3. United States 4,773

Boys' Doubles
1. Richard Leon/Nicola Petrillo, Venezuela 2,510
2. Paul Evans/Paul Delaney, England 2,482
3. Michael Mullin/Jeremy Sonnefeld, U.S. 2,465

Boys' All Events
1. Nicola Petrillo, Venezuela 3,766
2. Tommy Jones, United States 3,764
3. Jaime Gomez, Colombia 3,734
   Sang-Hun Lee, Korea 3,734

Boys' Masters
1. Myong-Jo Kim, Korea 3,586
2. Tommy Jones, U.S. 3,458
3. Duane Camacho, Guam 3,450

FIQ American Zone Youth Championships
Orlando, Fla., 1997

Girls' Team
1. United States 4,616
2. Colombia 4,423
3. Mexico 4,418

Girls' Doubles
1. Diandra Hyman/Jennifer Daugherty, United States . . 2,380
2. Janette Piesczynski/Tennelle Grijalva, United States . . 2,336
3. Clara Guerrero/Maria Salazar, Colombia 2,304

Girls' Singles
1. Tennelle Grijalva, United States 1,282
2. Maria Rodriguez, Mexico 1,270
3. Janette Piesczynski, United States 1,258

Girls' All Events
1. Janette Piesczynski, United States 3,646
2. Jennifer Daugherty, United State 3,581
3. Tennelle Grijalva, United States . . . . 3,529.

Girls' Grand Masters
1. Maria Salazar, Colombia 3,301
2. Tennelle Grijalva, United States 3,241
3. Janette Piesczynski, United States 3,226

Boys' Team
1. United States 4,921
2. Mexico 4,824
3. Puerto Rico 4,735

Boys' Doubles
1. Manuel Briseno/Marcos Baeza, Mexico 2,499
2. Junior Kato/Juliano Oliveira, Brazil 2,444
3. Juan Colon/Jean Perez, Puerto Rico 2,418

Boys' Singles
1. Chris Fernandez, Canada 1,340
2. (tie) Junior Kato, Brazil 1,297
   Celso Siado, Colombia 1,297

Boys' All Events
1. Shawn Evans, United States 3,803
2. Jean Perez, Puerto Rico 3,772
3. Eduardo Soria, Mexico 3,753

Boys' Grand Masters
1. Jean Perez, Puerto Rico 3,523
2. Marcos Baeza, Mexico 3,330
3. Alejandro Cruz, Mexico 3,327

Brunswick World Team Challenge

The American Bowling Congress and Prime/SportsChannel network made television bowling history by creating the National Team Challenge series in 1992. It consisted of 12 regional tournaments leading to the Grand Championship in June 1993.

One of original goals of the NTC was to rebuild interest in five-player team bowling, the format the industry was built on. To promote interest in team competition, the NTC featured the unique and increasingly popular Baker Scoring System which requires each player to roll two frames in one game combining for one score.

The initial concept was so successful it was expanded to the Brunswick World Team Challenge for 1993-94 with 15 United States events plus foreign franchises. The series was expanded in 1994-95 to 19 U.S. events for men and women and three Women's International Bowling. It expanded further in 1995-96 and 1996-97 to 22 U.S. events for men and six for women.

1996-97 Regional Winners
Open Division

Portland, Ore. (44 teams)
The Shoppe, Tacoma, Wash.
(Purvis Granger, Mike Clark, Lenny Blakey, Don Freund, Fred Mattson)

Hubbard, Ohio (51 teams)
Deer Acres, Bay City, Mich.
(Jim Tessner, Dale Hofmeister, Bill Froberg, Scott Weston, Chuck Bork)

Winter Haven, Fla. (60 teams)
Team Brunswick, Pittsburgh
(Jeff Poholski, Robert Alexander, Mike Chontos, Roger Kossert, Bruce Hollen)

Madison, Wis. (40 teams)
Linds Limited, Milwaukee
(Dale Traber, Gus Yannaras, Lennie Boresch, Ryan Lever, Steve Brinkman)

Harrisburg, Pa. (81 teams)
ESP Computer Software, Mechanicsburg, Pa.
(Darryl Bower, Ken Brewbaker, Steve Levering, Gary Bower, Roger Horst)

Orange, Calif. (60 teams)
Asher's Embroidery, Anaheim, Calif.
(Robert Smith, Mike DeVaney, Billy Myers Jr., Tim Mack, Barry Asher)

Ogden, Utah (42 teams)
IVM, North Salt Lake City, Utah
(Gerry Klinich, Anthony DeLahanty, Brett Wolfe, Russ Hunt, Joe Ciccone)

St. Petersburg, Fla. (112 teams)
Contour Power Grips, Milwaukee
(Dennis Rakauskas, Jace Peterson, Doug Becker, Brian Brazeau, Joe Natoli)

Las Vegas (70 teams)
Turbo 2-N-1 Grips, Chesterfield, Mich.
(Steve Fehr, Mika Koivuniemi, Bill Hoffman, Pat Healey Jr., Dave Bernhardt)

Fort Worth, Texas (80 teams)
Acme Pawn, Colorado Springs, Colo.
(Dave Husted, Mark Scroggins, Raleigh Gilchrist, Chris Barnes, Steve Anderson)

Indianapolis (80 teams)
TEAM USA
(Vernon Peterson, Bruce Steffani, Jerry Sikora, Brian Graham, Brad Angelo)

Tacoma, Wash. (60 teams)
Contour Power Grips, Spokane, Wash.
(Frank DeRemer, Bob Davidson, Dave Jacobsen, Roger LeClair, Matt Surina)

Windsor Locks, Conn. (80 teams)
Columbia Cuda C's, San Antonio, Texas
(Mike Lichstein, Patrick Allen, Bryan O'Keefe, Michael Mullin, Brian Boghosian)

Detroit (76 teams)
Lodge Lanes, Belleville, Mich.
(Dale Strike, Bob Goike, Kelly Bennett, Bob Jawor, Mike Moore)

St. Paul, Minn. (51 teams)
Ebonite Nitro/R's, Wichita, Kan.
(Sean Swanson, Lonnie Waliczek, Billy Murphy, Paul Fleming, Chad Murphy)

Atlanta (76 teams)
Trophies Unlimited, Richmond, Va.
(Paul Zevgolis, John Beasley, Kip Roberts, Trip Roberts, Wayne Sheridan)

Dublin, Calif. (72 teams)
Contour Power Grips, Tacoma, Wash.
(Bob Hanson, Todd Book, Jerry Ledbetter, Mike Kennedy, Mike Karch)

Vernon Hills, Ill. (71 teams)
Hammer, Fulton, N.Y.
(Mike Tryniski, Doug Kent, Mark McClain, Kurt Pilon, Rudy Kasimakis)

Kansas City (55 teams)
McGerr's Pro Shop, Lincoln, Neb.
(Brian Kretzer, Rick Miller, Sean Quinn, Mike Wolfe, Kevin McGerr)

Miami (71 teams)
ABBA Treb de Fox/Pollard's Bowl, Cincinnati
(Derwin Pitre, Don Scudder, Ron Pollard, Dave Wellage, Rick Pollard)

Baltimore (76 teams)
Maryland Crew, Burtonsville, Md.
(Lee Brosius, Rich Wilburn, Craig Jewell, Billy Oatman, David Hart)

Pittsburgh (84 teams)
Unique Embroidery, Lansing, Mich.
(Chris Jones, Scott Smith, Chris Sand, Chris Marshall, Lon Marshall)

Women's Division

Orange, Calif. (20 teams)
Reb's Pretty Girl International, West Hollywood, Calif.
(Laura Moriarty, Paula Vidad, Lauren Takahashi, Laurie
Soto, Anne Marie Duggan)

St. Petersburg, Fla. (18 teams)
Kinco Ltd., Jacksonville, Fla.
(Barbara Batt, Darlene Milton, April Costa, Sharri Johnson,
Dede Davidson)

Las Vegas (34 teams)
Hoinke Classic, Cincinnati
(Wendy Macpherson, Alisia Kellow, Regina Snodgrass,
Nancy Fehr, Tish Johnson)

Fort Worth, Texas (17 teams)
Team Brunswick, Wichita, Kan.
(Cindy Kesterson, Debbie Walker, Jodi Jensen, Lynda Norry,
Marci Williams)

Indianapolis (36 teams)
TEAM USA
(Lisa Duenow, Lesia Moos, Lucy Giovinco, Becky Kregling,
Kendra Cameron)

Baltimore (39 teams)
ConBow, Buffalo, N.Y.
(Sue Nawojski, Laura Colavito, Liz Johnson, Jennifer
Daugherty, Sue Jeziorski)

Silver Legacy Grand Championships
Reno, Nev. (Aug. 24-27, 1997)

OPEN DIVISION

1. Turbo 2-N-1 Grips, Chesterfield, Mich.	$25,000
2. TEAM USA	$15,000
3. Asher's Embroidery, Costa Mesa, Calif.	$10,000

Playoff results - Turbo 2-N-1 Grips def. Asher's Embroidery 372-368 and Turbo 2-N-1 Grips def. TEAM USA 347-327.

Other semifinalists — 4, Hammer, Fulton, N.Y., $8,000. 5, Acme Pawn, Colorado Springs, Colo., $6,000. 6, Linds Limited, Milwaukee, $5,500. 7, Brunswick, Pittsburgh, $5,000. 8, Ebonite Nitro/R's, Hopkinsville, Ky., $4,750.

Others — 9, McGerr's Pro Shop, Lincoln, Neb., $4,500. 10, Columbia Cuda C's, New City, N.Y., $4,250. 11, The Shoppe, Tacoma, Wash., $4,000. 12, Contour Grips, Milwaukee, $3,800. 13, Team Finland, $3,600. 14, ESP, Harrisburg, Pa., $3,400. 15, Contour Grips, Spokane, Wash., $3,200. 16, Trophies Unlimited, Richmond, Va., $3,000. 17, Maryland Crew, Burtonsville, Md., $2,800. 18, ABBA Treb de Fox/Pollard's Bowl, Cincinnati, $2,650. 19, Team Korea, $2,500. 20, International Voice Messaging, Salt Lake City, $2,350. 21, Contour Grips, Tacoma, Wash., $2,200. 22,

Unique Embroidery, Lansing, Mich., $2,050. 23., Deer Acres, Bay City, Mich., $1,900. 24, Lodge Lanes, Belleville, Mich., $1,750. 25, Team China, $1,600. 26, ABS Pro AM, Japan, $1,475. 27, Team Germany, $1,350. 28, Rock River Lanes, Ft. Atkinson, Wis., $1,225. 29, Ashi Bowling Service, Japan, $1,125. 30, Nippon Brunswick, Japan, $1,000.

WOMEN'S DIVISION

1. TEAM USA	$11,000
2. Team Korea,	$9,000
3. Reb's Pretty Girl International, West Hollywood, Calif.	$7,000

Playoff results — Team Korea def. Reb's Pretty Girl International 360-359 and TEAM USA def. Team Korea 369-348.

Other semifinalists — 4, Hoinke Classic, Cincinnati, $5,500. 5, Kinco Ltd., Jacksonville, Fla., $4,500. 6, Conbow, Tonawanda, N.Y., $3,500.

Others — 7, Nippon Brunswick, Japan, $2,800. 8, Team Brunswick, Wichita, Kan., $2,200. 9, Bowlers Edge, Glendale, Ariz., $1,700. 10, Contour Power Grips, Portage, Mich., $1,300. 11, Team China, $1,000.

1995-96 Regional Winners
Open Division

San Antonio (34 teams)
Boulevard Bowl, Edmond, Okla.
(Billy Young Jr., David Garber, Shane Hamilton, Pat Stinnett,
Mike Edwards)

Portland (46 teams)
The Shoppe, Tacoma, Wash.
(Don Freund, Mike Clark, Purvis Granger, Fred Mattson,
Lenny Blakey)

Hubbard, Ohio (46 teams)
Columbia Cuda C's, San Antonio, Texas
(Brian Boghosian, Jim Johnson Jr., Patrick Allen, Mike
Mullin, Mike Lichstein)

Wichita, Kan. (36 teams)
Columbia, Lincoln, Neb.
(Ryan Kretchmer, Bryan O'Keefe, Jeff Beasley, Rick Miller,
Kevin McGerr)

Vernon Hills, Ill. (64 teams)
Vise Grips, Vernon Hills, Ill.
(Davey Rosen, Vince Biondo, Larry Dilworth, Tony Cariello,
Dave Sill, Adam Colton)

Harrisburg, Pa. (68 teams)
Columbia/Turbo Grips, Dayton, Ohio
(Sean Quinn, Bob Bush, Bill Peters, Chris Nicewaner, Brian
Kretzer)

Orange, Calif. (68 teams)
Braasch Pro Shops, Orange, Calif.
(Joe Roussin, Rich Souddress, Mike McAleer, Jeff Carr, Andy Neeman)

St. Louis (52 teams)
Storm, Versailles, Ind.
(Rick Pollard, Al Runker, Dave Welage, Ron Pollard, Don Scudder)

Greeley, Colo. (44 teams)
Turbo 2-N-1 Grips, Chesterfield, Mich.
(Shawn Christensen, Bill Campbell, Gordy Kilpatrick, Scott Myers, Mike Miller)

St. Petersburg, Fla. (112 teams)
Brunswick, Pittsburgh
(Robert Alexander, Mike Chontos, Jeff Poholsky, Roger Kossert, Parker Bohn III)

Las Vegas (68 teams)
Vise Grips/Storm, Anaheim, Calif.
(Billy Myers Jr., Tim Mack, Robert Smith, Mike DeVaney, Barry Asher)

Fort Worth, Texas (88 teams)
Ebonite Nitro/R's, Hopkinsville, Ky.
(Billy Murphy, Paul Fleming, Sean Swanson, Lonnie Waliczek, Chad Murphy)

Indianapolis (80 teams)
Tri-State Bowling Supply, Cincinnati
(Dave Welage, Dean Lightbourn, Marc Massie, Nick Vogelgesang, Tim Weisbrod)

Tacoma, Wash. (60 teams)
Contour Power Grips II, Seattle
(Fred Conradi, Jeff Knapp, Dave Beckmann, Ken Darwin, Hugh Miller)

Cheektowaga, N.Y. (92 teams)
Vise Grips, Buffalo, N.Y.
(Jack Jurek, Brad Kiszewski, Brian Eaton, John Masiello, Mike Neumann)

Detroit (76 teams)
KR Industries, Chicago
(LeMire Schmeglar, LeRoy Johnson, Sherry Weatherly Jr., Mike Machuga, Bill Oatman)

Eagan, Minn. (60 teams)
Ebonite Omegas, Hopkinsille, Ky.
(Pat Healey Jr., Mika Koivuniemi, Bob Goike, John Gaines, Chris Barnes)

Norcross, Ga. (76 teams)
Don Carter's All-Star Lanes, Sunrise, Fla.
(Jim Queen, Tommy Evans, Paul Apolinario, Tony LeVance, Todd Agee, Dennis Rakauskas)

Dublin, Calif. (76 teams)
Todd's Bowling Supply, Las Vegas
(Ken Fernandez, Rick Berry, Tim Scott, Ricky Corona, Mike McGrath)

Pittsburgh (84 teams)
Turbo 2-N-1 Grips, Chesterfield, Mich.
(Steve Fehr, Brian Kretzer, John Hricsina, Ted Hannahs, Dave Bernhardt)

Kansas City (79 teams)
Vise Grips/Storm, San Antonio, Texas
(Lonnie Waliczek, Mark Dyson, Richard Howell, Steve Patterson, Joe Vito Buenrostro)

Baltimore (76 teams)
Pacific Storm, Fulton, N.Y.
(Rudy Kasimakis, Brad Angelo, Kurt Pilon, Doug Kent, Mike Tryniski)

Women's Division

Orange, Calif. (12 teams)
Brunswick Frameworx, Muskegon, Mich.
(Nedra Jerry, Sandi Smith, Laura Hardeman, Char Hammel, Cindy Coburn-Carroll)

St. Petersburg, Fla. (24 teams)
Windy City Omegas, Chicago
(Lisa Vint, Michelle Mullen, Pam Inloes, Lucy Giovinco, Marianne DiRupo)

Las Vegas (36 teams)
Ebonite Omegas, Hopkinsville, Ky.
(Kelly Everding, Lisa Skibinski, Tara Henderson, Leanne Barrette, Carolyn Dorin-Ballard)

Indianapolis (40 teams)
Sherman Towing, O'Fallon, Mo.
(Paula Stinski, Angie Goettel, Kim Kramer, Regi Jonak, Tracy Sherman, Pam Dobbins)

Concord/Dublin, Calif. (20 teams)
Contour Power Grips, Brea, Calif.
(Jenelle Poodry, Susan Heffern, Tammy Peltzer, Shannon Jaramillo, Rachel Walters)

Baltimore (48 teams)
Contour Power Grips, Detroit
(Marianne DiRupo, Lisa Bishop, Timi McCorvey, Kathy Haislip, Aleta Sill)

TREASURE CHEST CASINO GRAND CHAMPIONSHIPS
Kenner, La. (Aug. 24-27, 1996)

OPEN DIVISION

1, Ebonite Nitro/R's, Wichita, Kan. $25,000. 2, Columbia Cuda C's, San Antonio, Texas, $15,000. 3. Linds Limited, Milwaukee, Wis. $10,000.

Playoff results — Ebonite Nitro/R def. Linds Limited 392-385 and Ebonite Nitro/R's def. Columbia Cuda C's 510-380.

Other semifinalists — 4, Ebonite Omegas, Hopkinsville, Ky., $8,000. 5, Pacific Storm, Fulton, N.Y., $7,000. 6, Vise Grips/Storm, Anaheim, Calif., $6,000. 7, Turbo 2-N-1 Grips, Chesterfield, Mich., $5,500. 8, The Shoppe, Tacoma, Wash., $5,000.

Others — 9, Columbia, Lincoln, Neb., $4,500. 10, Boulevard Bowl, Edmond, Okla., $4,300. 11, Vise Grips, Buffalo, N.Y., $4,100. 12, Team Sweden, $3,900. 13, Storm, Versailles, Ind., $3,700. 14, Don Carter All-Star Lanes, Sunrise, Fla., $3,500. 15, Turbo 2-N-1 Grips, Denver, $3,300. 16, Contour Power Grips II, Tacoma, Wash., $3,100. 17, Team Finland/Brunswick, $3,000. 18, Storm/Vise Grips, San Antonio, $2,800. 19, Storm Dexter USA, Cambridge, Mass., $2,600. 20, Brunswick, Pittsburgh, $2,400. 21, Columbia/Turbo Grips, Dayton, Ohio, $2,200. 22, TEAM USA, $2,000. 23, Ebonite Chicago, Chicago, $1,800. 24, Todd's Bowling Supply, Las Vegas, $1,700. 25, Tri-State Bowling Supply, Cincinnati, $1,600. 26, Team Japan ABS, $1,500. 27, Vise Grips Inserts, Vernon Hills, Ill. 28, Strike Ten Entertainment, Racine, Wis., $1,300. 29, Team Japan Bench Warmers, $1,200. 30, Braasch Pro Shop, Orange, Calif., $1,100. 31, Team Germany, $1,000.

WOMEN'S DIVISION

1. Ebonite Omegas, Hopkinsville, Ky.	$11,000
2. TEAM USA	$9,000
3. Windy City Wolf Pack.	$7,000

Playoff results — TEAM USA def Windy City Wolf Pack 394-374 and Ebonite Omegas def TEAM USA 400-380.

Other semifinalists — 4, Contour Power Grips, Detroit, $5,500. 5, Brunswick Frameworx, Muskegon, Mich., $4,500. 6, Sherman Towing, O'Fallon, Mo., $3,500.

Others — 7, The Naccarato Group, Tacoma, Wash., $2,800. 8, Contour Power Grips/Fantastic Sam's, Brea, Calif., $2,200. 9, Team Canada/Hammer, $1,700. 10, Team Japan, $1,300. 11, Contour Collegiate All-Stars, $1,000.

1994-95 Regional Winners
Open Division

Portland, Ore. (42 teams)
No Fear, Eugene, Ore.
(Bob Humbert, Dean Bollinger, Marv LaVasseur, Jim Brockland, Scott Buckingham)

Hubbard, Ohio (56 teams)
Bowler's Choice Pro Shop, Buffalo, N.Y.
(Mike Neumann, John Masiello, Brad Kiszewski, Jack Jurek and Mike Eaton)

Vernon Hills, Ill. (63 teams)
Bass Open Pro Shops, Springfield, Mo.
(Brett Sterley, Randy Weimer, Greg Shields, John Hricsina, Randy Lightfoot)

Harrisburg, Pa. (72 teams)
Team Champions, Baltimore
(Lee Brosius, Mike Wheeler, Kurt Schmidt, Brian Bever, Bruce Hollen)

Fountain Valley, Calif. (60 teams)
Bowler's Depot, San Diego
(Steve Gagliano, Charlie Whitaker, Joel Reyes, Al Cullins, Mike Taylor)

St. Charles, Mo. (59 teams)
Hoinke Super Classic, Lincoln, Neb.
(Jim Dill, Tony Manna, Brian Himmler, Bryan O'Keefe, Kevin McGerr)

San Antonio (33 teams)
Showplace Lanes, Austin, Texas
(Jim Sneary, John Hood, James Roberts, Jimmy Thompson, Robert Lawrence)

St. Petersburg, Fla. (100 teams)
Saz's Barbecue Sauce, Milwaukee
(Doug Becker, Joe Natoli, Brian Brazeau, Jace Peterson, Ken Siarkiewicz)

Fort Worth, Texas (77 teams)
Ebonite Nitro/R's, Hopkinsville, Ky.
(Billy Murphy, Chad Murphy, Sean Swanson, Lonnie Walizcek, Paul Fleming)

Indianapolis (76 teams)
Super Hoinke Classic, Cincinnati
(Dave Welege, Marc Massie, Nick Vogelgesang, Charlie Standish, Tim Weisbrod)

Tacoma, Wash. (60 teams)
Team Storm, Tacoma, Wash.
(Layton Shirley, Peter Somoff, Purvis Granger, Lenny Blakey, Fred Mattson)

Cheektowaga, N.Y. (58 teams)
Turbo 2-N-1 Grips, Chesterfield, Mich.
(Mark Moore, Steve Fehr, Gene Stus, Ted Hannahs, Dave Bernhardt, Bob Learn Jr.)

Woodbury, Minn. (60 teams)
J.C. Body Shop, Schaumburg, Ill.
(Jerry Cullum, Kelly Plummer, Jamie Sensabaugh, Shawn Morris, Scott Salbeck, Tony Mazzocchi)

Edmond, Okla. (56 teams)
Madsen's B&B, Lincoln, Neb.
(John Losito, Randy Wilson Jr., Ryan Kretchmer, Rick Miller, Bryan O'Keefe, John Madsen)

Norcross, Ga. (76 teams)
Lou Scalia's Pro Shop, Davie, Fla.
(Larry Barwick, Rob Comito, Stan Garner, Dave Olm, Sam Zurich)

Dublin, Calif. (76 teams)
Ace Paving, Port Orchard, Wash.
(Bill Rowe, Frank DeRemer, Bob Davidson, Matt Surina, Curtis Messer)

Baltimore (76 teams)
Ebonite, Hopkinsville, Ky.
(Bill Rowe, Chris Barnes, Bob Goike, Steve Kloempken, John Gaines)

Kansas City (81 teams)
Brunswick Bayliners, Muskegon, Mich.
(Mike Machuga, Jeff Beasley, Mike Shady, Chris Barnes, Rick Miller)

Pittsburgh (79 teams)
(Mike Gordish, Bill Hoffman, Ted Hannahs, Dave D'Entremont, Rudy Kasimakis)

Women's Division

Las Vegas (28 teams)
Team Tulsa WBA, Tulsa, Okla.
(Patty Peachey, Nanci Johnson, Becky Weston, Claudia Whitmarsh, Terri McClure, Paula Drake)

Indianapolis (38 teams)
Contour Power Grips, Detroit
(Lisa Bishop, Carmen Allen, Jeanne Gebbia, Jodi Monday, Aleta Sill and Kathy Haislip)

Baltimore (39 teams)
Vise Grips, Bel Air, Md.
(Jeri Edwards, Brenda Norman, Jen Larson, Brenda Edwards, Kathy Zielke)

CIRCUS CIRCUS GRAND CHAMPIONSHIPS
Reno, Nev. (July 16-19, 1995)

OPEN DIVISION

1. TEAM USA	$25,000
2. Turbo 2-N-1 Grips, Chesterfield, Mich.	14,000
3. Ebonite International, Hopkinsville, Ky.	9,000
4. Brunswick Team Finland	6,750

Playoff results — Turbo 2-N-1 Grips def. Brunswick Team Finland 379-362, Turbo 2-N-1 Grips def. Ebonite International 335-331 and TEAM USA def. Turbo 2-N-1 Grips 370-363.

Other finalists — 5, Ebonite, Hopkinsville, Ky., $6,500. 6, Ebonite Omegas, Lincoln, Neb., $6,000. 7, Team Qatar, $5,250. 8, No Fear, Eugene, Ore., $5,000. 9, Turbo 2-N-1 Grips II, Chesterfield, Mich., $4,750. 10, Ace Paving, Port Orchard, Wash., $4,750.

WOMEN'S DIVISION

1, Contour Power Grips, Detroit	$10,000
2, Contour Grips/TEAM USA	$7,500

Playoff results — Contour Power Grips def. Contour Grips/TEAM USA 393-331.

Other Open Division — 11, Contour Power Grips/Saz's, Milwaukee, $4,500. 12, San Diego Storm, San Diego, $4,000. 13, Team Columbia, Lackawanna, N.Y., $3,500. 14, Columbia Super Hoinke, Cincinnati, $3,100. 15, Bass Pro Shop, Springfield, Mo., $2,700. 16, Scalia's Ebonite, Hollywood, Fla., $2,400. 17, Showplace Lanes, Austin, Texas, $2,200. 18, Madsen's B&B, Lincoln, Neb., $2,000. 19, Team Storm, Tacoma, Wash., $1,800. 20, Team Champions, Baltimore, $1,700. 22, Brunswick Hoinke, Cincinnati, $1,600. 24. J.C. Auto Body, Schaumburg, Ill., $1,500.

Other International (International teams not making the top 10 competed for a separate prize fund) — 21, Brunswick Team Canada, $4,500. 23, Japan ABS Pro Am, $3,500. 25,

Others — 3, Lane No. 1 Buzz Saws, Vallejo, Calif., $3,500. 4, Vise Grips, Bel Air, Md., $3,500. 5, Linds Collegians, Somerset, Wis., $2,500. 6. Team Tulsa WBA, Tulsa, Okla., $2,000.

1993-94 Regional Winners

Los Angeles (34 teams)
Bowlers Journal, Los Angeles
(Mike McGrath, Damon Cardwell, Tom Underwood, Ricky Corona, Tim Schwerdtfeger)

Denver (44 teams)
Saz's Barbecue Sauce, Milwaukee
(Joe Natoli, Brian Brazeau, Nile Konicek, Ken Siarkewicz, Jace Peterson)

Pittsburgh (39 teams)
Turbo 2-N-1 Grips, Detroit
(Kerry Kreft, Kurt Pilon, Mike Gordish, Ted Hannahs, Bob Learn Jr.)

Chicago (60 teams)
Brunswick Rhino Pros, Buffalo
(Pat Stefanik, Bob Santini, Mike Firzak, Bob Ujvari, Mike Faliero)

Oklahoma City (34 teams)
Boulevard Bowl No. 1, Edmond, Okla.
(Mike Ratliff, Shane Hamilton, Norm Duke, Joe Vito Buenrostro, Brian Berg)

St. Louis (60 teams)
Weber's Lanes, St. Charles, Mo.
(John Weber, Dennis Sherman, Kevin Toebbin, Dick Weber, Eugene McCune)

St. Petersburg (58 teams)
Pro Sports Systems, Vancouver, Wash.

(Don Sylvia, Kenny Lawson, Michael Cross, Robert Layman, Ernie Schlegel)

Dallas/Ft. Worth (80 teams)
Ebonite Nitro/R, Hopkinsville, Ky.
(Paul Fleming, Chad Murphy, Sean Swanson, Chris Barnes, Steve Kloempken)

Flint/Michigan (60 teams)
Ansara's Big Boy, Detroit
(Steve Roberts, Tony Stipcak, Mark Moore, Ken Kossick, Bob Chamberlain)

Seattle/Tacoma (64 teams)
Tabs Unlimted, Tacoma, Wash.
(Darrel Curtis, Mike Clark, Dave Hanson, Bob Hanson, Jim Kent)

Twin Cities (47 teams)
Sportstreet Classic, Milwaukee
(Gus Yannaras, Gary Daroszewski, Steve Brinkman, Lennie Boresch, Dale Traber)

Atlanta (76 teams)
River Lanes, Titusville, Fla.
(John Janawicz, Dave Oesch, John Joslyn, Ken May, Pete Couture)

New Jersey (68 teams)
Brunswick Rhino Pros II, Lackawanna, N.Y.
(John Masiello, Tom Baker, Jack Jurek, Brian Eaton, Mike Neumann)

Dublin California (76 teams)
Elma Lanes, Elma, Wash.
(Henry Dawson, Frank DeRemer, Bob Davidson, Matt Surina, Curtis Messer)

Baltimore (76 teams)
Country Club Lanes, Burlington, N.C.
(Chico Valenzuela, Mark Mosayebi, Dave Meurs, Jamie Reed, Curtis Odom, Bonnie Gibson)

GRAND CHAMPIONSHIP
Reno, Nev. (June 25-27, 1994)

1. Ebonite Nitro/R, Hopkinsville, Ky.	$25,000
2. Brunswick Rhino Pro II, Buffalo, N.Y.	15,000
3. Elma Lanes, Elma, Wash.	12,000
4. TEAM USA Men	9,000
5. Brunswick Scandinavia	6,500
6. Sportstreet Classic, Milwaukee	5,500
7. Finland	5,000

Playoff results (Three-game Baker Format matches) — TEAM USA Men def. Brunswick Scandinavia 607-526, Ebonite Nitro/R def. TEAM USA Men 526-522, Ebonite Nitro/R def. Elma Lanes 576-499 and Ebonite Nitro/R def. Brunswick Rhino Pro II 543-539.

Other U.S. Division teams — 5. Turbo 2-N-1 Grips, Detroit, $5,000; 6. Saz's Barbecue Sauce, Milwaukee, $4,200; 7. Country Club Lanes, Burlington, N.C., $3,600; 8. Boulevard Bowl, Edmond, Okla., $3,200; 9. Brunswick Rhino Pro I, Buffalo, N.Y., $2,800; 10. Weber's St. Charles Lanes, St. Charles, Mo., $2,400; 11. River Lanes, Merritt Island, Fla., $2,100; 12. Bowlers Journal, Los Angeles, $1,900; 13. Pro Sports Systems, Vancouver, Wash., $1,700; 14. Ansara's Big Boy, Detroit, $1,600; 15. TABS Unlimited, Tacoma, Wash., $1,500.

Other International Division teams — 4. Sweden, $4,500; 5. Canada $3,900; 6. Japan $3,300; 7. South Korea, $2,700; 8. TEAM USA women, $2,450; 9. Germany, $2,000; 10. Brazil, $1,750; 11. New Zealand, $1,500.

1992-93 ABC National Team Challenge
Regional Winners

Detroit (30 teams)
Goebel's Light Beer, Detroit
(Jeff Wells, Trey Edwards, Steve Roberts, Mike Lee, Quintin Greene, Ken Charrette)

Syracuse, N.Y. (18 teams)
Mt. Morris Lanes, Mt. Morris, N.Y.
(Mike Firzak, Mike Faliero, Pat Stefanik, Bob Santini, Bob Ujvari)

Chicago (38 teams)
Weber's Lanes, St. Charles, Mo.
(Jerry Anderson, Tom Flanagan, Kevin Bruenig, Randy Lightfoot, Leroy Bornhop)

Pittsburgh (40 teams)
AMF Sumo No. 2, Buffalo
(Jack Jurek, Mike Neumann, John Masiello, Brian Eaton, Tom Baker)

Twin Cities (32 teams)
Saz's Barbeque Sauce, Milwaukee
(Ken Siarkiewicz, Brian Brazeau, Joe Natoli, Joe Alivo, Jace Peterson)

Los Angeles (43 teams)
Bank-On-It, Chino, Calif.
(Doug Kempt, Martin Staggers, Walt Block, Mark Lowder, Dan Riera)

St. Petersburg, Fla. (46 teams)
Scime Signs, Windermere, Fla.
(Duane Podgorski, Dan Saile, Mark Scime, Rick Sotis, Bob Handley)

Ft. Worth, Texas (64 teams)
Kelly's Pro Shop, Omaha, Neb.
(Doug Laird, Dave Axon, Jay Watts, Brian Csipkes, Tom Kelly Jr., John Pearson)

Tacoma, Wash. (60 teams)
Wheatland Bowl, Colfax, Wash.
(Terry Stricker, Jeff Britton, Scott Olinger, Mike McPherson, Bruce Russell)

Atlanta (76 teams)
Thermocarbon, Altamonte Springs, Fla.
(Brad Briggs, Doug Becker, Mario Angelini, Todd Agee, Lenny Biondo)

New Jersey (60 teams)
Columbia 300, San Antonio, Texas
(Mike Lichstein, Rudy Kasimakis, Gary Shultis, Patrick Allen, Jimmy Johnson)

Baltimore (60 teams)
Ebonite Crush/R, Hopkinsville, Ky.
(Steve Kloempken, Chris Barnes, Russ Mills, Rob Causer, Doug Kent)

GRAND CHAMPIONSHIP
Reno, Nev. (June 25-27, 1993)

1. Brunswick Rhino Pro I, Buffalo	$10,000
2. Team Columbia, San Antonio	5,000
3. Brunswick Rhino Pro II, Buffalo	4,000
4. Thermocarbon, Altamonte Springs, Fla.	3,000

Playoff results — Brunswick Rhino Pro I (formerly Mt. Morris Lanes) def. Thermocarbon 548-498 (three games), Brunswick Rhino Pro I (formerly AMF Sumo No. 2) def. Brunswick Rhino Pro II 601-559 and Brunswick Rhino Pro I def. Team Columbia (formerly Columbia 300) 563-546.

Other results — 5. Columbia 300 (formerly Scime Signs), Windermere, Fla.; 6. Kelly's Pro Shop, Omaha, Neb.; 7. AMF Ninjas (formerly Weber's Lanes), St. Charles, Mo.; 8. Ebonite Crush/Rs, Hopkinsville, Ky.; 9. Complete Bowling Service (formerly Wheatland Bowl), Colfax, Wash.; 10. Saz's Barbeque Sauce, Milwaukee; 11. Goebel Light, Detroit; 12. Bank-On-It, Chino Hills, Calif.

Intercollegiate competition is comprised of 2,027 students in 135 U.S. university, college and junior college bowling programs. Intercollegiate membership provides competition rules and awards for high individual and conference performances. Bowlers compete for titles at the local, regional and national levels. Three prestigious national titles annually determined are the Intercollegiate Bowling Championships for teams and the Women's Intercollegiate Championships and Association of College Unions-International Championships for female and male individuals.

Intercollegiate Bowling Championships

The Intercollegiate Bowling Championships supply unique team competition for 32 teams (16 men's and 16 women's). The five-player teams bowl two four-game blocks and three blocks of eight Baker System two-game matches. The top-three scoring teams in both divisions advance to the tournament's stepladder finals.

Within each two-game Baker System match, a game victory earns teams 15 bonus points and a match victory earns teams 20 additional bonus points. Pinfall and bonus pins carry over throughout the tournament.

The field is cut to the six highest-scoring teams in both the women's and men's divisions. These teams continue competing in two two-game Baker System matches. The first two-game match comprises the finals competition. Match pairings are determined by tournament position and game and match bonus pins are awarded.

Teams compete in the finals for gold, silver and bronze medals. Tournament officials present the finalists' schools with trophies and the tournament champions with rings and trophies.

The tournament was the first national bowling championship to use the Baker System format. In the Baker System, a team's first player bowls the first and sixth frames, the second player bowls the second and seventh frames, the third player bowls the third and eighth frames, the fourth player bowls the fourth and ninth frames, and the fifth player bowls the fifth and 10th frames.

The 32 teams earn their Intercollegiate Bowling Championships berths through 10 automatic berth tournaments and three National Qualifier tournaments. The Young American Bowling Alliance conducts the Intercollegiate Bowling Championships in a different U.S. city each year. Through 1990, the tournament was titled the National Collegiate Bowling Championships.

Intercollegiate Bowling Championships Champions

Women's Division
1997.........................University of Nebraska, Lincoln, Neb.
1996 ....West Texas A&M University, Canyon, Texas
1995.........................University of Nebraska, Lincoln, Neb.
1994.......................Wichita State University, Wichita, Kan.
1993 ....William Paterson College, Wayne, N.J.
1992.......................West Texas State University, Canyon, Texas
1991.........................University of Nebraska, Lincoln, Neb.
1990.......................Wichita State University, Wichita, Kan.
1989.................Morehead State University, Morehead, Ky.
1988.................West Texas State University, Canyon, Texas
1987.................West Texas State University, Canyon, Texas
1986.......................Wichita State University, Wichita, Kan.
1985.................West Texas State University, Canyon, Texas
1984....................Indiana State University, Terre Haute, Ind.
1983.................West Texas State University, Canyon, Texas
1982 ....Erie Community College, Buffalo
1981 ....Arizona State University, Tempe, Ariz.
1980 ....Erie Community College, Buffalo
1979....................Penn State University, State College, Pa.
1978.......................Wichita State University, Wichita, Kan.
1977.......................Wichita State University, Wichita, Kan.
1976....................San Jose State University, San Jose, Calif.
1975.......................Wichita State University, Wichita, Kan.

Men's Division
1997..........Saginaw Valley State University, Saginaw, Mich.
1996.........................University of Nebraska, Lincoln, Neb.
1995.......................Wichita State University, Wichita, Kan.
1994.......................Wichita State University, Wichita, Kan.
1993.......................Wichita State University, Wichita, Kan.
1992.......................William Paterson College, Wayne, N.J.
1991 ....Saginaw Valley State University, University Center, Mich.
1990.........................University of Nebraska, Lincoln, Neb.
1989.....California State University-Fullerton, Fullerton, Calif.
1988 ....Erie Community College, Buffalo
1987.......................Wichita State University, Wichita, Kan.
1986 ....Erie Community College, Buffalo
1985 ....University of Wisconsin-La Crosse
1984 ....Buffalo State College, Buffalo
1983..........................Vincennes University, Vincennes, Ind.
1982 ....Washington State University, Pullman, Wash.
1981 ....Arizona State University, Tempe, Ariz.
1980 ....Wichita State University, Wichita, Kan.
1979 ....University of California-Berkeley, Berkeley, Calif.
1978..........................University of Minnesota, Minneapolis
1977.........West Liberty State University, West Liberty, W.Va.
1976 ....University of South Carolina, Columbia, S.C.
1975 ....University of Wisconsin-La Crosse

Intercollegiate Bowling Championships Records

Women's Division

18-Game Baker System Score, highest by five-player team
3,579	West Texas State University, 1992
3,540	Wichita State University, 1992
3,525	University of Nebraska, 1992

Four-Game Series, highest by five-player team
4,143	Wichita State University, 1994
4,128	West Texas State University, 1990
4,115	University of Nebraska, 1995

Four-Game Series, highest by individual
947	Robin Davis, West Texas State University, 1988
939	Jennifer Swanson, Sacred Heart University, 1995
932	Amy Knorowski, William Paterson College, 1990

Game, highest by individuals
300	Stacy Manley, California State University-Sacramento, 1992
298	Therese Abair, California State University-Fullerton, 1986
289	Lisa McGinnis, Morehead State University, 1988

Team Game, highest by five-player team
1,130	West Texas State University, 1992
1,122	University of Nebraska, 1997
1,120	William Paterson College, 1990

Team Game, highest in Baker System
289	San Jose State University, 1990
	Morehead State University, 1995
279	West Texas-A&M University, 1997

Three-Game Series, highest by individual
774	Stacy Manley, California State University-Sacramento, 1992
737	Kathy McNeil, Erie Community College, 1990
736	Robin Davis, West Texas State University, 1988

12-Game Baker System Score, highest by five-player team
2,456	University of Nebraska, 1992
2,449	Wichita State University, 1992
2,426	West Texas State University, 1992

12-Game Qualifying Score, highest by five-player team
12,042	University of Nebraska, 1997
11,909	West Texas State University, 1990
11,860	West Texas State University, 1992

24-Game Baker System Score, highest by five-player team
4,868	West Texas State A&M University, 1997
4,767	University of Nebraska, 1992
4,709	West Texas State University, 1992
4,666	West Texas State University, 1993

32-Game Baker System Score, highest by five-player team
6,394	West Texas A&M University, 1997
6,159	Wichita State University, 1996
6,035	West Texas A&M University, 1996

Men's Division

18-Game Baker System Score, highest by five-player team
3,807	Wichita State University, 1988
3,791	Wichita State University, 1992
3,774	S.W. Missouri State University, 1979

Four-Game Series, highest by five-player team
4,334	Wichita State University, 1990
4,320	Wichita State University, 1990
4,296	California State University-Fullerton, 1996

Four-Game Series, highest by individual
993	Ken Cobbley, University of Houston, 1990
992	Tony Manna Jr., University of Nebraska, 1994
967	Pat Healey Jr., Wichita State University, 1990

Game, highest by individual
299	Ken Cobbley, University of Houston, 1990
290	Tom Castellano, San Jose State University, 1980
	Lonnie Waliczek, Wichita State University, 1990
	Brian Weeks, Florida State University, 1993

Team Game, highest by five-player team
1,224	Erie Community College, 1990
1,209	University of Nebraska, 1990
1,205	University of Nebraska, 1990

Team Game, highest in Baker System
299	Erie Community College, 1988
298	St. John's University, 1993
289	Saginaw Valley State University, 1990

Three-Game Series, highest by individual
800	David Garber, Wichita State University, 1992
752	Steve Ewald, Michigan State University, 1993
747	Ken Cobbley, University of Houston, 1990

12-Game Baker System Score, highest by five-player team
2,599	West Virginia University, 1992
2,571	S.W. Missouri State University, 1979
2,563	Wichita State University, 1992

12-Game Qualifying Score, highest by five-player team
12,875	Wichita State University, 1990
12,613	University of Nebraska, 1990
12,397	San Jose State University, 1992

24-Game Baker System Score, highest by five-player team
4,957	Wichita State University, 1992
4,917	Saginaw Valley State University, 1990
4,905	West Virginia University, 1992

32-Game Baker System Score, highest by five-player team
6,297	University of Nebraska, 1996
6,282	Wichita State University, 1996
6,224	Arizona State University, 1997

Women's Intercollegiate Championships Champions

Individual Champions

1997 Janette Piesczynski, Erie Community College, 3,249
1996 Lisa Duenow, St. Cloud State University, 3,174
1995 Jennifer Swanson, Sacred Heart University, 3,157
1994 Karen Stroud, West Texas A&M University, 3,151
1993 Kim Wong, California State University-Fresno, 2,963
1992 Tammy Turner, West Texas State University, 2,930
1991 Linda Woods, University of Florida*, 2,896
1990 Linda Woods, University of Florida, 2,052
1989 Lynda Norry, San Jose State University, 1,855
1988 Dionne Lee, San Jose State University, 1,826
1987 Donna DiTrani, Wichita State University, 1,908
1986 Vicki Parker, Indiana State University, 1,690
1985 Michelle Mullen, University of Illinois, 1,824
1984 Suzette Mitchell, Virginia Tech University, 1,680
1983 Lori Wisnowski, Temple University, 1,735
1982 Melisa Day, Ball State University, 1,698
1981 Michele Citro, Penn State University, 1,691
1980 Terry Yoshihara, Hillsborough Community College, 1,784
1979 Sandi Tice, Erie Community College, 1,832
1978 Nikki Gianulias, Solano Community College, 1,739
1977 Lauren LaCost, Illinois State University, 1,681
1976 Lucy Giovinco, Hillsborough Community College, 1,734
1975 Debra Iwaniak, Canisius College, 1,697
1974 Debra Manning, Indiana State University, 1,675
1973 Susan Halloway, Indiana University, 1,752
1972 Diane West, Colorado State University, 1,739
1971 Barbara Duns, Mesa College, 1,629
1970 Michele Block, Ithaca College, 1,134
1969 Barbara Leicht, SUNY-Brockport, 1,143
1968 Brenda Rahn, University of Maryland, 1,122
1967 Pamela Fryer, Arizona State University, 1,136
1966 Judy Boeder, University of Wisconsin-La Crosse 1,070
1965 Lynne Robertson, Boston University, 1,638
1964 Frances Airing, University of Iowa, 1,773
1963 Janet Sheridan, SUNY-Cortland, 1,089
1962 Betty Jo Crow, University of Kansas, 1,090
* Defeated Dionne Lee of California State University-Fresno, 205-202, in tie breaker to win title

Doubles

1997 Debbie Rudd-Christy Lynette, University of Florida & Indiana State University 1,182
1996 Jennifer Swanson-Tammy Peltzer, Sacred Heart University-California State-Fullerton, 1,354
1995 Julie Johnson-Lisa Duenow, North Dakota State University & St. Cloud State University, 1,302
1994 Jennifer Swanson-Melinda Johnson, Sacred Heart College & Morehead State University, 1,152
1993 Colby Stejbach-Tina Fick, Erie Community College & Essex Community College, 1,131
1992 Kim Laird-Tammy Turner, Illinois State University & West Texas State University, 1,131
1991 Kari Murph-Pam Flowers, Morehead State University & Colorado State University, 1,177
1990 Jana Ohlendorf-Amy Hickman, Central Missouri State University & University of Florida, 1,126
1989 Juliann Brodziski-Lynda Norry, University of Wisconsin-La Crosse & San Jose State University, 1,273
1988 Betsy Peck-Lori Mason, Idaho State University & Arizona State University, 1,110

1987 Lynn Pruitt-Karen Senior, Indiana State University & University of Florida, 1,169
1986 Karen Coombs-Julie Bishop, Morehead State University & West Texas State University, 1,183
1985 Stacy Peterson-Rozalynd Monell, University of Florida & Wichita State University, 1,159
1984 Suzette Mitchell-Jan Schmidt, Virginia Tech University & Indiana State University, 1,152
1983 Debbie Horn-Mary Hardman, Oklahoma State University & Wichita State University, 1,100
1982 Melisa Adrian-Donna Kolb, Ball State University & Western Illinois University, 1,118
1981 Michele Zeiders-Carol Palangio, Penn State University & Robert Morris College, 1,124
1980 Terry Yoshihara-Michele Sullivan, Hillsborough Community College & West Texas State University, 1,193
1979 Sherry Allen-Candis Vegdahl, Wichita State University & St. Olaf College, 1,162
1978 Sue Schottke-Diane Johnson, SUNY-Buffalo & University of Montana, 1,109
1977 Lauren LaCost-LuAnn Calsetta, Illinois State University & SUNY-Farmingdale, 1,148
1976 Sue Schottke-Lori Gensch, Erie Community College & University of Wisconsin-Milwaukee, 1,113
1975 Lauren LaCost-Regina Loveall, Illinois State University & West Texas State University, 1,163
1974 Carol Ziegler-Ruthanne Bloyd, Virginia Tech University & Stephen F. Austin (Texas) College, 1,065
1973 Denys Jones-Nancy Young, Utah State University & Lee College, 1,090
1972 Ruth McCune-Sharon Seagraves, SUNY-Farmingdale & California State University-Chico, 1,136
1971 Diane Felton-Sandra Berousek, Colorado State University & University of Texas, 1,132
    Barbara Duns-Lynda Rusnak, Mesa College & SUNY-Farmingdale, Calif., 1,132
1970 Pamela Carver-Deborah Morey, Arizona State University & Appalachian State University, 1,117
1969 Constance Groeninger-Linda Skotnicki, Indiana University & University of Maryland, 1,048
1968 Norma Wallace-Jean Speer, University of Wisconsin-La Crosse & Washington State University, 1,117
1967 Pamela Carver-Susan Pfeffer, Arizona State University & Boston University, 1,148
1966 Lyle Griffith-Pat Karas, University of Kansas & Ithaca College, 1,007
1965 Janet Sheridan-Kim Kagaard, SUNY-Cortlane & University of Maryland, 1,146
1964 Lynne Robertson-Betty Jo Crow, University of Kansas & Boston University, 1,125
1963 Marjorie Pope-Diane Kopta, Washington State University & Portland State University, 994
1962 Frances Wolf-Betty Jo Crow, University of Iowa & University of Kansas, 1,075

Mixed Doubles

1997   Mindee Pullman-Dave Puffami, University of Utah
       & Morehead State University, 1,249
1996   Unavailable
1995   Jennifer Swanson-Chad Autore, Sacred Heart
       University, 1,319

Singles

1997   Marjorie Tassone, Arizona State University, 635
1996   Kelly Kulik, Morehead State, 702
1995   Andrea Rigby, University of Nebraska, 663
1994   Karen Stroud, West Texas A&M University, 682
1993   Liz Johnson, Morehead State University, 661
1992   Cindy Suber, Wright State University, 597
1991   Dionne Lee, California State University
       Fresno, 668
1990   Tracie Harook, Indiana State University, 668
1989   Kim Johnson, Washington State University, 681
1988   Jackie Sellers, Penn State University, 631
1987   Lisa McGinnis, Morehead State University, 659
1986   Karen Coombs, Morehead State University,
       661
1985   Rozalynd Monell, Wichita State University, 607
1984   Michelle Elkienbaum, University of Florida, 624

1983   Jan Speers, Linn-Benton Community College, 668
1982   Melisa Adrian, Ball State University, 575
1981   Linda Painter, Michigan State University, 596
1980   Terry Yoshihara, Hillsborough Community
       College, 608
1979   Valerie Bright, Penn State University, 610
1978   Lauren LaCost, Illinois State University, 585
1977   Sally Graybeal, Iowa State University, 599
1976   Diane Kerr, Bowling Green University, 606
       Pat McClellan, Penn State University, 606
1975   Sharon Swierczynski, Mott College, 583
1974   Lori Gensch, University of Wisconsin-
       Milwaukee, 554
1973   Susan Halloway, Indiana University, 622
1972   Diane Felton, Colorado State University, 584
1971   June Paciga, University of Illinois-Chicago, 554
1970   Michele Block, Ithaca College, 647
1969   Annette Fujii, California State University-Chico, 564
1968   Brenda Rahn, University of Maryland, 573
1967   Sandra Culp, Iowa State University, 545
1966   Judy Boeder, University of Wisconsin-La Crosse, 552
1965   Carla Rupert, Bowling Green University, 632
1964   Fran Wolf, University of Iowa, 626
1963   Janet Sheridan, SUNY-Cortland, 576
1962   San Lynn Merrick, Bowling Green University, 564

Women's National Intercollegiate Championships
Tournament Records

Game, highest by individuals
300   Kelly Kulick, Morehead State University, 1996
299   Jennifer Swanson, Sacred Heart University, match
       play, 1995
279   Donna DiTrani, Wichita State University, match
       play, 1987
278   Donna DiTrani, Wichita State University, doubles
       play, 1987
275   Laura Wolfgang, Penn State University, match
       play, 1989

Nine-Game Series, highest in all events
1,832   Sandi Tice, Erie Community College, 1979
1,784   Terry Yoshihara, Hillsborough Community College,
        1980
1,773   Fran Wolf, University of Iowa, 1964
1,752   Susie Halloway, Indiana University, 1973
1,741   Debbie George, Georgia State University, 1980

Six-Game Series, highest in all events
1,313   Becky Burkhammer, Montana State University,
        1996
1,290   Lisa Duenow, St. Cloud State University, 1996
1,286   Jennifer Moretti, Temple University, 1996
1,281   Andrea Rigby, University of Nebraska, 1995
        Lisa Duenow, St. Cloud State University, 1995
1,279   Dionne Lee, California State University-Fresno,
        1991

1,254   Sharon Owen-Todd, Morehead State University,
        1989
1,226   Jackie Sellers, Penn State University, 1988
        Jennifer Swanson, Sacred Heart University, 1995

Three-Game Series, highest by doubles team
1,354   Jennifer Swanson-Tammy Peltzer, Sacred Heart
        University & California State University-Fullerton,
        1996
1,306   Janette Piesczynski-Lisa Duenow, Erie Community
        College & St. Cloud State University, 1996
1,305   Jennifer Moretti-Becky Burkhammer, Temple
        University & Montana State University, 1996
1,302   Julie Johnson-Lisa Duenow, North Dakota State
        University & St. Cloud State University, 1995
1,287   Karen Stroud-Billie White, West Texas A&M &
        Mississippi State University, 1996

Three-Game Series, highest by individuals
702   Kelly Kulick, Morehead State University, 1996
700   Traci Maxam, University of Wisconsin-Whitewater,
       1996
681   Kim Johnson, Washington State University, 1989
676   Lynn Pruitt, Indiana State University, 1987
674   Jennifer Swanson, Sacred Heart University, 1995

Association of College Unions-International Championships Champions

All Events

1997 Aaron Walsh, West Texas A&M University, 3,078
1996 John Brockway, Kent State University, 3,169
1995 Mike Mullin, St. John's University, 3,199
1994 Brian Graham, University of Nebraska, 3,170
1993 Vince Biondo, Western Illinois University, 3,202
1992 Eric Cox, University of Florida, 3,285
1991 Chris Barnes, Wichita State University, 3,450
1990 Sanford Carvajal, San Diego State University, 3,127
1989 John Beldy, Bryant College, 3,134
1988 Tracy Lambert, Vincennes University, 3,030
1987 Mark Scroggins, West Texas State University, 3,228
1986 Scott Thomsen, Washington State University, 3,045
1985 Scott Thomsen, Washington State University, 2,976
1984 Jack Jurek, West Texas State University, 2,966
1983 Mike Jasnau, Wichita State University, 2,935
1982 Myrl Serra, Arizona State University, 3,074
1981 Bob Worrall, Northern Arizona University, 2,984
1980 Bob Worrall, Northern Arizona University, 2,456
1979 Dave Higgins, University of Oregon, 2,461
1978 Jeff Bellinger, South Carolina University, 2,374
1977 Ted Schmidt, Hillsborough Community College, 1,995
1976 Mark Schwabe, University of Wisconsin-Milwaukee, 2,116
1975 Nick Romanielo, South Connecticut State University, 1,981
1974 Ralph Welborn, Mt. Hood College, 1,987
1973 Lee Snow, Eastern Michigan University, 1,946
1972 Roger Dalkin, Georgia Tech University, 1,980
1971 Roger Dalkin, Georgia Tech University, 2,022
1970 Wayne Zmrhal, Northern Illinois University, 2,033
1969 Glenn Mueller, University of Wisconsin-La Crosse, 1,205
1968 Jack Connaughton, University of Wisconsin-La Crosse, 1,253
1967 Jack Connaughton, University of Wisconsin-La Crosse, 1,239
1966 Larry Bell, University of Oregon, 1,901
1965 Gary Gibson, Eastern Illinois University, 1,876
1964 Gunnar Voltz, University of Wisconsin-Oshkosh, 1,820
1963 Ted Akin, University of Texas-Arlington, 1,815
1962 George Pajar, Bowling Green University, 1,822
1961 Michael Flanagan, Washington University, 1,792
1960 Jerry Constantino, Bradley University, 1,189
1959 Fred Marcussen, Bradley University, 1,182

Doubles

1997 Adam Cardwell-Josh Chipps, University of Wisconsin-Whitewater & California State-Fresno, 1,261
1996 Stefan Gleason-Keith Butt, University of Florida & Essex Community College, 1,383
1995 Chad Autore-Mike Mullins, Sacred Heart University & St. John's University, 1,311
1994 Gary Schenk-Dave Paffumi, North Carolina State University & Morehead State University, 1,329
1993 Mark Taylor-Pete Borkowski, Sacred Heart College & Buffalo State University, 1,273
1992 Kevin Gurney-Vince Biondo, Washington State University & Western Illinois University, 1,348
1991 Chris Barnes-John Losito, Wichita State University & University of Nebraska, 1,404
1990 Rozell Moore-James Mack, George Washington University & Robert Morris College, 1,248
1989 Scott Johnson-Steve Todd, Morehead State University, 1,252
1988 George Gund-Mark Nelson, University of North Dakota, 1,249
1987 Tom Wannow-Chris Gibbons, University of Wisconsin-Milwaukee & University of Wisconsin-Stout, 1,216
1986 Scott Thomsen-Robert Warrick, Washington State University & Oregon State University, 1,291
1985 Derron Lax-Jack Jurek, University of Texas & West Texas State University, 1,240
1984 Jack Jurek-Mike Shequin, West Texas State University & Chemeketa Community College, 1,167
1983 Steven Roy Elkins-Darryl Paden, University of Florida & Columbus College, 1,233
1982 Myrl Serra-Tim Lynch, Arizona State University & Northern Colorado University, 1,255
1981 Tim Lundberg-Randy Horner, Kansas State University & Southwest Baptist College, 1,244
1980 Marty Schram-Mike Fogel, San Jose State University & University of Santa Clara, 1,189
1979 Doug Chung-Bill Stewart, University of Connecticut & Alfred Tech University, 1,194
1978 Bob Weeks-Dan Eberl, Cornell University & Erie Community College, 1,161
1977 David Buchanan-James Fichera, Alfred State College-Rochester Institute of Technology, 1,172
1976 Tom Porwoll-Ellis Mitchell, Florida State University & University of Alabama, 1,159
1975 Craig Elkins-Robert Pfeil, Santa Clara College & University of California-Davis, 1,203
1974 Jerry Novosel-Richard Ficken, Penn State University & University of Maryland, 1,152
1973 Gary Baker-Rudy Sedillo, University of Northern Colorado & University of Northern Arizona, 1,222
1972 Roger Dalkin-Ken Knowles, Georgia Tech University & Florida State University, 1,166
1971 Dirk Jackson-Ely Tomines, West Virginia University & Colorado State University, 1,139
1970 Frank Pontrick-Dave Slachter, Bellarmine College & Tulane University, 1,158
1969 Roger Dalkin-Joseph Hill, Georgia Tech University & Oklahoma State University, 1,191
1968 Jerry Steere-Pat Holseth, Florida State University & University of Minnesota, 1,168
1967 Jack Connaughton-Charles Atwood, University of Wisconsin-La Crosse & University of Miami, 1,197
1966 Dan Van Wolvelaere-Gerald Heverly, Northern Michigan University & Gettysburg University, 1,125
1965 Jack Hiatt-Bill Kring, Idaho State University & Washington State University, 1,219
1964 Dave Carney-Dick Stuttmeier, University of West Virginia & Georgia Tech University, 1,191

1963	Ted DeLuca-Joseph Moore, LaSalle College & Drexel Institute, 1,224
1962	Jerry Davis-Tony Servello, University of Arkansas & Texas A&M University, 1,217
1961	Mike Flanagan-Jerry Johnson, University of Washington & University of Idaho, 1,230
1960	Eugene Wodka-Jerry Constantino, University of Illinois & Bradley University, 1,249
1959	Ed Puletz-James Davis, University of Rhode Island & Pace College, 1,167

Singles

1997	Chad Dudley, Washington State University, 646
1996	Dan Goldstein, University of Illinois, 685
1995	Craig Tuholski, Mount Hood Community College, 2,969
1994	Robert Jakel, Illinois State University, 660
1993	Brian Aldridge, University of Cincinnati, 705
1992	Vince Biondo, Western Illinois University, 753
1991	Don Savant, University of Houston and John Losito, University of Nebraska, 704
1990	Brandon Keister, Vincennes University, 650
1989	Mark Fuhrman, Robert Morris College, 692
1988	Stan Kocon, Penn State University, 663
1987	Mark Scroggins, West Texas State University, 673
1986	Tim Sites, Wichita State University, 637
1985	Jack Jurek, West Texas State University, 653
1984	Gary Brobson, Akron University, 673
1983	Brad Briggs, Robert Morris College, 725
1982	Pete Peterson, University of Wisconsin-Parkside, 707

1981	Bud Loveall, West Texas State University, 629
1980	Don Garrett, University of Tennessee, 666
1979	Dave Higgins, University of Oregon, 716
1978	Jeff Bellinger, University of South Carolina, 694
1977	Jeff Bellinger, University of South Carolina, 642
1976	Mark Schwabe, University of Wisconsin-Milwaukee, 731
1975	Vic Martin, Armstrong State University, 611
1974	Richard Chang, University of California-Los Angeles, 624
1973	Jim Fiore, Rensselaer Polytechnic Institute, 598
1972	Mike Clemente, Michigan State University, 631
1971	Roger Dalkin, Georgia Tech University, 648
1970	Wayne Zmrhal, Northern Illinois University, 659
1969	Glenn Mueller, University of Wisconsin-LaCrosse, 618
1968	Jack Connaughton, University of Wisconsin-La Crosse, 683
1967	Jack Connaughton, University of Wisconsin-La Crosse, 614
1966	Larry Bell, University of Oregon, 592
1965	Gary Gibson, Eastern Illinois University, 679
1964	Dick Parks, Colorado State University, 630
1963	Ted Akins, Arlington State College, 656
1962	Jim Anderson, North Dakota State University, 643
1961	Paul Garrison, Oregon State University, 651
1960	James Nixon, University of Minnesota, 604
1959	Bob Carlson, Michigan College of M&T, 602

National Junior College Athletic Assn. (NJCAA)

Men's All Events

1997	Jamie Flynn, Vincennes University
1996	Mike Shockey, Vincennes University
1995	Mark Berry, Vincennes University
1994	Joe Ciccone, Erie Community College
1993	James Barnhart, Essex Community College
1992	David Bartlett, Vincennes University
1991	Dan Ruminski, Cuyahoga Community College
1990	Brian Eaton, Erie Community College
1989	Joseph Wojcik, Mohawk Valley Community College
1988	Tracy Lambert, Vincennes University
1987	Brad Kiszewski, Erie Community College
1986	Doene Moos, Vincennes University
1985	Ryan Shafer, Corning Community College
1984	Scott Zima, Erie Community College
1983	Bob Santini, Genesee Community College
1982	Paul Fabianski, Erie Community College
1981	Mark Hood, Merremac Community College
1980	Robert Morley, Vincennes University
1979	Ross Vandooser, Corning Community College
1978	Doug Mollo, Nassau Community College
1977	Keith Kolozsi, Sinclair Community College
1976	Ray Pagor, Cuyahoga West Community College
1975	Ron Bandy, Belleville Area Junior College
1974	Frank Walletitisch, Nassau Community College
1973	Frank Walletitisch, Nassau Community College
1972	Ron Gawel, Macomb Community College
1971	Rick Weyer, Erie Community College

Women's All Events

1997	Janette Piesczynski, Erie Community College
1996	Janette Piesczynski, Erie Community College
1995	Rachel Lamonica, Suffolk Community College
1994	Jessica Guernsey, Erie Community College
1993	Jessica Guernsey, Erie Community College
1992	Kendra Cameron, Essex Community College
1991	Tracy Owens, Vincennes University
1990	Kathy McNeill, Erie Community College
1989	Kathy McNeill, Erie Community College
1988	Ruth Jensen, Erie Community College
1987	Debbie Swan, Erie Community College
1986	Lynn Farr, Vincennes University
1985	Lynn Farr, Vincennes University
1984	JoAnn Haas, Erie Community College
1983	Peggy Funk, Erie Community College
1982	Sue Veley, Erie Community College
1981	Laura Harmon, Niagara Community College
1980	Laurie Brinkman, Erie Community College
1979	Sandi Tice, Erie Community College
1978	Mary Grace Hubert, Erie Community College
1977	Lucy Giovinco, Hillsborough Community College

Men's Team

1997	Erie Community College
1996	Vincennes (Ind.) University
1995	Vincennes (Ind.) University
1994	Erie Community College, Buffalo

Year	Winner
1993	Vincennes (Ind.) University
1992	Vincennes (Ind.) University
1991	Vincennes (Ind.) University
1990	Erie Community College, Buffalo
1989	Vincennes (Ind.) University
1988	Erie Community College, Buffalo
1987	Erie Community College, Buffalo
1986	Vincennes (Ind.) University
1985	Vincennes (Ind.) University
1984	Erie Community College, Buffalo
1983	Vincennes (Ind.) University
1982	Erie Community College, Buffalo
1981	Sinclair Community College, Dayton, Ohio
1980	Vincennes (Ind.) University
1979	Niagara Community College, Sanborn, N.Y.
1978	Erie Community College, Buffalo
1977	Erie Community College, Buffalo
1976	Niagara Community College, Sanborn, N.Y.
1975	Erie Community College, Buffalo
1974	Erie Community College, Buffalo
1973	Nassau Community College, Garden City, N.Y.
1972	Nassau Community College, Garden City, N.Y.
1971	Genesee Community College, Batavia, N.Y.

Women's Team

Year	Winner
1997	Erie Community College
1996	Erie Community College
1995	Hudson Valley (N.Y.) Community College
1994	Erie Community College, Buffalo
1993	Erie Community College, Buffalo
1992	Erie Community College, Buffalo
1991	Erie Community College, Buffalo
1990	Erie Community College, Buffalo
1989	Erie Community College, Buffalo
1988	Erie Community College, Buffalo
1987	Erie Community College, Buffalo
1986	Vincennes (Ind.) University
1985	Erie Community College, Buffalo
1984	Erie Community College, Buffalo
1983	Erie Community College, Buffalo
1982	Erie Community College, Buffalo
1981	Erie Community College, Buffalo
1980	Suffolk Community College, Selden, N.Y.
1979	Erie Community College, Buffalo
1978	Erie Community College, Buffalo
1977	Hillsborough Community College, Tampa

YOUTH COMPETITION

Coca-Cola Youth Bowling Championships

The Coca-Cola Youth Bowling Championships — conducted by the Young American Bowling Alliance and sponsored by Coca-Cola USA — is the premier international tournament for youth bowlers age 12-21.

Tournament qualifying begins at the league level with two-week qualifying windows in November and February. Centers with YABA Youth Division leagues are automatic qualifying sites.

The local scratch and handicap winners in the 12-21 age divisions advance to state or provincial competitions. Advancers from the state or provincial competitions receive scholarships and expense-paid trips to the international finals.

At the international finals, bowlers compete in girls' and boys' handicap and scratch events for $30,000 in scholarships. Scholarships for first-place finishers are $3,000, second place $2,000, third place $1,500 and fourth place $1,000. Individuals earning the highest four-game series or game in each division receive plaques.

Athletes competing in each division begin competition by rolling three four-game blocks. The field is cut to the top 24 scorers in each division and the pin totals are dropped. These semifinalists roll two more four-game blocks to decide the top-four finalists in each division. Finalists then compete in stepladder rolloffs.

A total of 272 bowlers from 50 U.S. states, Puerto Rico, six Canadian provinces and military commands in Europe, the Far East, the Caribbean and Brazil qualified to participate in the 1997 international finals.

From 1982-93, the event was known as the National Junior Bowling Championships.

Youth Bowling Championships Champions

Girls' Scratch Division*

1997	Tracy Castro, San Mateo, Calif.
1996	Amy Rocco, Phoenix
1995	Julie Johnson, Morehead, Minn.
1994	Pam Inloes, Modesto, Calif.
1993	Sarah Hillier, Flint, Mich.
1992	Elizabeth Johnson, Niagara Falls, N.Y.
1991	Laura Ross, Mahwah, N.J.
1990	Kelly Everding, Arvada, Colo.
1989	Allison Odaguchi, Winnipeg, Manitoba
1988	Kimberly Wong, Clovis, Calif.
1987	Stefanie Marek, Wilmington, Del.
1986	Dionne Lee, Modesto, Calif.

*Event was first offered in 1986.

Boys' Scratch Division

1997	Edward Smaglik, Milwaukee
1996	David Brown, Albany, Ga.
1995	Heath Brightbill, Mohnton, Pa.
1994	Keith Butt, Baltimore
1993	Mark Taylor, Fairfield, Conn.
1992	Michael Mullin, New City, N.Y.
1991	Jason Tamplet, Baton Rouge, La.
1990	Chris Williams, Anchorage, Alaska
1989	Paul Lavoie, West Warwick, R.I.
1988	Jack. Zuniga, Tulsa, Okla.
1987	Glenn Kelley, Lexington, Ky.
1986	John Belt, Corner, S.C.
1985	John Williams, New Orleans
1984	Jeffrey Vandergrift, Parkersburg, W. Va.
1983	Byron Brown, Acampo, Calif.
1982	Justin Hromek, Andover, Kan.

Girls' Handicap Division

1997	Jessica Orlik, Daphne, Ala.
1996	Tina Swearingen, Paducah, Ky.
1995	Maryorie Costoso-Ortiz, Bayamond, Puerto Rico
1994	Jennifer Ching, Kaneohe, Hawaii
1993	Heather Dunifer, Carmel, Maine
1992	Shawna McCarley, Vernal, Utah
1991	Melinda Warren, Victoria, British Columbia
1990	Rachel Zick, Guantanamo Bay, Cuba
1989	Jessie Wolfe, Kersey, Pa.
1988	Jennifer Bonner, Portage, Ind.
1987	Kristina Barker, Decatur, Texas
1986	Katrina Smith, Jonesboro, Ark.
1985	Christine Lennon, Rome, N.Y.
1984	Tori Pizzirusso, Massapequa, N.Y.
1983	Rhonda Roettger, Bigelow, Mo.
1982	Gale McColl, San Diego

Boys' Handicap Division

1997	Landon Pina, Rota, Spain
1996	Ben Lindley, Wilsonville, Ore.
1995	Jason Arrington, Anchorage, Alaska
1994	Donald Breese, Canton, Pa.
1993	Saqib Ali, Lethbridge, Alberta
1992	Kenneth Criscione, Fairfield, Conn.
1991	Nate Herbrandson, Widefield, Colo.
1990	Nestor Ortiz, Atlanta
1989	Steven Lacy, Meridian, Miss.
1988	Ray Goldal, Mayville, N.D.
1987	Jeff Carroll, Great Falls, Mont.
1986	Jeffrey Schlosser, Hanover, N.H.
1985	David Barbour, Duncan, Okla.
1984	Curt Ward, Livingston, Mont.
1983	Michael Barnes, Baltimore
1982	Mark Fyfe, Lancaster, Ky.

Youth Bowling Championships Records

Four-Game Series, highest by individuals
Girls' Handicap

1,016	Melissa Thomaczek, Syracuse, Kan., 1987
1,001	Me'Chell Thomaczek, Syracuse, Kan., 1986
993	Jennifer Bonner, Portage, Ind., 1988

Girls' Scratch

960	Cynthia Black, Taylor, Mich., 1995
951	Amy Dillon, Miami, 1995
933	Amanda Keller, Boring, Ore., 1995

Game, highest by individuals
Girls' Handicap

306	Jeanine Lenneman, St. Michael, Minn., 1986
301	Judy Wentworth, Gardiner, Maine, 1988
300	Jennifer Bonner, Portage, Ind., 1988

Girls' Scratch

300	Amanda Keller, Boring, Ore., 1995
279	Sarah Hillier, Flint, Mich., 1993
	Julie Johnson, Moorhead, Minn., 1996
	Shanna Hricko, Sunrise, Fla., 1996
	Shannon McDonald, Blue Springs, Mo., 1997

Four-Game Series, highest by individuals
Boys' Handicap

1,079	Rob Charles, Newark, Del., 1988
1,064	Mark Eramo, Grafton, Mass., 1988
1,046	Rob Charles, Newark, Del., 1988

Boys' Scratch

1,067	Rob Causer, Rochester, N.Y., 1988
1,051	Jason Stroud, Granite City, Ill., 1992
1,033	Rob Causer, Rochester, N.Y., 1988
	Dan Schmid, Antioch, Calif., 1997

Game, highest by individuals
Boys' Handicap

319	Keola Matsushige, Honolulu, 1997
309	Rob Charles, Newark, Del., 1988
	Alan Silva, Lewiston, Maine, 1987

Boys' Scratch

300	Randy Johnson, Coos Bay, Ore., 1988
	Ron Kator, Des Plaines, Ill., 1988
	Joe Klein, Maryland Heights, Mo., 1995

Professional Bowlers Association

The Professional Bowlers Association (PBA) is the acknowledged major league of men's bowling in the world today. Some 3,700-plus members, a far cry from the 33 famous charter members who banded together in 1958 to start the organizaion, now compete for nearly $8 million annually on the PBA national tour alone.

Early years found the PBA with only a few annual stops primarily in the East. Then in 1962, the Tour became a year-round operation with events in nearly every section of the country. ABC-TV began its popular "Pro Bowlers Tour" series which continues as the second-longest live sports series on network television behind only NCAA football.

The PBA was founded by Eddie Elias, an Akron, Ohio attorney and television sports interviewer. In 1972, Joe Antenora took over as Executive Director and later as Commissioner. In 1992, Mike Connor became only the second PBA Commissioner, with Mark Gerberich succeeding him in 1996.

1997 Statistics
(Through Nov. 11)

Earnings Leaders

Pos.	Name	City/State	Earnings	Pos.	Name	City/State	Earnings
1.	Walter Ray Williams Jr.	Stockton, Calif.	$207,235	6.	Doug Kent	Canandaigua, N.Y.	118,430
2.	Parker Bohn III	Jackson, N.J.	205,235	7.	Brian Voss	Atlanta	116,235
3.	Pete Weber	St. Ann, Mo.	184,984	8.	Tim Criss	Bel Air, Md.	102,725
4.	Amleto Monacelli	Barquisimeto, Ven.	131,205	9.	Steve Jaros	Bolingbrook, Ill.	94,134
5.	Norm Duke	Clermont, Fla.	125,270	10.	Wayne Webb	Las Vegas, Nev.	93,770

Average Leaders

1. Walter Ray Williams Jr., Stockton, Calif. 222.15
2. Pete Weber, St. Ann, Mo. 221.21
3. Parker Bohn III, Jackson, N.J. 220.69
4. Amleto Monacelli, Barquisimeto, Venezuela . . .219.71
5. Norm Duke, Clermont, Fla. 219.01
6. Brian Voss, Atlanta 218.94
7. Ricky Ward, North Fort Myers, Fla. 217.73
8. Steve Jaros, Bolingbrook, Ill. 217.19
9. Mike Aulby, Indianapolis, Ind. 217.12
10. Bob Learn Jr., Erie, Pa. 217.00

Most Cashes

1. Doug Kent, Canandaigua, N.Y. 23
2. Walter Ray Williams Jr., Stockton, Calif. 22
3. Tim Criss, Bel Air, Md. 21
   Bob Learn Jr., Erie, Pa. 21
   Steve Jaros, Bolingbrook, Ill. 21
6. Tom Baker, Buffalo, N.Y. 19
   Rick Steelsmith, Wichita, Kan. 19
8. Pete Weber, St. Ann, Mo. 18
9. Norm Duke, Clermont, Fla. 18
10. Amleto Monacelli, Barquisimeto, Venezuela 17
   Brian Voss, Atlanta 17

All-Time Records
(Through Nov. 11, 1997)

Average, highest season
225.49   Mike Aulby, Indianapolis, 1995.

Cashes, most consecutive
72   Dick Weber, St. Louis, 1960-64.

Cashes, most in year
34   Tommy Hudson, Akron, Ohio, 1977.

Earnings, Career
1. Walter Ray Williams Jr., Stockton, Calif. $2,036,023
2. Pete Weber, St. Ann, Mo.   2,012,014
3. Mike Aulby, Indianapolis   1,855,075
4. Marshall Holman, Medford, Ore.   1,690,744
5. Brian Voss, Atlanta   1,601,759
6. Amleto Monacelli, Barquisimeto, Venezuela   1,572,780
7. Mark Roth, Wall Township, N.J.   1,494,821
8. Dave Husted, Milwaukie, Ore.   1,478,641
9. Earl Anthony, North Plains, Ore.   1,441,061
10. Parker Bohn III, Jackson, N.J.   1,395,452

Earnings, year
$298,237   Mike Aulby, Indianapolis, 1989.
296,370   Walter Ray Williams Jr., Stockton, Calif., 1993.
273,753   Norm Duke, Edmond, Okla., 1994.
241,330   Walter Ray Williams Jr., Stockton, Calif., 1996.
236,232   Bob Learn Jr., Erie, Pa., 1996

Consecutive years with title
14   Earl Anthony, Cornelus, Ore., 1976-83.
12   Don Johnson, Las Vegas, 1966-77.
11   Brian Voss, Atlanta, 1987-97.
10   Mark Roth, Spring Lake Heights, N.J., 1975-84.
    Pete Weber, St. Ann, Mo., 1984-93.

Games, most in one year
1,300   Walter Ray Williams Jr., Stockton, Calif., 1993.

Earnings, most without title
$156,306   Pete McCordic, Houston, Texas, 1987.

Match, highest scoring
600   Tom Baker (300) vs. Pete Weber (300), Denver, 1981.
    Purvis Granger (300) vs. Norm Duke (300), Las Vegas, 1987.
    David Ozio (300) vs. Mike Edwards (300), San Antonio, 1993.
    Doug Wallace (300) vs. Norm Duke (300), Kennewick, Wash., 1995

Match Play, best 16-game record
16-0   Mike McGrath, Paramus, N.J., 1969.

Match Play, best 24-game record
22-2   George Pappas, Kansas City, 1974.

National Titles, career
41   Earl Anthony, Cornelius, Ore.
34   Mark Roth, Spring Lake Heights, N.J.
26   Dick Weber, St. Louis
       Don Johnson, Las Vegas
25   Mike Aulby, Indianapolis

National Titles, year
8   Mark Roth, Spring Lake Heights, N.J., 1978
6   Dave Davis, Bradenton, Fla., 1967
     Billy Hardwick, Memphis, 1969
     Don Johnson, Las Vegas, 1971
     Don McCune, Munster, Ind., 1973
     Earl Anthony, Cornelius, Ore., 1974
     Mark Roth, Spring Lake Heights, N.J., 1979
     Mike Aulby, Indianapolis, 1985

Television, lowest score
129   Steve Jaros, Lake Zurich, Ill., 1992

Television, highest scoring match
579   Mike Aulby (300) vs. David Ozio (279),
       Wichita, Kan., 1993
       Bob Learn Jr. (300) vs. Johnny Petraglia (279),
       Erie, Pa., 1996

Television, highest losing score
280   Norm Duke, Peoria, Ill., 1994

Television, highest three-game series
850   Bob Learn Jr., Erie, Pa., 1996

Television, highest four-game series
1,129   Bob Learn Jr., Erie, Pa., 1996

Tournaments, most consecutive
239   Harry Sullins, Ann Arbor, Mich., 1986-93

Winning Margin, highest in match play
172   Larry Laub (290) vs. Mark Estes (118),
       Waukegan, Ill., 1975

300 Games, most in tournament, overall
20   Mechanicsburg, Pa., 1993

300 Games, television
       Jack Biondolillo (rolled in Akron, Ohio), 1967
       John Guenther (rolled in San Jose, Calif.), 1969
       Jim Stefanich (rolled in Alameda, Calif.), 1974
       Pete McCordic (rolled in Torrence, Calif.), 1987
       Bob Benoit (rolled in Grand Prairie, Texas), 1988
       Mike Aulby (rolled in Wichita, Kan.), 1993
       Johnny Petraglia (rolled in Toledo, Ohio), 1994
       Butch Soper (rolled in Reno, Nev.), 1994
       C. K. Moore (rolled in Austin, Texas), 1996
       Bob Learn Jr. (rolled in Erie, Pa.), 1996
       Steve Hoskins (rolled in Rochester, N.Y.), 1997

300 Games, tournament
4   Walter Ray Williams Jr., Stockton, Calif., 1993
     Dave D'Entremont, Middleburg Heights, Ohio,
     1995

300 Games, year
8   Kelly Coffman, Topeka, Kan., 1994
     Dave D'Entremont, Middleburg Heights, Ohio, 1995
     Eric Forkel, Tucson, Ariz., 1995

Players of the Year
(As Voted by PBA Members)

1996 Mike Aulby	1985 Mike Aulby	1974 Earl Anthony
1995 Walter Ray Williams Jr.	1984 Mark Roth	1973 Don McCune
1994 Norm Duke	1983 Earl Anthony	1972 Don Johnson
1993 Walter Ray Williams Jr.	1982 Earl Anthony	1971 Don Johnson
1992 Dave Ferraro	1981 Earl Anthony	1970 Nelson Burton Jr.
1991 David Ozio	1980 Wayne Webb	1969 Billy Hardwick
1990 Amleto Monacelli	1979 Mark Roth	1968 Jim Stefanich
1989 Amleto Monacelli	1978 Mark Roth	1967 Dave Davis
1988 Brian Voss	1977 Mark Roth	1966 Wayne Zahn
1987 Marshall Holman	1976 Earl Anthony	1965 Dick Weber
1986 Walter Ray Williams Jr.	1975 Earl Anthony	1964 Bob Strampe
		1963 Billy Hardwick

Rookies of the Year

1996 Billy Myers Jr., Temple City, Calif.	1979 Mike Aulby, Indianapolis
1995 C.K. Moore, Chehalis, Wash.	1978 Joseph Groskind, Memphis
1994 Tony Ament, Garfield, N.J.	1977 Steve Martin, Kingsport, Tenn.
1993 Mark Scroggins, Amarillo, Texas	1976 Mike Berlin, Muscatine, Iowa
1992 Jason Couch, Winter Garden, Fla.	1975 Guy Rowbury, Ronan, Mont.
1991 Ricky Ward, Ft. Myers, Fla.	1974 Cliff McNealy, San Lorenzo, Calif.
1990 Brad Kizewski, Buffalo	1973 Steve Neff, Homosassa Springs, Fla.
1989 Steve Hoskins, Tarpon Springs, Fla.	1972 Tommy Hudson, Akron, Ohio
1988 Rick Steelsmith, Wichita, Kan.	1971 Tye Critchlow, Los Angeles
1987 Ryan Shafer, Horseheads, N.Y.	1970 Denny Krick, Tacoma, Wash.
1986 Marc McDowell, Madison, Wis.	1969 Larry Lichstein, Windsor Locks, Conn.
1985 Tom Crites, Tampa	1968 Bob McGregor, Lubbock, Texas
1984 John Gant, Pittsburgh	1967 Mike Durbin, Chagrin Falls, Ohio
1983 Toby Contreras, Kansas City, Mo.	1966 Bobby Cooper, Dallas
1982 Mike Steinbach, Alsip, Ill.	1965 Jim Godman, Reno, Nev.
1981 Mark Fahy, Chicago	1964 Jerry McCoy, Ft. Worth, Texas
1980 Pete Weber, St. Louis	

PBA Hall of Fame

Performance Category

Name	Year Inducted	Name	Year Inducted	Name	Year Inducted
Ray Bluth	1975	Jim Stefanich	1980	Marshall Holman	1990
Don Carter	1975	Earl Anthony	1981	Paul Colwell	1991
Carmen Salvino	1975	Wayne Zahn	1981	Roy Buckley	1992
Harry Smith	1975	Johnny Petraglia	1982	Steve Cook	1993
Dick Weber	1975	Bill Allen	1983	Wayne Webb	1993
Billy Welu	1975	Mike Durbin	1984	Brian Voss	1994
Buzz Fazio	1976	Larry Laub	1985	Walter Ray Williams Jr.	1995
Billy Hardwick	1977	George Pappas	1986	David Ozio	1995
Don Johnson	1977	Jim Godman	1987	Mike Aulby	1996
Dave Davis	1978	Mark Roth	1987	Dave Husted	1996
Dick Ritger	1978	Gary Dickinson	1988	Dave Ferraro	1997
Nelson Burton Jr.	1979	Tommy Hudson	1989	Amleto Monacelli	1997
Dave Soutar	1979	Joe Berardi	1990		

Veterans Category

Name	Year Inducted	Name	Year Inducted	Name	Year Inducted
Glenn Allison	1984	Mike McGrath	1988	Don McCune	1991
Joe Joseph	1985	Barry Asher	1988	Skee Foremsky	1992
John Guenther	1986	Jim St. John	1989	Mike Limongello	1994
Bob Strampe	1987	Andy Marzich	1990	Ernie Schlegel	1997

Meritorious Category

Name	Year Inducted	Name	Year Inducted	Name	Year Inducted
Frank Esposito	1975	Harry Golden	1983	Al Thompson	1991
Chuck Pezzano	1975	E.A. (Bud) Fisher	1984	Jack Reichert	1992
Eddie Elias	1976	Ted Hoffman Jr.	1985	Joe Antenora	1993
Chris Schenkel	1976	Dick Evans	1986	Chuck Clemens	1994
Steve Nagy	1977	Raymond Firestone	1987	Roger Zeller	1995
Lou Frantz	1978	John Jowdy	1988	Larry Lichstein	1996
Joe Richards	1978	John Archibald	1989		
Lorraine Stitzlein	1980	Joe Kelly	1989		

PBA Senior Tour

Once male bowlers turn 50 years of age and meet other eligibility requirements, they may compete on the PBA Senior Tour. More than 1,000 PBA members are classified as senior. Creation of the PBA Senior Tour allowed many bowlers who were unable to compete on the regular PBA Tour in earlier years due to family or employment obligations a second chance.

ABC Hall of Famer Bill Beach won the inaugural PBA Senior event in 1981 in New Orleans. One tournament per year was held in 1982 and 1983 with the tour expanded to two events in 1984 and 1985. The next year, the series began a gradual expansion that led to 16 events in 1997.

Final 1997 Statistics

Earnings Leaders

Pos.	Name	City/State	Earnings	Pos.	Name	City/State	Earnings
1.	Gary Dickinson	Edmond, Okla.	$109,240	6.	Earl Anthony	North Plains, Ore.	43,320
2.	Larry Laub	Tucson, Ariz.	59,255	7.	Dale Eagle	Lewisville, Tex.	40,025
3.	John Hricsina	Jackson, Tenn.	50,015	8.	Roger Tramp	Deltona, Fla.	39,615
4.	Gene Stus	Allen Park, Mich.	49,685	9.	Ron Winger	Tarzana, Calif.	38,542
5.	Pete Couture	Titusville, Fla.	45,425	10.	Johnny Petraglia	Manapalan, N.J.	35,000

Average Leaders

1. Gary Dickinson, Edmond, Okla. 224.45
2. George Pappas, Charlotte, N.C. 222.99
3. Earl Anthony, North Plains, Ore. 222.76
4. Pete Couture, Titusville, Fla. 222.37
5. Larry Laub, Tucson, Ariz. 221.93
6. Gene Stus, Allen Park, Mich. 220.87
7. Dale Eagle, Lewisville, Texas 220.65
8. John Hricsina, Jackson, Tenn. 220.38
9. Ron Winger, Tarzana, Calif. 219.55
10. Avery LeBlanc, Houma, La. 218.28

Most Cashes

1. Gene Stus, Allen Park, Mich. 16
2. Pete Couture, Titusville, Fla. 15
   Gary Dickinson, Edmond, Okla. 15
   John Hricsina, Jackson, Tenn. 15
   Larry Laub, Tucson, Ariz. 15
   Ron Winger, Tarzana, Calif. 15
7. Dale Eagle, Lewisville, Texas 14
   John Handegard, Las Vegas 14
   Dave Soutar, Bradenton, Fla. 14
10. Sam Flanigan, Columbus, Ohio 13
   Roger Tramp, DeHona, Fla. 13
   Dick Baker, Libertyville, Ill. 13

All-Time Records PBA Senior Tour

Cashes, season

15	Gene Stus, Allen Park, Mich., 1997
14	Gene Stus, Allen Park, Mich., 1993
13	Gary Dickinson, Edmond, Okla., 1994

Championship Round Appearances, season

8	Gene Stus, Allen Park, Mich., 1993
	Gary Dickinson, Edmond, Okla., 1997

Earnings, career

1. John Handegard, Las Vegas $388,946
2. Gene Stus, Allen Park, Mich. 332,895
3. Teata Semiz, Haskall, N..J. 312,115
4. Gary Dickinson, Edmond, Okla. 304,999
5. John Hricsina, Jackson, Tenn. 303,097
6. Dick Weber, St. Louis 219,324
7. Dave Soutar, Bradenton, Fla. 194,874
8. Dave Davis, West Palm Beach, Fla. 184,145
9. Ron Winger, Tarzana, Calif. 181,630
10. Tommy Evans, Fort Lauderdale, Fla. 176,886

Earnings, season

$109,240 Gary Dickinson, Edmond, Okla., 1997

High Score, 24th qualifier

4,105 Gene Stus, Jackson, Mich., 1994

Low Score, 24th qualifier

3,608 David Kail, Escondido, Calif., 1991

Match, highest scoring

598 Rich Holden (299) vs. Denny Torgerson (299), Jackson, Mich., 1994

Match-play Appearances, season

14 Pete Couture, Titusville, Fla., 1997

Match-play Record, 18-game format

16-2 Gene Stus, St. Charles, Mo., 1991

Match-play Record, 24-game format

20-4	Gene Stus, Oak Lawn, Ill., 1994
	Jackson, Mich., 1994

Television, highest games

300 Gene Stus, Allen Park, Mich., 1992

Ron Winger, Tarzana, Calif., 1993

Television, highest scoring match

537 Tommy Evans (290) vs. Teata Semiz (247), Sunrise, Fla., 1993

Television, highest four-game series

1,044 Teata Semiz, Lady Lake, Fla., 1991 (269, 279, 242, 254)

Television, highest losing game

257 Tommy Evans vs. Teata Semiz (279), Sunrise, Fla., 1993

Titles, season

3	Earl Anthony, Cornelius, Ore., 1990
	Gene Stus, Allen Park, Mich., 1991
	John Handegard, Las Vegas, Nev., 1991
	Larry Laub, Tucson, Ariz., 1997
	Gary Dickinson, Edmond, Okla., 1997

Titles, career

13	John Handegard, Las Vegas
9	Gary Dickinson, Edmond, Okla.
8	Teata Semiz, Wanaque, N.J.

Winning margin, largest in match play

149 Larry Laub (300) vs. Jim Moore, Jackson, Mich., 1994

Winning Margin, largest televised

112 Gene Stus (300) vs. Don Gilman (188), Lakewood, Calif., 1992

300 Games, most in tournament

16 Lady Lake, Fla., 1991

300 Games, most in year

45 1991

300 Games, most in year, individual

4	John Hricsina, Franklin, Pa., 1991
	Gene Stus, Allen Park, Mich., 1994

The Professional Women Bowler's Association was the first professional women's bowling organization. Formed in December 1959, the organization held its first Tournament in 1960. The PWBA is no longer operating. The Ladies Pro Bowlers Tour was formed in 1981.

1997 Statistics
(Through Nov. 11)

Earnings Leaders

1. Wendy Macpherson, Henderson, Nev. $135,325
2. Carol Gianotti-Block, Perth, Australia 115,250
3. Liz Johnson, Niagara Falls, N.Y. 90,350
4. Marianne DiRupo, Succasunna, N.J. 85,150
5. Carolyn Dorin-Ballard, N. Richland Hills,Texas .84,425
6. Leanne Barrette, Fremont, Calif. 61,975
7. Sandra Jo Odom, Coldwater, Mich. 59,327
8. Nikki Gianulias, Vallejo, Calif. 58,752
9. Anne Marie Duggan, Edmond, Okla. 56,525
10. Kim Adler, Las Vegas, Nev. 53,650

Average Leaders

1. Wendy Macpherson, Henderson, Nev. 214.68
2. Marianne DiRupo, Succasunna, N.J. 213.25
3. Carol Gianotti-Block, Perth, Australia 213.14
4. Carolyn Dorin-Ballard, N. Richland Hills, Texas .212.53
5. Liz Johnson, Niagara Falls, N.Y. 211.77
6. Nikki Gianulias, Vallejo, Calif. 211.23
7. Anne Marie Duggan, Edmond, Okla. 210.39
8. Leanne Barrette, Fremont, Calif. 210.20
9. Jackie Mitskavich, DuBois, Pa. 210.03
10. Jeanne Naccarato, Tacoma, Wash. 209.95

Earnings, Career

1. Aleta Sill, Dearborn, Mich. $821,462
2. Tish Johnson, Northridge, Calif. 773,415
3. Lisa Wagner, Bradenton, Fla. 716,183
4. Robin Mossonette, Newhall, Calif. 617,329
5. Anne Marie Duggan, Edmond, Okla. 607,516

6. Leanne Barrette, Fremont, Calif. 557,658
7. Cheryl Daniels, Detroit 532,449
8. Nikki Gianulias, Vallejo, Calif. 522,735
9. Wendy Macpherson, Henderson, Nev. 503,354
10. Lorrie Nichols, Algonquin, Ill. 488,221

All-Time Records

Earnings, year
$126,325 Aleta Sill, Dearborn, Mich., 1994
 124,722 Anne Marie Duggan, Edmond, Okla., 1994
 113,750 Robin Romeo, Newhall, Calif., 1989

Games, highest televised
300 Michelle Feldman, Skaneatales, N.Y., 1997
299 Paula Drake, Broken Arrow, Okla., 1987
297 Barbara Leicht, Albany, N.Y., 1987

300 Games, year
7 Tish Johnson, Panorama City, Calif., 1993
5 Kim Couture, Titusville, Fla., 1994

4 Betty Morris, Stockton, Calif., 1986
   Nikki Gianulius, Vallejo, Calif., 1986
   Debbie McMullen, Denver, 1991

Titles, career
30 Lisa Wagner, Palmetto, Fla.
28 Aleta Sill, Dearborn, Mich.
25 Pat Costello, Orlando, Fla.

Titles, season
7 Pat Costello, Orlando, Fla., 1976
6 Lisa Wagner, Palmetto, Fla., 1988

Players of the Year

1996 Wendy Macpherson, Henderson, Nev.
1995 Tish Johnson, Northridge, Calif.
1994 Anne Marie Duggan, Edmond, Okla.
1993 Lisa Wagner, Palmetto, Fla.
1992 Tish Johnson, Panorama City, Calif.
1991 Leanne Barrette, Yukon, Okla.
1990 Leanne Barrette, Yukon, Okla.
1989 Robin Romeo, Newhall, Calif.
1988 Lisa Wagner, Palmetto, Fla.
1987 Betty Morris, Stockton, Calif.
1986 Jeanne Maiden-Naccarato, Tacoma, Wash.
1985 Patty Costello, Scranton, Pa.
1984 Aleta Sill, Dearborn, Mich.
1983 Lisa Wagner, Palmetto, Fla.

Rookies of the Year

1996 Liz Johnson, Niagara Falls, N.Y.
1995 Krissy Stewart, Cape Coral, Fla.
1994 Tammy Turner, West Palm Beach, Fla.
1993 Kathy Edwards-Zielke, Budaiya, Bahrain
1992 Marianne DiRupo, Succasunna, N.J.
1991 Kim Kahrman, East Windsor, Conn.
1990 Debbie McMullen, Denver
1989 Kim Terrell-Canady, San Francisco
1988 Mary Martha Cerniglia, Springfield, Ill.
1987 Paula Drake, Broken Arrow, Okla.
1986 Wendy Macpherson-Papanos, Henderson, Nev.
1985 Dede Davidson, San Jose, Calif.
1984 Paula Vidad, Rancho Cucamongo, Calif.
1983 Anne Marie Duggan, Edmond, Okla.
1982 Carol Norman, Oklahoma City
1981 Cindy Mason, Sunnyvale, Calif.

Women's Professional Bowling Hall of Fame

Performance Category
Millie Ignizio 1995
Betty Morris 1995
Dotty Fothergill 1995
Donna Adamek 1995
Patty Costello 1995
Marion Ladewig 1995
Nikki Gianulias 1996
Lorrie Nichols 1996
Robin Romeo 1996

Lisa Wagner 1996
Cindy Coburn-Carroll 1997
Pat Costello 1997
Vesma Grinfelds 1997

Poineer Category
Helen Duval 1995
Laverne Carter 1995
Shirley Garms 1995
Doris Coburn 1996
Donna Zimmerman 1996

Jeannette Robinson 1996
Judy Soutar 1997
Loa Boxberger 1997

Builder Category
Georgia Veach 1995
Janet Buehler 1996
John Falzone 1996
John Sommer Jr. 1997
Pearl Keller 1997
Fran Deken 1997

Women's International Bowling Congress

The Women's International Bowling Congress is the largest women's sports organization in the world. WIBC exists to provide adult women league bowlers the opportunity to join together for a unified, representative voice in maintaining the integrity, credibility and popularity of the sport of bowling. WIBC provides uniform rules for bowling league and tournament competition, a free magazine subscription, and programs to increase women's interest and skill in bowling.

Season	Members	Associations	Leagues	Delegates	Season	Members	Associations	Leagues	Delegates
1996-97	1,797,773	2,570	86,955	3,156	1954-55	706,193	1,498	22,842	791
1995-96	1,916,761	2,714	92,334	3,036	1953-54	665,427	1,468	21,020	725
1994-95	2,035,755	2,713	97,054	3,058	1952-53	630,421	1,412	19,648	690
1993-94	2,191,064	2,705	100,545	3,168	1951-52	582,703	1,384	17,885	667
1992-93	2,403,186	2,700	108,855	3,437	1950-51	542,723	1,350	16,515	512
1991-92	2,523,357	2,735	112,990	3,592	1949-50	495,880	1,254	15,054	586
1990-91	2,711,909	2,771	119,612	3,391	1948-49	432,926	1,165	13,064	663
1989-90	2,859,570	2,784	123,907	3,321	1947-48	362,779	1,021	11,047	582
1988-89	3,026,468	2,787	129,421	3,133	1946-47	301,064	901	9,064	506
1987-88	3,184,196	2,797	115,494	3,568	1945-46	250,478	753	7,282	333
1986-87	3,351,411	2,792	137,547	3,549	1944-45	252,540	648	7,239	*
1985-86	3,555,679	2,809	146,467	3,450	1943-44	212,581	572	5,944	343
1984-85	3,713,751	2,824	153,435	3,737	1942-43	200,610	563	5,702	306
1983-84	3,886,718	2,807	157,607	3,737	1941-42	183,737	625	5,374	554
1982-83	3,947,229	2,805	160,269	3,772	1940-41	127,705	519	3,848	452
1981-82	4,064,861	2,807	163,639	3,466	1939-40	81,776	382	2,399	338
1980-81	4,112,012	2,818	165,887	3,459	1938-39	51,913	235	1,528	257
1979-80	4,187,053	2,818	168,718	3,328	1937-38	36,160	169	1,044	195
1978-79	4,232,143	2,806	168,227	3,506	1936-37	22,308	109	622	136
1977-78	4,209,220	2,788	165,720	3,272	1935-36	15,886	87	357	139
1976-77	4,043,631	2,778	160,457	3,235	1934-35	13,409	71	310	108
1975-76	3,870,947	2,745	154,376	3,159	1933-34	10,483	68	237	74
1974-75	3,692,694	2,724	146,318	2,899	1932-33	8,386	56	198	69
1973-74	3,531,061	2,720	139,548	2,701	1931-32	9,746	58	212	79
1972-73	3,343,965	2,745	132,298	2,502	1930-31	9,400	50	168	63
1971-72	3,184,711	2,766	126,977	2,483	1929-30	8,985	42	110	90
1970-71	3,058,977	2,766	123,040	2,525	1928-29	7,757	34	*	67
1969-70	2,988,077	2,784	121,302	2,418	1927-28	6,095	31	*	45
1968-69	2,968,268	2,810	121,281	2,272	1926-27	5,357	28	*	39
1967-68	2,941,739	2,866	122,730	2,181	1925-26	4,576	12	*	27
1966-67	2,896,693	2,910	123,139	2,250	1924-25	3,769	33	*	39
1965-66	2,821,747	2,943	121,127	2,035	1923-24	2,885	29	*	38
1964-65	2,736,393	2,890	118,320	1,689	1922-23	2,219	28	*	38
1963-64	2,607,370	2,881	114,713	1,881	1921-22	1,920	22	*	27
1962-63	2,453,783	2,803	108,851	1,723	1920-21	1,220	30	*	22
1961-62	2,212,339	2,683	96,368	1,464	1919-20	1,005	26	*	22
1960-61	1,906,098	2,450	80,309	1,282	1918-19	641	15	*	22
1959-60	1,543,362	2,158	63,587	1,064	1917-18	412	*	*	21
1958-59	1,231,529	1,915	48,293	1,017	1916-17	40	*	*	*
1957-58	1,005,157	1,727	36,727	894					
1956-57	865,603	1,629	30,059	853					
1955-56	764,456	1,562	25,561	838					

*Information not available. WIBC began chartering associations in 1918 and sanctioning leagues in 1929.

American Bowling Congress

The American Bowling Congress is the world's largest sports membership organization and is for bowlers aged 18 or older (under 18 with parents' consent), who live in the United States, Canada, Puerto Rico and on U.S. military bases abroad.

ABC provides its members with uniform rules and equipment specifications, rule counselings, league supplies, a yearly magazine, bowling awards and tournaments. ABC shares its headquarters in Greendale, Wis. with the Women's International Bowling Congress, Young American Bowling Alliance and USA Bowling.

Season	Members*	Associations	Leagues**	Season	Members*	Associations	Leagues**
1996-97	2,135,126	2,613	85,658	1941-42	875,000	1,317	21,009
1995-96	2,261,469	2,801	89,150	1940-41	746,000	1,216	18,123
1994-95	2,370,190	2,794	94,319	1939-40	602,000	1,000	14,305
1993-94	2,454,742	2,793	97,821	1938-39	483,000	799	11,799
1992-93	2,576,809	2,665	100,540	1937-38	446,000	705	10,212
1991-92	2,712,987	2,772	106,195	1936-37	307,000	532	7,249
1990-91	2,922,829	2,762	113,641	1935-36	251,000	474	5,865
1989-90	3,036,907	2,794	114,776	1934-35	203,000	391	4,715
1988-89	3,165,471	2,799	117,469	1933-34	158,000	339	4,023
1987-88	3,313,491	2,819	121,648	1932-33	140,000	327	3,610
1986-87	3,424,205	2,845	125,858	1931-32	187,000	349	4,518
1985-86	3,624,575	2,796	132,576	1930-31	215,000	352	5,098
1984-85	3,656,928	2,874	133,833	1929-30	210,000	322	4,806
1983-84	3,791,081	2,777	140,234	1928-29	139,000	279	2,817
1982-83	4,556,907	2,772	139,940	1927-28	110,000	283	2,240
1981-82	4,685,036	2,775	141,542	1926-27	94,000	248	1,881
1980-81	4,755,756	2,775	143,723	1925-26	76,000	235	1,455
1979-80	4,799,195	2,866	143,607	1924-25	64,000	170	1,193
1978-79	4,777,436	2,836	143,611	1923-24	51,000	161	926
1977-78	4,727,077	2,803	140,066	1922-23	58,000	159	800
1976-77	4,583,460	2,745	136,636	1921-22	30,000	140	721
1975-76	4,504,019	2,760	132,682	1920-21	24,350	111	649
1974-75	4,298,193	2,787	126,830	1919-20	25,885	111	648
1973-74	4,217,597	2,795	123,083	1918-19	13,620	101	271
1972-73	4,131,590	2,821	119,736	1917-18	15,760	111	388
1971-72	4,047,596	2,832	116,992	1916-17	16,740	101	441
1970-71	3,984,382	2,825	115,244	1915-16	16,440	102	424
1969-70	3,987,169	2,856	115,483	1914-15	10,520	105	282
1968-69	4,023,220	2,896	116,149	1913-14	8,900	97	280
1967-68	4,204,254	2,936	121,150	1912-13	7,690	93	298
1966-67	4,298,718	2,975	123,600	1911-12	6,370	81	311
1965-66	4,375,000	3,009	127,079	1910-11	7,270	100	288
1964-65	4,550,000	3,005	130,498	1909-10	6,785	116	302
1963-64	4,575,000	2,985	131,117	1908-09	6,640	111	298
1962-63	4,500,000	2,923	128,719	1907-08	6,640	113	277
1961-62	4,275,000	2,803	120,788	1906-07	6,075	108	236
1960-61	4,000,000	2,592	108,844	1905-06	4,895	70	177
1959-60	3,500,000	2,300	91,181	1904-05	3,155	85	162
1958-59	3,000,000	2,099	75,135	1903-04	1,850	85	143
1957-58	2,500,000	1,929	62,549	1902-03	2,020	45	136
1956-57	2,225,000	1,841	54,318	1901-02	1,100	42	126
1955-56	1,929,000	1,772	47,252	1900-01	1,000	38	67
1954-55	1,741,000	1,728	43,090	1899-00	750	21	41
1953-54	1,651,000	1,707	40,533	1898-99	600	19	30
1952-53	1,569,000	1,658	38,465	1897-98	500	19	29
1951-52	1,482,000	1,641	36,365	1896-97	375	18	26
1950-51	1,430,000	1,655	34,287	1895-96	300	13	10
1949-50	1,417,000	1,585	34,485				
1948-49	1,368,000	1,517	32,999				
1947-48	1,259,000	1,457	30,073				
1946-47	1,105,000	1,334	26,440				
1945-46	810,000	1,220	20,130				
1944-45	795,000	1,082	18,976				
1943-44	697,000	1,013	16,785				
1942-43	694,000	1,045	16,830				

*Membership totals are estimated until the 1965-66 season. Membership totals from the 1965-66 season to the 1982-83 season are playing strengths. Membership totals from 1983-84 to date are actual.

** League totals from the 1895-96 season to the 1902-03 season are estimated.

Young American Bowling Alliance

The Young American Bowling Alliance is the second-largest dues-paying youth sports organization in the world. YABA was formed in August 1982 when the American Junior Bowling Congress, Youth Bowling Assn. and the American Bowling Congress/Women's International Bowling Congress collegiate division merged.

YABA programs and services encourage healthy competition and members' physical fitness, good sportsmanship and positive citizenship. YABA provides playing rules, awards, membership opportunities and trained coaches and preserves members' amateur status.

Season	Members	Season	Members	Season	Members
1996-97	472,133	1979-80	770,460	1962-63	451,200
1995-96	484,375	1978-79	806,842	1961-62	442,511
1994-95	518,519	1977-78	853,650	1960-61	410,112
1993-94	555,675	1976-77	825,701	1959-60	330,280
1992-93	620,625	1975-76	821,281	1958-59	217,292
1991-92	637,757	1974-75	763,988	1957-58	181,198
1990-91	620,362	1973-74	751,748	1956-57	131,225
1989-90	693,537	1972-73	720,639	1955-56	93,767
1988-89	675,064	1971-72	679,833	1954-55	66,526
1987-88	665,705	1970-71	610,888	1953-54	46,090
1986-87	646,203	1969-70	535,277	1952-53	38,435
1985-86	663,411	1968-69	489,543	1951-52	31,607
1984-85	693,153	1967-68	442,331	1950-51	25,925
1983-84	744,244	1966-67	378,720	1949-50	24,139
1982-83	765,522	1965-66	349,388	1948-49	20,309
1981-82	686,178	1964-65	330,395	1947-48	13,683
1980-81	740,849	1963-64	313,848	1946-47	8,767

Awards, issued in past five seasons
Women

	1996-97	1995-96	1994-95	1993-94	1992-93
300 Games	714	713	622	495	373
299 Games	396	334	324	259	217
298 Games	169	148	156	120	117
800 Series	100	74	70	64	43
700 Series	*	9,055	7,554	4,637	*
100 Pins Over Average	*	17,025	21,500	26,000	20,059
Triplicates	*	15,344	26,200	40,000	19,858
All-Spare Game	*	12,255	20,700	30,500	14,996
Dutch 200 Games	*	1,455	1,700	2,500	1,237
Big 4 Splits	*	1,787	2,900	4,500	2,170
7-10 Splits	*	1,346	2,000	2,000	1,052
200 Averages	1,783	1,491	1,472	1,500	983
275 to 297 Games	*	8,129	7,272	5,430	*

Men

	1996-97	1995-96	1994-95	1993-94	1992-93
300 Games	32,276	30,630	29,032	25,387	20,542
299 Games	14,769	13,678	12,913	11,444	9,080
298 Games	6,085	5,691	5,456	4,700	3,999
800 Series	7,182	6,619	6,296	5,521	4,606
11-in-a-row	25,539	24,367	22,879	20,004	16,805
700 Series	170,235	163,448	151,838	130,445	113,093
100 Over Game	61,866	62,612	62,862	61,283	66,355
150 Over Series	92,733	89,964	85,639	79,156	72,055
Triplicate	18,842	20,371	20,488	21,014	22,647
All Spare Games	11,560	13,378	13,323	13,362	14,898
Dutch 200 Games	7,199	7,555	7,039	6,646	6,692
Big 4 Splits	4,635	4,904	4,431	4,263	4,408
7-10 Splits	4,703	4,822	4,547	4,595	4,327
Senior 75 Over Game	37,292	32,326	28,262	23,427	20,154
Senior 125 Over Series	25,643	22,135	18,847	15,418	13,589

Youth

	1996-97	1995-96	1994-95	1993-94	1992-93
300 Games	806	754	681	560	447
299 Games	302	274	253	124	127
298 Games	128	106	87	46	64
800 Series	143	113	109	83	66
700 Series	4,842	4,686	3,752	*	*

* Not available.

WIBC/ABC Bowling Center and Lane Certification Summary

Note: U.S. totals included in overall totals 1906-07 — 1946-47

Season	All Centers	All Lanes	U.S. Centers	U.S. Lanes	Season	All Centers	All Lanes	U.S. Centers	U.S. Lanes
1996-97	6,986	138,465	6,688	132,924	1950-51	6,638	56,004	6,514	54,943
1995-96	7,182	141,806	6,880	136,325	1948-49	6,097	50,145	6,019	49,555
1994-95	7,331	144,187	7,049	139,002	1947-48	5,747	46,004	5,667	45,296
1993-94	7,469	146,860	7,183	141,547	1946-47	5,446	44,513	5,382	44,028
1992-93	7,551	147,891	7,250	142,570	1945-46	4,874	40,146		
1991-92	7,713	149,650	7,395	144,351	1944-45	4,351	38,023		
1990-91	7,904	151,952	7,544	146,356	1943-44	4,335	37,104		
1989-90	8,025	153,163	7,671	147,775	1942-43	4,589	38,643		
1988-89	8,103	153,403	7,764	148,315	1941-42	5,096	39,812		
1987-88	8,279	155,324	7,923	150,152	1940-41	5,004	35,550		
1986-87	8,386	156,294	8,031	151,312	1939-40	4,848	31,996		
1985-86	8,503	157,706	8,149	152,882	1938-39	3,880	25,797		
1984-85	8,629	159,394	8,275	154,564	1937-38	4,323	26,496		
1983-84	8,720	159,877	8,351	155,089	1936-37	3,707	23,507		
1982-83	8,767	158,204	8,404	154,106	1935-36	3,343	21,670		
1981-82	8,850	158,704	8,481	154,090	1934-35	3,117	20,676		
1980-81	8,893	158,661	8,528	154,223	1933-34	2,944	19,846		
1979-80	8,951	158,769	8,591	154,412	1932-33	2,743	18,882		
1978-79	9,061	158,387	8,699	154,077	1931-32	2,583	18,114		
1977-78	9,068	155,997	8,698	151,725	1930-31	2,327	16,660		
1976-77	9,017	151,494	8,640	147,237	1929-30	1,986	14,507		
1975-76	8,993	147,500	8,607	143,380	1928-29	1,658	12,291		
1974-75	8,974	144,829	8,577	140,741	1927-28	1,422	10,350		
1973-74	8,998	143,345	8,595	139,267	1926-27	1,159	8,076		
1972-73	9,090	142,768	8,674	138,562	1925-26	944	6,436		
1971-72	9,257	143,630	8,818	139,023	1924-25	824	5,466		
1970-71	9,373	144,104	8,922	139,483	1923-24	687	4,301		
1969-70	9,612	146,234	9,140	141,492	1922-23	598	3,588		
1968-69	9,866	148,885	9,378	143,929	1921-22	525	2,777		
1967-68	10,255	152,741	9,707	147,526	1920-21	450	2,274		
1966-67	10,596	157,070	10,070	151,731	1919-20	409	2,065		
1965-66	11,025	161,894	10,457	156,219	1918-19	381	1,920		
1964-65	11,363	165,101	10,752	159,079	1917-18	370	1,780		
1963-64	11,453	165,033	10,839	158,996	1916-17	331	1,562		
1962-63	11,476	163,323	10,883	157,713	1915-16	278	1,283		
1961-62	11,163	153,449	10,610	148,535	1914-15	217	1,021		
1960-61	10,417	135,041	9,906	130,805	1913-14	180	803		
1959-60	9,467	111,802	8,997	107,908	1912-13	149	659		
1958-59	8,609	90,893	8,191	87,475	1911-12	120	492		
1957-58	7,904	76,486	7,475	73,081	1910-11	109	421		
1956-57	7,458	67,967	7,190	65,127	1909-10	90	347		
1955-56	7,190	63,210	6,957	60,654	1908-09	62	239		
1954-55	7,062	60,648	6,636	58,203	1907-08	33	134		
1953-54	6,911	58,982	6,634	56,861	1906-07	11	47		

State Lane Certification, 1996-97

State	Centers	Lanes	State	Centers	Lanes
Alabama	51	1,152	Tennessee	80	1,892
Alaska	25	454	Texas	214	5,661
Arizona	73	1,800	Utah	56	1,068
Arkansas	57	1,080	Vermont	21	346
California	312	8,862	Virginia	85	2,270
Colorado	105	2,109	Washington	134	2,640
Connecticut	36	1,242	West Virginia	49	910
Delaware	17	522	Wisconsin	437	5,427
Florida	212	6,158	Wyoming	39	461
Georgia	83	2,151	1996-97 Total	6,688	132,924
Hawaii	24	514	1995-96 Total	6,880	136,325
Idaho	64	850	Difference	-192	-3,401
Illinois	410	7,656			
Indiana	202	4,304			
Iowa	223	2,810	**Foreign (Regions)**		
Kansas	139	2,051		Centers	Lanes
Kentucky	82	1,721	Canada	219	4,201
Louisiana	52	1,366	Europe	44	678
Maine	15	276	Japan	7	142
Maryland	48	1,204	Outer Regions	15	306
Massachusetts	38	1,057	Pacific Area	13	214
Michigan	424	9,432	Saudi Arabia	1	24
Minnesota	270	3,511	1996-97 Total	299	5,565
Mississippi	33	566	1995-96 Total	302	5,481
Missouri	197	3,492	Difference	-3	84
Montana	83	896			
Nation's Capital	54	1,580	**Combined**		
Nebraska	131	1,566		Centers	Lanes
Nevada	31	910	1996-97 Total	6,986	138,465
New Hampshire	11	228	1995-96 Total	7,182	141,806
New Jersey	128	3,696	Difference	-196	-3,341
New Mexico	39	720			
New York	488	10,419	**Ancillary Data, 1994-95**		
North Carolina	102	2,458	New centers		48
North Dakota	83	842	New lanes		928
Ohio	442	9,493	Deleted centers		240
Oklahoma	80	1,602	Deleted lanes		3,820
Oregon	92	1,650	Avg. lanes per center		19.82
Pennsylvania	474	7,331	Lanes replaced, added		
Rhode Island	10	342	or certification reinstated		4,062
South Carolina	55	1,386	Centers affected by replaced, added		
South Dakota	77	776	or reinstated lanes		212

Top Five States for Certified Bowling Centers 1996-97 Season

	Centers	Lanes
New York	488	10,419
Pennsylvania	474	7,331
Ohio	442	9,493
Wisconsin	437	5,427
Michigan	424	9,432

Largest Centers

Lanes	Center
106	Showboat Lanes, Las Vegas
96	Palisades Palace, Wickcliffe, Ohio
94	Thunderbowl, Allen Park, Mich.
84	Stardust Bowl, Addison, Ill.
82	Carolier Lanes, North Brunswick, N.J.

Oldest Centers
(Still Active, First Year Certified)

Year	Center
1909	Elks Bowling Lanes, Fond du Lac, Wis.
1910	Holler House, Milwaukee
1912	Brown's Lanes, Cleveland
1912	Bert & Eddie Recreation, Milwaukee
1913	Klabba's West Side Lanes, Sheboygan, Wis.

American Blind Bowling Association (ABBA)
Ron Marcase, Executive Director
315 N. Main St.
Houston, Pa. 15342
(412) 745-5986

American Bowling Congress (ABC)
Gerald Tessman, President (thru April 30, 1998)
Max Weinstein, President (after April 30, 1998)
Roger Dalkin, Executive Director
5301 S. 76th St.
Greendale, Wis. 53129-1127
(414) 421-6400 • FAX: (414) 421-1194

American Recreation Centers (ARC)
Robert Crist, President
11171 Sun Center Dr., Suite 120
Rancho Cordova, Calif. 95670
(916) 852-8005 • FAX (916) 852-8004

American Wheelchair Bowling Association (AWBA)
George Snyder, Executive Secretary-Treasurer
6264 N. Andrews Ave.
Ft. Lauderdale, Fla. 33309
(954) 491-2886 • FAX: (954) 491-2886

AMF Bowling Companies Inc.
Doug Stanard, President and CEO
P.O. Box 15060
Richmond, Va. 23227
(804) 730-4000 • FAX: (804) 730-1313

Billiard & Bowling Institute of America (BBIA)
Claudia Handley, President
200 Castlewood Drive
N. Palm Beach, Fla. 33408
(561) 842-4100 • FAX: (561) 863-8984

Bowling Proprietors Association of America (BPAA)
Charlie Brehob, President
615 Six Flags Dr.
Arlington, Texas 76011
(817) 649-5105 • FAX: (817) 633-2940

Bowling Writers Association of America (BWAA)
Mike Hennessy, President
c/o Dave DeLorenzo, Executive Director
N8424 900 St.
River Falls, Wis. 54022
(715) 426-0383 • FAX: (715) 426-0997

Brunswick Corporation
Peter Larson, Chairman, CEO, President
One North Field Court
Lake Forest, Ill. 60045
(847) 735-4700 • FAX: (847) 735-4765

Brunswick Recreation Centers (BRC)
Fred Florjanic Jr., President
520 Lake Cook Road Suite 400
Deerfield, Ill. 60015
(708) 317-7300 • FAX: (708) 317-0237

BVL Fund
Helene Phillips, Executive Director
10760 Brewer House Road
North Bethesda, Md. 20852
(301) 881-8333 • FAX: (301) 881-4042

Canadian Tenpin Federation
Adrianne Bride, President
530 Home St.
Winnipeg Manitoba, Canada R3G 1X7
(204) 783-7453 • FAX: (204) 783-4856

Columbia 300
Mike Allbritton, President
5005 West Ave.
San Antonio, Texas 78213
(800) 531-5920 • FAX: (210) 349-8672

DBA Products
Remo Picchietti Sr., Chairman of the Board
One Sherwood Terrace
Lake Bluff, Ill. 60044
(708) 234-8100 • FAX: (708) 234-8160

Ebonite International, Inc.
William Scheid, President
P.O. Box 746
Hopkinsville, Ky. 42241
(502) 886-5461 • FAX: (502) 885-7791

Federation Internationale des Quilleurs (FIQ)
Gerald L. Koenig, President
1631 Mesa Ave., Suite A
Colorado Springs, Colo. 80906
(719) 636-2695 • FAX: (719) 636-3300

Heddon Bowling Service
Will Heddon, President
1025 N. Alternate 27
Lake Hamilton, Fla. 33851
(800) 523-0304 • FAX: (941) 439-5841

International Bowling Museum & Hall of Fame
Jerry Baltz, Executive Director
111 Stadium Plaza
St. Louis, Mo. 63102
(314) 231-6340 • FAX: (314) 231-4054

International Bowling Pro Shop and Instructors Association (IBPSIA)
Sue Haws, Executive Director
P.O. Box 5634
Fresno, Calif. 93755
(800) 659-9444 • FAX: (209) 275-9250

Ladies Pro Bowlers Tour (LPBT)
John Falzone, President
7171 Cherryvale Blvd.
Rockford, Ill. 61112
(815) 332-5756 • FAX: (815) 332-9636

Les Dames De 700 Bowling Club
Flora Mitchell, President
2029 E. Farm Rd. 94
Springfield, Mo. 65803
(417) 779-4555

Multi-Unit Bowling Information Group (MUBIG)
Rick Bourgeois, Acting President
12237 E. Milbum Dr.
Baton Rouge, La. 70815-6743
(504) 273-3294 • FAX: (504) 273-3294

Murrey International
Gordon W. Murrey Sr., President
407 West Rosecrans Avenue
Gardena, Calif. 90248
(310) 532-6091 • FAX: (310) 217-0504